HOLLYWOOD PLAYERS:
THE FORTIES

BY JAMES ROBERT PARISH

As author

THE FOX GIRLS*
THE PARAMOUNT PRETTIES*
THE SLAPSTICK QUEENS
GOOD DAMES
HOLLYWOOD'S GREAT LOVE TEAMS*
ELVIS!
THE GREAT MOVIE HEROES
THE GREAT CHILD STARS
THE GREAT WESTERN STARS

As co-author

THE EMMY AWARDS: A PICTORIAL HISTORY
THE CINEMA OF EDWARD G. ROBINSON
THE MGM STOCK COMPANY: THE GOLDEN ERA*
THE GREAT SPY PICTURES
THE GEORGE RAFT FILE
THE GLAMOUR GIRLS*
LIZA!
THE GREAT GANGSTER PICTURES
THE GREAT WESTERN PICTURES
FILM DIRECTORS GUIDE: THE U.S.
FILM DIRECTORS GUIDE: WESTERN EUROPE
THE DEBONAIRS*
THE SWASHBUCKLERS*

As editor

THE GREAT MOVIE SERIES
ACTORS' TELEVISION CREDITS: 1950–1972

As associate editor

THE AMERICAN MOVIES REFERENCE BOOK
TV MOVIES

*Published by Arlington House

HOLLYWOOD PLAYERS:
THE FORTIES

JAMES ROBERT PARISH
AND
LENNARD DeCARL

With
WILLIAM T. LEONARD and **GREGORY W. MANK**

Introduction by
JACK ANO

Editor
T. ALLAN TAYLOR

Research Associates
JOHN ROBERT COCCHI and **FLORENCE SOLOMON**

ARLINGTON HOUSE·PUBLISHERS
NEW ROCHELLE, NEW YORK

Library of Congress Cataloging in Publication Data

Parish, James Robert.
  Hollywood players.

  Includes index.
  1. Moving-picture actors and actresses—United States—
Biography. I. DeCarl, Lennard, joint author. II. Title.
PN1998.A2P3918   791.43′028′0922   75-33146
ISBN 0-87000-322-4

For KILROY

Who Was Always There in the Forties

Hollywood Players: The Forties

KEY TO THE FILM STUDIOS

AA   Allied Artists Picture Corporation

AIP   American International Pictures

AVCO EMB Avco Embassy Pictures Corporation

BV   Buena Vista Distributions, Co. Inc.

CIN   Cinerama Inc.

COL   Columbia Pictures Industries, Inc.

EL   Eagle Lion Films, Inc.

EMB   Embassy Pictures Corporation

FN   First National Pictures, Inc. (later part of Warner Bros.)

FOX   Fox Film Corporation (later part of Twentieth Century-Fox)

LIP   Lippert Pictures, Inc.

MGM   Metro-Goldwyn-Mayer, Inc.

MON   Monogram Pictures Corporation

PAR   Paramount Pictures Corporation

PRC   Producers Releasing Corporation

RKO   RKO Radio Pictures, Inc.

REP   Republic Pictures Corporation

20th   Twentieth Century-Fox Film Corporation

UA   United Artists Corporation

UNIV   Universal Pictures, Inc.

WB   Warner Bros., Inc.

Hollywood Players: The Forties

ACKNOWLEDGMENTS:

RESEARCH MATERIAL CONSULTANT:
  DOUG McCLELLAND

RICHARD BRAFF
MRS. LORAINE BURDICK
Cinemabilia (ERNEST BURNS)
HOWARD DAVIS
MORRIS EVERETT, JR.
Filmfacts (ERNEST PARMENTIER)
Film Fan Monthly
Films and Filming
Films in Review
Focus on Film
PIERRE GUINLE
MRS. R. F. HASTINGS
PETER HANSON
RICHARD HUDSON
KEN D. JONES
MILES KREUGER
DAVID McGILLIVRAY
ALBERT B. MANSKI
ALVIN H. MARILL

RESEARCH VERIFIER:
  EARL ANDERSON

JIM MEYER
MRS. EARL MEISINGER
PETER MIGLIERINI
NORMAN MILLER
Movie Poster Service (BOB SMITH)
Movie Star News (PAULA KLAW)
MICHAEL R. PITTS
DAVID RODE
Screen Facts (ALAN G. BARBOUR)
RICHARD SISSON
CHARLES SMITH
MRS. PETER SMITH
DON STANKE
Roz Starr Service
CHARLES K. STUMPF
Views and Reviews

And special thanks to Paul Myers, curator of the Theatre Collection at the Lincoln Center Library for the Performing Arts (New York City) and his staff: Monty Arnold, David Bartholomew, Rod Bladel, Donald Fowle, Maxwell Silverman, Dorothy Swerdlove, Betty Wharton, and Don Madison of Photo Services.

Contents

Introduction

The 1940's. America was at war and at peace, and by the end of the decade the visions of life we had accepted at the beginning would be ceasing to exist even in our imaginations.

At the start, everyone on the home front went to the movies and we all were under the Hollywood spell. Those of us who were kids usually demanded Royal Crown Cola because it was the drink of the Paramount stars (or so we believed), and our big sisters insisted on washing only with Lux—"the complexion bar of the Hollywood beauties."

But naivete was not limited to the young. There were few people, even among the adults, who did not accept the fantasies of America and the world that Louis B. Mayer and Jack L. Warner were choosing to bestow on us in the war years.

For the movie moguls, the Forties offered what one of their favorite public domain writers had once characterized as "the best of times and the worst of times." Hollywood itself was always at its best in exercising ingenuity and sometimes at its best in producing films and at its worst in the way it behaved.

The American motion picture industry was meeting the challenges of wartime with what it enthusiastically proclaimed was a selflessness and dedication little short of saintliness, an image persisting even now through late show re-runs of such incredible exercises in egomania such as *Thank Your Lucky Stars, Follow the Boys* and *Hollywood Canteen.* Self-sacrifice was the order of the day and, with characteristically pious

fanfare, Cecil B. DeMille obliged by contributing to the war effort the giant squid that had seen battle with John Wayne and Ray Milland in *Reap The Wild Wind.* Presumably, DeMille considered the rubber used in creating the blatantly artificial monster vital to the national defense.

What the Hollywood patriots were not so eager to publicize was the fact that they were threatening to halt all film production if legislation limiting salaries to no more than $25,000 annually went into effect in 1942. After all, Louis B. Mayer had reported earnings of $949,765 at the end of 1941 and so drastic a cut would leave him virtually impoverished. Executive privilege prevailed and salaries and profits rose ever higher as the war continued.

With so much money to be made, the moguls decided to increase production. In the full war years of 1942, 1943 and 1944, no fewer than 1,313 feature-length pictures went into release. Though many of them were grade-B efforts, there also were more so-called "important films" than ever before, and this meant that the mighty Hollywood ego had to be maintained.

The one thing that could not be sacrificed to the war effort was the glamour and excitement of the traditional Hollywood premiere.

Despite restrictions imposed by blackouts, brownouts and dimouts, the ceremonious Hollywood gala did continue. That most revered of California shrines, Grauman's Chinese Theatre, was shielded by a tent to disguise the glare of spotlights and flashbulbs from the enemy planes always expected overhead, while the outside of the Grauman temple was decorated with a special translucent paint that provided a celestial glow when exposed to ultra-violet light. It was an effect beloved by Louis B. Mayer.

As might be expected, Hollywood priorities always remained uppermost in the minds of the local establishment. The same Jack L. Warner who was to maintain that the controversial, pro-Russian *Mission To Moscow* was made at the personal request of his "good friend," President Roosevelt, and who was commissioned into the Air Force· as a Lieutenant Colonel at the outbreak of the war without being required to leave his studio domain, was considerably disturbed by the proximity of the Warner Bros. production facilities to the Lockheed aircraft plant, considered a vital target for those ever imminent Japanese bombers. To make matters worse, the Warner quonset hut sound stages could easily be mistaken from the air for the Lockheed installation. In what he later insisted was in the spirit of a practical joke, Lt. Col. Warner ordered studio artists to embellish the roof of his largest sound stage with a huge sign directing anyone who should pass overhead to Lockheed. By the time he was persuaded to remove the sign, the fear of aerial invasion by the Japanese had passed.

Not all problems could be so easily solved, however, and the one most pressing was the creation of stars and featured players for the pictures that were being ground out, assembly-line style, by the major studios.

Most of the able-bodied males were serving in the armed forces and the others were being overworked or were unreasonably temperamental by executive standards. The solution was to create new stars from the increasing ranks of contract players who were indentured to the studios in both the making of pictures and also maintaining the overtly patriotic Hollywood image on the grueling round of war bond drives and troop show personal appearances.

Despite the publicity of the times and the prominent billing that accrued almost overnight to the new discoveries, major stardom eluded most of them. For the most part they played opposite more secure box-office names in important features or they had starring roles in the also-ran attractions. Few had careers that outlasted the decade.

The opportunities for stardom were there, however, and it was axiomatic of the war years that anyone who really wanted to be in motion pictures had the chance. Apocryphally, a husky young 4-F arrived at the gates of Paramount studios and announced his intention to become a movie star. His name was Sonny Tufts.

It was also a time of renewal for faded stars. John Mack Brown, once Garbo's leading man in silent films, returned from poverty row westerns to don a tuxedo for Monogram's misguided attempt at a major feature, *They Shall Have Faith* (retitled *Forever Yours* when the company lost its faith in the picture). Nils Asther left service as a post office clerk to star in *The Man In Half Moon Street, Jealousy* and *Alaska,* while Erich von Stroheim became "the man you love to hate" in *Five Graves To Cairo, The Hour Before The Dawn* and grade-C horror movies for Republic.

Even more eagerly resuscitated were the prima donnas of the past who were supposed to provide established marquee value for movies more ostensibly showcasing the stars of tomorrow. Without exception, these comebacks were fated to last no longer than a single feature—though some of the ladies would, in later years, make more successful returns. Luise Rainer found herself bizarrely cast with William Bendix in *Hostages* and Elissa Landi starred in *Corregidor.* Gloria Swanson made *Father Takes a Wife* in 1941, with John Howard and Desi Arnaz representing the younger generation, and then retreated to cinematic obscurity until called upon nearly a decade later to attempt a self-parody in *Sunset Boulevard.* Ruby Keeler (absent since 1938) was tapped again in *Sweetheart Of The Campus,* and Pola Negri vamped her way to Utica, N. Y., for the world premiere of the less than memorable *Hi Diddle Diddle* in which she played second fiddle to Martha Scott and Dennis O'Keefe. Even early stagestar Elsie Janis, forever identified as "the sweetheart of the A. E. F.," returned for *Women In War.*

Another attempt at career renewal was made when veteran B-picture players changed their names in the hope of finding the new image that would make them major stars, a practice that had worked successfully with several of the minor players of the period— among them the stars we would know as Rita Hayworth and Jennifer Jones.

The veteran players were to have little luck with this ploy, though some did find modest moments of glory. After 15 years of playing bit roles and second leads in the humblest of minor movies, Jacqueline Wells became Julie Bishop and got to be Errol Flynn's gratuitously placed leading lady in *Northern Pursuit* before sliding back to the B's and eventually to the bit performer ranks. Then there was John Shepperd. Failing to score as a romantic lead in the early 1940's, he returned in the post-war years as Shepperd Strudwick and established himself as a reliable supporting player.

Ultimately, it fell to the overworked young contract players to serve as the bulwark of the motion picture industry in the Forties and, while some achieved stardom, nearly all in varying ways were to become victims of the prevailing Hollywood system.

The biggest and longest lasting of the new stars were those who had served apprenticeships in the 1930's—among them Grable, Bogart, Hayworth, Alan Ladd, Lana Turner, Paulette Goddard, Judy Garland, Mickey Rooney and, from England, Greer Garson. By this time, they all were professional enough to meet the standards demanded of them or shrewd enough to play for the kind of publicity that would turn even their failings to boxoffice advantage. Examples of the latter occurred when Rita Hayworth and Greer Garson were "forced" to retire from war bond drives after publicly collapsing from what was said to be physical exhaustion. Naturally, the nation's collective heart went out to these noble ladies for apparently having sacrificed even their health for the national defense.

Some personalities of the period were invented for political purposes. A wartime alliance with Latin America seemed essential and so the "good neighbor policy" was formulated, and with it came Saludos Amigos, rum and Coca-Cola cocktails, Chiquita Banana, Xavier Cugat, Latin jukebox rhythms and, inevitably, those most incredible of Hollywood creations—Maria Montez and Carmen Miranda.

The situation was, however, temporary. When the fear of Hitler's forces invading from the South faded, the Hollywood and Broadway tunesmiths switched their Latin rhythms from "Good Night, Good Neighbor" to the condescending cynicism of "South America, Take It Away." Simultaneously, the temperamental Latin movie queens found themselves unceremoniously reduced to shoddy productions and roles calculated to destroy whatever remaining popularity they held with the public. After all, as someone in power at Universal probably reasoned, young Peggy Morrison from Vancouver, Canada, was noticeably less schizophrenic than Montez and she could be made to seem just as exotic if brought to the public in Arabian sarong vehicles as Yvonne DeCarlo. It made little difference that De Carlo's talents lay in earthier directions or that more excitingly exotic types like Gail Russell, Cyd Charisse and Lucille Bremer were being wasted in ingenue roles. Stars in the 1940's generally were not allowed to create an image. They were made to fill the image preset for them by their studio.

The star who at first seemed to best fill the image for which she had been all too literally molded was Jane Russell—a Howard Hughes discovery and former big band singer who was thrust into the spotlight as a pin-up figure for three years before The Outlaw was finally released. The picture was a success but Russell proved something of a bust and, despite her superstar appearance in The Outlaw and much publicity to the contrary, she ultimately was destined to be just another Hollywood player who starred in B's and supported bigger names in the more important features.

If researchers today were to poll moviegoers of the Forties on the best remembered stars of the period there undoubtedly would be many surprises, since television was still to become the great leveler of mass taste and the popular personalities of the time were determined mainly by where you lived and where you saw movies.

This was because most major theatres were controlled by the film distributors and the system known as block booking wherein exhibitors contracted to play numerous films from a single studio. In cities of 100,000 population or more, there inevitably were downtown showcases for all the important pictures. However, the neighborhood double feature houses were not usually controlled by the large theatrical chains and they usually played lesser films with lesser stars. Inevitably, the small town and skid row markets had to settle for grade-C products from Republic, Monogram and PRC along with reissues from the ineptly named Film Classics, Realart and Dominant—companies specializing in films with big name stars that had not returned sufficient profits in original release. It was in these "orphan" areas, too, that the poverty row westerns (from which John Wayne and Robert Mitchum graduated) found their major audience, and it was here that such little chronicled names as William "Wild Bill" Elliott, Don "Red" Barry, Al "Lash" LaRue, Bob Steele and Charles Starrett were reigning heroes.

Movies of the time were made primarily in genres and within every genre the more successful pictures and players spawned low budget variations which sometimes proved fresher and more appealing than the originals.

Andy Hardy had his B-movie counterpart in Henry Aldrich and, even though the series was definitely on the wane in the Forties, The Thin Man tradition was being carried on in lively fashion for the neighborhoods by Jane Wyman and Jerome Cowan in Crime By Night and by Evelyn Keyes and Allyn Joslyn in Strange Affair, while out in the sticks audiences had to settle for William Gargan or Chester Morris with alternating combinations of Nancy Kelly, Jean Parker and Margaret Lindsay. Donald O'Connor and Peggy Ryan upheld the Rooney-Garland tradition in movies that played the neighborhoods, leaving June Preisser and Freddie Stewart to carry the rhythm to the hinterlands.

Ruth Terry, Betty Jane Rhodes and Grace MacDonald stood in for Grable and Hayworth in the small

13

towns; Vera Hruba Ralston and Belita briefly tried to copy Sonja Henie; and Johnny Coy and Marc Platt tapped in the Gene Kelly-Fred Astaire tradition. Ann Miller was the poor man's Eleanor Powell and, for those denied the supposedly classy pleasures of Maria Montez and Dorothy Lamour, strippers Ann Corio and Margie Hart were on hand with epics like *Jungle Siren, Sarong Girl* and, most aptly, *Swamp Woman.*

The Hollywood definition of "class" knew no boundaries and there was nothing ritzier at the time than a soprano. Gloria Jean, Mary Lee, Ann Blyth, Susanna Foster, Kathryn Grayson and Gloria Warren, at various times, served as the junior league Deanna Durbins of the neighborhoods, while Edith Fellows and Gale Storm carried the coloratura trills to the furthest farmlands.

War movies, of course, were popular everywhere. Errol Flynn, John Wayne and Ronald Reagan were winning Europe and Asia practically singlehandedly for the big city audiences, while in the lesser markets Tom Neal was "first Yank into Tokyo" and Alan Curtis, Tim Holt, and Preston Foster staunchly fought Hitler's madmen.

Abbott and Costello were the kings of service humor during the war years, inspiring practically identical antics from the B-movie team of Wally Brown and Alan Carney and the grade-C duo of William Tracy and Joe Sawyer. Even Jackie Gleason and Jack Durant tried copying the formula with *Tramp, Tramp, Tramp,* a sophomoric variation of *Buck Privates.*

The youngest major star of the era was Margaret O'Brien, who briefly found competition from Natalie Wood and Peggy Ann Garner and none at all from such would-be juvenile challengers as Sharyn Moffett, Patti Brady, Beverly Simmons, Luana Patten and Mary Jane Saunders. In reality, Margaret's main rival at M-G-M and in theatres for the favor of the family and moppet trades was Lassie, that classy collie who easily outdistanced such mongrel competition as Rusty, Pal and Shep. The canine's success brought a rash of animal stars ranging from Flicka, Thunderhead (son of Flicka) and Gallant Bess all the way down to Jim The Crow and those costumed lovebirds, Bill And Coo.

Boris Karloff and Lon Chaney, Jr., were the kings of horror but by this time their monster vehicles had degenerated, albeit profitably, to the B level. This sort of fright fare, appealing mainly to youngsters and action fans, usually alternated on weekends with the singing cowboy westerns starring Roy Rogers or Gene Autry and other low budget adventure films. Invariably, these pictures (seldom running more than 70 minutes) were accompanied by serials in 12 to 15

weekly chapters from Republic, Universal and Columbia. In the C markets, Kirby Grant and Monte Hale were the singing cowboy favorites and the horror stars, in shoddy efforts from PRC and Monogram, were George Zucco, Lionel Atwill and sometimes Bela Lugosi. The serials were the same everywhere—though the hinterland markets got them much later.

The separation of audience groups was so complete that a few players were able to bridge the A and B picture gaps by serving as stars in the pictures that went to the lesser theatres and as supporting players in the more important films.

The prime examples of the few players that had that ability were Kay Francis and Constance Bennett. Genuine superstars of the Thirties but no longer important boxoffice names for the major theatres, they remained popular personalities in the small towns where their old pictures were still playing. Consequently, Bennett could play a small supporting role in Garbo's *Two-Faced Woman* and simultaneously be a B-picture star in vehicles like *Law Of The Tropics, Sin Town* and *Paris Underground.* Even more remarkable was Francis who was bridging the A, B and C movie gaps by supporting the likes of Deanna Durbin and Jack Benny in the A's, nominally starring with small roles in B pictures made to showcase younger players and also reigning as the Bette Davis of the whistle stops in self-produced low budgeters like *Divorce, Wife Wanted* and *Allotment Wives.*

It was not until 1945 that some of the Hollywood players would begin to realize their vulnerability. Returning veterans were seeking to replace the wartime leading men and usually even the biggest names, like Gable, were having difficulty in re-establishing themselves as important boxoffice personages. But movies were still being made in assembly-line fashion and nobody, really, was out of work. It was a time of uncertainty, but it was also one of steady employment even for such bland and temporary leading man types as Tom Drake, Frank Latimore, William Prince, William Eythe and Sonny Tufts.

The real crisis would come on June 11, 1946: the date of the Supreme Court anti-trust decisions outlawing block booking and ordering the divorcement of the film companies from any of their previous operations in production, distribution and exhibition.

Reluctantly and only after futile court appeals, the moguls in charge decided to abandon exhibition. Then, without guarantee of playing time for their more routine pictures, they promptly cut back production and drastically reduced the ranks of contract players.

Still more blows were to come. A crippling series of labor difficulties and strikes in 1946 further limited production. The advent of television as a medium of mass entertainment would seriously cut into theatre attendance and, beginning in 1947, a series of anti-Communist investigations led by the publicity seeking House Un-American Activities Committee would destroy careers and expose to the public the most self-destructive and desperate elements of the motion picture industry.

More than 300 actors, writers, producers and directors would find their careers jeopardized, curtailed or destroyed. Among the more prominent victims, to varying degrees, were John Garfield, Larry Parks, Paul Muni, Edward G. Robinson, Marsha Hunt, Mady Christians, Edward Dmytrk, John Howard Lawson, Joseph Losey, J. Edward Bromberg, Herbert Biberman and Gale Sondergaard. Their guilt, often, was from suspicion only through their refusal to cooperate (in some cases temporarily) with the investigating committee. On the other hand, a former Communist like Sterling Hayden could reactivate a fading career by "heroically" revealing supposed knowledge of other Communists, and Lucille Ball could emerge professionally unscathed by capitalizing on her dumb blonde image and pleading youthful naivete.

For some the investigations served as a means of explaining career failures. Adolphe Menjou claimed that his anti-Communist stance caused him to lose employment as an actor, while Mrs. Lela Rogers, Ginger's mother, told the committee how she had forbidden her daughter to appear in Theodore Dreiser's *Sister Carrie* (later made with Jennifer Jones) because it was "open propaganda." Ginger's recent, disastrous appearance as a Parisian pickpocket in Sam Wood's *Heartbeat* was apparently predicated on the "fact," as explained by mother Rogers in her testimony, that "it's been a long time since you could get a good American story bought in the motion picture industry." This was a strange statement considering the movies of the time (*The Yearling, Life With Father, Miracle On 34th Street* and such then "controversial" works as *The Best Years Of Our Lives, Crossfire* and *Gentlemen's Agreement*), and the witnesses "friendly" to the committee and its aims (among them Sam Wood, Jack L. Warner, Robert Taylor, George Murphy, Robert Montgomery, Ronald Reagan, Gary Cooper, Leo McCarey, Walt Disney and, of course, the allegedly persecuted Menjou). The investigations would also serve as a major stepping stone in the career of the young, staunchly anti-Russian, Communist-fearing Congressman from California, Richard M. Nixon.

Ultimately, Hollywood would survive. Though movies like *The Search, Berlin Express* and *The Sealed Verdict* would make on-location filming the rule rather than the exception, this was due more to economic advantages than to any diminishment of Establishment power. Hollywood would continue as the center of the creative forces and employment pools for the film industry.

Finally forced to admit that television was competing for the mass audience, movie studios would become bolder and more mature in their presentations, while novelties like 3-D, Cinerama, CinemaScope, VistaVision, Stereophonic Sound and even Mike Todd, Jr.'s SmelloVision would be introduced in attempts to boost theatrical attendance.

But by this time the era of the Hollywood contract player was over. The bigger stars survived and, indeed, prospered more than ever before by demanding enormous salaries and percentages. Many of the former contract players drifted into television and a few, like Lucille Ball and Milton Berle, became home screen superstars. Some players headed for Broadway (Patricia Morison, Anne Jeffreys, Vivian Blaine, Robert Alda, Dane Clark) or for quick oblivion in summer stock (Veronica Lake, Susanna Foster, Tom Drake) while others, like June Haver, Louise Allbritton and Ella Raines, gradually drifted away from performing into private life.

At the same time, there would be the tragedies. Carole Landis, with a comedic flair to match Lombard's, could not pass as an imitation Grable and was considered unemployable, and became a suicide at 28. Barbara Payton, lacking film roles, turned to prostitution, while perennial screen convicts Lawrence Tierney and Tom Neal would find their movie roles turned to actuality behind prison bars. Maria Montez was to be found mysteriously dead in her bath at the age of 31. Alcoholism, degradation and early deaths lay ahead for Diana Barrymore, Gail Russell and Robert Walker.

For the Hollywood players the late Forties had brought awareness of their own vulnerability, the end of innocence and the beginnings of what often proved a cruel reality. Some survived, some did not . . . but their early innocence lives forever in the flickering shadows that constitute their contributions to our culture.

—JACK ANO

15

1

Robert Alda

When handsome Robert Alda first arrived in Hollywood in 1943, many people thought he resembled Cary Grant. Perhaps he bore a physical resemblance to Grant, but the similarity ends there. Cary Grant became a household term—but Robert Alda did not.

Grant was based at Warner Bros. at the same time Alda was there, and coincidentally, each of them starred in two of the studio's big musical fabrications: Grant played Cole Porter in *Night and Day* (1946) and Alda was introduced to film audiences as George Gershwin in *Rhapsody in Blue* (1945). Had Alda been allowed to apprentice in smaller roles before winning the starring part in *Rhapsody in Blue,* his performance in that picture and his career in general might have earned him a place of more enduring importance in film history. It is just possible that the engaging brashness of his own personality could have been captured, to be channeled into disciplined performing. As it was in 1948 his Warners' stay ended, and generally, he was considered washed up in show business.

But in 1950 he surfaced again as the singing gambler Sky Masterson in Broadway's *Guys and Dolls.* Since the '50s, he managed to keep his professional image in circulation, although the pickings frequently have been slim; and in recent years, the name Alda is better known to the younger generation through his son, the popular star Alan Alda.

Robert Alda was born on February 26, 1914, in New York City to Anthony and Frances (Tumillo) D'Abruzzo. His baptismal name was Alphonso Giuseppe Giovanni Roberto D'Abruzzo; when he went into show business he dropped the "o" from Roberto and wedded the first two letters from Alphonso and D'Abruzzo, which netted him the good marquee name, Robert Alda. Mr. D'Abruzzo was a barber who was not too happy about his son's ambitions to be an entertainer. So after graduating from Stuyvesant High School, Robert acceded to his father's wishes and attended New York University's architectural school at night; during the day he worked as a junior draftsman for an architectural firm. On September 31, 1932, he married Joan Brown, a Miss New York beauty contest winner, and they had a son, Alphonso, Jr., who is now known as Alan Alda. The marriage dissolved in the mid-fifties, gaining much publicity for the estranged couple. Alfie, as Alda Junior was then called, remained with his mother.

When Robert won an amateur singing contest, he felt encouraged to pursue a career in show business, and decided to accept an offer to do vaudeville rather than waiting around Broadway for that "big chance." He made his professional debut in an act called "Charlie Ahearn and His Millionaires," which played the RKO stage circuit in 1933. The following year Alda made his radio debut as a singer on WHN, and soon after became a straight man and singer in burlesque, working with such people as Bud Abbott, Rags Ragland, and Phil Silvers. One seasoned burlesque reviewer in 1937 reported that Alda "uncorks a good voice." He even entered television in its infan-

With Joan Leslie, Wilbur Mack (next right) and Brooks Benedict (right) in Rhapsody in Blue *(WB 1945)*

With Dolores Moran in The Man I Love *(WB 1946)*

cy, 1937, doing a modest variety program for CBS called "Alda and Henry," which was telecast *only* in Grand Central Station. (The "Henry" part of the act was none other than comedian Hank Henry.)

When Henry was drafted into the Army, Alda went out on his own again and for the next few years was involved primarily with hotel theatre productions in the Catskills on the "borscht" circuit. He also did a U.S.O. tour of Army camps throughout the United States. Upon returning to New York, he met the casting agent for Warner Bros., Steve Trilling, who was scouting for new talent on the east coast. Following Trilling's advice, the studio brought Alda to Hollywood for a screen test with the possibility of a contract at Warner Bros.

"Do not let anybody tell you," says Alda seriously, "that fate, destiny, luck, or whatever you want to call it, does not play an important part in the success of a career. When I finally reached Hollywood notice and was arranging for screen tests, it was John Garfield who called Warner Brothers' attention to me, because he had seen me act in a stock company. It's an old story now, my being on the spot when they were casting *Rhapsody in Blue.* Oh, they had plenty of stars from whom to draw. I had no illusions on that score. But what gave me the break was the fact they could not use a well-known screen actor for fear his personality would overshadow the portrayal of Gershwin. The point I want to bring out is the fact I was on the Warner lot when they were looking for an unknown of my physical qualities." John Garfield, who would have liked very much to play the role of Gershwin, would have been a much better choice. A week before shooting started on the film, Alda was told the plum part was his.

The Irving Rapper-directed film obviously did not meet the studio's desires; *Rhapsody in Blue* was held from release for nearly two years. During that time Alda was kept under contract but was not given any other acting assignments. When the 139-minute feature finally opened in June, 1945, it met with a cold shoulder from the press. Of Alda, Howard Barnes (*New York Herald-Tribune*) reported: "Robert Alda plays the difficult leading role and none too well. His tendency to be either stiff or sentimental evokes slight recollection of a musician whom this reviewer knew slightly." Bosley Crowther (*New York Times*) chided Alda's "opaque, mechanical way" of handling the showy part.

After that downbeat reception, Alda found that Warners' plans for him were not as great as he had hoped. The assignments he drew after *Rhapsody in Blue* were featured roles in less than memorable pic-

tures, although he was given both second and top male billing in his second and third features, the silly *Cinderella Jones* (1946) and *The Man I Love* (1947). His high billing in the latter film was only token, though, because Bruce Bennett had the important male role. That same year Bennett and Alda appeared together in *Nora Prentiss* (1947) with Ann Sheridan, and Alda was relegated to fourth billing, below Bennett this time. Alda's best film while at Warners was *Cloak and Dagger* (1946), in which he played Pinkie, an Italian partisan who helps O.S.S. man Gary Cooper locate an atomic scientist being held by the Nazis. Alda was to have co-starred with Claude Rains and Joan Caulfield in *The Unsuspected* (1947) but was replaced by Michael North, another actor whose screen career died in the 1940s. In *April Showers* (1948), a charming, if obvious, look at life on the vaudeville circuit, Jack Carson was the ham star of the picture, while Alda played the smaller part, the "other man" in Ann Sothern's life.

After Warner Bros. dropped Alda in the wake of industry retrenchment, he freelanced in several bad films, including *Mr. Universe* (1951), which featured two other Warners' refugees, Jack Carson and Janis Paige. The *New York Times* was kind: "Robert Alda, after some mighty sorry film assignments, makes the personable most of a racketeer who chisels in on the team property a la *Golden Boy.*" He also did some stock, toured with *A Hollywood Revue* with Carson and Paige, and hosted the television show "By Popular Demand" (1950).

Then, on November 24, 1950, he had his biggest success as Sky "Luck Be a Lady Tonight" Masterson in the Damon Runyon-based musical, *Guys and Dolls.* "I was lucky again," Alda admits. "If I had not been freelancing I would not have been able to accept the role in this musical fable of Broadway. When you are under contract to a studio it is not possible to take over a stage role when opportunity knocks." The stage role won Alda the Tony Award, the Donaldson Award, and a high spot on that year's Variety Poll. The *New York World Telegram and Sun* noted: "Robert Alda caps a picture career and long service in second stem clubs with a solid, winning appearance as the gambler whose religion has a pretty face. Sooner or later everybody is going to say Alda resembles Cary Grant, so we might as well too. Is that bad? He knows how to belt a ballad and sings like Vaughn Monroe might on a clear day. I hope the theatre hangs on to him." Alda later did the Las Vegas tab version of the show for three thousand dollars a week but lost out on the 1955 Samuel Goldwyn picturization to Marlon Brando.

During the Broadway run of *Guys and Dolls,* Robert was offered the male lead of Benny Fields in Paramount's *Somebody Loves Me* (1952), with Betty Hutton cast as Blossom Seeley; but either he could not or would not leave the show. Ralph Meeker finally played the part. No other major film offers came his way after the musical closed, so he turned to television as emcee on "What's Your Bid?" (1952) and "Can Do" (1956–57). He then starred in his own program, "The Robert Alda Show" (1953), and in his own series dealing with the O.S.S., "Secret File, U.S.A." (1954). He also was a frequent guest on Milton Berle's weekly television show. The famed comedian and he got along very well and worked together smoothly.

Before returning to Broadway to star opposite Linda Darnell in the ill-fated *Harbor Lights* (1956), he toured Italy's stages in *La Padrona di Raggio di Luna* and received the Italian Golden Wing Award for his performance. In *Harbor Lights* he played the role of Darnell's dashing ex-husband, originally intended for Dana Andrews. He was cast in Henry Denker's play, *Venus at Large*, with Menasha Skulnik, but the show never made it to Broadway. He was also going to produce and star in a musical, *Herald Square,* but it never came about, a fate also dealt to a proposed film biography of Russ Columbo for which he was wanted. Robert did, however, get married in 1956 to Flora Marino who bore him a son, Robert Jr.

While vacationing in Italy he encountered director Robert Z. Leonard who was packaging a film with French and Italian backing. The film was *Beautiful But Dangerous* (1958), starring Gina Lollobrigida, who was also a money partner. Alda was promptly cast in the feature and there began a new movie career in foreign-made pictures. He spoke Italian but his accent seemed funny to the Romans, so "I learned better Italian diction very fast." While in Italy, he also did television and radio. Because he had arrived on the Continent just at the time American actors were in demand, he managed to find work in European filmmaking for several years. However, the projects he was involved in were generally worse than many he had done in Hollywood. Soon, he was back in the United States to turn in a very creditable performance as a Seventh Avenue rogue in *The Gentlemen from Seventh Avenue* (1958) on "Playhouse 90," and the following year was hired by producer Ross Hunter to grace the remake of *Imitation of Life* as one of glittery Lana Turner's many swains.

By 1964 he was back on the New York stage costarring with Steve Lawrence and Sally Ann Howes in the musical *What Makes Sammy Run?* It was a very undisciplined cast—constantly breaking each other up on stage. New Yorkers saw him again in *My Daughter, Your Son* (1969), with Vivian Vance, and then as Robert Ryan's replacement in the revival of *The Front Page* (1970). At this time a dejected Alda stated, "I certainly don't see much of a future for Broadway. It makes me sick."

In 1973 he was making the rounds of summer stock touring in *Follies,* playing the role created on Broadway by John McMartin. He was also reunited in this Stephen Sondheim musical with his *Guys and Dolls* co-star, Vivian Blaine. His most recent feature films are the French production *The Serpent* (1974), in which he had a small role as an American CIA agent, an Italian-made feature or two, including *Off Shore* (1975), and then back in Hollywood, *I Will, I Will . . . For Now* (1976) which stars Elliott Gould.

Alda, unlike many other well-known performers with children in the business such as Henry Fonda, will have to settle for being known as his child's father. Alan Alda has been a very popular performer and TV series creator, especially noted for his starring role in the hit teleseries, "M.A.S.H." When Alan was ten and a half years old, he was stricken with polio and his parents would take turns days and nights applying the Sister Kenny hot packs and massaging the muscles of their son's paralyzed legs. Today there is no trace of his having been afflicted with the crippling disease.

Father and son enjoyed working together in the play *Luv* done at the Paramus Playhouse in New Jersey, and in the summer of 1974 Robert Jr. joined his father and brother in a production of *Come Blow Your Horn* in stock theatre. During the run of *Luv,* Papa Alda commented, "This is going to sound saccharine but we really do help each other. I'll suggest to Alan that it might be better if he turned his head this way and he'll do the same for me. There's no sense of competition." Perhaps no competition but there was compromise. Father and son each had his name first on the marquee on alternate days.

Today in his sixties, Robert Alda still has a great deal of energy and push and still retains a bit of the old ham in him—something that vaudevillians apparently never lose. His once familiar jet black hair has silver in it and it looks very handsome. Of the not always so glorious past, he reflects that he would not exchange his experience in small stock companies, his six-year term at Minsky's, nor his nightclub experience for the most coveted diploma from the best school of dramatic art. "I learned my trade in the best of schools—burlesque." Would he do it all over again? "I certainly would. I have had a happy life."

With Robert Douglas in Homicide *(WB 1949)*

20

ROBERT ALDA

Rhapsody in Blue *(WB 1945)*
Cinderella Jones *(WB 1946)*
Cloak and Dagger *(WB 1946)*
The Beast with Five Fingers *(WB 1946)*
The Man I Love *(WB 1947)*
Nora Prentiss *(WB 1947)*
April Showers *(WB 1948)*
Homicide *(WB 1949)*
Hollywood Varieties *(Lip 1950)*
Tarzan and The Slave Girl *(RKO 1950)*
Mr. Universe *(EL 1951)*
Two Gals and A Guy *(UA 1951)*
Beautiful But Dangerous *(20th 1958)*
Imitation of Life *(Univ 1959)*

A Soldier and A Half *(Italian 1959)*
A Che Sorvono Questi *(Italian 1959)*
Musketeers of The Sea *(Italian 1960)*
Force of Impulse *(Sutton 1961)*
Totte E Peppino *(Italian 1962)*
The Devil's Hand *(Crown International 1962)*
Cleopatra's Daughter *(Medallion 1963)*
Revenge of the Barbarians *(Italian 1963)*
The Girl Who Knew Too Much *(Commonwealth United 1969)*
Seven Steps From Murder *(Italian 1973)*
The Serpent *(Avco Emb 1974)*
Off Shore *(Italian 1975)*
House of Exorcism *(Italian 1975)*
I Will, I Will . . . For Now *(Brut 1976)*

2

Louise Allbritton

The lanky (5' 7¼") blonde, blue-eyed lady was a first-rate comedienne who graced the screen during the 1940s in a very mixed bag of B pictures at Universal. These films ranged from semi-dreary programmers to Westerns, escapist comedies, and the studio's special World War II forte, horror films. In all her work before the camera, she displayed more than ample charm, poise, and wit. For a time she was highly touted as the logical successor to the comedy crown of the late Carole Lombard, but she was seldom given the needed material to express her talents as a comic. While she was wasting away in Universal's production-line ventures, Irene Dunne, Rosalind Russell, and Jean Arthur were being showcased in glossy madcap comedies, the type of parts in which Louise would have excelled and through which she might have become a major cinema name.

She was born on July 3, 1920, in Oklahoma City, Oklahoma, to L. L. and Caroline Greer Allbritton. The family soon moved to Wichita Falls, Texas, where her father owned and operated the local traction system. Caroline Allbritton died when Louise was a youngster, leaving L. L. to cope with his daughter's snowballing theatrical ambitions. He packed her off to the University of Oklahoma, but after two years the determined young lady left the campus and traveled to California where she matriculated at the Pasadena Playhouse. While an apprentice there, she tried un-

successfully for film work. She remained at the Playhouse to perform lead roles in several of their major productions. The lack of studio interest in her potential was discouraging, and she began to rationalize that there was always life with father on a 100,-000-acre ranch some forty miles from Wichita Falls. However, during a Pasadena Playhouse production of *The Little Foxes,* Harry Cohn's Columbia Pictures signed her for a role in an upcoming Fay Wray-Paul Kelly film to be called *Just Another Dawn.* Retitled *Not a Ladies' Man,* it sneaked into double-bill theaters around the country in mid-1942. Shortly after that film's release, Louise joined Kay Harris and Marguerite Chapman in Columbia's misguided tribute to the airborne disciples of Florence Nightingale. Years later, when Louise was asked about her part in *Parachute Nurse* (1942), she replied, "It's a little vague. I played the parachute, I think."

Despite her inauspicious beginnings in films, Louise was determined to have a movie career and finally manipulated a seven-year contract from Universal.

Following Pearl Harbor, Hollywood developed a Pacific complex, producing more pictures with ocean background than there were ships at sea. For Universal, Louise was cast as an aviatrix with Don Terry, Leo Carrillo, and Turhan Bey in *Danger in the Pacific* (1942); she was romantically paired with Patric Knowles as Jane Little in a welter of frenzied Bud Abbott and Lou Costello shenanigans in the superior

Publicity pose for San Diego, I Love You *(Univ 1944)*

Who Done It? (1942). The publicity she received as the first lady on the silver screen to win a man from the glamorous Marlene Dietrich never took full account of her first important role as Shannon Prentiss in the film *Pittsburgh,* made the same year. In it, she played the daughter of a steel tycoon who marries and divorces John Wayne; her excellent performance as the unloved wife did not attract the notice it rightfully deserved.

As Edo Ives she was Donald O'Connor's cupid-baiting aunt in *It Comes Up Love* (1943), and withstood any inordinate amount of celluloid corn as attorney Elizabeth Christine Smith with a bemused Dennis O'Keefe in *Good Morning, Judge* (1943). Universal budgeted *Fired Wife* (1943) into a near-A status, and Louise gave a scintillating performance as Tig Callahan, a stage director secretly married to Robert Paige who is occupied fighting off a predatory woman. Diana Barrymore, who played the second female lead, gave little contest to Louise in either story or acting.

Universal of the 1940s was noted for several things: Actors being fired and finding almost instant stardom at other studios, moribund musicals, an occasional startlingly good A movie, and excellent horror films. The producers of *Frankenstein* (1931), *Dracula* (1931), and *The Invisible Man* (1933) profitably parlayed their monsters into various sequels that often were not as well conceived or produced. Long before Rosemary had her most unusual baby, Louise Allbritton, as Katharine Caldwell, became the wife of Dracula, in this case Lon Chaney, Jr. as Count Alucard (you know what it spelled backward). Together they took the matrimonial vows before a justice of the peace in *Son of Dracula* (1943). When she is killed, she rejoins the living as a vampire. Fellow Universalite Evelyn Ankers may have been princess of the lot's macabre features, but Louise displayed "undeniable charm" in her offering.

After a brief walk-on in Universal's all-star venture, *Follow the Boys* (1944), she was reteamed with Robert Paige, with whom she had made extensive personal appearances to promote their earlier *Fired Wife.* In *Her Primitive Man* (1944) she played Sheila Winthrop, a pert anthropologist who becomes involved with Paige, the latter posing as an aboriginal head hunter. Also along for the celluloid ride is Robert Benchley as a most perplexed publisher.

In the helter-skelter line-up of Universal films produced to entertain the troops, divert the people back home, and earn the studio many fast bucks, Louise was stationed in *This Is the Life* (1944). It was based on an unsuccessful play by Sinclair Lewis and actress

Fay Wray, *Angela Is 22.* This lack of success did not deter Universal from using their film version as a showcase for the talents of young Susanna Foster, which were bolstered by Donald O'Connor's breezy presence in uniting Harriet Jerret (Allbritton) with her estranged husband (Patric Knowles).

Louise's fine sense of comic timing was given a fine vehicle in the often hilarious *San Diego, I Love You* (1944), where she garnered laughs even when confronted by such scene stealers as Edward Everett Horton, Buster Keaton, Irene Ryan, and Eric Blore. Between fast-paced studio assignments she toured Army and Navy bases for the USO and made a quick trip to the Mediterranean war zone at Cassino, Italy.

Back at Universal she was astonished when the studio assigned her the brief role of Lillian Russell in their "major" musical, *Bowery to Broadway* (1944). She found it ironic that she should be portraying one of the all-time, highly publicized American beauties, since her nose had been broken twice while tomboying in Texas—the first time she hit a fire hydrant after being tackled in an otherwise all-male football game; and the second accident resulted from more rough-housing. If anything, Louise was lovelier than the original stage star of the nineties, and if audiences still preferred to recall Alice Faye's portrayal of *Lillian Russell* (1940) at Twentieth Century-Fox, Louise sang "Under the Bamboo Tree", just as creditably. After a slight part in a minor mishap featuring Peggy Ryan, *The Men in Her Diary* (1945), Louise surfaced with brisk, crackling delivery of lines as the cynical secretary to Franchot Tone in the pleasant *That Night with You* (1945). Universal, with their usual lack of imagination, followed her sparkling performance as Tone's gal Friday with a dreary supporting role in Maria Montez' unexotic *Tangier* (1946).

Offstage, however, Louise's life was blooming. On May 11, 1946, she and Charles Cummings Collingwood filed a marriage license and they were married two days later at the Little Church around the Corner in New York. Collingwood, born June 4, 1917 in Three Rivers, Michigan, was an Oxford Rhodes scholar, a United Press correspondent, and winner of the 1942 Peabody Award, as well as the Headliner's Club prize, for his accurate and dramatic reporting of the North African Allied invasion. Louise decided to put her marriage before her career. However, for her last fling at Universal she played Harriet Putnam, a wealthy lady farmer with designs on city-bred Fred MacMurray in *The Egg and I* (1947). This was the Claudette Colbert feature that introduced Ma and Pa Kettle (Marjorie Main and Percy Kilbride) to screen audiences. Allbritton managed to make her other

With Andy Devine in Danger in the Pacific *(Univ 1942)*

With Robert Paige and Evelyn Ankers in Son of Dracula *(Univ 1943)*

woman role (recommending her "new machinery" to MacMurray) a solid characterization.

Twentieth Century-Fox's *Sitting Pretty* (1948) introduced acerbic Clifton Webb as the world's most unlikely baby sitter, Lynn Belvedere, coping with the offsprings of screen couple Robert Young and Maureen O'Hara. Between offbeat child guidance sessions, Louise popped in as family friend Edna Philby. A supporting role in *Don't Trust Your Husband* (1948), and a similar role as Dr. Toni Neva, a scientist caught between FBI man Dennis O'Keefe and detective Louis Hayward in *Walk a Crooked Mile* (1948), led to the finale of Allbritton's Hollywood career as Rose of Cimarron in *The Doolins of Oklahoma* (1949), made back at her first studio, Columbia. Her final screen work to date is in the unreleased *Felicia* (1964).

Life for her as Mrs. Charles Collingwood took place for the most part in New York City, and, after a few television appearances, Louise starred on the small screen as Celia, with Scott McKay as Hank, in a nighttime soap opera "Stage Door," which told of the continuing heartaches, frustrations, and obstacles facing a young couple seeking to find success in the theater. For "Robert Montgomery Presents" she was in the telecast of "The Champion" with Richard Kiley, and also played in a comedy, "The Other Woman" for Circle Theatre. Offers of a husband-and-wife talk show similar to Dorothy (Killgallen) and Dick (Kollmar) never materialized for the Collingwoods, since he claimed to be a lousy actor and Louise maintained she was really too stupid. Both explanations seemed to be rather feeble excuses. But they were, and are, a handsomely matched pair. If the gab fest with the Collingwoods never crystalized, awards continued when, on the sixth annual Emmy Award Show, "See It Now" was an Emmy winner as the Best TV Program of News and Sports, citing *Christmas in Korea* with Charles Collingwood.

In the afternoon of Monday, July 5, 1954, another serial debuted. "Concerning Miss Marlowe" starred Louise as Maggie Marlowe, a middle-aged (!) actress devoting her enormous energies to a theatrical comeback. The following year an Emmy Award was presented to the Best Special Events Program—CBS's *A-Bomb Test Coverage* with Charles Collingwood. On November 13, 1955, Louise played another actress, Nora, in "Stage Fright" for TV's "Appointment with Adventure." Back in 1952 she had appeared on stage in *Rise By Sin,* which opened in New Haven and closed a week later in Washington, D.C. In 1955

she substituted for a vacationing actress in Broadway's *The Seven Year Itch.*

Great Britain's Lord Chamberlain declined to license Andrew Rosenthal's play *Third Person* because of the sub-theme of homosexuality entwined within the drama of post-war neurotics. The play had to be produced privately at London's Arts Theatre. On December 29, 1955, *Third Person* opened at New York City's President Theatre, featuring Louise Allbritton as Jean Moreland. Critics found it to be absorbing theatre and were generous in their recognition of Louise's quietly emotional performance and handsomely winning presence, which fully complemented Bradford Dillman's fine performance. After eighty-four performances in *Third Person,* Louise was featured in an episode in Alfred Hitchcock's video drama series. She played Renee Marlow, the object of Phyllis Thaxter's alcoholic jealousy. Meanwhile, husband Collingwood hosted such TV programs as "Adventure," "Odyssey," and "Conquest."

For the summer season of 1956, Louise traveled the citronella circuit starring in Edith Sommer's play, *A Roomful of Roses,* in which Patricia Neal had fared well on Broadway earlier in the year. Allbritton was splendidly elegant in the leading role of Nancy Fallon, and her playing was smoother than that of Miriam Hopkins who played the same role later in the year. Collingwood became president of the Broadcasting Union, New York local AFTRA, with assignments abroad; during that time, in 1958, Louise appeared on the London stage in N. C. Hunter's *A Touch of Sin.* She received critical notices as rewarding as those tossed to her co-stars, Sir Michael Redgrave and Diana Wynyard.

The Collingwoods had appeared as subjects on Edward R. Murrow's "Person to Person" TV interview show, and in 1959, Charles inherited the Murrow-moderator's job. Thereafter, Mrs. Collingwood was happy being Mrs. Collingwood. Despite the recurring presence of her nearly two dozen features on television late shows, Louise rarely recalls her film career. However, she has never forgotten going on a blind date with Carole Landis and meeting a dashing, *un*-Hollywood type, a genuine war correspondent who had landed on Utah Beach shortly after the Allied landing. This man witnessed the signing of Germany's surrender and later became CBS's Washington and then London correspondent, as well as her husband. Collingwood is also the author of *The Defector,* a novel of the Vietnam War, published in 1970.

LOUISE ALLBRITTON

Not a Ladies' Man   *(Col 1942)*
Parachute Nurse   *(Col 1942)*
Who Done It?   *(Univ 1942)*
Danger in the Pacific   *(Univ 1942)*
Pittsburgh   *(Univ 1942)*
It Comes Up Love   *(Univ 1943)*
Good Morning, Judge!   *(Univ 1943)*
Fired Wife   *(Univ 1943)*
Son of Dracula   *(Univ 1943)*
Follow the Boys   *(Univ 1944)*
Her Primitive Man   *(Univ 1944)*
Bowery to Broadway   *(Univ 1944)*

This is the Life   *(Univ 1944)*
San Diego, I Love You   *(Univ 1944)*
The Men in Her Diary   *(Univ 1945)*
That Night With You   *(Univ 1945)*
Tangier   *(Univ 1946)*
The Egg and I   *(Univ 1947)*
Sitting Pretty   *(20th 1948)*
Don't Trust Your Husband   *(UA 1948)*
Walk a Crooked Mile   *(Col 1948)*
The Doolins of Oklahoma   *(Col 1949)*
Felicia   *(Associated Producers 1964)* (Unreleased)

3

The Andrews Sisters

Sister acts were no novelty in the annals of American show business. Vaudeville's unbelievably bad Cherry Sisters collected a fine stipend for their creaking, amateurish routines. The Cherry Sisters were so uniquely offbeat that they became headliners on the two-a-day circuit in the early 1900s. In the 1920s there were the performing Duncan Sisters, Vivian and Rosetta. Radio brought recognition to the great Boswell Sisters, the King Sisters, the DeMarco Sisters, and the Lane Sisters. Later, television bolstered the vocal careers of the Lennon Sisters and Christine, Phyllis, and Dorothy McGuire. But when singing sister acts are mentioned, only one comes immediately to mind: The Andrews Sisters: LaVerne, Maxene, and Patty.

In the "halcyon" World War II years when the bands of Goodman, James, the Dorseys, Glenn Miller, Kemp, Kyser, Lombardo, et al., were the big items, and singers like the Eberles, the Helens (O'Connell and Forrest), Sinatra, Haymes, and Skinnay Ennis were on top, three sisters reigned supreme. Their domain in the swing era was quickly extended from radio, clubs, and recording sessions to the movies. It was Universal, that great provider of low budget, "hep" musicals, that contracted the popular trio and shoved them into one celluloid inanity after another. But if their silver screen outings revealed the girls to be pure camp in their naive frocks, frizzy hairstyles, and unsophisticated deportment, their movie appearances proved, then and now, that their verve and harmonics could not be beat or duplicated.

Their father, Peter, was Greek and owned a restaurant on Hennepin Avenue in Minneapolis, Minnesota. Their Norwegian mother, Ollie Sollie, gave birth to LaVerne on July 6, 1915, Maxene on January 3, 1918, and to baby Patty on February 16, 1920. The sisters entered many kiddies' contests and won first prize at Minneapolis' Orpheum Theatre on the same bill with an unknown ventriloquist named Edgar Bergen, who worked with a dummy called Charlie McCarthy. The teenage sisters were signed by Larry Rich and toured with his orchestra, playing the vaudeville circuits and living in cheap theatre hotels. After eighteen months with the Rich band they joined Joe E. Howard's vaudeville act, and they sang with Ted Mack's band. While working in Chicago in nightclubs like the High Hat, they were spotted at the Royal Frolics by Leon Belasco, who signed the blooming trio for his orchestra. With Belasco's unit they made their first recordings on March 18, 1937, as vocalists with the band, singing "There's a Lull in My Life," "Wake Up and Live," "Turn Off the Moon," and "Jammin.' "

Later, in New York, the girls accepted a radio job at fifteen dollars a week. Dave Kapp, one of the Kapp brothers of Decca Records, heard their broadcast from the Hotel Edison over a taxi radio. Another man, Lou Levy, heard the same broadcast; Levy would soon become their manager and set up a recording session with Kapp at Decca Records.

Levy taught the girls the words of an old Yiddish song, "Bei Mir Bist Du Schoen," and persuaded the

Publicity pose ca. 1944

Kapp Brothers of Decca to record it with "Joseph, Joseph" on the flip side. The 78 r.p.m. recording was never released, because the Kapps, realizing the three sisters could easily become the sensation of the recording industry, wanted their first record to be much stronger.

Lou Levy had the girls sing "Bei Mir Bist Du Schoen" to composer Sammy Cahn over the telephone; within an hour, Cahn, who was working at Warner Bros.' Brooklyn studio, wrote the English lyrics from Jacob Jacobs' original Yiddish lyrics which were set to music by Sholom Secunda. Decca decided to feature the George Gershwin song "Nice Work if You Can Get It" from the film *Damsel in Distress* (1937) as the flip side to the re-worked *"Bei Mir."* The sisters cut the record (De 1562) on November 24, 1937, for which they received a flat fifty dollars and *no* royalties. Until the record was released, the girls had performed radio spots for ten or fifteen dollars, but when "Bei Mir" was distributed, the Andrews trio became an overnight sensation with a new Decca contract paying them five cents* royalty on every re-

*In 1941, *Time* Magazine termed them "the Juke Box Divas" and noted that Decca Records paid the sisters two cents a copy for the eight million records then sold.
**The country of Argentina banned the film and the Harvard *Lampoon* called it the most frightening picture of the year.

cord sold. "Bei Mir" sold over a million copies, and Warner Bros. featured the song in the 1938 film with Priscilla Lane, *Love, Honor and Behave.*

Throughout 1938 and 1939 the Andrews Sisters turned out record after record hit for Decca, including "Hold Tight, Hold Tight," "The Beer Barrel Polka," "Well, All Right," and, inevitably, they were signed for motion pictures by Universal. Their film debut in 1940 was in a trifle, a confused picture with the Ritz Brothers, set in a convention hall, on an ocean liner, and in a spooky, haunted house. This mishmash, for reasons perhaps known best to Universal, was called *Argentine Nights.*** The girls sang "Hit the Road," "Oh, He Loves Me," and "Rhumboogie" and recorded the songs for Decca. Their recordings soared in sales and boosted the public's interest in catching the Andrews Sisters' act on film. By the close of 1940 they had made recordings of "Beat Me, Daddy, Eight to the Bar," "I'll Be with You in Apple Blossom Time," and "Mean to Me."

Universal brought them back to the screen as novelty interludes for Bud Abbott and Lou Costello's hilarious *Buck Privates* (1941), in which the sisters sang "You're a Lucky Fellow, Mr. Smith," "Bounce Me Brother, with a Solid Four," and the infectious "Boogie Woogie Bugle Boy from Company B." They also recorded all these songs for Decca. Their next

Maxene, LaVerne and Patty Andrews with Lou Costello in In the Navy *(Univ 1941)*

Ernest Truex with Maxene, Patty and LaVerne Andrews in Private Buckaroo *(Univ 1942)*

assignment from Universal was again with Abbott and Costello in a less successful comedy, *In the Navy* (1941), in which they were joined by crooner Dick Powell. But for their third profitable romp with Bud A. and Lou C., *Hold that Ghost* (1941), they belted the songs "Aurora" and "Sleepy Serenade," recording the first in March, 1941, for Decca and the latter in May.

In 1941, Maxene married the trio's manager, Lou Levy. The sisters' performance schedule was breathtaking—boxoffice-breaking appearances at New York's Paramount Theatre, personal appearances across the country, their radio show "Club Fifteen," which ran for five years, and more films for Universal.

In *Give Out, Sisters* (1942), which gave the girls running characterizations as a team out to better their careers by posing as wealthy socialites, they introduced one of their greatest hits, "The Pennsylvania Polka." In *Private Buckaroo* (1942) they harmonized to "Three Little Sisters" and to "Don't Sit under the Apple Tree with Anyone Else but Me," which become one of their most important special theme songs.

Recently, film scholars and enthusiasts have wondered what direction the Andrews Sisters' movie career would have taken if they had been under contract to MGM, Paramount, Warners, or in fact, to any studio other than Universal. The mindless, escapist films they did for Universal added relaxation to the tensions building during the war years. The stories were mere wisps of plot, designed to hold together the Andrews' forte, singing.* And one had to face it, as surely the lively sisters did, they were personalities, not actresses. Their charm was based on their snappy, ingenuous way of performing and always being one shade too brassy, but never strident. Thus, the casual song-and-dance fare of Universal proved a far better showcase for them than the more sophisticated vehicles of the other major studios.

Some of the Andrews Sisters finest songs were featured in their Universal films. In *Always a Bridesmaid* (1943) they operated a questionable "lonely hearts" club over the radio to the consternation of the DA's office and the local police; in *How's About It?* (1943) they were elevator operators singing "The Beer Barrel Polka" ("Roll out the Barrel"). For the Universal all-star *Follow the Boys* (1944) they did a bang-up rendition of "Shoo-Shoo Baby." For *Swingtime Johnny* (1944) the sisters were on a swing shift in a shell casing factory reprising "Boogie Woogie Bugle Boy"

---

*None of the Andrews Sisters read music. "We hear it in our minds," Maxene once said. "You see, musically educated vocalists sing what they read. We sing what we feel—from the heart."

In Moonlight and Cactus *(Univ 1944)*

with Mitch Ayres and His Orchestra. Their final screen effort at Universal was a bomb called *Her Lucky Night* (1945).

For Warner Bros.' *Hollywood Canteen* (1944) they sang "Gettin' Corns for My Country." In Walt Disney's full-length feature cartoon, *Make Mine Music!* (1946), made in 1944, the Andrews Sisters provided voice backing for the "A Love Story" segment, in which two hats fall in love in a department store window; they sang "Johnny Fedora and Alice Blue Bonnet." They had appeared with Bing Crosby on the radio often and, in Paramount's 1947 *The Road to Rio,* they popped out of nowhere in a shipboard scene to join Mr. C in "You Don't Have to Know the Language."

In 1948 LaVerne married Lou Rogers, and the sisters were back at Disney's Burbank studio doing the voice-overs for a segment of *Melody Time,* singing "Little Toot," which related the joy of a young tugboat rescuing a steamer during a storm and becoming a hero to his pappy-tugboat. Their mother died the same year, and shortly after her death their father passed away.

In 1950 Maxene and Lou Levy were divorced; Maxene was awarded custody of their two children, Aleda Ann and Peter. The following year Maxene underwent major surgery in Santa Monica, California,

while Patty and LaVerne filled their previously booked engagements as a duo for the first time. Maxene's ex, Lou Levy, continued as their agent. Maxene, explaining the arrangement, said: "We love our work too much to break up, and each of us has too great an investment to sacrifice it. We sisters are a corporation, with Lou and each of us owning an equal amount of stock."

Patty, who had married Martin Melcher on October 19, 1947, separated from him on August 2, 1949, and their divorce became final on March 30, 1950. When the sisters took off for a fantastically successful engagement at London's Palladium, Melcher met Doris Day. Melcher and Day were married on April 3, 1951, and on Christmas day of that year, Patty married Walter Wescheler in Beverly Hills, California. Patty quipped with reporters that she had married the sisters' pianist, "because he knows all of our arrangements by heart. This way we won't lose our library." They combined their honeymoon trip with the sisters' tour to Las Vegas.

Nineteen fifty-four was a fateful year for the Andrews Sisters. Patty decided to go solo and worked up an act with husband Wescheler. In July, she appeared at the Ramona Room at the Last Frontier in Las Vegas. LaVerne slipped in to catch her baby sister's first solo effort but did not go backstage afterward to visit. In

November, Patty took her sisters to Superior Court in Long Beach, California, demanding an equitable settlement of their mother's estate; LaVerne and Maxene ignored Patty in court. On December 21st Maxene made headlines after an apparent suicide attempt resulting from her deep depression over the break-up of the act and the incident in Superior Court. Maxene denied the headlines, as did LaVerne, who said, "She loves life too much to want to end it!"

Though the sisters appeared on television, and again in clubs and on records, the break was made permanent in 1967 with LaVerne's illness. Patty and Maxene continued to perform as a duo until May 8, 1967, when the oldest sister, LaVerne, died in Los Angeles of cancer at age fifty-four. Lou Rogers, her husband of eighteen years, was at her bedside. The following year sister Maxene retired to become dean of women at Nevada's Tahoe Paradise College, also assisting in the drama and speech department. Patty never quit, explaining: "I'll never retire. Last year I did a "Lucy" TV show and a few other dates. Show business is my life. I'll never leave it!"

In 1969 Patty appeared with a dozen other veteran performers playing themselves in a mishmash called *The Phynx,* which was released the following year by Warner Bros. In 1971, during the nostalgia craze, Patty was signed for the stage musical *Victory Canteen* with a book by TV writers Milt Larsen and Bob Lauher and music by Richard and Robert Sherman (who did the songs for Disney's film *Mary Poppins* [1964]). Patty enthused about the project: "I've never done a book show before. It's one phase of show business we promised each other we'd never do. I'm not worried about it, though. I was always the one doing the talking when the sisters worked and that was like doing a show. Musically, too, I'm right at home. This is a play about the 40s and canteen life. Well, let me tell you, we lived it." Patty was cast as Mom Davis, but the show, which opened at Hollywood's Ivar Theatre on January 27, 1971, did not work. However, late in 1973, Kenneth Waissman and Maxine Fox, who had produced *Victory Canteen,* found a new show-book by Will Holt and, recruiting the Shermans again for the score, came up with another nostalgia piece called *Over Here!* They also recalled Patty, who was joined now in the venture by Maxene. The two Andrews Sisters were back in business, starring in their first Broadway show. The diverting, vulgar *Over Here!* had an extensive shake-down on the road in Philadelphia and opened to glowing notices for the girls in New York City. Clive Barnes, of the *New York Times,* thought the best part of the evening came after the final curtain when Patty and Maxene, somewhat plumper than in their heyday, came onstage in glittering gowns and Patty casually asked the enthralled audience, "Do you want to hear some of the old ones?"

And they sang the old ones, erasing the past thirty years for many in the audience. Their recordings have sold many millions and their new venture endeared them to a new generation. (Part of the team's revival vogue was due to Bette Midler's recent mimic rendition of their "In the Mood.") *Over Here!* closed in January, 1975. An announced road tour of the musical was cancelled when the two sisters publicized their feud with the show's producer. Later the "misunderstanding" was clarified and they agreed to do the show in summer stock. Currently the two sisters, who maintain very separate offstage lives, are involved in an autobiography project covering their show business years to date.

Recently the girls were asked to explain the phenomenon of their Forties' fame. Said Patty, "We were such a part of everybody's life in the Second World War. We represented something overseas and at home—a sort of security."

THE ANDREWS SISTERS

Argentine Nights *(Univ 1940)*
Buck Privates *(Univ 1941)*
In the Navy *(Univ 1941)*
Hold That Ghost *(Univ 1941)*
Give Out, Sisters *(Univ 1942)*
Private Buckaroo *(Univ 1942)*
What's Cooking? *(Univ 1942)*
Always a Bridesmaid *(Univ 1943)*
How's About It? *(Univ 1943)*

Follow the Boys *(Univ 1944)*
Moonlight And Cactus *(Univ 1944)*
Hollywood Canteen *(WB 1944)*
Swingtime Johnny *(Univ 1944)*
Her Lucky Night *(Univ 1945)*
Make Mine Music! *(RKO 1946)* (Voices only)
The Road to Rio *(Par 1947)*
Melody Time *(RKO 1948)* (Voices only)
The Phynx *(WB 1970)* (Patty only)

4

Evelyn Ankers

When one speaks of typical 1940s Hollywood film, the frame of reference is likely to be the first half of that hectic decade when World War II was raging and the movie industry was at its most prolific and imaginative. Then, Hollywood was turning out features to amuse, divert, and inspire both the patrons on the home front and the troops in the various global theaters of battle. While the Big Four (MGM, Warner Bros., Paramount, Twentieth Century-Fox) churned out the glossiest films, it was often the lesser studios (Universal, RKO, Columbia, Monogram, PRC, Republic, United Artists) in their proletarian efforts which came closer to representing the real flavor of those complicated times.

Perhaps no second-class studio was as near to the masses as Universal, which, in a prime year, 1941, cranked out fifty-eight features, three serials, and sixty short subjects. It must be admitted that a good deal of the company's resources was used to produce films in *quantity* with appropriately enticing titles. For example, in that same year, 1941, they released *Six Lessons from Madame LaZonga* (with Lupe Velez), *Bury Me Not on the Lone Prairie* (with Johnny Mack Brown), and *Man Made Monster* (with Lon Chaney, Jr.).

For its prime vehicles, the company relied upon moneymakers Deanna Durbin, Abbott and Costello, and Olsen and Johnson, with occasional class appearances by such stars as Irene Dunne (*Unfinished Business*), Margaret Sullavan (*Back Street*), Marlene Dietrich (*The Flame of New Orleans*), and Loretta Young (*The Lady from Cheyenne*).

But to decorate the bulk of its annual product, the studio relied upon a few well-chosen players, who, through sheer dint of constant reappearance, came to be the spokesmen for Universal. If Jane Frazee (with Gloria Jean breathing down her neck) was Queen of the studio's B musicals, then Evelyn Ankers was Queen of the remaining bread-and-butter Universal pictures.

In a four-year period (1941–45), Evelyn appeared in sizeable roles in twenty-seven Universal features. This vital blonde lady may have adorned strictly meat and potatoes movies, but she was always elegant in the most flattering sense of that word. Many critics have categorized her as Hollywood's successor to Fay Wray, since Evelyn graced many of Universal's horror films (*The Ghost of Frankenstein,* 1942; *Son of Dracula,* 1943; *The Mad Ghoul,* 1943; etc.) and was the most attractive screaming heroine of the World War War II celluloid period. But she was also an accomplished comedienne, as her favorite film, *All By Myself* (1943), attests. As with most second-string leading ladies of the lesser studios, it is always interesting to imagine what she might have brought to prime vehicles at the major lots, and how it might have altered her spot in cinema history. But such thinking is dealing in fantasy. In reality, she did all right by herself and especially for a problem-plagued public.

Evelyn Ankers was born in Valparaiso, Chile, on August 17, 1918, of English parents. Her father was a

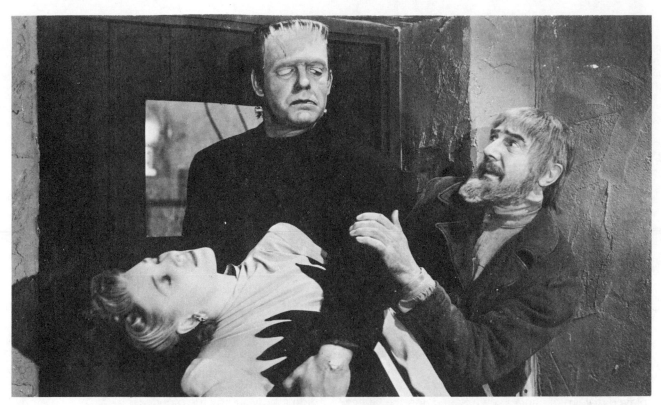

With Lon Chaney, Jr. and Bela Lugosi in The Ghost of Frankenstein *(Univ 1942)*

In The Pearl of Death *(Univ 1944)*

mining engineer, shuttling around South and Central America. In Columbia at the age of ten, Evelyn, fluent in Spanish, made her stage debut in *The Daughter of Dolores*. A few years later the family returned to England, where she attended Latymer and Godolphyn Schools to study, then teach, dancing. When she had to give up her dance career for health reasons, Evelyn concentrated on singing and acting. Commenting on her feature film debut she said: "After seeing myself in my first film, *Belles of St. Mary's*, in 1936, I decided I needed a *lot* more training and was accepted at the Royal Academy of Dramatic Art." Subsequently she played small roles in several Alexander Korda films and made a highly successful stage appearance on London's West End with Vivien Leigh in *Bats in the Belfry*.

In 1939, the globe-trotting actress accepted a promising film offer in Buenos Aires. When it did not materialize, she made good use of her time in Argentina to start "The Evelyn Ankers Hour" on radio.

She was offered the female lead in Gabriel Pascal's film production of Shaw's *Major Barbara*, and returned to England for filming. But the war had temporarily cancelled production (Deborah Kerr eventually played the role), and Evelyn sailed for the States. Armed with a letter of introduction to Broadway producer Gilbert Miller, she was given the part of the maid Lucy Gilham in the thriller, *Ladies in Retirement*. The story revolves around the murder of retired actress Leonora Fiske (Isobel Elsom), by her housekeeper (Flora Robson); Evelyn's character discovers that murderess Robson had walled up her employer in an old oven, and she let loose a scream that reverberated throughout the theatre. As might be expected, this nightly vocal exercise riveted audience attention on her performance. When the show reached Los Angeles, her interest-gathering part brought her to the attention of Universal, who soon signed her to a seven-year contract.

Her first brush with the cinematic supernatural was Universal's biggest money-maker of 1941, a picture sensitively directed by George Waggner from Curt Siodmak's taut script. The studio had assembled a brilliant cast for the film, including Claude Rains, Warren William, Ralph Bellamy, Patric Knowles, Bela Lugosi, Maria Ouspenskaya, Lon Chaney, Jr. (in the title role), and the lovely Miss Ankers. *The Wolf Man*, although dismissed as "just another monster movie" when it was first, released, has become a classic in its genre. It is still intriguing new generations with its ominous, atmospheric fog, sharp visual photography, and the sincerity of the performances by the widely diversified cast. Ankers' sensitive, wholly convincing Gwen—from her first meeting with Chaney in a won-

derfully cluttered antique shop where she sells him a walking stick with a silver werewolf's head, to the final scenes in the heavily fog-shrouded marsh, where she pierces the setting with commendable screams upon encountering werewolf Chaney—is an excellent balance for the flamboyant, snarling monster of the resident ghoul-maker, Chaney.

Recalling her experiences during the filming of *The Wolf Man*, Evelyn still cringes when she speaks of being chased by a huge male bear that had escaped from its chain. It chased her to the top of a ladder, where an electrician pulled her onto his platform, and then blinded the bear with a Kleig light while its keeper retrieved him. On the same picture, she was playing a scene in the "English" woods, where she was required to scream and faint—and actually did pass out completely from the "fog" fumes; she was almost forgotten in the special-effects haze until someone on the set asked what had happened to their heroine. In 1972, Evelyn told cinema writer Doug McClelland, one of her most ardent champions: "With all that, it was a pleasure and an honor to work with the marvelous players we had in *The Wolf Man*. Still, when that picture was over, I was always glad that the gray hairs didn't show among the blonde."

On September 6, 1942, she married Richard Denning, a Paramount contractee,* whom she had met in a bowling alley where he was leading his studio's bowling team, the Demons, to victory. They were a matched pair and easily one of the film capital's most handsome couples. Two weeks later, Denning joined the Navy submarine service as a first-class petty officer, and Evelyn continued contributing above average performances for Universal as Elsa, Dr. Frankenstein's (Sir Cedric Hardwicke) daughter in *The Ghost of Frankenstein* (1942); Kitty, a Limehouse girl in *Sherlock Holmes and the Voice of Terror* (1942); supporting Diana Barrymore as Nancy Mitchell in *Eagle Squadron* (1942); and the enduring wife of double agent Ralph Bellamy in *The Great Impersonation* (1942).

Her versatility deserved far more than the B features Universal tossed her way, but she persevered and maintained a standard of excellence in her acting. One of her showiest movie parts was Ilona, the *Weird Woman* (1944), in which she pulled out all stops when she is going insane from voodoo, registers one of her most blood-curdling screams, falls off a roof, and, for a climax, hangs herself. Her voice training showed when the year before she sang "I Dreamt

---

*Denning, who had gained recognition in Columbia's *Adam Had Four Sons* (1941), had the distinction of being replaced by Sonny Tufts in *So Proudly We Hail* (1943), when he went off to military service.

I Dwelt in Marble Halls" as Isabel Lewis, a concert singer pursued by *The Mad Ghoul* (George Zucco) and his zombie creation (David Bruce).

She would occasionally escape Universal's family of monsters with supporting roles, such as Liz Campbell, enamoured of Franchot Tone in *His Butler's Sister* (1943)—with deadpan Pat O'Brien as the hilarious butler and Deanna Durbin as his sister, the maid; as a flip WAF in *Ladies Courageous* (1944); or as Bonnie Latour dancing and singing "Just Because You Made Those Goo-Goo Eyes" in Universal's all-star mishmash *Bowery to Broadway* (1944). She was pregnant while she was making this last film, and on October 23, 1944, her daughter Diana Dee (Dee-Dee) was born.

Following his discharge from Naval service, Denning's career resumed on a satisfactory pace, but Evelyn was getting sick and tired of "the lousy parts I was getting in lousy pictures." Once she was released from her Universal pact, she played the title role in *Queen of Burlesque* (1946) at PRC; made *Black Beauty* (1946) with her husband for Fox; was romanced as Laura Reed by crooked Alaskan salmon fisherman Paul Kelly in *Spoilers of the North* (1947); sought eternal youth in *Tarzan's Magic Fountain* (1949) with Lex Barker; and finished her career in

feature films by playing the distaff part in *The Texan Meets Calamity Jane* (1950).

Evelyn made a rare return to picturemaking with Brandon Films' *No Greater Love* (1960), a Lutheran-sponsored featurette with Evelyn as a converted nurse. She made infrequent television appearances during that medium's earlier years, although she had danced on the first live TV show in 1934 in England and worked in one of the early "Mr. District Attorney" segments with John Howard during the 1940s in the States.

Richard Denning and his wife were staunch supporters of the Beverly Hills Lutheran Church, keeping apart from the Hollywood brouhaha and partygoing binges. Evelyn explained her retirement from films by saying, "I only did them [the nothing roles] in the first place because of the money and that was my downfall." Her new incentive in life was to devote herself full time to being a wife and mother.

Denning became Lucille Ball's "My Favorite Husband" on radio and then gained national recognition in the 1950s as Jerry North in the video series "Mr. and Mrs. North," with Barbara Britton (another ex-Paramount beauty) as his wife Pam. Evelyn appeared in a few of the "North" episodes, and on September 29, 1953, appeared as Lady Montagu to aid Sam Mul-

With Patric Knowles in All by Myself (*Univ 1943*)

With Anne Gwynne (seated left), Diana Barrymore, and Loretta Young in Ladies Courageous *(Univ 1944)*

ford (Cecil Kellaway) in his fight against taxation in the American colonies in *Sam and the Whale* for the "Cavalcade of America" series.

In 1958, the Dennings left for England where Richard made thirty-nine episodes of a TV series called "The Flying Doctor." After a trip around the world the family returned to their home in Corona del Mar, and Evelyn indeed retired. Before she made the Lutheran-sponsored *No Greater Love,* her last professional appearance had been on January 28, 1958, in an episode for the "Cheyenne" TV series. She played a saloon owner who enlists the help of Cheyenne (Clint Walker) to prevent her daughter—arriving from a Boston school—from discovering her unladylike occupation. It was a theme generously borrowed from *Lady for a Day* (1933).

Daughter Dee-Dee, a graduate of San Diego State College, is married, and Evelyn is living in tropical bliss. Husband Richard can be seen as the governor of Hawaii on TV's "Hawaii Five-O," a part he accept-

ed in 1968 when Lew Ayres turned it down. Denning was available in Maui and bore a striking resemblance to Governor John Burns.

The Evelyn of today has some sharp thoughts of her past: "As far as the picture business, as a whole, is concerned, both my husband and I feel it has gone completely to pot. Here [in Hawaii] we live a life more like we think God intended us to live: Quiet, clean, healthy, but most of all peaceful—away from the man-made rat race!" The once monster-menaced Evelyn, looking back on the years when she was pursued by the entire Universal horror stable except the Mummy and Dr. Hyde, says: "They were a memorable experience, profitable but strenuous, and I'm very happy they are over and behind me. It was always nerve-wracking and a tremendous effort for me." But, in fair retrospect, her cool beauty and bright talent brought a fine balance and artistry to many films that hardly deserved her presence.

EVELYN ANKERS

Belles of St. Mary's   *(MGM—British 1936)*
Land Without Music   *(Capitol—General 1936)*
Rembrandt   *(UA—British 1936)*
Fire Over England   *(UA—British 1937)*
Knight Without Armour   *(UA—British 1937)*
Over The Moon   *(UA—British 1937)*
Wings of the Morning   *(20th—British 1937)*
Claydon Treasure Mystery   *(20th—British 1938)*
Murder in the Family   *(20th—British 1938)*
The Villiers Diamond   *(20th—British 1938)*
Second Thoughts   *(20th—British 1938)*
Coming of Age   *(Col—British 1938)*
Burma Convoy   *(Univ 1941)*
Hold That Ghost   *(Univ 1941)*
Hit the Road   *(Univ 1941)*
Bachelor Daddy   *(Univ 1941)*
The Wolf Man   *(Univ 1941)*
The Ghost of Frankenstein   *(Univ 1942)*
Eagle Squadron   *(Univ 1942)*
The Great Impersonation   *(Univ 1942)*
Sherlock Holmes and the Voice of Terror   *(Univ 1942)*
North to the Klondike   *(Univ 1942)*
Pierre of the Plains   *(MGM 1942)*
Captive Wild Woman   *(Univ 1943)*
You're A Lucky Fellow, Mr. Smith   *(Univ 1943)*
Hers to Hold   *(Univ 1943)*

All by Myself   *(Univ 1943)*
His Butler's Sister   *(Univ 1943)*
Son of Dracula   *(Univ 1943)*
Keep 'Em Slugging   *(Univ 1943)*
The Mad Ghoul   *(Univ 1943)*
Ladies Courageous   *(Univ 1944)*
Jungle Woman   *(Univ 1944)*
Follow the Boys   *(Univ 1944)*
The Invisible Man's Revenge   *(Univ 1944)*
Pardon My Rhythm   *(Univ 1944)*
The Pearl of Death   *(Univ 1944)*
Bowery to Broadway   *(Univ 1944)*
Weird Woman   *(Univ 1944)*
The Fatal Witness   *(Rep 1945)*
The Frozen Ghost   *(Univ 1945)*
Black Beauty   *(20th 1946)*
The French Key   *(Rep 1946)*
Queen of Burlesque   *(PRC 1946)*
Flight to Nowhere   *(Screen Guild 1946)*
Last of the Redmen   *(Col 1947)*
The Lone Wolf in London   *(Col 1947)*
Spoilers of the North   *(Rep 1947)*
Parole, Inc   *(El 1949)*
Tarzan's Magic Fountain   *(RKO 1949)*
The Texan Meets Calamity Jane   *(Col 1950)*
No Greater Love   *(Brandon Films 1960)*

5

Jean Pierre Aumont

Over the years, Katharine Cornell and her husband Guthrie McClintic introduced several actors in their stage productions who later would become famous. One of these young players was Jean Pierre Aumont. Four days after Aumont arrived on these shores Miss Cornell signed him for the part of Marcel Dutry in her production of Henri Bernstein's *Rose Burke*. The play opened at the Curran Theatre in San Francisco on January 19, 1942. Recalling his theatre debut in America, Aumont said recently: "I could read English but spoke scarcely a word when I landed here. I didn't understand English and I had to learn the language phonetically. In the play I did with Katharine Cornell I played my whole part learning the lines phonetically. On opening night I played the part not understanding a word I was saying, and I've never gotten such good reviews since."

The assistant stage manager for *Rose Burke* was a young actor who also understudied Aumont and Philip Merivale. Fearing he would have to play the part onstage and fake a French accent, he helped Aumont with his English and saw to it that the Frenchman was always ready for a performance. His name was Gregory Peck. Aumont's stage debut led to an eight-week tour that ended in Toronto, where Miss Cornell wisely decided to close *Rose Burke*. During the show's Los Angeles engagement Jean Pierre was signed by Metro-Goldwyn-Mayer for his American film debut.

Assignment in Brittany (1943), his initial Hollywood picture, was a war story in which he portrayed the role of Captain Pierre Matard, who is masquerading as Bertrand Corlay, a pro-Nazi native of a Brittany village. Matard is seeking the location of a hidden Nazi submarine base while evading detection from Corlay's mama (Margaret Wycherly) and his fiancee (Susan Peters). Aumont was compared to a younger Jean Gabin and critics predicted he would devastate the female audience with his touseled blond hair, blue eyes, and six feet, 168 pounds of Gallic charm. His effect on the opposite sex, like the 1930s' Charles Boyer, was immediate on and off the screen.

Jean Pierre Salomon was born in Paris, France, on January 5, 1909, to Alexandre Salomon and his wife Suzanne Berr. After being dismissed from several prep schools, Jean Pierre enrolled at the Paris Conservatory of Dramatic Art at the age of sixteen, where he was sponsored by actor Louis Jouvet. It was an immense relief to Jean Pierre's father, a wealthy Paris department store executive. Six years later, in 1931, Jean Pierre made his first film, *Echec et Mat,* and within three years had made seven additional features. Then, he made a sensational stage debut on April 10, 1934, at the Comedie Champs-Elysees, Paris, as Oedipus in Jean Cocteau's *La Machine Infernale*.

From 1934 until the outbreak of World War II, Aumont divided his talent between films and stage. He appaeared in some twenty-six features, including sev-

With Billy Roy and Gene Kelly in The Cross of Lorraine *(MGM 1943)*

With Adolphe Menjou and Eduardo Ciannelli in Heartbeat *(RKO 1946)*

eral with Simone Simon: Gogol's *Taras Bulba* (1936) with Harry Baur, *Cheri-Bibi* (1937) which MGM had made in 1931 with John Gilbert, as *The Phantom of Paris* and *S.O.S. Sahara* (1938). On the French stage he was Pelleas in *Pelleas et Melisande,* and Orlando in *As You Like It,* with Annabella as Rosalind. His versatility was impressive as he proved in the French version of such American and British stage hits as *White Cargo, Romance, Design for Living,* and *Outward Bound.*

Before France capitulated to the Third Reich, Jean Pierre served with the French Third Mechanized Division from September, 1939, to July, 1940, distinguishing himself in fierce fighting at Adrennes for which he was awarded the Croix de Guerre with two Palms. At the same time he had become the leading stage and screen idol of France.

Aumont's second and best American film was taken from Hans Habe's novel about the French Resistance Movement, *A Thousand Shall Fall,* directed by the ebullient Tay Garnett and called *The Cross of Lorraine* (1944). Aumont had met the fiery and beautiful Maria Montez and, after a three-month courtship, married her on July 13, 1943. (His first marriage in France to Blanche Montel had been dissolved in 1940.) Four weeks later, Aumont left to join the Free French forces in North Africa. Especially proud of his war record for which he was awarded the Legion of Honor, he values the following letter dated December 9, 1943:

From: Charles de Gaulle:

My felicitations for showing in a beautiful film the active participation of all the French people resisting the foe under the sign of the Cross of Lorraine.

It is good that this silent and bloody war be brought under the eyes of our faithful friends of foreign lands, particularly the United States.

Will you accept, Monsieur, the expression of devoted sentiments.

C. de Gaulle

to: Monsieur Jean Pierre Aumont
    Hotel Aletti
    Alger.

Returning from the war, Aumont made an offbeat and not well received comedy for RKO with Ginger Rogers called *Heartbeat* (1946), and he and Maria Montez became the parents of a daughter, Marie-Christine. After appearing as Rimsky-Korsakoff in Universal's 1947 splashy Technicolor bid for culture, *Song of Scheherazade* ("Don't say it, sigh it" suggested the ads), he decided to make his permanent home in France. In Europe, he could return to his previous eminence in the theatre and escape the glamorous but weak parts that Hollywood offered him. In England he appeared as Prince Leopold of Saxe-Coburg in Cavalcanti's film, *The First Gentleman* (1948). Back in France he quickly regained his past popularity on the screen in *Hans Le Marin* (1948) (with Montez), and added to his professional prestige in January, 1948, by playing the part of Pierre Renault in his own play, *L'Empereur de Chine.*

After acting in his own production for five months, Aumont returned to the States to tour the summer theatre circuit as Otto in Noël Coward's comedy *Design for Living,* and in the fall in he signed with the Theatre Guild to appear in the English adaptation (by Philip Barry) of his play *L'Empereur de Chine.* The outing was retitled *Figure of a Girl.* The show was reworked on the road and moved to Broadway on February 9, 1949, at the Lyceum Theatre for thirty-one performances as *My Name Is Aquilon.* It marked Jean Pierre's and Lilli Palmer's Broadway debuts, but the thin comedy, geared to Aumont's immeasurable charm, had very little conviction.

Returning to France, he made several films including Mme. Nicole Vedres' compelling and challenging *La Vie Commence Demain* (1950), and *La Vendetta Del Corsaro* (1951), shot in Italy with Maria Montez. He also wrote another play, *L'Ile Heureuse* (1951), which had a Paris presentation. On September 5, 1951, Maria Montez died tragically, and Aumont was nearly inconsolable. He entered his daughter in the convent school of Notre Dame de Ruci-Malmaison before returning to the States for the role of Marc, the charming and promiscuous magician in MGM's delightful *Lili* (1953), and to enter the television area in "No Time for Comedy."

On Sunday, May 3, 1953, "Omnibus" presented the first George Bernard Shaw play to be televised, *Arms and the Man,* with Nanette Fabray, Kent Smith, Martita Hunt, Walter Slezak, Mischa Auer, and Aumont in the part of Bluntchli. He followed his excellent performance in the Shavian satire with an equally fine performance in the televised version of *Crime and Punishment.* Film work continued in Sacha Guitry's *Si Versailles m'Etait Conte* (a.k.a. *Royal Affairs in Versailles,* 1954) with many of France's leading stars, plus Claudette Colbert and Orson Welles, as Captain Eric Evoir; with Paulette Goddard in the low-class *Charge of the Lancers* (1954); and in Jolivet's *Dix-huit Heures D'Escale* (1954). And in the spring of 1955 he again met Grace Kelly.

The Eighth Film Festival in Cannes was made memorable by the pairing of Oscar-winner Grace Kelly and Jean Pierre Aumont, who had been selected as her "official" escort. They had met two years before in New York, and now the gossip columns were soon awash with breathless tidbits of a new romance. Under the heading, "Grace's Riviera Romance," the May 30, 1955, issue of *Life* Magazine published a series of intimate pictures, taken with a telescopic lens by a French photographer for Paris *Match;* according to *Life,* the photos were "a warmhearted record of two pleasantly happy people having an unashamedly good time." The pictures did record a good deal of hand-holding and hand-kissing in a Riviera restaurant. Encouraged by Aumont's comment that after renewing their acquaintance, he was deeply in love with Grace, reporters and photographers besieged the pair.

Ironically, it was Jean Pierre who drove Miss Kelly to visit Prince Rainier in Monaco, and he was the only one permitted by the Prince to take photographs of Grace during her afternoon in the palace that would become her future home. The coolly sedate Miss Kelly parried with reporters questioning her marriage plans with, "A girl has to be asked first." Jean Pierre, not given to such reticence, was declaring, "I adore Grace. Any man would be proud to marry her. She is a wonderful woman!" Grace's rebuttal: "There is no truth to the rumors about a romance, but there would have been two years ago."

The idyll continued from Cannes to Paris, where the future Princess of Monaco stayed at the elegant Hotel Raphael and was escorted everywhere by Aumont. In the City of Light, they were seen together at the theatre, to see the French version of *The Country Girl* and *Intermezzo.* They dined and danced together, and even in a quiet corner of the Club Regance they were pursued by the press. During the following six days, Aumont's attitude toward the press cooled noticeably, because of an accusation in print that he was using the situation for publicity. The besieged pair escaped Paris, the press, and gossip mongers for a quiet weekend at Les Rochers, Aumont's home in Malmaison, where they were surrounded by his family, Montez' sister, Lucita, and his daughter, Maria-Christine.

The affair ended when Aumont said goodbye to Miss Kelly at Orly Airport and told the press that marriage was too personal a matter to discuss publicly. But he dropped out of the cast of Jean-Louis Barrault's *Orestes* and left ahead of schedule for America.

Back in the States, he starred in Albert Husson's *Les Payes du Ciel,* which he had done on the Paris stage two years before. The English translation by Louis Kronenberger, drama critic for *Time* Magazine, was called *The Heavenly Twins,* and although Aumont played father, son, and a grandfather's clock with a

With Philip Reed in Song of Sheherazade *(Univ 1947)*

With Joan Hopkins in Affairs of a Rogue *(Col 1949)*

good deal of verve and hilarity, neither he nor his co-star Faye Emerson could make much out of the frenzied fantasy produced by the Theatre Guild.

In 1956 he appeared as Jacques De Lisle in the Twentieth Century-Fox film version of Samson Raphaelson's play *Hilda Crane.* On March 27th of that same year, at the age of forty-six, he was married by Judge Frank Kearney in Santa Barbara, California, to twenty-three-year-old Maria Luis Pierangeli, known professionally as Marisa Pavan. A month later, Grace Kelly married Rainier II, Prince of Monaco.

He did an occasional television show, such as "Climax," but his film roles became infrequent and, for the most part, were unmemorable. He was in such pallid fare as MGM's *The Seventh Sin* (1957) with Eleanor Parker; he reigned over the French court (filmed in Madrid's Palacio Real) as a much stronger King Louis XVI than that doomed monarch had actually been in *John Paul Jones* (1959); and he was wasted as Lionel Durand in *The Enemy General* (1960). He was caught between two volcanos and salvation-seeking convicts in what Hollis Alpert termed "a monumental pile of hash" in *The Devil at Four O'Clock* (1961). After little more than a walk-on in Anatole Litvak's implausible and soggy *Le Conteau dans la Plaie* in 1962, released in America as *Five Miles to Midnight* (1963), he wisely returned to the

stage. He appeared in *A Second String* on Broadway, in the title role of *The Affairs of Anatol* at the Boston Arts Festival, and returned to Paris to co-star with Melina Mercouri in *Flora* at Le Theatre des Varietes.

He came back to New York for his best American stage performance as Prince Mikhail Alexandrovich Ouratieff in the musical version of *Tovarich,* starring with Vivien Leigh (with whom he had been romantically linked following Montez' death). His performance as Mikhail was a constant delight and his singing of "I Go to Bed" proved to be the show's musical highlight. His Mikhail was awarded by the *Variety*-New York Drama Critic's Poll and remains one of his favorite parts.

While rehearsing *Tovarich,* his film *Seven Capital Sins* (1962) was released. In that picture, written and directed by Roger Vadim, he played an erring husband in the episode *Pride.*

In the summer of 1964 he toured with Eva Gabor in *Tovarich,* and the following year he made the summer theatre circuit with his wife, Marisa, in the Anita Loos stage version of *Gigi,* in which he was Gaston Lachaille. With less promising roles offered him, Aumont and Marisa devised a nightclub act which debuted at New York's Plaza Hotel's Persian Room in the summer of 1965 to glowing reviews.

The couple and their two sons made their home at

Malmaison, where Aumont had lived with Montez, courted Grace Kelly, written his memoirs (*Souvenirs Provisoires*) and five plays (including a dramatization of Irwin Shaw's novel, *Lucy Crown*), and proved that the age difference between him and Marisa really did not matter. Their theatrical activities continued on both continents; Aumont appeared as the aging, impotent Comte de Maldorais gallantly dying in defense of his castle in Sidney Pollock's *Castle Keep* (1969), a picture which Judith Crist called "a pretentious piece of pap." The film was arty and allegorically confusing, but the acting, especially Aumont's, was excellent.

In 1970 the Lincoln Center Repertory Theatre revived Tennessee Williams' quixotically allegorical play *Camino Real,* and although he was not lavishly praised for his performance, the part of Jacques Casanova remains one of Aumont's favorites. The next season he played Dag Hammarskjold in the Phoenix Theatre production of *Murderous Angels,* while continuing to make television appearances. In his early sixties, he made an indelible impression as the bittersweet homosexual movie star in Francois Truffaut's *Day for Night* (1973). Onstage, he joined with Tammy Grimes in the feckless comedy *Perfect Pitch* by Samuel Taylor, which had an unpromising tryout in Washington, D.C. in June, 1974. At least Aumont received pleasant reviews. ("Plays with charming sophistication" said *The Hollywood Reporter)*

Thereafter he joined with Lynn Redgrave in a laundered version of *The Happy Hooker* (1975), the "true" story of famous call girl Xaviera Hollander. Aumont had a cameo as a compassionate lover. Back in Europe, the seemingly inexhaustible and scarcely aging performer joined with Claude Dauphin and Fausto Tozzi in a new rendition of Dumas' *The Man in the Iron Mask* (1975) and then whisked off to Rome to make *Catherine and Cie* (1975) with Jane Birkin and Jean-Claude Brialy. As in past decades, Aumont remains the charming Continental.

JEAN PIERRE AUMONT

Echec Et Mat   *(French 1931)*
Faut-Il Les Marier   *(French 1932)*
Jean De La Lune   *(French 1932)*
Eve Cherche Un Pere   *(French 1933)*
Dans Les Rues   *(French 1933)*
La Merveilleuse Tragedie De Lourdes   *(French 1933)*
Le Voleur   *(French 1933)*
Un Jour Viendra   *(French 1933)*
Les Yeux Noirs   *(French 1935)*
Les Beaux Jours   *(French 1935)*
Lac Aux Dames   *(French 1936)*
La Porte Du Large   *(French 1936)*
Taras Bulba   *(French 1936)*
L'Equipage   *(French 1936)*
Cargiason Blanche   *(French 1937)*
Le Messager   *(French 1937)*
Cheri-Bibi   *(French 1937)*
Maria Chapdeleine   *(French 1937)*
Drole De Drama   *(French 1937)*
La Femme Du Bout Du Mone   *(French 1938)*
Le Paradis De Satan   *(French 1938)*
Hotel Du Nord   *(French 1938)*
La Belle Etoile   *(French 1938)*
S.O.S. Sahara   *(French 1938)*
Bizarre Bizarre   *(French 1939)*
Song of the Street   *(Mayer-Burstyn 1939)*
Assignment in Brittany   *(MGM 1943)*
The Cross of Lorraine   *(MGM 1944)*
Heartbeat   *(RKO 1946)*
Song of Scheherazade   *(Univ 1947)*
Siren of Atlantis   *(UA 1948)*
The First Gentleman   *(Col—British 1948)*
Hans Le Marin   *(French 1949)*
Affairs of a Rogue   *(Col 1949)*
Three Men and a Girl (a.k.a., Golden Arrow)   *(Renown 1949)*
La Vie Commence Demain   *(French 1950)*

L'Homme de Joie   *(French 1950)*
L'Amant de Paille   *(French 1950)*
La Vendetta Del Corsaro (a.k.a., The Pirates' Vengeance)   *(Italian 1951)*
Ultimo Incontro   *(Italian 1951)*
Les Loups Chassent La Nuit   *(French 1951)*
Lili   *(MGM 1953)*
Moineaux De Paris   *(French 1953)*
The Gay Adventure   *(UA 1953)*
Si Versailles M'Etait Conte (Royal Affairs in Versailles)   *(French 1954)*
Dix-Huit Heures D'Escale   *(French 1954)*
Charge of the Lancers   *(Col 1954)*
Mademoiselle de Paris   *(French 1955)*
Hilda Crane   *(20th 1956)*
The Seventh Sin   *(MGM 1957)*
John Paul Jones   *(WB 1959)*
Domenica D'Estate   *(Italian 1959)*
The Enemy General   *(Col 1960)*
The Devil at Four O'Clock   *(Col 1961)*
The Blonde of Buenos Aires   *(Argentinian 1962)*
The Horse Without a Head   *(BV 1962)*
A Summer Sunday (a.k.a. Always on Sunday)   *(Italian 1962)*
Le Conteau Dans La Plaie (a.k.a., Five Miles to Midnight)   *(French 1962)*
Les Sept Peches Capitaux (Seven Capital Sins)   *(French 1962)*
Vacanes Portugaises   *(French 1963)*
Una Deomenica D'Estate   *(Italian 1963)*
Cauldron of Blood (a.k.a., Blind Man's Bluff)   *(Spanish 1967)*
Castle Keep   *(Col 1969)*
L'Homme Au Cerveau Greffe   *(French 1972)*
La Nuit Americaine (a.k.a. Day for Night)   *French 1973)*
Porgi L'Altra Guancia (Turn the Other Cheek)   *(Italian 1974)*
The Man in the Iron Mask   *(French 1975)*
The Happy Hooker   *(Cannon 1975)*
Catherine and Cie   *(Italian 1975)*

6

Diana Barrymore

The quintessence of superstars, Joan Crawford, knows the demanding, rigorous road to stardom and, even more importantly, the precarious balance, the in-fighting, and the personal sacrifice required to remain there. Crawford started at the bottom and once she reached the heights of stardom, stayed there, in one of screenland's longest major careers.

Diana Barrymore started at the top and rapidly descended to the bottom. Was it only coincidence that her brief bid for movie fame took place at pedestrian Universal, where her once illustrious father, John Barrymore, made one of his embarrassing final films, *The Invisible Woman* (1941)?

Blanche Oelrichs Thomas preferred being known by her pen name, Michael Strange. She was a dark and beautiful, temperamental but talented woman who, on August 5, 1920—less than forty-eight hours after her divorce from Leonard Thomas became final —married her famous lover of three years, John Barrymore. On March 3, 1921, seven months after the hurried nuptials, John Barrymore's first child was born. Blanche named their daughter Joan Strange Blythe (the legal surname of the Barrymores), but, at the christening, whimsically changed it to Diana.

Diana, of course, attended the very best schools, from Brearley to Miss Hewitt's where she was considered a bad influence on her fellow pupils and was asked to leave after one term. At the Garrison-Forest

school in Baltimore, she became re-acquainted with her illustrious father, who introduced his teenage daughter to the wonders of a Brandy Alexander. A few years before, while she was attending Miss Thomas' School in Connecticut, Diana had made her stage debut at the age of fourteen, playing the third wise man in a Christmas play at the Rowayton Methodist Church. This otherwise unmemorable amateur sketch garnered some notice in the press as the debut of a "new Barrymore."

With four generations of theatre artistry supporting it, the name was magic: Barrymore! Diana soon learned the value of the trade name, and although she entered the American Academy of Dramatic Art as Diana Blythe she saw to it that all present knew she was a *Barrymore*.

On November 29, 1938, armed with a letter from David O. Selznick, she made a screen test at Paramount's old Astoria studio (with some fifty other aspirants) for the coveted role of Scarlett O'Hara in MGM's upcoming *Gone with the Wind*. Richard Carlson appeared as Ashley Wilkes in the test. The following summer she officially entered the world of theatre in Ogunquit, Maine, as the ingenue Alice Sycamore in George Kaufman and Moss Hart's *You Can't Take It with You;* she followed that by playing in *The Greeks Had a Word for It, Madame sans Gene* (with Cornelia Otis Skinner), *Springtime for Henry* (with Edward Everett Horton), and even played Juliet opposite Philip Faversham's Romeo. When the new

With Louise Allbritton and Robert Paige in a publicity pose for Fired Wife (Univ 1943)

season opened, William A. Brady signed her for the part of Ann in the touring company of *Outward Bound,* starring the legendary, if unpredictable, Laurette Taylor, as well as Florence Reed and Bramwell Fletcher. Years later, Miss Reed would observe that to know Diana's life is to weep, and that it could be summed up in two words: "Nobody cared."

Outward Bound opened its tour in the birthplace of the Barrymores, Philadelphia. Reviews of Diana's performance were fair, noting that she played her part with conviction but was hardly a seasoned Barrymore. She had youth and beauty, and the blue-blooded social register heritage of the Oelrichs to underscore her elaborate debut into society at the exclusive River House on December 3, 1938. She had all the arrogance and pride of the Barrymore clan, but very little of their talent.

Outward Bound eventually played Chicago at the Harris Theatre. Next door, was the Selwyn Theatre, where John Barrymore had opened on May 8, 1939, for a record-breaking thirty-four weeks in *My Dear Chilren,* his first stage appearance since his theatrically historic *Hamlet* had closed on April 28, 1925. John enthused over his daughter's arrival in the Windy City by telling reporters, "I worked like hell on *Hamlet* and *Richard III,* but she's the best thing I ever pro-

duced." Commenting on her performance in *Outward Bound,* critic Ashton Stevens said she did not need her birthright to stay on the stage, and her father told her, "It is right that your name is Barrymore."

For her Broadway debut, she was not asked to read for the part. Any new Barrymore could conquer. On December 2, 1940, she appeared as the young actress and mistress of Charles Dickens, Caroline Bronson, in a short-lived play *The Romantic Mr. Dickens.* Her notices were predominately good. The play closed in six days, and she signed for the part of Marianne in Zoë Atkin's *The Happy Days.* Burns Mantle (*New York Daily News*) reported that Diana "again reveals the poise and the simple, direct approach that will one day help her a lot." The comedy lasted a brief twenty-three performances. During the summer of 1941 she returned to summer stock in White Plains, New York, and while playing her Aunt Ethel's role of Mme. Trentoni in *Captain Jinks of the Horse Marines,* she received a big red apple from her father which was the traditional Barrymore family reward for a good performance. Diana now felt she had arrived and was, in truth, a full-fledged Barrymore.

On October 28, 1941, Diana opened as Linda Kincaid, the insufferable granddaughter of the ruthless founder of a vast railroad fortune, in Edna Ferber's

With Kay Francis and Andy Devine in Between Us Girls *(Univ 1942)*

With Gavin Muir and Brian Donlevy in Nightmare *(Univ 1942)*

multi-generational family saga, *The Land is Bright.* During the show's run of seventy-nine performances Louis Shurr negotiated a star film contract with Walter Wanger, which stipulated that Diana was to receive a thousand dollars weekly for a period of six months and was limited to three pictures a year. Diana was then twenty years old, and the contract was a great concession to a minor talent with a big, exploitable name.

Her first picture for Universal-based Wanger was *Eagle Squadron* (1942), in which she played an English girl, Anne Partridge. Her performance opposite Robert Stack was wooden; the uniform she wore as a member of the A.T.S. assigned to the Royal Air Force made her appear shapeless and emphasized her bow legs. While Diana was attending the preview of *Eagle Squadron* at Hollywood's Pantages Theatre on Friday night, May 29, 1942, John Barrymore died. Father and daughter had been estranged before his death but two months before they had performed a credible balcony scene from *Romeo and Juliet* on Rudy Vallee's radio program. On March 5, 1942, they had made a broadcast of a scene from *Julius Caesar,* with John as Brutus, Lionel as Caesar, and Diana as Calpurnia.

During the filming of *Eagle Squadron,* she had dis-cussed with John her mother's deep opposition to her planned marriage to Bramwell Fletcher, who was nearly twice her age. (Fletcher had been in the 1931 Warner Bros.' production of *Svengali* with John, playing Little Billie.) John, for a rare change, was in agreement with his ex-wife, Michael Strange. Fletcher was recently divorced from Helen Chandler, a shining actress who had debuted on the stage at the age of nine in *Richard III* with John Barrymore. Miss Chandler's personal life was beset with alcoholic problems.

Against all opposition, she did marry Bramwell Fletcher on July 30, 1942. The lavish wedding took place in the show-place home of Basil and Ouida Rathbone, which Diana had rented and where she and Fletcher had lived during their engagement. The marriage lasted as long as her film career, which, even then, was quickly and very noticeably declining.

Her best opportunity onscreen was in *Between Us Girls* (1942), in which she was surrounded by such pros as Kay Francis, Robert Cummings, John Boles, and Ethel Griffies. Aided by the makeup miracles of Perc Westmore, she played Queen Victoria, Sadie Thompson, and Joan of Arc, in addition to masquerading as a teenager to help her mother (Francis) land a husband (Boles). However, in this, her first juicy role, she strained for laughs, and her inexperience could not carry such a large, demanding role. Theodore Strauss, in the *New York Times* complained, "No doubt even the offspring of royal families must be allowed their little indiscretions, but why display them?"

In *Nightmare* (1942), she played Leslie Stafford, English girl who discovers her husband (Henry Daniell) knifed in the back in the opening shot; this strange, erratic film included Nazi spies in England, stocky Brian Donlevy attempting to help the country, and Diana's glaringly amateurish acting. After *Fired Wife* (1943), in which she played the role of Eve Starr, out to snare Hank Dunne (Robert Paige) from his wife Tig Callahan (Louise Allbritton), the handwriting was on the screen. Her next film appearance was a minor role as Claire, the owner of a gambling house in a western, *Frontier Badman* (1943). Then, the disgruntled studio asked her to play another minor role, this time in a Sherlock Holmes film, or, as an alternative, to stooge for Abbott and Costello in one of their slapstick comedies. She refused, claiming she would not sell the Barrymore name so cheaply (even though her offscreen performances were pulling the once proud family name through a good deal of mire). After six months of suspension (she was then receiving fifteen hundred dollars weekly) she returned to the studio at the promise of an important role in *Ladies Courageous* (1944), but the part went to sterling Geraldine Fitzgerald, and Diana was cast as Nadine Shannon, the bitchy heavy. The gooey heroine of this patriotic offering was none other than queenly Loretta Young.

Diana's brief screen career ended effectively with this film, and in December, 1943, she and Bramwell Fletcher returned to New York and signed for the leads in a touring company of *Rebecca*. She did return to Hollywood, but this time with a thousand-dollar-a-week contract to appear on the Jack Carson NBC radio comedy show. Her flamboyant after hours debauches and increasingly promiscuous love affairs, however, took their professional and personal toll. Her marriage to Fletcher ended after she drunkenly confessed her string of amours and made a halfhearted suicide attempt. A few hours after her divorce was final, she flew to Boston to meet John R. Howard, the professional tennis player. They were wed on January 17, 1947, but the stormy marriage was soon on the rocks, culminating in a drunken melee that ended in a Louisville, Kentucky jail and blaring headlines. By June, Diana was appearing in summer stock as Joan of Lorraine, hardly an appropriate vehicle for one so prone to escapades. It would take Diana three years to rid herself of Mr. Howard, who was later convicted on a charge of violating the Mann Act and participating in white slavery.

Her leading man in *Joan of Lorraine* was Robert Wilcox, recently released from an alcoholism clinic. Wilcox, after a few dozen B pictures in Hollywood and a two-year marriage to Florence Rice, had returned to the stage and the bottle. For three years, Diana and Wilcox lived together, appeared on the stage in assorted touring companies, and drank heavily together. On October 17, 1950, they were married by a justice of the peace in Newark, New Jersey. Earlier in the year, Diana, who had aged beyond her years, arrived drunk for the CBS premiere of "The Diana Barrymore Show." The late evening talk show's first guest were to have been Nina Foch and Earl Wilson, and the program could have established Diana as a TV personality. The following week, the show was revamped to star Faye Emerson, who made it, her plunging V neckline, and herself, a smashing video success.

More touring shows—on a lower echelon—with Wilcox followed, plus a season in vaudeville that included playing the venerable Palace, where her Aunt Ethel had once enthralled audiences in Sir James Barrie's *Twelve Pound Look*. Diana was a good mimic and did impressions of many famous people, including her aunt. Marion Spitzer, author of *The Palace*, calls Diana "the doomed bearer of a great name." In 1955, when author Gerold Frank first approached Diana to solicit her life story, he was so appalled by the miserably impoverished, wretched surroundings in which he found her, he could not believe the drunken woman before him was the love child of Michael Strange and the great and handsome John Barrymore.

Both Diana and Wilcox unsuccessfully tried Alcoholics Anonymous, and went on tour in a dismal, cheap farce, *Pajama Tops*, in which she screamed, overacted, and was more often than not drunk onstage. The marriage continued as a living nightmare and Diana's profligacy increased. Wilcox died on June 11, 1955, on a train en route to his home in Rochester, New York, and early the following year Diana entered a Westchester county sanitorium for alcoholism. Later that year, she appeared at the Provincetown Playhouse in New York City for thirty dollars a week in *The Ivory Branch*. She rehearsed and played the show cold sober.

To publicize her book (with Gerold Frank), *Too Much, Too Soon*, she appeared on Arlene Francis' "Home" show on April 15, 1957. She wore a black dress in an attempt to disguise her overweight figure, but she looked matronly, dissipated, and old beyond her thirty-six years. There was a flurry of renewed interest in Diana following the publication of the book (later made into a movie by Warner Bros. with Dorothy Malone playing Diana and Errol Flynn rather touching in his role as John Barrymore), and she signed for a revival of *A Streetcar Named Desire*. As the tragic Blanche DuBois she was more than credible, and she appeared in subsequent revivals as other Williams heroines—as Maggie in *Cat on a Hot Tin Roof* and as Catherine Holly in *Garden District*. She developed an unrequited love for the plays' author, Tennessee Williams, whom she called "that damned monkey on my back." Above all, she stayed sober.

For Christmas, 1959, Williams gave Diana a large bottle of champagne. She lived with the hope that he would write a great play and a great part for her which would establish her as one of the "great" Barrymores, but the dream never materialized. On January 25, 1960, a maid found her dead in bed in her second floor rear apartment at 33 East 61st Street in New York City. Three telltale empty bottles on the floor beside her bed, combined with sleeping pills, produced, according to the coroner, heart failure—a climax to a life of failure—a life that was either too little, too late, or, more likely, too much and too soon.

DIANA BARRYMORE

Eagle Squadron   *(Univ 1942)*
Between Us Girls   *(Univ 1942)*
Nightmare   *(Univ 1942)*

Fired Wife   *(Univ 1943)*
Frontier Badmen   *(Univ 1943)*
Ladies Courageous   *(Univ 1944)*

7

William Bendix

Like Barry Fitzgerald, Cass Daley, and Billy De Wolfe, who contributed to the pleasure of 1940s moviegoers through a contractual stay at Paramount, burly William Bendix was never a cinema star in the accepted sense of the term, but neither was he merely a featured player. His soulful, often inarticulate screen characters continually blossomed forth in new celluloid guises to provide ample justification for someone else's starring vehicle to exist. He had an amiable knack for making his star co-players shine onscreen, yet always making his own unique presence felt. On occasion he broke out of his movie mold as second banana by starring in a stark drama (*The Hairy Ape,* 1943), or in an unpretentious comedy (*Don Juan Quilligan,* 1945), amply demonstrating on each outing that his acting talents were far more versatile and subtle than casting agents or even he cared to admit.

He has been described as Brooklyn's reincarnation of the Neanderthal man—built like a barrel with a face resembling several uncharted miles of bad roads held up by a concrete, lantern jaw under a bulbous nose rivalling Jimmy Durante's famous appendage.

Although touted as the pride of Flatbush Avenue, William Bendix was actually born in a flat on Third Avenue at Forty-fifth Street in Manhattan on January 14, 1906. His father, Max, was a violinist and sometime conductor for the Metropolitan Opera Orches-

tra. At the age of five, Bendix appeared in a film made at Vitagraph's Brooklyn studio. Later he became a bat boy for the New York Giants, running errands for the great Babe Ruth, and he even played semi-professional baseball. After his marriage in 1927 to his childhood sweetheart, Therese Stefanotti, he managed a grocery store in Orange, New Jersey, until the depths of the Depression closed that enterprise and, with astonishing fortitude, he turned to acting.

When he had been sixteen, Bendix had made a half-hearted attempt at acting with the Henry Street Settlement House Players. In 1936 he joined the New Jersey Federal Theatre at $17.50 per week, first appearing as Shad Ledue, a neo-storm trooper in *It can't Happen Here,* and then in minor roles in *The Emperor's New Clothes, Created Equal,* and *Laugh that Off.* Bendix made his Broadway debut at the Maxine Elliott Theatre on August 9, 1937, as George B. Shaw in *The Trial of Dr. Beck.* After portraying cab drivers in a series of six flops that included *Run, Sheep, Run* (1938) and *Miss Swan Expects* (1939), he was jokingly dubbed "the taxicab driver of Show Biz."

His excellent performance as Krupp, a waterfront cop, in the Theatre Guild's two-year run of William Saroyan's Pulitzer Prize play, *The Time of Your Life* (1939), brought recognition. After a season of summer stock, in which he was Mickey in *Golden Boy,* detective Mullins in *Mr. and Mrs. North,* and Mr. Kimber in *George Washington Slept Here,* he accepted an offer to make pictures in Hollywood. He signed

With Joe Sawyer and Jack Norton in Taxi, Mister *(UA 1943)*

With Stanley Clements and Allen Martin, Jr. in Johnny Holiday *(UA 1949)*

with fun factory entrepreneur Hal Roach for three hundred dollars a week plus a percentage of the gross over six hundred dollars, but his film career took him to almost every other major studio. For Roach he made a couple of shorts plus two features, *The Brooklyn Orchid* (1942) and *Taxi, Mister* (1943). The latter film again cast him as a cabbie, Tim McGuerin, hopelessly in love with Sadie, an ex-burlesque queen.

In *Woman of the Year* (1942), the first (and definitely the best) of the nine films combining the inestimable talents of Katharine Hepburn and Spencer Tracy, Bendix was a standout in his first major film in the relatively small role of "Pinkie" Peters, a bartender. As Private Aloysius "Smacksie" Randall, a tough marine, in Paramount's *Wake Island* (1942), the first of many serious combat films done in semidocumentary style, Bendix was directed by John Farrow. He played the part very effectively; tossing his lines out with fine comic scorn. When his foxhole partner, Robert Preston, complains of the distinct possibility of being blown to bits by the Japanese, Bendix carps, "What d'ya care? It ain't your island, is it?" His performance was nominated for an Oscar for Best Supporting Actor, but the Award went to Van Heflin for his part in *Johnny Eager.*

Although not as effective as its original 1935 version, the Paramount remake of Dashiell Hammett's *The Glass Key* (1942), featured a cast that included Brian Donlevy, Alan Ladd, Veronica Lake, and Bendix. As Jeff, he gave a superb performance as the hired, psychopathic mauler. Four years later, as "White Suit" in Twentieth Century-Fox's *The Dark Corner,* he would convincingly play a similar, if more vicious, killer. After *The Glass Key,* Paramount signed him to a non-exclusive contract that allowed him to work for other studios.

Often, his performances as a heavy were more memorable than his standard dumb-guy-with-the-heart-of-gold roles. He was Brannigan, a dim-witted cop in Bud Abbott and Lou Costello's *Who Done It?* (1942); Alan Ladd's buddy, Johnny Sparrow, in *China* (1943); and he did an exceptionally good job as Janoshik, a deeply political Czech Underground leader masquerading as a stupid washroom attendant, in Paramount's version of Stefan Heym's novel *Hostages* (1943). This was the picture that was heralded as Luise Rainer's triumphant return to the screen. It did not live up to its initial expectations.

After his first feature for Twentieth Century-Fox, in which he sprouted Brooklynese homilies as Taxi Potts in one of the best war films of that era—Richard Tregaskis' *Guadalcanal Diary* (1943)—he appeared on the March 29, 1943 broadcast of "DuPont's Cavalcade of America" in "The P-T Cook Writes Home."

Bendix's sincerity as Gus Smith, the seaman who has his leg amputated in Alfred Hitchcock's powerful *Lifeboat* (1944), was considered by many filmgoers as a more finely etched performance than that offered by fellow players Tallulah Bankhead and Walter Slezak.

Bendix's greatest oncamera challenge came with the starring role in Eugene O'Neill's *The Hairy Ape* (1944). The film version, directed by Alfred Santell, lost a good deal of the play's power, but gained most of its strength from Bendix's performance as the steamship stoker Hank who, slighted by a snobbish rich girl (Susan Hayward), obsessively seeks revenge by trying to find "someplace in the world where I belong." The film also gained for him his best movie reviews. The O'Neill tragedy was followed by William's appearance in drag with Dennis O'Keefe in the screwball comedy *Abroad with Two Yanks* (1944), and his supporting roles, first with Brazil's fruit-conscious bombshell Carmen Miranda in *Greenwich Village* (1944), then with Fred Allen in the rowdy comedy *It's in the Bag* (1945). And he was, of course, *Don Juan Quilligan,* running a barge between Brooklyn and Buffalo with a wife in each port.

In the midst of this steady film activity, Bendix became radio's Chester A. Riley in 1944. Five years later, Universal put *The Life of Riley* (1949) on the screen with Bendix and Rosemary De Camp as his wife Peg. Miss De Camp continued as Riley's patient wife when Jackie Gleason starred as Chester A. in the teleseries that won an Emmy in 1949.

William's film assignments continued. In *Two Years Before the Mast* (1946), he was first mate Amazeen who signed Richard Henry Dana (Brian Donlevy) aboard the Pilgrim, cracked the whip over the crew, and gave Alan Ladd thirty lashes for insubordination, before he was shot by the captain (Howard da Silva) while swimming to join the mutinied crew. In *A Bell for Adano* (1945), Bendix was the cynical Sergeant Borth. Also for Twentieth Century-Fox, he gave a credible appearance in the generally soggy *Sentimental Journey* (1946), and in *The Blue Dahlia* (1946), was again Alan Ladd's buddy, this time as Buzz Wanchek. For Universal, he offered a couple of staunch support roles in *White Tie and Tails* (1946), and as Deanna Durbin's guardian in *I'll Be Yours* (1947). Later in 1947, he appeared as himself in *Variety Girl,* as the perplexed cop Victor O'Brien in Bob Hope's *Where There's Life,* and as a more dignified law enforcer, Lieutenant Damico, with horn-rimmed glasses, in *The Web.*

Although movies about baseball background invariably had failed at the boxoffice, Bendix was full of joy and anticipation for his role as his childhood idol

Advertisement for The Hairy Ape *(UA 1944)*

for whom he had once run errands, the great slugger, Babe Ruth. But *The Babe Ruth Story* (1949) was a resounding flop, and Bendix later declared, "I was thrilled that I was asked to play the lead, as I knew the Babe real well. But it was a terrible movie. I was so sick about it that I went to the hospital with ulcers!"

In RKO's *Race Street* (1948), George Raft is killed on the hilly streets of San Francisco, as he protects Bendix, who plays a police lieutenant, Barney Runsom. Bendix was excellent but the picture was not. In 1948, he was back in *The Time of Your Life,* starring James Cagney, not in his original stage role of policeman Krupp, but as Nick, the gentle bartender and owner of Nick's Pacific's Street Saloon, Restaurant, and Entertainment Palace. (He had played Nick in the road company version of the show.)

One of Bendix's best roles was Army Captain Blake in RKO's fast-paced, if confused, thriller *The Big Steal* (1949). In this film, he hid his villainy under the guise

of being the good guy, while competing with Robert Mitchum in killing Patric Knowles and acquiring a fat Army payroll. He was William Holden's sidekick Wahoo (Reuben) Jones in his first Western, *Streets of Laredo* (1949). Then, complete with armor and a long wig with bangs, William portrayed the very amusing Sir Sagramore in Bing Crosby's *A Connecticut Yankee in King Arthur's Court* (1949).

After several minor roles in B pictures, his performance as Joe Farrow in RKO's *Gambling House* (1950) won critical applause and so impressed iconoclastic Howard Hughes (then head of the studio) that he signed Bendix to a seven-year contract with full rights to work in television. William appeared in supporting roles in four films for RKO before Hughes left the studio. Meanwhile, William returned to Paramount as Petty Officer Boyer in *Submarine Command* (1951), and as Detective Lou Brody, a sympathetic cop in William Wyler's *Detective Story* (1951).

Bill Bendix's greatest show business success came when he succeeded Jackie Gleason in the television show "The Life of Riley," which debuted January 2, 1953, on NBC and continued for 217 segments over eight seasons. As the affable, not-too-bright Chester A. Riley, he coped with a series of instant crises (often of his own creation) that resulted from the foibles of everyday life and almost always climaxed with a "revoltin' development." Produced and directed by Irving Brecker, with ex-Paramounter Marjorie Reynolds as Bendix's onscreen wife Peg, the show was even more successful on television than it had been during its seven years on radio. With his television series, Bendix gained more national recognition than he had received from any of his many films. With a weekly salary plus ten percent of the gross for the "Riley" series, he also gained financial independence. The "Riley" video show was filmed on Stage Five of the Hal Roach, Jr. studio, where years before Bendix had started his film career making a few shorts for Roach Sr., such as *The McGuerins of Brooklyn* with Max Baer.

Bill said of "Riley," "I like to think of Riley as friendly and human, over-anxious to please, unwitting perhaps, bumbling and bungling, inclined to go to extremes and often misguided—but not stupid." Wise or stupid, it is as Chester A. Riley that Bill Bendix is fondly remembered by his fans.

As his film career dwindled to one unimportant picture a year, his television career gained prominence. In a touching love story, "Kyria Katina," he underplayed and interpreted with surprising tenderness the role of an Irish-American motor vehicle inspector in love with a Greek widow. As Carol Ledbetter in a "Ford Theatre's" installment, *Segment,* he was excellent as a husband driven to a near-breaking point by his nagging wife Mildred (Rosemary De Camp). For a "Schlitz Playhouse" episode called *Ivy League,* he was Bill, a tough ex-marine enrolled as a college freshman; and in *A Quiet Game of Cards* he played dangerously high stakes in a poker game for "Playhouse 90," with such acting pros as Barry Sullivan, Gary Merrill, Franchot Tone, and E. G. Marshall. His television acting was nearly always credible. He also did guest spots on several shows, and was the surprised star of Ralph Edwards' "This Is Your Life."

He joined Alan Ladd for the last time in *The Deep Six* (1958), made some films in England (the best of which was Robert Siodmak's *The Rough and the Smooth,* (1959), and, completely changing his professional pace, entered the nightclub scene with Rose Marie and Harold Lloyd, Jr. in a comedy, dancing, and juggling act in Las Vegas. His television appearances continued on most of the major drama shows,

and, in 1960, he signed for another video series. The short-lived (seventeen segments) "Overland Trail," starring Doug McClure, features Bill Bendix as a stagecoach driver.

The musical version of Eugene O'Neill's *Ah, Wilderness,* produced by David Merrick, opened in Boston on September 9, 1959, as *Take Me Along.* With the all-star cast of Jackie Gleason, Walter Pidgeon, Eileen Herlie, Robert Morse, and Una Merkel, the play moved to Broadway and was a rousing success. A year later, restless Gleason left the show, and on October 24, 1960, William Bendix stepped into the role of Sid Davis, professionally replacing Gleason for the second time. He performed a commendable soft shoe dance with Walter Pidgeon and delighted audiences with his singing of "Little Green Snake," a lyric measuring the evils of drink for his none-too-sober nephew. When *Take Me Along* closed on Broadway, Bendix headed another company in 1961 at the Meadowbrook Dinner Theatre in New Jersey. The following year he signed for the lead in Ira Levin's play *General Seeger,* directed by George C. Scott and co-starring one-time Hollywood star Ann Harding. Bill left the faltering show during the Detroit tryout and was replaced by Scott. *General Seeger* lasted for two performances on Broadway.

Bendix was back tending bar in MGM's rib-tickling comedy *Boys' Night Out* (1962), and in 1963 played in another MGM film, *The Young and the Brave.* Then, for Universal, he appeared with Kirk Douglas in *For Love or Money* (1963) as another good-natured detective. During the 1962 summer season he had toured the summer circuit in *The Gazebo.* The following year he traveled as the star (along with former screen beauty Nancy Carroll and television's Will Hutchins) in Sumner Arthur Long's prefabricated comedy *Never Too Late,* playing the part of Harry Lambert, the middle-aged unexpected and highly embarrassed father-to-be. In the summer of 1964 he had a brief tour in the play *Take Her, She's Mine,* and that autumn he signed for a proposed television series called "Bill and Martha" (Martha Raye). When CBS cancelled the "Bill and Martha" series, Bendix sued the network and its president, James T. Aubrey, for $2,658,000, maintaining he was capable of completing his contract and was not, as the network publicly insisted, in poor health. The suit was settled out of court for an undisclosed amount, seemingly to Bendix's satisfaction.

William's last two films were Paramount's *The Law of the Lawless* (1965), in which he played a sheriff, and *Young Fury* (1965) another low-budget Western, in which he was a blacksmith.

On December 8, 1964, he was taken to the hospital, and, on December 14th, after a week of battling lobar pneumonia, he died. His wife of thirty-seven years and his daughters Lorraine and Stephanie buried him on the grounds of the San Fernando Mission.

Chester A. Riley would have called Bendix's death at the age of fifty-eight a "revoltin' development," and undoubtedly would have disagreed with Therese Bendix's summation of the character and the man who played him. Therese had once observed: "Chester Riley and Bill Bendix are alike in a lot of ways. Bill's bluff manner doesn't let outsiders know what he's like at all. He has the kindness and desire to help others that Riley is noted for. Sometimes when I watch a Riley show I say to myself, 'You'd think the writers lived with us.'"

WILLIAM BENDIX

The Brooklyn Orchid   *(UA 1942)*
Woman of the Year   *(MGM 1942)*
Wake Island   *(Par 1942)*
The Glass Key   *(Par 1942)*
Star Spangled Rhythm   *(Par 1942)*
Who Done It?   *(Univ 1942)*
China   *(Par 1943)*
Hostages   *(Par 1943)*
The Crystal Ball   *(UA 1943)*
Taxi, Mister   *(UA 1943)*
Guadalcanal Diary   *(20th 1943)*
Lifeboat   *(20th 1944)*
The Hairy Ape   *(UA 1944)*
Abroad with Two Yanks   *(UA 1944)*
Greenwich Village   *(20th 1944)*
Don Juan Quilligan   *(20th 1945)*
It's in the Bag   *(UA 1945)*
A Bell for Adano   *(20th 1945)*
Two Years Before the Mast   *(Par 1946)*
Sentimental Journey   *(20th 1946)*
The Blue Dahlia   *(Par 1946)*
The Dark Corner   *(Par 1946)*
White Tie and Tails   *(Univ 1946)*
I'll Be Yours   *(Univ 1947)*
Blaze of Noon   *(Par 1947)*
Calcutta   *(Par 1947)*
Where There's Life   *(Par 1947)*
Variety Girl   *(Par 1947)*
The Web   *(Univ 1947)*
The Babe Ruth Story   *(AA 1948)*

The Time of your Life   *(UA 1948)*
Race Street   *(RKO 1948)*
Johnny Holiday   *(UA 1949)*
Cover Up   *(UA 1949)*
The Life of Riley   *(Univ 1949)*
The Big Steal   *(RKO 1949)*
The Streets of Laredo   *(Par 1949)*
A Connecticut Yankee in King Arthur's Court   *(Par 1949)*
Kill the Umpire!   *(Col 1950)*
Gambling House   *(RKO 1950)*
Submarine Command   *(Par 1951)*
Detective Story   *(Par 1951)*
Blackbeard the Pirate   *(RKO 1952)*
Macao   *(RKO 1952)*
A Girl in Every Port   *(RKO 1952)*
Dangerous Mission   *(RKO 1954)*
Crashout   *(Filmakers 1955)*
Battle Stations   *(Col 1956)*
The Deep Six   *(WB 1958)*
Idol on Parade   *(Col 1959)*
The Rough and the Smooth (a.k.a., Portrait of a Sinner)   *(Renown 1959)*
Boys Night Out   *(MGM 1962)*
The Young and the Brave   *(MGM 1963)*
For Love or Money   *(Univ 1963)*
The Phony American   *(German 1964)*
Johnny Nobody   *(Medallion 1965)*
Law of the Lawless   *(Par 1965)*
Young Fury   *(Par 1965)*

Turhan Bey

While most of the world was dealing with the chaos and grimness of World War II, Hollywood engaged in its own battle to create elaborate exotica to distract the weary world. What other era could have given the movie-going public such stars as Maria Montez, Acquanetta, Vera Hruba Ralston, or Turhan Bey? He was a perfect romantic concoction, tailor-made for the needs of 1940s' escapist fare with his scrutable charm that was one-third Charles Boyer and two-thirds Jon Hall.

In 1529 and 1683 the Turks had besieged Vienna; by the twentieth century, however, they were no longer forcing entry to the city on the Danube, but were established diplomatically in the Turkish Embassy within the inner city of Wien. To a member of that Embassy and his lovely Czechoslovakian wife, who had been raised in Vienna, a son was born on March 30, 1920. Turhan Gilbert Selahettin Schultavey probably would have followed his father's Moslem religion but for the elder Schultavey's possible disillusion when his prayers to Allah—who, it was taught, would restore an earnest worshipper's broken body to wholeness—did not work for him. Turhan's father had lost his right arm in World War I, and, perhaps reflecting on the absence of restorative miracles, he abandoned services at the mosque and never insisted that his son follow the teachings of Islam.

Turhan's early fascination with photography won him a place with an archaelogical expedition to Tibet, an enterprise he later believed to have been motivated more by a German interest in the geopolitics of the more remote sections of Asia, than by an interest in the region's archaeology. After Hitler's Austrian Anschluss, Turhan, with his mother and grandmother, migrated to America, settling in Los Angeles. (Turhan's parents had separated.) The young Turkish-Austrian entered former actor Ben Bard's School of Dramatic Art, to improve his command of the English language. Accidentally, he found himself involved with acting at Bard's school and on discovering great joy in acting, he enrolled at the Pasadena Playhouse. He was found there by a Warner Bros. talent scout, given a screen test and the role of Ahmed in Errol Flynn's *Footsteps in the Dark* (1941). His name was deemed professionally unsuitable, and Hollywood's expertise in renaming such people as Archie Leach, Marion Morrison, Lucille Langehanke and Lucille Le Sueur (Cary Grant, John Wayne, Mary Astor and Joan Crawford) was once again enlisted—this time the result was Bey.

Bey, complete with turban, was properly menacing in Warners' *Shadows on the Stairs* (1941). After playing another exotic role, Retana, in RKO's first Falcon epic, *The Gay Falcon* (1941), he returned to Universal, which was now his home studio, for its serial, *Junior G-Men of the Air* (1942). As Axis agent Araka,

With Susanna Foster in Bowery to Broadway *(Univ 1944)*

With Virginia Mayo and George Brent in Out of the Blue *(EL 1947)*

pursued by Huntz Hall and Billy Halop, he appeared in thirteen episodes.* He was a mysterious Chundra in *Bombay Clipper* (1942), and Juma in *Drums of the Congo* (1942), a low-grade B movie that combined spies, savages, and two bombs (one was the script). His mystical appearance and well-modulated voice made him a natural for an annual outing in Universal's Maria Montez-Sabu-Jon Hall Technicolor fairy tales, beginning with 1942's *Arabian Nights* in the small role of the captain. His other roles in the genre included Tamara in *White Savage* (1943), Jamiel, a faithful slave, oozing a good deal of sex and laughter, in *Ali Baba and the Forty Thieves* (1944), and a dash-

ing bandit chief, Herua, wooing Queen Naila (Montez) in *Sudan* (1945). These annual color-splashed fantasies at Universal were impossibly fanciful in script, outrageous in acting, but highly profitable in distribution.

The initial success of Universal's 1932 horror film *The Mummy* led to the studio's resurrection of the property with *The Mummy's Hand* (1940). In the 1942 movie, *The Mummy's Tombs* George Zucco, the expiring ancient High Priest, turned over his struggles with the Mummy Kharis (Lon Chaney, Jr.) to Turhan, who played a younger High Priest of Karnak, Mehemet Bey. Within the sixty-one-minute story Turhan is killed by Chaney over the love for a lovely Egyptian girl who, alas, disintegrates before the audience's eyes as horribly as Margo went to dust in *Lost Horizon* (1937). In 1943's Universal serial, *Adven-*

*During the summer of 1941, among other screen ventures, he appeared as Hassen with Richard Arlen and Andy Devine in a tinny Western-gone-Arabian called *Raiders of the Desert*.

With Evelyn Ankers, Keye Luke, and C. Montague Shaw in Burma Convoy *(Univ 1941)*

60

With Alan Curtis, Samuel S. Hinds (rear), Thomas Gomez, Ethan Laidlaw (at desk), Susanna Foster, Chuck Hamilton, Andy Devine, and Eddie Polo (under light) in Frisco Sal *(Univ 1945)*

tures of Smilin' Jack, which boasted a cast that included Tom Brown, Rose Hobart, Sidney Toler, and Keye Luke, Turhan was another Axis plotter, Kageyama. As Eric Iverson, he was Evelyn Ankers' accompanist on a concert tour, pursued by George Zucco as *The Mad Ghoul* (1943). Warners gave Bey a sympathetic part of a modern Turk aiding George Raft in *Background to Danger* (1943), Eric Ambler's tale of intrigue in wartime Turkey, which was immeasurably helped by the film industry's first "odd couple," Sydney Greenstreet and Peter Lorre. For Universal's star-strewn *Follow the Boys* (1944), Bey was one of several members of the Hollywood Victory Committee; and as music student Franz he was kept busy trying to release Susanna Foster from the hypnotic powers of evil Dr. Hohner (Boris Karloff in his first Technicolor picture). This latter film, *The Climax* (1944), was based on Edward Locke's melodrama and permitted Universal to reuse the finely designed sets from their *The Phantom of the Opera.*

Universal loaned Bey to MGM for the important role of Lao Er, Katharine Hepburn's bewildered Chinese peasant husband in the superfilm version of Pearl Buck's *Dragon Seed* (1944). *Dragon Seed* was certainly the pinnacle of Bey's Hollywood career and should have assured him better roles from his home studio, Universal. However, that studio shuttled him into their impoverished cavalcade of show business, *Bowery to Broadway* (1944), as Ted Barrie, singing away with C. Lee Sweetland's dubbed-in voice. Indeed, had Bey been at almost any other studio in Hollywood, his charm, liquid speaking voice, and more than passable acting would have garnered him far better parts. Handled properly and given proper development by a major studio he conceivably could have equated the success of silent screen star Sessue Hayakawa.

As if hoping to awaken Universal to the untapped continental sex-appeal talent in their back yard, critics, upon the release of *Dragon Seed,* stated that Bey was deserving of a far better movie fate than Universal was providing. Bey, commenting on his good notices in the Pearl Buck film, said, "I'm an ersatz lover. If Clark Gable, James Stewart, and the rest of the big lovers of the screen hadn't gone into the War, I would still be playing some despicable villain in B pictures." His candor did not impel Universal to give him anything other than trite parts such as Dude, a San Francisco cafe owner of the gay nineties, in *Frisco Sal* (1945), where his presence and charisma saved the Susanna Foster film from oblivion. Offscreen he received more publicity than for any of his onscreen emoting. He met Lana Turner.

Hollywood's mother superior, Louella O. Parsons—to whom everyone in the industry seemingly and strangely "confided"—was glowingly playing her favorite role of cupid-in-print in 1945 when Lana told her, "My romance with Turhan is the most beautiful thing in my life." The moody and temperamental Turhan and ever-between-marriages Lana had met at a party at the home of Bey's good friend Maria Montez, and for over a year romance flourished, to the point of making plans for an August, 1946, wedding. At a swank party at Ann Rutherford's home, Steve Crane, from whom Lana was awaiting a final divorce decree, started fighting with Bey, apparently for romancing his ex-wife. Crane came out of the battle sporting one black eye, and the Turkish Romeo's face was badly scratched. Two weeks later, Turhan ended a telephone conversation with Lana, "I'll talk to you tomorrow." He never called back. Louella, suddenly the outraged matchmaker, was pompously taking Turhan to task in print for deserting Lana, shedding glycerin tears in the press while Lana was busy dating Robert Hutton, Rory Calhoun, and Peter Shaw. Mutual friends claimed religious differences split Bey and Turner.

Turhan's last Universal assignment was *A Night in Paradise* (1946) as Aesop of fable fame, with the still beautiful Merle Oberon as Princess Delerai. However, the film was more paradise lost than found.

In 1947, he met Linda Christian, but the Acapulco-based romance was brief and, instead, became a long and lasting friendship, especially after Tyrone Power deserted the ubiquitous Lana Turner for wedlock with Linda. Onscreen, Turhan was heavily romantic as Greenwich Village artist David in Eagle-Lion's farce *Out of the Blue* (1947). For his role of a phoney mystic in Eagle-Lion's *The Amazing Mr. X* (1948), Turhan became adept at minor magic tricks after training in feats of illusion with magician Harry Mendoza. After the same company's tepid and overly stiff *Adventures of Casanova* (1948) with Lucille Bremer, in which he was Lorenzo, Casanova's (Arturo de Cordova) reckless aide, he joined the Army as a private at Camp Roberts. In the service, he won the respect of his associates by performing the most menial jobs and remaining a typical G.I. without expecting any special star-status treatment.

When he returned to Hollywood there had been a volcanic change in the industry that had started in 1947 with televised sports. The desertion of movie houses for entertainment in the living room had seriously crippled the one-time world capital of films. The generally mindless, escapist movies which had been Turhan's primary vehicle during the 1940s were no longer accepted by a more sophisticated and war-weary public. Bey came full cycle in Columbia's 1953 release of *Prisoners of the Casbah*. He was again Ahmed as he had been in his first Warner Bros. film of 1941.

With the industry's lack of interest in his Turkish charm, Turhan drifted back into commercial photography for a living. He based himself for a time in Miami and then returned to Vienna. In 1952, he produced *Stolen Identity*, a feature starring Francis Lederer. But his interest in the film business waned. According to reports, he seldom reflects on his Hollywood years, now, preferring to relish the indefinable Viennese "gemutlichkeit."

TURHAN BEY

Footsteps in the Dark   *(WB 1941)*
Raiders of the Desert   *(Univ 1941)*
Burma Convoy   *(Univ 1941)*
Shadows on the Stairs   *(WB 1941)*
The Gay Falcon   *(RKO 1941)*
Junior G-Men of the Air   *(Univ 1942)* (Serial)
The Falcon Takes Over   *(RKO 1942)*
A Yank on the Burma Road   *(MGM 1942)*
Bombay Clipper   *(Univ 1942)*
Drums of the Congo   *(Univ 1942)*
Arabian Nights   *(Univ 1942)*
Destination Unknown   *(Univ 1942)*
The Unseen Enemy   *(Univ 1942)*
Danger in the Pacific   *(Univ 1942)*
The Mummy's Tomb   *(Univ 1942)*
Adventures of Smilin' Jack   *(Univ 1943)* (Serial)
White Savage   *(Univ 1943)*

The Mad Ghoul   *(Univ 1943)*
Background to Danger   *(WB 1943)*
Follow the Boys   *(Univ 1944)*
The Climax   *(Univ 1944)*
Dragon Seed   *(MGM 1944)*
Bowery to Broadway   *(Univ 1944)*
Ali Baba and the Forty Thieves   *(Univ 1944)*
Frisco Sal   *(Univ 1945)*
Sudan   *(Univ 1945)*
A Night in Paradise   *(Univ 1946)*
Out of the Blue   *(El 1947)*
The Amazing Mr. X (a.k.a., The Spiritualist)   *(El 1948)*
Adventures of Casanova   *(El 1948)*
Parole, Inc.   *(El 1949)*
Song of India   *(Col 1949)*
Prisoners of the Casbah   *(Col 1953)*

Vivian Blaine

When vivacious Vivian Blaine opened on Broadway on November 24, 1950, as Adelaide, Damon Runyon's nasal peach of a doll, in *Guys and Dolls*, it became the role for which she would always be remembered. She played it for thirteen hundred performances on Broadway, eighteen months in London, starred in the movie version, and in 1966, repeated it at New York's City Center with Hugh O'Brien as her new co-star. In the musical, her delivery of Frank Loesser's "Adelaide's Lament" ("A person can develop a cold") always stopped the show. The role itself later became Vivian's personal lament, because she could never live it down and would always be identified with it. She later admitted that *Guys and Dolls* almost ruined her life because after it was all over, "I was like Edgar Bergen without Charlie McCarthy. I was practically typecast out of business. I worked, but it was always another version of Adelaide. We're friends again, Adelaide and i, but for a long time Adelaide over-bloomed."

To further the irony, Vivian's Adelaide in the film *Guys and Dolls* (1955) is her only noteworthy screen appearance. Under contract to Twentieth Century-Fox for six years during the 1940s, she floundered badly in a series of musicals as an unsuccessful *new* prototype of Alice Faye. The studio even had her sounding like Alice Faye. "Boy, was that the kiss of death," says Blaine. "You're either yourself or nobody." In the Fox totem pole of blonde musical stars, Blaine was the third girl. Alice Faye was number one,

followed by Betty Grable in second spot. After Faye retired from films and Grable unquestionably became number one, Blaine remained in third position, because by then June Haver had appeared on the scene and quickly proved to be popular with movie audiences. Haver was prettier than Vivian and, in a lilting Irish way, she possessed a stronger film personality. Through this tenure at Darryl F. Zanuck's playground, Vivian remained stifled by the competition. What she could have achieved at a less well-endowed studio is pure speculation, but it is a cinch Vivian would not have had to wait for the Broadway stage to solidify her image for public consumption.

Bright, blue-eyed Vivian was born Vivian S. Stapleton in Newark, New Jersey on November 21, 1921. Her father, Lionel Pierre Stapleton, was a theatrical booking agent who found his daughter nightly singing jobs (for one to five dollars) while she was still attending Southside High School. Actually, she had begun performing in vaudeville in Newark when she was just three years old. By the time she was thirteen, her parents divorced and her mother, Wilhelmina, had to struggle to make a living by turning her parlor into a beauty salon.

By the time Vivian was fourteen she was making her own living as girl vocalist with a number of small bands playing the Jersey area. After high school she attended the American Academy of Dramatic Art for

With Michael (Stephen) Dunne in Doll Face (20th 1946)

a while, and then wisely decided to concentrate on her singing career. She obtained short-term stands with one band after another, using a variety of names, such as Vivianne Lane, Vivian Stevens, and Vivian Stevenson, before inventing and sticking with Blaine. Her unrealized goal was to sing with a really big band such as Benny Goodman's outfit. "Band singing," Vivian told a writer for *Film Fan Monthly*, "is totally different from singing in a Broadway show. All band singing is one-two-three-four on the beat, with no change, for people to dance to. But I was always working on phrasing, which is the secret to good singing, and understanding the lyrics and trying to have a sound of my own. When the big bands broke up, the singers who were able to make a go of it were the ones who could do these things well."

By 1940 Vivian was singing in New York clubs such as the Cafe de la Paix and the Glass Hat Cafe in the Belmont-Plaza. While performing at Manhattan's Governor Clinton Hotel, she was spotted by Twentieth Century-Fox talent scout Myer Mishkin and soon after given a studio screen test, in which she sang "What do You Think I Am?" "I was—quote—'discovered'—unquote," said Vivian. "I didn't know what Hollywood would want with me. But mother and the Twentieth Century-Fox talent scout drove me out of my mind. Would I please go for six months? Six months became six years." She started out at the usual one-hundred-dollar-a-week salary, but first had to go on a strict diet. She weighed somewhere between 130 and 140 pounds, but in time slimmed herself down to a trim 103.

After small roles in three minor Fox films, she did nothing but take drama lessons at the studio and then toured for the USO for six months. She was finally noticed when cast as the ingenue opposite Laurel and Hardy in *Jitterbugs* (1943), one of the comedy team's later and lesser efforts. Vivian refers to the comedy duo as "two of the dearest men I've ever known." The film, essentially a B picture, attracted Hollywood agent Manuel "Manny" Frank. He became her agent and pushed for her as much as was possible. By the mid-1940s he had boosted her Fox salary to one thousand dollars a week. After her mother died, Vivian leaned on Frank for support, and though he was twenty years her senior, they married on January 10, 1945.

Then came the film that finally put her name in movie lights, albeit small ones. The picture was *Greenwich Village* (1944), with Don Ameche, and her first of four pictures with Brazil's own Carmen Miranda, then under studio contract. It took this fifth movie to make Vivian a "star," much the same as Janet Blair, who also became a screen name in her fifth film. Blaine and Blair had other similarities: Both were born in 1921 and both began as band vocalists. Alice Faye was to have starred in this color production of *Greenwich Village,* but she was pregnant with the child who would become Phyllis Faye Harris. Betty Grable was then assigned to do it, but she in turn, was expecting Vicky Elizabeth James. So Vivian got the role by default, although it was not as simple as all that, since several other candidates were tested for the part. Had not June Haver been busy filming *Irish Eyes Are Smiling* (1944), she undoubtedly would have inherited the part.

Vivian was determined to get the *Greenwich Village* bid. She marched into the front office saying she wanted a star part or she would quit. "Imagine telling Zanuck what to do," says Blaine. "I still shudder at the memory of my brashness." However, she got the part and the studio went about turning her into a celebrity. They dyed her original brownette hair an off-color red and publicized her as "The Cherry Blonde." Of the Walter-Lang-directed film, Vivian, billed below Miranda, said, "We both had our separate images. I sat in the picture window, sang the song, and kissed the pretty boy, and she was the lady with the fruit on the top of her head." The *New York Herald-Tribune* remarked that "an ambitious newcomer, Vivian Blaine, is given a chance to show her 'cherry blondeness' and sing in a major role. But Miss Blaine is not a sensation. Miss Blaine has neither the voice nor the style of a finished star." The same newspaper, reviewing Vivian's next musical with Carmen Miranda (still billed over Blaine), *Something for the Boys* (1944), said: "If you can care what happens to Vivian Blaine, the heiress to a broken down southern plantation, and Michael O'Shea, playing a staff sergeant on maneuvers, *Something for the Boys* might suit your fancy. I couldn't care for a minute." Such reviews helped to seal Vivian's fate in Hollywood.

Warner Bros. considered borrowing Vivian for *Rhapsody in Blue* (1945), which was to star Robert Alda as George Gershwin, but finally decided to give the part to contract player Joan Leslie. However, in 1945, Vivian played the chanteuse of a Barbary Coast saloon in *Nob Hill,* starring George Raft and Joan Bennett. She appeared in her best Fox film, *State Fair,* a musical remake of the 1933 picture that had starred Janet Gaynor, Will Rogers, and Lew Ayres. Vivian played the role* originally done by Sally Eilers, and co-starred with Jeanne Crain, Dana Andrews, and Dick Haymes in this spunky musical which boasted a wonderful original score by Rodgers and Hammer-

---

*In the cheap Fox 1962 remake, Ann-Margret inherited Vivian's part.

With Vera-Ellen and June Haver in Three Little Girls in Blue *(20th 1946)*

stein. She played her part well (as a band singer who is romanced by farm boy Haymes), soloing and dueting four songs: "I Owe Ioway," "Isn't It Kinda Fun?," "It's a Grand Night for Singing," and the lovely "That's for Me." The film's other song, "It Might As Well Be Spring," won the Oscar as best original song of 1945.

In 1946, Vivian was seen in three musicals: *Doll Face* and *If I'm Lucky,* both with Miranda and Perry Como, and *Three Little Girls in Blue,* co-starring with competitor June Haver, who by this period was starring in all her vehicles. In this remake of *Three Blind Mice* (1938), Haver looked beautiful, Vera-Ellen danced superbly, and Vivian, as the older of the three sisters, was lovely and underplayed convincingly.

It was at this point that Vivian realized: "Things were slowly coming to a halt. I realized I was getting no place. I saw myself going down, down, down. So I asked for my release and got it. It was all very amicable." One thing she did enjoy doing and continued to do after leaving Fox was singing at the studio's New York flagship theatre, the Roxy, when they had a stage show with films. She appeared there several times between 1945 and 1950.

"One day I'm a star, the next I'm a big fat nothing," said Vivian about leaving Hollywood and the security of a studio contract. "A few night club offers came in, but I was too frightened to take them. I'd lost confidence. I was weeping all over the house like a Niobe character. Then Manny, bless him, laid down the law. 'Either,' said he, 'you go out on the road, get the self-assurance you need, and give your talent a chance, or else take up needlepoint.' " She stopped crying (and gaining weight) and went to work. She opened at the Copacabana in New York on April 6, 1948, along with a couple of newcomers, Dean Martin and Jerry Lewis. "To say I laid an egg would be an understatement," claims Vivian. "The kindest review I received was: 'Vivian Blaine looks gorgeous in her California suntan. She sings too.' "

However, her old assurance and drive quickly returned and she continued doing club dates here and in England. She also ventured into summer stock, doing *Bloomer Girl, Light up the Sky,* and *One Touch of Venus.* Then she auditioned for the female lead in a new Broadway musical, *Guys and Dolls,* based on a story and characters by Damon Runyon and a book by Jo Swerling and Abe Burrows. She was considered too strong for the role of the Salvation Army girl Sarah Brown (the part went to Isabel Bigley), and she quickly forgot about it. Sometime later she literally bumped into one of the producers of the show, who told her

With William Bendix in Greenwich Village *(20th 1944)*

With Carmen Miranda and Phil Silvers in Something for the Boys *(20th 1944)*

about a new role that had been written into the play. The character's name was Adelaide, the moll of Broadway gambler Nathan Detroit (Sam Levene). She auditioned for the show again and made her own special niche in Broadway history in her New York stage debut, as well as winning a Donaldson Award for her work. *Life* Magazine said that Vivian's performance as a tough but virtuous dumb blonde "has helped make this a bright season for Broadway musicals." She later duplicated her triumph in the London production.

On an evening off from *Guys and Dolls* in November of 1951, Vivian dropped by the Palace Theatre to see Judy Garland perform her one-woman show, and ended up replacing her on that great stage. It was one of Garland's bad nights and her voice was almost completely gone. A hand tapped Vivian on the shoulder as she sat watching Judy and asked her to go backstage. When she did, she was told that Garland could not continue that night and could she possibly entertain the audience for a while. "It all happened so fast," recalled Vivian. "I just started to sing 'I Don't Care.' What a laugh, singing that song. I never cared more. That audience paid four eighty to see Judy Garland not Vivian Blaine. I tried to make every note I sang a haymaker, everything I had went into it."

On one of her vacations from *Guys and Dolls,* Vivian returned to Hollywood and made her first film in six years. She was a wave in MGM's *Skirts Ahoy* (1952), a romantic comedy with music starring Esther Williams. It was definitely one of Miss Williams' lesser efforts. But *Daily Variety* said, "The distaffers [Williams, Joan Evans, Blaine] acquit themselves well, particularly Vivian Blaine." Back in the show in New York she did daytime duty for MGM as a guest star in *Main Street to Broadway* (1953).

Vivian once again returned to California to do the film verson of *Guys and Dolls* for Samuel Goldwyn at MGM. She claims that Goldwyn had always promised her the role and that he kept his word. Perhaps he did, but the "truth" of the matter is that Vivian was, per usual, third in line for the assignment. Goldwyn's first choice was Marilyn Monroe, and when he was unable to hire her screen services, he offered it to Betty Grable. Because of some ridiculous misunderstanding between Goldwyn and Grable (he claimed she did not keep an appointment with him because of a sick dog), he signed Vivian to repeat her role. Of course, she was very good as Adelaide, but the combination of Grable, Marlon Brandon, Frank Sinatra, and Jean Simmons would have been a powerhouse of a cast. As it was, Miss Simmons, in her quiet British way, stole the picture from everybody, including Vivian.

The only film offers to come her way after the cinema version of *Guys and Dolls* were other dumb blonde parts. When Red Skelton filmed *Public Pigeon Number One,* based on his "Climax" TV outing (CBS, September 8, 1955), Vivian joined with Janet Blair as his oncamera co-stars. The lackluster venture was made at RKO, but when that studio went out of theatrical distribution, Universal released the film in 1957 with negligible results. On television Vivian starred with Bob Hope and Greer Garson in *The Awful Truth* and in the demanding title role in *Dream Girl* (1955) for "Hallmark Hall of Fame." In the latter, she was regretably miscast (but no more so than Betty Hutton in the 1948 Paramount film version). Returning to New York, she was thrilled to break away from the "Adelaide" image when she succeeded Shelley Winters as the dope addict's wife in *A Hatful of Rain* (1956) on Broadway and in the subsequent national tour, playing opposite Ben Gazzara and, later, Steve McQueen.

She divorced Manny Frank in a three-minute court hearing in Arkansas on December 10, 1956, later explaining, "I think he knew only after the divorce that he loved me. We kept in touch, but had to keep the relationship in focus until he died." In March, 1957, the *New York Daily News* headline read, "Bandleader's Wife Names Vivian Blaine." Mrs. Arthur "Cow Eyes" Engler accused Vivian of stealing her musician husband from her. Vivian promptly denied the charges, claiming only that they were friends who occasionally had lunch or dinner together. "As far as the world is concerned," she said at the time, "I'm a woman involved and I never had any intention of being one." The publicity deeply distressed her and the public did not believe her, siding, as usual, with the wronged wife. She was also kept busy denying a breach of etiquette during her London engagement of *Guys and Dolls.* There, the other parts of the triangle were Queen Elizabeth and the Duke of Edinburgh.

After another Broadway run, this time with David Wayne in the short-lasting musical *Say Darling* (1958), she married Milton R. Rackmil, president of Universal Pictures and Decca Records. Immediately after the May 9, 1959 wedding, she announced that she was quitting show business then and there. She did stay out of the entertainment spotlight until she divorced Rackmil on July 25, 1961. She made it back to Broadway as the middle-aged actress with whom young Alan Arkin becomes involved in *Enter Laughing* (1965). The *New York World Telegram and Sun* applauded her for "brilliantly setting up every scene in which she appears." In truth, there were not that

many. Since then, she had appeared in such revivals as *Panama Hattie, Light up the Sky, Born Yesterday, Gypsy, Rain, Cactus Flower, The Unsinkable Molly Brown, I Do, I Do,* and she even has played Blanche DuBois in *A Streetcar Named Desire.* Much of this work came after Vivian appeared on the 1971 Tony Awards telecast. She and Sam Levene were scheduled to duet "Sue Me" from *Guys and Dolls,* but as Vivian says, "I think he got sick deliberately so I could sing 'A person can develop a cold.'"

The audience went wild over her delivery, and in 1972 she succeeded Jane Russell (who had succeeded Elaine Stritch) in the Stephen Sondheim musical, *Company,* singing the wonderful and popular, "The Ladies Who Lunch." It was around this time that she filmed a cameo spot in *Richard* (1972), a would-be spoof of President Nixon, filmed in and around New York City. It is her last motion picture work to date.

In the summer of 1973, solid trouper Vivian toured with her old *Guys and Dolls* co-star Robert Alda in *Follies,* playing the role Alexis Smith had originated on Broadway. After a bus-and-truck tour with *Twigs* she wed garment industry executive Stuart Clark in December, 1973. The summer of 1974 saw her headlining a stock company of *Hello, Dolly!*

Early 1975 found Vivian joining with Kay Medford, Celeste Holm, Wesley Addy in a stock revival of *Light up the Sky.* But her greatest triumph of recent years was yet to come. In May, 1975 she opened a cafe act at Brothers and Sisters Club in New York. In a season where cabaret performances were generally excellent, Vivian received plaudits from the critics. *Women's Wear Daily* reported, "Truly dazzling in diamonds and sequins, Ms. Blaine has lost neither her looks nor her voice during her absence [sic] from the public. And whether it's a Helen Morgan-style slouch on the piano or a little dishing with the boys in the audience . . . Ms. Blaine is all entertainment. . . . Vivian Blaine's talent is matched only by her sense of humor." In the fall of 1975 she joined Milton Berle in the Broadway show, *The Best of Everybody.*

Had Vivian's show business career merely consisted of her stint in Hollywood during the hurly-burly 1940s, she would be just a dimly recalled name today. However, with her never-say-die attitude, she chose to salvage her career whatever way possible and became a winner with her *Guys and Dolls* casting. Says the ex-Faye/Grable/Haver challenger: "Broadway represents a greater challenge than Hollywood. I enjoy walking on stage and being able to sustain a character all night without somebody yelling, 'Cut,' because an electric light blew out or something." Regarding her recent decades behind the footlights: "In Hollywood I was always looking over my shoulder to see where the next knife was coming from. I'm not sorry when I think about it now and I wasn't sorry then."

The Vivian of today is a very much "up" individual. "I think positively. I'm the type of person who says that the glass is half-full rather than half-empty. You have to have faith. And I do believe in a being—a presence or divine guidance. Today, more than ever, I believe it is important for actors to maintain a positive image that they can project. There seems to be so little gracious living (no thanks to the current mania for 'telling it like it is'), everything's so mundane, so cut and dried. I think people crave and cherish what little illusion they can find, and they flock to the theatre to get it."

VIVIAN BLAINE

Girl Trouble   *(20th 1942)*
Through Different Eyes   *(20th 1942)*
He Hired the Boss   *(20th 1943)*
Jitterbugs   *(20th 1943)*
Greenwich Village   *(20th 1944)*
Something for the Boys   *(20th 1944)*
Nob Hill   *(20th 1945)*
State Fair   *(20th 1945)*

Doll Face   *(20th 1946)*
If I'm Lucky   *(20th 1946)*
Three Little Girls in Blue   *(20th 1946)*
Skirts Ahoy   *(MGM 1952)*
Main Street to Broadway   *(MGM 1953)*
Guys and Dolls   *(MGM 1955)*
Public Pigeon Number One   *(Univ 1957)*
Richard   *(Aurora 1972)*

10

Janet Blair

Vivacious, strawberry blonde Janet Blair, who became known as the wide-eyed girl from Altoona, Pa., is one of the true triple-threat performers in show business, and the pity is she has not gone further with her impressive talents than she has. An excellent singer, dancer, and actress, she is as comfortable in comedies or dramas as she is in musicals. Laboring at Columbia Pictures from 1941 through 1948, she is best remembered for her fifth film, *My Sister Eileen* (1942), which starred irrepressible Rosalind Russell. Because Harry Cohn's studio was so involved in promoting love goddess Rita Hayworth throughout the 1940s, Janet received the short end of the company's publicity stick. She received less attention at Columbia than did two of her contemporaries, Vivian Blaine and Gloria De Haven, at their respective studios, Twentieth Century-Fox and MGM. By 1950, Janet, who had emerged from energetic ingenue to accomplished torch singer, became the road-show Mary Martin and invariably began replacing star performers on stage and television. By this juncture the public had nearly forgotten the quasi-classic *My Sister Eileen,* and Janet was often being confused with such singers as Martha Wright and Mindy Carson, two other hinterlands performers. Nevertheless, she has never stopped her entertainment activities, because "If I weren't working, I'd be performing free for friends."

Janet was born to Florence and Fred Blair Lafferty on April 23, 1921, in Altoona, Pennsylvania. She was named Martha Janet Lafferty by her parents. She later took her professional name from both her own and her father's middle names. Mr. Lafferty was in the fruit and produce business and was soloist and choirmaster of their local church. Mrs. Lafferty was also musical, playing the organ and piano exceptionally well. The Laffertys had two other children, Fred Jr. and Ann Louise. Speaking of her childhood, Janet once remarked, "I was so homely that nobody paid any attention to me. So I decided to be the best singer and the best dancer and the best actress, even if I killed myself trying."

In the pre-World War II era of the big bands, Hal Kemp and his orchestra came through Altoona to play their sweet arrangements, and Janet's mother invited Kemp's business manager, Alex Holden, an old friend of the family, to dinner. He heard Janet sing and had her audition for Kemp. Shortly afterward, Janet briefly replaced Nan Wynn, who suddenly left the band, at an engagement at the Stanley Theatre in Pittsburgh. After high school graduation Janet went to New York to study voice, and, before long, she was back with the Hal Kemp orchestra permanently as his new female vocalist. She toured with the band in a series of one-nighters across the country.

While performing in Los Angeles she made a

With Andrew Tombes, Penny Singleton, and Arthur Lake in Blondie Goes to College *(Col 1942)*

With Tommy and Jimmy Dorsey in The Fabulous Dorseys *(UA 1947)*

screen test for Twentieth Century-Fox and made a band short for Warner Bros. Gordon Jenkins, representing NBC, also made her a radio offer, but she remained with the Kemp band for another year. She left the band in the summer of 1940, some months before Kemp's death (December 19, 1940) in an automobile accident on his way to San Francisco. Her reason for leaving the group? She had screen-tested for Columbia and was signed to a hundred-dollar-a-week contract. "I look back on it now," Janet said some time later, "and I'm amazed at how well I really did—and only because I didn't know what to do, so I just acted natural."

Janet was originally given a role in the Fred Astaire-Rita Hayworth musical, *You'll Never Get Rich* (1941), but was dropped from the cast before filming began because a Columbia executive felt that "this girl can be an actress if we're careful. So let's not type her by putting her in a musical. Let's make her work." So, instead, Janet made her film debut in the comedy-mystery *Three Girls in Town* (1941), sharing the billing with two knowledgeable veterans, Joan Blondell and Binnie Barnes. *Variety* thought that "ingenue Janet Blair catches attention in the fast company." The *New York Daily News* said, "Janet Blair is a new and prominent face on the Columbia lot, but this film won't do much for her." The latter verdict was correct.

She then played a coed in *Blondie Goes to College* (1942), the tenth in that series, and was given the female lead in *Two Yanks in Trinidad* (1942), headlining Pat O'Brien and Brian Donlevy. She obtained this latter role because someone on the lot suggested Janet to director Gregory Ratoff. He immediately ordered that she be sent to see him. At the time, so the story goes, she was posing for cheesecake photography in a bathing suit, but threw on a coat and ran to his office. Ratoff requested she remove her coat, adding, "I want to look you over to see if you're the girl for the part." A stubborn Janet refused to take off the coat and said, "I'm either the girl or I'm not, regardless of the coat." "That's the girl for me!" declared a surprised Ratoff. "That's just the fire and punch I'm looking for." So Janet got the role and sang the title song. Unfortunately the picture was not much to remember.

Janet's first loanout film was Universal's *Broadway* (1942), in which she was the "romantic interest." The film, a remake of the studio's earlier (1929) version of the Broadway play about show business and the speakeasy era, was notable largely because ex-hoofer George Raft, in the lead, played himself. Then came Janet's big break in *My Sister Eileen.* The studio wanted to use a contract player for the role of Rosalind

Russell's naive sister. Penny Singleton had been considered, but she was indelibly branded as the *Blondie* girl, and Russell, who knew of Blair, recommended her for the important assignment. When the Alexander Hall-directed comedy was through shooting, Russell went to the studio's front office and demanded that Janet be given star billing along with herself and Brian Aherne.

The critics loved this film about two sisters from Ohio determined to make it big in New York while sharing a street-level Greenwich Village apartment. And more importantly, the reviewers were finally impressed by Janet's performance as the dewy-eyed miss who aspires to be an actress. She is the innocent to whom Russell says, "Something tells me you weren't ready to leave Columbus." The *New York Morning Telegraph* reported, "Miss Blair as the blonde Eileen who raises most of the Cain, is not only a looker but an interesting personality as well, and should go a considerable distance in her movie career."

However, she did not go that "considerable distance," because Columbia kept her in bland, pleasant ingenue or romantic-interest roles that, generally, just displayed her cute face with its tilted nose and radiant smile. She did get to sing some Cole Porter ditties in *Something to Shout About* (1943), produced and directed by Gregory Ratoff. The best thing about this backstage musical was the Porter song "You'd Be So Nice to Come Home To," which she dueted with co-star Don Ameche. The *New York Times* summed the film up perfectly: "Even Janet Blair who's been coming along promisingly seems hopelessly bewildered in the trite story of a songstress from Altoona [no less] who finds herself involved in the intrigue surrounding a big-time musical. The intrigue, not too surprisingly, stems from a lady backer [Cobina Wright, Jr.] who also fancies herself as the star performer of the show until the first night audience gives her come-uppance, and flash—Miss Blair gets the big chance." Janet received the 1943 *Look* Magazine award as the year's most promising actress.

After her marriage to musician Lou Busch in July of 1943 (he had been pianist for the Hal Kemp band), she co-starred with Cary Grant in *Once upon a Time* (1944), but played second fiddle to a dancing caterpillar, and another scene-stealer, Ted Donaldson (as her young brother). This picture was followed by the best of her film musicals, *Tonight and Every Night* (1945), a color film in which she supported Rita Hayworth in wartime London and got to sing the title song (reprised less successfully by dubbed-in Hayworth). She and Miss Hayworth performed an enjoyable song-skit together called "The Boy I Left Behind." The *New York Herald-Tribune* passed judgment on

Publicity pose ca. 1946

Janet's performance as the girl who dies in the blitz with, "Miss Hayworth is less successful in sustaining the light burden of fun in the show than Miss Blair."

In 1946, Janet did two inconsequential films, *Gallant Journey,* a heavy-handed aviation drama with Glenn Ford; and *Tars and Spars,* of which Janet remarked, "Alfred Drake and I were doing the romantic leads and getting along fine until Sid Caesar came in, did a fifteen-minute bit, and stole the picture." Her only 1947 release was her second loanout, a mild musical at United Artists about Tommy and Jimmy Dorsey called *The Fabulous Dorseys.* The reason Janet did not appear in more films was that, unlike fellow contractees (Nina Foch, Margaret Lindsay, Lynn Merrick, Marguerite Chapman, Jeff Donnell, Ann Miller, Jinx Falkenberg, et al.), she was often on suspension from the studio for refusing to accept lousy roles.

Janet's last year under contract to Columbia was 1948, and by this time her salary was up to an unremarkable $750 per week. She appeared in three releases that year. *I Love Trouble* was a fast moving mystery with Franchot Tone. She played straight lady to Red Skelton's sometimes funny antics in *The Fuller Brush Man* and, finally, graced the swashbuckler, *The Black Arrow,* as Lady Joanna. Referring to her role in the latter film, Janet said: "My chief function was to stand around and look pretty. I remember that Louis Hayward, in one sequence, was standing on a moat wall and fighting the villains off with a sword. My line of dialogue in this situation was: "Jump, Richard. It's your only ch*awnce.*' Then I kept on looking pretty."

Janet and Columbia parted unamicably, but, on thinking back over her film career, she holds no grudge against Hollywood or the studio for not giving her more opportunity. She explains: "Columbia offered me a new contract with a heavy bonus. I could have taken it, sat beside a swimming pool, and continued to make money. But I decided if I couldn't make some of my dreams come true, I'd better quit dreaming." Referring to Harry Cohn, Columbia's autocratic studio head: "He could be the most terrifying tyrant, or he could be a petulant child. If your films made money, he was very charming and very happy. But if they didn't . . . ."

Janet left Hollywood and headed for New York where she auditioned for Ethel Merman's replacement in *Annie Get Your Gun* and for *Miss Liberty.* She lost out on both musical accounts, but in the summer of 1949 she toured with Francis Lederer in *For Love or Money,* her legitimate stage debut. She declined a later offer from Tommy Dorsey to tour with his band, declined joining The Eddie Cantor Show which was then playing Chicago, and also turned down the opportunity to become Mary Martin's understudy in *South Pacific* on Broadway. Janet has explained the latter refusal with, "I love Mary, but I didn't intend to serve as understudy to anybody." Instead, she decided to build her own nightclub act to play only the "classier saloons" and contacted the Blackburn Twins, dancers she had seen in the MGM film, *Words and Music* (1948). The twins happily agreed to join her and after two weeks of rehearsal, the combined act opened in Chicago. They then toured, finally coming to New York. "I spent twenty-five thousand dollars on costumes, special material, arrangements, and everything else needed in an act," recalls Janet. "It was an education, all right." *Billboard* voted the act the best of 1949.

As luck would have it, Oscar Hammerstein II saw the show at the Waldorf in New York and liked it very much. The family of his partner, Richard Rodgers, had seen Janet as a guest on Milton Berle's television show and urged that she be considered for the lead in the first national company of *South Pacific.* Hammerstein later told her that he had vetoed her previously because he believed she "spoke like a bass and sang like a soprano," but he had since changed his mind. Janet re-auditioned for the hit show and sang "It Never Entered My Mind." When she came off the stage, Joshua Logan, the show's director, rushed up to her and said, "You are Nellie!" Janet played Nellie Forbush in *South Pacific* from 1950 to 1953—1,263 times—and never missed a performance.

Janet had divorced her first husband in 1950, but in 1953 (on October 5th) she wed Nick Mayo, stage manager for *South Pacific.* It was the second marriage for each. The Mayos waited some time before having children because of their careers. Their first child, Amanda, was born February 22, 1959, and a son, Andrew, came along two years later.

Janet made her Broadway debut in *A Girl Can Tell,* a comedy by F. Hugh Herbert, which opened on October 29, 1953, at the Royale Theatre. Her husband, again, was the stage manager. The play was not as successful as Herbert's previous *The Moon Is Blue,* and many critics thought that show's Barbara Bel Geddes more suited to the Herbert brand of comedy than Janet was. When the show closed, Janet went on the road again in Nick Mayo's production. *Broadway Highlights,* with Jack Cassidy and Richard Eastham. The show was composed of thirty-eight production numbers from various hit Broadway musicals. In 1955, Janet played the Ethel Merman role of Reno Sweeney in *Anything Goes* for the Pittsburgh Light Opera Company.

Janet had previously appeared on television variety shows, but in 1955 branched out to such heavy dramatic fare as "Kitty Foyle." She also starred in such video specials as "One Touch of Venus" and "A Connecticut Yankee." Then, in 1956, there was much publicity when she was chosen to replace Nanette Fabray as Sid Caesar's third television spouse, beating out such competition as Polly Bergen, Edie Adams, and Gisele MacKenzie. She accepted the part because Caesar convinced her that she would have the opportunity of doing a lot of different things in a number of formats of which she never had considered herself capable. The other reason she accepted was for the money. Janet also knew and liked Caesar, her *Tars and Spars* film co-worker. At the time, a jubilant Janet informed one interviewer, "The studio won't let me tell you how much, but it's enough to make me very happy." She reportedly received a higher salary than her predecessor, Nanette Fabray.

Four days after signing the contract for "The Sid Caesar Hour" she did her second film with Red Skelton, *Public Pigeon Number One,* made for RKO but released by Universal in 1957. It was her first film in many years and she should never have done it. Considering that her contemporary, Vivian Blaine, was also in the frail comedy and received billing ahead of her, it was a definite downward step. "The Sid Caesar Hour" also proved a bad choice for her, as she found herself sharing oncamera time with very competent Shirl Conway and Pat Carroll, not to mention egocentric star Caesar. Janet was simply miscast in that environment. What was needed was somebody gaudier and more clownish. She quit the show the following year, saying it was a purely professional split and that she and Caesar were still friendly.

Janet quit another show in 1957. She was cast opposite ex-MGM star Howard Keel in the New York City Center's revival of *Carousel.* Her reason for dropping out was that Keel attempted to assume directorial privileges. She detailed, "He had preconceived ideas on how Julie should be played because he had played it [*Carousel*] so often before." She was not upset about this episode for long, because television variety show emcee Ed Sullivan signed her for six appearances on his Sunday night program for $50,000.

In the summers of 1958 and 1959 Janet became a very popular television performer. She and John Raitt were the stars of "The Chevy Show" on NBC; she became Dinah Shore's summer replacement, and the show was a big success. When asked what it was "really" like competing with Dinah, Janet responded, "Dinah is an institution. Competing with her would

be like competing with Crosby or Sinatra. It's impossible. There's no competition between us. We're keen friends." Janet had another big victory, this time in London, playing the Judy Holliday role, Ella Peterson, in *The Bells Are Ringing* (1959).

After returning to the States, England beckoned her professionally again, this time to star in the film, *Burn, Witch, Burn* (1962). The film dealt with the powers of mesmerism, and was originally called *Conjure Wife.* It had been filmed before as *Weird Woman* (1944) with Universal's Evelyn Ankers in Janet's role. The new edition has since become a minor classic in the horror genre, but at the time the movie received poor United States distribution despite critical approval. The *New York Times* observed, "Miss Blair looks unglamorous and never more appealing." Another 1962 film was *Boys' Night Out,* playing Tony Randall's wife and unmercifully out-acting distaff co-stars Kim Novak and Patty Paige.

For want of better offers, Janet continued appearing around the country in variety shows, such as *Annie Get Your Gun* and *The Sound of Music,* and won the Composers and Lyricists Award of Merit for outstanding contribution to stage, film, and television in 1964. By 1964, forty-three-year-old Janet had a new nightclub act and performed throughout the country at such night spots as the Riviera in Las Vegas and the Waldorf in New York. Janet's last feature film appearance, thus far, was as the wife of Buddy Ebsen in *The One and Only Genuine Original Family Band* (1968). It was not one of Walt Disney's most successful films; the title, among other ingredients, was in desperate need of a change. "I had a supporting role," said Janet of this 110-minute feature, "and much of it, in fact most of it, was edited before it was released. Blink your eyes and you miss me." Such has been the film career of the 1940s' Miss Potential.

Janet and Nick Mayo divorced in the late 1960s after years of a sometimes tumultuous marriage, and though quite affected by the break-up, she threw herself back into the business of performing by doing a road company version of the musical *Mame.* "I got the compensation in the applause and the love of the audiences," she said. "But then I realized I had just receded into being my old selfish self again. So I moved back to Los Angeles with the children."

After playing a very fussy lady with heart trouble who unwillingly shares a hospital room with Dolores Del Rio on "Marcus Welby" (1970), she won the role of Betty Smith, Henry Fonda's wife, on the television series, "The Smith Family" for ABC. She recalls the producers liked her but felt they had to have Fonda's approval. He was then up in Oregon filming *Some-*

With Tom Powers, Franchot Tone, and Janis Carter in I Love Trouble *(Col 1948)*

times a Great Notion (1971). They were going to send Janet up there to see him, but as it turned out the trip was unnecessary. Fonda phoned the producers, saying, "I wouldn't think of putting an actress of Miss Blair's quality in such an embarrassing position. She's fine with me, sight unseen." "That dear, wonderful man. Every woman needs a Henry Fonda," says Janet. The television series lasted two half seasons and her role was far from challenging, with her weekly stints being relegated to such weary lines as, "How did things go today, dear?" But the show did make her a permanent fixture in many homes for a year, and now she is recognized everywhere she goes. That is the wonder of present-day television compared to other entertainment mediums.

Janet continued to keep her name in show business circles by performing in a few productions of *Mame*

each year, and she did a dinner theatre production of an English play, *Who Killed Santa Claus* in 1973. She also replaced Dorothy Collins in the Los Angeles production of *Follies* for the last few weeks of its short run.

Today, when not on stage, in front of a camera, or presiding over her children, she performs volunteer work for the Crippled Children's Society and is a member of their board of directors. She is still a bundle of energy and would like to be working more, particularly behind the footlights. What Janet needs to cap her decades of "showladyship" is an original starring vehicle of her own on Broadway. It would once and for all prove that she is not a carbon copy of any major star and should not be classified as *just* a road-show heroine, but a fine actress in her own right.

JANET BLAIR

Three Girls About Town   *(Col 1941)*
Two Yanks in Trinidad   *(Col 1942)*
Blondie Goes to College   *(Col 1942)*
Broadway   *(Univ 1942)*
My Sister Eileen   *(Col 1942)*
Something to Shout About   *(Col 1943)*
Once Upon a Time   *(Col 1944)*
Tonight and Every Night   *(Col 1945)*
Tars and Spars   *(Col 1946)*

Gallant Journey   *(Col 1946)*
The Fabulous Dorseys   *(UA 1947)*
I Love Trouble   *(Col 1948)*
The Fuller Brush Man   *(Col 1948)*
The Black Arrow   *(Col 1948)*
Public Pigeon Number One   *(Univ 1957)*
Burn, Witch, Burn   *(AIP 1962)*
Boys' Night Out   *(MGM 1962)*
The One and Only Genuine Original Family Band   *(BV 1968)*

11

Ann Blyth

"As an actress," says demure but dynamic Ann Blyth, "I have always believed that the truer challenge, the deeper obligation, begins after the camera stops. My role as a woman in my community and in my home has always overshadowed the excitment of any part I have ever played on stage or screen." Petite Ann (5' 2", 103 pounds) never allowed Hollywood mores to change her way of thinking or her essential lifestyle. A sincerely religious girl, she has often been referred to as a "goody-goody." Notwithstanding this epithet, she does exemplify the "nice girl" image.

Her screen career had three parts: The first as an overly sweet, always compatible Peggy Ryan type for mid-1940s Universal entries which generally featured Donald O'Connor and Ryan; the third as a mid-1950s successor to Kathryn Grayson and Jane Powell as MGM's operetta star; and the second, the most intriguing of all, personified by her indelible portrait of Veda Pierce, that bitchy stinker in Joan Crawford's Oscar-winning *Mildred Pierce* (1945). In this piece of contra-casting, she made the grade in 1940s' Hollywood and won an Oscar nomination as Best Supporting Actress, to boot.

This pretty Irish colleen type was born on August 16, 1928, in Mt. Kisco, New York. After her parents, Nan Lynch and Harry Blyth, separated, she moved, together with her mother and sister, Dorothy, to a fourth floor walk-up apartment on New York City's East Thirty-first Street. They later moved to a nicer apartment at 307 East Forty-ninth Street, where they lived while Ann attended Catholic schools and, later, Manhattan's Professional Children's School.

From a very early age, determined Ann (with or without her mother's prodding) had her sights set on becoming an actress. Her mother complied with Ann's wishes by providing her with singing and acting lessons. By the time Ann was nine years old, she was a member of New York's Children's Opera Company and was a fairly well-established radio performer. She appeared on such programs as Jean Hersholt's "Dr. Christian" series, "The Sunday Show," "Our Barn Children's Show," and seemingly on any radio soap opera that needed a child.

Then, one day, while eating her lunch at the Professional Children's School, director Herman Shumlin spotted her and cast her as Babette, Paul Lukas and Mady Christian's daughter, in Lillian Hellman's Broadway play, *Watch on the Rhine* (1941). She was billed as Anne, with an "e," and remained with the hit drama for two years, first on Broadway and then on tour. "It meant so much for so many reasons," Ann remembers. "It meant that for the first time in years my mother wouldn't have to work so hard." While on tour and playing the Biltmore Theatre in Los Angeles, director Henry Koster, then with Universal Studio, saw her and decided to give her a screen test. She performed a scene from *Peg O' My Heart* and was signed to a term contract. [When Warner Bros.

With Howard Duff in Red Canyon *(Univ 1949)*

With Ruth Warrick in Swell Guy *(Univ 1947)*

filmed *Watch on the Rhine* (1943), they cast many of the play's original members, but Ann was not asked. She had already outgrown the role, which went to Janis Wilson.]

Ann's first film was a teenage musical, *Chip Off the Old Block* (1944), with Donald O'Connor and Peggy Ryan, followed by two other pleasant, low-budget O'Connor-Ryan outings. She was also part of an all-star cast in *Bowery to Broadway* (1944). Ann recalls attending the preview of her first film with her mother: "She probably realized I had a lot to learn, but there for the first time on the screen was her daughter. Her daughter made little impression on anyone else. Nobody recognized me outside. Nobody asked me for an autograph."

Nothing much happened to Ann in Hollywood until *Mildred Pierce*. Al Rockett, her agent, learned that Warner Bros. was not happy with any of their contract players for the role of the young murderess in *Pierce* and, with some difficulty, got his client a test for the part. Much to everyone's amazement, she landed the plum job. Surprising many people with her strong, calculating performance that gave dynamic Joan Crawford a run for her screen time, Ann explained at the time, "Most people forget I'm a stage

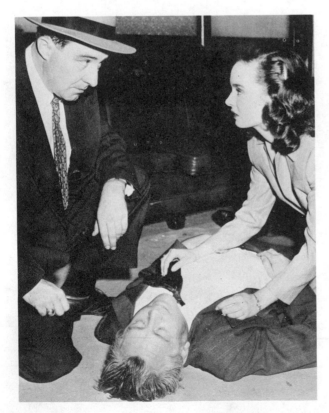

With Paul Bryar and James Dunn in Killer McCoy *(MGM 1947)*

actress." There were, however, a few dissenters to her acting in this film. The *New York Times* carped, "Ann Blyth interprets Veda with such devastating emphasis that she is quite incredible on the whole." Ann certainly did play it with a great deal of emphasis—under director Michael Curtiz' prodding—but in so doing made the role one of the two most famous spoiled brats the screen has ever witnessed. The other was Bonita Granville's performance in *These Three* (1936). Sadly for nominated Ann, that year's Best Supporting actress Oscar went to Anne Revere of *National Velvet*.

Quite happy with her screen work, Warners borrowed Ann again for *Danger Signal* (1945) to appear with her scoundrelly *Mildred Pierce* co-player, Zachary Scott. But filming began, while she was on a short vacation at Lake Arrowhead, she was hurled from a toboggan sled and broke her back. Mona Freeman replaced her in *Danger Signal* (with minimal effect). The doctors' prognosis was poor: They suspected that Ann might never walk again. She spent seven months in bed and another seven months in a brace, but with great will power and even greater belief in God, she recovered. However, she had another of life's tricky hurdles to overcome. While Ann was still recuperating, her mother died, at the age of fifty. Ann, then only eighteen, moved in with her aunt and uncle who lived in the San Fernando Valley. During this time, Universal used her to good advantage, wheelchair and all, in one of the female cameo roles in the prison drama *Brute Force* (1947). Her first starring role was opposite Sonny Trufts in *Swell Guy* (1947), and since then, she has always had top female billing except for one time when she took second billing to waning star Claudette Colbert in *Thunder on the Hill* (1951).

After a loanout assignment to MGM for *Killer McCoy* (1947), opposite another bundle of dynamite, Mickey Rooney, she co-starred with Charles Boyer in the suspenseful melodrama, *A Woman's Vengeance* (1948). The *New York Times* said that "Ann Blyth, as the little lady whom he [Boyer] marries after his first wife is dead, acts—and is treated by him—as though she were one of Andy Hardy's girl friends." Jessica Tandy, as Boyer's sister-in-law, stole the film. In *Another Part of the Forest* (1948) she played the same character Bette Davis had performed in *The Little Foxes* (1941) but at an earlier age. Ann imbued her characterization with a determination that was reminiscent but more far-reaching than her Veda of *Mildred Pierce*.

For whatever distinction it is worth, Ann become one of the very few actresses to ever play a mermaid oncamera in the sometimes amusing *Mr. Peabody* and the Mermaid (1948), opposite William Powell. Ann was scheduled to do two drama for Universal: Rogue's Regiment (1948) and Abandoned (1949), but ex-MGMer Robert Montgomery asked for her for his film Come Be My Love, later released as Once More My Darling (1949). The studio, thinking of Wanda Hendrix's rise after she appeared with Montgomery in Ride the Pink Horse (1947), agreed and released Ann from her two other commitments. Ann was replaced, respectively, by Marta Toren and Gale Storm. But the Montgomery film, directed by Mr. M., did nothing to further Ann's career. As the debutante who chases middle-aged movie star Montgomery, the New York Herald-Tribune remarked that "her role requires a solemn, furious enthusiasm delivered in a steady stream of breathless dialogue, and there are mighty few actresses who could prevent this type of thing from becoming irritating. Certainly Miss Blyth is not one of them."

She enjoyed working on loan at Paramount with Bing Crosby and Barry Fitzgerald in Top o' the Morning (1949), and had a very dramatic, if soggy, role in Samuel Goldwyn's Our Very Own (1950). In the latter film, she plays an adopted girl who does not find out that she is adopted until she is eighteen. She then goes in search of her real mother, played by Ann Dvorak. Miss Dvorak's performance is worth the entire film and more. Around this time, Ann was one of an all-celebrity cast, including William Holden, in a religious documentary called You Can Change the World.

At the 1950 Oscar ceremonies, Ann, hoping to change her screen image and also praying for the lead in a musical, wore a lowcut, flaming red dress and sang "My Foolish Heart," an Oscar contender for best song, in a very torchy rendition. For the moment, she was highly applauded, but it failed to change her celluloid stereotype. However, this performance did lead her to obtain the role of Caruso's wife in MGM's The Great Caruso (1951), with bombastic Mario Lanza in the title assignment. She sang in the film a new version of "Over the Waves," called "The Loveliest Night of the Year." MGM paid Universal $50,000 for Ann's oncamera services. Ann made four (!) other 1951 releases, the most interesting of which was Thunder on the Hill, a relatively well-acted drama about a wrongfully convicted murderess (Blyth) and a nun (Claudette Colbert) who sets out to prove her innocence. Ann was generally convincing in the picture, but tended to overplay her part. The role, however, represented a good change of pace for her. Coincidentally, the following year Ann replaced Claudette Colbert as Robert Mitchum's leading lady in One Minute to Zero (1952) at RKO; presumably,

Miss Colbert read the finished script, and, rightfully, declined.

The Russian countess in A World in His Arms (1952), with Gregory Peck co-star, was Ann's final role for Universal. Her contract with them ended in December, 1952, and she signed with MGM, who promised her leads in the musical operettas Rose Marie (1954) and The Student Prince (1954). Ann would be challenging MGM's own sopranos Kathryn Grayson and Jane Powell and was determined to become a top musical performer in her own right. As with everything she has done in her life, she tackled her new quest with industrious diligence. However, while Ann's voice is a pleasant one, deeper sounding than either Grayson's or Powell's, as a singer she was never in their class, especially not in Grayson's. Where she did have an edge over those two Culver City veterans was in the area of believably acting emotions. Ann was an actress who sang, the others were primarily singers. However, Jane Powell was the most versatile of the trio, because she could also dance quite well.

Ann's first contract film for MGM was the non-musical All the Brothers Were Valiant (1953), starring Robert Taylor, but then she filmed two operettas. Rose Marie (1954) was an awful third remake, and

With Robert Cummings in Free for All (Univ 1949)

despite the presence here of CinemaScope and color, one longed for Jeanette MacDonald and Nelson Eddy's 1936 version, which also had a completely different story line. The best thing about the 1950s' rendition was Howard Keel's deep-throated singing. Not one of the best things was Ann's abrasive French accent.

The Student Prince (1954) almost never got (re)made. It was to have been lensed before *Rose Marie* with Metro's resident tenor Mario Lanza in the lead. Lanza and Ann had already recorded the songs, but Lanza never showed up for the shooting. The studio filed suit against the singer and cancelled the production after more than $700,000 had been spent. When Dore Schary's regime decided to go through with the production some time later, and differences had been settled with temperamental Lanza, he was by then far too overweight to play the lead. They then went in search of an actor to play the role and mouth the songs to Lanza's recorded voice. Edmund Purdom, who would later substitute for Marlon Brando in Twentieth Century-Fox's *The Egyptian* (1954), was hauled into service and he became a "star" for a short period of time. It must be acknowledged in Purdom's favor that he was an ideal visual choice for the part and hardly any Hollywood star in recollection has ever mouthed another singer's voice as well as he did, including Larry Parks in his Jolson films. As for Blyth, Kathy was her perfect role and she had the right spirit, warmth, and tenderness to make the heroine credible. Her final scene with the prince (Purdom), whom she loves but will never see again, was exquisitely modulated down to the final catch in her throat.

Ann's only other MGM musical was the plastic, sequinned *Kismet* (1955), in which Vic Damone faltered as the pale romantic lead. Not even the verve of Howard Keel (as the Poet) or Dolores Gray (as the bored Lalume) could buoy the script from total ineffectuality. Ann's vacant-looking Marsinah was no asset to the Vincente Minnelli-directed film. The costumed *The King's Thief* (1955) with Purdom and David Niven, and *Slander* (1957) were programmers, though Ann had some moving moments in the latter picture, which dealt with a slut magazine that was blackmailing performer Van Johnson. Ann played his troubled wife. In 1956, a declining MGM cancelled her exclusive contract at her request. She agreed to do some films for them at some later date, but she never did.

On June 27, 1953, Ann wed Dr. James Vincent McNulty. She was twenty-four, he was thirty-five. She had been introduced to him by his brother, singer-comedian Dennis Day. About their courtship, Ann coyly says, "I never knew if he was going to kiss me or take my pulse." Their marriage ceremony was performed by a Cardinal with a special benediction from Pope Pius XII. Among Ann's bridesmaids were Betty Lynn, Jane Withers, and Joan Leslie. The McNultys have five children and reside in apparent contentment, a rare domestic scene in Hollywood.

The Buster Keaton Story (1957) at Paramount was a travesty. Donald O'Connor was inappropriately cast as the renowned screen comedian, and Ann was little better as the ineffectual love interest. *The Jazz Age* was the original title of Ann's last film to date, which was released as *The Helen Morgan Story*, a property which Warner Bros. had owned for some fifteen years. Ann desperately wanted to play the torch singer lead, but the studio and the film's director Michael Curtiz (who had helmed *Mildred Pierce*) thought she was wrong for the pivotal part. After forty or more other actresses had tested for the part, Ann maneuvered a test for herself. One company official, upon hearing that Ann was being tested, exclaimed, "This kid can't even smoke—much less act drunk! She's about as sexy as a cream cheese and jelly sandwich."

But again, Ann's persistence paid off, and she was co-starred in the picture with fast-rising Paul Newman, the latter playing a composite character of all the men in Helen Morgan's life. Ann *did* lose out in singing the role, though. The studio decided her voice was too high-pitched for Morgan's (which was not actually the case). Gogi Grant, another strong-voiced singer, but less classical, recorded the songs superbly with Ann mouthing them equally well. Not long before the film was released, on April 16, 1957, to be exact, Polly Bergen starred on television's "Playhouse 90" in the same role and received solid notices for her telling performance. By contrast, her performance made Ann's version pale. The *New York Post* judged: "Ann Blyth makes a good pretense of putting forth the songs. Her emotional acting gamut is a narrow one, turning simply from large, rolling, glistening tears or a set gloomy expression to the dazzling smile that has long been her trademark. If she doesn't quite convince you she's Helen Morgan, at least she manages to become sufficiently awry-eyed to turn aside suspicions that she might still be Ann Blyth."

Ann made her dramatic television debut in 1954, playing the Elizabeth Taylor role in the video version of *A Place in the Sun,* co-starring with John Derek and Marilyn Erskine. She also appeared in the television adaptation of *The Citadel,* recreating the role Rosalind Russell had essayed in the 1938 Metro venture. Ann's other occasional television stints include the role of a saloon owner on "Wagon Train," as a guest on "The Bell Telephone Hour," with Howard Keel, and the "Perry Como Show." Her ambition to sing on the musical stage was realized when she began appearing in such summer stock musicals as *The Sound of Music, The King and I,* and *Carnival.* In 1966-67 she replaced Shirley Jones, on tour, in *Wait until Dark,* and most recently was seen as Nellie Forbush in *South Pacific* with Fernando Lamas. These days her radiant smile and charming way grace a television commercial for Hostess Twinkies.

Ann has fond memories of her feature-film days, but she still prefers the satisfaction derived from her roles as wife and mother. Through the years, she, along with Jeanne Crain, probably has received more coverage as a Hollywood mother than anyone else. A devout Catholic, Ann and her husband were invested with the rank of Lady and Knight of the Holy Sepulchre by Cardinal Cooke. She is totally against abortion and completely for organized religion. She insists, "Going to mass makes me feel good. I gain a great deal from going to church, whether it be Sunday, Monday, or Thursday."

ANN BLYTH

Chip Off the Old Block   *(Univ 1944)*
The Merry Monahans   *(Univ 1944)*
Babes on Swing Street   *(Univ 1944)*
Bowery to Broadway   *(Univ 1944)*
Mildred Pierce   *(WB 1945)*
Swell Guy   *(Univ 1947)*
Brute Force   *(Univ 1947)*
Killer McCoy   *(MGM 1947)*
A Woman's Vengeance   *(Univ 1948)*
Another Part of the Forest   *(Univ 1948)*
Mr. Peabody and the Mermaid   *(Univ 1948)*
Red Canyon   *(Univ 1949)*
Once More, My Darling   *(Univ 1949)*
Top O' The Morning   *(Par 1949)*
Free for All   *(Univ 1949)*
You Can Change the World   *(Documentary 1949)*
Our Very Own   *(RKO 1950)*

The Great Caruso   *(MGM 1951)*
Katie Did It   *(Univ 1951)*
The Golden Horde   *(Univ 1951)*
Thunder on the Hill   *(Univ 1951)*
I'll Never Forget You   *(20th 1951)*
Sally and Saint Anne   *(Univ 1952)*
One Minute to Zero   *(RKO 1952)*
The World in His Arms   *(Univ 1952)*
All the Brothers Were Valiant   *(MGM 1953)*
Rose Marie   *(MGM 1954)*
The Student Prince   *(MGM 1954)*
The King's Thief   *(MGM 1955)*
Kismet   *(MGM 1955)*
Slander   *(MGM 1957)*
The Buster Keaton Story   *(Par 1957)*
The Helen Morgan Story   *(WB 1957)*

12

Eddie Bracken

Bucolic, bombastic, sappy, engaging. These are some of the contrasting qualities Eddie Bracken has displayed in his long-enduring show business career. Like another less talented but more famous Paramount contractee, Sonny Tufts, Bracken was displayed by that studio onscreen as America's typical civilian on the World War II home front (and heaven help us, was the obvious implication). His two best film parts came in 1944 in a pair of Preston Sturges comedies (*The Miracle of Morgan's Creek* and *Hail the Conquering Hero*), in which the sometimes whiny, always pudgy Bracken was his most ingratiatingly comic.

Edward Vincent Bracken entered show business at the age of six, playing the purser of *The Good Ship Leviathan* for the Knights of Columbus in Astoria, New York, where he was born on February 7, 1920. His father was the foreman of the East River Gas Company, Joseph L. Bracken, and his mother, Catherine, demonstrated appliances for Con Edison. In Astoria, he attended Our Lady of Mt. Carmel School, studied acting with the Homer sisters, and eventually attended New York's Professional School for Actors. Before his ninth birthday he made his film debut as the snooty rich boy in Hal Roach's famous *Our Gang* comedies, and after four such Roach two-reelers, he returned to Manhattan to appear in six episodes for

Fox Film's comedy series, *The New York Kiddie Troupers.*

He made his Broadway debut as a Western Union boy in *The Man on Stilts* on September 9, 1931. Various small roles followed: As Hank Parkes in *The Lady Refuses* (1933), as a boy in *The Drunkard* (1934), as Alfred in *Life's Too Short* (1935), as Cadet Brown in *So Proudly We Hail* (1936), and, at sixteen, as a thirty-five-year-old plumber in Norman Bel Geddes' flop, *Iron Men* (1936). A Hollywood offer to play Huckleberry Finn fizzled (Jackie Moran got the role in David O. Selznick's 1938 *The Adventures of Tom Sawyer*). But Bracken thumbed his way to Hollywood only to discover that storming the studio gates was a quixotic gesture, and he returned to New York, where George Abbott signed him to succeed Frank Albertson in the role of Billy Randolph in the highly successful stage comedy, *Brother Rat.*

Abbott's genius for directing youths was never more successful than in a first play by a high school lecturer, Clifford Goldsmith, which introduced a new type of teenage hero to the world, namely Henry Aldrich. *What a Life* opened at the Biltmore Theatre in New York on April 13, 1938, romped through 538 performances, and became a successful radio show; eventually, Paramount developed a Henry Aldrich series for the screen. On Broadway, Eddie played the role of Bill while understudying Ezra Stone as Henry, and, in July, 1938, he subbed for Stone as the fight-

With Gil Lamb and Dorothy Lamour in Rainbow Island *(Par 1944)*

With Dona Drake in The Girl from Jones Beach *(WB 1949)*

ing, cribbing, disaster-prone Henry. When the national touring company of *What a Life* was formed, Bracken was given the lead role. He made a perfect Henry, and the enormously successful road company included Butterfly McQueen in her original role of Mary, and, in the part of Barbara Pearson, played on Broadway by Betty Field, a competent young actress named Connie Nickerson. Elated with his road tour success, Bracken had three thousand pictures of himself printed with his name on the bottom and passed them out generously to anyone within reach. He was also prolific in becoming engaged to this girl or that, but finally bought a ring for Connie Nickerson. After playing a summer theatre engagement of *What a Life* at Bass Rocks Theatre (which Bracken also directed), they were married on September 25, 1939.

Mr. Abbott's next venture, *Too Many Girls,* opened on Broadway at the Imperial Theatre on October 18, 1939, and introduced Cuban Desi Arnaz. In the top comedian spot, as Jo Jo Jordan, was Abbott's road company "Henry," Eddie Bracken. Understudying the three male leads, Arnaz, Bracken, and Richard Kollmar, was a red-headed chorus boy named Van Johnson. When the show was sold to RKO, Abbott was engaged to write and direct the screen version of the Rodgers and Hart musical. He took Arnaz, Eddie, six girl dancers, and Van Johnson to Hollywood. RKO

added Lucille Ball and Ann Miller to the "hep" cast. Bracken had returned to Hollywood to stay for the forties decade.

Paramount filmed *What a Life* in 1939 with Jackie Cooper as Henry Aldrich and Betty Field, making her screen debut, in her original Broadway role. (Bracken's role of Bill had been deleted from the film.) In 1941, Paramount signed Eddie to a contract and assigned him the part of Dizzy Stevens in their sequel to the popular *What a Life,* called *Life with Henry.* Eddie's brisk playing and crack-voiced mugging would have been perfect for the lead role, but that was still in the amiable if ineffectual hands of Cooper. As Dizzy, Bracken walked away with the acting honors in the sequel. The cast also included as Henry's parents the director of the silent epic *Ben-Hur,* Fred Niblo, and the garrulous and over-glittery Hedda Hooper. Paramount continued the Aldrich series on a B budget, first testing the original Henry, Ezra Stone, but finally signing Jimmy Lydon for the series of nine additional Henry Aldrich misadventures. The production values and sadly declining scripts of these nine films hardly equaled Metro's highly profitable Andy Hardy series. Mercifully, Bracken escaped the programmer skein when the studio put Charles Smith into the continuing part of Dizzy Stevens.

Bracken was shuttled into a routine flop, *Reaching*

With Florence MacMichael in Young and Willing *(UA 1943)*

With Boyd Irwin, Russell Hicks, Richard Hageman, and Priscilla Lane in Fun on a Weekend (UA 1947)

for the Sun (1941), and went from playing Bob Hope's pal Bert in the slapstick Caught in the Draft (1941) to being dumb-dumb sailor Barney Waters in Paramount's remake of Clara Bow's The Fleet's In (1942). In the latter film, two boisterous, bouncy gals, Betty Hutton and Cass Daley, made their motion picture debuts. Eddie's hayseed, countrified comedy lead was a good balance for the bombastic belting by Hutton of "Arthur Murray Taught Me Dancing in a Hurry." Oddly enough, Paramount saw them as a weird team in which the dominating blonde bombshell Hutton usually gave out with something more raucous than "Hearts and Flowers" in her energetic pursuit of the somewhat bewildered, little-boyish Bracken. For the studio's multi-star musical Star Spangled Rhythm (1942), Eddie was again a gob, Jimmy Webster, with Hutton as the movie studio telephone operator madly in love with him. Earlier in the year, he was cast as Jack Mitchell with bouncy, acrobatic June Preisser in a musical murder mystery Sweater Girl (1942), a movie notable only for the song "I Don't Want to Walk Without You, Baby".

Out of the Frying Pan (1941) had been an infectious Broadway comedy. Its screen version served as a showcase for several of Paramount's young talents, including Eddie, Susan Hayward, Barbara Britton, and William Holden. It was filmed under the title Young and Willing and followed the premise of a groups of kids trying to break into show business. As part of a special deal with United Artists, Young and Willing (1943) was among a group of films made by Paramount but released by United Artists. Eddie and Betty Hutton were together again as second leads in support of Mary Martin and Dick Powell in a Technicolor splash of fluff, Happy Go Lucky (1943), dipped in Caribbean calypso and made notable by Hutton's powerhouse singing of "Murder He Says." Then both Eddie and Barbara, who had shown their proficiency at tossing off double entendres, came under the direction of Paramount's resident director and writer genius, the myth-smasher and irreverent creative force, Preston Sturges.

Sturges had won fame as the playwright of Strictly Dishonorable (1929), emerging as a satirical scripter in Hollywood, where he ferociously attacked many American idols and overblown dreams. He wielded his assault on politics in The Great McGinty (1940), on greed, celebrities, and experts in Christmas in July (1940), and pretentious Hollywood producers and "message" films in Sullivan's Travels (1941). For The Miracle of Morgan's Creek (1944) (called by some the greatest film script ever composed), he let loose with salvos at such revered institutions as marriage, motherhood, and instant celebrities. It became the screen's

89

comedy hit of the year. As Trudy Kockenlocker, Betty Hutton was effective in her first non-singing role, and Eddie appeared as a meek, frightened, incredulous stammering 4-F idiot Norval Jones who becomes a national hero after marrying pregnant Hutton (she cannot recall who sired her male sextuplets that provides Sturges' "miracle"). The public's reception to Bracken's inspired, nervous performance provided one of the genuine benchmarks of his career.

Bracken's second Sturges satirical hero was Woodrow Lafayette Pershing Truesmith, a World War I hero's son who is 4-F. Sturges aimed his well-laced barbs in *Hail the Conquering Hero* (1944) at America's mindless devotion to hero-worship and blowhard politicians. If less than endearing in his cloying part, Eddie fulfilled Sturges' idea of the fraudulent hero, while Franklin Pangborn, William Demarest, and Raymond Walburn contributed first-rate performances that bolstered the comic script.

After Sturges, it was back to Paramount's wardrobe of uniforms for Bracken, first as Merchant Marine Toby Smith in a Technicolor tongue-in-cheek grimace of Dorothy Lamour's sarong-sagas, *Rainbow Island* (1944), and then as wealthy socialite J. Newport Bates enlisting in the Navy with his chaperone Sonny Tufts in a silly, unlikely, and less interesting *Bring on the Girls* (1945). For the studio's hodge podge *Duffy's Tavern* (1945), Eddie played himself, and in the boring, trite tale of kleptomania and romance, *Hold that Blonde* (1945)—in which bland Veronica Lake was seen without her usual teammate, Alan Ladd—Eddie was timid, well-heeled Ogdon Spencer Trulow III. Using the gimmick of Bing Crosby's voice dubbed for his vocalizing, Eddie was Herbie Fenton, a Western Union delivery boy turned into an overnight bobbysox sensation, in a mild musical, *Out of This World* (1945), which featured Diana Lynn tossing off the "Minute Waltz" as leader of an all-girl orchestra.

Bracken entertained servicemen in camps and hospitals throughout the South Pacific and in the United States, returning to complete his Paramount contract as Henry Haskell in the tepid *Ladies' Man,* which was not tossed out into release until 1947. For two years, Eddie appeared on his own radio show from Hollywood, "The Eddie Bracken Show" (in 1934 he had been a gag writer for NBC's Bob Hope radio show and made his audio acting debut as Dizzy on NBC's "Henry Aldrich Show").

By 1949, Eddie's career was fading as fast as the decade. He was Chuck Donovan, an advertising agent, in Warners' *The Girl from Jones Beach* (starring Virigina Mayo) and, in Judy Garland's last MGM film, *Summer Stock* (1950) he was another hayseed, Orville Wingait, who loses Judy to toothy Gene Kelly.

Preston Sturges produced a revival of the farce *Room Service* on the West Coast for the 1951–52 season and Bracken, back on the stage at the Players Theatre, shone brilliantly in the part of the playwright (played in the 1938 RKO Marx Brothers' film version by Frank Albertson). After Twentieth Century-Fox's episodic *We're Not Married,* in which he was cast opposite Mitzi Gaynor in one of the segments, Eddie returned to the stage in the touring company of George Axelrod's comedy, *The Seven Year Itch,* playing the leading role of Richard Sherman on Broadway in 1955.

Things were going less and less well for the hyperdynamic Bracken, who was geared to cope only with success. On television he was a guest on a special AGVA "Comedy Hour Show" with Bob Hope, Bing Crosby, and Billy Daniels, and appeared in the "Gulf Playhouse" telecast of "A Question of Rank" (1952) and "Mr. Berger" (1952), "Ford Theatre's "It Happened in a Pawn Shop" (1953), and as a collector of pin-up pictures in Korea for the "Video Theatre" production, "The Corporal and the Lady" (1953). On "Schlitz Playhouse," in "Simplon Express" (1953), he was Peter Wade, an amateur sleuth involved in a plot to blow up a tunnel. Finally, in a "Studio One" drama he played Billy Cascade, half of a down and out vaudeville team with Jack Whiting as the other half of the team. Replacing Burgess Meredith as Sakini in the national touring company of *The Teahouse of the August Moon,* he continued working in the theatre through summer stock, and during the next several years was frequently seen on television on many anthology series.

Alternating between theatre and television, Bracken managed to keep professionally occupied, but it was often as a creature of another time and place. Talking about his chosen profession he said, "This is the business I'm in and I'm in it to put my five kids through school and to provide food and clothes for me and my family. If that sounds as if I think too many actors are overly idealistic, it's true." Since their marriage in 1939, Eddie and Connie Bracken had become the parents of two sons, David and Michael, and three daughters, Susan, Carolyn, and Judith, the latter girl named for George Abbott's daughter.

Based on Don Marquis' delightfully droll *The Lives and Times of Archie and Mehitabel,* Columbia Records produced an album "archy and mehitabel," sub-titled "A Back-alley Opera," with music by George Kleinsinger and lyrics by Joe Darion. The narration was by David Wayne, and Carol Channing played the "free soul queen of Shinbone Alley," with Eddie as her mentor, the cockroach poet archy. Released in the spring of 1955, the album was a huge success and Bracken's career would include archy in various forms for the next several years. He found himself everywhere observing that "sometimes I think Mehitabel is too *toujours gai*," followed by Mehitabel's constant reply, "There's a dance or two in the girl yet!" On April 13, 1957, he reprised the cockroach role in a misguided, unexciting Broadway musical *Shinbone Alley* with Eartha Kitt as the bitchy, immoral alley cat Mehitabel. The show expired after forty-nine performances. With Tammy Grimes as Mehitabel, Eddie repeated his role of the philosophical insect for television's "Play of the Week" on May 16, 1960. Nine years later, again with Carol Channing, Eddie supplied the voice of Archy in the cartoon film version of Marquis' *Lives and Times of . . . The* poorly distributed feature, entitled *shinbone alley,* was slipped into release by Allied Artists in 1971.

For NBC's special version of *Strawberry Blonde* with David Wayne and Janet Blair, Eddie played Carson's 1941 film role of Hugo Barnstead. In January, 1960, he and Carroll and Harris Masterson produced a dull, humorless beatnick musical starring Larry Parks, Betty Garrett, and himself, which struggled through five performances after opening at the Martin Beck Theatre on February 10th. For the record, the flop's name was *Beg, Borrow or Steal.* The following February (1961) he directed an implausible play, *How to Make a Man,* which contained less comedy than a comic book, in which Barbara Britton, Peter Marshall, Vicki Cummings, and other talented players survived for twelve tattered performances. Undaunted Bracken continued onward. For TV's "Rawhide" in March of 1963 he was Morris G. Stevens, an accident-prone scholar attempting to make peace between the Indian and the white man. Later in the year he toured in the play *Come Blow Your Horn.* On October 25, 1965, he replaced Art Carney as Felix Unger, the sedate, prissy half of Neil Simon's hilar-ious *The Odd Couple,* and, with Jack Klugman as the slob Oscar, played in the comedy for two years on Broadway, finally leaving the Simon show to tour in Robert Anderson's three-sketch play *You Know I Can't Hear When the Water Is Running.* His daughter was featured in the cast and his wife Connie understudied the female lead. It was also at this time that Eddie returned to radio, as host of a show originating from station WBIC at Bay Shore, Long Island.

Ambitious plans to create a circuit of ten winter and summer theatres under Eddie Bracken Ventures, Inc. collapsed after two years at a loss of over two million dollars. The greatest loss was the Coconut Grove Playhouse in Miami, for which Bracken had paid successful entrepreneur Zev Bufman nearly $750,000 in 1970. Bufman successfully operated Miami's sole legitimate playhouse, a veritable lighthouse within the cultural desert of the Miami area, but by the end of 1971, Bracken Ventures Inc. had hit the bottom of the financial barrel. Eddie, explaining the loss of Cape Cod's Falmouth Playhouse, Skowhegan's Lakewood Theatre, the Hyde Park Playhouse and others, said: "It was a problem of growth that was too fast, and gross mismanagement. A lot of enthusiastic sales pitches were made to me by people I had trusted, and the money kept going out instead of in. I'm stuck in a Gargantuan mess. My agent once said an actor is not a very good businessman, and I guess I set out to prove him wrong. So far he's been dead right."

For Bracken, the collapse of his ambitious theatre empire must have seemed like one of his old Paramount films in which he was usually cast as a befuddled, confused, and perplexed schnook, upon whom the fates descended with mounting fury against a roly-poly little man totally incapable of combating them.

EDDIE BRACKEN

Too Many Girls *(RKO 1940)*
Life with Henry *(Par 1941)*
Reaching for the Sun *(Par 1941)*
Caught in the Draft *(Par 1941)*
The Fleet's In *(Par 1942)*
Sweater Girl *(Par 1942)*
Star Spangled Rhythm *(Par 1942)*
Young and Willing *(UA 1943)*
Happy Go Lucky *(Par 1943)*
The Miracle of Morgan's Creek *(Par 1944)*
Hail the Conquering Hero *(Par 1944)*
Rainbow Island *(Par 1944)*
Bring on the Girls *(Par 1945)*
Duffy's Tavern *(Par 1945)*

Hold that Blonde *(Par 1945)*
Out of this World *(Par 1945)*
Ladies' Man *(Par 1947)*
Fun on a Weekend *(UA 1947)*
The Girl from Jones Beach *(WB 1949)*
Summer Stock *(MGM 1950)*
Two Tickets to Broadway *(RKO 1951)*
We're Not Married *(20th 1952)*
About Face *(WB 1952)*
A Slight Case of Larceny *(MGM 1953)*
Wild, Wild World *(Sokoler 1961)*
A Summer Sunday (a.k.a. Always on Sunday) *(Italian 1962)*
shinbone alley *(AA 1971)* (Voice only)

13

Scott Brady

When Brooklyn-born Scott Brady first arrived in Hollywood just after the Second World War, he was known only as Lawrence "Dillinger" Tierney's kid brother. However, soon enough, with his Irish good looks and with a little help from his established brother, he was on his way to becoming a movie star in his own right. After doing little more than a walk-on in one of his brother's pictures, he was signed to a term contract by the now defunct Eagle-Lion Studios. It was a small company that manufactured low-budget films, and Brady appeared in four features for them. Two of those pictures, *Canon City* (1948) and *He Walked by Night* (1948), were excellent programmers with a memorable stark style. The attention Brady received for his performances went to his and his agent's heads, and he bought his way out of Eagle-Lion and into the Universal-International players' stable where he soon discovered that while Audie Murphy, Jeff Chandler, and later Tony Curtis and Rock Hudson, were being promoted, he was still considered a nobody. At that time Brady was a more consummate actor than those other gentlemen and at 6' 2" was still one of the best looking men on the Hollywood scene. More times than not Universal cast him as a heavy, roles he played quite convincingly, but that marvelously smiling glint in his eyes gave a hint of much more.

Scott Brady's career never fulfilled its early promise. As it developed he became a post-World War II casualty in the California theatrical battleground.

Blue-eyed Scott was born on September 13, 1924, in Brooklyn to Lawrence and Maria Tierney. His real name was Gerald Kenneth Tierney, and he was always called Jerry. His father was chief of New York's aqueduct police force. (After he retired from that office he decided to go into show business himself, making his theatrical debut in the road company of *A Streetcar Named Desire.*) Tierney Sr. passed away on February 13, 1964, four years after his wife's death. Brady's older brother, Lawrence Tierney (born on March 15, 1919), would hit his Hollywood peak when he successfully played the title role in RKO's *Dillinger* (1945). From that time on, however, Lawrence had a highly variable career due to his drinking problem and his scrapes with the law. Brady's younger brother, Edward, made an unsuccessful attempt to become an actor under the name of Edward Tracy. The youngest Tierney also had his problems with the law, having once been jailed on a morals charge. It seemed that having had a policeman for a father did not set any law-abiding example for this family. Scott, himself, was slapped with a narcotics charge in 1957, but accused the police narcotics office of framing him on a phoney dope charge. He made the headlines again in 1963 when he was involved with a well-known bookie in some illegal trotting horse activities.

Though he was born in Brooklyn, Scott grew up in Westchester and attended Roosevelt and St. Michael's High Schools there, earning letters for basketball, football, and track. He was, and still is, very

With John Russell in Undertow *(Univ 1949)*

With James Millican and Charles D. Brown in In this Corner *(EL 1948)*

sports-minded. His ambition then was to be a football coach. After graduation, however, he enlisted in the Navy and saw service in China and Japan, mostly as a naval aviation mechanic on the U.S.S. *Norton Sound*. He became light heavyweight boxing champion at his naval base during his gunnery training at Pensacola, Florida. His boxing skill later helped him land his first major screen role as an ex-Navy boxer in *In This Corner* (1948) at Eagle-Lion.

After his release from the Navy in April, 1945, he traveled to California with seven hundred dollars in his pocket. Brady once told columnist Hedda Hopper, "I had the Navy discharge me in California so I could see my brother, Lawrence, but I wasn't thinking of becoming an actor. I'd asked my brother about that and he said he wouldn't advise anybody to do it— that it's about the most heartbreaking work in the world." Brady thought it was then too late for college, so he took on a number of odd jobs not really knowing what he was going to do with his life. He worked as a cab driver, a laborer, and also had a job in a lumber yard. But one afternoon he was having lunch at a local cafe and was spotted by producer Hal B. Wallis, who offered him a screen test.

Scott photographed well, but sounded like a Dead End kid. The test was a flop, but it gave him an incentive to become a success as a film actor. He enrolled in the Bliss-Hayden drama school in Beverly Hills under the G.I. Bill, which paid for his tuition and provided him with sixty-five dollars a month spending money. His brother Lawrence was also a great help to him. "Consider the edge I have over other fellows who want to get into this business," Brady once mused. "Larry didn't only take me to saloons. He brought me on all the sound stages, introduced me to everyone he knew, kept shoving me forward so I could meet people and learn."

When Scott was appearing in the drama school's production of *Heaven Can Wait*, his older brother sent agent Johnny Darrow to see the show. This meeting led to Scott's contract at Eagle-Lion. The fledgling actor, at this point, decided to change his name, because he did not want people saying that he was capitalizing on his brother's fame. He chose his new name from a story a friend wrote about a boxer hero called Scott Brady. Speaking of his brother Lawrence, who was his greatest booster, Scott would say, "He's a great actor, a thinking actor, unlike me. I rush into each scene like a bull in a china shop and hope it comes out all right. Larry is analytical, sensitive. He studies the other actors, the whole scene and his place in it—before the cameras roll. Larry's moodiness is part and parcel of his greatness. He personifies what we mean by 'black Irish.' One minute he's up

on cloud nine, the next he's down. Today everything's going great, sensational, terrific—but tomorrow, wham! Everything is gloomy." It was once suggested that perhaps Twentieth Century-Fox star Gene Tierney—also a Brooklynite—was a relation of theirs, but Brady replied that as much as he would like to think so, it just was not true.

Brady walked into his Eagle-Lion pact at three hundred dollars per film. Of *In This Corner*, Brady says, "it wasn't released, it escaped." The picture was shot in nine days, and when he read his first line in his first scene, he blew it and the director said, "O.K. kiddo, that's your screen test." Nevertheless, Scott was quite good as Sherbondy, a prison escapee in his next film, *Canon City*. It was an Alan Ladd type role, a sympathetic baddie. *He Walked by Night* (1948) was a solid follow-up film about a cold, calculating killer, exceptionally well-played by Richard Basehart. Brady plays a detective who finally helps capture him.

After *Port of New York* (1949), shot in Manhattan, Brady and his ambitious agent, Johnny Darrow, concluded that it would be much better to buy up his Eagle-Lion contract and move on to greener pastures. That company petitioned an injunction to prevent the actor from working elsewhere, but the affair was finally settled, costing Scott a good deal of money. He then signed a contract for two pictures a year, with Universal. Scott, unfortunately, never made a film for them that even approached *Canon City* and *He Walked by Night*.

His first feature for Universal was the Yvonne DeCarlo vehicle, *The Gal Who Took the West* (1949). He and John Russell played feuding cousins and the only aspect Scott did not like about making this Western was that he had to wear "elevated" boots. Although Brady is 6'2", Russell is 6'4", and it was decided that they should both be the same height as they were rivals for Yvonne's affections. Russell and he were reunited in *Undertow* (1949), with Brady playing the lead, a man accused of a murder he did not commit. In *Kansas Raiders,* (1950) which starred Audie Murphy, Marguerite Chapman, and Brian Donlevy, and featured Tony Curtis, Scott was forever blowin' the hair out of his eyes and lettin' the tobacco juice streak down his chin.

Scott had been well aware of the limitations of his Universal pact and negotiated a one-picture-a-year deal with Twentieth Century-Fox, to run concurrent with his other acting contract. Under that Fox contract, though, he made only two films at the Pico Boulevard lot: A straight lead role with humor in *The Model and the Marriage Broker* (1951), in which Thelma Ritter stole the whole show, and *The Bloodhounds of Broadway* (1952), where Scott played a

With Charles Coburn, Yvonne De Carlo, and John Russell in The Gal Who Took the West *(Univ 1949)*

Runyonesque gambler. He received $25,000 for each of his Fox films.

Back at Universal, Brady was allowed to display some of his bent for comedy in *Bronco Buster* (1952), in which he was generally mean and rugged. In *Untamed Frontier* (1952), he was back at being the heavy, beating Shelley Winters unmercifully. Of doing this scene, he says: "I've known Shelley for years. We're old friends from our Schwab's counter days. I said, "Sister, you've had this coming to you for years and years.' Then I laid it on." He kept asking Universal producers for more hero roles, but inevitably they were assigned to Rock Hudson, such as the lead in *The Golden Blade* (1953). In that case, it was just as well, because this "Bagdad" swashbuckler was a miserable affair for all concerned.

While Scott was making films for both Universal and Fox, Hal B. Wallis offered him the role of Terry Moore's beau in Paramount's *Come Back Little Sheba* (1952). It paid $30,000 for only two weeks of work, and as much as he wanted to accept it, he had to turn it down because of his prior commitments. The role eventually went to Richard Jaeckel. The one thing Brady's rash of Universal programmers did for him was to give him plenty of space in fan magazines. For many years, these publications referred to him as Hollywood's number one bachelor.

Brady did not sign a new agreement with Universal after his contract expired; instead, he made limited deals with other studios, such as Republic, Lippert, Columbia, and Fox again. At Republic he had the opportunity to co-star in Western with two of the screen's leading ladies (each living through leaner days): *Johnny Guitar* (1954) with Joan Crawford and *The Maverick Queen* (1956) with Barbara Stanwyck. His roles in both features were quite similar, even down to his characters' names. In the former he was The Dancin' Kid and in the latter Trucolor venture, he was The Sundance Kid. In the latter film, Howard Petrie played Butch Cassidy. Scott's role in *Johnny Guitar* is one of his better ones: he was cocky, swaggering, energetic, and sexy, and lost Crawford to resolute Sterling Hayden, who played the taciturn title role. He also gets killed oncamera in each of these sagebrush tales. Of working with Crawford, Brady says it was not so bad, "but as an alternative you could join the Marine Corps. Joan's all right, so long as you report for work on time, know your lines, and always stand at attention." He considers Stanwyck his favorite leading lady, as do most male stars. "That gal is dynamite and I love her." As an actress, he prefers Anne Bancroft, "I worked with her in a western [*The Restless Breed*, 1957] before she made it big." *The Restless Breed*, directed by Allan Dwan,

95

was one of five Westerns Scott did for Fox's budget unit in the late 1950s.

After appearing in a poor Korean war romance, *Battle Flame* (1959), Brady did not make another feature until 1963, when he supported Tab Hunter and Frankie Avalon in the inane *Operation Bikini*. He did, however, work continuously on television from 1953 on, primarily doing westerns. In 1957, he filmed a "Playhouse 90" episode called *Lone Woman,* in which he played a man who weds a beautiful Cheyenne Indian, played by Kathryn Grayson in one of her rare departures from the musical field. In 1959 Brady had his own syndicated video series, "Shotgun Slade," as a detective on horseback. It lasted for seventy-eight episodes.

Scott also interspersed some stage work between films and television, appearing with David Niven and Diana Lynn in Otto Preminger's production of *The Moon Is Blue* in San Francisco. He played the role William Holden undertook in the 1953 film. He also toured in stage productions of *Detective Story* and *Picnic*. The role of the drifter Hal in *Picnic* is one that perfectly suited Brady (as it had Ralph Meeker on Broadway). At this time he still had his marvelous physique which was a necessary quality for the role. Scott made his Broadway debut at the Imperial Theatre on April 23, 1959, as the ruthless card sharp in the musical *Destry,* co-starring with Andy Griffith and Dolores Gray. The part was originally set for John Ireland, who backed out of the project. The distaff critic of the *Gotham Guide Review* said of Brady, "He's one of the handsomest men who have ever appeared on Broadway—so good looking that you forget to notice if he's a good actor—but he is." New York's *Daily Mirror* said that he "is as slick as a well-oiled gun barrel and as sinister as a rattlesnake." Scott has not returned to Broadway, but did tour in the national company of Gore Vidal's *The Best Man,* playing Senator Joe Cantwell, but, surprisingly, Don "My Favorite Secretary" Porter received first billing over Brady. "The stage is fun," Brady has said, "but picture work is easier and a lot more lucrative. Broadway is a gas. But even if you get the work, who can afford it?"

In December, 1962, Brady played the title role on *The Floyd Gibbons Story,* a segment of ABC-TV's "The Untouchables," dealing with the patch-over-one-eye headline hunter of the 1920s and 1930s. It had been decided beforehand that if the show was hailed a good one, Desilu and ABC would turn it into a series for Brady called "The World of Floyd Gibbons." Brady remained under contract with Desilu until the future of the series was decided, but it never materialized and Scott went back to doing more video guest spots and many more minor films. Several of these films have played only drive-ins or have been sold directly to television. He also appeared in five of A. C. Lyles' mini-budgeted Westerns for Paramount.

In 1967, at age forty-three, Hollywood's one-time number one bachelor finally got married. After dating Mary Lizabeth (Lisa) Tirony for many years he finally decided to settle down. Years before, he had been a steady companion of Dorothy Malone, and it was assumed that someday they would wed, but their relationship evolved into one of deep friendship. Brady was also romantically linked with Gwen Verdon for a long time. The Bradys have two sons, Timothy (Timber) and Terence, and Brady says, "I don't want my boys to be actors. They'd meet too many kinky broads."

Today, Scott Brady is no longer the trim, good-looking, devil-may-care Irish rogue. He is badly overweight—almost in the same category with Broderick Crawford—and is balding, but he has become one of television's most competent character actors, playing, more times than not, heavies and policemen. He has had guest spots on almost every television show aired on the little screen, and he will often take even a small supporting part. "To tell you the truth," he admits, "I can't afford to turn down many parts, not with kids to send to college." Feature filmmaking is not at its briskest, especially in Hollywood, but Scott still can be seen in some minor independent productions, and through his good friend, producer Mike Frankovich, has also had supporting assignments in three of latter's major productions for Columbia studios: *Marooned* (1969), *Doctors' Wives* (1971), and *Dollars* (1971). *Dollars* gave him one of the sturdiest roles of his career to date. Reviewing the Warren Beatty-Goldie Hawn picture for the New York *Daily News,* Wanda Hale declared, "The big surprise is a great performance by Scott Brady as Sarge, fat and balding." The Long Island *Press* termed him "superb." He then turned up in the fall of 1974 as a semi-regular role on NBC-TV's "Police Story" which thanks to a new vogue in cops shows, has done quite well in the ratings.

Brady now refers to himself as an "ex-star," and even though his acting career has never reached any aesthetic or commercial heights, it certainly has been a steady one, for he never stops working. (His brother Lawrence works very little these days, but will occasionally be seen in a small television role or in an out-of-town theatre production.) Brady sums up his professional past and present by saying, "I'm perfectly happy with the career choice I made."

SCOTT BRADY

Born to Kill   *(RKO 1947)*
In This Corner   *(EL 1948)*
Canon City   *(EL 1948)*
He Walked by Night   *(EL 1948)*
The Gal Who Took the West   *(Univ 1949)*
Port of New York   *(EL 1949)*
Undertow   *(Univ 1949)*
I Was a Shoplifter   *(Univ 1950)*
Kansas Raiders   *(Univ 1950)*
Undercover Girl   *(Univ 1950)*
The Model and the Marriage Broker   *(20th 1951)*
Bronco Buster   *(Univ 1952)*
Untamed Frontier   *(Univ 1952)*
Yankee Buccaneer   *(Univ 1952)*
Bloodhounds of Broadway   *(20th 1952)*
Montana Belle   *(RKO 1952)*
A Perilous Journey   *(Rep 1953)*
El Alamein   *(Col 1953)*
White Fire   *(Lip 1954)*
The Law vs. Billy the Kid   *(Col 1954)*
Johnny Guitar   *(Rep 1954)*
They Were so Young   *(Lip 1955)*
Gentlemen Marry Brunettes   *(UA 1955)*
The Vanishing American   *(Rep 1955)*
Terror at Midnight   *(Rep 1956)*
The Maverick Queen   *(Rep 1956)*
Mohawk   *(20th 1956)*

The Storm Rider   *(20th 1957)*
The Restless Breed   *(20th 1957)*
Ambush at Cimarron Pass   *(20th 1958)*
Blood Arrow   *(20th 1958)*
Battle Flame   *(AA 1959)*
Operation Bikini   *(AIP 1963)*
Stage to Thunder Rock   *(Par 1964)*
John Goldfarb, Please Come Home   *(20th 1964)*
Black Spurs   *(Par 1965)*
Destination Inner Space   *(Feature Film Corp. of America 1966)*
Castle of Evil   *(World Entertainment 1966)*
Red Tomahawk   *(Par 1967)*
Fort Utah   *(Par 1967)*
Journey to the Center of Time   *(Goldstone Enterprises 1967)*
Arizona Bushwhackers   *(Par 1968)*
Nightmare in Wax   *(Crown International 1969)*
Satan's Sadists   *(Independent International 1970)*
Marooned   *(Col 1969)*
They Ran for Their Lives   *(Independent International 1970)*
Cain's Way (a.k.a., Cain's Cutthroats)   *(MDA Associates 1970)*
Five Bloody Graves   *(Independent International 1970)*
Hell's Bloody Devils   *(Independent International 1971)*
Doctors' Wives   *(Col 1971)*
$(Dollars)   *(Col 1971)*
Bonnie's Kids   *(General Film 1972)*
The Loners   *(Fanfare 1973)*
Wicked, Wicked   *(MGM 1973)*

14

Barbara Britton

Attractive, keen Barbara Britton became a nationally known household name, not as a Paramount ingenue of the 1940s who went on the make some thirty features, but as the Betty Furness of the cosmetic world. She was television's most popular salesgirl, "*The* Revlon Girl," seen every Tuesday night on the quiz program "The $64,000 Question." Barbara replaced Wendy Barrie as Revlon's nail polish pitch lady and remained with the sponsor for twelve years, huckstering cosmetics on such later television shows as "The $64,000 Challenge" and "Bid 'n' Buy." Her stardom as an actress came again, not in theatrical films, but as Pam North, the distaff side of the famous amateur detective duo of "Mr. and Mrs. North," on televison. With this 1952 series she established herself as a pert comedienne of no mean capabilities. The following year she had the dubious honor of being in the first, full-length, natural vision three-dimensional film, *Bwana Devil.* Certainly this bizarre professional career with its odd twists is not what she had in mind when she began in the acting craft, but then. . . .

She was born Barbara Brantingham in Long Beach, California, on September 26, 1919. She attended Polytechnic High School and then Long Beach City College, where she was a speech major and hoped to become a drama and speech teacher. While in college, she represented Long Beach on a float in the Tournament of Roses and her picture appeared in the papers. From the photo alone she received calls from three separate Hollywood talent agencies. The scout from Paramount also came to see her in a school production of *The Old Maid* and was surprised to find that she had some natural dramatic ability. He offered her a studio screen test. Barbara did her audition opposite Richard Denning, who, years later, would be her "Mr. and Mrs. North" video partner. Dampening her spate of good luck were the attitudes of her parents. Coming from solid Quaker and Methodist stock, they strongly objected to a possible acting career for their daughter. However, she finally convinced them that acting could be as harmless as teaching and won their reluctant approval. Blue-eyed, five-foot-five Barbara made her film debut in *Secret of the Wastelands* (1941), a Hopalong Cassidy western, in which she spent most of her screen time hidden behind horn-rimmed glasses and a five gallon hat.

If Paramount was topheavy in the early 1940s with female stars (Claudette Colbert, Barbara Stanwyck, Dorothy Lamour, Paulette Goddard, Madeleine Carroll, Mary Martin, Veronica Lake, and the fast-rising Susan Hayward), it also had an over-healthy contingent of starlets (including Betty Brewer, Eva Gabor,

With Macdonald Carey in Wake Island *(Par 1942)*

Frances Gifford, Helen Gilbert, Margaret Hayes, Bernice Kay, Jean Phillips, Eleanor Stewart, and Barbara). Besides this imposing roster, there were also in the middle-ground players, such as Frances Farmer, Ellen Drew, Betty Field, Susanna Foster, Diana Lynn, Constance Moore, Patricia Morison, Martha O'Driscoll, and June Preisser. Therefore, it was hardly any wonder that Barbara had a difficult time getting her screen career into orbit. She was used as a bit player in a number of films and was kept busy posing for cheesecake. She was the only female in *Wake Island* (1942), but her first major role was in the remake of *Mrs. Wiggs of the Cabbage Patch* (1942), starring Fay Bainter. The following year she gave a moving performance as Lieutenant Rosemary Larson, a young nurse in the stirring and patriotic *So Proudly We Hail* (1943), an all-star women-in-war story. As Sister Clothilde in *Till We Meet Again* (1944), she had star billing with Ray Milland and received better notices than he did. The *New York Times* reported, "Miss Britton, as the novice, was convincing and she gave evidence of being able to give a competent performance as a hunted woman. But she did not give depth to the role of a fearful, yet brave woman who had been torn from her lifelong seclusion and security." While filming this Frank Borzage-directed feature, Barbara was constantly aware of how important the picture was to her future career. The combined pressure of that haunting thought, the long-working hours, and her Hollywood Canteen and other benefit work, came to a head when she was playing a scene where shots were fired into a wall next to her. Barbara fell apart and suffered a minor nervous breakdown.

In her search for help, a naturopathic physician, Dr. Eugene Czukor, was recommended to her. Her condition rapidly improved with the doctor's treatment, and she married him on April 2, 1945. She firmly believes that physicians make the best husbands, and offering a case in point, she has said, "Look at Irene Dunne." The Czukors have two chil-

With Ray Milland in Till We Meet Again *(Par 1944)*

With Helen Spring, Ann E. Todd, and Art Baker in a publicity pose for Cover-Up *(UA 1949)*

dren, a son, Teddy, and a daughter, Chris. They have also lost two children, a daughter, and a son, the latter dying two days after birth from a respiratory illness.

Barbara ended her exclusive contract with Paramount after appearing in their remake of the Western classic *The Virginian* (1946) with Joel McCrea and Brian Donlevy, and in the minor melodrama *They Made Me a Killer* (1946) with Robert Lowery. She enjoyed making the awful *Captain Kidd* the previous year because of her costar, Charles Laughton. She has always remembered the advice that the British actor gave her regarding a performer's speaking voice: "Read the Bible aloud three hours daily."

By 1950, Barbara's non-locomotive screen career was slipping, as her non-essential sister role (to Ronald Colman) in *Champagne for Caesar* attested. However, her professional career seemed to brighten the next year, when she signed a non-exclusive contract with Universal. Unfortunately, that company saw fit to cast her as decoration in a few unimpressive westerns. In the three films she made for Universal, *The Raiders* (1952), *Ain't Misbehavin'* (1955), and her last feature to date, *The Spoilers* (1955), she was cast as "the other woman." In between these programmers, at least, the independently-produced, but United Artists' released, *Bwana Devil* (1953), gave her a good deal of publicity because of the film's 3-D process. She recalls that making the film was "an exciting experience." *Bwana Devil* was slaughtered by the critics, but the film made a bundle of money. Even a boxoffice hit, however, did not help her stagnating movie career, particularly when she was a thirty-three-year-old quasi-ingenue.

Like many other Hollywood performers, she turned to the Broadway stage for public and critical attention. Her performance in George Bernard Shaw's *Getting Married*, which played a limited engagement at New York's ANTA Playhouse in 1951, earned her the role of Pam North in the "Mr. and Mrs. North" television series. The show began on CBS-TV; then, after a two-season hiatus, it was brought back by NBC. In its final season (1955) the series was syndicated. Between her role in this persistently popular series and her role as the video spokeswoman for Revlon, Barbara was able to earn a hefty salary. On "The $64,000 Question" she would work only one day a week—three hours of rehearsal and the show—and would collect one thousand dollars weekly for her efforts. This one-day-a-week salary arrangement applied to any Revlon-sponsored show on which she appeared. With this schedule she found time to appear on the television soap opera "Date with Life." Since her work time was restricted to New York, her husband agreed to move their home base to Manhattan. She does not regret leaving California, stating that "Hollywood is the most provincial town in the world. It's a one-industry community."

It was not always clear sailing for Barbara with her Revlon sponsor. From time to time, there would be rumors that the company intended to replace her. Kathryn Grayson was one performer who did receive an offer from the company: One million dollars for five years. Miss Grayson was affronted by the proposal because she believed that film stars should not be salesladies.

Barbara returned to the Broadway stage in 1956 in *Wake Up Darling,* a comedy by Alex Gottlieb, staged by Ezra Stone, and co-featuring Barry Nelson. She played a young actress, and all her reviews commented favorably on her extraordinary beauty. The *New York Post* said she was " a beautiful girl with an intelligent sense of humor." The *World-Telegram* found her "startlingly lovely, but her wide success in TV has an odd effect on her stage acting. She performs with radiant omnivorous enthusiasm which suggests any minute she will pick up a box of her sponsor's product and try to sell it to you. It is kind of frightening, from such a pretty girl." Barbara returned to Broadway again in February, 1961, in *How to Make a Man,* a dismal and quick failure directed by ex-movie star Eddie Bracken. She left her Revlon post when Carl Reiner offered her the role of his TV wife in the proposed series "Head of the Family." After the pilot was aired in 1960 and did not sell, she made yet another pilot. This one was called "You Can't Take It with You," and was made up of original stories concerning a zany family taken from the George Kaufman-Moss Hart play. It did not find an on-the-air sponsor either.

For the past several years, Barbara has been appearing in stock and in dinner theatres, headlining such shows as *Born Yesterday, The Rainmaker, Once More with Feeling,* and *Forty Carats.* She is also a charter member of an organization offering religious-psychiatric service to those in need of guidance. She prefers working in the legitimate theatre, but says that "TV and movie audiences are much larger, and, let's face it, the pay is better."

Today, Barbara looking amazingly slim and chipper, can *still* be found on television selling something, and, as always, is a very convincing saleslady. "Commercials," she says, "are very often sort of stilted and can sound like they are part of a magazine ad. You've got to say a lot of things that aren't too natural and make them come out like they're the most natural things in the world." Barbara always does them naturally and with a great deal of enthusiasm.

BARBARA BRITTON

Secret of the Wastelands   *(Par 1941)*
Louisiana Purchase   *(Par 1941)*
The Fleet's In   *(Par 1942)*
Reap the Wild Wind   *(Par 1942)*
Beyond the Blue Horizon   *(Par 1942)*
Wake Island   *(Par 1942)*
Mrs. Wiggs of the Cabbage Patch   *(Par 1942)*
Young and Willing   *(UA 1943)*
So Proudly We Hail   *(Par 1943)*
The Story of Dr. Wassell   *(Par 1944)*
Till We Meet Again   *(Par 1944)*
The Great John L   *(UA 1945)*
Captain Kidd   *(UA 1945)*
The Virginian   *(Par 1946)*
They Made Me a Killer   *(Par 1946)*
The Fabulous Suzanne   *(Rep 1946)*
The Return of Monte Cristo   *(Col 1946)*

Gunfighters   *(Col 1947)*
Albuquerque   *(Par 1948)*
Mr. Reckless   *(Par 1948)*
The Untamed Breed   *(Col 1948)*
Loaded Pistols   *(Col 1949)*
I Shot Jesse James   *(Screen Guild 1949)*
Cover-Up   *(UA 1949)*
Champagne for Caesar   *(UA 1950)*
Bandit Queen   *(Lip 1950)*
The Raiders   *(Univ 1952)*
Ride the Man Down   *(Rep 1952)*
Bwana Devil   *(UA 1953)*
Dragonfly Squadron   *(AA 1954)*
Ain't Misbehavin'   *(Univ 1955)*
Night Freight   *(AA 1955)*
The Spoilers   *(Univ 1955)*

15

Geraldine Brooks

In the flood of new faces at 1940s' Warner Bros., there were, among others, Dorothy Malone, Joan Leslie, Martha Vickers, Janis Paige, Andrea King, Faye Emerson, Joan Lorring, Geraldine Brooks, and Lauren Bacall. Unquestionably, Miss Bacall had such a unique screen charisma that she would have surfaced even without the studio support of husband Humphrey Bogart. But how does one account for the non-emergence of Geraldine Brooks, a petite (5'2") blue-eyed, brown-haired beauty, who displayed a particularly radiant smile, and, even more importantly, demonstrated such a marvelous ability at powerhouse acting. Had she checked into the Burbank studio earlier in the 1940s, she just might have won the coveted role of Veda in *Mildred Pierce* (1945), taking it away from Ann Blyth, and established herself as the talented young lady she was. Instead, Geraldine was cast by the post-World War II Warners into conventional roles, publicized as just another starlet, subjected to over-makup for the camera, and then dumped by the company in their recession shuffle. To date, Geraldine has made only fourteen features with not one comedy among them. It has remained for television to provide her with recurring showcases to exhibit her persistent, clear beauty and her knack for adding dimension to emotionally dramatic roles.

Geraldine was trained from infancy for a theatrical career. (She began taking dancing lessons when she was two years old.) She comes from a very well-known theatrical family and was born Geraldine Stroock, a Dutch name, on October 29, 1925, in New York City. Her father, James Stroock, owns Brooks Costume Company, New York's top theatrical costumers. Her mother, Bianca, was a well-known costume designer and stylist. As a child, Geraldine could alwasy be found playing in the costume shop. Her older sister, Gloria Brooks, is also an actress. Geraldine's theatrical heritage is extensive. Morris Gest, the stage producer, is a cousin, while two aunts, Helen Rook and Rosa Olitzka, were also in show business. Miss Rook was a member of the Ziegfield Follies and Miss Olitzka was a contralto who sang with the Metropolitan Opera from 1900 to 1910.

Geraldine was named after opera diva Geraldine Farrar. "All during my growing up days," says Geraldine, "famous persons were everyday visitors to our house. I took it all for granted." During grammar school she also attended the Hunter modeling school and, later, Julia Richman High School, from which she was graduated in 1942. She was president of the drama club there, directing and appearing in many shows. She was accepted at Syracuse University, but decided to study acting at the American Academy of Dramatic Art, instead, and, later, at the Neighborhood Playhouse. Thanks to a gift from her father (a five percent royalty interest from the phenomenally successful Broadway musical *Oklahoma!*), money was not an inhibiting problem while she studied and looked for acting jobs.

She had appeared in some summer stock productions, such as *Junior Miss,* before she was called in to replace an ailing actress in the pre-Broadway tryout of *Follow the Girls* with Gertrude Niesen and Jackie Gleason. Miss Niesen was starred as a burlesque

With Joan Bennett in The Reckless Moment *(Col 1949)*

With Ross Ford in a publicity pose for Challenge to Lassie *(MGM 1949)*

With Joan Crawford in Possessed *(WB 1947)*

queen, Bubbles LaMarr, who is found working in a servicemen's canteen. Geraldine was seen in the small role of Catherine Pepburn. *Women's Wear Daily* said of her performance, "A line of praise is due Geraldine Stroock for her imitation of Katharine Hepburn, which is perfection in face, mannerism, and voice." Geraldine had had the opportunity of observing Hepburn many times at the Stage Door Canteen and received an exit ovation during the show's first performance in New Haven. While the play was in Boston, the great Hepburn herself saw it and "climbed three flights of stairs to my dressing room to compliment me," recalls Geraldine. After the May 8, 1944 Century Theatre debut of *Follow the Girls,* Geraldine remained with the Broadway production for nine months.

Next, the Theatre Guild cast Geraldine as Juliet in their proposed revival of *Romeo and Juliet,* but when they cancelled the production, she was assigned instead to play Perdita in *The Winter's Tale.* During this period she received a few film contract offers but did not accept any, because there were no definite roles mentioned, that is, until Warner Bros. offered her the part of Julie, the hysterical niece who commits suicide in *Cry Wolf* (1947). She was the thirty-third young actress tested for the role in this Errol Flynn-Barbara Stanwyck thriller. For the movies she dropped her real surname and took on Brooks, the

name of her father's company. Unlike most newcomers who started out at a seventy-five- to one-hundred-dollar-a-week contract, Geraldine's weekly salary began at eight hundred fifty dollars and rose to twelve hundred dollars.

In a similar vein to her role in Cry Wolf was her part as Raymond Massey's sensitive daughter in *Possessed* (1947), which most critics agree is one of the better, if not the best, of Joan Crawford's screen performances. It would have been hard for any supporting actress to hold her own against Crawford's harrowing performance as the catatonic registered nurse, but Geraldine did just that. The *New York Herald-Tribune* called her a very promising young actress. "Her portrayal of a sane teenager in bedlam is definitely refreshing," the reviewer added.

She was given the lead in *Embraceable You* (1948), in which she was the young girl injured by tough guy Dane Clark who later comes to love her. This picture went nowhere, and other Warners films went from bad to worse, but two of her loanouts were quite good. *Live Today for Tomorrow,* retitled *An Act of Murder* (1948) after its initial release, dealt quite intelligently with the subject of euthanasia. Geraldine played Frederic March's daughter and was a "standout," according to *Variety.* The other outside assignment of note was at Columbia where she supported Joan Bennett and James Mason in the excellent, overlooked suspense tale, *The Reckless Moment* (1949). However, once again, despite her sterling work, she was taken for granted in a thankless part as the star's daughter. MGM even borrowed Geraldine to co-star with Lassie in one film and then her Warners' contract terminated.

At loose ends, Geraldine promptly accepted an offer from director William Dieterle to play Anna Magnani's younger sister (typecasting again) in the Italian film *Volcano.* In this 1950 film, she was an island fishermaid and wore no makeup at all. While they were on location, Roberto Rossellini was filming *Stromboli* (1950) on a neighboring isle with Ingrid Bergman as his star. "The only reason Anna Magnani wanted to make *Volcano,*" Geraldine explains, "was because Rossellini was making *Stromboli.* They were once very thick. Rossellini was like a shadow over *Volcano.*" Reviewing *Volcano,* which did not have American release till 1953, the *New York Times* reported, "It does nothing to improve the reputations of Miss Magnani or the Hollywood-schooled Miss Brooks." Geraldine was in no great hurry to return to television-tormented Hollywood, so she signed to do another Italian picture, *No Sognato Il Paradiso,* which was released in the United States as *Streets of Sorrow* in 1952, a full year before *Volcano* was viewed in this country. She was also going to do a film a year for three years in Italy, but, after appearing with Glenn Ford in *The Green Glove* (1952), set in post-World War II France, she became disillusioned with Continental filmmaking and returned to America to ply her craft on stage and on television.

In the summer of 1952, Geraldine appeared in *The Petrified Forest* with Gene Raymond and, also in stock, starred in *The Voice of the Turtle.* That fall she returned to Broadway, but with only featured billing as the American wife in Arthur Laurents' *Time of the Cuckoo,* starring Shirley Booth. Live and filmed television then took up most of her time until she joined the Actors' Studio in 1956. The studio's famed "method" style of acting came easily to Geraldine, because as a child she always talked to inanimate objects. "When they told me to be a tree and to imagine sap running through me," she said, "I could do it because that is what I had been doing all my life."

On the subject of talent, Gerladine states that it has nothing whatsoever to do with brains. "I have met a lot of dumb actors who were very good. You have to be tuned in emotionally, but you don't need to be intelligent. I don't agree for a minute that you have to be smart to play a dumb blonde." While studying at the Studio she dubbed the voice of Giulietta Masina in the English-language version of *La Strada* (1956).

Her next feature film was a distinct come-down, the low-budgeted United Artists release, *Street of Sinners* (1957), with George Montgomery. The Hollywood *Reporter* judged, "Miss Brooks, as a martini-soaked woman, created a character of genuine tragedy." Since then, Geraldine has appeared in *Johnny Tiger* (1966), an undernourished feature starring Robert Taylor, in which she played a doctor helping Seminole Indians on a Florida reservation. Her one television film so far has been *Ironsides* (1967), which was the pilot for the popular series.

In 1962, Geraldine was nominated for an Emmy for her performance in *Call Back Yesterday,* a segment of the "Bus Stop" series on ABC-TV. But television audiences probably remember her best for her roles as E. G. Marshall's only romantic interest on "The Defenders" and her appearance on the last episode of "The Fugitive," when the one-armed man, Lieutenant Gerard (Barry Morse) and Richard Kimble (David Jansen) finally come together. On television in 1971, she played Amelia Earhart, the famed aviatrix, in a "You Are There" segment, and in the 1973–74 mini-series, "Faraday and Company," she was excellent as Dan Dailey's secretary and old flame. Her most recent stage appearances have been in Dore Schary's Broadway play *Brightower* (1970) as Robert Lansing's long-suffering wife, a road tour of *The Rothschilds* (1972), with both Theodore Bikel and Jan Peerce, and as Golde, Teyve's (Norman Atkins) wife, in the Jones Beach production of *Fiddler on the Roof* (1974). *Brightower* closed after only one performance, but Geraldine won a Tony nomination as best actress of the year for her performance.

Recently, she co-starred with Dean Martin in *Mr. Ricco* (1975), a Paul Bogart-directed feature in which she portrayed a divorcee who becomes deeply involved with tough guy Martin.

In 1961, Geraldine divorced her television writer husband Herbert Sargent, whom she had wed on March 8, 1958. In June of 1964, she married Budd Schulberg, author of *What Makes Sammy Run?* and the screenplay of *On the Waterfront* (1954). Schulberg was an old friend of Geraldine's family and had even babysat with her when she was small. The Schulbergs now live mostly in California; after the 1965 riots in the Watts section of Los Angeles, they opened a writers workshop there for underprivileged blacks. "Many are smart and some brilliant," claims Geraldine. For the workshop she types manuscripts, teaches drama classes, doing anything and everything.

The very talented and versatile Geraldine recently collaborated (with Schulberg) on *Swan Watch* (1975) a book tracing the story of two years spent with the swans on the property of the authors' Westhampton, N.Y. home. The volume contains fifty photographs taken by Geraldine, with text by Budd.

Geraldine used to worry very much about goals in life, but not anymore. She is quite happy with her present of work and her hobby of writing poetry for children. Had Warner Bros., or any studio in Hollywood for that matter, given her the opportunity of playing good roles in top films, she would have undoubtedly been among the elite leading ladies of the movie industry. Heavy drama has always been her forte but she likes and wants to play comedy. "I've always played tragedy," she says," and my disposition isn't like that; I'm sort of sunny, I think."

GERALDINE BROOKS

Cry Wolf   *(WB 1947)*
Possessed   *(WB 1947)*
Embraceable You   *(WB 1948)*
An Act of Murder (a.k.a., Live Today for Tomorrow)   *(Univ 1948)*
The Younger Brothers   *(WB 1949)*
The Reckless Moment   *(Col 1949)*
Challenge to Lassie   *(MGM 1949)*

This Side of the Law   *(WB 1950)*
Volcano   *(Italian 1950)*
No Sognato Il Paradiso (Streets of Sorrow)   *(Italian 1951)*
The Green Glove   *(UA 1952)*
Street of Sinners   *(UA 1957)*
Johnny Tiger   *(Univ 1966)*
Mr. Ricco   *(UA-MGM 1975)*

16

Rod Cameron

There is no truth in the persistent rumors that Rod Cameron was the model for the comic strip character Dick Tracy, or that he posed for any of the sculpturing on Mount Rushmore. He just *looks* like he is capable of doing both.

Cameron's energetic, hard-working rise in the film firmament is a reflection of a Hollywood long since dead, where by persistence a person could break into the movie industry, and by dint of effort under the studio "star" system make a name for himself in the business.

The rugged six-foot four-inch actor was born Roderick Cox on December 7, 1912. Educated in Canada and New York, the young Cox drifted from job to job, including working as a sand hog during the construction of the Holland Tunnel in Manhattan, and eventually discovered a different career in California.

Cameron's first onscreen bit was in a scene with superstar Bette Davis in *The Old Maid* (1939) at Warner Bros. Glowing with excitement over his small bit with Davis, he invited all his friends and family to the premiere of *The Old Maid,* only to discover that director Edmund Goulding had cut the scene from the picture. Rather than return to construction work that had brought him to the west coast, he found a berth at Paramount doing bit parts, acting as a stand-in for Fred MacMurray and becoming Paramount's leading man for a long line of screen tests of female hopefuls.

In Paramount's *Christmas in July* (1940), one of Preston Sturges' comic delights, Rod had a brief turn. He then received a screen credit as Corporal Underhill in Cecil B. DeMille's first all-Technicolor film dealing with the Riel Rebellion in Canada, *Northwest Mounted Police* (1940). Cameron's early desire to be a Royal Candian Mountie materialized only as far as the Paramount lot. Rod augmented his meager wages by doubling for aging cowboy star Buck Jones in Universal's serial *Riders of Death Valley* (1941), which had an impressive cast: Dick Foran, Monte Blue, Lon Chaney, Jr., Noah Beery, Jr., Charles Bickford, and Leo Carrillo.

Cameron's Paramount days see-sawed from bit parts to billed roles and then to secondary leads, such as Sam Daniels in *The Monster and the Girl* (1941), Tom Reed in *No Hands on the Clock* (1941), Jesse James in the Dalton Trumbo-scripted *The Remarkable Andrew* (1942), and a "sailor" in *The Fleet's In* (1942). Small parts in *Wake Island* (1942) and *True to the Army* (1942) gave way to a recognized performance as Jim Lawrence in Paramount's less-than-exciting *The Forest Rangers* (1942), starring Fred MacMurray, and the part of Sam Welch in Dorothy Lamour's *Riding High* (1943).

For Universal, Rod played a Kentucky hillbilly, Rube Tedrow, with Colonel Carson's raiders on Makin Island in *Gung Ho!* (1943), and was cast as the pastor in Columbia's *Commandos Strike at Dawn* (1943). It was a logical move for athletic Cameron to

Publicity pose ca. 1946

move over to action studio Republic, where he participated in the serial *G-Men vs the Black Dragon* (1943), in which he played the role of Rex Bennett helping our ally—China—to combat the deadly Japanese Black Dragon Society. Cameron may have lacked the finesse of a polished performer, but in such slug-'em-and-run adventures he was more than capable of using his fists realistically and mouthing the rapid dialog. This escapade at Republic was followed by fifteen more chapters of a new cliffhanger, in which he was again Rex Bennett, American undercover agent, joining the Gestapo to persuade the Arab nations to join the Allied cause. *Secret Service in Darkest Africa* (1943) was undisputably over-involved in plot, what with a sacred dagger of Solomon and a forged sacred Moslem scroll, but audiences thrived on the vicarious adventures of hero Rod as he outwits the Gestapo and, in a final sword fight with the Nazi villain (Lionel Royce), ends the Hitler spy ring in North Africa.

After other small parts in *Honeymoon Lodge* (1943) and *No Time for Love* (1943), the latter also starring Fred MacMurray, he played Kelso, helping town marshal Richard Dix to clean up the town in *The Kansan* (1943). Because Johnny Mack Brown had left Universal for Monogram, Universal signed Rod Cameron for a string of B westerns with Fuzzy Knight as his sidekick. These hasty efforts did little for his career. However, Walter Wanger came to his rescue and cast him opposite luscious Yvonne De Carlo in *Salome, Where She Danced* (1945), in which he played newspaperman Jim Steed. Walter Slezak was in the cast and stole each reel, but Cameron also gave a solid performance. James Agee (*The Nation*) thought *Salome, Where She Danced* was one of 1945's best films and one of the funniest deadpan parodies the screen had yet invented.

Rod was toplined with De Carlo (also born in Canada) in *Frontier Gal* (1945). Rod played Johnny Hart, a man married to a saloon owner who rejoins his family after six years in jail. The *New York Times* called the would-be adventure tale a "corn-fritter," and the New York *World-Telegram* said of Cameron, he "is good-humored and assured as her [Yvonne De Carlo's] rough guy." In *Swing Out, Sister* (1945) Rod played, of all things, a symphony conductor. He was back in form as lumberjack Dan Corrigan in *River Lady* (1948), which also starred De Carlo. For Twentieth Century-Fox he was Bob Yauntis in an implausible epic called *Belle Starr's Daughter* (1948) but managed to give the most convincing performance in the movie. Ruth Roman played the title role. He starred in such kiddie matinee fare as *The Plunderers* (1948), *Stampede* (1949), and was Johnny Tremaine hunting down Walter Brennan in *Brimstone* (1949). Brennan, playing a bandit, also stole the film with his usual fine performance.

In 1950, Rod, who could certainly be termed a well-known movie veteran by this point, married Angela Alves-Lico, bought a home in North Hollywood where he pursued his hobby of wood carving (and occasionally working in ivory), and played terrific boogie-woogie on the piano. To the amazement of some people in Hollywood, Rod became an avid Bible student and immersed himself in juvenile welfare at various boys' schools and orphanages, especially St. Mary's School for Indian Children. His daughter, by a first and very early marriage, was growing up rapidly and Rod's interest in children's welfare in some ways compensated for his several years' lack of cohesive homelife. For Republic, a studio at which he could have done much more work in years past and become a real western-action star, he played Gunner McNeil, a deep-sea diver blowing up a submerged wreck in *The Sea Hornet* (1951). He continued at that studio as Web Calhoun in an Indian war in the Dakota's Black Hills in *Oh Susannah!* (1951), and was seen trying to make peace with the Indians as Kirby Frye in *Cavalry Scout* (1951). Leading roles continued in Republic's *Ride the Man Down* (1952), in which he played Will Ballard, supported by a strong cast that included Brian Donlevy, Ella Raines, Chill Wills, and Barbara Britton. After *Woman of the North Country* (1952) and *Fort Osage* (1952) as Tom Clay, wagonmaster in a routine trek to California, Rod went to India to film *The Jungle* (1952)

Frank Capra was selected to head the American delegation for 1952's International Film Festival in India, where America's film entry was Cecil B. DeMille's *The Greatest Show on Earth.* Capra did an excellent job of offsetting Communist control of the Festival, and, hearing that an American film company was shooting a jungle picture in Salem, he invited all who could come to meet him in Madras. On February 9, 1952, Capra met Marie Windsor, Cesar Romero, Rod Cameron and his wife Angela, film producer Ellis Dungan and director William Berke at the Madras airport. The American delegation supported Capra's sub rosa fight to lessen Communist commandeering of the Festival. On February 22nd, when the Festival ajourned to Delhi, Capra again asked the American film unit to join him, and Romero, the Camerons, and cameraman Clyde De Vinna drove five hours to meet Capra. As Capra later wrote, "They are big attractions and the best good-will ambassadors the U.S. could send anywhere." The following day Cameron, Windsor, and Romero sat on a jeep to lead a Parade of Stars before fifty thousands people at the Sports Stadium.

If the three American actors helped to save the India International Film Festival for Capra, the film they made entirely in India left much to be desired other than the exquisite photography by De Vinna.

When Cameron returned to the States he was approached by Revue Studios for a TV series, "City Detective," in which he appeared as Lieutenant Bart Grant. Deep-voiced, low-keyed Cameron was quite effective in the recurring role as the law enforcer who tracks down metropolitan crime. The series ran for sixty-five episodes (1953–55). Cameron also appeared on other major TV shows, including a tropical romance yarn on "The Loretta Young Show" with Phyllis Kirk.

Rod continued making features at fast-declining Republic, but they were strictly programmers. On February 3, 1956, he was featured as Nevada state trooper Rod Blake on the segment *Killer on Horseback* for TV's "Star Stage." It was a pilot film for a proposed series which debuted a year later as "State Trooper." The show reflected a higher-than-average budget and had carefully planned segments. It ran for 104 episodes over a three-year period, with Cameron then going into "Coronado 9" (39 episodes) as a former Naval Intelligence officer now involved in private investigation.

The easy-going Cameron surprised the film colony in 1960 by divorcing his wife Angela Alves-Lico and marrying her mother Dorothy. They managed to keep their marriage a secret for over a year while Rod continued appearing on television in several segments of the "Laramie" series and as a wealthy Texan in the TV debut of the series "Burke's Law," playing another rich Texan, Grover Johnson, on the Perry Mason telecast of *The Case of the Bouncing Boomerang*. On the screen he was seen as Sheriff Corey with Rory Calhoun in *The Gun Hawk* (1963).

In 1964 he went to Spain and filmed *El Sandero del Odio* and *Las Pistoles no Discuten*. Back in the States he played the lead in *Requiem for a Gunfighter* (1965), with a parcel of old Western favorites: Johnny Mack Brown, Lane Chandler, Raymond Hatton, Edmund Cobb, and Bob Steele. For Bob Hope's TV comedy, *Have Girls Will Travel,* Cameron was cast as Tiny (!). Others in the show were Jill St. John, Rhonda Fleming, Mr. Hope, and Sonny Tufts. In the "Bonanza" episode, *Ride The Wind,* (1966) Rod was Curtis Wade trying to keep the Pony Express running against violent Indian attacks. He was Trooper Major Rogers for 1966's "Iron Horse" and the following year played Martin Blaine trying to re-open an abandoned silver mine on "Hondo."

By 1972, sixty-year-old Rod was still active in television on the series "Alias Smith and Jones" as Sher-

With Anne Gwynne in Panhandle *(AA 1948)*

With Dan Duryea in River Lady *(Univ 1948)*

111

With Fred MacMurray in The Forest Rangers *(Par 1942)*

iff Grimly in the first episode, where Roger Davis replaced the later Peter Duel as Hannibal Heyes. In September of 1972, Rod played bounty hunter Luke Billings on the "Alias Smith and Jones" series that was filmed in Utah's Arches National Park, with Marie Windsor and Buddy Ebsen in the supporting cast. Rod also returned to his native Canada in the late 1960s for a Canadian television show, "Star Hunt," that featured an up-and-coming American singer, Glen Campbell.

Rod has been on the screen for thirty-five years and retirement is just not in his vocabulary.

Recently he reminisced, "In the old Hollywood, acting was fun. The atmosphere was looser. We used to play practical jokes on each other. . . . Once I went with a film crew into the High Sierras. After I finished my part, I fell asleep under a tree. When I woke up, I was all alone—the whole company had packed up and gone, leaving me there. I spent half the night trying to hitch a ride back to Los Angeles. . . . Yep, those were the good old days!"

ROD CAMERON

The Old Maid   (WB 1939)*
Heritage of the Desert   (Par 1939)
Christmas in July   (Par 1940)
If I Had My Way   (Univ 1940)
Northwest Mounted Police   (Par 1940)
Rangers of Fortune   (Par 1940)
Stagecoach War   (Par 1940)
Those Were the Days   (Par 1940)
The Quarterback   (Par 1940)
Henry Aldrich for President   (Par 1941)
The Monster and the Girl   (Par 1941)
I Wanted Wings   (Par 1941) (Voice only)
Nothing But the Truth   (Par 1941)
Among the Living   (Par 1941)
The Parson of Panamint   (Par 1941)
The Night of January 16th   (Par 1941)
Buy Me That Town   (Par 1941)
Pacific Blackout (a.k.a., Midnight Angel)   (Par 1941)
The Fleet's In   (Par 1942)
The Remarkable Andrew   (Par 1942)
Star Spangled Rhythm   (Par 1942)
Priorities on Parade   (Par 1942)
Wake Island   (Par 1942)
True to the Army   (Par 1942)
The Forest Rangers   (Par 1942)
Gung Ho!   (Univ 1943)
Commandos Strike at Dawn   (Col 1943)
G-Men vs the Black Dragon   (Rep 1943) (Serial)
Secret Service in Darkest Africa   (Rep 1943) (Serial)
Riding High   (Par 1943)
The Good Fellows   (Par 1943)
Honeymoon Lodge   (Univ 1943)
No Time for Love   (Par 1943)
The Kansan   (UA 1943)
Mrs. Parkington   (MGM 1944)
Beyond the Pecos   (Univ 1944)
The Old Texas Trail   (Univ 1944)
Boss of Boomtown   (Univ 1944)
Riders of the Santa Fe   (Univ 1944)
Trigger Trail   (Univ 1944)
Salome, Where She Danced   (Univ 1945)
Frontier Gal   (Univ 1945)
Renegades of the Rio Grande   (Univ 1945)
Swing Out, Sister   (Univ 1945)
*Scene deleted from release print

The Runaround   (Univ 1946)
Pirates of Monterey   (Univ 1947)
River Lady   (Univ 1948)
Panhandle   (AA 1948)
Strike It Rich   (AA 1948)
Belle Starr's Daughter   (20th 1948)
The Plunderers   (Rep 1948)
Stampede   (AA 1949)
Brimstone   (Rep 1949)
Stage to Tucson   (Col 1950)
Dakota Lil   (20th 1950)
Short Grass   (AA 1950)
The Sea Hornet   (Rep 1951)
Oh Susannah!   (Rep 1951)
Cavalry Scout   (Mon 1951)
Ride the Man Down   (Rep 1952)
Woman of the North Country   (Rep 1952)
Wagons West   (Mon 1952)
Fort Osage   (Mon 1952)
The Jungle   (Lip 1952)
San Antone   (Rep 1953)
The Steel Lady (UA 1953)
Southwest Passage   (UA 1954)
Hell's Outpost   (Rep 1954)
Headline Hunters   (Rep 1955)
Santa Fe Passage   (Rep 1955)
The Fighting Chance   (Rep 1955)
Double Jeopardy   (Rep 1955)
Passport to Treason   (Astor 1955)
Yaqui Drums   (AA 1956)
Spoilers of the Forest   (Rep 1957)
The Man Who Died Twice   (Rep 1958)
Escapement (a.k.a., The Electronic Monster)   (AA 1960)
The Gun Hawk   (AA 1963)
Las Pistoles no Discuten (a.k.a., Bullets Don't Lie)   (Spanish, 1964)
El Sandero Del Odio (a.k.a., Bullet and the Flesh)   (Spanish, 1964)
The Bounty Killer   (Emb 1965)
Requiem for a Gunfighter   (Emb 1965)
Winnetou and His Friend Old Firebrand   (German 1967)
The Last Movie   (Univ 1971)
Evel Knievel   (Fanfare 1971)
Redneck   (German 1975)
The Kirlian Force   (Mars 1975)
Jesse's Girls   (Manson 1975)

17

Macdonald Carey

Many actors gain fame because their images differ from the norm, whether in looks, personality, or talent. Macdonald Carey was not one of these. His modicum of stardom came because he was so typical; the perfect upper middleclass type—sort of a tough Franchot Tone. Only moderately attractive, Macdonald seemed the right choice to play doctors, lawyers, detectives, and even insurance agents. As Carey himself admits, "It's the curse of my face." Carey's name was also a hindrance to his early career in Hollywood. Movie-goers, columnists, and reviewers had difficulty remembering his correct name. Many would call him Carey MacDonald, Donald Carey, Donald MacCarey, etc. There was also a long standing confusion between Carey and Wendell Corey, the latter also a Paramount contract player. The two actors appeared in the same film only once, playing the notorious James brothers in the western, *The Great Missouri Raid* (1950). One reviewer said, "Corey and Carey draw their six-guns, sit their horses and descend on banks and trains as though they had never heard of a drawing room drama." But through the years, Carey did appear in a number of westerns, such as *Streets of Laredo* (1949), *Outlaw Territory* (1953), and he even portrayed rugged Jim Bowie in Universal's *Comanche Territory* (1950). Somehow it was always difficult to accept him in these outdoors parts; he seemed more comfortable in a suit and tie or in a sport shirt, slacks, and golf jacket.

He was born Edward Macdonald Carey on March 15, 1913, in Sioux City, Iowa, to Charles and Elizabeth Macdonald Carey, of Catholic Irish and Scottish descent. His father was an investment counsellor. (Besides Carey, Sioux City was also the birthplace of the cinema star, Blanche Sweet.) Carey attended lower grade and Central High schools in Sioux City, singing bass baritone in the choir and taking leads in Gilbert and Sullivan operettas. Concentrating on stagecraft and acting through school, he received his B.A. and M.A. degrees from the University of Iowa. His first professional theatrical internship was in Shakespeare. Upon graduation in 1936, he joined the Globe Players, doing condensed versions of the Bard's works at the Texas Centennial. Other celebrities-in-the-making in the company were Martha Scott and David Wayne.

When he was unable to obtain any further legitimate stage work, Macdonald accepted radio soap opera jobs in Chicago, and played a young country doctor on the "Young Hickory" series. He then moved to New York and continued in radio, being heard on such programs as "The First Nighter," "Lights Out," "John's Other Wife," and "Stella Dallas." On one radio program he met stage producer Cheryl Crawford, who helped him to win a summer stock job in Maplewood, New Jersey. This, in turn, led to his being discovered by Moss Hart, who was then casting his *Lady in the Dark,* starring Gertrude

With Betty Hutton in Dream Girl *(Par 1948)*

With Wanda Hendrix in Song of Surrender *(Par 1949)*

Lawrence. Hart liked him and had him read for the musical. Kurt Weill, the show's composer, admired his voice and also thought him the right type for the role of Charley Johnson, the advertising man. After Gertrude Lawrence gave her approval, the part was his, and he made his Broadway debut at the Alvin Theatre on January 23, 1941. The show also brought stardom to two other unknowns, Danny Kaye and Victor Mature.

When Paramount bought the hit *Lady in the Dark,* they also took Carey and signed him to a seven year contract. Unfortunately, when the studio finally got around to filming it (December, 1942, but not released till February, 1944), Carey was in the Marines and Ray Milland, with the role built up, played his part opposite Ginger Rogers. Carey's first film for the studio was to have been *Take a Letter, Darling* (1942) with Rosalind Russell and Fred MacMurray, but the executives decided to star him in a quickie first, the Damon Runyonesque melodrama, *Dr. Broadway* (1942). Once again, as on Broadway, Carey did not have to wait around playing small roles before he was pushed into the limelight. He was given first star billing in this his debut film. He received very decent reviews for his role as the Times Square physician. The advertisement for the film read, "He can bust a jaw . . . or mend a heart . . . and what a bedside manner!" He had the second male lead in *Take a Letter, Darling,* playing a much-married millionaire. Bosley Crowther (*New York Times*) was not much impressed with Macdonald's performance, referring to him as "a newcomer, who makes one think of Mischa Auer trying to be serious—just walks around."

Carey was among the performers who tested for the prize role of Robert Jordan in *For Whom the Bell Tolls* (1943) but, of course, the role went to Gary Cooper. When not auditioning for such tempting parts, he was given oncamera kissing lessons with many of the lot's starlets. "The only one who's still around," says Carey, "is Barbara Britton." She played his young wife in the best role of his young career in *Wake Island* (1942). This John Farrow-directed picture stands out as one of the better war films of that era, with Carey playing a pilot who destroys a Japanese cruiser twelve miles from Wake Island. Not long after making this picture Macdonald joined the Marines himself, but before doing so he was lent to Universal to appear with Teresa Wright and Joseph Cotten in Alfred Hitchcock's excellent *Shadow of a Doubt* (1943), in which he played a government man. In addition, for his own studio, he did a minor musical called *Salute for Three* (1943), with Betty Rhodes and Dona Drake,

about an all-girls' orchestra who open a serviceman's canteen.

His intermission as a first lieutenant ended in 1945 and he came back to Paramount with a job awaiting him. Unfortunately, his comeback was in the asinine comedy, *Suddenly It's Spring* (1947), starring Paulette Goddard and Fred MacMurray. He subsequently starred opposite Goddard in two other awful movies: *Hazard* (1948), a so-called comedy, and *Bride of Vengeance* (1949), a very heavy costume drama with many unintentional laughs. In the latter film, Carey made a ridiculous Cesare Borgia, Lucretia's brother, with Paulette, of course, as Lucretia. The *New York Herald-Tribune* scoffed, "Macdonald Carey leers through the part of the Bull of Rome, stabbing his chief General when no other victims are handy."

On loanout to Universal for *South Sea Sinner* (1950), a remake of Marlene Dietrich's *Seven Sinners* (1940), Carey remembers this tawdry picture rather painfully, for two reasons: "One because the critics rapped Wendell Corey, not me, and Corey, poor guy, had nothing to do with the movie. Second, because there was a piano player in it named Liberace—and, by sheer coincidence, there's a line in *Anniversary Waltz* [a play Carey did on Broadway in 1954] which reads that one of the horrors of TV is the danger of having Liberace in your living room!"

Two of his last films under his contract to Paramount are his favorites: *The Great Gatsby* (1949), in which he plays F. Scott Fitzgerald's narrator, Nick Carraway, to the leads of Alan Ladd and Betty Field, and *The Lawless* (1950) his pet film and perhaps his best screen work. Of *Gatsby,* the *New York Times* said that he did "a fair imitation of a youthful father time." In the 1974 David Merrick production of Fitzgerald's famous novel, Sam Waterston undertook the Carraway part. In *The Lawless,* directed by Joseph Losey and co-starring Gail Russell, Macdonald was a crusading newspaperman who fights bigotry against Mexican-Americans in California. The *New York Herald-Tribune* judged that he played the part with "great skill and sympathy." *The Great Missouri Raid* ended his Paramount tenure. About this time Hollywood secretaries made a list of the ten worst-dressed men in filmdom. Carey made the list because "He's still wearing Marine Corps fatigues." He was in good company, though, because Adolphe Menjou, usually on the best-dressed list, was also included.

His subsequent three-picture deal at Twentieth Century-Fox cast him opposite three of that studio's then top leading ladies: Betty Grable in *Meet Me after the Show* (1951), Claudette Colbert in *Let's Make it Legal* (1951), and Anne Baxter in *My Wife's Best*

Friend (1952). The latter two comedies are prime examples of the special type of role Carey projected best: the harassed husband with marital problems.

Plans were in preparation for Macdonald to co-star with Anna Magnani, in Italy, in a Vittorio DeSica-directed film called *Half a World Away,* but the project fizzled. He did, however, travel to Spain to co-star with Maureen O'Hara in *Fire over Africa* (1954) and to Africa to do *Odongo* (1956) with Rhonda Fleming. While he was in Spain, Moss Hart tracked him down and offered him the lead in a new Broadway comedy, *Anniversary Waltz,* which opened in New York on April 7, 1954, with Carey in the role of a TV-hating husband. (Kitty Carlisle was the wife, with Warren Berlinger and Mary Lee Dearring as the tolerant kids.) The *New York Daily News* labeled Carey "charming and funny as the husband who boils quickly and cools fast." Although he was now firmly established on Broadway, he hastened to tell interviewers that it did not mean he was no longer interested in filmmaking. "I'm very much interested," he insisted. "What I mean is that I've fallen into a rut; two ruts to be exact. One is comedy, the other western. I got plenty of offers to do movies that fall into those categories and I

don't like it." He added, "This feeling of wanting to come to Broadway is shared by a lot of people in Hollywood, by the best of them."

Anniversary Waltz would prove to be Carey's last Broadway appearance to date, but he attempted to return in *Tin Wedding,* a Theatre Guild attraction with Maureen Stapleton, and a play called *Memo* with Fred Clark and Pippa Scott. Neither one made it to the Great White Way. Carey also lost out to Don Ameche for the male lead in the musical *Goldilocks.*

In 1952, Carey wisely began accepting television assignments. The movies were feeling the new medium's impingement, and Carey's film roles were becoming fewer and fewer. After guest-starring on many video shows, he got his own series, the TV title role in "Dr. Christian" in 1956. The radio and movies' Dr. Christian, Jean Hersholt, appeared in the series' first two episodes, but Carey's younger Dr. Mark was not the small town doctor of the original. The same year that the series aired, Carey turned in one of his better small screen performances as a temporary pilot on "The Alcoa Hour's" production of Arthur Hailey's *Flight Into Danger.* In the summer of 1959 he turned down the series "Peck's Bad Girl" (starring Patty Mc-

With Paulette Goddard in Hazard *(Par 1948)*

Cormack) which, unsurprisingly, went to Wendell Corey, but he did do the series "Lock Up", which ran for two season on NBC and in which he played an attorney. Another television series which did not pan out for him was "Mr. Blandings," playing the role Cary Grant did in the feature film, *Mr. Blandings Builds His Dream House* (1948). One of Carey's many television roles in the fifties was that medium's first version of *Miracle on 34th Street* with Teresa Wright. He played John Payne's film role.

In 1958 Macdonald returned to feature filmmaking in a low-budget Western at Republic. Audrey Totter was the co-star of *Man or Gun*. The following year he and Marsha Hunt were the parents in the generation gap story *Blue Denim*, and he gave a poor showing as Patrick Henry in the overblown spectable *John Paul Jones* (1959). After two nondescript films made in England and Italy respectively, he was in another British film, *The Damned* (a.k.a., *These Are the Damned*) (1962), directed by ex-Hollywoodite Joseph Losey. This latter film, which has gained its own cult reputation, was an interesting venture, which dealt with the aftermath of a nuclear war. Back in Hollywood, Carey participated in *Tammy and the Doctor* (1963) in which Sandra Dee and Peter Fonda had the title roles It is Carey's last feature film to date, except for the dubbing of Christ's voice in *The Redeemer* (1965), a Spanish film.

Carey married Elizabeth Heckacher, a Philadelphia socialite with dramatic aspirations, on May 4, 1941. They met while he was doing radio and she was in drama school in New York. She relinquished her ambitions and became a housewife and thereafter the mother of six children: three boys and three girls. When the children were small they were known around Hollywood as "Father Carey's Chickens." Their eldest daughter, Lynn (born in 1946), has appeared in the film *Lord Love a Duck* (1966) and has since had her own rock singing group. "With six kids around the house," says Carey, "you can't have an actor's ego long." Domesticity, however, did turn sour, and in 1971 the Careys divorced.

Carey, who was once Vice President of the Screen Actors Guild, has been, since 1967, a regular member of the daytime soap opera "The Days of Our Lives" on NBC-TV. He plays the role of Dr. Tom Horton for which he won an Emmy in 1974. Along with the late Ann Sheridan and Joan Bennett, Carey is one of the growing number of once-name film performers who turned to rigorous television serial work for their livelihood. He was nominated for an Emmy as best daytime actor for the 1972–73 video season and won the following year. He has also appeared on three made-for-television movies, *Gidget Gets Married* (1972), *Ordeal* (1973), and *Who Is the Black Dahlia?* (1975), and has guested on such nighttime series as "Owen Marshall" and "The Magician." Summer stock audiences have recently seen him in *The Music Man, Guys and Dolls,* and *A Thousand Clowns*, proving once again that he is a far more versatile performer than generally conceded.

The six-foot, brown-eyed Carey still lives in Beverly Hills. He is a very pleasant, affable man who has kept working through the years, more because of his reputation as a steady, reliable and thoroughly professional actor, than because of any extraordinary acting gift. His career has made a complete cycle, though. He started on radio soap operas and now, more than three decades later, is doing them again on television. But as he says, "I'm an actor who likes to work and what's the difference whether it's in the daytime or at night."

As for his private life, he admitted in mid-1975, "I love Lois [Crane]! She's the end and a new beginning." He met the socialite, formerly wed to a wealthy businessman, in July, 1973 at a charity benefit. As she recalls, ". . . I turned around and saw Mac standing by my side with that beautiful smile—and that was it. That was the start—it's still going strong. Mac lives just over the hill from me, so we see each other often."

MACDONALD CAREY

Dr. Broadway   *(Par 1942)*
Take A Letter, Darling   *(Par 1942)*
Wake Island   *(Par 1942)*
Star Spangled Rhythm   *(Par 1942)*
Shadow of a Doubt   *(Univ 1943)*
Salute for Three   *(Par 1943)*
Suddenly It's Spring   *(Par 1947)*
Variety Girl   *(Par 1947)*
Hazard   *(Par 1948)*
Dream Girl   *(Par 1948)*
Streets of Laredo   *(Par 1949)*
Bride of Vengeance   *(Par 1949)*
The Great Gatsby   *(Par 1949)*
Song of Surrender   *(Par 1949)*
South Sea Sinner   *(Univ 1950)*
Comanche Territory   *(Univ 1950)*
The Lawless   *(Par 1950)*
Copper Canyon   *(Par 1950)*
Mystery Submarine   *(Univ 1950)*

The Great Missouri Raid   *(Par 1950)*
Excuse My Dust   *(MGM 1951)*
Meet Me after the Show   *(20th 1951)*
Cave of Outlaws   *(Univ 1951)*
Let's Make it Legal   *(20th 1951)*
My Wife's Best Friend   *(20th 1952)*
Count the Hours   *(RKO 1953)*
Outlaw Territory (a.k.a., Hannah Lee)   *(Realart 1953)*
Fire over Africa   *(Col 1954)*
Stranger at My Door   *(Rep 1956)*
Odongo   *(Col 1956)*
Man or Gun   *(Rep 1958)*
Blue Denim   *(20th 1959)*
John Paul Jones   *(WB 1959)*
Stranglehold   *(Rank 1962)*
The Devil's Agent   *(British Lion 1962)*
The Damned (These are the Damned)   *(Col 1962)*
Tammy and the Doctor   *(Univ 1963)*
The Redeemer   *(Spanish 1965)* (Voice only)

18

Jack Carson

If the 1940s produced excesses on the battlefront, Hollywood was guilty of its own unbridled indulgences. One of the more unrestrained semi-major personalities who rose to eminence on the movie scene during that decade was Jack Carson. On screen he was a ham. He knew it, and capitalized on his heavy-handed approach to acting in order to become a prominent member of the Warner Bros. stock company. He was a veteran of vaudeville and proudly claimed that his corn-ball act with college pal Dave Willock contributed to vaudeville's demise and burial. What he did not so readily admit, and what movie producers scarcely noted, was that he was far more than a younger, more versatile Alan Hale. When handed a non-song-and-dance straight role, he had the makings of a subtle dramatic performer.

John Elmer Carson was born on October 27, 1910, in Carman, Manitoba, Canada, but the family soon migrated to Milwaukee, Wisconsin, and it was that city Jack claimed as his "home town." He was educated at St. John's Military Academy in Delafield, Wisconsin. He was in and out of Illinois College, and eventually spent three years at Carleton College, where he played football and made his first stage appearance as Hercules in a college play. His performance was noticed when his 6'2", 220 pound frame clad in a tiger skin tripped and knocked down most of the set. After Carleton, he decided his father's

insurance business was not for him. He tried working as a salesman and then as a railroad construction laborer. But then he decided to try what pleased him. He leaped into vaudeville with his Carleton chum, Dave Willock.

He and Willock plied the circuit for a spell, and even got booked into the Paramount Theatre in New York where their act, satirizing the gay, worn-thin Nineties (augmented with a newsreel skit they authored), was not met with any rave reviews. In fact, during their stay at that august theatre, so Carson claimed, vaudeville actually died.

Carson decided to head west, and once on the coast he aligned himself with a little theatre group, landed several radio jobs, and signed a featured player contract with RKO, after making an unbilled screen debut in United Artists' *You Only Live Once* (1937) and appearing as Potts, a hard-boiled press agent, in Tay Garnett's *Stand In* (1937). His "featured" roles for RKO were mainly unmemorable minor parts, although he gained attention in the star-studded *Stage Door* (1937) as Milbank, the blind date, and as the assistant director of the Hollywood Bowl in *Music for Madame* (1937). Infrequently RKO tossed him a small but showy assignment, as, for example, Butch Connors, Fred Astaire's buddy in *Carefree* (1938) or as Ginger Rogers' loud-mouthed ex-flame in *Having Wonderful Time* (1938). But, after his last 1938 RKO casting as a roustabout in *Bringing up Baby* and as a sailor in the park in Ginger Rogers' *Fifth Avenue Girl*

With Cary Grant in Arsenic and Old Lace *(WB 1944)*

With Dennis Morgan, Bill Goodwin, and Doris Day in It's a Great Feeling *(WB 1949)*

With Joseph Crehan, Dennis Morgan, Ann Sheridan, and Marie Wilson in Shine On Harvest Moon *(WB 1944)*

(1939), he determined that freelancing was certainly preferable to the assembly line shuttling at RKO.

For the next two years his freelance work was little more effective than the RKO sojourn, although he made an impression as Sweeney in *Mr. Smith Goes to Washington* (1939), and came on very strong as Jack Tyndall, a saloon blowhard, in Universal's *Destry Rides Again* (1939). He was amusing as policeman Tom Gerrity competing with Stuart Erwin for Una Merkel's hand in *Sandy Gets Her Man* (1940). He was a deadly serious G-man, Ross Waring, helping FBI partner Ralph Bellamy track down the notorious Ma Barker (Blanche Yurka) in *Queen of the Mob* (1940). In his role as a ship's mate Jack spent some time on Catalina Island making Paramount's *Typhoon* (1940). He returned to RKO for the role of Freddie, a pompous stuffed shirt, engaged to Ginger Rogers, who loses her to Ronald Colman in *Lucky Partners* (1940). Carson would later claim, "I had a whole career losing Ginger Rogers at RKO." At Metro-Goldwyn-Mayer he was involved in the endless production of *I Take This Woman* (1940), which went through the regimes of three directors, wasted the talents of Spencer Tracy, Hedy Lamarr, and Carson, and justifiably failed at the boxoffice. As William Powell's rival for the affections of Myrna Loy in the wacky comedy *Love Crazy* (1941), Carson was exceptionally good in the role of Ward Willowby.

After playing the oafish Hugo Barnstead in Warner Bros.' remake of James Hogan's play *One Sunday Afternoon*, released as *The Strawberry Blonde* (1941), Carson was finally established on screen and earned a long-term Warners' contract. He attributed much of his success in this period film to James Cagney who kept telling him to relax oncamera or he would be a nervous wreck. Whenever Carson would freeze in his part Cagney would deliberately blow one of his own lines until Carson could regain his composure. "You're pressing too hard, kid. Play the scene easy," Cagney told him. Carson's praise for Cagney's aid was combined with equal praise for Bette Davis' assistance during the filming of *The Bride Came C.O.D.* (1941), which also had Cagney in its star lineup, where Carson played Allan Brice, a stuffy orchestra leader prevented from eloping with Davis by Cagney.

In Warners' eyes, Carson was heir apparent to fill the stereotyped role of the big, bluff affable guy most likely to lose the girl, or to play the counterpart of the egocentric, strutting boor whose enflamed self approval has far outdistanced his poverty of intelligence. A third "type" destined to become a Carson speciality was the well-met pal with a heart of gold who supplies mindless comedy relief. Karl Dane, among others, had filled this multi-faceted niche during the silent film era, and later Jack Oakie strutted through the early days of sound pictures paced by Nat Pendleton, Frank McHugh, and Allen Jenkins. However, few actors in this genre could equal Carson's nimble playing and versatility. Except for Edward Everett Horton, and, possibly, Oakie, no one in films could match the confused perplexity of a Carson double take. His dumbfounded expression at the disappearance of a football while demonstrating his once famous Statue of Liberty play as the has-been football star in *The Male Animal* (1942) remains one of the delights of that film. At the same time, his versatility

With Penny Edwards, Dennis Morgan, and Dorothy Malone in a publicity pose for Two Guys from Texas *(WB 1948)*

permitted a fine performance as the tragic vaudeville hoofer, Albert Runkel, in Vincent Sherman's tautly directed *The Hard Way* (1942).

Warners' attempt to team Carson with Jane Wyman in several minor comedies was a desperate decision that promoted neither of their careers, although Jack received star billing as "Our No. 1 Comedy Star" in his role as a meddling, addled detective in *Make Your Own Bed* (1944). He and Wyman were teamed in a half-dozen films and in *Hollywood Canteen* (1944), another Warners' musical star-burst, they dueted "What You Doin' the Rest of Your Life?"

Carson could justly claim to being a work horse during the early 1940s, when he was seemingly forever in front of the cameras, emcee-ing radio's "Camel Caravan" and rehearsing and broadcasting a weekly radio show with Jane Morgan, Mel Blanc, Arthur Treacher, Elizabeth Patterson, and his college buddy, Dave Willock. The program was CBS' "The Jack Carson Show." Three years before he had met singer Kay St. Germain on a radio show and married her. (He had been previously wed to Betty Ann Linde, his one-time vaudeville partner.)

It was Warners' ace director, Michael Curtiz, who saw in Jack a talent beyond the stock roles the studio's repertory kept him in. Curtiz assigned him the lead opposite Rosalind Russell as Harold Pierson in the film version of Louise Randall Pierson's autobiography, *Roughly Speaking* (1945). From his entrance halfway into the 117 minute film, he dominated the picture. His splendid performance as the husband with the wild moneymaking schemes was a constant

delight that virtually saved the pedestrian story. It remained his favorite screen role. Reaction to this performance in *Roughly Speaking* bewildered Jack. "Guys I've known for years came up to me after seeing *Roughly Speaking* with 'Why didn't you tell me you could act?' At first I was sore as a hornet—and that's good and sore. Then I realized they weren't to blame. They were simply following the old Hollywood custom of typing a guy and leaving him to rot. In the four years I'd been at Warners' I'd done little more than good roles. They weren't bad parts necessarily, but I always portrayed the perennial goof-ball, the good-natured meat-head who tossed lines back and forth, usually with Ann Sheridan and Dennis Morgan. I'd get laughs if I was lucky (and most of the time my luck held) but I registered no further with audiences than 'that funny-faced guy, What's-His-Name.'"

Director Curtiz also cast him in *Mildred Pierce* (1945), as the rejected but staunch friend of Joan Crawford. His relaxed and effective performance was an asset in the film that won Crawford an Academy Award. Several more team efforts with Dennis Morgan followed, such as *Two Guys from Milwaukee* (1948), then a musical *The Time, The Place and The Girl* (1946), and a role as the alcoholic member of "The Three Happy Tymes" in another vaudeville epic with Ann Sothern, *April Showers* (1948). Then Carson had the historical distinction of being Doris Day's leading man in her film debut, *Romance on the High Seas* (1948). He again supported Day in *My Dream Is Yours* (1949) and *It's A Great Feeling* (1949). His last

123

Warners' contract role was as medicine showman Chris Malley, giving fine backup to Cary Cooper, Lauren Bacall, and Patricia Neal in *Bright Leaf* (1950).

In 1945, Carson had been "invited" to join the Army, but during the physical examination doctors discovered he had a heart murmur. The hefty, manly Carson who had once tackled football's all-time bone crusher Bronko Nagurski in a college game, received the shock of his life. He fainted. His apparently happy home life with Kay St. Germain and their two children, Jack, Jr. and Germain, collapsed in 1948 and Jack walked out. On April 3, 1950, Kay won a divorce, custody of both children, a sizable cash settlement, and a tax-free annual $15,000. She charged "desertion."

Leaving Warner Bros. for another freelancing experiment, Carson discovered a new field he embraced with enthusiasm at a time when most of his colleagues in Hollywood were very reluctant to even admit its existence. He entered the television scene enthusiastically, playing the lead in *Room Service* and starring in the "Four Star Revue." In this situation comedy he was a big, well-meaning chap getting into perpetual unsolicited trouble with a regular cast of Betty Kean, Jack Norton, and March and Sweeney. At the same time, for Columbia Pictures, Jack was Biff Jones in *The Good Humor Man* (1950), a slapstick film that featured Lola Albright. She was a capable, hardworking actress who was later to gain recognition as television's "Peter Gunn"'s girlfriend, Edie Hart. In addition, she became Carson's third wife when they were married by Reverend Errol B. Sloan of the Christian Church at the Little Brown Church in the Valley on August 1, 1952.

In 1951, Carson returned to the stage, appearing at London's Palladium and in his first stage revue, *Texas, L'il Darlin'* before an enthusiastic Dallas audience. In the spring of 1951 he signed for the role of President Wintergreen in a revival of George S. Kaufman and Morrie Ryskind's satire on national politics, with music by George Gershwin. The show was *Of Thee I Sing.* Carson stated, "I suppose it's the ham in me, but I've wanted all my life to be in a musical and here it is. I was sticking my chin out when I took on Billy Gaxton's original role but I've always done that and it hasn't worked out too badly." It is said that Carson accomplished the amazing feat of making the usually dour George S. Kaufman guffaw with laughter at some of his improvised onstage antics. Following out-of-town tryouts, the Pulitzer Prize-winning musical opened at New York's Ziegfeld Theatre on May 5, 1952, but lasted a meagre thirty-two performances. Evidently real-life Washington had become funnier than the pseudo-Washington of the show.

Carson's compulsive work habits kept him working

in television and before the cameras as Jeff Clayton in *Mr. Universe* (1951), as Windy Webbe encouraging Esther Williams to swim the English Channel in *Dangerous When Wet* (1953), and, giving one of his best movie portrayals, as Libby, the acerbic studio press agent, in the remake of *A Star Is Born* (1954). In addition, Carson was seen with Dorothy Lamour on "Suspense" in *Conversation at the Inn,* on "U.S. Steel Hour" in *Goodbye, But It Doesn't Go Away,* as Calvin Botz with Allen Jenkins and Mabel Albertson in *Here Comes Calvin,* and with Dennis O'Keefe and Constance Towers he recalled Christmas past with tear-filled eyes on his own "Jack Carson Show."

His film career dwindled to about one release yearly but his work on television increased on most of the major drama programs in such roles as crude, nouveau riche Harry Mauldon with Patricia Morison in *The Trophy,* or guest-playing with wife Lola Albright on the "Bob Cummings Show." In the fall of 1956 Carson signed with Max Gordon for a new Broadway-bound comedy by Mannie Manheim and Arthur Marx called *Everybody Loves Me,* in which he played Gordy Williams, a frequently divorced, egomanic TV comic. His performance, however, was too forcibly amiable to stress the deep bitterness of the character and the weakly scripted play closed on the road. Back on television, Jack played a quick-buck artist named King, singing "The Boasting Song" with Basil Rathbone on "U.S. Steel Hour"'s musical version of *Huck Finn.* Also, he did a creditable job as Eugene Skinner on *Tunnel of Fear* for "Climax," and alternated on George Gobel's variety show.

On November 10, 1958 Lola Albright divorced him. The dissolution of Carson's third marriage was attributed to a conflict of careers. Jack wanted a wife, at home, and Lola wanted a career. The same year film audiences saw him as the confused, empty-headed, tactless Captain Hoxie flying off into space on an misfired missile in Leo McCarey's *Rally 'Round the Flag, Boys!.* A high spot in Carson's film career was his subtle performance as Gooper Pollitt in MGM's whitewashed *Cat on a Hot Tin Roof* (1958). He played Bert Mosley, a low-grade politician running for the office of district attorney, in Warner Bros.' confused and inept *The Bramble Bush* (1960), and he turned in an exceptionally fine performance as Big Tim O'Brien, a corrupt political boss in *King of the Roaring Twenties* (1961).

During the summer of 1962 Carson returned to the theatre but, on August 26th he collapsed during a dress rehearsal of the play *Critic's Choice* on the stage at Andover, New Jersey. His final professional work was for Walt Disney's *Sammy, the Way-Out Seal* (1963). After the film was completed, Carson entered a hospital for a stomach malignancy. He never mentioned his illness, and on New Year's Day watched the Rose Bowl Game and chatted pleasantly with his fourth wife, the former Sandra Tucker, to whom he was married in 1961. Frank Stempel, Carson's agent for over twenty-five years, talked with the actor on the morning of January 2, 1963. After his conversation with Stempel, his wife returned to the room and found Carson dead.

Death took no holiday in Hollywood from mid-December until the end of January, 1963. Charles Laughton and Thomas Mitchell died before Christmas, 1962, and Jack Carson died four hours before Dick Powell on January 2, 1963. All these stars were victims of cancer. Before January ended, directors Frank Tuttle and Mia Farrow's father, John, succumbed to heart attacks. Hollywood was rightfully in mourning throughout the early part of 1963.

Services for fifty-two year old Carson were held in a replica of Anne Laurie's church (the original being in Glencairn, Scotland) at the Wee Kirk o'the Heather in Forest Lawn Memorial Park, Glendale, California, where Dr. Raymond Lindquist of the Hollywood Presbyterian Church eulogized Carson for his surprising religious faith. Dr. Lindquist told the mourners that Jack had completed eight chapters of a book based on his religious convictions, the theme being how well man utilizes his God-given responsiveness. Pallbearers for the ebullient Carson included his long time friend and ex-vaudeville partner Dave Willock, and his buddy from Warners, Dennis Morgan, of whom Jack once said, "I was the guy in the movie who never won the girl, but I never complained because I usually lost her to my buddy Dennis Morgan —and he was from Milwaukee, too!"

JACK CARSON

You Only Live Once   (UA 1937)
Stand In   (UA 1937)
It Could Happen to You   (Rep 1937)
Reported Missing   (Univ 1937)
Too Many Wives   (RKO 1937)
On Again Off Again   (RKO 1937)
A Damsel in Distress   (RKO 1937)*
High Flyers   (RKO 1937)
Music For Madame   (RKO 1937)
Stage Door   (RKO 1937)
The Toast of New York   (RKO 1937)
This Marriage Business   (RKO 1938)
The Saint in New York   (RKO 1938)
The Girl Downstairs   (MGM 1938)
Condemned Women   (RKO 1938)
Carefree   (RKO 1938)
Go Chase Yourself   (RKO 1938)
Crashing Hollywood   (RKO 1938)
Law of the Underworld   (RKO 1938)
Everybody's Doing It   (RKO 1938)
Night Spot   (RKO 1938)
Having Wonderful Time   (RKO 1938)
Maid's Night Out   (RKO 1938)
Quick Money   (RKO 1938)
She's Got Everything   (RKO 1938)
Vivacious Lady   (RKO 1938)
Bringing Up Baby   (RKO 1938)
Fifth Avenue Girl   (RKO 1939)
The Kid From Texas   (MGM 1939)
The Escape   (20th 1939)
Mr. Smith Goes to Washington   (Col 1939)
The Honeymoon's Over   (20th 1939)
Legion of Lost Flyers   (Univ 1939)
Destry Rides Again   (Univ 1939)
Shooting High   (20th 1940)
The Girl in 313   (20th 1940)
Sandy Gets Her Man   (Univ 1940)
Alias The Deacon   (Univ 1940)
Enemy Agent   (Univ 1940)
Queen of the Mob   (Par 1940)
Typhoon   (Par 1940)
Love Thy Neighbor   (Par 1940)
Parole Fixer   (Par 1940)
Lucky Partners   (RKO 1940)
Young As You Feel   (20th 1940)
I Take This Woman   (MGM 1940)
Love Crazy   (MGM 1941)
*Scenes deleted from release print

Mr. and Mrs. Smith   (RKO 1941)
The Strawberry Blonde   (WB 1941)
The Bride Came C.O.D.   (WB 1941)
Blues in the Night   (WB 1941)
Navy Blues   (WB 1941)
The Hard Way   (WB 1942)
Gentleman Jim   (WB 1942)
The Male Animal   (WB 1942)
Larceny, Inc   (WB 1942)
Wings for the Eagle   (WB 1942)
Thank Your Lucky Stars   (WB 1943)
Princess O'Rourke   (WB 1943)
Make Your Own Bed   (WB 1944)
Hollywood Canteen   (WB 1944)
Shine on Harvest Moon   (WB 1944)
The Doughgirls   (WB 1944)
Arsenic and Old Lace   (WB 1944)
Roughly Speaking   (WB 1945)
Mildred Pierce   (WB 1945)
The Time, The Place and The Girl   (WB 1946)
One More Tomorrow   (WB 1946)
Two Guys From Milwaukee   (WB 1946)
Love and Learn   (WB 1946)
Always Together   (WB 1948)
Two Guys From Texas   (WB 1948)
Romance on the High Seas   (WB 1948)
April Showers   (WB 1948)
My Dream Is Yours   (WB 1949)
John Loves Mary   (WB 1949)
It's a Great Feeling   (WB 1949)
The Good Humor Man   (Col 1950)
Bright Leaf   (WB 1940)
The Groom Wore Spurs   (Univ 1951)
Mr. Universe   (EL 1951)
Dangerous When Wet   (MGM 1953)
A Star Is Born   (WB 1954)
Red Garters   (Par 1954)
Phffft!   (Col 1954)
Ain't Misbehavin'   (Univ 1955)
The Magnificent Roughnecks   (AA 1956)
The Bottom of the Bottle   (20th 1956)
The Tattered Dress   (Univ 1957)
The Tarnished Angels   (Univ 1957)
Rally 'Round the Flag, Boys!   (20th 1958)
Cat on a Hot Tin Roof   (MGM 1958)
The Bramble Bush   (WB 1960)
King of the Roaring Twenties   (AA 1961)
Sammy the Way Out Seal   (BV 1963)

Marguerite Chapman

19

Although it has been used frequently by critics to disparage a performer, the word "competent" is really a compliment. Webster's Dictionary defines this descriptive adjective as: "Answering to all requirements, adequate; capable; fit." Marguerite Chapman fulfilled this definition admirably during the 1940s at Columbia where she, along with Nina Foch, Lynn Merrick, Jeff Donnell, Janis Carter, et al. were the stalwart female players who peppered feature after feature with their very able and amiable presences. Though they were all outshined by the studio's top female attractions (Jean Arthur, Rita Hayworth, and to a lesser degree, Janet Blair), these other girls were the backbone of the lot's productions.

Marguerite was neither gutsy nor overly saccharine in her screen portrayals, but was a well-modulated, dark-haired ingenue, who exemplified the best of middle class America. In the hectic forties, she made nineteen features for Columbia. When she arrived at the Gower Street studio she filled a gap left by the departure of the still active Margaret Lindsay—that of queen of the company's programmers. When Marguerite left the studio in 1948, she was replaced, in effect, by Barbara Hale. Marguerite's career was not the boisterous type that the public doted on, or one that cinema scholars clamored to chronicle, but it was a steady, dependable stint of screen acting that reflects what 1940s Hollywood was all about: ensemble playing by stock company performers at still

proud major studios. Thanks to such as Marguerite Chapman, the decade's films were a good deal brighter than they might have been.

Marguerite Chapman was born in Chatham, New York, on March 9, 1921. She was educated at the public schools of Chatham and White Plains. After completing school she operated a switchboard in White Plains, and then took a job modeling for the prestigious John Robert Powers agency in Manhattan. At the suggestion of womanizer Howard Hughes, Marguerite, then thriving as a relatively well-paid mannequin, went to Hollywood and entered motion pictures. She made her screen debut at Twentieth Century-Fox in their Jones Family series feature *On Their Own* (1940). The same studio's Charlie Chan series was both one of its major sustaining financial successes and a further training ground for several of Hollywood's later stars. In *Charlie Chan at the Wax Museum* (1941), Marguerite was cast as Mary Bolton, a reporter, with Sidney Toler as Chan. The programmer is one of the best films in that series. Marguerite was given the small part of Cecilia Grange in the Harold Lloyd production for RKO featuring George Murphy and Lucille Ball, *A Girl, a Guy and a Gob* (1941). She won her "break" in Warner Bros.' *Navy Blues* (1941), directed by Lloyd Bacon and starring Ann Sheridan, Martha Raye, three Jacks (Oakie, Hal-

With Jerome Cowan in One Way to Love *(Col 1945)*

ey, and Carson), and Jackie Gleason. It was saddled with an undistinguished score by Johnny Mercer and Arthur Schwartz.

Although *Variety* quite rightly said that *Navy Blues* floundered on a reef of frequent boredom, it did have the saving grace of six lovely starlets in the cast who were widely advertised as "The Navy Blues Sextet." The young beauties comprising this special group were sent to Honolulu for the world premiere of the picture in mid-summer of 1941, and then returned to make a cross country junket in September starting in Dallas, Texas. The six went on to various major cities and finally to New York City where Sherman Billingsley gave them a well-planned, well-publicized party at his famous Stork Club. "The Navy Blues Sextet" (wryly called the modern Floradoras) included Claire James, Peggy Diggins (who later became a WAC photographer in London), Lorraine Gettman, Katherine (Kay) Aldridge (who later became Republic's serial queen), Georgia Carroll (who eventually joined a band as vocalist and married its leader, Kay Kyser), and five foot, seven inch Marguerite, who, with her blue eyes and reddish-brown hair, decorated the celluloid very prettily indeed.

Navy Blues and the lengthy promotional tour should have led Marguerite on to better things at Warners, but her roles in Jimmy Durante's *You're in the Army Now* (1941) and *The Body Disappears* (1941) with Jeffrey Lynn and Jane Wyman, gave her no leeway. Having completed these assignments, Marguerite made a hurried trip to the hospital for an appendectomy. While there, she was visited regularly by her favorite escort, actor Don Alvarado, a handsome Latin who had some success in silent films, notably *The Bridge of San Luis Rey* (1929).

After recuperating, Marguerite signed with Republic for twelve episodes of the serial *Spy Smasher* (1942), in which she played Eve Corby, daughter of Admiral Corby (Sam Flint) and fiancée of the hero (Kane Richmond). Following the dozen segments of mayhem, spying, murder, and submarine disaster in this cliffhanger, Marguerite turned to a less athletic pursuit and joined Harry Cohn's acting stable at Columbia. She played straight lady to Joe E. Brown in *The Daring Young Man* (1942), headed the contingent of aerial Florence Nightingales in *Parachute Nurse* (1942), and turned in a polished performance as Melinda Matthews, a press agent helping Edmund Lowe solve murders by rattlesnake venom in *Murders in Time Square* (1943). She played to good advantage

With Joe E. Brown in The Daring Young Man *(Col 1942)*

128

with George Sanders and Gale Sondergaard in *Appointment in Berlin* (1943), despite the *New York Times* characterizing her as a "lukewarm Nazi."

For Columbia's 1943 film starring Edward G. Robinson, *Destroyer* (the *USS John Paul Jones II*), Marguerite was Captain Edward G.'s daughter, Mary Boleslavski, who weds young Glenn Ford. To promote this William Seiter-directed feature, Marguerite undertook another tour of the country, making personal appearances with the picture's openings and guesting at shipyards and bond-selling functions. Her personal appearances delighted the press and she enchanted the Navy Yards and shipyards by telling their workers, "This is my way of paying tribute to my four brothers in uniform. Three are in the Navy and one in the Army." Her four brothers nicknamed her "Slugger" and Marguerite seldom, if ever backed off in defense. Her romance with Barret O'Shea was a thing of the past when she left to tour with appearances for *Destroyer*. In addition she was determined to override several Hollywood directors' opinions that she was just another pretty face, as well as a wooden-style mannequin.

Marguerite demonstrated a flair for lighthearted fare in *My Kingdom for a Cook* (1943) which is noted for being Charles Coburn's first real solo-starring vehicle. One of her sturdiest roles at Columbia was as Lisa Elenko in the Zoltan Korda-directed *Counter-Attack* (1945). Shorn of any glamour, she was exceedingly effective as the girl guerrilla helping Paul Muni, a wounded Soviet paratrooper who stands off seven German prisoners while they are all trapped in a cellar. It was a tense, well-executed script by John Howard Lawson, but once again, Marguerite failed to captivate the New York critics. Bosley Crowther (*New York Times*) chided, "her main contribution and performance is that of holding a gun." Archer Winsten (*New York Post*) concurred, "[she] fills the part of a girl fighter by the simple expedient of doing and saying little. Since she looks the part, she's all right."

After the fine comedy-drama *Pardon My Past* (1945) with Fred MacMurray, it was downhill for Marguerite at Columbia. She was only the second female lead (supporting Janis Carter) in *One Way to Love* (1945). In 1948, she made the western scene in *Relentless*, as Luella Purdy, a lovely prairie flower helping Robert Young prove he is innocent of murder while being pursued in glorious Technicolor by Akim Tamiroff and Mike Mazurki. She remained in the

With Willard Parker in Relentless *(Col 1948)*

West with Randolph Scott in a scenically stunning movie, *Coroner Creek,* also 1948 and also for Columbia. Her final fling at Columbia was in 1948's *The Gallant Blade,* in which she appeared as Nanon de Lartiques with Larry–*The Jolson Story*–Parks as the unlikely "Blade" out to save both France and Marguerite, and ends up turning the swashbuckling yarn into a yawning bore.

Marguerite was among the many who left Columbia in the 1948 industry recession. Later that year, on December 29th, she married Hollywood attorney G. Bentley Ryan. They were wed in Santa Barbara; but they separated two weeks before their first wedding anniversary, in December, 1949. The twenty-seven year-old "Slugger" Chapman won an interlocutory decree from lawyer Ryan on February 20, 1950, claiming extreme cruelty, charging that Mr. Ryan left home after a minor disagreement for some five weeks at a time and was critical of everything she did. Marguerite received her legal divorce from the forty-one year-old Ryan on March 10, 1951, plus a settlement of $10,000. Prior to the divorce proceedings she made a delightful film for Glen McCarthy, the RKO release *The Green Promise* (1949) in which she trenchantly played farm girl Deborah Matthews, oldest daughter of impoverished farmer Walter Brennan. For Universal, she was Kate in *Kansas Raiders* (1950), with Audie Murphy as Jesse James, Brian Donlevy as Quantrill, and a cast that included Scott Brady, Richard Long, Dewey Martin, and Anthony Curtis, known more recently as "Tony."

With parts becoming less attractive in subgrade films, Marguerite turned her talents to television. On April 2, 1951 she debuted in "Bigelow Theatre's" *The Lady's Companion* where she mistakenly hired a companion who turns out to be the very male Robert Paige. On "Ford Theatre" in *Life, Liberty and Orrin Dooley,* she was an Oklahoma country girl to whom ex-G.I. Will Rogers, Jr. returns, and she played a fashion magazine editor on the *My Boss and I* segment of "Hollywood Opening Night." She also played Elsa Purvis, whose son Tommy Rettig saves her career-torn marriage with husband George Nader in *The Tin Bridge* on "Your Play Time."

Marguerite went to England to make *The Last Page*

(a.k.a. Man *Bait*) (1952) with George Brent. Back in the States she stopped off at Twentieth Century-Fox for a featured role in *Bloodhounds of Broadway* (1952) with Mitzi Gaynor and Mitzi Green. Marguerite was Yvonne, wanting mink more than love. But television occupied most of her professional time, and she was seen on the small screen with David Niven in "Four Star Playhouse"'s *The Book,* as Barbara Nicholson in the telecast of Richard Tregaskis' *Unfair Game,* and as a career-wife in marital trouble with Douglas Kennedy on *Clair.* For 1954's "Playhouse" she was a lady lawyer defending Vera Miles on a murder charge in *Such a Nice Little Girl,* and was again involved in a murder case as Liza with Dick Powell and John Hubbard in *The Contest* for "Four Star Playhouse."

For Billy Wilder, Marguerite returned to Twentieth Century-Fox to play Miss Morris, the secretary in Fox's top grosser for 1955, *The Seven Year Itch.* Then she temporarily abandoned motion pictures for her increasingly more interesting and challenging career on television. She was extremely effective as Myra Saunders on *Private Worlds* for "Climax" and for the same anthology series played the self-centered Mrs. Carter in the episode, *The Healer.* For the next three years (1955–58) she appeared on most of the major drama telecasts and by the close of the fifties (from *Dead Ringer* on "Studio One" with Gig Young to a "Rawhide" series episode with Dan Duryea, *Incident with the Executioner*), Marguerite offered consistently good performances. Not only had she outlasted many of her flashier contemporaries, but she had improved as an actress. Her last film to date was the Edgar Ulmer-directed *The Amazing Transparent Man* (1960) in which she was the girl friend of a deranged scientist (James Griffith), who dreams of controlling the world via an army of invisible men.

Marguerite is now Mrs. J. Richard Bremerkamp and has become a talented artist, with several of her canvases displayed in West Coast galleries. She should have received better assignments during her cinema heyday. Her natural talent was refined by studying acting with Josephine Hutchinson. Then too, her fierce ambition and sensuous beauty should have made the road to movie fame a lot easier.

MARGUERITE CHAPMAN

On Their Own *(20th 1940)*
Charlie Chan at the Wax Museum *(20th 1940)*
A Girl, A Guy and a Gob *(RKO 1941)*
Navy Blues *(WB 1941)*
You're in the Army Now *(WB 1941)*
The Body Disappears *(WB 1941)*
Spy Smasher *(Rep Serial 1942)*
Submarine Raider *(Col 1942)*
Parachute Nurse *(Col 1942)*
The Spirit of Stanford *(Col 1942)*
The Daring Young Man *(Col 1942)*
A Man's World *(Col 1942)*
Murder in Times Square *(Col 1943)*
Appointment in Berlin *(Col 1943)*
My Kingdom for a Cook *(Col 1943)*
One Dangerous Night *(Col 1943)*
Destroyer *(Col 1943)*
Strange Affair *(Col 1944)*

A Thousand and One Nights *(Col 1945)*
Counter-Attack *(Col 1945)*
Pardon My Past *(Col 1945)*
One Way to Love *(Col 1945)*
The Walls Came Tumbling Down *(Col 1946)*
Mr. District Attorney *(Col 1947)*
Relentless *(Col 1948)*
Coroner Creek *(Col 1948)*
The Gallant Blade *(Col 1948)*
The Green Promise *(RKO 1949)*
Kansas Raiders *(Univ 1950)*
Flight to Mars *(Mon 1951)*
The Last Page (a.k.a., Man Bait) *(Lip 1952)*
Sea Tiger *(Mon 1952)*
Bloodhounds of Broadway *(20th 1952)*
The Seven Year Itch *(20th 1955)*
The Amazing Transparent Man *(AIP 1960)*

20

Dane Clark

Dane Clark always hoped to follow in the footsteps of his screen idol Humphrey Bogart, but he never did. He did, however, become a minor-league John Garfield, without having Garfield's particular charisma. Clark projected a cockiness that was quite similar to Garfield's but was more animated and energetic than the established star. Clark's greatest attribute as an actor was and always has been his direct, no nonsense, ungimmicky playing. Even later in his career, after having studied at the Actors' Studio in New York, he never lost his direct approach. A short and wiry man—he is just under 5'9"—he was quite acceptable in tough-guy roles as had been other more famous, shorter performers (James Cagney, Edward G. Robinson, and George Raft), but as Clark himself has said, it was a little ridiculous to see him onscreen beat up six-foot-two muscled men. Under contract to Warner Bros., the home base of the cinema's rough guys, he spent most of his early screen career in uniform. In his first six films for that studio he either played a soldier or a sailor and thereafter ended up in B films playing mostly tough guys. After the mid-1940s, Clark never again appeared in a major film.

Bernard Zanville, his real name, was born on February 18, 1915, in New York City, where his father owned a sporting goods store. His major interest as a boy was baseball, and he was good enough at the game to make the minor leagues, but instead he chose to receive a B.A. degree from Cornell University and a law degree from St. John's. Due to the Depression, work was difficult to find and when a job with an important law office failed to materialize, he became disgusted and decided to take any type of job that was offered to him. He worked on a road gang, he boxed, and he even did some modeling before turning to the theatre. A job writing for the radio led to some anonymous radio acting which, in turn, led him to Orson Welles' flowering Mercury Theatre, where he made his Broadway debut in the company's production of *Panic* in 1935. That same year he followed this up with a small role in Sidney Kingsley's *Dead End*, and understudied and played bit parts in touring companies of *Dead End*, *Of Mice and Men*, *Waiting for Lefty*, *Stage Door*, *Sailor Beware*, and *Golden Boy*. *Lefty* and *Golden Boy* were produced by the renowned Group Theatre of which John Garfield was also a member. The *Golden Boy* tour in 1938 starred Phillips Holmes, Jean Muir, and in a featured part, another future Hollywood performer, Richard Conte.

Clark drifted to Hollywood in the early 1940s to do some short films for the Army. While there he was able to get some bit parts in such films as *Pride of the Yankees* (1942), *Wake Island* (1942), and *Tennessee Johnson* (1942). Warner Bros. then cast him as Johnnie Pulaski, a member of the Merchant Marine, in *Action in the North Atlantic* (1943), starring his idol, Humphrey Bogart. Says Clark, "The original idea was

With Janis Paige in Her Kind of Man *(WB 1946)*

to sign me for just the one picture and then drop me. But as the rushes started coming through, Bogey got interested and began throwing more and more plums at me. As a result, before the picture was released, the presumption was that I would remain at Warners."

Bogart also had a hand in renaming him. After *Action in the North Atlantic,* in which he still used his real name, the studio decided a new name tag was in order. "The idea of changing my name was shocking," Clark admits, "but it was the code of Hollywood at the time." He anxiously hoped nobody would come up with a name like Gig Young for him, even though it seemed the entire studio made a game of it. Bogart came up with the selection "Zane Clark" but the nickname of Zany did not appeal to serious-minded Bernard Zanville. Eventually the monicker was modified to Dane Clark. To this day, however, he has never changed his name legally. He was first billed as Dane Clark in *Destination Tokyo* (1943), playing the role of Tin Can, a Greek. He was Dennis Morgan's jovial sidekick in both *The Very Thought of You* (1944) and in *God Is My Co-Pilot* (1945). In the former film, he was a wolfish soldier with a quick eye for attractive Faye Emerson, and he recalls that he was criticized for overacting in it. "I had to bark like a dog when I saw a girl," says Clark. "They were always giving me lines like 'you woman, you.' How can you underplay when you're making sounds like a dog?" Clark definitely had his share of bad dialog. In *Hollywood Canteen* (1944), in another wolfish soldier role, he dances with Joan Crawford, who, as a Canteen hostess, was playing herself. The scene read (and played), Clark: "Did anybody ever tell you that you're a dead ringer for Joan Crawford?" His head jerks up. "You are?" he says, "you are!" He then faints dead away. End of scene.

Dane's most memorable screen performance came early in his career, as John Garfield's war buddy in *Pride of the Marines* (1945). The film was a true account of Al Schmidt, a blinded war veteran, and his rehabilitation problems. One of the highlights of the drama is when his pal Clark tells him to his face, "You have no guts!" The *New York Times,* among others, commended Clark for his "vivid" performance. But then his Warners' career started going downhill. In the first of his two 1946 films, *Her Kind of Man,* he finally reached first billing only to have the sinister Zachary Scott steal the gangster melodrama from under him. In his other film that year, *A Stolen Life,* he had the opportunity of working with Bette Davis, whom he had always admired. He was quite pleased with his assignment as a rude, arrogant, and deadly honest artist because he was able—for a few oncamera moments anyway—to dominate the indomitable Miss Davis. His role as Karnok is interest-

ing but completely superfluous to the film, in which Glenn Ford was *the* leading man. The *New York Times* said of Clark here, "He snarls and makes passes at Miss Davis with a rare lack of gentility. Just what he proves or what happens to him is never adequately explained. For all we know, he is still residing in the lady's New York studio, eating, drinking and shouting insults at her badly frightened maid."

Warners considered him for the Al Jolson role in a remake of *The Jazz Singer* but shelved the idea until the early 1950s when Danny Thomas played the role. Clark should have played the role that went to John Garfield in *Gentlemen's Agreement* (1947), Elia Kazan's picture about anti-Semitism. The role of Dave, a young Jew, would have boosted Dane's sagging career. Instead, he was cast in a few potboilers, *That Way with Women* (1947), a feeble remake of George Arliss' *The Millionaire* (1931), and *Embraceable You* (1948), an undistinguished love story with Geraldine Brooks, she being another misused studio stock company player.

Deep Valley (1947), directed by Jean Negulesco, was Clark's only good film for Warners in the late 1940s. Playing a convict, Dane and Ida Lupino, as a farm girl, turned in solid performances which elevated this rather grim drama. Although *Whiplash* (1948) was not a good film, it was colorful and had an amenable cast including Alexis Smith, Zachary Scott, and Eve Arden. Clark portrayed a moody artist turned boxer who falls in love with elusive Alexis. The latter had to play their scenes together in stocking feet because in heels she towered over Clark. By 1949, Warners was dropping many of their contract players and since Clark was among those to be let out to pasture, he was only given a supporting role in *Backfire* (1950), and then a part in an undistinguished Western, *Barricade* (1950), which terminated his seven year contract.

Next to *Pride of the Marines,* Clark's best 1940s movie part was in the backwoods drama, *Moonrise* (1948), which had been made on loan to Republic Pictures. Under Frank Borzage's guidance, Clark provided one of his best dramatic efforts as a man running from the law after unwittingly committing murder. Gail Russell was his girl. The picture was not a success, for it was considered too arty, and even a prestige name like Ethel Barrymore (as his grandmother) did not help matters at the boxoffice. Clark continued to make minor films, both here and abroad, until 1957. He even co-starred with the Harlem Globetrotters in the basketball yarn *Go, Man, Go* in 1954, which he co-produced, but most of his post-Warners pictures were melodramas or westerns that generally had him escaping the authorities. For example, in the British-made *Paid to Kill* (1954), he was a

With Faye Emerson in The Very Thought of You *(WB 1944)*

With Fay Bainter and Ida Lupino in Deep Valley *(WB 1947)*

businessman who hires an assassin to kill him so his wife can reap the insurance benefits. But when circumstances change and he no longer wants to die, he tries to alter his plans.

Seeking some way to exapnd his acting skills, Clark returned to Broadway in October, 1951 to co-star with Martha Scott in *The Number,* at the Biltmore Theatre, an exposé of gambling rackets with Clark as a small time gambler. The *New York Times* admitted he "plays the heel with enthusiasm and unction." After losing the lead in the Jose Ferrer-directed *Stalag 17* on Broadway, he went on tour with Robert Young and Nancy Kelly in Clifford Odets' *The Country Girl,* playing the director, Bernie Dodd, which William Holden would play on the screen. In summer stock, he was the boxer in *Heaven Can Wait* which had been filmed in 1941 as *Here Comes Mr. Jordan,* and he also appeared in *One Sunday Afternoon.* Good notices followed him in *The Fragile Fox,* a war drama, which opened at the Belasco Theatre in New York in October, 1954. As a bitter platoon commander he shared the stage with Don Taylor and James Gregory and the *New York Herald-Tribune* commented, "Mr. Clark enters with a seething contempt and an insolent stare; he turns an apology into a compounded insult; he stretches his mouth taut and his fingers tense as he whiplashes tension into his every scene. Whether you believe in the evening's villains or not, you can't help believing in this actor's breathless, staccato firebrand."

The following year he received a terrible shock while on stage in the Los Angeles production of *The Shrike,* when his leading lady, Isabel Bonner (also the playwright's wife), had a heart attack onstage and died in his arms. In 1962, at New York's Theatre De Lys, he replaced Eli Wallach in the dramatic anthology *Brecht on Brecht,* appearing with such stage stalwarts as Viveca Lindfors, Anne Jackson, and Lotte Lenya. He also replaced Jason Robards on Broadway in *A Thousand Clowns* in 1965, delivering a more honest performance than his predecessor.

High-powered Clark has always been a natural performer for television, able to convey intense emotions quickly, broadly, and effectively, to home viewers. He has appeared in that medium steadily since 1950 and has had two of his own series, "Wire Service" and the syndicated "Bold Venture." As a reporter on "Wire Service," he alternated as star with Mercedes McCambridge and George Brent. This 1956 sixty-minute series was re-run three years later, with the Dane Clark segments entitled "Deadline for Action." He found that making the production-line series became a grind, but said, "Everybody's doing it so I just grit my teeth and bear it." "Bold Venture" (1958–59), which lasted thirty-nine episodes, was an outgrowth of the Humphrey Bogart film *To Have and Have Not* (1944) and the "Bold Venture" radio series, which starred Bogie and his wife, Lauren Bacall. Whereas most of the radio show took place on a boat, the filmed series had Clark, as adventurer Slate Shannon, mostly on *terra firma.* His interpretation of the pivotal part differed from Bogart's, and Clark explained, "As

With Alexis Smith and Jeffrey Lynn in Whiplash *(WB 1948)*

an actor, I can't even carry his coat. Bogey was a giant!" Clark knew the series was typecasting him again and limiting the type of feature film roles he might be offered. "I simply haven't the time to do anything else. But I will not make a quickie B picture anymore; they're out."

He stuck to his guns and continued working on television even though he considered the medium "a good place to visit but not to stay." He appeared in the video version of Hemingway's *The Killers* (1959) and gave his finest acting performance in *No Exit*, Jean-Paul Sartre's allegory about three people, a man and two women, locked up for eternity in one room in hell: Colleen Dewhurst and Diana Hyland expertly played opposite Clark. Most recently, looking quite fit in a new toupee, he has been guest-starring on such series as "Police Story," "Mod Squad," and "Mannix," generally playing a cop, just as his one-time 1940s Twentieth Century-Fox-based competitor, Richard Conte, always seems to be a Mafia man. Clark was Lieutenant Arthur Tragg of the Los Angeles Police Department in the ill-fated "New Adventures of Perry Mason" on CBS in 1973. His made-for-television features include *The Face of Fear* (1971) in which he had a small role as a bartender, *The Family Rico* (1972), and *Say Goodbye, Maggie Cole* (1972), starring Susan Hayward.

Clark was married in 1941 to Margo Yoder, an artist who is well-known for her portraits of clowns. The only time he has ever had any adverse publicity was when his name was found in prostitute Pat Ward's little black book during the scandalous Mickey Jelke vice trial in the 1950s. Clark claimed he simply did not know the woman. In 1972, Dane, no longer wed to Miss Yoder, married Geraldine Frank.

Typecast almost by choice as the pugnacious ruffian, Clark readily admits that a good portion of his feature films were poor, but the gum-chewing actor will take credit any good performance he gave in them. As he says, "It's not difficult to be good in a movie directed by George Stevens, Billy Wilder or Elia Kazan." But Clark never had a chance to work with the top flight directors on screen or on television (re "Bold Venture," he once snapped, "Eugene O'Neill this ain't"). Often in the late 1960s, Clark could be seen pounding the beat along agents' row on New York's West 57th Street, job searching with a furious determination. He returned to the screen briefly in 1970 in a small role in *The McMasters* starring Burl Ives, Brock Peters, and David Carradine. More recently he made a feature called *Days in My Father's House* which has yet to be released.

Although he has never made it big as a Bogart or a Garfield, he still loves his chosen profession. "If I were kept away from greasepaint," he says, "I'd be a miserable bum. When they don't want me as an actor anymore, I'll starve to death. That's all I can do or all I want to do." Meanwhile Clark, the best exponent of the chip-on-the-shoulder guy of the Depression days, is thriving and continues doing what he likes and does best: Acting (as well as being a TV spokesman for a national gasoline company, in mid-1974). In the fall of 1975, Dane joined with Lloyd Bridges in the teleseries "The Metro Man" a spinoff from the successful "Police Story" program.

DANE CLARK

AS BERNARD ZANVILLE:
Sunday Punch   (MGM 1942)
Pride of the Yankees   (RKO 1942)
The Glass Key   (Par 1942)
Wake Island   (Par 1942)
Tennessee Johnson   (MGM 1942)
Action in the North Atlantic   (WB 1943)

AS DANE CLARK:
Destination Tokyo   (WB 1943)
The Very Thought of You   (WB 1944)
Hollywood Canteen   (WB 1944)
God Is My Co-Pilot   (WB 1945)
Pride of the Marines   (WB 1945)
Her Kind of Man   (WB 1946)
A Stolen Life   (WB 1946)
That Way With Women   (WB 1947)
Deep Valley   (WB 1947)
Embraceable You   (WB 1948)

Whiplash   (WB 1948)
Moonrise   (Rep 1948)
Without Honor   (UA 1949)
Backfire   (WB 1950)
Barricade   (WB 1950)
Never Trust a Gambler   (Col 1951)
Highly Dangerous   (Lip 1951)
Fort Defiance   (UA 1951)
The Gambler and the Lady   (Lip 1952)
Go, Man, Go!   (UA 1954)
Black Out   (Lip 1954)
Paid to Kill (a.k.a., Five Days)   (Lip 1954)
Thunder Pass   (Lip 1954)
Port of Hell   (AA 1954)
Time Running Out   (French-British 1955)
Toughest Man Alive   (AA 1955)
Massacre   (20th 1956)
The Man Is Armed   (Rep 1956)
Outlaw's Son   (UA 1957)
The McMasters   (Chevron 1970)
Days in My Father's House   (Unreleased)

21

Steve Cochran

While Senator Kefauver's crime commission was attempting to clean up America's underworld, Steve Cochran was cleaning up in Hollywood as a gangster on film. In contrast to the cinema's big four celluloid hoodlums (Cagney, Robinson, Raft, Bogart), Cochran was a husky six-footer with penetrating green eyes. He may not have had the intensity of manner or professional endurance of the other four, but he was by far the sexiest bad guy in the movies during the late 1940s and through the 1950s. His screen villains were suave, and when he sported a moustache he bore more than a slight resemblance to Clark Gable. If he lacked Gable's charismatic screen presence, his acting ability and own brand of macho allowed him to surpass such past film mobsters as Bruce Cabot, Lloyd Nolan, Alan Baxter, and Robert Lowery.

Cochran once described the secret of his success as a film gangster to publicist-columnist Joe Hyams, in the *New York Herald-Tribune.* "I don't act like a hood. I'm basically a decent person and I let this come through in my portrayals. After all, a guy has to make a living some way, even if he's a gangster. Robinson, Bogart, Widmark and Cagney, who were the most successful film gangsters, played their men with terrible intensity. Every once in a while one of them would break down on screen and admit he loved his mother. It came as a shock. I love my mother right from the start. When I become tough it's even more of a shock to the audience." "Once, in New York, a girl he was dating at the time introduced him to a man

who was closely associated with Murder, Inc. "I try to model my gangster portrayals after him," explained Cochran. "Gentle, polite and nice until the time comes for action; then, Bam!"

He was born Robert Alexander Cochran on May 25, 1917, in Eureka, California, but grew up in Laramie, Wyoming. His father, after whom he was named, was a lumberman from Indiana; his mother, Jessie Rose, hailed from Missouri. He made his first stage appearance in high school in *Once There Was a Princess,* but, at the time, he was more interested in athletics, particularly basketball. After high school, he worked as a cowpoke and then as a railroad station hand, later saying, "It was like a western movie." He then entered the University of Wyoming and while on the campus basketball team, broke training by painting the town red with a girlfriend. As a result of the escapade, he was removed from the basketball squad and soon afterward joined the dramatic club. He soon liked acting so much that he decided to become a professional, and quit college in 1937 to give Hollywood a try.

In Los Angeles, Cochran soon discovered that it was not a simple task to make the right connections in order to obtain a movie job. All he did was starve, so he returned home and took odd jobs as a carpenter and department store detective until he made his summer stock debut with the Cedo Players of Wyo-

With Jinx Falkenburg in The Gay Señorita (*Col 1945*)

ming in 1939. He continued doing stock and other work in the theatre, and eventually was signed on by the WPA Federal Theatre in Detroit. After that, he returned to the west coast and acted with the Shakespeare Festival in Carmel. During his two seasons with them, he played Orsino in *Twelfth Night*, Malcolm in *Macbeth*, Horatio in *Hamlet*, and the title role in *Richard III*. Cochran never had the opportunity to play Shakespeare again.

When the U.S. entered the war (he was not accepted into service because of a heart murmur), he organized and directed shows for west-coast Army camps and then toured with them. By this time, he felt he had enough stage experience to try his luck on Broadway. Due to the war, acting jobs were rather easy to come by and he was soon employed doing stock all over the east coast. He appeared as an extra in *Stage Door Canteen* (1943), and among the other extras was his good friend, Ruth Roman, with whom he would later star in films.

In 1944, he appeared on Broadway in *Broken Hearts on Broadway* and in *Hickory Stick*. In the latter play he had a leading role as a returned war veteran, who comes home "minus 12 feet of intestine from a bullet wound, and with an idea." The *New York Sun* was among those who disapproved of the play script, but did commend Cochran for his "manly and convincing performance." Richard Basehart was also in the cast of the J. B. Daniels-directed play. Then, Cochran went on the road as Constance Bennett's leading man in the Theatre Guild's touring production of *Without Love,* which had starred Katharine Hepburn and Elliott Nugent on Broadway in 1942. Unpredictable, shrewd movie mogul Samuel Goldwyn caught the show one night and signed Cochran to a term film contract. Steve began his Hollywood career as a split personality: Half his contract was owned by Goldwyn and the other half by Harry Cohn's Columbia.

Cochran shuffled back and forth between Columbia and the Goldwyn studios during his first two filmmaking years. He supported Danny Kaye and Virginia Mayo in *Wonder Man* (1945) and in *The Kid from Brooklyn* (1946), playing heavies in both these Goldwyn features. For Columbia, he had less prestigious assignments, appearing in two *Boston Blackie* detective yarns and in the minor musical *The Gay Senorita* (1945), with Jinx Falkenburg. In 1946, he had a small role as Virginia Mayo's extra-marital lover in *The Best Years of Our Lives,* one of the finest American films ever produced, and considered by many as the best film of the forties. His association with this William Wyler-directed feature was enough to elevate him to larger roles; but he would never again appear in a film of such high quality.

Copacabana (1947) was another minor musical and was basically a vehicle for fading stars Groucho Marx and Carmen Miranda (in a dual role). *A Song Is Born* (1948) reunited Steve with Danny Kaye and Virginia Mayo. This was a remake of the Barbara Stanwyck-Gary Cooper comedy, *Ball of Fire* (1941). Steve was a gangster again and played the role Dana Andrews performed in the original. Regardless of the fact that *Ball of Fire* was a better picture, Cochran was far more convincing than Andrews in the gangster role.

When Cochran's Goldwyn contract expired, no great film offers came his way, so he decided to return to New York and "starve some more." Starve he did not. He played the male lead in the subway circuit production of *John Loves Mary* and auditioned for Mae West's revival of *Diamond Lil.* Miss West was impressed by his macho sex appeal and quickly decided to cast him as Juarez, one of her leading men. *Diamond Lil* opened on Broadway at the Coronet Theatre on February 5, 1949. Ward Morehouse (*New York Sun*) stated, "Steve Cochran is in the blood and thunder tradition in his performance as the scheming Brazilian." Romantic rumors began percolating about Cochran and West being "that way," but it was merely publicity. Cochran said, "I was eleven years old when Mae was in the original *Lil* in 1928." Years later, he added, "Mae and I are still good friends. I learned a lot from her."

Warner Bros., having discharged a good number of their World War II vintage contract players, had to revitalize its actor roster and decided that Steve was just the right type of performer to add to their players' stable. He was signed to an exclusive contract, fitting perfectly into their continuing cycle of melodramas and gangster films. His first role for them made him a real Hollywood name. The film was Raoul Walsh's *White Heat* (1949), and starred James Cagney with, of all people, Virginia Mayo as the leading lady. It proved to be the best violent film of the late 1940s. Cochran played one of Cagney's hoods who makes a play for the leader's wife (Mayo). *Variety* called him a "good looking, double crossing mobster's aide," while the *New York Times* plainly stated that he was "ugly."

Steve frankly admitted he fitted into this type of blood-and-guts film, because "my face has always aroused suspicion." As Nick Prenta in *The Damned Don't Cry* (1950), he was admirably showcased as the leader of a mob and David Brian's major rival. Joan Crawford is used as a pawn by Brian, to eliminate Cochran, but instead, Crawford falls in love with him. Steve's forcefulness in the part was memorable. The following year, Cochran appeared in two movies with his old pal, Ruth Roman. In *Dallas* (1950), starring Gary Cooper, he and Roman did not have a single

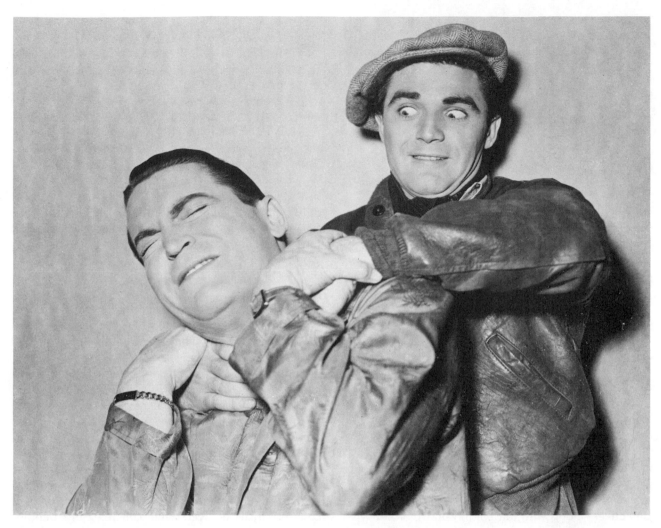

With Chester Morris in a publicity pose for Boston Blackie's Rendezvous (Col 1945)

scene together. Their second film, *Tomorrow Is Another Day* (1951), had Ruth receiving top billing. In this movie, directed by Felix E. Feist, Steve is an ex-convict who believes he has killed Roman's boyfriend. He and Ruth marry and try to build a life together while escaping from the authorities. It was a taut film in which both leads were shown to their best advantage.

In 1951, there were seven Steve Cochran films in release. His favorite film was among these. *Storm Warning,* which dealt with the Klu Klux Klan in the South, was a throwback to such Warner Bros. films of the 1930s as *Black Legion* (1936) and *They Won't Forget* (1937). As Doris Day's stupid, egomaniac husband, Cochran joins the KKK and gets carried away with their mob violence. Steve said of this memorable part, "Playing a character like this gave me a chance to interpret just about every emotion: Love, hate, fear, cowardice, pride, and shame. A role with more realism and vitality than any I had played before." Few movie-goers who saw this picture would forget Coch-

ran's sadistic portrayal, in the course of which he slugs Day and her oncamera sister, Ginger Rogers.

In 1953, Cochran concluded his Warner Bros. contract. His last two films for the Burbank studio were musicals: *She's Back on Broadway* (1953) and *The Desert Song* (1953). In the former, he co-starred with Virginia Mayo for the sixth and final time, and, as if in celebration of their sextet of picture-making, he finally won her in the last reel. In *The Desert Song,* yet another cinema rendering of the Sigmund Romberg operetta, he supported Kathryn Grayson and Gordon MacRae between beautifully sung interludes.

The main interest of *Carnival Story* (1954) was the fact that it was lensed on location in Munich with two separate casts. The English version starred Steve and Anne Baxter, while Curt Jurgens and Eva Bartok undertook the same roles in the German edition. Later that year, he was in *Private Hell 36* (1954), a suspenseful melodrama helmed by Don Siegel, in which two detectives find some missing money and decide

141

Publicity pose ca. 1948

to keep it. Howard Duff and Steve Cochran as the detectives, along with Ida Lupino and Dorothy Malone, gave taut performances. After this low-keyed picture, Steve told the press:"I just don't care to play heavies any more. I tell them to go and find another actor. For years Hollywood offered me heavy roles and nothing else. It got to be an obsession with me. There was no chance to do anything else. I don't work as much now, but I make just as much money and I'm a lot happier. I left Warner Brothers recently because I wasn't growing. I had some pleasant assignments there in movies like *Storm Warning* and *She's Back on Broadway,* but the last few parts were so bad I had to get out. I had a good role in *Carnival Story,* but my new producing-acting venture is my most exciting experience yet."

Steve founded his own producing company (Robert Alexander Productions), and *Come Next Spring* (1956), distributed by Republic, was the first film. He had always been an avid home moviemaker and used to film his own stories but not for release; one of his friends, actor Edward Norris, appeared in many of them. Having his own company gave him the chance to cast himself as a hero. The R. G. Springsteen-di-

rected movie dealt with a man who, after wandering for eight years, returns home to Arkansas to his wife (Ann Sheridan) and family. It was a lovely, unpretentious movie which never received its full due with critics or the public.

Steve's next picture was *Slander* (1957) for MGM. He probably accepted this assignment because the role was a different kind of villain for him. He played the ruthless publisher of a scandal sheet called *Real Truth* Magazine who blackmails people to get sensational stories. This is the film in which he does prove he loves his mother from the start. His mama, beautifully played by Majorie Rambeau, kills him at the finish because she can no longer bear his dirty dealings or the thought that she brought him into the world. Steve's performance was not successful, however, as his use of a rather clipped accent along with a phony effeteness was just not sufficiently believable.

In 1957, he also made his only foreign language film, *Il Grido.* It was released in the States as *The Outcry* in 1962. The black-and-white picture, directed by Italy's Michelangelo Antonioni, took seven months to complete. It was Antonioni's autobiographical story set in the Po Valley, focusing on a man's mental disintegration because of his inability to communicate with those he loves. Of working in this Continental production, Steve said: "Eventually I learned the language and mouthed the part. Initially, Betsy Blair [his co-star] was my go-between. I spoke to her in English and she relayed it to Antonioni in French. I had two scripts, one in Italian and one in English." In its delayed American release, Cochran received outstanding reviews: "Remarkably sensitive" *(New York Times),* "astonishingly good" *(Saturday Review),* "excellent" *(Variety).*

Despite the favorable notices from *Il Grido,* it seemed too late by the early 1960s to salvage the downward curve of Cochran's career. The rest of his films ranged from poor to awful, with the exception of *The Deadly Companions* (1961), a gritty little western starring Maureen O'Hara and directed by Sam Peckinpah. With the era of the major gangster film over, Steve was relegated to playing nasty characters in minor films which were neither popular nor critical successes. His own production company planned a number of features: *The Tom Mix Story,* starring Cochran as Mix, *Klondike Lou,* written by Joe Hyams and Robert Stevens, and a movie called *Tell Me in the Sunlight.* The latter film was the only one made and it received a very limited release in 1967. It was to be Steve's last movie. He was also mentioned as the leading contender for the film biography of Jack Dempsey's life, but it never came about.

Cochran's screen career was on the wane. Age and

With Carmen Miranda, Groucho Marx, and Gloria Jean in Copacabana *(UA 1947)*

too much good living, which give him a bloated, dissipated look, were taking their toll. Yet, he was never idle. He always managed to find work either on television or back on the stage. On television, he could be found playing bad guys again on such shows as "The Untouchables" and "Naked City." His best video part, in the sixties, was surprisingly enough on a segment of the "Stony Burke" series, starring Jack Lord, in an episode called *Death Rides a Pale Horse* (1963). Steve was effective as a crooked broncho-riding rival of Lord. On the stage, Cochran had the opportunity to play some fine parts around the country primarily in summer stock; among them were Starbuck in *The Rainmaker* and the tough cop in *Detective Story.*

Steve was also no trifler when it came to the making of headlines. If his vocation was acting, his strongest avocation was women. His reputation as a ladies' man came close to rivaling that of Errol Flynn's. He once remarked, "Despite all their faults, I like women. I'll settle for the sex anytime." He married three times and had a daughter, Xandra, by his first wife, artist Florence Lockwood. Years later, Xandra took off and eloped, disappearing out of his life. He told reporters that he did not even know her married name. He and Miss Lockwood divorced in 1946, and he wed actress Fay McKenzie the same year, in Acapulco. This marriage lasted only two years. He did not marry again until 1961, when he wed a girl just about his own daughter's age. Heddy Jonna Jensen was only nineteen, and they married in Las Vegas. They divorced in 1964. Through the years, womanizer Cochran was linked romantically with such women as actresses Denise Darcel, Dorothy Hart (who was in *Raton Pass,* 1951, with him), belly dancer Nejia Ates, and Darryl F. Zanuck's daughter, Susan. He had a swinging time with blonde actress Barbara Payton, who enjoyed the same activities as he did: Drink and sex. At one point he was engaged to Gloria Howard, who was the star witness in a $250,000 jewel theft case.

As if his romantic escapades were not enough, he made the news in other ways. In 1952, at a party at his home, he clobbered middleweight boxer Buddy Wright with a baseball bat; in 1953 he was arrested for reckless driving and for evading arrest. It required a gun shot to make him stop his car. In August, 1960, his forty-foot yacht, *Rogue,* wandered off course and smashed into the Los Angeles breakwater. Cochran was below at the time, in his cabin entertaining three girls. Fortunately, the Coast Guard was nearby and rescued the passengers when the boat began to sink.

While Steve was in South Africa in late 1964, filming *Mozambique* (1966) with Hildegarde Neff, a jockey had him arrested because his wife, who was a bit player in the film, visited Cochran in his hotel room on more than a few occasions. The irate husband demanded $5,600 in damages, but the judge dismissed the case. Soon afterward, back in the States, singer Ronnie Rae claimed that while at Steve's abode, he hit her, ripped off her sweater, and tied and gagged her. The district attorney's office refused to issue a complaint.

Then, in 1965, Cochran placed an advertisement in the trade paper *Variety* for a six-girl crew to accompany him on a boat trip. The girls he hired left him in Acapulco. He then placed another ad, this time in a Mexican paper, stating that he would pay the girls seventy pesos (about $5.83) a day. He received 180 applications but he took only three because there were "no real lookers." The trio of girls were twenty-one, nineteen, and fourteen years of age. The vessel left Acapulco on June 3rd, but encountered a hurricane off the coast of Oaxaca. The boat was badly damaged and Steve was forced to remain at the helm for two days and nights combatting the storm. Completely exhausted and in considerable pain, he collapsed and died on June 15, 1965, at the age of forty-eight. The girls were not rescued until June 21st, by which time they were in a state of total hysteria at being adrift with a decomposing corpse. An autopsy revealed that Cochran died of acute infectious edema, an accumulation of liquid in the lung tissues. His body was shipped to California and his divorced wife, Jonna (as she now called herself), filed a petition to be named executor of the estate, which consisted of stocks and bonds, $12,000 in cash, and properties worth $138,000.

Had Steve lived, his career would certainly have had a rebirth in the 1970s. The success of *The French Connection* (1971) and *The Godfather* (1972) began a series of crime pictures both here and abroad in which he would undoubtedly have found a good deal of work. The one actor who possibly could have replaced Steve Cochran in films was Ray Danton. Smoother in his good looks than Cochran, Danton also had a suave sexiness and was at his best playing hoods, but he relied too heavily on an "acting" voice which gave him a fake quality, in contrast to Cochran who was totally believable in his underworld characterizations. "With this puss of mine," Cochran had once said, "I could play a corpse and be accused of overacting. The big secret in playing a gangster in movies is to really believe that the character you are playing is doing no wrong."

STEVE COCHRAN

Stage Door Canteen   *(UA 1943)*
Wonder Man   *(RKO 1945)*
Boston Blackie Booked on Suspicion   *(Col 1945)*
The Gay Señorita   *(Col 1945)*
Boston Blackie's Rendezvous   *(Col 1945)*
The Kid from Brooklyn   *(RKO 1946)*
The Best Years of Our Lives   *(RKO 1946)*
The Chase   *(UA 1946)*
Copacabana   *(UA 1947)*
A Song is Born   *(RKO 1948)*
White Heat   *(WB 1949)*
The Damned Don't Cry   *(WB 1950)*
Highway 301   *(WB 1950)*
Dallas   *(WB 1951)*
Raton Pass   *(WB 1951)*
Inside the Walls of Folsom Prison   *(WB 1951)*
Jim Thorpe—All American   *(WB 1951)*
Storm Warning   *(WB 1951)*
Tomorrow is Another Day   *(WB 1951)*
The Tanks are Coming   *(WB 1951)*

The Lion and the Horse   *(WB 1952)*
Operation Secret   *(WB 1952)*
She's Back on Broadway   *(WB 1953)*
The Desert Song   *(WB 1953)*
Back to God's Country   *(Univ 1953)*
Shark River   *(UA 1953)*
Carnival Story   *(RKO 1954)*
Private Hell 36   *(Filmmakers 1954)*
Come Next Spring   *(Rep 1956)*
Slander   *(MGM 1957)*
The Weapon   *(Rep 1957)*
Il Grido (a.k.a., The Outcry)   *(Italian 1957)*
Quantrill's Raiders   *(AA 1958)*
I, Mobster   *(20th 1959)*
The Beat Generation   *(MGM 1959)*
The Big Operator   *(MGM 1959)*
The Deadly Companions   *(Pathe-America 1961)*
Of Love and Desire   *(20th 1963)*
Mozambique   *(WB-7 Arts 1966)*
Tell Me in the Sunlight   *(Movierama Color Corp. 1967)*

22

Richard Conte

In the 1940s, Italian-descended Richard Conte struggled hard to be the "new" John Garfield as he plied his craft at Twentieth Century-Fox. Unfortunately, he was consistently overshadowed at Darryl F. Zanuck's toyland by the more beefcakey Victor Mature, the more sinister Richard Widmark, the more handsome William Eythe, and the vastly more popular and handsome Tyrone Power. Many industry observers at the time would certainly have given odds that Conte's more American-featured counterpart at Warner Bros., Dane Clark, would have merged the bigger name performer (and he did for a time).

For example, during the well-publicized sweepstakes for the role of Don Corleone in *The Godfather* (1972), Richard Conte was among the leading contenders to portray the Mafia leader. The choice role went to Marlon Brando, who took an Academy Award for his performance. In this Paramount blockbuster, Conte was assigned the featured role of Barzini and scored with a low-keyed, vividly sinister playing of the Mafia chieftain of a rival family in the unholy brotherhood. His onscreen scenes were brief and his lines very few, but all were very telling. About the casting, he candidly said: "In the beginning they thought of me for the Godfather, not Brando. I'm not saying it sorrowfully, or anything like that, but they should have had an Italian for it. I wasn't aware of it till it was a little late, and if I'd known, I'd have pursued it. But I'm objective, even fatalistic about things. I wasn't happy with Brando's performance, but I

thought it was a great movie. Trouble is—I got shot—so I can't be in the sequel." Conte believes the movie was good for him and felt rewarded when Brando said to him, "I can't question some of those scenes you did." But the brutally honest Conte adds: "It was rewarding to hear something like that—but it's just as rewarding if it comes from the waiter or the butcher or the elevator guy. It doesn't have to be Brando. The subtleties may escape some people, but as long as they've enjoyed it, it doesn't matter."

Nicholas Peter Conte was born March 24, 1914, to parents of Italian extraction in Jersey City, New Jersey. His father, a barber, had a love of music and kept the young boy daily practicing the piano, encouraging his artistic bent for drawing. Young Conte graduated from Dickinson High School, but admits, "I had no ambition as a kid. I was a kind of drifter, a guy who hung around street corners. It took me five years to finish the four-year high school course." He flunked every subject in his freshman year and, after graduating, had no idea what he wanted to do. "I was unemployed for six months after graduation, then my father got me a job driving a truck delivering barber's supplies. I had never driven before and smashed the truck the first day. I was fired."

With little enthusiasm he learned barbering from his father, ran messages on Wall Street, sold refrigerators at Gimbel's, was a shoe salesman, and, for three

With Susan Hayward in House of Strangers *(20th 1949)*

dollars a night, played piano at christenings and weddings. Finally, during the summer of 1935 Conte became a jack-of-all trades at the Pinebrook (Connecticut) Country Club. Referring to this changing point in his life, Conte recalls: "I waited on tables, cleaned the silver, and worked in the barber shop. Then they said I would also have to help entertain. I said I didn't have time, but they gave me a part to read anyway. I got interested in reading it, then I got all emotional and worked up, and Sanford Meisner of the Group Theatre and Playhouse, who was putting on the show at the resort, asked how I would like to study with them. I had never seen a show in my life and I refused them. But when I saw the crowd that turned out for their play, and started to identify myself with those people on the stage, I changed my mind and they gave me a scholarship. It was a whole new wonderful world."

He spent the next two years completely engrossed in and dedicated to the theatre. The spartan life included board and lodging and he was soon rewarded with walk-ons in the Group Theatre productions such as *Waiting for Lefty* (1935). In 1939 he toured in Odets' *Golden Boy,* starring Phillips Holmes and Betty Furness, in which he played the small role of Frank

Bonaparte, and later the lead. On April 18, 1940, he opened at the National Theatre in New York City with John Garfield, Burl Ives, Harry Carey, and Aline MacMahon in an *Outward Bound*-type fantasy called *Heavenly Express,* which collapsed after twenty runs. By the end of 1941, he had survived twenty-nine performances as Gino Sarellis, a Chicago bad boy passing counterfeit money in the flop *Walk into My Parlor,* and in Baltimore, Maryland, on January 12, 1942, the gods smiled on him when *Jason* opened.

Samson Raphaelson's *Jason* was selected as one of the ten best plays of the 1941–42 season, and clocked 125 performances after it opened January 21, 1942, at the Hudson Theatre in New York despite an astonishing reshuffling of actors in the lead part of the fastidious critic, priggish Jason Otis. Originated by actor Alexander Knox, Jason was played in February by George Macready and, finally, by the great Lee J. Cobb. Critics covering the show for each change of the leading character were unanimous in praising Nicholas Conte's bravura performance of the half-charlatan, half-genius gypsy. (Playwright Raphaelson had drawn the role as a caricature of William Saroyan in whose antic play, *My Heart's in the Highland,* 1939, Conte had made his official stage debut.)

With James Stewart in Call Northside 777 *(20th 1948)*

Conte's consistent performance as Mike Ambler, the messenger and *Jason's* protagonist, was played with spirit and conviction and improved after Cobb took over the lead. The one-time ambitionless kid from Jersey City was compared to a modern Valentino; the acerbic George Jean Nathan tagged him as the outstanding young actor of the year. After a nine-month stint in the Army, from which he was released with an honorable medical discharge, Conte signed a contract with Twentieth Century-Fox, for whom he had first appeared as a hobo in their *Heaven with a Barbed Wire Fence* (1940).

At the end of April, 1943, Conte arrived in Hollywood and on May 21, 1943, married radio actress Ruth Strohm. As "Richard" Conte he was Marine Captain Davis in Twentieth's film version of Richard Tregaskis' novel *Guadalcanal Dairy,* a film that today still retains its original power to grip audiences. Although most of Conte's films would be made after this decade, he is emphatically a sterling product of the 1940s. If he was out of the Army, Fox kept him in uniform as Angelo Canelli in Lewis Milestone's extraordinary war film of the treatment and trial of a group of American fliers by the Japanese in *The Purple Heart* (1944). He was expertly cast as Nicolo in Henry King's film version of John Hersey's *A Bell for Adano* (1945), and as Private Bartek, a crew member of Rickenbacker's crashed plane, awash on a raft in the Pacific Ocean in *Captain Eddie* (1945).

He was out of uniform as Chris Conlon, a private eye suspected of three murders in *The Spider* (1945). His acting was one of the best things about the film and critics were beginning to see in Conte the rough-hewn charm of Cagney and Bogart. However, Twentieth Century-Fox did not give him the type of roles offered the bad boys at Warners. Nevertheless, Richard was fortunate in being part of one of the best American films to come out of World War II, Lewis Milestone's controversial *A Walk in the Sun* (1946), from Harry Brown's novel that concentrated on the action of a single platoon after the Salerno, Italy landing by the American armed forces. His portrayal of the brash, glib machinegunner Rivera was outstanding in an excellent cast that provided—and still does —a stimulating film experience. He was also in the tense film drama, *13 Rue Madeleine* (1946), by documentary-prone Louis de Rochemont. Made on location in New York, Quebec, and Boston this espionage film sends James Cagney, Conte, Annabella, and Frank Latimore on a top priority mission to France.

Conte's first onscreen romance was in *The Other Love* (1947). In this film adaptation of Erich Maria Remarque's unpublished story "Beyond," he was

With Barbara Stanwyck in The Other Love *(UA 1947)*

Paul Clement, having an affair with dying pianist Barbara Stanwyck. He fared better in uniform. During one overly-tender love scene, he nearly swallowed one of Miss Stanwyck's earrings!

His 5'10½", darkly handsome presence never gained him the stardom he deserved, but his acting was admirably realistic as Frank Wiecheck in *Call Northside 777* (1948), as Martin Rome, a cop-stalking killer in *Cry of the City* (1948), and as Max Monetti in *House of Strangers* (1949). He gave a sharp performance as Nick Garcos in the robust thriller *Thieves' Highway* (1949), with his old friend, Lee J. Cobb, and closed the forties by appearing as Dr. Alexander Meade for MGM in Wallace Beery's last film, *Big Jack* (1949), released after Berry's death.

With the change in the players' roster at Fox, Richard left the studio and signed a contract with Universal-International for two pictures a year, most of them saved from quick oblivion by his enlivening presence. In 1952, he spent two and a half months vigorously training as a boxer for his role of Filipe Rivera in *The Fighter* for United Artists. In addition, he made personal appearances with the film. The year before, Richard and his wife Ruth adopted a baby boy whom they named Mark and who has now graduated from U.C.L.A.

Conte's efforts to escape typecasting as a gangster was difficult, but he played one of Lillian Roth's (Susan Hayward) three husbands, Tony Bardeman, in *I'll Cry Tomorrow* (1955), and was miraculously given a chance to show his flair for comedy with Judy Holliday in Columbia's *Full of Life* (1956). As an harassed husband, married in a civil ceremony but required to go to confession after a seven-year lapse in order to be eligible for a remarriage within the Catholic Church, Conte was splendid, even when confronted with a 320-pound scene stealer, Salvatore Baccaloni, and the soaring talents of blonde Judy Holliday. Following *Full of Life,* he made four more films for Columbia, a studio that had rejected him in 1946 for the lead in *The Jolson Story.* The quartet of pictures included the boxoffice disappointment *They Came to Cordura* (1959), starring Rita Hayworth and Gary Cooper, and as one of many guest stars in *Pepe* (1960), a film built around the talents of the Mexican comedian, Cantinflas. Conte sang "Hooray for Hollywood" with Sammy Davis, Jr. and Joey Bishop.

He joined Frank Sinatra's "Rat Pack" for Warner Bros.' *Ocean's Eleven* (1960) in which, as Anthony Bergdorf, he has a fatal heart atack while Sinatra and his clan rob five Las Vegas clubs. If the picture itself was relatively bad, Conte was given a remarkably atrocious line for his death scene, which he delivered with as straight a face as he could, "You can give it to me straight, Doc. Is it Big Casino?"

Richard appeared on television from the early 1950s onward, being a guest on most of the major drama shows. On "G.E. Theatre" he was in the *Rashomon*-type episode, *The Eye of the Beholder,* with Martha Vickers, as artist Michael Gerard seeking a twentieth-century Madonna for a model. Richard was an ex-gunfighter trying to forget his shady past and retire, but challenged by a gun-happy kid (John Barrymore, Jr.) on *End of a Gun* for "Twentieth Century-Fox Hour." Finally, as Cayetana Ruiz, he was a wounded gangster aided in his recovery by the nursing of Sister Cecelia (Eleanor Parker) in A.E. Hotchner's adaptation of Ernest Hemingway's story, *The Gambler, the Nun and the Radio.*

His film roles shrunk to one or two annually, although as Reid, trying to cure his drug addiction in *Synanon* (1965), his playing was true and intense, and he was a fine Barabbas in George Stevens' pretentiously arty and endless *The Greatest Story Ever Told* (1965). With his pal Frank Sinatra he made three

more films: As Tony Moreno, an expert machinist repairing a World War II German submarine for an *Assault on a Queen* (1966), and as Lieutenant Dave Santini in two Miami Beach-filmed fiascos, *Tony Rome* (1967) and *The Lady in Cement* (1968). For Warners' overly-glamorized version of Arthur Hailey's *Hotel* (1967) (not as grand a hotel as Vicki Baum's), Conte was an unscrupulous house detective blackmailing alcoholic Duke of Lambourne (Michael Rennie), who has killed a child in a hit-and-run accident. Along with several other cast members in roles encompassing everything from seducers to thieves, and what-have-you, Conte turned in a sincere performance.

Richard's talent was seemingly always in demand. His many television appearances often varied from his usual role as a stereotyped hoodlum, but his brooding face still menaced the home screens on NBC's "Bold Ones" in *The Trial of a Mafiosa.* After *The Godfather* opened in the U.S., Conte went to London to promote the Paramount picture. While there, the divorced actor, who had by then just married Shirlee Colleen Garner (known professionally as Shirley Krieger), started his honeymoon. He was fifty-eight and she was thirty-six. After his promotional duties in London, Conte and his second wife continued their honeymoon in Italy and Sicily, visting ancestral homes and discovering relatives a long way from Jersey City, New Jersey.

Within the mid-Seventies, Richard completed a skein of pictures in Italy, including: *Big Guns* (1973) with Alain Delon, *The New Mafia* (1973) with Henry Silva, *The Inspector Is Killed* (1973), *My Brother Anastasia* (1974) in which he portrayed Albert Anastasia, and others. He then went over to Spain to complete contractual commitments on gangster features.

Then on Tuesday, April 15, 1975 he died in Los Angeles from a heart attack and paralyzing stroke. He had been in intensive care at the U.C.L.A. Medical Center for thirteen days. He was buried at Westwood Village Mortuary. He died leaving no will, necessitating his wife, Shirlee, to file a petition for letters of administration for his estate valued at some $70,000, including $5,000 annual income from all sources.

The obituaries of Richard Conte referred to him as an actor noted for "portraying gangsters and world-weary heroes." Even in death he could not escape the typecasting description.

RICHARD CONTE

Heaven With a Barbed Wire Fence   *(20th 1940)*
Guadalcanal Diary   *(20th 1943)*
The Purple Heart   *(20th 1944)*
A Bell for Adano   *(20th 1945)*
Captain Eddie   *(20th 1945)*
The Spider   *(2th 1945)*
A Walk in the Sun   *(20th 1945)*
Somewhere in the Night   *(20th 1946)*
13 Rue Madeleine   *(20th 1946)*
The Other Love   *(UA 1947)*
Call Northside 777   *(20th 1948)*
Cry of the City   *(20th 1949)*
Whirlpool   *(20th 1949)*
House of Strangers   *(20th 1949)*
Thieves' Highway   *(20th 1949)*
Big Jack   *(MGM 1949)*
The Sleeping City   *(Univ 1950)*
Under the Gun   *(Univ 1950)*
The Hollywood Story   *(Univ 1951)*
The Raging Tide   *(Univ 1951)*
The Raiders   *(Univ 1952)*
The Fighter   *(UA 1952)*
The Blue Gardenia   *(WB 1953)*
Desert Legion   *(Univ 1953)*
Slaves of Babylon   *(Col 1953)*
Highway Dragnet   *(AA 1954)*
Target Zero   *(WB 1955)*
New York Confidential   *(WB 1955)*
The Big Combo   *(AA 1955)*
The Big Tip-Off   *(AA 1955)*
The Case of the Red Monkey   *(AA 1955)*
Bengazi   *(RKO 1955)*
I'll Cry Tomorrow   *(MGM 1955)*

Full of Life   *(Col 1957)*
The Brothers Rico   *(Col 1957)*
This Angry Age   *(Col 1958)*
They Came to Cordura   *(Col 1959)*
Pepe   *(Col 1960)*
Ocean's Eleven   *(WB 1960)*
Who's Been Sleeping in My Bed?   *(Par 1963)*
The Eyes of Annie Jones   *(20th 1964)*
Circus World   *(Par 1964)*
Synanon   *(Col 1965)*
The Greatest Story Ever Told   *(UA 1965)*
Assault on a Queen   *(Par 1966)*
Tony Rome   *(20th 1967)*
Hotel   *(WB 1967)*
Sentence of Death   *(Italian 1967)*
The Lady in Cement   *(20th 1968)*
Operation Cross-Eagles   *(Yugoslavian 1970)*
Explosion   *(AIP 1970)*
The Godfather   *(Par 1972)*
The Big Family   *(Italian 1972)*
Big Guns   *(Gaumont 1973)*
Pete, Pearl and the Pole   *(Italian 1973)*
The Inspector Is Killed   *(Italian 1973)*
The New Mafia (a.k.a., The Boss)   *(Italian 1973)*
Anna: The Pleasure, the Torment   *(Italian 1974)*
My Brother Anastasia   *(Col 1974)*
Shoot First, Die Later (a.k.a., The Corrupt Cop)   *(Italian 1974)*
The Spectres   *(Spanish 1975)*
The Evil Eye   *(Spanish 1975)*
The Citizens Needs Self Protection   *(Italian 1975)*
The Police Accuse   *(Italian 1975)*
Who Are You Satan? (a.k.a., The Exorcist #2)   *(Italian 1975)*

23

Tom Conway

Many performers have suffered in their show business endeavors because of more successful brothers or sisters in the profession. For example, there have been Steve Forrest and Dana Andrews; Tommy Noonan and John Ireland; Peter Graves and James Arness; Sally Blane and Loretta Young; Marion Hutton and Betty Hutton; and Tom Conway and George Sanders.

Tall handsome, impeccably groomed Conway had the makings for his own special niche in movies, but he always seemed to be following on the heels of his more illustrious brother, debonair George Sanders. In fact, when Sanders tired of playing the suave sleuth in the 1940s *Falcon* series, RKO promptly substituted Conway in the low-budget entries, and he proved to be even more ingratiating in the pivotal assignment than his brother. While acerbic, blase Sanders, renowned as the "professional cad," continued to gain fame and riches (which he promptly lost) over the years from his array of cinematic portrayals, Conway could never muster a sufficient aura of self-identity to convince producers to think of him as anything but a less-expensive alternative to his brother. It was a burden as tough as anything an actor has had to endure in Hollywood's typecasting syndrome, and it finally drove Conway to total defeat and self-destruction.

Thomas Charles Sanders was born on September 15, 1904, in St. Petersburg (Leningrad), Russia, the son of the British consul and his Russian wife. At the outbreak of the Russian Revolution, the family left frozen Russia for England where Conway was sent to various boarding schools. After graduating from Brighton College, he left for South Africa to work as a laborer in the mines and as a tour guide to the Rhodes Tomb. For six years he tried ranching in South Africa, until a severe case of malaria forced him to return to England, where, after a succession of uninteresting jobs, he decided to enter the acting profession.

Changing his name to Conway to avoid any reflected fame from the theatrical success of his brother George (born July 3, 1906), he spent several seasons touring the English provinces, as well as acting with the Manchester Repertory Company and making frequent broadcasts on the BBC. In 1939, he followed his brother to Hollywood, signed a Metro-Goldwyn-Mayer contract, and made his film debut in a minor Nick Carter mystery *Sky Murder* (1940), which starred Walter Pidgeon.

Urbane, attractive Conway was next featured by Metro in their remake of *The Trial of Mary Dugan* (1941), with Laraine Day and Robert Young, which in many ways surpassed the original version with Norma Shearer. He was Mr. Blanton in *Lady Be Good* (1941), city slicker Morgan Pell in Wallace Beery's *The Bad Man* (1941), and the villainous Medford who kidnaps Jane (Maureen O'Sullivan) and Boy (Johnny Sheffield) in *Tarzan's Secret Treasure* (1941). With Bud Abbott and Lou Costello he appeared as Maurice Craindall in a fanciful, confused, and silly script that

With Ralph Dunn in The Falcon Strikes Back *(RKO 1943)*

With June Vincent and Richard Stapley in The Challenge *(20th 1948)*

Florenz Ziegfeld would have never recognized as his *Rio Rita* in its 1942 Metro remake.

Hollywood in the 1940s found boxoffice gold in producing B-budget series films that required minor investment and netted substantial profits. Each studio had at least one series that kept their contract players steadily employed and provided a testing ground for new performers. Under the block-booking system, where theatres were required to take a series if they wanted to play the studio's classier productions, such series proved to be economically profitable ventures. Paramount had Henry Aldrich and Hopalong Cassidy; Metro thrived for two decades on Andy Hardy and Dr. Kildare; Blondie helped to pay Harry Cohn's bills at Columbia; Fox's profitable Charlie Chan moved to Monogram; and RKO featured Dr. Christian and Simon Templar, the Saint, played by George Sanders.

Leslie Charteris, the prolific author of *The Saint* books, and RKO came to a parting of the ways, and in

1941 the studio dropped *The Saint* series in favor of a story by Michael Arlen called *Gay Falcon*. Another series was born in *The Gay Falcon* (1941), again with Sanders. The ofttime cantankerous Sanders tired of the quickie series after the first four films, and RKO hit upon an unusual casting feat by replacing Sanders with his own brother, Tom Conway.

RKO was astonished when Conway attained a greater success as The Falcon than his brother had enjoyed, his pictures outgrossing Sanders' four adventures. George was conveniently killed off in *The Falcon's Brother* (1942), and Conway, as Tom Lawrence, took over, starring in nine of the sixteen *Falcon* pictures. The high point of Conway's movie career was as a second-string star of these bottom-of-the-bill features, although many of his performances beyond *The Falcon* role were both effective and persuasive because of his suave charm. He was fine as the psychiatrist paying with his life for trying to help Simone Simon from turning into a vicious cat destroying her

154

With Robert Osterloh and Steve Brodie in I Cheated the Law *(20th 1949)*

"enemies" in *The Cat People* (1942), a terrifying movie highlighted by Jacques Tourneur's excellent direction of DeWitt Bodeen's script.

Nevertheless, Conway was a sincere, plodding actor who never attained the success of his brother Sanders. His well-modulated English voice was fine on radio as "Sherlock Holmes" and "The Saint," but his film career was delegated largely to playing "other men" parts or cosmopolitan heavy assignments. Tom was warm and outgoing and in many ways more handsome than his coldly-restrained, cynical brother, but the younger George forged ahead in his film career with a good deal more drive and talent than his older brother. While George was establishing himself as a first-rate actor, winning an Oscar for his venomous performance as Addison de Witt in 1950 in *All About Eve,* Tom added a touch of sophisticated elegance to *One Touch of Venus* (1948) and was on-camera briefly as Gene Nelson's stuffy Uncle Bennington in Warner Bros.' cornball musical, *Painting the Clouds with Sunshine* (1951).

Tom was best man for his brother when George married Georgia, otherwise Zsa Zsa, Gabor. Tom arrived on the chartered plane taking the wedding party to Las Vegas with a shotgun over his shoulder telling the group, "Just in case the old boy gets cold feet." The precaution was unnecessary. George went through five marriages while Tom married Lillian Eggers, a former New York model, in 1941 and, after their divorce in 1953, married pert English actress Queenie Leonard. Conway was responsible for Zsa Zsa's bombshell appearance on a television panel show, "Bachelor's Haven." Nevertheless, that show propelled her into a show business career; of course, she was aided immeasurably by a decollete black Balenciaga gown worn as background to a staggering display of diamonds to which she referred, "Oh, these, they're just my working diamonds." Gabor became an "in" person.

With another of the Gabors, Eva, Tom appeared as the Maharajah of Kim-Kepore in a Columbia programmer, a tedious episodic bit of fluff called *Paris Model* (1953). For Walt Disney's animated feature, *Peter Pan* (1953), his sonorous voice was heard as the narrator. Although he continued making films both in the U.S. and in England, his important assignments came with television as Inspector Mark Sabor in many half-hour shows of "Cases of . . ." For the "Twentieth Century-Fox Hour" Tom appeared on October 17, 1956, with Joan Fontaine, Michael Wilding, and Elsa Lanchester in *Stranger in the Night,* based on R. A. Dick's *The Ghost and Mrs. Muir*

(which in turn was a 1947 feature). He was Gerry Monte in the RKO film based on a true, unsolved murder, *Death of a Scoundrel* (1956), which starred his brother as Clementi Sabouria and featured his sister-in-law, Zsa Zsa. In October of 1957 he was Max Collodi, a music hall ventriloquist, in Alfred Hitchcock's televised mystery, *The Glass Eye,* with Jessica Tandy and Rosemary Harris. Tom continued to make minor and infrequent television appearances through 1961, highlighted by his performance in *The Fifth Caller* with Eva Gabor, Elsa Lanchester, and Michael Rennie. The same year he was back at Disney's factory for *One Hundred and One Dalmatians* as the voice of the collie who rescues the horses from a blinding snowstorm in the English countryside.

Tom's flamboyant, high-styled living increased to the extent of even heavier drinking than before and neither film nor television parts were offered to him. In Twentieth Century-Fox's ridiculous farce *What a Way to Go!* (1964) he was seen briefly as Lord Kensington (with ex-wife Queenie Leonard as Lady Kensington), and during the same year played Guy Penrose in television's "Perry Mason" segment, *The Case of the Simple Simon.*

A year later he was found in poor health in a two-dollar-a-day hotel room in Venice, California, drunk, broke, and saddled with impaired eyesight despite an operation in January, 1965, for cataracts in both eyes. He had not communicated with his brother for several years because of a disagreement between them, an impasse that contrasted sharply with their once closer relationship. His faded career and poor eyesight compounded by marathon drinking and squandering over one million dollars earned during his twenty-nine-year career was dismissed with, "I have nothing to grumble about really. It's just a temporary setback. Friends in West Hollywood have offered me space in their house." After national headlines appeared on September 14, 1965, offers of help came from all over the country, from people with fond memories of the once handsome *Falcon* and from fellow actors.

He spent the next four months in a county hospital and an additional three months in a convalescent sanitarium, where he told reporters, "Now that I'm on the wagon I find the old brain works better. I've got a million damn things cooking. It will be more or less a cold start, but acting-wise, I think I'm at my peak." *The Case of the Simple Simon* was to be his last on-camera performance.

At the age of sixty-three, he died from cirrhosis of the liver on April 22, 1967. It was a sad ending to a once promising career.

TOM CONWAY

Sky Murder   *(MGM 1940)*
The Trial of Mary Dugan   *(MGM 1941)*
Free and Easy   *(MGM 1941)*
The People vs. Dr. Kildare   *(MGM 1941)*
Wild Man of Borneo   *(MGM 1941)*
Lady Be Good   *(MGM 1941)*
The Bad Man   *(MGM 1941)*
Mr. and Mrs. North   *(MGM 1941)*
Tarzan's Secret Treasure   *(MGM 1941)*
Rio Rita   *(MGM 1942)*
Grand Central Murder   *(MGM 1942)*
The Falcon's Brother   *(RKO 1942)*
The Cat People   *(RKO 1942)*
The Falcon and the Co-Eds   *(RKO 1943)*
The Falcon Strikes Back   *(RKO 1943)*
The Falcon in Danger   *(RKO 1943)*
The Seventh Victim   *(RKO 1943)*
I Walked with a Zombie   *(RKO 1943)*
A Night of Adventure   *(RKO 1944)*
The Falcon Out West   *(RKO 1944)*
The Falcon in Hollywood   *(RKO 1944)*
The Falcon in Mexico   *(RKO 1944)*
Two O'Clock Courage   *(RKO 1945)*
The Falcon in San Francisco   *(RKO 1945)*
Whistle Stop   *(UA 1946)*
Criminal Court   *(RKO 1946)*
The Falcon's Adventure   *(RKO 1946)*
The Falcon's Alibi   *(RKO 1946)*
Fun on a Weekend   *(UA 1947)*

Repeat Performance   *(EL 1947)*
Lost Honeymoon   *(EL 1947)*
The Checkered Coat   *(20th 1948)*
The Challenge   *(20th 1948)*
Thirteen Lead Soldiers   *(20th 1948)*
Bungalow 13   *(20th 1948)*
One Touch of Venus   *(Univ 1948)*
I Cheated the Law   *(20th 1949)*
The Great Plane Robbery   *(UA 1950)*
Painting the Clouds with Sunshine   *(WB 1951)*
Confidence Girl   *(UA 1952)*
The Bride of the Gorilla   *(Realart 1952)*
Paris Model   *(Col 1953)*
Tarzan and the She-Devil   *(RKO 1953)*
Peter Pan   *(RKO 1953)* (Voice only)
Park Plaza 605 (a.k.a., Norman Conquest)   *(Eros, 1953)*
Prince Valiant   *(20th 1954)*
Three Stops to Murder   *(Astor 1954)*
Barbardos Quest (a.k.a., Murder on Approval)   *(RKO—British 1955)*
Breakaway   *(RKO—British 1956)*
The She-Creature   *(AIP 1956)*
The Last Man to Hang   *(Col 1956)*
Death of a Scoundrel   *(RKO 1956)*
Operation Murder   *(Associated British Producers 1957)*
Voodoo Woman   *(AIP 1957)*
The Atomic Submarine   *(AA 1959)*
Twelve to the Moon   *(Col 1960)*
One Hundred and One Dalmatians   *(BV 1961)* (Voice only)
What a Way to Go!   *(20th 1964)*

24

Wendell Corey

There used to be a superstition in Hollywood that if you died in your first film it was good luck for the performer. Wendell Corey died in his first two features (*Desert Fury,* 1947, and *I Walk Alone,* 1948) so luck certainly should have been on his side. However, that "luck" gave him only about ten good years on the big screen. He was one of those actors who was not exceptionally good-looking and had no strong screen personality, but was talented enough to be able to play a variety of roles. He could be the hero, the killer, the detective, the weakling, or the best friend. His best screen moments occurred when he played the cynic. Delivering an acerbic line, Corey's blue eyes would twinkle and he would come alive on the screen. These roles did not come his way very often and audiences never really got to know him as a movie personality. He was often confused with Macdonald Carey. In fact, in the late 1940s, there was a group of actors who could have interchanged movie roles without much difficulty: Corey, Carey, Frank Lovejoy, and Barry Sullivan: All talented but all unexciting in the terms of stardom.

The youngest son of a Congregational minister, the Reverend Milton R. Corey, Wendell was born on March 20, 1914, in Dracut, a little town near Lowell, Massachusetts. His family tree can be traced back to two American presidents, John Adams, and John Quincy Adams. He had one brother, Milton, Jr., who

would become a jewelry manufacturer, and two sisters, Dorothy, who became a school teacher, and Julia, who became a proficient sculptress. Wendell was graduated from grammar school as class president and majored in English and history at Central High in Springfield, Massachusetts, where he sang in the school glee club, went out for track, and became an excellent tennis player. He never gave the world of the theatre a thought. He had decided to become a laywer, but his parents hoped he would follow in his father's footsteps and take up the ministry.

By the time he completed high school, he still had not decided which profession to enter, so he got a job selling washing machines and refrigerators. One night he stopped by at a Springfield Repertory Theatre rehearsal to pick up a friend who was working there; the amateur group needed somebody to play the role of a Swedish janitor in *Street Scene,* and Corey was recruited, rather against his will. "I spoke with a Swedish accent that I am sure no United Nations Assembly would ever recognize," he said. "Fortunately, no Swedes were in the audience, so I got by." He retained his job and worked with the group at night for a year, for the acting "bug" had hit him. When the year was up, he quit his sales post and joined the Mountain Park Casino Players in Holyoke and made his professional debut in 1935 in their production of *The Night of January 16th.*

He continued doing stock and then toured New England as part of the Federal Theatre. In stock he

With Mary Astor in Any Number Can Play *(MGM 1949)*

With Janet Leigh in Holiday Affair *(RKO 1949)*

played in *Winterset,* in *Personal Appearance* with Helen Twelvetrees, and played Alfred Doolittle in *Pygmalion* at the Copley Theatre. Reviewing the latter play, the Boston *Herald Traveler* reported he gave a "lugubrious performance." During this period he met actress Alice Nevin Wiley and they were married in 1939. She gave up her theatrical ambitions and the couple had four children: Lucy, Jonathan, Jennifer, and Bonnie Alice.

Wendell Corey made his Broadway debut on May 26, 1942, in *Comes the Revelation* at the Jolson Theatre. The play lasted a mere four days. Between the years 1942 and 1945, he appeared in eleven Broadway shows, none of them hits. Among them were *The Life of Riley* (1942), *Strip for Action* (1942), *Manhattan Nocturne* (1943), *Follow the Girls* (1944), and *The Wind Is Ninety* (1945). Between Broadway shows he would produce, direct, and act in stock.

Then came the right part in the right play: Clark Redfield, the cynical newsman, in *Dream Girl,* starring Betty Field and written by her husband, Elmer Rice. It opened at the Coronet Theatre on December 14, 1945, to unanimously rave reviews, and Corey was given a 1946 Theatre World Award as a promising stage personality. George Freedley, reviewing for the *New York World-Telegram,* wrote, "Wendell Corey gives an outstanding performance as the newspaperman, contriving to add reticence, manliness, and a certain homely charm to a brisk comic attack." Referring to his *Dream Girl* role, Corey once stated: "It was really a fluke. I tried out for *The Rugged Path,* but I wasn't right for the part. Bob Sherwood, Garson Kanin, and Spencer Tracy were awfully nice about it, however. They all agreed that I was a natural for this stint in *Dream Girl.* They went so far as to tell Elmer Rice that I'd fit into this. I read twice for him. It's the best part I've ever played."

His performance in *Dream Girl* attracted powerful producer Hal B. Wallis, who had left Warner Bros. to set up an independent film unit at Paramount. Wallis invited Corey to Hollywood for a screen test. Wendell was promptly signed to a contract and became a member of Wallis' stock company, which included Lizabeth Scott, Burt Lancaster, Kirk Douglas, Kristine Miller, and, occasionally, Barbara Stanwyck. Wallis tested him for the second male lead in *The Strange Love of Martha Ivers* (1946), but the part went to Kirk Douglas. Prior to going to the coast, though, Wendell opened his own summer theatre in Yardley, Pennsylvania, where he produced, directed, and starred in such plays as *Over 21* and *White Cargo.*

Corey's first film role was as John Hodiak's latent homosexual henchman in *Desert Fury,* released by Paramount in 1947. The cast of this tough melodrama included Lizabeth Scott, Burt Lancaster, and Mary Astor. The Baltimore *Evening Sun* judged: "Miss Scott and the Messrs. Hodiak and Lancaster are the nominal stars but it is Miss Astor and Mr. Corey, a newcomer from the stage, who deserve that dubious billing. He obliges with a performance that is right in every phase." At this same time, Paramount, was casting the film version of *Dream Girl* (1948) to star Betty Hutton, but, as was generally the case, Corey's stage role went to another actor. Macdonald Carey played the part in the Mitchell Leisen-directed film.

Before the start of his second film, Corey went off to the London stage and co-starred with Margaret Sullavan in *Voice of the Turtle* (1947). He returned to Hollywood for Hal Wallis' *I Walk Alone,* released by Paramount in 1948. In this abrasive gangster tale, he appeared with Lizabeth Scott, Burt Lancaster, Kirk Douglas, and Kristine Miller. Wendell was (just) another mobster in this one, wherein the *New York Times* found him "wan" and the *New York Herald-Tribune* called him "somber." Wallis then lent him to Universal for Sabu's *Man-Eater of Kumaon* (1948), which was guaranteed to do nothing for his career, and then to MGM for *The Search* (1948). In *The Search,* a well-constructed beautifully made, somber feature about a war orphan in post-World War II Europe, Corey played Montgomery Clift's Army buddy. Under Fred Zinnemann's direction, it was one of the best films of the year, and, Corey, in a supporting role, was excellent. This role was a telling example of how well he could play a nice-guy cynic.

By 1949 Wendell began receiving star billing in films, primarily in support of some of the screen's first ladies. He was the police lieutenant in Loretta Young's *The Accused* (1949), and starred with Barbara Stanwyck in both *File on Thelma Jordan* (1950) and *The Furies* (1950). He had previously appeared with Stanwyck in *Sorry, Wrong Number* (1948), in which Burt Lancaster played the homicidal maniac. In *Thelma Jordan,* Wendell had his largest role to date, that of an attorney lured by Stanwyck into a web of murder and deception. The children used in the film were Corey's own. He and Stanwyck played well together and proved it, once again, in *The Furies,* Corey's last film for Hal B. Wallis. In the latter picture he also demonstrated that he could portray a self-assured gambler in the best Clark Gable tradition. It was one of his best and most worthwhile screen assignments, because it gave him tremendous scope and freedom to maneuver the tart dialog.

Nineteen fifty turned out to be Corey's most important cinema year. Besides the two Stanwyck features, he went to Columbia to co-star with Margaret Sullavan in *No Sad Songs for Me,* a mature tearjerker

With Sabu in Man-Eater of Kumaon *(Univ 1948)*

about a young wife and mother facing death from incurable cancer. The film was quite admirable in its restraint. The *New York Times* found Corey's performance to be "forthright and genial" and that "the acting support especially of Wendell Corey, as the spouse, is of an accomplished order to match that of Miss Sullavan." His other 1950 release was the remake of *Craig's Wife* (1936), now called *Harriet Craig* to assure its star, Joan Crawford, a more specific title role. Rosalind Russell had played it in the earlier version, but Crawford was, somehow, far more believable in the part of a selfish and possession-minded woman. Corey's role onscreen was originally played by John Boles. The *New York Mirror* thought Corey was "splendid as the husband who loves this impossible woman until his eyes are opened." The *New York Times* could not sympathize with his character because "he is such an impossible dunce as Wendell Corey plays him, such a simpering, apologetic dope who goes around sucking a pipe as though it were a lemon lollipop, that he plainly deserves all the misery to which he is subjected."

In 1951 Wendell received first billing as Frank James to Macdonald Carey's Jesse James in *The Great Missouri Raid,* but it was not until 1954 that he appeared in another important film, Alfred Hitchcock's *Rear Window,* which starred James Stewart and Grace Kelly. Wendell was a wry New York detective in this brilliant suspense story, which, thanks to scripter John Michael Hayes, gave him some excellent dialog to work with. He followed this appearance with a cold-blooded performance as Rod Steiger's henchman in Hollywood's hatchet job on itself, *The Big Knife* (1955).

Between film assignments Wendell found time to appear on the stage and on television. He toured as Linus, the older brother, in *Sabrina Fair* (1954), and as Lieutenant Barney Greenwald in *The Caine Mutiny Court Martial* (1954–55). His role in the latter had been enacted originally on Broadway by Henry Fonda, and then followed by Barry Sullivan. On television, Corey was seen in such diverse offerings as *The Animal Kingdom* (1952), the video version of *The Tale of Two Cities* (1953), *Donovan's Brain* (1955) for "Studio One," and as the prosecuting attorney in *The Rack* (1955) for "The U.S. Steel Hour," a role which he later repeated the following year for MGM in the screen version starring Paul Newman.

Besides *The Rack,* Corey had other good feature film roles in 1956. He was a psychopath in *The Killer Is Loose,* of which the *New York Herald-Tribune* said "he deserved a better fate," a soldier in *The Bold and the Brave,* and the sheriff in *The Rainmaker,* starring Katharine Hepburn and Burt Lancaster. He was also

busy in other media. He played the title role in *The Lou Gehrig Story* on CBS-TV's "Climax" and starred on Broadway in *Night of the Auk.* Had Corey cared more about his career than his pocketbook, he would have stayed in New York and found more work in the legitimate theatre, but he preferred the good life of California. He went the way of many film folk and signed to do his first television series, "Harbor Command," which premiered on ABC-TV on October 11, 1957. The same year he was reunited with Lizabeth Scott in *Loving You,* a superior Elvis Presley effort. After thirty-nine episodes of playing Captain Ralph Baxter on "Harbor Command," Corey did another video series, "Peck's Bad Girl" (1959) for CBS. It was a short-lived summer entry, and afterward, he returned to Broadway for a limited run in *Jolly's Progress* (1959). He also did summer stock at the Oqunquit Playhouse in Maine and appeared in a smallish role in Bob Hope's wacky film, *Alias Jesse James* (1959). After that, Wendell did not appear in another motion picture until 1964 (*Blood on the Arrow*), by which time his film career was nosediving into grade C films.

During 1962 and 1963, Corey was President of the Academy of Motion Pictures Arts and Sciences, succeeding to the office after the death of Valentine Davies. *Films in Review*'s correspondent, reviewing the Oscar show for 1963, stated of the telecast that Wendell "is not of presidential calibre" and that "he reads a few lines of greeting, without sincerity, clarity or force." What the reviewer failed to mention (or know) was that Wendell was inebriated. It was not common knowledge outside the industry, but Corey had become an alcoholic. It did become quite obvious to the educated television viewer when watching segments of his third video series, "The Eleventh Hour" (1962–63) for NBC. He was barely able to get through some of his scenes. In this series (until he was replaced by Ralph Bellamy) he played a psychiatrist, with actor Jack Ging as his younger associate. He enjoyed doing a dramatic series again, because as he explained, "In domestic comedy shows, nothing changes. The same faces, the same furniture." He also liked his onscreen character because "what Dr. Bassett has learned in books isn't half as important as what he knows and feels. What he has mostly is good solid horse sense."

Corey hopped on the bandwagon of stars turned politicians in 1965, and won a seat on the Santa Monica City Council. He campaigned the following year for a Republican nomination for Congress but was unsuccessful. At six foot, two inches, dark-haired, blue-eyed Corey always had appeared rather slender, despite his 180-pound weight, but by the time of the

Jane Russell mini-Western, *Waco* (1966), Corey looked positively cadaverous oncamera, and his somnambulent performances in *Women of the Prehistoric Planet* (1966), *Buckskin* (1968) (another A. C. Lyles Western), or *The Astro-Zombies* (1969) confirmed the fear that the once vigorous performer was living on borrowed time. Wendell died of a liver ailment, November 8, 1968, at the Motion Picture Hospital. He was only fifty-four years old and was bured in his family plot in Beckett, Massachusetts. His last feature was something called *The Starmaker,* made in 1968, but never released.

Just as Corey's personality was locked into the 1940s, so was he an actor who belonged, primarily, in the theatre where his versatility was well used. Nevertheless, he enjoyed filmmaking—of any type—much more than his theatre work. He once said, "I'm not one of those guys who knocks making movies. I guess that's because I'm not stage struck. Don't get me wrong—acting is a good life. But I'd just as soon stick to films."

WENDELL COREY

Desert Fury   *(Par 1947)*
I Walk Alone   *(Par 1948)*
Man-Eater of Kumaon   *(Univ 1948)*
The Search   *(MGM 1948)*
Sorry, Wrong Number   *(Par 1948)*
The Accused   *(Par 1949)*
Any Number Can Play   *(MGM 1949)*
Holiday Affair   *(RKO 1949)*
File on Thelma Jordan   *(Par 1950)*
No Sad Songs for Me   *(Col 1950)*
The Furies   *(Par 1950)*
Harriet Craig   *(Col 1950)*
The Great Missouri Raid   *(Par 1951)*
Rich, Young and Pretty   *(MGM 1951)*
The Wild North   *(MGM 1952)*
Carbine Williams   *(MGM 1952)*
My Man and I   *(MGM 1952)*
The Wild Blue Yonder   *(Rep 1952)*
Jamaica Run   *(Par 1953)*
Hell's Half Acre   *(Rep 1954)*

Laughing Anne   *(Rep 1954)*
Rear Window   *(Par 1954)*
The Big Knife   *(UA 1955)*
The Killer Is Loose   *(UA 1956)*
The Bold and the Brave   *(RKO 1956)*
The Rack   *(MGM 1956)*
The Rainmaker   *(Par 1956)*
Loving You   *(Par 1957)*
The Light in the Forest   *(BV 1958)*
Alias Jesse James   *(UA 1959)*
Blood on the Arrow   *(AA 1964)*
Agent for H.A.R.M.   *(Univ 1966)*
Waco   *(Par 1966)*
Picture Mommy Dead   *(Emb 1966)*
Women of the Prehistoric Planet   *(Realart 1966)*
Cyborg 2087   *(Feature Film Corp. of America 1966)*
Red Tomahawk   *(Par 1967)*
Buckskin   *(Par 1968)*
The Astro-Zombies   *(Geneni Films 1969)*
The Starmaker   *(Unreleased)*

25

Laird Cregar

Anyone standing six feet, three inches in his socks, with a body weighing some three hundred pounds, has to be noticed. If this mountainous mass of humanity could not be ignored, neither could his name, which provided many odd pronunciations until he would explain, "It's a contraction of the Scottish Mc-Gregor, pronounced Cree-gar as in cee-gar. Just accent the second syllable or remember 'Cigar!'" However his name was pronounced, Laird Cregar was one of the major Hollywood discoveries of 1940, bursting on the screen like a comet and leaving it just as rapidly four years later. Some movie followers say he was just a younger Sydney Greenstreet or that the more recent Victor Buono in his more serious moments overreached him in screen effect. Neither is true. Cregar was his own man, and a very tormented one at that, a person who desperately wanted to be a handsome leading man no matter what nature and Twentieth Century-Fox's front office preordained. In the 1940s, when many of the screen's once so vivid personalities were going mushy and fuzzy, Cregar was a breath of fresh air with his energy, dynamism, intensity, and individualism.

Samuel Laird Cregar was born in Philadelphia, Pennyslvania, on July 28, 1916, the youngest of six boys. At the age of eight he was sent to England and enrolled at the Winchester Academy where his father, Edward M. Cregar, had played cricket before the King and Queen of England. During summer vacations from Winchester he was a page boy with the Stratford-on-Avon Players, occasionally serving as a super in their productions. He later admitted, "From that time on all I've ever wanted to do was go on the stage."

Returning to the family fold he was sent to Episcopal Academy in Philadelphia and later attended the Douglas Adams School in Longport, New Jersey. His preoccupation with the theatre drove him, at age fourteen, to find jobs as an usher in various theatres. A few years later he found jobs in various local stock companies in the Philadelphia area. He spent a year with Jasper Deeter's notable Hedgerow Theatre in suburban Rose Valley, Pennsylvania.

In 1936 Cregar was awarded a scholarship to Gilmore Brown's famed Pasadena Community Playhouse, but only had thirty dollars of the three-hundred-dollar tuition. While desperately seeking the balance of the entrance fee he learned that Rotary International gave financial assistance to those qualifying for a professional career. Cregar stalked the Rotary board meeting like an impatient Goliath, staging a dramatic appeal for their assistance after it became apparent that Rotarians held large doubts about the classification of "acting" as a profession. His histrionics convinced the brotherhood and he was given his tuition for Pasadena. Living expenses were something else, but he fortuitously met a newly wed couple, owners of a sedan who let him sleep in the back seat,

In I Wake up Screaming *(20th 1941)*

With Monty Woolley and Gracie Fields in Holy Matrimony *(20th 1943)*

and he depended on another friend for his one meal a day—dinner. During the lean two years at Pasadena he played a variety of good roles but no movie scout approached him. He registered at employment agencies for any kind of work. "But," explained the actor, "whenever I went to a place for a job they seemed scared of my size." His five brothers were successful in the business world and were all larger than Samuel Laird, one of them a towering six feet, seven inches.

Cregar returned East in 1938 and worked for a paltry salary at the Federal Theatre, appearing as Samuel Cregar when billed as "a Mate" in two Eugene O'Neill plays, *Bound East for Cardiff* and *The Moon of the Caribees*. He played Stand-up-Steadfastly Snat in *A Moral Entertainment* in Bryn Mawr College's Goodhart Hall for the Federal Theatre. He saved what money he could and supplemented his income by selling bed sheets at Gimbel's store in New York and bellowing "immediate seating in the balcony" in front of Manhattan's Paramount Theatre. He later returned to Pasadena for a good part in *The American Family*, but still no film offers came his way.

Robert Morley had given one of his finest performances in the title role of Leslie and Sewell Stokes' play *Oscar Wilde*, as presented on the Broadway stage. Cregar read the play and decided to create self-employment by finding someone willing to back him in a west-coast production with himself in the showy title role. Arthur Hutchinson accepted Cregar's proposition and produced the play that met with astounding success when it opened at Hollywood's El Capitan Theatre. Cregar soon became the talk of the town and the initial engagement was extended to six weeks. In San Francisco there was the same enthusiastic acclaim for Cregar and during the two week engagement there he received flattering offers from five studios in Hollywood. John Barrymore wrote the young actor an unabashed fan letter saying that Cregar was the most gifted young actor he had seen in the past twenty years in the theatre.

Warner Bros., for whom he had done an unbilled bit in a courtroom scene in the film version of an Erle Stanley Gardner murder mystery, released as *Granny Get Your Gun* (1940), wanted him to sign for Bette Davis' film *The Letter* (1940), but instead he signed a lucrative seven-year contract with Twentieth Century-Fox. He said his rationale for signing with Darryl F. Zanuck's studio was "because at that time [1940] there was only one other character man, John Carradine, under contract and, of course, we two couldn't ever vie for roles."

For his film debut, Fox cast him as Medard Chouart "Gooseberry" Grosielliers, a roaring, brawling, voyager-fur trapper helping Pierre Esprit Radisson (Paul Muni) found the Hudson's Bay Company in *Hudson's Bay* (1940), a film that had more geography per reel than sturdy characterization or engrossing plot. He played the small role of Natalio Curro in Rouben Mamoulian's Technicolored *Blood and Sand* (1941), which starred Cregar's close friend Tyrone Power. Then Laird displayed a fine flair for comedy as Mr. Spettigrew in *Charley's Aunt* (1941), with Jack Benny and Kay Francis. The *New York Times* recorded that "Laird Cregar's swashbuckling parent and Edmund Gwenn's hot-footed old codger are wickedly comic portraits both," Cregar's career boomed after playing Ed Cornell, a sinister detective pathetically in love with a murdered girl and willing to hang an innocent man for her murder out of insane jealousy in *I Wake up Screaming* (a.k.a., *Hot Spot*) (1941). He emerged as a first-rate villain, a position he reinforced on loanout to Paramount for *This Gun For Hire* (1942) as Willard Gates, a nightclub owner involved in a plot to sell poison gas to Japan. The gun he hires is 5'4" Alan Ladd, but, revolted at the function of a hired assassin, Ladd double-crosses him. Commenting on his showy role as Willard Gates, Cregar admitted, "I didn't like it because it's a mammoth man who is afraid of violence. You've no idea how much physical work it requires of a large man to quake like jelly." Nevertheless he quaked more than adequately. Earlier in the year he had been seen in RKO's *Joan of Paris* (1942) as Herr Funk. Ladd had first made his screen name in that Michele Morgan picture.

Versatile Cregar returned to his home lot as Warren, a con man in a nefarious business with Mrs. Mabel Worthington (Spring Byington) using Gene Tierney as bait for their swindling activities. For one sequence in *Rings on Her Fingers* (1942) the studio wardrobe department had to make a bathing suit to cover his three-hundred-pound frame, just for a brief shot of Cregar diving off a ten-foot board and swimming across a pool. Cregar enthused about his role as Warren as "It's a peerless part, one of those once-in-a-lifetime roles that permits an actor to go hammy in the story." Mr. Cregar could, on occasion and with little provocation, go hammy even without a script or with less than rigid directorial reins.

Between films Laird worked assiduously at the Hollywood Canteen as a busboy, and played the part of Sheridan Whiteside with a good deal of bravado and great critical acclaim in a Los Angeles stage production of *The Man Who Came to Dinner*. He explained his ability to switch from stage to screen: "In the theatre I always underplay my parts. For the camera I just do them naturally." Whatever his technique, he brought great talent to several hackneyed roles on the screen, such as Major Sam Carter, a scarfaced marti-

With Edmund Gwenn and Jack Benny in Charley's Aunt *(20th 1941)*

net of a training officer getting the first batch of officers graduated in *Ten Gentlemen from West Point* (1942), and as the former pirate who became Governor of Jamaica, Captain Henry Morgan, in Tyrone Power's *The Black Swan* (1942). In this Henry King-directed feature he created an impressive portrait far beyond the demands of the part, but was outshone by red-bearded George Sanders as buccaneer Captain Billy Leech. Hidden behind massive whiskers as Sam Weaver, a prospector, Laird brought creative authority as a player to *Hello, Frisco, Hello!* (1943), the Alice Faye musical.

Hollywood has always had periodic cycles with each studio rushing into production the prevalent genre which, in turn, is embraced and strongly supported at the boxoffice by the trend-following public. The horror film binge gave way to the gangster era, then the studios discovered boxoffice gold in biographies of famous men, from composers to politicians with an occasional brush with the classics. In the forties the "Satan cycle" began (bolstered by an ethereal messenger), presenting the Prince of Evil as one an audience could blithely cope with, embrace, and even enjoy, as long as he remained *on* the silver screen. Laird, with his mellifluous voice, was a humorous, roguish Devil in Ernst Lubitsch's *Heaven Can Wait* (1943). Massively suave as "His Excellency," sporting a well-trimmed goatee and unctuous speech he consigned souls to hell from his swanky reception room via a trap door (and poof went Florence Bates) and spent most of the film listening to Don Ameche's life story before deciding his fate on an elevator that went to Heaven or Hell.

Nunnally Johnson's *Holy Matrimony* (1943), based on Arnold Bennett's *Buried Alive,* was enhanced by a fine performance from Cregar as Clive Oxford, an art dealer, involved in a hilarious law suit with Monty Woolley, and the quite wonderful import from the British musical halls, Gracie Fields. Cregar's niche in film history, however, did not arrive until 1944, when he played Jack the Ripper in the John Brahm-directed *The Lodger.*

Mrs. Marie Belloc-Lowndes' classic· thriller was adapted for the screen by Barre Lyndon, expertly photographed by Lucien Ballard, and directed in a crescendo of shock and excitement by Brahm. *The Lodger* had been previously filmed in England by Alfred Hitchcock in 1926 with Ivor Novello as a pseudo-Jack-the-Ripper known as "The Avenger." Hitchcock was forced to compromise on the ending of his silent picture because Novello, being England's leading matinee idol, could not be shown as such a fiend, and the denouement was a cop-out of mistaken identities. In 1954 Fox trotted Jack out again with Jack Palance as The Lodger, retitled *Man in the Attic,*

and in 1960, there was a British-made exploitation-biography of the famed killer entitled *Jack the Ripper,* starring Lee Patterson. But no one has equaled Cregar's performance as the Bible-quoting doctor stalking the fog-bound, gas-lit streets of London's Whitehall, venting his hatred of women upon prostitutes or an actress, then pausing to wash the blood from his hands in the Thames. Alton Cook (*New York World-Telegram*) called the film "a magnificent example of its type and a magnificent picture as well."

A brilliant cast including Merle Oberon, Sir Cedric Hardwicke, George Sanders, Sara Allgood, Doris Lloyd, and Helena Pickard (in a vivid bit as a faded music hall star), surrounded Cregar. With his carefully drawn psychotic portrait of *The Lodger,* neatly suggesting the apprehension, fear, and torment of Jack-the-Ripper with terrifying realism, Cregar dominated the entire picture and was superb. Although the real-life Jack-the-Ripper was never caught, Cregar's dramatic death scene was one of the film's highlights. Cregar said that "*The Lodger* was such a plum part it keeps an actor in fear that what he does next will in no way live up to it. Maybe the fact that villainy is my special forte—although I hate to be symbolized such —comes from being a direct descendant of John Wilkes Booth." Nothing has come to light during the years to substantiate any of the Cregar blood lines running back to or from the Booths, Junius, Edwin, or John Wilkes.

His fear of typecasting was well founded. His studio saw him as a younger Sydney Greenstreet, and critics suggested that since he was such a skillful, revolting menace, he might find himself confined to such roles in the future. Cregar's last film confirmed all of these suspicions. In an elaborate, over-worked version of Patrick Hamilton's novel *Hangover Square* (1945), reset in turn-of-the-century London in a Barre Lyndon script again directed by John Brahm, Cregar played George Harvey Bone, a schizophrenic composer suffering lapses of memory during which periods he commits brutal murders.

The actor, always conscious about his weight, had gone on a crash diet, the results being visible in the unreeling of *Hangover Square.* The climax of the film was expertly done, with Cregar wildly playing his concerto as flames sweep through the room and the ceiling crashes down on the piano and mad composer.

On the morning of December 9, 1944, he suffered a heart attack, after undergoing an abdominal operation a few days before (as a result of the crash diet that removed one hundred of his three hundred pounds), and by evening he was dead—a victim of his vanity and the pressures of studio typecasting.

He was only twenty-eight years old.

LAIRD CREGAR

Oh Johnny, How You Can Love   *(Univ 1940)*
Granny Get Your Gun   *(WB 1940)*
Hudson's Bay   *(20th 1940)*
Blood and Sand   *(20th 1941)*
Charley's Aunt   *(20th 1941)*
I Wake Up Screaming (a.k.a., Hot Spot)   *(20th 1941)*
Joan of Paris   *(RKO 1942)*
Rings on Her Fingers   *(20th 1942)*

This Gun For Hire   *(Par 1942)*
Ten Gentlemen from West Point   *(20th 1942)*
The Black Swan   *(20th 1942)*
Hello, Frisco, Hello!   *(20th 1943)*
Heaven Can Wait   *(20th 1943)*
Holy Matrimony   *(20th 1943)*
The Lodger   *(20th 1944)*
Hangover Square   *(20th 1945)*

26

Cass Daley

While classically trained Grace Moore, Lauritz Melchior, Rise Stevens, et al., were overwhelming Metropolitan Opera patrons with well-modulated arias, moviegoers of the frantic forties were being treated to a more frenetic type of song performance by the likes of Betty Hutton, Martha Raye, Judy Canova, and Cass Daley. This quartet of memorable film players had several career traits in common: each was more energetic than beautiful, none could resist a facial contortion or body gymnastic if it meant a possible laugh, and all—very surprising to some—were terrific singers. Miss Daley never atttained the fame of these other comic songsters, but in her own way she was just as vital to the well-being of the movies she populated.

Like blonde bombshell Hutton, Cass was a Paramount contractee, and, as with the dynamic Hutton, she always seemed to be compensating for imaginary talent deficiencies by giving more energy to her film appearances than anyone had a right to expect. If Paramount persistently linked Hutton with Eddie Bracken on film, athletic, bombastic Cass was generally paired "romantically" with fellow player Gil Lamb, the latter best described as a more frantic, less egocentric version of the later Woody Allen.

If one spotted Cass's name in the screen credits of a picture, it was inevitable that, soon, the former band vocalist, famed for her toothy grin, raucous comedy songs, and Plain-Jane looks, would be capering front and center to create her own special brand of song and dance nonsense. Seen today, her vintage film performances might seem to some like freakish displays of misguided slapstick, but her specialty routines were as valid to the jitterbug-prone 1940s as any "meaningful" bit that Alice Cooper might concoct for the relevant 1970s.

Bill Daley was a Philadelphia streetcar conductor whose wife Louise presented him with a dark-haired daughter on July 17, 1915. They named her Catherine, and the young child was in and out of many of the City of Brotherly Love's schools because of her parents' persistent passion for moving. It became obvious at an early stage that Catherine was not destined for beauty contest competitions. She became overly self-conscious of her thin, wiry appearance and, especially, of her widely spaced, protruding teeth. "I guess it gave me something of an inferiority complex. The kids used to call me 'Bucky' and 'Horseteeth' but I got over it." She developed a passion for performing, mimicking recordings of the "boop-boop-a-boop" girl, Helen Kane and, as soon as she was old enough, she entered a staggering series of amateur vaudeville shows. She would return home with certificates for shoe repairing, flowers, or dresses, prizes won for belting out songs while maintaining a stiff upper lip, trying to shield her protruding teeth.

When Cass was six years old, Louise Daley divorced her spouse and married Herman Burkart, a steel construction worker. However, finances in the

In Crazy House *(Univ 1943)*

With Johnny Coy and Eddie Bracken in Ladies' Man *(Par 1947)*

home continued at a low ebb and, at fourteen, Cass went to work in a hosiery mill as a stocking trimmer. She soon lost this job when she provided co-workers with a too accurate imitation of the mill's boss. Soon, however, she landed a job in a Camden, New Jersey nightclub, The Old Mill, doubling as hat check girl and singer. When an airplane hanger at the Camden airport was opened for a Walkathon Contest, Cass was hired as a singer during the fifteen minute intermissions, singing the blues.

"Until then I'd never done comedy, I was strictly a blues singer. But one day—I'll never forget it as long as I live—the audience started laughing, and I couldn't figure out why until I discovered that the emcee was on his stomach holding a candle behind me so they could see right through my dress. Well, in that day, that was shocking. But it was funny! The emcee was just getting started in the business. His name was Red Skelton."

Cass soon decided to make the worst of what nature had given her, abandoned any hope of glamour of replacing Helen Morgan atop a piano, and became an instant comedienne. From the Camden Walkathon, she found a job in a Westchester, New York, nightclub. There she met real estate insurance agent and sometime-talent agent Frank Kinsella. Kinsella

persuaded her to stress comedy with her singing that Cass claimed at the time "was not good—but loud." Kinsella bought her a dilapidated trumpet that her stepfather Burkart gagged up with improbable plumbing attachments and Cass was all set with her burlesque routine, a one-note trumpet solo after singing her own wild version of "The Music Goes Round." Kinsella became her full time manager and the close seven year association resulted in marriage in 1941.

The revised *Ziegfeld Follies of 1936* returned in 1937 with several cast replacements, among them Cass Daley for Judy Canova. In this stage revue starring Fannie Brice, Bobby Clark, and later, Gypsy Rose Lee, Cass sang a whirlwind blues number, "You Don't Love Me Right", as well as "Harlem Waltz," while Cherry and June Preisser did their acrobatic dancing. With Bobby Clark as Major Bones and Fannie Brice as Myrtle Appenshaw, Cass was Elvira Mackintosh in a hilarious sketch, "Amateur Night," that had been played in the original *Follies* by Judy Canova. The exuberant, boisterous Miss Daley sang with many of the top name bands, and in 1938 she did a tour of the British music halls.

During the summer of 1939, Cass appeared at the St. Louis Municipal Opera Company in *Naughty Marietta* and *Rio Rita.* In the fall of that year, she signed

With Matt McHugh and Gil Lamb in Riding High *(Par 1943)*

with Brown and Henderson's road tour of their New York success, *Yokel Boy*. Cass replaced Judy Canova as "Judy" and Joe Penner was starred in the original Buddy Ebsen part. The show opened in Philadelphia on January 6, 1941, and four days later comedian Penner died at the age of thirty-six in his sleep at the Ritz Carlton Hotel. Thus ended the promising tour. Cass returned to radio where her comedic charms had enlivened the "Kraft Music Hall," "The Edgar Bergen-Charlie McCarthy show," Jack Benny's program, and many others. She continued playing vaudeville where, while she was doing a five-shows-a-day in Cleveland, Ohio, Paramount signed her to a film contract.

Paramount had just come under the aegis of B. G. (Buddy) DeSylva, who had once been part of the music publishing and producing firm of DeSylva, Henderson and Brown. DeSlyva put two of his recent "discoveries" into a Paramount musical, *The Fleet's In* (1942). In short order, hoydenish Betty Hutton and mayhem-prone Cass Daley stole the show, purportedly a starring vehicle for Dorothy Lamour. The film quickly became a riotous showcase for the manic singing and clowning of Hutton and Daley, who burst upon the screen singing a Victor Schertzinger (who directed the film) and Johnny Mercer song, "To-morrow You Belong to Uncle Sam (But Tonight You Belong to Me)."

Cass's film debut was followed by a spot in the multistar Paramount *Star Spangled Rhythm* (1942) where, as Mimi, she belted a Harold Arlen-Johnny Mercer number, "He Loved Me Till the All-Clear Came." For 1943's drab Technicolor release, *Riding High,* which again supposedly starred Dorothy Lamour, Cass was Tess Connors running a dude ranch and she sang "Willy the Wolf of the West." Her highly energetic teaming with loose-limbed Gil Lamb and the ever-delightfully addled Victor Moore saved the film from obscurity. Said the *New York Times,* "Miss Daley, the girl with the dentures, screams and tortures amusingly a couple of comedy numbers." Paramount loaned her to Universal for the zany antics of Olson and Johnson's *Crazy House* (1943) when both as Sadie Silverfish and herself, she convulsed audiences with her "Lament of a Laundry Girl."

Cass's broad comedy was a natural for radio, and on that medium she was a regular on the Frank Morgan show and NBC's "Maxwell House Coffee Time," as Morgan's boisterous niece Cassandra. Listeners soon came to identify the defiant tag line, "I said it and I'm glad!" with Cass. As a summer replacement for the Fitch Bandwagon show with Alice Faye and

173

Phil Harris, came "The Cass Daley Show," featuring Cass, Larry Keating, and Freddy Martin's Orchestra. One of the highlights of Cass' radio career occurred on February 15, 1945, when she took part in a colossal Armed Forces radio service broadcast entitled *The Wedding of Dick Tracy*, with Bing Crosby as Tracy, Dinah Shore as Tess Trueheart, Bob Hope as Flattop, Frank Morgan as Flintheart, the Andrews Sisters as the Summer Sisters, Jimmy Durante as the Mole, Judy Garland as Little Snowflake, Frank Sinatra as Shaky, and Cass as Gravel Gertie.

Back at Paramount, Cass appeared as herself in *Duffy's Tavern* (1945), joining Bing Crosby, Dorothy Lamour, Betty Hutton, Diana Lynn, and Billy De Wolfe in a satirical version of "Swinging on a Star." She was Fanny the drummer, a frenetically energized member of Diana Lynn's all-girl orchestra in *Out of This World* (1945), and again as herself in *Variety Girl* (1947). With Eddie Bracken in *Ladies' Man* (1947), she did a raucous, hilarious imitation of Carmen Miranda singing "Mama Yo Quiero" with Spike Jones and his City Slickers. For Bing Crosby's *Here Comes the Groom* (1951), she joined Dorothy Lamour, Louis Armstrong, Phil Harris, and Crosby singing "Misto Christofo Columbo" in an airplane sequence.

Sporadically Cass returned to vaudeville, appearing at the nation's top houses, and bringing down the house at New York's Paramount Theatre with her booming, exuberant singing while going through seemingly impossible contortions. *Life* Magazine had run a two page spread in their weekly "Speaking of Pictures" section, featuring Cass in repose and in a repertoire of grimaces in which she mangled her rubberized facial muscles into fantastic expressions worthy of a chamber of horrors.

Between radio, motion pictures, and frequent vaudeville bookings, Cass made some twenty or more recordings for Decca, including "Put the Blame on Mame," "A Good Man Is Hard to Find," "It's the Last Time I'll Fall in Love," and, with Hoagy Carmichael, she waxed "The Old Piano Roll Blues" and "Aba Daba Honeymoon" among others. After playing "Minnie Redwing" in Paramount's dull musical Western satire, *Red Garters* (1954), in which she joined Rosemary Clooney, Guy Mitchell, and Buddy Ebsen in the song "Ladykiller," Cass retired to Newport Beach, where her son Dale Kinsella was born. Tiring of kitchen and nursery, Cass eventually returned to the screen in Paramount's 1967 *The Spirit Is*

Willing as Felicity Twitchell, spending the entire Sid Caesar film roaming around as a red nightgowned bed-bonneted ghost.

"Moving to Newport Beach was probably the worst mistake I ever made," Cass admitted in 1973. "I became terribly domestic. I was playing house, I had a new baby who, incidentally, is doing great. He's been working in the White House for the past two summers and soon graduates from law school." In the 1940s Cass was proclaimed the number one comedienne by the Hooper Ratings, but by the 1960s she was just a name, among others, on the Late, Late Show. In 1970, she came out of retirement again, this time to join a large cast of comics in Warners' fiasco, *The Phynx*, and to play the role of Mrs. Remley with Glen Campbell and Joe Namath in *Norwood* (1970).

During the summer of 1972, Cass joined a revue, or nostalgic vaudeville show, produced by Stan and Darren M. Seiden called *The Big Show of 1936*, with Allan Jones doubling as master of ceremonies. The show played eight performances at the Felt Forum of New York City's Madison Square Garden. The acts included The Ink Spots (singing "If I Didn't Care"), Arthur Tracy the Street Singer, comic Vince Barnett, Jackie Coogan doing a monologue, Beatric Kay revitalizing the songs of the Gay Nineties, deadpan ex-MGM singer Virginia O'Brien doing wonders to the song "In a Little Spanish Town," Carl Stevens of the original Borrah Minnevich Harmonica Rascals, and petite and still shapely Sally Rand doing her famous fan dance on the dimly lit stage with two pink luminescent fans. And after thirty-three years away from the New York stage, still performing acrobatic contortions was the warm, boisterous, super-energized Cass Daley, letting loose three songs that hit the roof and would have challenged the vocal power of Ethel Merman. In the 1974 Los Angeles stage revival of *The Front Page* with Hugh O'Brian and Bert Convy, Cass was among the large cast, playing the scrubwoman.

Just as her life took many strange turns, so death came to her in an odd way. Her demise was the result of a "freak" accident. She died on March 22, 1975 in her Hollywood apartment. According to her husband, Robert Williamson, who discovered the body, she had tripped and fallen in the living room, shattering a goblet on the coffee table and a piece of glass imbedded in her neck, severing her jugular vein. For someone who had been nearly forgotten by Hollywood, her death rated a large-size obituary.

CASS DALEY

The Fleet's In *(Par 1942)*
Star Spangled Rhythm *(Par 1942)*
Riding High *(Par 1943)*
Crazy House *(Univ 1943)*
Duffy's Tavern *(Par 1945)*
Out of This World *(Par 1945)*
Ladies' Man *(Par 1947)*

Variety Girl *(Par 1947)*
Here Comes the Groom *(Par 1951)*
Red Garters *(Par 1954)*
The Spirit Is Willing *(Par 1967)*
The Phynx *(WB 1970)*
Norwood *(Par 1970)*

27

Billy De Wolfe

Brooks Atkinson, reviewing *John Murray Anderson's Almanac* (1953), described the antic clowning of Billy De Wolfe's belated Broadway debut: "Except for a few geniuses left over from vaudeville and burlesque of thirty years ago, the theatre is starved for low comedians. Mr. De Wolfe is the most likely new figure to appear here in recent years. He can act. He moves." Broadway was discovering what the other media had known for years; whether in low comedy or high camp De Wolfe's comedic contributions were nearly always hilarious. His special creation was that of a blowzy, middle-aged matron burdened with an armload of bundles, suffering from anguished feet and a massive thirst who stops at a cocktail bar to have a wee snort (with water on the side) to help her get up the hill: Mrs. Murgatroyd.

In the 1940s Billy was under contract to Paramount who astutely assigned him to bridge low spots in a variety of studio musicals and comedies. In front of the cameras, moustachioed De Wolfe could be funny, perplexed, or just useful to push along a story's plot. Generally the funster was given asexual characterizations to portray, but sometimes, as in *Blue Skies* (1946), for which he was named *Motion Picture Herald's* "Star of Tomorrow," he made at least a feeble effort at romancing the second female lead, here Olga San Juan. But generally it was only when he was engulfed in one of his routines that he came alive above and beyond the expected double takes, wry comments, and shrugs of the shoulders. If audiences hardly ever stopped to ponder the one-dimensional, unrealistic aspects of his onscreen roles, they were well assured that when De Wolfe popped up onscreen there would be no sluggish moments, that his co-players would suddenly spring to life as if exhilarated by his mere presence, and that when he disappeared from the storyline for a breather he would soon return for an encore of antics. Unlike other such 1940s screen comedians as Jack Oakie and Phil Silvers, who performed their comedy moments with little, if any subtlety, Billy, in his own peculiar unisex manner, integrated his acerbic dialog with the main plotline and made his presence not so much a comedy relief as a hilarious joy.

William Andrew Jones was born February 18, 1907, in Wollaston, Massachusetts, to bookbinder Robert Ellis Jones and his wife Ada Gaynor. They took their nine-week-old son back to their home in Pwllheli, Wales—a small town that defies pronounciation and which Billy suggests can only be "coughed." When the boy was nine years old his parents returned to Massachusetts to become American citizens. Young William was educated in Quincy, Massachusetts, raised by his Aunt Laura and later found employment as an usher in the Quincy Theatre at $7.50, until the manager of Jimmy Connor's band saw him rehearsing a routine in the theatre and hired him at fifty dollars a week as a dancer with the band.

In Blue Skies *(Par 1946)*

With William Holden and Joan Caulfield in Dear Ruth *(Par 1947)*

The theatre manager told him he would never succeed in show business with a name like William A. Jones, so Billy took the manager's last name, De Wolfe.

He toured vaudeville circuits with his own act, De Wolfe and Kindler and played in a dancing act at New York's Hippodrome. Then, forming a new act, De Wolfe, Metcalf and Ford, he signed for four weeks in London. However, Billy stayed five years. When his partners returned to America, De Wolfe remained on as a single, playing the English provinces, the Palladium, the Continent and, in 1938, his act was included in Cochran's revue, *Revels in Rhythm,* at the Trocadero in London. Back in America in 1939, he became a major nightclub performer with his eccentric dancing and satirical routines, from the boozing Mrs. Murgatroyd to his expert satire on a cheap nightclub, in which he played each part from the master of ceremonies to the very bored gum-chewing chorines to an overbearingly rude waiter. As alternates to these skits, he could display the rigors of getting into and out of a girdle, or an irate sailor trying to bathe under an unwilling shower. Performing his stylized buffoonery in white tie and tails Billy was soon earning five thousand dollars a week in the nation's top clubs from New York's Rainbow Room to Houston's Shamrock, and Chicago's Palmer House.

On January 20, 1942, he enlisted in the U.S. Navy as Seaman First Class William A. Jones and was soon transferred as musician second class to Great Lakes Naval Training Station, Illinois. Before enlisting in the Navy he had made an impressive film debut in *Dixie* (1943)* Paramount's imaginative biography of minstrel man Dan Emmett (Bing Crosby) in which De Wolfe as Mr. Bones, a riverboat cardsharp in pre-Civil War New Orleans, cheats Crosby out of his savings and then joins him in forming a new style minstrel act with Lynn Overman and Eddie Foy, Jr.

After his stint with the Navy, he returned to Paramount in 1945 as a psychiatrist listening to boisterous Betty Hutton bellow her indecisions and perplexities about men in the song "The Hardy Way" in Paramount's star-studded, but leaden *Duffy's Tavern* (1945). In *Miss Susie Slagle's* (1945), which had sat on the completion shelf for some time, he was Ben Mead, who brought greatly needed comic relief to this sudsy soap opera set in a 1910 Baltimore boarding house. The film was saved from total oblivion by Lillian Gish's glowing performance as the dispenser

*De Wolfe, a frequent performer at the Stage Door Canteen, was appearing at the Rainbow Room in New York when Bing Crosby spotted his act and suggested he come to California. For *Dixie,* makeup artist Wally Westmore suggested he wear a moustache, which became his trademark and was later described by Walter Winchell as "a seagull in flight."

of loving knowledge to a group of Johns Hopkins Medical School students.

Paramount had done quite well with Cornelia Otis Skinner and Emily Kimbrough's *Our Hearts Were Young and Gay* (1944) and determined to equal that success in a sequel, *Our Hearts Were Growing Up* (1946). Diana Lynn and Gail Russell repeated their assignments, but the new adventures lacked the charm and originality of the first. However, De Wolfe's wacky Greenwich Village artist, Roland Du Frere, provided several very funny scenes. With the hyper-energetic Betty Hutton as Pearl White, he played Timmy, a Shakespearean ham, in *The Perils of Pauline* (1947). The role of prissy, ineffectual Albert Kummer was a natural for De Wolfe when Paramount filmed Norman Krasna's stage hit *Dear Ruth* (1947) with Joan Caulfield in Virginia Gilmore's stage role. He played Ruth's torch-carrying fiance Kummer three times on "Lux Radio Theatre" and repeated the part of the flustered suitor in Paramount's less successful two film sequels, *Dear Wife* (1949) and *Dear Brat* (1951). Away from Paramount, he worked at Warner Bros., ably supporting Doris Day in two musicals. He was Larry Blair in a far-fetched remake of *No, No, Nanette* called *Tea for Two* (1950) and was "Lefty" Mack in *Lullaby of Broadway* (1951). Two years later he returned to the screen in Twentieth Century-Fox's

version of Irving Berlin's *Call Me Madam* (1953). As State Department attache Pemberton Maxwell, he is sent into a snit by Ethel Merman's "hostess with the mostest" when she tells him they will get along just fine, "as long as you remember I am the Madam and you're just one of the boys."

With his filmmaking activities becoming sporadic at best, DeWolfe turned to television, where, on December 23, 1951, he did his bit on Ed Sullivan's "Toast of the Town" along with guests Gloria Swanson and Julie Harris. But it was onstage that he gained his greatest acclaim. John Murray Anderson's last Broadway show was *Almanac,* which debuted at the Imperial Theatre in New York on December 10, 1953. The glittering harlequinade showcased Hermione Gingold, Harry Belafonte, and De Wolfe. Cyril Ritchard directed the revue's hilarious sketches that were acted with consummate buffoonery by Gingold and De Wolfe. In one spot they were two tippling spinsters extravagantly lying to each other aboard the European Express. In the show's best skit, "Dinner for One," she was a grande dame and he her butler who grows progressively clumsy, spilling the wine and dropping dishes until his wildly distorted drunken staggering reduces the elegant dinner to shambles. De Wolfe's caricature of the oversexed, excessively manly hero of the play *Picnic* (played with an ego-

With Mona Freeman in Isn't It Romantic? *(Par 1948)*

centric, strutting gait, throwing his bare chest into a semi-globular shape Charles Atlas would have admired) nearly always stopped the show. For his versatile performance in *John Murray Anderson's Almanac,* Billy received the 1954 Donaldson Theatre Award.

He had appeared in a Royal Command Performance in London in 1948 and returned to the Palladium in 1955 with his Mrs. Murgatroyd sketch. Although the boozing old dame remained the public's favorite De Wolfe characterization, he would claim, "I've been trying to kill off the old girl for years. Strangers waylay me and insist that I entertain their women's club—'and be sure to bring along Mrs. Murgatroyd,' they giggle. Almost every mail contains requests from dramatic groups for rights to the material. Millinery agents want to put out Mrs. Murgatroyd hats. I'm haunted by the dame!"

On March 1, 1957, he returned to Broadway at the Winter Garden Theatre in the twenty-sixth and last edition of *The Ziegfeld Follies* that brought England's most talented comedienne, Beatrice Lillie, back to mainstem theatre after four years' absence. The long critical carping that Lillie was always better than her material continued with the last *Follies,* and was also applicable to De Wolfe. The venture lasted 123 performances but did nothing to increase the prestige of Lady Peel nor Mr. De Wolfe.

New York City Center's 1962 light opera spring schedule included four Frank Loesser musicals, including his Pulitzer Prize smash *How to Succeed in Business Without Really Trying,* and someone had the wisdom to hire Billy for the role of pompous J. B. Biggley. With Warren Berlinger as the young man who succeeds, Billy returned to London as J.B., president of World Wide Wicket Company, singing the praises of "Old Ivy" in *How To . . .* which was the opening attraction (March 28, 1963) at the refurbished Prince's Theatre renamed the Shaftesbury. Later, he played Biggley in summer stock (with Jerry Van Dyke as the youthful success) at Kenley, Ohio, and developed a personal vendetta for the town of Eaton, Ohio.

He received his first speeding ticket* in Eaton and for two years (1972–73) on the Mike Douglas and Johnny Carson talk shows related his running battle with this Ohio city. "I've been blasting Eaton wherever I go. So now they're going to have a Billy De Wolfe

Day during the Preble County Pork Festival. Well, they should. I was not going 84 miles an hour! I know because I was driving behind two elderly little people and everyone knows elderly little people don't speed. But they love me now in Eaton and Officer Kinney who gave me the ticket has now been promoted to lieutenant."

Television became Billy's forte after appearing in the film *Billie* (1965) as Mayor Davis, supporting maturing Patty Duke, Jim Backus, and Jane Greer in Ronald Alexander's screen adaptation of his own play, *Time Out for Ginger.* In a February, 1965 telecast of ABC's "Burke's Law," he joined Martha Raye, Macdonald Carey, and Don Rickles as Artemis Newpenny in an amusing whodunit. Later that year, he was the inspector investigating aged, would-be bank robbers Claude Rains, Bert Lahr, Ken Murray, and Cyril Delevanti in "Chrysler Theatre"'s *Cops and Robbers* (1965). As the fussy boss of Lewis and Clarke, disc jockeys, in the series "Good Morning World" (1967) he contributed much-needed comedy to the short-lived program. In the CBS series "The Queen and I" (1969) he was Nelson, a meddlesome officer interfering with Larry Storch's frantic efforts to save an aged ship from the scrapyard.

Helen Hayes and Lillian Gish were the two dotty sisters bent on homicide with Christian burial in ABC's special telecast, April 2, 1969, of *Arsenic and Old Lace.* After administering their lethal elderberry wine and last rites to thirteen family-less men they agreed to go to a sanitarium, Happy Dale. The prissy, tightlipped superintendent of Happy Dale arrives to sign the old girls into the asylum, but the sisters learn he, too, is alone in the world and they offer the unsuspecting disciplinarian a glass of their arsenic-spiked homemade wine as the play ends. Billy was properly fatuous and pompous as the fourteenth victim, Mr. Witherspoon, a part he could play in his sleep. For the next two years he was Doris Day's fuss-budget, quarrelsome neighbor Jarvis on her TV series. In Walt Disney's feature *The World's Greatest Athlete* (1973), Billy had a thankless role in a nearly funless comedy.

When the revival of *Irene* was announced in 1973, Billy was selected for the role of Madam Lucy but ill health, and his aging battle with hypochondria forced him to relinquish the role for which George S. Irving received a Tony award. Then on March 5, 1974, the sixty-seven year old De Wolfe died in Los Angeles, of lung cancer. He left personal property in value of $230,225.00, with a Hollywood public administrator later announcing that the only heir he had been able to find was a "possible" half-sister, Virginia Durham, living in Mesa, Arizona. Eventually, his sizeable collection of show business memorablia was donated to the University of Southern California.

*Lifelong bachelor Billy, who was more finicky about his way of life than any devout spinster, was a devout automobile worshiper with a passion for motoring. "I'm noted for driving from Coast to Coast, you know. The first car I ever had I named 'Daisy Dodge,' then there was 'Polly Pontiac,' and now 'Clara Cadillac.' I always said if their was a bridge to London, I'd be on it.

De Wolfe's death emphasized once again how essentially private was this very public figure who had been entertaining the world for over four decades. Any audience that could disassociate him from his ever-popular Mrs. Murgatroyd, would recall him as the immaculately dressed, precisely-speaking (who else said "t-iss-oo" like he did?), upper-crust denizen who saved so many show business outings from dullness. Although in his last years he self-kiddingly called himself an "elderly character actor," he resented growing old, with the accompanying loss of energy, and the necessity of giving way to fresh talent. De Wolfe craved attention and public adulation so desperately that it often mattered little to him where he was performing or in what format. "As long as it's show business, I'm happy," he confessed.

Just as in many ways, he replaced and embellished the same role played in the past by the late, great Edward Everett Horton and by the elegantly effete Franklin Pangborn, so types like Paul Lynde have come along to fill in the gap left by De Wolfe. But he would have been pleased and comforted to know that he was and is irreplaceable.

BILLY DE WOLFE

Duffy's Tavern   *(Par 1945)*
Miss Susie Slagle's   *(Par 1945)*
Blue Skies   *(Par 1946)*
Our Hearts Were Growing Up   *(Par 1946)*
The Perils of Pauline   *(Par 1947)*
Dear Ruth   *(Par 1947)*
Variety Girl   *(Par 1947)*
Isn't It Romantic?   *(Par 1948)*

Dear Wife   *(Par 1949)*
Tea for Two   *(WB 1950)*
Dear Brat   *(Par 1951)*
Lullaby of Broadway   *(WB 1951)*
Call Me Madam   *(20th 1953)*
Billie   *(UA 1965)*
The World's Greatest Athlete   *(BV 1973)*

Bobby Driscoll

28

The 1940s, with its prolific array of feature films, saw a number of superb performances by male child actors. There was Roddy McDowall in *How Green Was My Valley* (1941), Skippy Homeier in *Tomorrow the World* (1944), Claude Jarman, Jr. in *The Yearling* (1946), Ivan Jandl in *The Search* (1948), and at the end of the traumatic decade, Bobby Driscoll in *The Window* (1949). Bobby's performance in this finely conceived film must be acknowledged as one of the finest acting jobs ever offered by an adolescent on-screen. Indeed, he was the star of the suspense movie. The other young performers mentioned above were all surrounded by veteran players and were generally in support of these stars. In *The Window*, the very able cast, including Barbara Hale, Arthur Kennedy, Ruth Roman, and Paul Stewart, were in support of Bobby. He carried the film with amazing results. This slightly-built boy, with his freckled, turned-up nose, his wide-open, gray-eyed look and his charming eagerness, captivated the critics. The *New York Times* applauded him: "The striking force and terrifying impact of this RKO melodrama is chiefly due to Bobby's brilliant acting." The *New York Herald-Tribune*, reviewing this film which was based on the old "cry wolf" fable, said: "Bobby Driscoll gives an amazing controlled performance as a nice young brat who sees and talks too much for his own good. Any of the overplaying or boyish cuteness so often displayed by Hollywood juveniles would have reduced an intelligent screenplay to run-of-the-mill pulp. Driscoll

steers a difficult dramatic course with a skill far beyond his years." The Academy of Motion Picture Arts and Sciences even gave Bobby a special Oscar (statuette) as the outstanding juvenile performer of 1949, as a result of his performance in *The Window*. Just a few short years later Bobby could no longer get acting jobs and the once-child celebrity turned to drugs. This desperate move literally killed him.

Born in Cedar Rapids, Iowa, on March 3, 1937, he and his parents, Isabelle and Cletus Driscoll, moved to California in 1943. A Los Angeles barber suggested to Mrs. Driscoll that the boy should be in the movies. The barber's own son was an actor and recommended Bobby to his boy's agent. The agent, in turn, took Bobby and Mrs. Driscoll to MGM, where they were then casting Margaret O'Brien's *Lost Angel* (1943) and Bobby was hired on the spot for a small role. His pixie face was his fortune.

Other studios rapidly hired the resourceful young actor, and, at six years of age, he was making five hundred dollars a week. Twentieth Century-Fox cast him in *The Sullivans* (1944) and *Sunday Dinner for a Soldier* (1944), both with Anne Baxter; Republic hired him for *The Big Bonanza* (1945) and *Identity Unknown* (1945), and Paramount cast him in a bit part in the much-delayed release, *Miss Susie Slagle's* (1945). But in RKO's *From This Day Forward* (1946), he made his mark as Rosemary DeCamp and Harry

With Gene Holland, George Nokes, and Luana Patten in Song of the South *(RKO 1946)*

With Eddie Cantor and Joan Davis in If You Knew Susie *(RKO 1948)*

Morgan's son. In Paramount's *O.S.S.* (1946), starring Alan Ladd, he made a very strong impression as a boy working with the French underground who comes to Ladd's timely aid. Bobby did not come across as a personality child player, such as Butch Jenkins would be some years later, but he emerged as an actor, and it was all instinctual. In close-ups, one could observe the boy thinking in character. Three other child actors at this time were Dean Stockwell (who became a good friend of Bobby's and tried helping him out in later years), Claude Jarman, Jr., and Peter Miles (the brother of moppet actress Gigi Perreau). Miles was probably the closest to Driscoll in character interpretation, though a bit slicker in his acting style and with less reality to his performances. Stockwell, good as he was, usually played with an attitude of toughness or cockiness; Jarman, Jr. was sensitive. None of these other child stars had Bobby's range.

Universal gave Bobby fourth billing in *So Goes My Love* (1946), a comedy-drama of Brooklyn domesticity in the 1860s. It starred Myrna Loy as the "perfect wife" and Don Ameche as an inventor, thereby providing little challenge to the talents of either star. Nevertheless, Bobby shone in his role. The *New York Herald-Tribune* approved of his "natural portrayal." Frank Ryan, that film's director, said of Bobby, "He has a fabulous memory and an innate ability to hold his own in scenes with established stars. Oh, I know that people insist kids can steal scenes from the greater actors in Hollywood, but if they don't have it on the ball, they're out of luck." Miss Loy stated, "He has so much charm. If Don Ameche and I aren't on our toes all the time, we know that the audience will be looking at the youngster and ignoring us. That's bad in this business." Don Ameche took a great liking to the boy and spent a good deal of offcamera time with him. "He's got a great talent," said Ameche, "I've worked with a lot of child players in my time, but none of them bore the promise that seems inherent in young Driscoll. Moreover, he works at his job, doesn't loaf and disappear between scenes. I think he will go far."

He did go far—for a time. At age nine, he became the first human actor ever signed to a contract by Walt Disney. He and little Luana Patten became known as Disney's "sweetheart team." They co-starred in *Song of the South* (1946) and, later, in *So Dear to My Heart* (1948). *Song of the South* was the first occasion on which Disney incorporated live action with his animated characters. It was a real thrill, especially for children, to see cartoon animals talking to real people. Audiences loved it. There were some outcries in later years that the film depicted racial bias and, therefore, it was not released again until 1972.

At one point during his Disney years, Driscoll went to Los Angeles Supreme Court to have his three-hundred-dollar weekly salary court approved. The young breadwinner announced, "I'm going to save my money and go to college, then become a G-Man."

Regarding his performance in the endearing *So Dear to My Heart,* the *New York World-Telegram* offered, "Bobby Driscoll impetuously swarms through his share of the picture and fills it with the eager charm of an idealized childhood." Bobby's own childhood was not quite as ideal, however. He suffered from too little discipline and too much adulation. "The other kids didn't accept me," he later complained ruefully, "They treated me as one apart."

Then came his huge screen success in *The Window,* and next he played Jim Hawkins to Robert Newton's Long John Silver in Disney's remake of *Treasure Island* (1950). Many agreed that Bobby's boyish lead was a far more engaging characterization than the too precious performance by Jackie Cooper in the 1934 MGM film of the Robert Louis Stevenson classic.

By now, Driscoll was in his early teens and screen work was growing scarce for him. He played a boy who runs away from home in *When I Grow up* (1951), and was a teenager in *The Happy Time* (1952), a domestic comedy about a French-Canadian family; but that was only one film a year. Likewise, he did only one picture in 1953 and it was to be his final foray for Disney. He was the voice and image model for the cartoon title character in *Peter Pan*. Suddenly, Bobby found that he was no longer needed in films. Had George Stevens produced *Shane* (1953) a few years earlier, Bobby would have been wonderful as the rancher's boy, played by the late Brandon De Wilde.

In 1954, an acne-prone Bobby did only two television programs, a "Loretta Young Show" and a "Fireside Theatre." His teenage social life was also difficult. "I really feared people," he later told a reporter. "I tried desperately to be one of the gang. When they rejected me, I fought back, became belligerent and cocky and was afraid all the time." His career picked up a bit in 1955 when he returned to the screen as Cornel Wilde's young sidekick in MGM's *The Scarlet Coat,* but it was only a brief part. He also played the boy in the television adaptation of *Ah, Wilderness!* for CBS. This part was one among a number of video roles which all failed to establish him in any new adult mold.

When Bobby was only sixteen he began smoking marijuana and using harder drugs; by the following year was addicted to heroin. In 1956 he was arrested

With Paul Stewart in The Window *(RKO 1949)*

on narcotics charges and was also suspected of being a trafficker in drugs. The narcotics charge against him was eventually dropped. He lied at the time to the press, "It's ridiculous. I've never had any marijuana in my life." By 1957, it seemed as if he were straightening out his personal life, and he even tried for a film comeback. He was determined to succeed as an adult actor, but even though he was twenty years old he would still play younger roles because of his baby face. "I want to continue as an actor. After all, it's what I'm best qualified to do," he said. "It gives me the most satisfiaction and I think I can give more to society and humanity by acting than I can doing anything else." He even joined the Drama Study Group in Hollywood and appeared in a low budget juvenile delinquency drama, *The Party Crashers* (1958) with Connie Stevens, using the name Robert instead of Bobby. Like another has-been player in the picture, Frances Farmer, who was vainly struggling to reaffirm a place in the movie business, Bobby would never make another film.

Driscoll, on the professional outs with Hollywood, later married a girl named Marjorie, had a son, and worked at odd jobs such as a gas station attendant and as a clothing salesman. But he failed at these jobs. It was very difficult for him when people recognized him, especially people connected with show business. It was also very embarrassing to these people who remembered him or had worked with him. Bobby remarked, "I've worked in gas stations before, but there's no real hard luck story to it. I won't say I can't use the money because who can't." He also swore that his own children would never be allowed to become actors. When he was asked about his own movie childhood, he snapped, "I blanked out that part of my life. I have found that memories aren't very useful." When his wife divorced him, Driscoll found himself once more battling his drug addiction.

In 1959, he was again arrested on narcotics charges. When needle marks were found on both his arms, he was jailed as an addict. In 1961 he was arrested for burglarizing an animal clinic and taking $450.00. Bobby called it a "bum beef." He did plead guilty, though, to forging a forty-five-dollar check which he tried cashing at a liquor store. Finally, he entered California's Chino Penitentiary for drug addiction. He remained there for over a year and upon release found work as a carpenter until his parole was relinquished in 1964 and he could leave California, hopefully to forget his past successes and failures. His mother said, "Bob washed his hands of his family and the movie industry and left for New York in hopes of getting work."

Other than his attempts to see some agents and producers, very little else is known about Bobby's life in New York, but it was probably his own hell on earth. "Bobby called us once and said he was having a hard time getting work," his mother later recalled. "None of the studios in New York would hire him because he had once been on drugs."

Bobby Driscoll died in New York at age thirty-one, alone and unmourned. He was found on March 30, 1968, in an abandoned tenement in Greenwich Village. His body was discovered by children playing in the ruins. He was penniless, without identification, and was buried in a New York pauper's grave. Nobody recognized him or claimed his body. His cause of death was "occlusive coronary arterio-sclerosis," or hardening of the arteries, which is common to long-time heroin users. No needle marks or drugs were found on him, but beside the body were two empty beer bottles and some religious pamphlets. His parents had heard from him only on the rarest of occasions, by phone, but had not seen him since he left California. When Cletus Driscoll became seriously ill in 1968, he had a desire to see his only son again. Bobby's mother tried endlessly to reach him in New York but could not locate him. Mr. Driscoll died on October 9, 1968, never again seeing his son or knowing that he, himself, had outlived him. Mrs. Driscoll finally took her plight to the F.B.I. and even asked the Walt Disney Studio for help in locating her son. Some time later, she received a letter from a Los Angeles County agency stating that her son was dead. His identity was traced through his fingerprints. When *Song of the South* was re-released in 1972 all this information became publicized and those who remembered the adorable little tyke on the big screen were stunned and saddened. His mother responded that she was delighted *Song of the South* was being re-issued, but "it's painful to see him there on the screen. He was such a fine boy."

Obviously, Bobby found it difficult to fit into society. He called himself an introvert and said that "most addicts are. I'm not really sure why I started using narcotics," he admitted on one occasion. "I was 17 [actually, 16] when I first experimented with the stuff. In no time at all I was using whatever was available . . . mostly heroin, because I had the money to pay for it." The boy who was so dear to so many hearts wrote his own epitaph when he ruefully concluded, "I was carried on a satin cushion and then dropped into the garbage can."

BOBBY DRISCOLL

Lost Angel   *(MGM 1943)*
The Sullivans   *(20th 1944)*
Sunday Dinner for a Soldier   *(20th 1944)*
The Big Bonanza   *(Rep 1945)*
Identity Unknown   *(Rep 1945)*
Miss Susie Slagle's   *(Par 1945)*
From this Day Forward   *(RKO 1946)*
So Goes My Love   *(Univ 1946)*
O.S.S.   *(Par 1946)*
Song of the South   *(RKO 1946)*

If You Knew Susie   *(RKO 1948)*
So Dear to My Heart   *(RKO 1948)*
The Window   *(RKO 1949)*
Treasure Island   *(RKO 1950)*
When I Grow Up   *(EL 1951)*
The Happy Time   *(Col 1952)*
Peter Pan   *(RKO 1953)* (Cartoon voice and image)
The Scarlet Coat   *(MGM 1955)*
The Party Crashers   *(Par 1958)*

29

Dan Duryea

Through most of his Hollywood career, nasal mono-tone-voiced Dan Duryea was a typecast staple of the film industry. Beginning with his first screen role, as the weasel-like nephew in Samuel Goldwyn's *The Little Foxes* (1941), he ran the gamut of playing un-scrupulous, selfish characters (*Mrs. Parkington,* 1944, *The Valley of Decision,* 1945, *Another Part of the Forest,* 1948), gangsters (*Ball of Fire,* 1941, *Larceny,* 1948, *Criss Cross,* 1949), blackmailers (*The Woman in the Window,* 1944), *Too Late for Tears,* 1949), pimps (*Scarlet Street,* 1945); murderers, outlaws, thiefs, and just plain crooks. Duryea, himself, once stated, ''It's a darn good living and my fan mail goes up everytime I tee off on a girl. I love to do comedy and straight dramatic parts but it's silly to turn down a really good heavy part. It pays well and the audiences remember the killer a lot longer than they do the hero.''

By 1948 Duryea was earning over one hundred thousand dollars a year; but the previous year a new actor appeared onscreen, portraying a maniacal gangster. He was blond, as was Duryea, and he was physically more attractive. He had what appeared to be a greater acting range and his first movie part was a tour-de-force. His performance dimmed anything Duryea had done or would do in the villainy depart-ment. The actor was Richard Widmark and the mo-tion picture was *Kiss of Death* (1947).

The slim, six-foot-one Duryea was born in White Plains, New York, on January 23, 1907, to Richard Hewlett Duryea, a textile salesman, and his wife Ma-bel. Young Dan was a member of the drama club at White Plains High School and majored in English at Cornell University. In his senior year at Cornell, he succeeded Franchot Tone as president of their drama society. After graduation he did not venture into pro-fessional theatre; instead, he became a man in a gray flannel suit. He decided the advertising field would be a safer way to make a living. Through a commuter acquaintance he met Helen Bryan and they were married on April 15, 1932. Duryea lasted only about six years in the hectic advertising profession, because he suffered a heart attack. If it had not been for that, he might never have became an actor.

In 1935, after some insignificant summer stock jobs (one of which paid only five dollars a week), Duryea contacted a Cornell classmate, Sidney Kingsley, whose new play *Dead End* was being produced that season on Broadway. Kingsley made sure that Dan received a bit part in the show and he played it for eighty-five weeks at forty dollars a week. Toward the end of the play's run he was elevated to the lead role, Gimpy the crippled architect. ''From that time on I never had to worry about a job,'' Duryea admitted. He then appeared on Broadway in *Missouri Legend* (1938) as Bob Ford, that ''dirty little coward who shot

With William Trenk, Ella Raines, and Richard Gaines in White Tie and Tails *(Univ 1946)*

With Howard Duff in Johnny Stool Pigeon *(Univ 1949)*

Mr. Howard and laid poor Jesse James in his grave." The play lasted only six weeks, even though it had an unusually strong cast: Dean Jagger as Jesse, Dorothy Gish, Mildred Natwick, Karl Malden, and Jose Ferrer.

Then came the play that took him to Hollywood. It was Lillian Hellman's *The Little Foxes* (1939), starring Tallulah Bankhead. Miss Hellman and the play's director, Herman Shumlin, saw Duryea as Bob Ford in *Missouri Legend* and agreed he would be right for the role of Leo Hubbard, a part quite similar to that of Bob Ford. Years later, Duryea stated, "I wish I could once again have Lillian Hellman's words come out of my mouth. I haven't had words like those or scenes like those since then. As for Tallulah Bankhead, she is fantastically the greatest woman I've ever known." He played Leo for the play's entire Broadway run (410 performances) and then toured with it for another year. He received consistently fine notices. Sam Goldwyn bought the screen rights to *The Little Foxes* and hired Duryea to recreate his role with Bette Davis in the lead.

Once in Hollywood, Duryea never appeared on the Broadway stage again. In 1963 he was to be in the Broadway production of *A Case of Libel*, but never opened in it, since his differences with director Sam Wanamaker resulted in his leaving the cast after a week's rehearsal. At the time, Duryea was quoted as saying, "I wanted to use Broadway so I could make more money in the movies." Appearing in a hit Broadway show would certainly have helped his sagging career at that time.

The Little Foxes movie was the beginning of a lucrative, if unsensational, screen career. "That picture started me off on the road to hell as a bad man, and ever since then, I've been portraying the most hateful screen characters you can think of. The trouble is that when producers think of me, they invariably say, 'Here's a guy who's been a louse for years. What else can he be but a bad guy?'" Duryea's few professional departures into the realm of "nice guy" were not memorable experiences.

Sam Goldwyn continued to hire Duryea after *The Little Foxes*. He cast him as a gangster in Billy Wilder's *Ball of Fire* (1941), starring Gary Cooper and Barbara Stanwyck, and as the cynical reporter in *Pride of the Yankees* (1942), in which Gary Cooper was sterling as disease-plagued ball player Lou Gehrig. Duryea's telling performance in the latter film should have proven to producers that he was capable of delivering a witty line and equally capable of displaying subtlety. However, the moviemakers felt that subtlety was not his strong selling point, whereas his sneer was, what with the accompanying flat voice, his taut lips, and mocking glances. In 1943, freelancing Dur-

yea was given a sympathetic role in the war drama *Sahara* in which Humphrey Bogart and his British-American fighting unit are stranded in the desert. "*Sahara*," Duryea would later reflect, "is a picture which practically nobody remembers my being in; one of the few pictures I didn't play a heel and maybe for that reason." The following year he was a denizen of London's East End in Clifford Odets' *None But the Lonely Heart*, in which Cary Grant went dramatic and tried to outdo the theatrics of Ethel Barrymore. She won an Oscar; Grant did not.

It is most likely that three films which Duryea made in the mid-1940s secured his position in Hollywood and with the fickle public. The first was *The Woman in the Window* (1944), directed by Fritz Lang and starring a revitalized Joan Bennett and always dependable Edward G. Robinson. The *New York Times* reported, "Dan Duryea is so good in the role of the blackmailer that you feel like actually hissing him." The second film was *Scarlet Street* (1945), also directed by Lang, and again, starring Bennett and Robinson. Here, Duryea played a pimp in cahoots with low-lifer Bennett; Robinson was the timid, unrecognized artist. Duryea urges her to drain the poor guy of his money, driving Robinson to larceny and embezzlement. Then they steal his paintings and sell them as Bennett's own work. Said the *New York Times*, "Only Dan Duryea hits a proper and credible stride, making a vicious and serpentine creature out of a cheap, chiseling tinhorn off the streets." It was in this picture that Duryea belted Joan Bennett, and his fan mail promptly doubled. Women moviegoers endorsed his ungentlemanly onscreen behavior, in which he blew smoke in her face, rifled through her handbag for loose change, and explored the cache of her powder compact for the five dollars she was hiding. Here was a vicious woman being put down by an equally unpalatable character. Hardly a charming or dashing villain, Duryea was playing a slimy and obnoxious creature. It was to be the peak of his movie career. The other film, also released in 1945, guaranteed Duryea's post as Hollywood's resident bad guy In *Along Came Jones*, a not very funny comedy-western, Duryea shoots Gary Cooper. Of course, he does not kill the hero, but what could be worse than plugging good old 'Coop'? Heroine Loretta Young saves Coop in the nick of time, by shooting Duryea right between the eyes. Said one New York reviewer, "Duryea is as ugly as a snake in the role of the slick and fast-shooting evildoer."

Now at his cinema peak, Duryea signed a long-term, exclusive contract with Universal. His first film for that studio was *Lady on a Train* (1945), with the inestimable Deanna Durbin, followed by *Scarlet*

190

Street. Most of his films at this studio were routine melodramas or routine westerns. However, he did one very routine comedy, *White Tie and Tails* (1946) with Ella Raines, because the studio felt that audiences were so used to his being an oncamera wrongdoer that the plots of the films became predictable as soon as he strolled into view. Duryea wanted to do comedy. He put it this way, "If I can make the switch successfully it'll be as good as a twenty year annuity. Audiences get tired of a face fast enough without that face looking the same in the same kind of parts all the time." The comic premise of the film (butler Duryea pretends to be the master of the house) did not work, and the experiment with Duryea's career was quickly forgotten.

Occasionally, Duryea did get a meaty role, but, of course, each one involved him in his old milieu. In *Another Part of the Forest* (1948), he was again playing one of the Hubbards from *The Little Foxes.* This time he was Oscar Hubbard in Lillian Hellman's earlier generation drama. He was also in a top acting company in this stately drama: Fredric March, Florence Eldridge, Edmond O'Brien, Betsy Blair, and Ann Blyth. As good as Duryea was, March and Eldridge commanded the attention and rightfully so.

In 1949, Dan played one of his nastiest villains in *Criss Cross*, with Yvonne De Carlo and Burt Lancas-ter. By this point De Carlo and Duryea were somewhat of a team, having appeared together in three films in two years, the others being *Black Bart* (1948) and *River Lady* (1948). His performance in *Criss Cross* is undeniably one of his best. At the end of the film he kills both De Carlo and Lancaster and then is done in himself.

His film roles away from Universal were no better. In 1948 his contract with Universal was revised. He would do one picture annually for them for the next four years and be able to freelance at other studios. He played a crooked private investigator in Dorothy Lamour's *Manhandled* (1949) at Paramount. He hits Lamour in this one and attempts to throw her off a roof. "It's not enough that I twice punch the lady in the jaw and want to throw her off the roof, but I run along the edge looking for a straight drop to make sure that there is no fire escape or other obstruction to break her fall." He was teamed with a much tougher babe, Lizabeth Scott, in *Too Late for Tears* (1949). He blackmails her and she, in turn, poisons him. He had the title role in *Al Jennings of Oklahoma* (1951), the true-life saga of the train robber who was eventually pardoned by Teddy Roosevelt. Al Jennings, himself, lived to see the film and, reportedly, liked it very much.

The film that Duryea liked best in this busy period

With Peter Lorre, Broderick Crawford, and June Vincent in The Black Angel *(Univ 1946)*

of his career was *Chicago Calling* (1951), a little drama about a man whose estranged wife and daughter have been injured in a car crash and who is desperately trying to reach them via long distance telephone. This was the closest Duryea ever came to having a tour-de-force part, but it was a small film that never became a big-time audience pleaser. Back at Universal he was Jimmy Stewart's pal in *Thunder Bay* (1953) ("I'm legal and almost likeable this time"), and in *Foxfire* (1955), which united busty Jane Russell with well-muscled Jeff Chandler, Dan was an inebriated medic. He emerged as the only stable item in this otherwise pretty dreadful love story.

In 1952, television called, but it was not a redemption for Duryea, because he was still very busy with feature filmmaking. Instead, it was an additional outlet to ply his craft. He did several guest spots on the "Schlitz Playhouse of Stars" and was then offered his own series, "The Adventures of China Smith" for ABC. He filmed twenty-six half-hour segments and the show was a lucrative enterprise for him. In 1955, he filmed another twenty-six segments playing the same title character in "The New Adventures of China Smith." In the former series he played an Irish soldier of fortune in a Far East locale; in the later segments the scene was shifted to the San Francisco area. From 1955 onward, Duryea was a very active television performer, appearing in over seventy-five shows. He guest-starred on many anthology series, western shows, adventure programs, and even on a few situation comedies, including "December Bride" in 1955. He was a guest on NBC's "Wagon Train" at least seven times. For "G. E. Theatre" in 1957 he portrayed a simple backwoodsman in *The Road that Led Afar* and received an Emmy nomination.

In the mid-1950s, Hollywood provided Duryea with a few more change-of-pace assignments. He was the good brother to Cornel Wilde's bad one in *Storm Fear* (1955). In *Battle Hymn* (1956) he was the comic relief. This film was the true story of Colonel Dean Hess, played by Rock Hudson, who rescued thousands of war orphans in Korea. "You should see me in this picture," Duryea told the press at the time, "I'm a real sweet guy. The cigar smoking sergeant is the best role I've had in a long time, comic and sympathetic for a change; I'm a good character in this picture. They say my pictures don't make money unless I am a menace to society, but I'll bet on *Battle Hymn* being a boxoffice winner. They'll have to do a lot of convincing now to get me to play a bad guy again." The convincing must have been good, or at least the money was, for he then was seen as a jewel thief in *The Burglar* (1957), a train robber in *Night Passage* (1957), a racketeer lawyer in *Slaughter on Tenth Avenue* (1957), and, later on, as the evil head

of a military school in MGM's puerile *Platinum High School* (1960).

During this active filmmaking period, Duryea commented, "New villains are coming along all the time and I figure most people are beginning to get tired of the old faces like mine." But there was no villain to replace Duryea onscreen because he was unique.

The early 1950s brought Jack Palance and Lyle Bettger to the screen, but as good as they were in their nasty roles, they lacked the special combination of the weakness and vulnerability that was at the heart of Duryea's people. Bettger came closest to emulating the Duryea figure. He was blond, tight-lipped, killed with a sneer, and could die like a coward. As for Richard Widmark, he had decided that he preferred a career as bad good guys rather than good bad guys.

In 1958, Universal cast Duryea against type in a little gem of a movie called *Kathy O*. He played an harassed publicity agent assigned to promote a movie star brat, played by Patty McCormack of *The Bad Seed* fame. Dan's non-subtle performance came in handy in this captivating comedy drama. *Kathy O* would be his last decent film until he did the prestigious *The Flight of the Phoenix* (1965) with James Stewart, for director Robert Aldrich. He was one of the distraught passengers in this plane crash-in-the-desert drama.

In between these two pictures, he was only in minor westerns such as *Taggart* (1964), *He Rides Tall* (1964), and *The Bounty Killer* (1965). However, he did manage to keep to his famous image. In *He Rides Tall,* Indians come and demand his bride-to-be (Jo Morrow) and he replies quite simply, "I guess this is goodbye, Honey," and they scalp her right in front of him.

After the Aldrich film, which was more of an artistic than commercial venture, Duryea did a spaghetti western entitled *The Hills Run Red* (1967), and a cameo part in an international co-production, *Five Golden Dragons* (1967). His final theatrical feature was just about his worst, the inept *The Bamboo Saucer* (1968). In 1967, he appeared in two television feature films for NBC, *Stranger on the Run* with Henry Fonda, and *Winchester '73*. The latter, with Tom Tryon and John Saxon, was a remake of the well-remembered film Duryea had done with James Stewart for Universal back in 1950. Dan, now so much older, did not recreate his original role. Unexpectedly, he showed up in the recurring role of wandering confidence man Eddie Jacks in ABC's highly successful nightime soap opera, "Peyton Place." It was to be his last acting role.

Helen Duryea, Dan's wife of thirty-five years, died on January 21, 1967, of a heart ailment. They had two sons: Peter, born in 1939, and Richard, born in

1942. Both boys were born on July 14th. Peter is an actor and appeared with his father in *Taggart* and *The Bounty Killer*. Richard is a talent manager. Duryea would not allow his sons to see many of his movies when they were children. He did not want them to think of him as "the guy who took pot shots at Gary Cooper."

Duryea was a soft-spoken family man. The tight-lipped sneer was for public consumption only. Publicity agents always made mention that his real-life personality was quite the opposite from his screen personality. He lived a quiet life on his well-manicured estate in the Hollywood Hills or at his summer place at Lake Arrowhead. He enjoyed gardening and boating, and participated in many community functions.

When his boys were in school he joined the PTA, showed films for his sons' friends, and was scoutmaster. Occasionally in public places, some smart aleck would demand proof of his toughness. Duryea stated, "When I can't smile my way out of a fight, I usually run like hell in the other direction, but, now and then, I've had to flatten a wise guy to protect my reputation as a heel."

Duryea died of cancer on June 7, 1968. He had undergone surgery for a malignancy several months before. He is buried at Forest Lawn Memorial Park and left his six-figure estate to his two sons. Peter has stated, "I think Dad was secretly glad someone was going to carry on the name in the profession."

DAN DURYEA

The Little Foxes   *(RKO 1941)*
Ball of Fire   *(RKO 1941)*
Pride of the Yankees   *(RKO 1942)*
That Other Woman   *(20th 1942)*
Sahara   *(Col 1943)*
Man from Frisco   *(Rep 1944)*
Mrs. Parkington   *(MGM 1944)*
Ministry of Fear   *(Par 1944)*
None But the Lonely Heart   *(RKO 1944)*
The Woman in the Window   *(RKO 1944)*
Main Street After Dark   *(MGM 1944)*
The Great Flamarion   *(Rep 1945)*
The Valley of Decision   *(MGM 1945)*
Along Came Jones   *(RKO 1945)*
Lady on a Train   *(Univ 1945)*
Scarlet Street   *(Univ 1945)*
The Black Angel   *(Univ 1946)*
White Tie and Tails   *(Univ 1946)*
Black Bart   *(Univ 1948)*
River Lady   *(Univ 1948)*
Larceny   *(Univ 1948)*
Another Part of the Forest   *(Univ 1948)*
Criss Cross   *(Univ 1949)*
Manhandled   *(Par 1949)*
Johnny Stool Pigeon   *(Univ 1949)*
Too Late for Tears   *(UA 1949)*
One Way Street   *(Univ 1950)*
Winchester '73   *(Univ 1950)*
The Underworld Story   *(UA 1950)*
Al Jennings of Oklahoma   *(Col 1951)*

Chicago Calling   *(UA 1951)*
Thunder Bay   *(Univ 1953)*
Sky Commando   *(Col 1953)*
Terror Street   *(Lip 1953)*
World For Ransom   *(AA 1954)*
Ride Clear of Diablo   *(Univ 1954)*
Rails into Laramie   *(Univ 1954)*
Silver Lode   *(RKO 1954)*
This Is My Love   *(RKO 1954)*
The Marauders   *(MGM 1955)*
Foxfire   *(Univ 1955)*
Storm Fear   *(UA 1955)*
Battle Hymn   *(Univ 1956)*
Night Passage   *(Univ 1957)*
The Burglar   *(Col 1957)*
Slaughter on Tenth Avenue   *(Univ 1957)*
Kathy O   *(Univ 1958)*
Platinum High School   *(MGM 1960)*
Six Black Horses   *(Univ 1962)*
He Rides Tall   *(Univ 1964)*
Walk a Tightrope   *(Par 1964)*
Taggart   *(Univ 1964)*
Do You Know This Voice?   *(British Lion 1964)*
The Bounty Killer   *(Emb 1965)*
The Flight of the Phoenix   *(20th 1965)*
Incident at Phantom Hill   *(Univ 1966)*
The Hills Run Red (a.k.a., A River of Dollars)   *(UA—Italian 1967)*
Five Golden Dragons   *(Commonwealth United 1967)*
The Bamboo Saucer (a.k.a., Collision Course)   *(World Entertainment 1968)*

30

Wild Bill Elliott

Few of the legendary heroes of the Old West have received greater coverage in the fantasy-fact-fictional history of the American West than James Butler Hickok. A Union scout and spy, he had killed a traitorous federal soldier in Springfield, Missouri, a year before becoming United States Marshal at Fort Riley, Kansas. He acquired the nickname "Wild Bill" ten years before when, as a stagecoach driver over the rugged Santa Fe Trail, he killed a ferocious bear with a Bowie knife in the Raton Pass. For a year, Hickok toured the East with Buffalo Bill's Wild West Show, and on August 2, 1876, Jack McCall, a minor desperado seeking fame in reflected glory, shot Hickok in the back in Deadwood in the Dakota Territory. The colorful, handsome, quite mannered Hickok's life was ended before he reached the age of forty, and McCall's murderous feat attained a place in the same historical niche as "the dirty little coward who shot Mr. Howard"—Bob Ford. But Hickok's life and adventures enflamed the imagination of writers and provided the screen with many interpretations of "Wild Bill," none more successful than a rangy, six-foot-two man named William "Wild Bill" Elliott, who became the matinee idol of kiddies and adventure-loving adults in the 1940s.

Elliott was born Gordon Nance on his father's ranch near Pattonsburg, Missouri, on October 15, 1903. When he was ten years old, his father, Roy

Nance, became an agent-commission man at the famous Kansas City stockyards, a favorite meeting place for range riders of the West. It was from them that young Gordon learned bronco busting, roping, and how to ride a horse as expertly as the cowboys who taught him. At age sixteen he was competing in rodeo contests; he took top place in the American Royal Horse and Livestock Show and won first place in competition with the men who taught him rodeo riding. He spent six years working rodeos, during which time he graduated from high school and attended Rockingham College.

It was his admiration for William S. Hart, whom he first saw on the screen at the age of nine, which most influenced Gordon's career. Reports claim that his mother told him a fortune teller had predicted he would be a film star, so, with his desire to emulate Hart, Gordon trekked to Hollywood and soon joined the Pasadena Community Playhouse. A talent scout spotted Gordon, changed his name to Gordon Elliott, and got him a bit part as a dancer in *The Plastic Age* (1925), in which Gilbert Roland and Clark Gable also had bits. Gordon continued to work onstage and to do occasional small roles in films. He had the nominal lead in *The Private Life of Helen of Troy* (1927) and a featured role in *Western Society* (1928) for Fox, in which he played the part of Roy Schyler, the polo-playing brother of Dorothy Sebastian, whose Santa Barbara polo team wins against great odds when Tom Mix and his famous horse, Tony, rescue the game.

With George "Gabby" Hayes in Calling Wild Bill Elliott *(Rep 1943)*

Elliott continued to work in the film industry, taking jobs as they came along. He primarily played bit parts or extras and hardly ever received billing. His stage training at Pasadena, where he continued to study, held him in good stead when the talkies emerged, but fame was elusive, although work seemed to be steady. Among his early talking roles were the part of George Halloway in Columbia's musical *Broadway Scandals* (1929), a minor role as Dorothy Mackaill's boyfriend in First National's dismal sound version of William Vaughn Moody's *The Great Divide* (1930), and as one of a number of house guests involved in murder in RKO's *The Midnight Mystery* (1930) starring Betty Compson.

During the early years of the talkies Elliott jumped from major studio to poverty row for work, but the parts dwindled to such a low level as a dance extra, in *City Streets* (1931) and in *Merrily We Go to Hell* (1932), both Paramount releases. The humiliation of such work, after nominal leads and feature roles in the late 1920s, must have been great. Still, Elliott kept at his trade and it must have been lucrative enough to have kept him from losing the optimism needed to believe in the nearness of stardom.

By 1932, Gordon had the security of a Warner Bros.' stock contract which kept him continually active in dozens of bit parts for the next five years, with

occasional loanouts to other studios. He also turned up in the genre he loved best, westerns, in a couple of Dick Foran sagebrush entries as the villain. He also went to Twentieth Century-Fox in 1937 to support Smith Ballew in *Roll Along Cowboy.*

Stardom finally came, however, in 1938 when Columbia Pictures, like Republic, known for casting new faces in serial leads, cast Elliott as the star of the fifteen-episode chapter-play, *The Great Adventures of Wild Bill Hickok* with Gordon taking the opportunity to emulate his idol William S. Hart. Hart had portrayed the famed westerner in Paramount's *Wild Bill Hickok*(1923), and the legendary lawman returned to the screen over the years played by J. Farrell Mac-Donald (*The Last Frontier*), Gary Cooper (*The Plainsman*), Roy Rogers (*The Young Bill Hickok*), Richard Dix (*Badlands of Dakota*), Bruce Cabot (*Wild Bill Hickok Rides Again*), Robert Culp (*The Raiders*), and Don Murray in the remake of *The Plainsman;* Howard Keel became a singing Hickok in *Calamity Jane,* and on TV, Guy Madison would find a new career as Wild Bill.

The success of the serial, *The Great Adventures of Wild Bill Hickok,* with a supporting cast that included Monte Blue, Frankie Darro, Kermit Maynard, and Chief Thundercloud, prompted Columbia to sign Elliott as their top western star and to rush him into

With Linda Stirling and LeRoy Mason in The San Antonio Kid *(Rep 1944)*

196

With Andy Clyde, Vera Ralston, and Gail Patrick in The Plainsman and the Lady *(Rep 1946)*

another, less successful and more hastily conceived serial, *Overland with Kit Carson* (1939). By this time he was being billed as Bill Elliott and Columbia soon teamed him with popular Tex Ritter in a series of well-paced, lively features. In the studio's hastily made horse operas, Elliott was soon established as a first-rate western star; he stayed with features after one more serial, *The Valley of Missing Men* (1942), with Slim Summerville as his sidekick, Missouri.

Republic next signed Elliott, now billed as "Wild Bill" Elliott for a series of B outdoor films co-starring George "Gabby" Hayes and Anne Jeffreys. Despite the competition of such on-the-lot stars as Roy Rogers and Gene Autry, Elliott had the advantage of an ingratiating personality, a sincere acting style, and an ability to read lines convincingly. Along with his expert horsemanship and daredevil stunting (although he was frequently doubled by Tom Steele), these qualities insured Elliott's position in the annual list of top ten cowboy stars at the boxoffice, a post he maintained for fourteen consecutive years.

His first Republic release was *Calling Wild Bill Elliott* (1943), but his greatest success came the following year when studio president Herbert J. Yates selected him to portray Fred Harmon's comic strip hero, Red Ryder. Four years earlier Republic had produced a serial based on the character with Donald

"Red" Barry who finally rebelled as being typed as "Red," but to whom the tag would cling for his entire film career despite the fact that he was not a redhead. The Elliott-Red Ryder series began with *Tucson Raiders* (1944), with fine character actress Alice Fleming as the Duchess and Bobby Blake as Little Beaver, Red's constant sidekick. (The three appeared in all sixteen Red Ryder films and Blake outdistanced the series to appear in later years as the cold-blooded murderer in *In Cold Blood,* 1968, and to give excellent performances in *Tell Them Willie Boy Is Here,* 1970, and *Busting,* 1974. The Elliott series films were action-packed and flavorful with their contingent of Republic supporting players, but after the second production season, Elliott was moved to A productions and Allan "Rocky" Lane took over the Red Ryder role.

Contrary to popular belief, Elliott was quite happy playing Red Ryder and he did not take kindly to being chosen over Randolph Scott for the lead in the Joseph Kane-directed *In Old Sacramento* (1946). The increase in salary, however, and a better opportunity to play a William S. Hart-type character, changed his mind. In fact at the end of *In Old Sacramento,* Elliott was shot and killed onscreen, a shock to his young fans, but certainly a throwback to the Hart westerns of the 1910s.

Elliott, now billed as William Elliott for Republic's class A productions, succeeded quite well in portraying the "good-bad-man" made famous by Hart. Although Hart portrayed the West as it was, austere and without frills, Elliott's westerns did have a streamlined look, but he kept as close to Hart's formula as he could without turning off the post-war audiences who had long been fed on the pseudo-westerns of Gene Autry, Roy Rogers and countless other cowboys whose concepts of the old West were without much merit or substance.

Wearing well-tailored costumes, colorful without being ostentatious, Elliott's deadpan, no-nonsense acting certainly approached his idol, and for a time Elliott tried, without success, to convince Republic to star him in a picture about Hart's exciting life. The actor did, have a trademark which would no doubt have given Hart great pause, that of guns reversed in their holsters. That trademark, along with his famous tag line, "I'm a peaceable man, but . . ." made Elliott a great favorite with both adult and youth audiences of the late 1940s. Republic was pumping plenty of money, and perhaps unfortunately putting Vera Ralston into the star's pictures. By 1948 Bill formed his own production company with Dorrell and Stuart McGowan, and, subsequently, produced two of his starring features, *Hellfire* (1948), in color, and *The Showdown* (1950).

Unfortunately, Elliott appeared on the scene too late as a western star to maintain an audience hold as did John Wayne or Randolph Scott. With the encroachment of television, his popularity began to fade and he moved to the Monogram/Allied Artists fold where he did his last sixteen films: Eleven westerns and five detective thrillers. For this last series, he reverted back to Bill Elliott for billing purposes.

Bill's Monogram westerns certainly held up better than most of the B competition of the period, and *Topeka* (1953) compares favorably to William S. Hart's *The Return of Draw Egan* (1916); both have the theme of an outlaw reformed by the love of a good woman, a premise which was a favorite of both cinema stars. As the 1950s progressed budgets became more stringent and scripts, in turn, suffered. After *Vigilante Terror* (1954), Bill spent his last three years onscreen in modern-dress detective films, culminating with *Footsteps in the Night* (1957), which offered him as a police lieutenant on the track of a killer.

Retiring from the screen, Bill spent most of his time on his Las Vegas ranch with his wife and daughter, Barbara. He had married Helen Josephine Myer, a one-time model and hostess at I. Magnin's Shop in 1927. He also hosted a local "Western Theatre" video program, showing some of his old features (*a la* Tim McCoy and Max Terhune). Bill also was a TV spokesman for a national cigarette firm and was involved in several TV projects, including the lead in an unsold video series pilot, "The Marshal of Trail City."

Gordon Nance, alias William, Bill, and "Wild Bill" Elliott, died of cancer on November 26, 1965, at his Las Vegas ranch. He left behind his second wife, Dolly Moore (his first marriage ended in divorce in 1961) and millions of fans.

Of all the western stars in the post-1920s period, William Elliott certainly must rank as one of the best. His realistic approach to the Old West was in sharp contrast to the slick, shallow westerns of the singing cowboys and their countless imitators which glutted and eventually destroyed the B western film market. Unlike most western players, Elliott did manage to appear in adult fare, which were generally well-made and usually a credit to their genre. That he survived as a western star for two decades is proof of the popularity and believability of Elliott's characterizations.

GORDON "WILD BILL" ELLIOTT

The Plastic Age (B. P. Schulberg 1925)
Napoleon Jr. (Fox 1926)
The Drop Kick (FN 1927)
The Private Life of Helen of Troy (FN 1927)
The Arizona Wildcat (Fox 1928)
Beyond London's Lights (FBO 1928)
The Passion Song (Excellent 1928)
Restless Youth (Col 1928)
Broadway Scandals (Col 1929)
She Couldn't Say No (WB 1930)
Sunny (FN 1930)
The Midnight Mystery (RKO 1930)
The Great Divide (FN 1930)
City Streets (Par 1931)
Delicious (Fox 1931)

The Magnificent Lie (Par 1931)
Palmy Days (UA 1931)
Convicted (Artclass 1931)
Merrily We Go to Hell (Par 1932)
Lady with a Past (RKO 1932)
Night After Night (Par 1931)
One Hour With You (Par 1932)
Vanity Fair (Hollywood Exchange 1932)
The Rich Are Always With Us (FN 1932)
Jewel Robbery (WB 1932)
Crooner (FN 1932)
Private Detective 62 (WB 1933)
The Keyhole (WB 1933)
Gold Diggers of 1933 (WB 1933)
The Little Giant (FN 1933)

Twenty Million Sweethearts   *(FN 1934)*
Case of the Howling Dog   *(WB 1934)*
Here Comes the Navy   *(WB 1934)*
Registered Nurse   *(FN 1934)*
A Modern Hero   *(WB 1934)*
Wonder Bar   *(FB 1934)*
Gold Diggers of 1935   *(FN 1935)*
G-Men   *(WB 1935)*
Doctor Socrates   *(WB 1935)*
Moonlight on the Prairie   *(WB 1935)*
Dangerous   *(WB 1935)*
Broadway Hostess   *(FB 1935)*
Secret Bride   *(WB 1935)*
Devil Dogs of the Air   *(WB 1935)*
Go Into Your Dance   *(FN 1935)*
A Night at the Ritz   *(WB 1935)*
Alibi Ike   *(WB 1935)*
Broadway Gondolier   *(WB 1935)*
Bright Lights   *(FN 1935)*
I Live for Love   *(WB 1935)*
Stars Over Broadway   *(WB 1935)*
The Story of Louis Pasteur   *(WB 1935)*
Ceiling Zero   *(WB 1935)*
The Traveling Saleslady   *(FN 1935)*
While the Patient Slept   *(WB 1935)*
The Woman in Red   *(FN 1935)*
The Girl from Tenth Avenue   *(FN 1935)*
The Goose and the Gander   *(WB 1935)*
The Walking Dead   *(WB 1936)*
The Singing Kid   *(FN 1936)*
The Murder of Dr. Harrigan   *(FN 1936*
The Big Nose   *(WB 1936*
Down the Stretch   *(FN 1936)*
Murder by an Aristocrat   *(FN 1936)*
The Case of the Velvet Claws   *(FN 1936)*
Two Against the World   *(WB 1936)*
Polo Joe   *(WB 1936)*
Bullets or Ballots   *(FN 1936)*
Trailin' West   *(FN 1936)*
Romance in the Air   *(WB 1936)*
The Case of the Black Cat   *(FN 1936)*
Fugitive in the Sky   *(WB 1937)*
Midnight Court   *(WB 1937)*
Melody for Two   *(WB 1937)*
Speed to Spare   *(Col 1937)*
Guns of the Pecos   *(FN 1937)*
Love takes Flight   *(Grand National 1937)*
Roll Along Cowboy   *(20th 1937)*
Wife, Doctor and Nurse   *(20th 1937)*
Swing it, Professor   *(Conn-Ambassador 1937)*
Boy of the Streets   *(Mon 1937)*
Boots and Saddles   *(Rep 1937)*
You Can't have Everything   *(20th 1937)*
Valley of Hunted Men   *(Pathe 1938)*
Tarzan's Revenge   *(20th 1938)*
Lady in the Morgue   *(Univ 1938)*
The Devil's Party   *(Univ 1938)*
The Great Adventures of Wild Bill Hickok   *(Col 1938)* (Serial)
In Early Arizona   *(Col 1938)*
Frontiers of '49   *(Col 1938)*
Lone Star Pioneers   *(Col 1939)*
The Law Comes to Texas   *(Col 1939)*
Taming of the West   *(Col 1939)*
Overland with Kit Carson   *(Col 1939)* (Serial)
Return of Wild Bill   *(Col 1940)*
Pioneers of the Frontier   *(Col 1940)*
The Man from Tumbleweeds   *(Col 1940)*

Prairie Schooners   *(Col 1940)*
Beyond the Sacramento   *(Col 1940)*
Wildcat of Tucson   *(Col 1940)*
North from the Lone Star   *(Col 1941)*
Across the Sierras   *(Col 1941)*
The Return of Daniel Boone   *(Col 1941)*
Son of Davy Crockett   *(Col 1941)*
Hands Across the Rockies   *(Col 1941)*
King of Dodge City   *(Col 1941)*
Roaring Frontiers   *(Col 1941)*
Lone Star Vigilantes   *(Col 1942)*
Bullets or Bandits   *(Col 1942)*
North of the Rockies   *(Col 1942)*
The Devil's Trail   *(Col 1942)*
Prairie Gunsmoke   *(Col 1942)*
Vengeance of the West   *(Col 1942)*
The Valley of Vanishing Men   *(Col 1942)* (Serial)
Calling Wild Bill Elliott   *(Rep 1943)*
The Man from Thunder River   *(Rep 1943)*
Wagon Tracks West   *(Rep 1943)*
Bordertown Gunfighters   *(Rep 1943)*
Overland Mail Robbery   *(Rep 1943)*
Hidden Valley Outlaws   *(Rep 1944)*
Mojave Firebrands   *(Rep 1944)*
Tucson Raiders   *(Rep 1944)*
Marshal of Reno   *(Rep 1944)*
The San Antonio Kid   *(Rep 1944)*
Cheyenne Wildcat   *(Rep 1944)*
Vigilantes of Dodge City   *(Rep 1944)*
Sheriff of Las Vegas   *(Rep 1944)*
Bells of Rosarita   *(Rep 1945)*
Great Stagecoach Robbery   *(Rep 1945)*
Lone Texas Ranger   *(Rep 1945)*
Phantom of the Plains   *(Rep 1945)*
Marshal of Laredo   *(Rep 1945)*
Colorado Pioneers   *(Rep 1945)*
Wagon Wheels Westward   *(Rep 1945)*
California Gold Rush   *(Rep 1946)*
Sheriff of Redwood Valley   *(Rep 1946)*
Sun Valley Cyclone   *(Rep 1946)*
Conquest of Cheyenne   *(Rep 1946*
In Old Sacramento   *(Rep 1946)*
The Plainsman and the Lady   *(Rep 1946)*
Wyoming   *(Rep 1947)*
The Fabulous Texan   *(Rep 1947)*
Old Los Angeles   *(Rep 1948)*
The Gallant Legion   *(Rep 1948*
Hellfire   *(Rep 1948)*
The Last Bandit   *(Rep 1949)*
The Savage Horde   *(Rep 1949)*
The Showdown   *(Rep 1950)*
The Longhorn   *(Mon 1952)*
Waco   *(Mon 1952)*
Fargo   *(AA 1952)*
The Maverick   *(Mon 1952)*
Kansas Territory   *(Mon 1952)*
The Homesteaders   *(AA 1953)*
Rebel City   *(AA 1953)*
Topeka   *(AA 1953)*
Bitter Creek   *(AA 1954)*
The Forty-Niners   *(AA 1954)*
Vigilante Terror   *(AA 1954)*
Dial Red O   *(AA 1955)*
Sudden Danger   *(AA 1955)*
Calling Homicide   *(AA 1956)*
Chain of Evidence   *(AA 1957)*
Footsteps in the Night   *(AA 1957)*

31

Faye Emerson

The iron fist in the velvet glove. Five feet, four inches of blonde lightning with a razor-edged mind and sparkling wit, combined with the tenacity of an angry bull dog—that's Faye Emerson. A dominating woman who became Queen of Television, a talent for acting wasted in Hollywood B pictures but shining brightly in the theatre, three unsuccessful marriages and a strong philosophy for living ("You've got to get up on your big hind legs and fight if you want to stay human. You've got to kick over an ash can occasionally or slug a cop. Picking on somebody bigger than you gives you a wonderful feeling of being eight feet tall.") This philosophy underscored her zestful battle with life. Today, in her late fifties, overweight and gray, there is little resemblance to the once glamorous First Lady of Television. She is now "happily," solitarily retired at Palma on the island of Majorca, spending her time puttering about her spacious Spanish-type home with its large garden, contemplating writing her memoirs, but mostly, "Having a marvelous time." "I don't regret anything I ever did, but I know that I'll never go back. There's no particular reason why I wouldn't go back. It's just that I worked for about 25 years and I thought it was time to take some time off and think about life—and have some life for myself."

Faye Margaret Emerson was born July 8, 1917, in Elizabeth, Louisiana. She never tried to hide the date,

reasoning that there was, "No sense in being coy about it, everybody knows it anyway." She spent most of her childhood in California, attending the Academy of San Luis Rey at Oceanside, the Point Loma High School and, later, San Diego State College. Her first stage experience was with the St. James Repertory Theatre in Carmel, California in 1935 (in *Russet Mantle*) and while appearing in *Here Today* at San Diego's Municipal Theatre in 1941 she was offered contracts by two Hollywood studios. She chose Warner Bros. where, during the next six years, she appeared in two dozen features in roles ranging from fair to worse. After her first year with Warners she divorced William Wallace Crawford, Jr., a San Diego automobile dealer whom she had married on October 29, 1938, retaining custody of her son, William Wallace Crawford, III, whom she nicknamed Scoop.

At Warners she became one of several contract players the studio kept busy in minor, unimportant, dreary roles in similar films. From a bit part in *Man Power* (1941) as a nurse, she donned a nurse's uniform again for *The Nurse's Secret* (1941), a remake of Mary Roberts Rinehart's *Miss Pinkerton* which had starred Joan Blondell in 1932. She was in five other 1941 studio ventures, including *Wild Bill Hickok Rides* in which the sophisticated Constance Bennett went slumming. Faye was Violet Murphy in a sub-B bomb of a film with Ronald Reagan and Ann Sheridan called *Juke Girl* (1942). She appeared as Gladys Wayne, a newspaper editor's secretary helping young

200

With George Meeker and Craig Stevens in Secret Enemies *(WB 1942)*

With Gene Lockhart, Dennis Morgan, and Bruce Cabot in The Desert Song *(WB 1943)*

brash reporter Van Johnson expose a political frame-up in *Murder in the Big House* (1942). The picture was re-released in 1945 as *Born for Trouble* to capitalize on Johnson's MGM success, but it hardly had improved in the succeeding three years.

The quality and depth of the Emerson career at Warner Bros. is almost typically exemplified in a fizzle entitled *Lady Gangster* (1942). Robert Florey, the director of the film, had august film credits as a writer of such vehicles as *Oil for the Lamps of China* (1935) and *Murders in the Rue Morgue* (1932). However, as director of this Emerson opus he requested his name removed from the film, and the director credited for the hopeless and hapless *Lady Gangster* is the nonexistent "Florian Roberts."

Dennis Morgan's offkey singing was equalled only by Faye's miscasting as the native flower girl, Hajy, a sexy lookout for the Riffs in Warners' second version of *The Desert Song* (1943). Then, as Susan McMartin, she had the diminished female lead in a virtually all male cast headed by John Garfield and Gig Young in *Air Force* (1943). Her career continued in a series of secondary roles, first as Cary Grant's wife in *Destination Tokyo* (1944), and then in a masterpiece of miscasting, as Irene, the sluttish ex-girl friend of Zachary Scott in *The Mask of Dimitrios* (1944), in which she slinked around a Far Eastern nightclub in a preposterous black wig. Along the way Faye turned in a spirited but ignored performance as Eleanor Parker's parachute factory co-worker in *The Very Thought of You* (1944), in which she was the smiling victim of Dane Clark's wolfish passes. Trying to escape the wretched parts Warners consistently tossed her, she maintained a firm regime of dramatic and diction lessons and rigid dieting to retain her svelte figure.

At a Hollywood party in 1943 Faye met Elliott Roosevelt and they discovered many mutual interests, including politics—a subject upon which the volatile Faye could expound with intelligence and force. Before she married the docile Elliott she astonished a swank movie colony dinner party by smashing a glass to the floor, flinging several choice invectives at the heads of the anti-FDR contingent there, and punctuating her flamboyant exit by slamming the French doors. Her deceptive regal coolness (with that winsome smile) erupted at Warners when she, justifiably, rebelled at her dreary roles and stormed the studio's front office demanding to know if the company intended to continue casting her as a silver screen whore. They replied by assigning her the role of Tili Weiler, resident hostess of *Hotel Berlin* (1945), in which she gave an ultra fine, warm performance as the Nazi informer recanting in a dramatic defense of her Jewish lover. During the filming of the Peter Godfrey-directed *Hotel Berlin,* she married Air Force

Colonel Elliott Roosevelt on December 3, 1944 at Grand Canyon, Arizona. She became his third wife, following Elizabeth Donner and Ruth Goggins from whom he was divorced on April 18, 1944.

Faye completed three more minor films for Warners, including *Nobody Lives Forever* (1946), in which she and Walter Brennan played support to John Garfield and Geraldine Fitzgerald, and then walked out on her contract when she was handed what she termed "possibly the worst script ever written." At FDR's fourth inaugural she displayed equally stringent values when she snubbed a pleasant, unimposing gray-haired man to whom she had not been introduced and whom she considered a "masher," only to see him sworn in as vice-president Harry S. Truman. She settled into the Roosevelt clan with considerable ease, despite a current waggish paraphrasing of FDR's "nothing to fear but fear itself" speech: "That marriage will last if Elliott realizes he has nothing to fear but Faye herself."

Life with the Roosevelts was blessed for sparkling Faye because of her thoughtful mother-in-law, Eleanor. The unbelievably busy Eleanor Roosevelt made a life-long friend of Faye, accepting her son Scoop as her grandchild and, in her nightly rounds, reading to the young boy at Hyde Park. Faye worked in summer stock in 1946 and on September 15, 1946, Jim Ameche announced a new radio chatter show, "At Home with Faye and Elliott." Transmitted over forty-two stations, the first broacast included Hildegarde singing and bantering small talk with the young Roosevelts and Anna Sosenko. Future guests included Orson Welles, Lucille Ball and Desi Arnaz, Toots Shor, Earl Wilson and his wife, and Martha Scott. On July 14, 1947, Faye opened at Oquinquit, Maine's summer theatre, in *State of the Union,* wearing a newly designed John Frederics' hat when Elliott and his mother attended the second night's performance.

In early 1948, Faye and Elliott left Hyde Park to take a suite in a New York hotel, Elliott to work on a volume of his father's letters and Faye rehearsing at the Music Box Theatre for her Broadway debut. Eleanor Roosevelt was in London for the unveiling of FDR's statue in Grosvenor Square and missed Faye's opening on April 28, 1948 at the Booth Theatre where she played Ilona Szabo, the tempestuous, amorously amoral operetta star in Ferec Molnar's *The Play's the Thing.* Faye was sleek and alluring and made an impressive debut as the sole female in the cast headed by Louis Calhern. The show played 244 performances at the Booth, closing on December 18, 1948, at which point Faye returned to Hyde Park.

On the day after Christmas, at four A.M., Elliott Roosevelt rushed his wife to a doctor's office for treatment of what the Poughkeepsie, New York, sheriff maintained the following day was a self-inflicted razor slash of the wrist. Faye Emerson Roosevelt was taken to Vassar Brothers Hospital in Poughkeepsie and released on December 28, 1948. Both Faye and Elliott confirmed the early morning affair was pure accident; Faye had cut her wrist reaching into a drawer for aspirin but striking several razor blades instead. The papers had a field day with the incident, even calling Faye's mother, Mrs. John C. Young, in San Diego to confirm the story. In a few days the overblown accident was dismissed. Faye had quickly discovered that being a Roosevelt brought headlines. During the war the press was agog over G.I.s being bumped on a military plane to make room for Faye and her dog. In addition, expense accounts of Johnny Meyer, Howard Hughes' press agent, being investigated by a Senate committee, revealed $132 for hard-to-get nylons charged off to Faye.

While Faye was making the film *Guilty Bystander* (1950) in New York with Zachary Scott, she announced, "I'm sorry to say that Mr. Roosevelt and I have been separated for some time and I plan a divorce when I have finished my current motion picture. Elliott and I parted on friendly terms." On January 5, 1950, she flew to Cuernavaca, Mexico, where at noon on January 14th, Judge Alfonso Roqueni signed the divorce decree.

Meantime, Faye made her splash in the medium that was to make her most famous. Early in 1950 when CBS had to cancel the 11 P.M. debut of "The Diana Barrymore Show," because the star arrived drunk, the television network recalled Faye's brilliant ad-libbing at the Democratic National Convention, rushed her in as a replacement on the Ansonia Shoe-sponsored video gab show, and she premiered with guests Paul Winchell and his dummy Jerry Mahoney. Fine camera work heightened Faye's polished delivery, natural charm and wit, and emphasized the dramatic appeal of her startling plunging neckline gown. Soon she was heading her own "The Faye Emerson Show" and *Life* Magazine was reporting, "Faye Emerson's decollete makes TV melee."

In February, 1950, the energetic Faye was brightening television with her blonde charm and low-cut gowns on "Celebrity Time" with fellow guests Max Baer and Slapsie Maxie Rosenbloom. In addition, she appeared on "Philco Playhouse" in *Home Town* with Barry Nelson, on "Ford Theatre's" televised production of the play *Skylark* with Lee Bowman and Alan Baxter, and on "Billy Rose's Playbill" in *George III Once Drooled in This Plate.*

In the summer of 1950 she was back on Broadway with the Festival Theatre Repertory in a two-week engagement at the Fulton Theatre of *Parisienne* with

With Eduardo Ciannelli and Peter Lorre in The Mask of Dimitrios *(WB 1944)*

Francis Lederer and Helmut Dantine. At the close of her television show on November 7th, she leaned forward conspiratorially, displaying her best cleavage, and told the audience, "Because you are all my friends I want you to meet the man I am going to marry." She introduced orchestra leader Skitch Henderson. In order to avoid any legal complications, she became Mrs. Lyle Cedric Henderson in Cuernavaca, Mexico, on December 12, 1950.

She was nominated for a 1950 television Emmy Award as the Most Outstanding TV Personality but lost to Groucho Marx. However, in 1951, she was tagged "Television's First Lady." In January, 1951, *Look* Magazine called her "Television's Most Appealing Female Personality" and in Boston she was voted an award as "The Outstanding Woman of Achievement." Her energies abounded throughout the 1950s, touring with the American Shakespearean Festival Theatre and Academy production of *An Evening with Will Shakespeare,* hostessing a weekly television show, "Faye Emerson's Wonderful Town," with name guests honoring various American cities. The program was backed oncamera by Henderson's orchestra. She also found time to appear on such anthology shows as the "U.S. Steel Hour" in Taylor Caldwell's *Hope for Harvest,* and to make a cameo appearance as herself in Tay Garnett's MGM film, *Main Street to Broadway* (1953).

In September, 1954 she was writing a syndicated column for the newspapers commenting on the world —hers, ours and yours—and occasionally scratching the veneer of momentary idols. On Liberace she wrote, "Such dimpling and winking. Such tossing of curls and fluttering of eyelashes and flashing of teeth —such nausea!" On television she was *Melissa* on "Studio One," giving up life and love for devotion to her sociologist father, Marion Burnett. Then, bored with her life as a college professor's wife she was seen urging him to run for state governor in *The Fifth Wheel* on the "U.S. Steel Hour." She even popped up on such panel shows as "What's in a Word?", "What's My Line," and "The Show of Shows." Punctuated with her quick, roaring, hearty laughter, she called herself, "The Grand Old Lady of Television."

With a fusilade of pistol shots, the curtain rose on *The Heavenly Twins* on Broadway in 1955 as Faye, playing Lucille Miremont, kills her faithless husband (Jean Pierre Aumont). The comedy misfired despite sparkling performances from both stars. The following season Faye had no better luck with the play *Protective Custody,* in which she was a foreign correspondent brainwashed by Soviet psychiatrist Fritz Weaver. When the play folded in Washington,

D.C., Faye acquired additional financing and brought the show into New York. It opened on December 28, 1956 at the Ambassador Theatre, but closed after three performances. Faye voiced her opinion of New York critics on nationwide television.

She lost the 1956 Emmy Award for "Best Female Personality, Continuing Performance on Television" to Dinah Shore. The next year she did a cameo role in Elia Kazan's film, *A Face in the Crowd* (1957), and, for the Theatre Guild, starred onstage in Arnold Moss' adaptation of George Bernard Shaw's *Back to Methuselah* with Tyrone Power and Arthur Treacher. Faye gave possibly her best performance onstage to date as Eve and her varied sisters down through the ages. For the summer of 1958 she was on the straw-hat circuit in three of Noël Coward's one-act plays, entitled *Tonight at 8:30.*

Her work on television continued as Dorothy Hilton in *Call It a Day* on the "U.S. Steel Hour" and her own show, "Ladies of the Press," for which she received the New York area Emmy Award. She toured in *State of the Union* and *Biography* in 1960 and the next summer she toured with Reginald Gardiner in *The Pleasure of His Company.* Later in 1961 she joined the National Repertory Theatre and toured extensively as Lady Penelope Gray, lady-in-waiting, in Maxwell Anderson's *Elizabeth the Queen,* and played the lead in *Mary Stuart* with Eva Le Gallienne as Elizabeth in both productions.

After a 1962 summer tour of the vintage *The Vinegar Tree,* and a few guest appearances on television, 1963 was an entire year without Faye on television. She had divorced Skitch Henderson in 1957 and, unburdened of family ties, she left for Europe. For a while she lived in Switzerland, then moved to the island of Majorca growing not so gracefully old and writing her memoirs. While seldom looking back at her past, this one-time best dressed woman has stated that her favorite TV show was with Mike Wallace, and she sums up her film career this way: "I never really liked pictures anyway. Maybe that's why I wasn't a big success in them." On her marriages her ratings are: The first, complete incompatibility; the second with Elliot Roosevelt "was the happiest," and, with Skitch Henderson, "I couldn't work out our mutual problems. My divorces were all quiet. I never took a cent of alimony. I'm the breadwinner. Bad as divorces are, you can at least have the good manners to be civilized about them!"

One thing about Faye, she was almost always impeccably civilized and added a good deal of joy and glamour to America's entertainment.

FAYE EMERSON

Man Power   *(WB 1941)*
The Nurse's Secret   *(WB 1941)*
Blues in the Night   *(WB 1941)*
Affectionately Yours   *(WB 1941)*
Bad Men of Missouri   *(WB 1941)*
Nine Lives are Not Enough   *(WB 1941)*
Wild Bill Hickok Rides   *(WB 1941)*
Juke Girl   *(WB 1942)*
Murder in the Big House   *(WB 1942)*
The Hard Way   *(WB 1942)*
Lady Gangster   *(WB 1942)*
Secret Enemies   *(WB 1942)*
The Desert Song   *(WB 1943)*
Air Force   *(WB 1943)*
Find the Blackmailer   *(WB 1943)*
Destination Tokyo   *(WB 1943)*

The Very Thought of You   *(WB 1944)*
In Our Time   *(WB 1944)*
Between Two Worlds   *(WB 1944)*
Hollywood Canteen   *(WB 1944)*
The Mask of Dimitrios   *(WB 1944)*
Uncertain Glory   *(WB 1944)*
Crime by Night   *(WB 1944)*
Hotel Berlin   *(WB 1945)*
Danger Signal   *(WB 1945)*
Nobody Lives Forever   *(WB 1946)*
Her Kind of Man   *(WB 1946)*
Guilty Bystander   *(Film Classics 1950)*
Main Street to Broadway   *(MGM 1953)*
A Face in the Crowd   *(WB 1957)*

32

Dale Evans

Cowgirls—not to be confused with Western movie heroines or leading ladies such as Barbara Stanwyck who dip back into the genre—have always been more of an oddity on the silver screen than was ever the case in the real American Old West. In silent films there were Texas Guinan and, more importantly, Ruth Roland of the serials. In the talkies there were some minor cowgirl leads like Ruth Mix and Dorothy Page, and on television, there would be Gail Davis of "Annie Oakley," but none ever gained the acceptance or popularity of Dale Evans, whom Republic billed as Queen of the Cowgirls. If moviegoers had any skepticism about giving her special film billing, Miss Evans' marriage in 1947 to Roy Rogers, King of the Cowboys, ended any such possible reluctance.

Dale Evans was born Frances Octavia Smith in Uvalde, Texas on October 31, 1912, five days before her future husband Roy was born in Duck Run, Ohio. The Smiths moved to Osceola, Arkansas where she attended high school and fell in love with a senior classman, Thomas Fox, with whom she eloped to Blitheville, Arkansas in January, 1927. On November 28, 1927, she gave birth to Thomas Fox, Jr. and, following the early death of her young husband in 1929, she sought and found singing jobs to support herself and her young son.

While she was singing on Louisville, Kentucky's radio station WHAS, Joe Eaton, the program director,

changed her professional name from Frances Fox to Dale Evans. With her new name she returned to Dallas, Texas, singing on radio station WFAA's "The Early Birds" program, and met and married pianist and arranger Robert Dale Butts. After two years in Dallas, the Butts family moved to Chicago, where Dale found a job as vocalist with Anson Weeks' orchestra, touring the country with that group for a year, then returning to Chicago as staff singer for station WBBM. By 1940 Dale had her own show, "That Girl from Texas" on WBBM, while singing every night at the Drake, Blackstone, or Sherman Hotel and, finally, at Chicago's famous supper club, Chez Paree.

In 1941 an agent persuaded Dale to test for the ingenue lead opposite Bing Crosby in *Holiday Inn*. Paramount was less than enthusiastic about her screen test and her obvious inability to dance, and gave the role to Marjorie Reynolds. Through agent Art Rush, Dale did land a job as vocalist on the Edgar Bergen-Charlie McCarthy show for a forty-three week run and also appeared on the radio shows of Jack Carson, Garry Moore, and Jimmy Durante. The telltale Paramount screentest was eventually passed on to Twentieth Century-Fox who in turn signed Dale to a one year contract at four hundred dollars a week. During the Fox year, she was cast in a bit role in *Orchestra Wives* (1942), starring Glenn Miller's band, and after a small part as Ruth with Don Ameche and Joan Bennett in *Girl Trouble* (1942), Twentieth did not take up her option.

With Roy Rogers and Estelita Rodriguez in Susanna Pass *(Rep 1949)*

With George "Gabby" Hayes and Hardie Albright in Sunset in El Dorado *(Rep 1945)*

According to her agent, her son Tommy presented a professional problem for a rising, young actress in Hollywood, and he persuaded fledgling Dale to pass her fourteen-year-old boy off as her brother. The rationale was that she would never succeed on the screen if it became generally known she was the mother of a teenager. Dale reluctantly accepted the ten percenter's advice and kept Tommy in the background. Nevertheless, she and Tommy joined the Westwood Baptist Church as mother and son. While out of film work, Dale did close to six hundred shows for the U.S.O. and the Hollywood Victory Committee. She then signed a one year pact with Republic studios, making her debut for that company with Vera Vague in *Swing Your Partner* (1943).

Dale's second assignment for Republic was as Gloria Winston, the wilful daughter of Henry Hull, with Donald "Red" Barry in *The West Side Kid* (1943), and the reviewers noticed her favorably. Dale then appeared as "Cuddles" Walker, the second female role in *In Old Oklahoma* (1943), with John Wayne and Martha Scott, followed by her role with the Hoosier Hot Shots in something called *Hoosier Holiday* (1943). She ended her first year with Herbert J. Yates' studio singing "Baby, You're So Good to Me" as Jean

Foster with Al Pearce and his Gang in *Here Comes Elmer* (1943).

Dale's first effort in 1944 was in the amusing farce, *Casanova in Burlesque,* playing the role of Barbara Compton in the havoc of burlesque performers trying to make Shakespeare's plays the thing. Then, fortuitously, Republic cast Dale opposite their boxoffice western champ, Roy Rogers. He had been with the studio since 1938, riding to fame (in competition with Republic's Gene Autry) on his beautiful palomino horse Trigger, for whom he paid $2,500.

The public enthusiastically accepted the pairing of Dale and Roy in their initial joint film, *The Cowboy and the Senorita* (1944). For the next few years they were teamed together in a variety of westerns, including *The Yellow Rose of Texas* (1944), *Song of Nevada* (1944), *Utah* (1945), and, with most of Republic's other western heroes, ("Wild Bill" Elliott, Don "Red" Barry, Robert Livingston, Allan "Rocky" Lane) in *Bells of Rosarita* (1945). She was given time off from the Rogers' adventures to make a comedy with Arthur "Blondie" Lake and Lionel Stander titled *The Big Show-Off* (1945), but returned to the cinema range with Roy, Roger Pryor, and the Sons of the Pioneers in *The Man from Oklahoma* (1945). As a matter of fact, the singing Sons of the Pioneers, formed in 1936, were very far from the actual wild, wild West. Robert Nolan was a Canadian; Len Slye (Rogers) was from Ohio; Verne Tim Spencer was from Missouri; and Hugh and Carl Farr had only some vague western lineage. During the 1940s, the Sons of the Pioneers, whose recordings of "Cool Water" and "Tumbling Tumbleweed" would sell several million copies, appeared in most of the Rogers-Evans horse operas during the 1940s.

Besides her active film career, Dale made inroads in the recording field. Her rendition of "Aha, San Antone," one of her own compositions, made for her contract employer, RCA Victor, sold over a quarter-million copies.

In 1945, Roy Rogers' Championship Rodeo appeared in New York's Madison Square Garden and other major cities, grossing over a million dollars. The same year, Dale realized her marriage to Robert Dale Butts was floundering and they were divorced. Roy and Dale, in 1946, turned out eight westerns for Republic—all money-earners—and that year Roy's wife of ten years, Arlene Wilkins Rogers, died of a blood clot eight days after the Caesarian birth of Roy Rogers, Jr. whom they nicknamed "Dusty."

Left with two daughters, Linda Lou and adopted Cheryl, and Roy Jr., the cowboy star was desolate but returned to a heavy work schedule as an antidote. During the summer of 1947, Roy again toured the

With Roy Rogers in Lights of Old Santa Fe *(Rep 1944)*

208

With Dorothy Christy, Roy Rogers, Mary Lee, and John Hubbard in The Cowboy and the Senorita *(Rep 1944)*

country with his Rodeo. On Wednesday, June 18, 1947, he led a parade down the Atlantic City boardwalk for the fiftieth anniversary of that city's famed Steel Pier, where Dale was headlining the wharf's vaudeville show as "the singing queen of westerns," with Ed Sullivan as the master of ceremonies. Roy, Dale, Trigger, and the Sons of the Pioneers continued with the rodeo to overflow crowds. That autumn, while sitting on their horses waiting for their entrance cue at Chicago's Stadium, they decided to get married. With Roy's three children and Dale's Tom, the newlyweds moved into a rambling Spanish-style house in the Hollywood Hills that originally had been built by Noah Beery.

Their Republic films were filled with western music, which led former western star Buck Jones to lament that the general acceptance of the Rogers-Evans type of western movie would mean that "children will get the wrong idea that all you need to stop an Indian or a rustler is a loud voice accompanied by a hillbilly band." Nevertheless, Roy was the top western moneymaker at the boxoffice, branching out with his own radio show in 1948 over NBC. Then, in 1951, Roy and Dale entered television with their NBC program, plus appearing in various "specials"

and as guests on several top video variety shows. Dale's last feature with Roy (and Pinky Lee) was Republic's *Pals of the Golden West* (1951). In the eight years since Republic's head of production Armand Schaeffer heard her sing on Edgar Bergen's radio show and signed her to a one-picture deal, she made forty feature films for the studio, including a remake of *Slippy McGee* (1948), playing Mary Virginia Hunter, who had been played in the silent version by Colleen Moore.

After their last film together the Rogers moved to the San Fernando Valley. On August 26, 1950, Dale became the mother of a baby girl they named Robin Elizabeth, but before leaving the hospital Dale and Roy were told the child was afflicted with Mongolism. They refused the doctor's advise to institutionalize the child and took her home, but two days before Robin Elizabeth's second birthday she died of complications following a case of mumps. Dale was overwrought at her daughter's death and wrote a book, *Angel Unaware* (1953), detailing their love for the fragile child. Taking her title from the Book of Hebrews in the New Testament, "Be not forgetful to entertain strangers, for thereby some have entertained angels unawares," the book's sales were phenomenal. Dale has contributed all royalties from *Angel Unaware* to the National Association for Retarded Children.

Dale and Roy have stretched their firm belief in God's true love to encompass all phases of their daily lives, augmenting their family with adopted children: Sandy and Dodie. In 1954, Roy and Dale, with Trigger, made a successful tour of the British Isles and were part of Billy Graham's Crusade at London's Harringay Arena. By 1956, Roy and Dale had completed 101 segments of their television series and, in 1958, were once again part of Billy Graham's Crusade at a sunrise Easter Service in Washington, D.C., followed by a visit to the National Presbyterian Church with President and Mrs. Eisenhower. The same year Roy was slowed down with a heart-artery constriction but he and Dale did two TV specials for Chevrolet from their Charsworth, California ranch, joined on the September 27th telecast by Edie Adams, Audie Murphy, and Connie Francis.

During their British Isles tour they returned with another adopted daughter, eleven-year-old Marion, and, in 1955, they had increased their household by adopting a Korean orphan, whom they renamed Debbie. That year Dale also wrote *My Spiritual Diary*, reflecting the fact that she and Roy were spiritual leaders in their community. She admitted, "I would love to be an evangelist, but I think God has revealed to me that I can serve him best by just remaining at my post."

Tragedy continued to plague the Rogers' clan when, on August 17, 1964, Debbie was killed in a bus crash six miles south of San Clemente, California. Debbie was standing up front in the bus talking with Reverend Lawrence Elton White who was driving the church bus home after delivering food and clothing in Tijuana, Mexico. A tire blew and the bus bumped and careened along the rough shoulder of the road, stopped finally by a palm tree at the edge of a forty-foot bluff. Debbie and seven others were killed. Dale, informed of the accident, cried, "I've heard it, but I can't accept it. I just can't. Roy's in the hospital [recovering from neck surgery], and I can't tell him of this until I'm certain." Later, Dale wrote a book *Dearest Debbie* (1965), with all royalties going to World Vision, Inc.

The Rogers' family suffered another loss the following year when their adopted son Sandy, PFC John David Rogers, died on October 31, 1965. Sandy, stationed with the Third Armored Division at Gelhausen, Germany, had complained of feeling ill after dinner at the enlisted men's club, after being goaded by his buddies to drink an undetermined amount of liquor to which he was not accustomed. He was taken to the hospital and the clinical autopsy report gave cause of death as "asphysia due to aspiration of vomitus." The eighteen-year-old Sandy had choked to death while vomiting. Somehow, Roy and Dale's faith sustained them and Dale composed another book called *Salute to Sandy* (1965). In 1966, they entertained troops in Vietnam for the enjoyment of the men stationed there, and in memory of Sandy. When they returned, Dale was given "The Texan of the Year" award from the Texas Press Association.

Dale was selected as California's "Mother of the Year" in 1967, and in June, Roy opened a museum near their home in Apple Valley, California. There, in the eighteen-thousand-square-foot museum with a stockade exterior, Trigger (who died on July 3, 1965, at age thirty-three) rears on his hind legs wearing a specially made silver saddle, a wonder of the art of taxidermy, surrounded with trophies and memorabilia from Dale and Roy's careers. In 1973, Roy and Dale held a ground-breaking ceremony at Victorville, California for a group of buildings that is to be known as the Roy Rogers Western World commercial center. The first phase of the project has been estimated at $3.2 million dollars.

Today, in their sixties, Dale and Roy have mellowed, glowing in the love of their fourteen grandchildren, radiating the confidence and love that has sustained them throughout the years with their deeply religious devotion to church, God, and the family of man. Dale's record albums are still best sellers from "The Bible Tells Me," "Faith, Hope and Charity," "Jesus Loves Me," "Sweeter as the Years Go By" to "Peter Cottontail and other Eastern Favorites" and a Christmas album sung by both her and Roy. Roy has branched out into real estate and many other ventures including his chain of Roy Rogers' Restaurants featuring Pappy Parker's Fried Chicken. Dale's other books *Christmas Is Always, No Two Ways about It, To My Son, Time Out, Ladies,* and her best-selling autobiography, *The Woman at the Well,* attest to a full life.

Dale's feeling that the past is only a prologue, a foundation for the building of tomorrow, combined with her religious convictions and faith, creates a bright future for both Mr. and Mrs. Roy Rogers. They are never loath to entertain strangers and, thereby, discover more "angels unaware." As for the secret of their long-standing successful marriage, Roy says, "We still like and respect each other and I guess that's been one of the biggest assets in our marriage."

DALE EVANS

Orchestra Wives   *(20th 1942)*
Girl Trouble   *(20th 1942)*
Swing Your Partner   *(Rep 1943)*
The West Side Kid   *(Rep 1943)*
In Old Oklahoma   *(Rep 1943)*
Hoosier Holiday   *(Rep 1943)*
Here Comes Elmer   *(Rep 1943)*
Casanova in Burlesque   *(Rep 1944)*
The Cowboy and the Senorita   *(Rep 1944)*
San Fernando Valley   *(Rep 1944)*
Song of Nevada   *(Rep 1944)*
The Yellow Rose of Texas   *(Rep 1944)*
Lights of Old Santa Fe   *(Rep 1944)*
The Big Show-Off   *(Rep 1945)*
Utah   *(Rep 1945)*
Hitchhike to Happiness   *(Rep 1945)*
Bells of Rosarita   *(Rep 1945)*
The Man from Oklahoma   *(Rep 1945)*
Don't Fence Me In   *(Rep 1945)*
Sunset in Eldorado   *(Rep 1945)*
Along the Navajo Trail   *(Rep 1945)*

Song of Arizona   *(Rep 1946)*
My Pal Trigger   *(Rep 1946)*
Rainbow over Texas   *(Rep 1946)*
Out California Way   *(Rep 1946)*
Roll On, Texas Moon   *(Rep 1946)*
Home in Oklahoma   *(Rep 1946)*
Under Nevada Skies   *(Rep 1946)*
Helldorado   *(Rep 1946)*
Apache Rose   *(Rep 1947)*
Bells of San Angelo   *(Rep 1947)*
The Trespasser   *(Rep 1947)*
Slippy McGee   *(Rep 1948)*
Down Dakota Way   *(Rep 1949)*
Susanna Pass   *(Rep 1949)*
The Golden Stallion   *(Rep 1949)*
Twilight in the Sierras   *(Rep 1950)*
Trigger, Jr.   *(Rep 1950)*
Bells of Coronado   *(Rep 1950)*
South of Caliente   *(Rep 1951)*
Pals of the Golden West   *(Rep 1951)*

33

William Eythe

Early in William Eythe's theatrical career he appeared in a summer stock production of *Caprice* (1941) with the illustrious Ruth Chatterton. Miss Chatterton stated at the time, "I have seen and played with a great many young actors in the course of my career. I have never seen one with so much natural ability. He knows instinctively the right thing to do." Elliott Norton, writing for the *Boston Post,* put it this way, "William Eythe has the most unusual acting talent of any young man seen in the summer or winter theatre circuits in a good many years. He is not only a good actor, but he may very well, if he puts his mind to it, become one day a great actor."

William Eythe never became a great actor and there is little evidence, even if he had put his mind to it, that he ever would have emerged as one. He showed promise on the New York stage, but when Hollywood took him up, he was generally lost among all-star casts. Even though he appeared in some of Twentieth Century-Fox's most important films of the 1940s, only his role as the farm boy soldier who carries on a telepathic discourse with his mother and girlfriend in *The Eve of St. Mark* (1944) has left much of an impression. This is both unfortunate and ironic, for Eythe was an attractive and extremely charming young man. He possessed an ambition and personality strong enough to make him attractive to the right people in theatrical business—male or female. This strength of personality, however, never came across on screen. The charm was evident in *A Royal Scandal*

(1945) with Tallulah Bankhead, but for the most part he was only a younger and bouncier version of Warner Bros.' Jeffrey Lynn.

William John Joseph Eythe was born on April 7, 1918, in Mars, Pennsylvania, a small town some twenty-five miles from Pittsburgh. "The main industry of the community is the dairy business," said Eythe. "Local society has its fling on Saturday night when the farmers make their weekly visit to town. The usual occupation of boyhood, trying to evade school, kept me fairly busy until I was nine. After that I had plenty to do."

At age nine he appeared in *Peter Rabbit* in school. He fought against doing the role but finally did it to please his mother, Katherine. Bill's father, Carl S. Eythe, was a contractor; he also had an older brother, Howard, known as "Dutch," and a sister, Ruth. After his first taste of theatrics, Bill decided this was what he wanted to do, but he was more interested in directing than acting. He began his directing career when he was eleven years old, making imaginary Westerns in the hills around his home. He used a shoe box for a camera and held a megaphone. When he was short of actors he would act himself. During one of these Westerns, while trying to leap from one tree to another, Bill missed his foothold. Filming came to a halt. For seven months he was confined to bed with two broken legs in casts. When he recovered he turned an

With Dana Andrews in Wing and a Prayer *(20th 1944)*

With Tallulah Bankhead in A Royal Scandal *(20th 1945)*

213

old barn into a theatre and wrote original plays which he also directed for Eythe Productions. He found this less risky to his body.

At Mars High School he did some dramatics, but preferred working on costumes and set designs. He did the sets for their production of *Seventeen* and also held down boxoffice duty. In 1933 the family moved to Baltimore where Bill continued high school, returning to Mars in time to be graduated in 1936. Bill then stayed out of school for a year and worked at the Mars dairy store. "The place didn't make any money," he admitted. "Maybe it was because I spent all day in the back room painting stage and costume designs."

He saw his first professional stage production at this time at the Nixon Theatre in Pittsburgh. It was *Winterset,* with Burgess Meredith and Margo. He barged backstage to see the two stars and asked their advice about getting into theatre work. They suggested the School of Drama at Carnegie Tech as one of the best schools in the country for theatre. He entered Carnegie Tech in 1937 as a drama major but concentrated on sets and costumes. (Bill's brother, "Dutch," had gained fame there as an All-American football halfback. Dutch later became a coach at a boys' military school.)

One of the reasons Bill preferred set design was that he stammered. Edith Skinner, who had operated the Provincetown Playhouse, was now a speech instructor at the school and helped him greatly by forcing him to speak before audiences. When he began doing plays it was noticed that he had a natural gift for acting. He joined the student organization called "The Scotch and Soda Club" and produced amateur musicals for them. He wrote the songs, designed the sets and costumes, and also acted. Bill was graduated in 1941. He always remained loyal to Carnegie Tech and later stated, "It's professional. I've seen better plays there than I have on Broadway, and Carnegie Tech people are everywhere. While I was in Paris I stopped backstage at the Theatre Montparnasse. The stage manager walked up to me and said, 'You're William Eythe, aren't you? Well, I'm from Carnegie Tech, myself.'" While in college Bill had worked at odd jobs for expense money. "And believe me, they were odd," he said. He did fashion shows on musicals for a department store and lectured on astronomy at Buhl Planetarium. To win this job he spent many hours doing research, wrote a lecture about the heavens, and memorized it. He knew nothing else about astronomy.

After college, Bill produced *Lend an Ear,* a musical revue, at the Pittsburgh Civic Playhouse while also singing and dancing in it. He also performed it in Cohasset, Massachusetts, where he worked in stock with such stars as Ruth Chatterton, Nancy Carroll, Grace George, and Conrad Nagel. The Shuberts became quite interested in *Lend an Ear* and hoped to take it to Broadway, but its author, Charles Gaynor, insisted on the original cast or nothing. Therefore, the play did not make it to the Great White Way, at least not yet.

After a summer of playing the borscht circuit in the Catskill Mountains, Eythe returned to Pittsburgh and opened his own stock company, The Fox Chapel Players. It was composed mainly of Carnegie Tech students and disbanded after one performance of *Liliom,* due to lack of operating capital. Bill admitted, "We shot a bit too high."

While appearing in a stock production of *Ladies in Retirement,* a Twentieth Century-Fox talent scout spotted him and offered him a screen test. Eythe insisted he was not ready yet, that he needed far more experience. The scout promised to keep in touch but Bill thought no more of it and proceeded on a tour with Ruth Chatterton. He finally made his move to New York and auditioned for Oscar Serlin, who was producing Molnar's *The King's Maid* starring Margo. Serlin, who was once a talent scout for David O. Selznick, was then looking for a juvenile, but thought Eythe was too young. However, he was sufficiently impressed with him to give him a small role in the show. The play flopped but Serlin and Eythe became close friends and when Serlin later produced John Steinbeck's *The Moon is Down* on Broadway, he gave Bill an important role in it. That drama opened at the Martin Beck Theatre on April 7, 1942, with a cast that included Ralph Morgan, Otto Kruger, Maria Palmer, and Lyle Bettger. As Lieutenant Tonder, the neurotic young Nazi officer, Eythe received very favorable notices. The *New York Daily News* offered, "William Eythe does well as a hysterical German boy, in search of feminine companionship, who gets himself stabbed with a lady's shears." The *Daily Worker* thought his performance "stands out as a fine piece of emotional acting." But the *New York World Telegram* felt that the "Germans at the Martin Beck are too nice for comfort or belief." Bill had a few occupational problems in this play. Onstage he had to lapse into hysteria and a German officer would cuff him on each cheek to snap him out of it. The actor playing that role was nearsighted, and in Baltimore, where the show tried out, the player misjudged his slap and the blow punctured Bill's left eardrum. Opening night in New York the same thing happened and his right eardrum was shattered. For two weeks he was completely deaf, getting his cues only through laborious lip-reading.

The Twentieth Century-Fox scout kept his promise and showed up again. This time, Bill jumped at the chance for a screen test. He performed a scene from *The Moon Is Down* and was signed to an exclusive long term contract. He left for the west coast on June 20, 1942, after his Broadway run ended, accompanied by fellow actor Chuck Gordon who was driving out there. Eythe spent his first day at the studio going from wardrobe to makeup for his movie debut in *The Ox-Bow Incident* (1943), starring Henry Fonda. Fox had purchased the screen rights to *The Moon Is Down* (1943) but cast German actor Peter Van Eyck in the role Eythe had originated. However, Bill did appear in a number of top Fox productions, such as *The Song of Bernadette* (1943), *Wing and a Prayer* (1944), *Wilson* (1944), and *The Eve of St. Mark.* Reviewing his performance in the latter picture, the *New York Times* commented, "William Eythe is completely at a loss to create a flesh and blood soldier. The best he can turn is a walking rhapsodist."

Only when top Fox star Tyrone Power turned down *A Royal Scandal* did Eythe win the option to play opposite Tallulah Bankhead, proving to directors Otto Preminger and Ernst Lubitsch that he had the fluidity of language to handle the role as Catherine the Great's handsome swain. But in this heavy-handed

Publicity pose ca. 1944

With Charles Coburn and Joan Bennett in Colonel Effingham's Raid *(20th 1945)*

production he was completely overshadowed by the iconoclastic Bankhead. And in *Colonel Effingham's Raid* (1964), it was Charles Coburn as the cantankerous veteran soldier who held the limelight. Eythe received top billing for the first time in *The House on 92nd Street* (1945), Louis de Rochemont's semi documentary study of Nazi espionage in the United States. There were no big names in this superior film, but the cast was uniformly good, including Eythe as a young German-American sent to the homeland on a spy mission. Eythe's last major film on the Fox lot was the musical, *Centennial Summer* (1946), and, again, in this Technicolor Jerome Kern songfest, he got lost in the crowd of name players including Jeanne Crain, Cornel Wilde, Linda Darnell, Constance Bennett, and scene-stealing Walter Brennan. The little singing Bill did in this picture was dubbed, even though it was a known fact that he *could* sing and dance himself. It was to be his only film musical.

Eythe's problems on the Fox lot could not be merely attributed to the fact that he was just another handsome, but vapid, newcomer who filled a needed gap in the studio stable during the World War II years when the major names were away in military service. Eythe was his very own worst enemy. He was very self-centered, knew it, accepted it, and did not care to change. This did not endear him to his co-workers, the technical talent, or to the top Fox brass. Around the studio he was known as "s--t in the mouth" Eythe. The actor had a more professional, self-serving way of explaining the sad waste of his potentials at the Darryl F. Zanuck playground. "Hollywood was fine until they found out I wasn't a silent accepter of any old part."

Bill's close relationship with Lon McCallister was also a thorn in the studio's side. They were two young actors working at the same studio, although McCallister was not a contract player, and they became very close. The topper to this relationship, as far as the studio was concerned, was when a movie magazine ran a story with pictures of their last evening together before McCallister went into the army. One photograph even revealed Eythe giving McCallister a friendship ring. This was all too glossy looking and Darryl F. Zanuck at Fox exploded. He set down a dictum that thereafter the two actors were not to be mentioned in the same press release or story.

Perhaps in hopes of punishing Eythe and thus whipping him into shape, or just as an expedient method of using up the contractual time he owed to Fox, Eythe was farmed out to England to do *Meet Me at Dawn* (1948). However, it did not turn out to be punishment for Eythe, because he enjoyed the venture. It got him away from California and Hollywood,

which he claimed was "dominated by directors who only worry about production figures and think any deviation from the rule is sheer radicalism." While abroad, he traveled throughout the Continent and visited the film studios in various countries. Part of the time he was accompanied by McCallister. Of his trip overseas, Eythe remarked, "I learned a lot. The main thing was that European picture makers have a respect for their audience. They never think of making a film for the fourteen year old mind, exclusively, like we do. Their pictures are adult and have a realism that is different from the flat patterns and over-worked characters that constantly turn up in our films."

On the social scene, Eythe had not been seriously linked with any Hollywood actress, preferring to spend most of his non-working hours in the company of pal McCallister. Thus it was much to the surprise of the movie colony when in 1947 Eythe wed Buff Cobb (Mrs. Patricia Cobb Chapman), who was the granddaughter of the late author and humorist, Irvin S. Cobb. The marriage was short-lived, though, for the couple divorced in February, 1949.

In 1946, Bill co-produced a production of *The Glass Menagerie* with Franklin Gilbert at the Las Palmas Theatre in California and he played the role of the soul-searching son in it. He then attempted reassembling the original East coast cast of *Lend an Ear* for a new production, but found that many of the founding players now had other jobs or committments. He formed his own producing company, Mars., Inc. and brought the *Lend an Ear* composer and author, Charles Gaynor, to California. With Franklin Gilbert again as co-producer, Eythe directed and played one of the leads in the West-coast version of *Lend an Ear*. The intimate revue ran for eight months in Hollywood, and on Broadway (National Theatre: December 20, 1948) it ran for two years. The show turned out to be a springboard for a number of very talented performers, including Carol Channing, Gene Nelson, Yvonne Adair and Tommy Morton. Gower Champion was the show's dance director.

Having launched *Lend an Ear* so successfully, Eythe then hoped to produce the film, *The Perfect Round,* based on the Henry Morton Robinson novel, and to star Dorothy McGuire, with location shooting in the Hudson Valley. But the project never came to fruition. His last two film roles were in two minor efforts. He was the hero, a young detective, in Paramount's *Special Agent* (1949), and, in *Customs Agent* (1950) with Marjorie Reynolds, he played the title role of an agent who pretends to be a drunk and a dope peddler in order to apprehend the criminals. Eythe thought it was a "wonderful role." It was a good part, which he played well, but the Seymour Friedmandirected picture was only a run-of-the-mill action yarn.

It was in 1950 that Eythe received a frantic call from Lehman Engel, musical director of the in-coming Broadway show, *The Liar* directed by Alfred Drake. Dennis Harrison, playing the title role of Lelio Bisognosi, was relinquishing his part and they needed somebody to replace him immediately, because the show had to open within a few days. Back in 1941, Engel had directed *The Beggar's Opera* at Carnegie Tech and in an emergency Eythe had taken over the lead role with only a twenty-four-hour notice and had enjoyed a great success. Now he was needed again.

The Liar part was a long and taxing undertaking. Eythe insisted that not only could he not sing well (he always said this) but that he no longer had the inspiration to act onstage, and besides he had lost his knack for being a quick study. But Engel was persuasive and finally Eythe agreed to tackle the assignment. *The Liar* opened at the Broadhurst Theatre on Broadway on May 11, 1950. The *New York World Telegram* reviewed, "In a little more time Eythe would have conquered it entirely, for he has the flourish, the stamina and the charm and can talk a song better than most people sing one." The *New York Post* was less enthusiastic: "William Eythe who has the title role, tailored for Mr. Drake, is a competent enough juvenile but he lacks the proper romantic style and humorous flourish, and his performance is more industrious than deft. The best I can say for him is that he strives manfully to fabricate an air of satirical bravado that is not forthcoming." The show had a limited run, but in December of the same year, Eythe opened on Broadway in yet another musical, *Out of This World,* which starred Charlotte Greenwood, and boasted songs by Cole Porter. In his second-billed role Eythe was, according to *Variety,* "more or less incidental in the nonsinging dual part of a reporter-bridegroom and of Jupiter in the guise of same."

Eythe made occasional forays into television work, appearing on such shows as "Lights Out," "Tales of Tomorrow," "Schlitz Playhouse," and "Ford Theatre," but none of his appearances were memorable. In 1956, he, Huntington Hartford, and Lon McCallister produced a theatrical revue, *Joy Ride,* but it closed in Chicago.

It seemed that Eythe's career had burned itself out. He became a very heavy drinker, often gulping down alcohol until he passed out. His father died on February 8, 1956, and his own death followed about a year later. On January 16, 1957, he entered a Los Angeles hospital for treatment of hepatitis. He died of complications arising from that condition ten days later.

WILLIAM EYTHE

The Ox-Bow Incident   *(20th 1943)*
The Song of Bernadette   *(20th 1943)*
The Eve of St. Mark   *(20th 1944)*
Wing and a Prayer   *(20th 1944)*
Wilson   *(20th 1944)*
A Royal Scandal   *(20th 1945)*
The House on 92nd Street   *(20th 1945)*

Colonel Effingham's Raid   *(20th 1946)*
Centennial Summer   *(20th 1946)*
Meet Me at Dawn   *(20th 1948)*
Mr. Reckless   *(Par 1948)*
Special Agent   *(Par 1949)*
Customs Agent   *(Col 1950)*

34

Betty Field

"I just want to do as many utterly different parts as I can get," Betty Field once said. "Variety teaches you to act and it keeps you fresh in your approach." Betty Field knew what she wanted out of a theatrical career and generally found it. She proved herself skillful in a wide range of roles. She progressed from child actress to ingenue to leading lady to character actress and along the way became one of America's outstanding actresses, especially on the stage. She was equally adept at comedy and serious drama. Her stage career began in a string of George Abbott Broadway comedies, and then she stunned audiences as Mae, the rancher's alluring wife who falls victim to the mentally retarded Lennie, in the film version of *Of Mice and Men* (1939). Betty always took acting seriously and always remained a New York stage actress at heart. She had a persistent loyalty to the theatre and when she signed a movie contract with Paramount in 1938, she insisted on a six-month Broadway clause to provide time for stage work. She was *not* one of those actresses who *only* spoke of returning to the stage after movie success came her way. She actually did return. Betty once candidly told *Screenland* magazine, "I'm not an outstanding personality and I'm certainly no beauty. Acting ability is all I've got to trade on."

Betty was born on February 8, 1918, in Boston, Massachusetts, the only child of Katherine Frances Lynch and George Baldwin Field. Her father, a salesman, was a descendant of Priscilla and John Alden. Her parents divorced when she was quite young. Thereafter, mother and daughter traveled to many Spanish-speaking countries where the girl learned to speak Spanish fluently. When her mother remarried, she settled down with her mom and step-father in Newton, Massachusetts, but then came a succession of movies that took the family to Morristown, New Jersey, and later to Forest Hills, New York. While Betty was attending high school in New Jersey she was allowed to go to Newark on Saturday afternoons to see matinees of Rowland G. Edwards' stock company. There she watched such actresses as Gale Sondergaard and Florence Reed perform. She soon decided to follow their professional example. "They were wonderful creatures to me," Betty later said. "Not quite human."

Betty would hang around the Newark theatre stage door to meet members of the company. She hounded the producer's secretary for small roles and after much persistence she was rewarded with a walk-on part in *The Shanghai Gesture,* starring Florence Reed. She received one dollar per performance, playing a Chinese girl behind a screen. Thereafter she played extra roles for the company in a number of other shows.

Betty quit high school after only two years and entered the American Academy of Dramatic Art, in New York, in October of 1932, realizing she needed

With Alan Ladd in a publicity pose for The Great Gatsby *(Par 1949)*

training as well as talent. She was the first in her acting class to obtain a professional job and played a maid in *The First Mrs. Fraser* at the Stockbridge Summer Theatre in Massachusetts. Betty was not present at the school's graduation ceremony because she had been engaged by Gilbert Miller for the London production of *She Loves Me Not* (1934). Miller had to rewrite the role of Frances Arbuthnot, the debutante, because Betty looked so young. (No other actress of the right age was willing to go to London for the little money offered.) The British hated *She Loves Me Not,* and, as Betty would recollect, ''My memory is that I entered London and left it between a lunch and a dinner and no one was aware I ever had been there.''

Once back in the States, she landed five theatre jobs in a row—all understudies—and she never got to step into any of the roles onstage. George Abbott then called her in to understudy and play a small role in *Page Miss Glory.* It was her first Broadway show and opened on November 27, 1934. She played a reporter and had two lines, ''Where's your necktie?'' and ''What's going on here, anyhow?'' This began her long professional association with Abbott and his successful Broadway comedies. She appeared in *Three Men on a Horse* (1935), *Boy Meets Girl* (1936), and she had her first important Broadway role as the hotel

manager's secretary in *Room Service* (1937), with Sam Levene. In 1938, she created the role of Barbara Pearson, Henry Aldrich's loyal girl friend, in *What a Life.* Paramount immediately signed her to a seven-year contract which contained that reluctantly given six-month stage work proviso. Before going to Hollywood, though, Betty had another Broadway success as Clare in *The Primrose Path* (1939).

Betty would have two distinct film careers. The first, starting in 1939 and lasting a decade, was as an ingenue and leading lady. The second, spanning from 1955 through 1968, was as a character actress. She was successful in both. Her first two films for Paramount were as ingenues of the stickiest sort. She re-created her original role in the film version of *What a Life* (1939) and played the baby-talking Lola, the young vamp, in *Seventeen* (1940). In both pictures she played opposite pleasant but undynamic Jackie Cooper. As Lola, her character was so nauseating in conception that not even Betty could make her palatable to film-goers. Paramount undoubtedly would have kept her whiling away the years in a series of young lady roles, had it not been for *Of Mice and Men.*

Eugene Solow, scripting the movie version of *Of Mice and Men,* phoned Sam and Bella Spewack and

With Fredric March in a publicity pose for Victory *(Par 1940)*

220

With Priscilla Lane in Blues in the Night *(WB 1941)*

With Robert Cummings in Kings Row *(WB 1941)*

asked the playwrights to suggest someone for the part of the all-important farm girl. They told him that Betty Field, a Hollywood newcomer, would be dandy for it. Betty was promptly tested and producer Hal Roach borrowed her from Paramount for the role. The National Board of Review chose her performance as one of the best of the year and the *New York Sun* reported, "Miss Field, with the unexpected force of her performance, immediately becomes an important actress in the dramatic field." At the age of twenty-two, Betty was already proving that she was one of the most versatile and capable actresses in tinsel land.

After her third picture she kept her promise to herself and returned to the Broadway stage to work again for George Abbott, this time in *Ring Two* (1939). It was her eighth and last Abbott assignment. The play ran only a few performances, but playwright Elmer Rice saw her in it and cast her in the lead of his new comedy, *Two on an Island* (1940). Brooks Atkinson, writing in the *New York Times,* noted, "She gives the whole play a captivating radiance." He also commented about the "modest sunniness" of her personality and the "grace of her acting." She also appeared in Rice's *Flight to the West* (1940) and *A New Life* (1943). Offstage, on January 12, 1942, Betty married the forty-nine-year-old playwright, and they had three children: John Alden, Judith, and Paul. Years later the children would act in summer stock with their mother.

In Holywood, Paramount cast her in *Victory* (1940), a diluted translation of Joseph Conrad's novel, which now boasted a happy ending. Betty was cast as Alma, a stranded member of a theatrical troupe who falls in love with Fredric March, a recluse on a Dutch East Indies island. The public never endorsed this sombre presentation and although Betty received some laudatory reviews (William Boehnel of the *New York World-Telegram* stated: "Betty Field can hardly be improved upon as the girl he befriends.") she could hardly wait to return to the Broadway stage.

Her first color film was *Shepherd of the Hills* (1941) with John Wayne. During the making of this Henry Hathaway-directed feature, she gained the reputation of being a hermit, for she seemingly never trod the social circuit. In point of fact, she was not a hermit, but was very concerned with her career. She preferred living quietly with her mother and spending most of her spare time reading play scripts. Paramount then loaned her out to Warner Bros. for what turned out to be two of her best parts. She received only second billing in *Blues in Night* (1941) which had a good blend of gangsterism and music. Priscilla

Lane had the female lead in the movie, but Betty had the choicest part as a despicable villainess, and never once allowed herself audience sympathy in the proceedings. *Cue* magazine reviewed, "Betty Field in a tragic, trollopy role, gives a tight, beautifully moulded performance." *PM* said she was directed to "play it as Messalina." The *New York Post* commented that "Betty Field puts on the vocal swagger so heavy that she sounds like a thin Mae West half the time." Betty, in this screen role, went far beyond anything she had done in the past. If one recalled her early comedies, this metamorphosis was all the more striking.

Her best-remembered screen role is probably as Cassie, Claude Rains' tormented daughter, in *Kings Row* (1942), based on the lushly constructed Henry Bellaman best selling novel about the 1890s in a small midwestern town. It was a very absorbing story similar to the later, *Peyton Place* novel and film. Under Sam Wood's guidance this 127-minute feature had strong direction and a richly ingratiating cast, all except for Robert Cummings, who, in the pivotal male lead, verged too often on the ludicrous. *Variety* judged that Betty "gives an irresistably touching performance. It is glowing, sensitive and a deeply persuasive portrayal." Not everyone was enamoured by her celluloid interpretation. The *New York Times* decided that her performance as "Cassie the crackpot . . . . takes the prize for village idiocy." Thereafter Betty was tested for and was a strong contender for the plum role of Maria in *For Whom the Bell Tolls* (1943), but lost it to Vera Zorina, who, in turn, lost it to Ingrid Bergman. Betty would have had no trouble capturing the accent, especially since she spoke Spanish fluently, but her quality was far too American for the vital role. Betty also had one detriment as a performer: her voice. She had a flat, unhurried manner of speech which sometimes came out with an annoying singsong quality.

Betty's only 1943 release was the supernatural *Flesh and Fantasy*. She gave a lovely performance as the ugly girl who hides behind a beautiful mask in this three-part film. Her co-star in the episode was Robert Cummings, less insipid as her would-be lover than in *Kings Row*. To conclude her Paramount contract, which she did not wish to renew, she joined Joel McCrea in *The Great Moment* (1944). While she photographed amazingly like Anita Louise in this Preston Sturges-directed feature (one of his rare directorial excursions away from comedy), she acted pure Fieldian. After appearing as the kindly school teacher, opposite Fredric March, in *Tomorrow the World* (1944), and as the bedraggled but optimistic farmer's wife, opposite Zachary Scott, in *The Southerner*

(1945), she returned to the Broadway stage to succeed Margaret Sullivan in the smash hit, *The Voice of the Turtle.*

This take-over stage venture was followed by the greatest achievement of her entire theatrical career: Georgina Allerton in Elmer Rice's *Dream Girl.* She played a twenty-three-year-old virgin who acts out a wide variety of daydreams. *Dream Girl* ran for 348 performances after it opened at the Coronet Theatre on December 14, 1945 with Mr. Rice also directing and co-producing the project. The part of Georgina is one of the most complex ever written for a woman and rivals *Hamlet* as the longest stage role. She is in front of the footlights, either in reality or in her daydreams, for all but two or three minutes of total playing time. It had always been thought that Elmer Rice wrote the play with Betty particularly in mind, but she later crisply remarked, "My husband wrote it, offered me the job, and I took it." For her performance, Betty received the New York Drama Critics Circle Award as the best actress of the year (1945–46) confirming what the critics had stated in print. *PM* called her "the most accomplished actress of her age now on Broadway." The *New Yorker* said, "She is a very subtle humorist at acting, and her performance is certainly one of the most impressive of the year." Along with Hedvig in Ibsen's *The Wild Duck,* Georgina was her most personally rewarding part. Betty was no longer under contract to Paramount when they filmed *Dream Girl* (1948) and the role went to Betty Hutton, thus making it a distorted, low-brow adaptation.

Betty did not appear on the screen again until 1949. For her old studio, Paramount, she played Daisy Buchanan in *The Great Gatsby.* Daisy is a very hard role to cast properly. She should be beautiful, but more importantly, have the ability to project the charm, the sadness, the vagueness, and the carelessness of the "disenchanted" high society female of the 1920s. The producer and co-author of the screenplay, Richard Maibaum, said, "We chose Betty Field because we decided her quality and her ability were more important than any other factors involved. We could think of no other actress who could manage what one of the London critics has called the 'disharmonic chatter' so typical of the period." The *Dallas Morning News* said of Betty's screen emoting here opposite Alan Ladd, "Betty Field, from the stage, plays Daisy with a vast skill, turning several sharp scenes and making the enigmatic woman understandable." In 1926, Florence Eldridge had played Daisy on the stage and the same year a silent film version premiered with Lois Wilson in the part. The 1974 filmization had Mia Farrow in the telling part.

Of all three versions, perhaps the 1949 one was least heralded, for it was geared as just another Alan Ladd vehicle. *The Great Gatsby* should have led to more delectable movie roles for Betty, but it did not, for she chose to return once again to Broadway. Her celluloid ingenue days were finished.

Betty's versatility as an actress was never more challenged than in the ensuing years onstage. She was a weary ex-dancer in *The Rat Race* (1949) (Debbie Reynolds played it in the film version); she replaced Jean Arthur as *Peter Pan* (1950), co-starring with Boris Karloff; she and Burgess Meredith replaced Jessica Tandy and Hume Cronyn in *The Fourposter* (1952); and she was in her husband's *Not for Children* (1951). Another highly acclaimed role was that of Mildred Tynan in Dorothy Parker and Arnaud d'Usseau's *Ladies of the Corridor* (1953), in which Betty played an alcoholic. She was particularly brilliant in a scene where she berates herself in front of a mirror and ultimately commits suicide by flinging herself out of a hotel window. In 1956 she appeared off-Broadway as Irina, the actress, in Chekhov's *The Seagull.* The *New York World Telegram and Sun* observed, "She doesn't seem to be playing Chekhov at all. In its way, her performance is consistent. It is light, quick and controlled. In going resolutely after every conceivable laugh, she makes Madame Arkadina seem not so much the mercurial artist of some magnitude, and of some personal involvement, but a giddy entertainer from the Moscow music halls." She was "althogether delightful" in *Waltz of the Toreadors* (1958) and she then co-starred with Helen Hayes, Kim Stanley, and Eric Portman in Eugene O'Neill's *Touch of the Poet,* which debuted at the Helen Hayes Theatre on October 2, 1958. As the witty Yankee patrician she only had one scene, but most of the critics used "brilliant" to describe her work. She also received a personal salute from O'Neill's widow: "Dear Miss Field," the note read, "Deborah is a particular pet of mine and I am very happy you are playing her. Success and good wishes. [Signed] Carlotta Monterey O'Neill."

When Betty returned to Hollywood filmmaking, it was quite evident what had been only an illusion onstage. She, in her late thirties, had lost* all shades of her once-blooming youth, and had taken on a hard, blowsy look. But as a character actress she

---

*A recent *Esquire* magazine article on *Crying* contains an anecdote regarding Betty. Writer Gloria Emerson reports, "I only just found out from a friend how he had once found her [Betty] weeping in front of a television set, watching herself in an old film like *Kings' Row,* suddenly seeing what her eyes and mouth and skin had once been."

proved superb. She was Kim Novak's earnest mother in *Picnic* (1955) which was directed by her old stage manager, Joshua Logan; she was a robust Grace, the diner owner, in the Logan-directed *Bus Stop* (1956) starring Marilyn Monroe; and she was quite moving as Nellie Cross, Hope Lange's suicide-bent mother, in *Peyton Place* (1957). Other supporting roles followed, such as Elizabeth Taylor's uncomprehending friend in *Butterfield 8* (1960) and as prisoner Burt Lancaster's in-name-only wife in *Birdman of Alcatraz* (1962). Certainly her least impressive film performance was as one of John Ford's *Seven Women* (1966). In Betty's last motion picture, the largely New York-lensed *Coogan's Bluff* (1968), starring Clint Eastwood and directed by action ace Don Siegel, she played an old floozie (and looked it). Although she had only one scene in the film, she gave an incisive portrayal.

For whatever soul-satisfying reasons, Betty never stopped working as an actress. If it was not in films or on the stage, it was on television. Her first exposure to this medium was in NBC's production of *Six Characters in Search of an Author* in 1950. One of her best video roles was as the librarian who finds romance on her first visit to a neighborhood cafe in *Happy Birthday* (1956) on NBC's "Producer's Showcase." Other TV-adapted theatrical plays that she enhanced were *They Knew What They Wanted* (1952), *Ah, Wilderness* (1959—which also starred Helen Hayes, Burgess Meredith, and Lloyd Nolan), *Uncle Harry* (1960), and *All Summer Long* (1961). In 1968 she was excellent as a witch cult priestess on a segment of the "Judd for the Defense" television series.

She and Elmer Rice divorced in 1956 and the following year she married lawyer and criminologist Edwin J. Lukas, cousin of the actor, Paul Lukas. This marriage also ended in divorce. On March 22, 1968 she married Raymond Olivere, an artist, with three children of his own. One of the reasons Betty did not work in Hollywood more often was because of her children. They lived in the East and she liked being near them as much as possible. Broadway saw her again in the all-star *Strange Interlude* (1963), as the Massachusetts mother in William Inge's *Where's Daddy?* (1966) as the Cockney landlady in the revival of Harold Pinter's *The Birthday Party* (1971), and as the taciturn nurse in Edward Albee's *All Over* (1971). Mexico and South America saw her as a member of the touring New York Repertory Theatre (1961–62), and the rest of the United States had chances to observe her stage work when she toured in many diversified roles, such as Amanda in *The Glass Menagerie* (1964), Birdie in *The Little Foxes* (1968), and as the unhappy mother in *The Effect of Gamma Rays on Man-in-the-Moon Marigolds* (1971). It all proved the remark Betty once made, "I'm only unhappy when I'm not working."

The day before she was to leave for Hollywood to make the movie *The Day of the Locust* (1974) and to do an "ABC Movie of the Week" she was stricken with a cerebral hemorrhage and died on September 13, 1973 in Hyannis, Massachusetts. She and her husband had spent the summer vacationing in Provincetown. Geraldine Page replaced her in the film.

Betty was never and could never have been a movie star in the traditional sense, because the theatre always came first with her, and she made no pretense of this loyalty when dealing with Hollywood producers. A performer of her versatility should have tried the classics, but the opportunity never came. In her early years she expressed a desire to play Cleopatra in Shaw's *Caesar and Cleopatra,* but the occasion never arose. However, she was not one to brood about parts she did not get. Her newest role was far more important to her. She once told an interviewer, "I think it must be awful not to work. My only point in being idle is to rest so that I can work more."

BETTY FIELD

What a Life *(Par 1939)*
Of Mice and Men *(UA 1939)*
Seventeen *(Par 1940)*
Victory *(Par 1940)*
Shepherd of the Hills *(Par 1941)*
Blues in the Night *(WB 1941)*
Are Husbands Necessary? *(Par 1942)*
Kings Row *(WB 1942)*
Flesh and Fantasy *(Univ 1943)*
The Great Moment *(Par 1944)*
Tomorrow the World *(UA 1944)*

The Southerner *(UA 1945)*
The Great Gatsby *(Par 1949)*
Picnic *(Col 1955)*
Bus Stop *(20th 1956)*
Peyton Place *(20th 1957)*
Hound Dog Man *(20th 1959)*
Butterfield 8 *(MGM 1960)*
Birdman of Alcatraz *(UA 1962)*
Seven Women *(MGM 1966)*
How to Save a Marriage—And Ruin Your Life *(Col 1968)*
Coogan's Bluff *(Univ 1968)*

35

Barry Fitzgerald

Long a fixture among the supporting players' ranks in Hollywood and even longer a member of the famed Abbey Players, Barry Fitzgerald did not hit his cinema stride until he won a Best Supporting Actor's Academy Award for his shamrock performance in Leo McCarey's *Going My Way* (1944). He was fifty-six years old when he was launched by Paramount as their resident ''leprechaun'' (he was 5' 3"). To his credit, the fame which came to him at such a mature age did not change his natural shyness, and his unaffected attitude saved his Irish-brogued presence from ever becoming too cloying. Fitzgerald's phenomenal movie fame was typical of the frantic forties, which saw a sudden fondness for ethnic flavor oncamera, whether Mexican (Tito Guizar), Brazilian (Carmen Miranda), Gallic (Jean Pierre Aumont), or Gaelic (Fitzgerald, his brother Arthur Shields, Sara Allgood, et. al.).

Fitzgerald (no relation to Warner Bros.' Geraldine F.) was born William Joseph Shields in Dublin, Ireland on March 10, 1888, the son of the *Evening Telegraph* columnist Adolphus William Shields and the former Fanny Ungerland. From Taylor's Endowed School, young William went to Civil Service College and became a junior executive in the Unemployment Insurance Division of the British Civil Service. Explaining his status in later years, he recalled, ''It was the one profession into which most of the families of

our grade in my young days tried to stow away their progeny, as it gave a fair living and a certain social status.''

Friendship with an actor from the celebrated Abbey Theatre, and goading by his brother Arthur who was studying there, finally led William Joseph to venture backstage at the theatre where he was induced to be part of a mob in a walk-on. ''They put a coat and a hat on,'' Fitzgerald would later recollect, ''and I went out there, tremblin' and shiverin'. I stayed the rest of that week and began to like it.'' Nevertheless, like it or not, practical William Shields held on to his dull, tedious Civil Service job.

His first speaking part with the Abbey Players was in 1915 in Richard Sheridan's *The Critic,* and consisted of four words, ''T'is meet it should.'' However, terrified by stagefright, he muffled his cue and changed the words to ''T'is sheet it mould.'' His terror produced the heartiest laughter of the evening and launched his career as a comedian. The Abbey gave him small parts, then larger ones, but he clung to his Civil Service post for fourteen more years until he felt reasonably assured his life could be supported by his acting. At the age of forty-one he became a full-time member of the renowned Dublin Theatre group, having long since adopted the name of Barry Fitzgerald to mask his double life of actor and civil servant.

He performed in plays by Pirandello, Molnar, Strindberg, and the contemporary Irish dramatists Dunsany, Yeats, Synge, and Sean O'Casey, O'Casey

With Cary Grant in None But the Lonely Heart *(RKO 1944)*

in 1929, wrote *The Silver Tassie* especially for Fitzgerald and persuaded the actor to play it on the London stage. Fitzgerald resigned from the Civil Service and shared an apartment in London with O'Casey, but *The Silver Tassie* failed and Fitzgerald found employment in Cochran's musical comedies. The training, discipline, and freedom to develop roles at the Abbey appealed to him more than the commercial theatre and he returned to Dublin to join the players on a tour of America.

During his first Abbey Theatre tour of America in 1932, Fitzgerald told the press: "The Abbey Theatre is a healthy part of Irish life. It receives seven-hundred fifty pounds annually as a subsidy from the government. We use it as a political clearing house. If it hadn't been for the Abbey, Dublin might have exploded more times in the past than it has. Ever since it was founded by Yeats and George Moore around 1898, it has been the mouthpiece for Irish nationalism. Sometimes our Dublin audiences get pretty excited, but we don't mind that. A vocal protest is a healthy sign. Such plays as *Kathleen-ni-Houlihan* have had a great political influence. Our seats are priced so that almost anyone can attend. Many a fellow has become an Irish nationalist after attending an Abbey performance. That was true in my case."

Two years later, Fitzgerald was back in the States playing shiftless, if lovable, "Captain" John Boyle in O'Casey's *Juno and the Paycock* and Fluther Good in *The Plough and the Stars*. At the concluding performance of *Juno* at the Golden Theatre, an unprecedented tribute was presented to Fitzgerald on stage by Channing Pollock. It was a testimonial scroll proclaiming him the greatest character comedian in the world. The scroll read: "In token of his distinctive contribution to the theatre in his widely varied interpretations of such roles as Captain John Boyle, Fluther Good, Michael James, and James Duffy and many others, we present this scroll with our signatures attached expressing our conviction that he is the most versatile character comedian in the world today." The scroll was signed by Mayor Fiorello La Guardia, Eva Le Gallienne, Walter Winchell, William Phelps, Whitney Bolton, and the theatre critics from all the New York City newspapers. Fitzgerald was astounded by the award, saying hesitantly with deep emotion, "There are no stars in the Abbey Theatre. Sometimes we get big parts, and we are grateful. Other times we are cast in small roles. Each of us tries our best. Any attainment you good people may extol me for is but reflected glory."

Barry had made his film debut as the orator in *Juno and the Paycock*, directed by Alfred Hitchcock in 1930. Later, Fitzgerald would play the lead role of the "Captain" more than two hundred times on the stage in repertory. His first Hollywood film production was for master director John Ford in a part he had performed on the stage, Fluther Good, in Dudley Nichols' screen adaptation of O'Casey's *The Plough and the Stars* (1936). The play was set against a background of the Irish Easter Rebellion of 1916 and for the production Ford used other fine players from Dublin's Abbey Theatre to surround and showcase leading lady Barbara Stanwyck.

Fitzgerald remained in Hollywood for several undistinguished films where his natural talents were significant if wasted, and, on January 10, 1939, he was back on Broadway at the Cort Theatre as Canon Matt Lavelle in Paul Vincent Carroll's *The White Steed.* His acting was brilliant as the crippled clergyman, but he found that "this is the most tiring role I have ever played. Ever since the play opened it has been more of a drain on my strength and energy than you would believe. When you are able to move about, you can act with your whole body, express yourself with all sorts of gestures. But Canon Lavelle is paralyzed and so I can only use my face and hands and voice, and it is surprisingly wearing." It was also not-so-surprisingly a great performance. The following January, he and Sara Allgood were back on Braodway with *Juno and the Paycock,* and Fitzgerald tied with Alfred Lunt for the critics' choice of the best male performer of the 1939–40 season.

Of Eugene O'Neill's filmed plays only John Ford's expertly handled *The Long Voyage Home* (1940) found favor with the playwright. Ford's combination of several one-act plays by O'Neill set aboard the S.S. *Glencairn* was distinguished by several fine performances, among them Barry Fitzgerald as Cocky and John Wayne as Ole Olson. Barry then returned to the New York stage in Louis d'Alton's play *Tanyard Street* at the Little Theatre, playing the part of a grumbling hypochrondriac, Mosey Furlong. However, Fitzgerald's crisp playing and the talents of Margo, Lloyd Gough, and Barry's brother, Arthur Shields, could not rescue the play beyond twenty-three performances.

Barry returned to the West Coast and to films. Although lensed five times before, Robert Rossen's powerful screenplay of Jack London's novel *The Sea Wolf* (1941) was expertly cast by Warner Bros. and skillfully directed by Michael Curtiz. In a film brimming with vivid performances from Edward G. Robinson, John Garfield, Gene Lockhart, and Ida Lupino, Barry's portrayal of the menacing "Cooky" of the ship, "Ghost," who loses his leg to a shark, was well defined and truly played. At the end of 1941 he was part of another power-packed cast in John Ford's Twentieth Century-Fox version of Richard Llewellyn's

With Tom Dillon and Arthur Shields in Easy Come, Easy Go *(Par 1947)*

With Paulette Goddard and Sonny Tufts in I Love a Soldier *(Par 1944)*

With Bing Crosby and Hume Cronyn in Top o' the Morning *(Par 1949)*

novel *How Green Was My Valley* and gave a stand-out performance as Cyfartha. Sara Allgood was present to portray the warm-hearted mother of a brood that included Roddy McDowall and Maureen O'Hara.

The next two years were a general waste of Barry's talents in unmemorable films, and then, in 1944, he signed a contract with Paramount and was cast as irascible Father Fitzgibbon in *Going My Way,* which starred Bing Crosby. There was general rejoicing about Fitzgerald's great performance as the petulant, crotchety old priest who wins a new lease on life. As a gimmick within the film, Barry's real-life mother was brought from Ireland for a cameo assignment as his onscreen mother. The New York Film Critics hailed *Going My Way* as the best picture of the year and Barry's performance as the best of the year. The following March, the Academy of Motion Picture Arts and Sciences awarded him an Oscar for the Best Supporting Actor of the Year over Hume Cronyn, Clifton Webb, Claude Rains, and Monty Woolley. (Interestingly, Barry had been nominated in the Best Actor category for the same role—in that division, Bing Crosby won the prize for his priest characterization.)

Over at RKO, Barry managed to give a telling performance against Ethel Barrymore's Oscar-winning role and the exceptionally controlled dramatic acting of Cary Grant in *None But the Lonely Heart* (1944). Paramount seemed intent on merely exploiting Fitzgerald's onscreen cuteness, and cast him in supporting roles of Mike Guinan, Texas Guinan's (Betty Hutton) father dreaming of fantastic financial windfalls in *Incendiary Blonde* (1945), and again with Hut-

ton, he was starred as Jerry B. Bates, a masquerading millionaire serving table at *The Stork Club* (1945). For the home lot's all-star *Duffy's Tavern* (1945), he played Bing Crosby's father.

His luck always seemed to be better away from Paramount. At Twentieth Century-Fox he appeared in Rene Clair's extraordinarily cast film of Agatha Christie's play *Ten Little Indians,* retitled for the screen, *And Then There Were None* (1945). He was Judge Quincannon, blithely murdering most of the cast in cadence with the child's nursery rhyme, "Ten Little Indians" His scene with Walter Huston (as Dr. Armstrong) was a gem as the two professionals tried desperately to outwit one another. Two more supporting roles at Paramount, Terence O'Feenaughty in *Two Years Before the Mast* (1946) and Michael Fabian in *California* (1946), made way for a reunion with his *Going My Way* co-star, Bing Crosby, in what Paramount hoped would be a duplication of the Award-winning Leo McCarey triumph. However, *Welcome Stranger* (1947), in which Crosby was the new young doctor in town, did not equal its predecessor.

Nothing Barry would do on the screen ever matched his performance in *Going My Way,* but the parts were not as bright and the pictures were a good deal duller. After a series of mild comedies he was back with Crosby again as Officer Brian McNaughton, a kindly if not too bright Irish cop trying to help Crosby locate the stolen Blarney Stone in *Top O' the Morning* (1949). It was the type of role audiences expected from Barry, much more so than the previous year's outing in high melodrama at Universal, where, as Lieutenant Dan Muldoon of the New York homi-

230

cide squad, he followed the clues to a bathtub murder in *The Naked City.* (The *New York Times* complained of his performance, "It is just a combination of standard Fitzgerald and Sherlock Holmes.")

If Barry was generally, irrepressible onscreen, he was equally so offcamera. Much to the consternation of his Paramount bosses, he rode to work on his motorcycle, defying protests that it was a dangerous sport. At age fifty he started to study the piano and in a few years was playing Bach, Beethoven, and Brahms in a rented bungalow he shared for several years with his stand-in, aide, and friend, Angus D. Taillon, a Scottish-named Iroquois Indian.

Fitzgerald's wealth of expression was given full play in yet another John Ford picture, *The Quiet Man* (1952), shot largely on location in Ireland. John Wayne and Maureen O'Hara were the stars, but Barry shone as the matchmaking-bookmaker whose thirst for the brew almost equalled his ability to make wry quips. He was especially memorable in the sequence in which he surveys a bedroom the morning after a wedding night, only his eyes and facial muscles conveying his suspicion of a riotously bawdy night. While in Europe, Barry traveled to Italy where he, along with Lois Maxwell and Una O'Connor, appeared in the Rome-lensed *Il Filo D'Erba* (1952). Back in Hollywood, Fitzgerald was the sensitive uncle in *The Catered Affair* (1956), starring Bette Davis, Ernest Borgnine, and Debbie Reynolds.

Barry then returned to Ireland. For Rank's 1958 film *Rooney,* he gave a charming performance as a grand-father spending his life's savings to help his grand-daughter. The next year, he participated in the Paul Rotha-directed documentary, *The Cradle of Genius,* dealing with the history of the Abbey Theatre. Barry's last screen role was, fittingly, another Irish comedy, *Broth of a Boy* (1959), in which he played Patrick Farrell.

Away from his Paramount contract, Barry was heard on NBC's radio series, "His Honor, the Barber" (1945); for CBS's "Video Theatre" he was seen in *The Man who Struck It Rich* and repeated his stage role in *The White Steed* on "G.E. Theatre" in 1954. For Alfred Hitchcock's video series, he appeared in the episode, *Santa Claus and the 10th Avenue Kid.*

On January 4, 1961, the battlin' bantam Irishman died in Dublin after an illness of several months. He had had brain surgery just two years before. This jovial man with his mischievous blue eyes and a stubborn, agressive jaw contributed many hours of pleasure to audiences around the world. He once said, "You can dig deeper into human nature and in everyone there is a strata of humanity from which warm, human laughter can be brought to the surface. Humanity is a grand thing!" He could bring laughter to the surface in any of his oncamera bar-room brawls by agreeing to take on any man in the house, and then reveal his great acting artistry in performances such as Father Fitzgibbon, basing his character on his observation of clerical friends, not on his own experience in the Catholic Church—Barry was a Protestant!

BARRY FITZGERALD

Juno and The Paycock *(Wardour 1930)*
When Knights Were Bold *(General Film Distributors 1936)*
The Plough and the Stars *(RKO 1936)*
Ebb Tide *(Par 1937)*
Pacific Liner *(RKO 1938)*
Bringing Up Baby *(RKO 1938)*
The Dawn Patrol *(WB 1938)*
Four Men and a Prayer *(20th 1938)*
The Saint Strikes Back *(RKO 1939)*
Full Confession *(RKO 1939)*
The Long Voyage Home *(UA 1940)*
San Francisco Docks *(Univ 1940)*
The Sea Wolf *(WB 1941)*
How Green Was My Valley *(20th 1941)*
Tarzan's Secret Treasure *(MGM 1941)*
Two Tickets to London *(Univ 1943)*
The Amazing Mrs. Holliday *(Univ 1943)*
Corvette K-225 *(Univ 1943)*
I Love a Soldier *(Par 1944)*
Going My Way *(Par 1944)*
None But the Lonely Heart *(RKO 1944)*
Incendiary Blonde *(Par 1945)*

And Then There Were None *(20th 1945)*
Duffy's Tavern *(Par 1945)*
Stork Club *(Par 1945)*
Two Years Before the Mast *(Par 1946)*
California *(Par 1946)*
Welcome Stranger *(Par 1947)*
Easy Come, Easy Go *(Par 1947)*
Variety Girl *(Par 1947)*
The Sainted Sisters *(Par 1948)*
The Naked City *(Univ 1948)*
Miss Tatlock's Millions *(Par 1948)*
The Story of Seabiscuit *(WB 1949)*
Top O'the Morning *(Par 1949)*
Union Station *(Par 1950)*
Silver City *(Par 1951)*
The Quiet Man *(Rep 1952)*
Il Filo D'Erba *(Italian 1952)*
Tonight's The Night *(AA 1954)*
The Catered Affair *(MGM 1956)*
Rooney *(Rank 1958)*
Broth of a Boy *(Kingsley-International 1959)*

36

Geraldine Fitzgerald

Geraldine Fitzgerald was singularly fortunate in her first two American-made films. She made an auspicious Hollywood debut as Isabella Linton, the desperate girl who makes a fool of herself over Heathcliffe (Laurence Olivier) in William Wyler's unforgettable *Wuthering Heights* (1939), and immediately followed that role with a deeply moving performance as Bette Davis' devoted friend in *Dark Victory* (1939). She was Oscar-nominated for her performance in *Wuthering Heights*, but lost out in the Best Supporting Actress category to Hattie McDaniel of *Gone with the Wind.*

Her two 1939 American features were very distinguished productions and no young actress could have had a more successful beginning to her film career. However, Geraldine never became a goddess of the silver screen as was expected. One of the reasons for this was that she fought the contract system before she was in the position to do so. While under contract to Warner Bros., she felt she was being exploited and turned down many roles, resulting in her suspension a number of times. This type of action had worked for Bette Davis, a good friend of Geraldine's, but Miss Davis was already an important money-earner for the studio and Geraldine was not. As Geraldine told columnist Rex Reed: "Humphrey Bogart always told me movies were like a slot machine. If you played long enough, you'd eventually hit the jackpot, which he did with *Maltese Falcon*. But I was a fool. I stuck to my Irish logic instead of saying yes to everything. I fought Jack Warner for better parts, and I finally lost."

Geraldine was born in Dublin on November 24, 1914, to Edward and Edith Fitzgerald. Her father was a prominent attorney with his own law firm and, quite often in the years ahead, handled Geraldine's contract problems in Hollywood. Her aunt, Shelah Richards, was a noted Abbey Theatre actress. Geraldine says that Sean O'Casey wrote all of his female roles for her aunt and that Barry Fitzgerald (no relation) was so in love with her that he never married. Another distant relative was James Joyce. Joyce used the name of her father's firm, D. & T. Fitzgerald, in *Ulysses.*

As a child, Geraldine witnessed many dramatic events of the Irish revolution and was moved to London during the worst part of the uprising. During her girlhood she never thought about acting, for she had hopes of becoming a painter. After attending convent school, she entered the Dublin Art School in 1928. "I really wasn't very good," she has said.

Her entrance into the theatre world came about purely accidentally. As she remembers: "I'd gone with Aunt Shelah to a rehearsal at the Gate Theatre and the director saw me with her and mistook me for some established actress and shouted, 'You're late—get on stage immediately!' I read, he signed me, and months later I asked him how long he'd been fooled. 'Not very long, dear,' he said, 'I knew instantly you'd never read before'—but he seemed to see a promise."

At the Gate she played everything from walk-ons to romantic leads and character parts. Other members of the company were Orson Welles, James Mason,

Publicity pose ca. 1940

and Michael MacLiammoir. While at the Gate, British film studios noticed her and cast her in a number of films, most of which were anything but noteworthy except for *Turn of the Tide* (1935) and *The Mill on the Floss* (1937). Reviewing the latter picture, the London *Daily Telegraph* printed: "Miss Fitzgerald reveals charm, repose, an attractive speaking voice and a technique already remarkably mature—a combination of qualities which should take her a long way." By this point, Geraldine had already lost her once thick Irish brogue.

In 1938 she and her husband, Edward Lindsay-Hogg, whom she had married two years earlier, traveled to New York, she to pursue acting and he to write songs, which he did as a hobby. A wealthy Irish horseman, Lindsay-Hogg was also president of the Irish Red Cross. The couple had a son, Michael, born in 1940, who is now a very successful television director in London and who was director of the Beatles' film, *Let It Be* (1970). Geraldine's Gate Theatre chum, Orson Welles, then hired her for his Mercury Theatre in New York and she made her Broadway debut with the company on April 29, 1938, in Shaw's *Heartbreak House.* The Mercury Theatre was having more than its share of financial troubles and finally disbanded. "So we all ended up in Hollywood in the competitive star system," says Geraldine.

Many movie offers came her way and she decided to accept Warner Bros.' bid if they agreed to give her six months off every year to pursue her theatrical career. She returned to her family in Dublin while the studio made up its mind. They finally acquiesced to her demands and she was signed to an agreement that began with *Dark Victory.* Prior to that vehicle, which starred Bette Davis and George Brent, she was borrowed by Samuel Goldwyn for *Wuthering Heights,* named the best picture of 1939 by the New York Film Critics over *Gone with the Wind.* She received sensational reviews for her performance as Isabella. The *New York World-Telegram* admitted "the real joy of the film is Geraldine Fitzgerald, who is both beautiful and forthright." The *New York Daily News* agreed, saying that she "walks away with most of the acting honors." But *Dark Victory* is the film most people remember her for, especially her final scene in the flower garden with the dying, blind Bette Davis.

Geraldine was among those considered for a plum role in *Gone with the Wind,* and when Warners seemed unlikely to loan Olivia de Havilland for the part of Melanie, it appeared that Geraldine might

With Donald Woods, Janis Wilson, and Bette Davis in Watch on the Rhine *(WB 1943)*

234

have the assignment. Had it been offered to her she probably would have rejected it because she naturally preferred the role of Scarlett. At any rate, in her third film, *A Child Is Born* (1940), a rather morbid remake of Loretta Young's *Life Begins* (1932), Geraldine had the lead role. However, it was during the production of this Lloyd Bacon-directed feature that she became truly disenchanted with the studio system. To her dismay, the once-naive miss discovered that each film turned out on the production line was not conceived as a piece of art. She was so dismayed by her realization that she rebelled whenever possible against the assembly-line style of filmmaking. She was to have starred opposite Laurence Olivier in *The Prime Minister,* a film of Disraeli's life, but the picture was never made. She was set to appear opposite Errol Flynn in *The Sea Hawk* (1940), but at the last minute rejected it and was replaced by Brenda Marshall. *Forgive Us Our Trespasses* with John Garfield and Fay Bainter, *Underground* with Garfield, *Lost Beauty* with George Brent, and *Captain Hornblower* were also film projects that never materialized. The studio did film *Captain Horatio Hornblower* in 1951 with Virginia Mayo in the role that Geraldine was scheduled to do. *Underground* was filmed in 1941 without Ger-

aldine or Garfield. Bette Davis, Miriam Hopkins, and Geraldine were the three original Bronte sisters in Warners' *Devotion* (1946), but were replaced, respectively, by Ida Lupino, Olivia de Havilland, and Nancy Coleman. Miss Coleman also replaced Geraldine in *Dangerously They Live* (1941) with Garfield. Instead, Geraldine played a role quite similar to her *Dark Victory* one in *'Til We Meet Again* (1940), a remake of the Kay Francis and William Powell vehicle, *One Way Passage* (1932), with Merle Oberon as the fatally ill heroine this time. The *New York Herald-Tribune* said that Geraldine gave "a customarily brilliant account of herself." She was also quite good as Jeffrey Lynn's wife in *Flight from Destiny* (1941) and in the prestigious, but unsuccessful, *Shining Victory* (1941), a love story about a psychiatrist and his assistant.

The Gay Sisters (1942), starring Barbara Stanwyck, was the first of her "monster" roles, as she calls them, and she loved doing it. "I wore a monocle and stamped all over the place in my high heels," she says. She loathes playing noble heroines, "If I had my way I would like to play an absolute monster. The public likes monsters." She was back in a sympathetic role supporting Bette Davis again in *Watch on the*

With Charles Coburn, Stanley Ridges, Thomas Mitchell, and Sidney Blackmer in Wilson *(20th 1944)*

With Harold Vermilyea and Alan Ladd in O.S.S. (Par 1946)

Rhine, 1943's best film, playing Marthe de Brancovis, wife of Fascist George Coulouris. "I would much rather have Coulouris' part," she said at the time.

Warners then re-negotiated her contract and instead of having six months' freedom each year she was allowed one picture a year for any other studio. She quite wisely chose *Wilson* (1944) at Twentieth Century-Fox. The picture was nominated for numerous awards and was highly acclaimed. Geraldine portrayed the second Mrs. Wilson (to Alexander Knox's president) and was beautifully coiffured and gowned for the important role. After being loaned to Universal for another colorful "monster" role in *Ladies Courageous* (1944) (a part originally intended for Diana Barrymore), Geraldine stayed on at the studio for *The Strange Affair of Uncle Harry* (1945) as George Sanders' long-suffering sister. She concluded her Warners' pact with the fascinating but overlooked *Three Strangers* (1946) and *Nobody Lives Forever* (1946) in which she finally got to co-star with John Garfield.

Two 1940s films that she made for Paramount gave Geraldine ample opportunity to display her versatility. She had a showcase role in *O.S.S.* (1946) as an agent of the Office of Strategic Services who, along with Alan Ladd, is ordered to destroy rail lines being used by the Nazis. It was a generally taunt, moving film and provided Geraldine with her best role as a leading lady. The other film was *So Evil, My Love* (1948), with Ray Milland and Ann Todd, in which Geraldine played a sweet dipsomaniac. One New York film critic said that she gave the picture's best performance, underplaying her part as the frightened, heartbroken wife, for all it was worth. "She manages to attract a little sympathy in a bird-like portrayal of a woman who would like nothing better than to kill her husband, but who hasn't the courage or the will to do it."

Geraldine had turned down the British-made picture *So Well Remembered* (1947), which Martha Scott did in her place, but in 1951, she accepted an English offer to make *The Late Edwina Black,* released in the U.S. as *The Obsessed.* Geraldine accepted this minor film job because, frankly, she had no other offers at the time. She did not appear on the screen again until 1958.

Geraldine and Lindsay-Hogg were divorced on August 30, 1946, and the following month she married Stuart Scheftel, whom she had met at the home of lyricist Howard Dietz. Scheftel, grandson of the founder of Macy's, was once the director of the *New York Post,* had conceived the *Sports Illustrated* Magazine, and had even helped pay for the Pan American building. The Scheftels have a daughter named Susan, born in 1951, for whom Geraldine turned down professional assignments between 1951–55 because she wanted to spend more time with her daughter than her career had allowed when her son was a youngster.

However, as time passed, Geraldine could not stay away from show business. "I knew I wouldn't remain happy if I divorced myself from the entertainment world on a permanent basis." She appeared in a number of plays that were quick failures, such as *Hide and Seek,* which opened on Broadway on April 2, 1957, but she was generally always praised for her portrayals by the critics. Earlier, she had been in the cast of *The Doctor's Dilemma* (1955) at the Phoenix Theatre in downtown New York and the *New Yorker* Magazine termed her the most appetizing woman ever to take the part of Mrs. Dubedat. She played Goneril to Orson Welles' *King Lear* at the City Center and Gertrude in *Hamlet* for the Connecticut Shakespeare Festival. In 1961, she was directed by her son, Michael, as the Queen in *The Cave Dwellers.* "He really has a great deal of talent—and I'm speaking as an actress, not as a mother."

Surprisingly, Geraldine has not done much in television over the years. Her Elizabeth Barrett Browning in the video special "The Barretts of Wimpole Street" (1955) lacked the needed romantic fervor. She also appeared in specials of "Dodsworth" (1956) and "The Moon and Sixpence" (1959). She was on the evening soap opera "Our Private World" (1965) for CBS. This tearjerker was an offshoot of the daytime show "As the World Turns," but it was unable to survive beyond one summer. In 1970, she did the daytime soap opera "The Best of Everything" for ABC, co-starring with Gale Sondergaard. However, this show was not a success either.

It was not until 1958 that Geraldine returned to Hollywood, this time to play Gary Cooper's prim, shrewish wife in *Ten North Frederick,* directed by Philip Dunne. Had there not been so much publicity about the oncamera May-December romance in the film between Suzy Parker and Cooper, Geraldine's fiercely cold portrayal might have netted her a Best Supporting Actress nomination. Her other film chores have been few and far between. She was in the Zulu action tale, *The Fiercest Heart* (1961) and then surprisingly overplayed her roles as a social worker in *The Pawnbroker* (1965) and as a crazy preacher in *Rachel, Rachel* (1968). Her tendency, recently, is to play for all it's worth. This approach can work on the stage but onscreen it becomes somewhat overbearing. She was Jacqueline Bisset's mother in *Speed Is of the Essence,* but when the MGM film was released as *Believe in Me* (1971), Geraldine's role had been deleted. Her most recent film appearances have been as

Jeff Bridges' patient mother in *The Last American Hero* (1973), Oscar-winning Art Carney's semi-senile old flame in *Harry and Tonto* (1974) a featured spot in *Cold Sweat* (1975), and a part in *Echoes of a Summer* (1975).

In the late 1960s, Geraldine's husband earned a dollar a year as chairman of Mayor Lindsay's Youth Council Board and Geraldine joined the bandwagon by starting a Theatre of the People in which plays were performed on the streets of New York. She and a Franciscan monk, Brother Jonathan Ringcamp, formed a modernized version of *Everyman* and staged it on the streets. "Street theatre is not a copy of any existing theatre," she says. "It has its own needs and its own solutions. It's truly for every man." They even wrote a satirical rock opera version of *Macbeth* and performed it with neighborhood people in the cast. "The Theatre should belong to everyone," she explains.

The Scheftels live luxuriously on East 79th Street in New York, and Geraldine spends much of her time writing or performing in all media, including college tours and resident theatres such as the Long Wharf in New Haven, where she recently appeared opposite E. G. Marshall in Ibsen's *The Master Builder.* She toured colleges in *The Honorable Estate,* a stage production consisting of separate vignettes on love and marriage. A play that she wrote, with the title, *The End Is Here, Baby,* was performed at Lincoln Center in 1968. She has also been writing film scripts and hopes to see them produced. One such scenario was based on Edna O'Brien's novel, *The Country Girls,* which, at one time, Sam Spiegel was interested in producing.

There have been several highlights in Geraldine's recent past. In 1971 she starred in an off-Broadway revival of *Long Day's Journey into Night.* Her interpretation of the drug-addicted mother brought critics and audiences to their feet. Her portrayal of Mary Tyrone was decidedly different from that of either Florence Eldridge (on Broadway in 1956) or that of Katharine Hepburn (in the 1962 film version). Geraldine made her a very strong, definitively Irish woman. Both she and her co-star, Robert Ryan, were hailed as two of the finest actors working in theatre. If Geraldine's performance as native American Carrie Chapman Catt on television's "The American Parade: We the Women" (1974) did not gain acceptance (her accent was "out of sync with the rest of the show" said

Variety), she more than made up for it when, in May, 1974, she made her nightclub debut in New York's showcase room, Reno Sweeney, with what she termed as "an evening of street songs." Said the enthused *New York Times'* reporter. "Miss Fitzgerald's singing voice is a limited instrument, but one is scarcely aware of this, because she acts singing. It is her eyes that hold one's attention—dancing, gleaming, vital eyes that accent, underline, and project the varying emotional values of her performance. In the easy, informal flow of her program, she blends music and theater and her own warm personality to create an exceptional evening in a supper club." It is said this innovative move for Geraldine is a warmup for her musical stage bow in a version of *Juno and the Paycock.*

Then late in 1974 at the Long Wharf Theatre at New Haven, Geraldine was Essie the mother, with Teresa Wright as Lily the maiden aunt in a rousing production of Eugene O'Neill's *Ah, Wilderness!* which received a tremendous reception. In 1975, besides performing in several features, Geraldine was on television in *Forget-Me-Not Lane,* a seriocomic drama adapted by Peter Nichols from his 1971 London stage hit. Donald Moffat co-starred. In the summer of 1975 Miss Fitzgerald, along with Eileen Heckart, Fred Gwynne, and others, performed for the American Shakespeare Theatre, Connecticut in Thornton Wilder's *Our Town.*

Geraldine's once auburn hair is now touched with gray, but the emerald eyes are still alive and vibrant. She is a petite five feet three inches, an intelligent, honest woman, totally without pretensions. As she told Rex Reed of her early film career. "I don't think anyone remembers me from those days. I was at Warner Brothers at a time when you had to look like Joan Crawford or Garbo or you may as well have stayed home. Warners was the cheapest studio—they wouldn't pay for us to wear eyelashes or have our teeth capped—but they gave us good scripts, and now I think it has paid off. The old Warner movies look better on the late show than the others because we were allowed to be ourselves." She admits: "I made a mistake trying to fight Hollywood because, it's an invisible adversary," adding: "No one had ever thrown away good breaks with such monotonous frequency. I had to sit by and watch everyone else play parts that I knew could have been mine."

GERALDINE FITZGERALD

Open all Night   *(Radio 1934)*
The Lad   *(Univ—British 1935)*
Turn of the Tide   *(Gaumont 1935)*
The Ace of Spades   *(Radio 1935)*
Three Witnesses   *(Univ—British 1935)*
Lt. Daring, R.N.   *(Butcher's 1935)*
Blind Justice   *(Univ—British 1935)*
Debt of Honour   *(General Film Distributors 1935)*
Radio Parade of 1935   *(Radio 1935)*
Department Store   *(Radio 1935)*
Cafe Mascot   *(Par—British 1936)*
The Mill on the Floss   *(British Lion 1937)*
Wuthering Heights   *(UA 1939)*
Dark Victory   *(WB 1939)*
A Child is Born   *(WB 1940)*
'Till We Meet Again   *(WB 1940)*
Flight from Destiny   *(WB 1941)*
Shining Victory   *(WB 1941)*

The Gay Sisters   *(WB 1942)*
Watch on the Rhine   *(WB 1943)*
Ladies Courageous   *(Univ 1944)*
Wilson   *(20th 1944)*
The Strange Affair of Uncle Harry   *(Univ 1945)*
Three Strangers   *(WB 1946)*
O.S.S.   *(Par 1946)*
Nobody Lives Forever   *(WB 1946)*
So Evil, My Love   *(Par 1948)*
The Obsessed (a.k.a., The Late Edwina Black)   *(UA 1951)*
10 North Frederick   *(20th 1958)*
The Fiercest Heart   *(20th 1961)*
The Pawnbroker   *(Landau 1965)*
Rachel, Rachel   *(WB 1968)*
The Last American Hero   *(20th 1973)*
Harry and Tonto   *(20th 1974)*
Cold Sweat   *(UA 1975)*
Echoes of a Summer   *(Bryanston 1975)*

37

Nina Foch

One of the more amazing aspects of 1940s cinema was the staggering number of ingenues hired by the Hollywood film factories to decorate their assembly line features. However, it was rare, and this was particularly true at the lesser studios, that a starlet made a sufficiently deep impression to last beyond her term contract, let alone to remain in the public's favor over the year. A pleasant exception to this seemingly unwritten law was Nina Foch, who rose from the Columbia Pictures' salt mines to become a seasoned, respected actress.

Consuelo Flowerton was the famous World War I "Poster Girl," a beautiful woman who crossed the stage in several musical comedies and appeared as Olympe in Nazimova's *Camille,* Metro's 1921 film production that featured Rudolpho Valentino as Armand. She appeared in several silent features and, after completing *The Sixth Commandment* (1924) with William Faversham and Charlotte Walker, returned to Holland with her husband, the noted Dutch composer and symphony conductor, Dirk Fock. In Leyden, Netherlands, on April 20, 1924, they became the parents of a daughter they named Nina Consuelo Maud Fock. When the child was two, her parents were divorced and her mother took her to New York. Nina grew up in her mother's native Manhattan where she had a thorough musical education at her

father's insistence and made a creditable debut in her early teens as a concert pianist at Aeolian Hall.

Occasionally, Consuelo Flowerton returned to the stage in such fare as *Lysistrata,* supporting Blanche Yurka with Ernest Truex and Miriam Hopkins, and she continually encouraged her gifted daughter. Nina studied painting and sculpturing at Parsons School of Design and the Art Student's League, graduated from New York's Lincoln School, and entered the American Academy of Dramatic Art, eventually studying acting with such future stars as Stella Adler and Lee Strasberg. Her talents, inherited and developed, were seemingly endless, but it was acting that captured her active and agile mind. After appearing with several little theatre groups, she landed a small part in a touring company of *Western Union, Please,* starring deadpan comedian Charles Butterworth. By the time she was nineteen and had long since changed her last name to Foch, she had signed a contract with Columbia Pictures.

Her screen debut was truly bizarre, playing with Bela Lugosi in *The Return of the Vampire* (1943), followed by a featured role in *Nine Girls* (1944), a murder mystery with Ann Harding. She made five more B films including the offbeat *Cry of the Werewolf* (1944), before Columbia assigned her the role of Constantina in their lavish misrepresentation of the life of Chopin. In *A Song to Remember* (1945) Cornel Wilde played the composer, Merle Oberon portrayed

With George Raft in Johnny Allegro *(Col 1949)*

With Glenn Ford in The Undercover Man *(Col 1949)*

George Sand, and Paul Muni passed through a considerable number scenes as Chopin's teacher. Columbia may have had Rita Hayworth, Janet Blair, Adele Jergens, et al., to provide the sex allure onscreen, but in *A Song to Remember,* Nina proved that she was definitely an asset in the acting department.

In the title role of *My Name Is Julia Ross* (1945), she gave a thoroughly brilliant performance. "She knows how to vary the typical heroine's wide-eyed terror with calm deliberation," reported the *New York Herald-Tribune.* The *New York Daily News*'s Wanda Hale labeled Nina "up and coming." In this modest feature she is the girl being driven to near madness and suicide by Dame May Whitty and George Macready. It was several cuts above the average B film in which Nina had been previously involved. But the glare of her obvious acting ability seemed only to blind Columbia's pundits and she was assigned to program features doing what she could with the low-class material tossed to her.

In 1947 she returned to Broadway. Richard Rodgers and Oscar Hammerstein II, with Joshua Logan, produced Norman Krasna's comedy, *John Loves Mary,* and, through the courtesy of Columbia Pictures, Nina played the lead of Mary McKinley with William Prince as John. The play opened at New York's Booth Theatre on February 4, 1947. The delightful comedy was a hit and continued its run through the year to become a near-staple for many summers on the straw-hat circuit. Columbia remade *Blind Alibi* (1939) as *The Dark Past* in 1949, and Foch played Betty, the loyal girl friend of gangster William Holden. She then played Judith Warren, the patient wife of treasury agent Glenn Ford, in *The Undercover Man,* and was romanced by an ex-convict turned florist, George Raft, in *Johnny Allegro.* Both of the latter films were released in 1949.

Nina's eighteen-month stint in *John Loves Mary* had given her career an impetus and direction that nothing in Hollywood could have provided, and in the spring of 1949 she returned to the stage, touring as Lissie McKaye in Jean Paul Sartre's *The Respectful Prostitute,* preceded by a curtain raiser, *Hope Is the Thing with Feathers.* On October 3, 1949, she opened at the Empire Theatre on Broadway in *Twelfth Night,* then opened and closed in Albany in *Congressional Baby,* and later, on April 26, 1950, was a stunning Dynameme in *A Phoenix Too Frequent* at the Fulton Theatre in New York.

Nina had certainly never been known for reticence, nor has she ever sidestepped a challenge, and in television she saw a vivid opportunity to extend her acting talents. She offered Harry Cohn, the irascible head of Columbia Pictures, half of her earnings if he would permit the new adventure. Cohn released her from her contract without charge. Her entrance into the new medium of television was alternated with summer stock in *The Philadelphia Story, Light up the Sky,* and other plays, but she discovered that television offered her a gratifying selection of roles. She later said, "The standards of acting TV are better than in any other medium. TV shows the actor's true worth. It separates the men from the boys. It's a good, tough, hard profession where nobody has any personal ego to be buttered." During the year 1950, she plunged into video work and ended the year by opening Christmas eve in *King Lear* at the National Theatre, performing as Cordelia.

On television she was seen on "Pulitzer Prize Playhouse" in video productions of *Ice-Bound, The Buccaneer,* and *The Skin of Our Teeth.* Meanwhile, her career in films greatly improved at MGM when she sparkled as Milo Roberts, the wealthy American sponsor of artist Gene Kelly, in the award-winning, Vincente Minnelli-directed *An American in Paris* (1951). In a light-hearted comedy of the reformation of three hoodlums, Nina was quite fine as Linda Kovacs in *St. Benny the Dip* (1951) at United Artists, and as Joyce Laramie complicating Glenn Ford's life in Metro's *Young Man with Ideas* (1952), she gave the best offering of the film.

In 1951, for the twentieth anniversary opening of the summer season at the Westport Country Playhouse in Connecticut, Nina joined Kim Hunter, Karl Malden, and Scott McKay in Philip Barry's *The Animal Kingdom.* She appeared on "Schlitz Playhouse of Stars" as a historian with no time for romance with Charlton Heston in the telecast of Sinclair Lewis' *World So Wide.* Then, in *The Jungle* on "Pulitzer Prize TV Playhouse" she returned to Guadalcanal with her World War II hero-husband (Robert Preston).

For Metro-Goldwyn-Mayer's remake of *Scaramouche* (1953), a lavish, Technicolor swashbuckler that was far less exciting than Rex Ingram's silent film version, Nina was a regal and lovely Marie Antoinette. Finally, in her last work at the Culver City studio she reached the peak of her screen career with *Executive Suite* (1954). As Erica Martin, secretary to the president of a large furniture company whose death sets off a battle for executive control, her performance was cool perfection as an almost alarmingly efficient and dedicated employee. Her work was rewarded with her one and only Academy Award nomination. She lost the Oscar to Eva Marie Saint (*On the Waterfront*). The loss of the prize did not affect Nina's positive philosophy: "Either you can be an adolescent all your life and be safe, or you can grow up and risk failure." If she lost the acting accolade,

With Stephen Crane and Osa Massen in Cry of the Werewolf *(Col 1944)*

she won a wedding ring by marrying actor James Lipton, Dr. Grant of CBS-TV's soap opera, "The Guiding Light." The marriage ended five years later and Nina then married Dennis Brite. Her only child, a son, Schuyler Dirk Brite, was born in 1962 when Nina was thirty-eight.

Nina was propelled into further acting marathons by her desire and determination to be not just an actress, but one of the best. On "Producer's Showcase," in State of the Union, she was effective as Kay Thorndyke with designs on Margaret Sullavan's political, presidential-hopeful husband (Joseph Cotten), and as Sophie Teale Nina added a good deal of zest to the musical telecast Roberta with Gordon McRae and Agnes Moorehead.

Her determination to grow as an actress made her join the American Shakespeare Festival Theatre at Stratford, Connecticut, alternating in the Bard's roles from Isabella in Measure for Measure to a hell-fired Katharine in The Taming of the Shrew. Asked why she wanted to play such roles, she replied, "Because there are certain parts I want to have played in my lifetime," and then added, regarding Shrew, "Shakespeare should never be politely done because he is bawdy and lusty enough to make Jayne Mansfield look like vanilla beans."

After playing Pharoah's daughter Bithiah in Cecil B. DeMille's massive The Ten Commandments (1956), she continued her hectic pace appearing on most of television's top drama programs, including an excellent portrayal of Brita, in the "Alcoa Theatre" TV version of the film A Double Life, with Shelley Winters (repeating her screen role) and Eric Portman. In A Night of Rain Nina was seen plotting with her younger lover (Roddy McDowall) to get rid of her husband, and then she played the lead on "Wagon Train" in The Clara Beauchamp Story, insulting an Indian chief and precipitating warfare.

In 1958 she became an assistant to famed director George Stevens on all dramatic phases of the film The Diary of Anne Frank, taking on the interesting if ambiguous task of helping other players polish their performances and develop a deeper concept of their roles. Her television credits increased during the following years, and after appearing in the star-choked epic, Spartacus (1960), as Glabrus' wife Helena, she was back on Broadway in A Second String. Three

years later (1963), she divorced Dennis Brite, intensified her television activity, and in 1964 went to Tampa, Florida, to film Sterling Silliphant's Where's a Will, There's a Way, playing Samantha in that segement of "Route 66."

In 1967 she was at Malibu Beach with Claire Bloom and Maximilian Schell, filming a TV adaptation of Henry James' novel, Washington Square, called A Time for Love, when she married her third husband, Michael Dewell. For the first play (the TV special, A Night at Ford's Theatre) done on the stage of the historic Ford's Theatre since the assassination of Abraham Lincoln on April 14, 1865, she was director John Houseman's assistant. In 1968 she made the telefilm Prescription Murder, and in March, 1969, as Duchess Sophia, she was escorted by Robert Conrad and Ross Martin to reclaim a royal icon in a "Wild, Wild West" episode. She was a wealthy widow covering up a murder on "Gunsmoke," and then played a part in the telefeature Gidget Grows Up (1969), with Karen Valentine and Paul Lynde.

If Nona Foch's main passions today are painting and spending time with her son, she is still to be seen frequently on television in parts provided by such dramatic shows as "Hawaii Five-O," and "Owen Marshall, Counsellor at Law." Always she is devilishly attractive and slick in her professional way. Otto Preminger's embarrassing feature Such Good Friends (1971) was a gabby, flabby affair for which Elaine May wisely used a pseudonym for screen credit of the script. The picture did contain a few good performances and a standout in the less than compelling picture was Nina Foch as Mrs. Wallman, a primly pushy mother. For the producers of the "Flipper" and "Gentle Ben" video series, Nina not too long ago completed a Florida-made feature called Salty (1974), and is currently teaching acting classes in Hollywood.

Tireless in work, candid in speech, Nina still contends that women are as intelligent (if not more so) than men but feels many of her sex withold their knowledge rather than scratch a man's ego. Her dream of success is the personal satisfaction that comes only through the fulfillment of her ideals as an artist, and through helping others realize their artistic potentials. She has come a long way on the path to her goal.

NINA FOCH

The Return of the Vampire   *(Col 1943)*
Nine Girls   *(Col 1944)*
Cry of the Werewolf   *(Col 1944)*
She's a Soldier Too   *(Col 1944)*
Strange Affair   *(Col 1944)*
She's a Sweetheart   *(Col 1944)*
Shadows in the Night   *(Col 1944)*
A Song to Remember   *(Col 1945)*
My Name is Julia Ross   *(Col 1945)*
Prison Ship   *(Col 1945)*
I Love a Mystery   *(Col 1945)*
Boston Blackie's Rendezvous   *(Col 1945)*
Escape in the Fog   *(Col 1945)*
Johnny O'Clock   *(Col 1947)*
The Guilt of Janet Ames   *(Col 1947)*
The Dark Past   *(Col 1949)*
The Undercover Man   *(Col 1949)*

Johnny Allegro   *(Col 1949)*
An American in Paris   *(MGM 1951)*
St. Benny the Dip   *(UA 1951)*
Young Man with Ideas   *(MGM 1952)*
Scaramouche   *(MGM 1952)*
Fast Company   *(MGM 1952)*
Sombrero   *(MGM 1953)*
Executive Suite   *(MGM 1954)*
Four Guns to the Border   *(Univ 1954)*
You're Never too Young   *(Par 1955)*
Illegal   *(WB 1955)*
The Ten Commandements   *(Par 1956)*
Three Brave Men   *(20th 1957)*
Cash McCall   *(WB 1959)*
Spartacus   *(Univ 1960)*
Such Good Friends   *(Par 1971)*
Salty   *(Salt Waters Distributors 1974)*

38

Susanna Foster

Among the various genres running rampant in the 1940s, ranging from zany comedies to war features, was the teenage movie. During their brief glory these films enriched the studios that were involved with them and spawned and fostered precocious young talents. The decade either produced or furthered the careers of Judy Garland, Jane Powell, Deanna Durbin, Donald O'Connor, Peggy Ryan, Margaret O'Brien, Ann Blyth, Gloria Jean, and Susanna DeLee Flanders Larson who became Susanna Foster. She was discovered, promoted, exploited, and discarded by Hollywood, all within a brief six-year period (1939–45).

She was born in in Chicago on December 6, 1924, and when she was six months old her parents moved to Minneapolis. There, she entered school, skipping grades frequently because of her remarkable intelligence, and soon was singing in theatres and conventions in Minneapolis and St. Paul, and on the radio. Operatic star Mary McCormick predicted a great future for the child, and, after hearing her sing, Merle Potter, drama editor for the *Minneapolis Star,* and Carl Johnson, an orchestra leader, persuaded Susanna to make some recordings, "Italian Street Song," and "Ah, Sweet Mystery of Life." The two men sent the demonstration records to Metro-Goldwyn-Mayer in Culver City, California, and, sight unseen, Susanna was signed to a one-year contract. Mr. and Mrs. Les-

ter Larson left Minneapolis for Hollywood with twelve-year-old Susie and two younger daughters.

Metro had recently released Deanna Durbin, who transfered to Universal and attained enormous popularity and stardom. MGM readied *B Above High C* for their new young soprano, but that picture was never made, and after a year of collecting a salary and not appearing onscreen, Susanna was dropped by the studio. Now at liberty, Susanna studied voice with Gilda Marchetti, who stressed the Italian Bel Canto method of strengthening the lower tones without sacrificing the upper range of her voice. Miss Marchetti's brother, Milo, then arranged an audition with Paramount Pictures. They signed Susanna to a new contract and cast her as Allan Jones's and Mary Martin's daughter, Peggy, in an ersatz biography of Victor Herbert, *The Great Victor Herbert* (1939), with Walter Connolly in the title role. Susanna made an impressive film debut and her remarkable voice excelled in the number "Kiss Me Again," in which she hit B flat above high C.

Her second Paramount effort was as Toodles La Verne, a burlesque singer rescued by Allan Jones from a raid on the show and taken to a camp for children run by Jones's father. Filmed as *The Hard Boiled Canary,* the picture, which also included newcomer Dolly Loehr (later Diana Lynn) in its cast, was released as *There's Magic in Music* (1941). Interestingly enough, Susanna received more critical notice for her acting than for her singing. The *Canary* opus

A publicity pose with David Bruce for That Night with You *(Univ 1945)*

With Jackie Cooper and Walter Abel in Glamour Boy *(Par 1941)*

was followed by supporting Jackie Cooper in a hackneyed Hollywood fable, based on the remake of Cooper's 1931 Paramount hit *Skippy,* called *Glamour Boy.* As Jane Winslow in this 1941 film, Susanna sang "Love Is Such an Old Fashioned Thing" and "The Magic of Magnolias." Her Paramount contract ended with a brief cadenza in the studio's all-star *Star Spangled Rhythm* (1942). Forty days after leaving Paramount, Susanna signed with Universal.

A frequent ploy of the Hollywood factories was to employ an actor or actress of comparable talent or physical appeal as a threat to the enlarged egos of their top stars. Universal's leverage for controlling Deanna Durbin was in Susanna. But it was at Universal that Susanna was given her best and most memorable role of Christine Dubois in the remake of Gaston Leroux's thriller, *The Phantom of the Opera* (1943). The new version of Lon Chaney's silent classic (1925), stressed the operatic background of Leroux's novel rather than the cringing horror of the original and was produced in magnificent Technicolor, sumptuous sets, and brilliant costumes, all of which were acknowledged with Oscars at the Sixteenth Annual Academy presentations.

The original story of *The Phantom of the Opera* was considerably altered, as were the names of the lead-

ing characters. Chaney's Erik became Claude Rains's Enrique Claudin (Rains gave a magnificent performance), the bedeviled heroine Christine Dane (played in the silent edition by Mary Philbin) became Christine Dubois (Susanna Foster), and the romantic lead, Raoul de Chagny, played in the Chaney film by Norman Kerry, was relegated to second place in favor of enlarging the role of the baritone played by black-haired, moustachioed Nelson Eddy. The altered script was easier to follow than the Chaney classic. Also, the addition of operatic sequences (based on the music of Tchaikovsky and Chopin, and sung exquisitely by Eddy and Foster), beautifully mounted and filmed, enhanced the chills when Susanna rips the light blue mask from the Phantom, as he is engrossed playing the organ in his subterranean lair, to reveal a face of seared flesh, acid-burned to ghastly scars and a twisted mouth. Susanna was splendid as Christine, and her singing and acting were not again equalled in her brief career.

From her success in the grade A *The Phantom,* mercurial Universal assigned her the role of Connie Allen in support of Donald O'Connor and Peggy Ryan, in an unlikely fable of teenagers inaugurating a separate shift in a defense plant, called *Top Man* (1943). Here, she sang "Wrap Your Troubles in Dreams, and

With Claude Rains in Phantom of the Opera *(Univ 1943)*

Dream Your Troubles Away." The following year, Susanna returned to the Paris Opera—oncamera that is—as aspiring singer Angela, hypnotized out of her voice by mad Boris Karloff in his first Technicolor film. Universal smartly used the sets from the previous year's *Phantom* for the Karloff chiller, *The Climax,* directed by George Waggoner. With Edward Ward, Waggoner also wrote two songs for Susanna to sing: "Now at Last" and "Some Day I'll Know," plus the operatic sequences. As Peggy Fleming, Susanna helped Donald Cook and Jack Oakie battle their way from *Bowery to Broadway* (1944), and she was just part of the Hollywood Victory Committee sequence for *Follow the Boys* (1944).

The translation of a bad play to the screen rarely makes a good movie, but Universal bought Sinclair Lewis' and Fay Wray's flop play, *Angela Is Twenty-One,* and, with Susanna in the title role, released the picture as *This Is the Life* (1944). It set no boxoffice records. Turhan Bey and Alan Curtis feuded for the affections of *Frisco Sal* (1945), a songstress in San Francisco's bawdy Barbary Coast of the gay nineties. Susanna's performance as Sal was acceptable and she sang three songs, "Beloved," "Good Little, Bad Little Lady," and "I Just Got In."

Between pictures, Susanna trained at the Los Ange-les County Hospital and graduated as a nurse's aide. Her final Universal picture was with Franchot Tone, one of Deanna Durbin's frequent co-stars. The film was *That Night with You* (1945) in which Susanna, as flirtatiously delightful Penny, sings "Once Upon a Dream." After finishing that film, she convinced Universal that her value to them would increase if she studied voice abroad, and the studio loaned her $26,000 to go to Europe to study. When she returned, she repaid the studio most of their loan but refused their screen assignments. Silver-voiced, acid-tongued Miss Foster explained her decision to leave Universal and motion pictures. "It was the same old thing. They wanted me to sing while Sonja Henie skated in *The Countess of Monte Cristo.* Sonja was to be the Countess and I, the maid, and she comes up to here on me. She should have been the maid!" (The film was made for 1948 release with Olga San Juan in Susanna's vacated role.) Universal released Susanna from further contractual commitments, and she signed with Edwin Lester to star in his west-coast stage production of Victor Herbert's *Naughty Marietta.* Her co-players were Wilbur Evans and Edward Everett Horton.

Wilbur Evans, a native of Philadelphia, had won the first Atwater Kent Radio Contest while as a scholarship student at the Curtis Institute of Music. He made his grand opera debut in *Tristan and Isolde*, his New York debut as Prince Danilo in the Carnegie Hall production of *The Merry Widow*, and scored a personal success on Broadway in *Mexican Hayride* and *Up in Central Park*. In 1948, Evans was asked to go to the west coast to sing the male lead in *Naughty Marietta*, because they were having difficulty with the star (Susanna), and it was thought he could handle her. Said Evans, "I handled her so well that in five weeks I asked her to marry me. But it took Susie six months to give in." Evans, age forty-three, had divorced his first wife, Florence Monroe, in 1946, and on October 23, 1948, Susanne Larson became Mrs. Wilbur Evans, two months before her twenty-fourth birthday. The ceremony was performed by Chief Magistrate James J. Clothier in the office of Register of Wills at Philadelphia's City Hall, and the newlyweds honeymooned at Atlantic City.

The Evans became a splendid singing and acting team billed as "America's Singing Sweethearts" (shades of Jeanette MacDonald and Nelson Eddy!) and as the wildly imaginative and presumptive "Singing Lunts." Together they appeared in operettas for the Cleveland Light Opera Company and toured in *The Merry Widow*. Later, Evans was signed for the role of Emile in the London production of *South Pacific*, which he played for 792 performances with Mary Martin (and later Julie Wilson). Wilbur and Susanna already had a son, Michael David, when, during the *South Pacific* engagement at London's Drury Lane Theatre, their second son was born. They named him Philip, in honor of the Duke of Edinburgh.

When Evans signed for the lead opposite Shirley Booth in the short-lived musical *By the Beautiful Sea*, the family returned to the United States. In 1955, he was appointed director of the Valley Forge Music Fair, a summer theatre presenting well-tested musicals. Susanna appeared as Fiona MacLaren in *Brigadoon* and sang the role of Magnolia in *Show Boat*. The following year the alleged "Singing Sweethearts" went through a bitter divorce case.

Susanna created a national stir by asking a radio audience for the whereabouts of her ex-husband and for a part-time job to support her teenage sons beyond her day employment at the Wall Street office of Merrill, Lynch, Pierce, Fenner & Smith. In April, 1962, the bitterness between Evans and his ex-wife flowed into the press when he charged in court that Susanna had turned "beatnik," preferred to dress in blue jeans and "otherwise inhabit an unrealistic world in which she is content to act the part of a Bohemian clad in the best beatnik style." Evans further charged that Susanna had squandered a $25,000 trust fund and maintained her westside apartment in a "slovenly, slipshod" fashion, and, furthermore, one of his sons told him that she had spent the night with a soldier from Fort Dix, New Jersey. The war of the Evanses came to a standoff.

Susanna, commenting on her film career, has said, "I made a dozen pictures in Hollywood in five years and only in one did I approach—even remotely approach—being in the least satisfied. That was *Phantom of the Opera* with Nelson Eddy and Claude Rains. It, at least, had some taste." Although she has received offers for plays, television, and nightclub tours over the years, the hardboiled canary replies, "I want to do what I want to do and that does not include anything in show business." One of the last times in recent years that Susanna was spotted in public, she was working as a check-in attendant at a Manhattan Turkish bath.

SUSANNA FOSTER

The Great Victor Herbert   *(Par 1939)*
There's Magic in Music (a.k.a., The Hard Boiled Canary)   *(Par 1941)*
Glamour Boy   *(Par 1941)*
Star Spangled Rhythm   *(Par 1942)*
Phantom of the Opera   *(Univ 1943)*
Top Man   *(Univ 1943)*

The Climax   *(Univ 1944)*
Bowery to Broadway   *(Univ 1944)*
Follow the Boys   *(Univ 1944)*
This Is the Life   *(Univ 1944)*
Frisco Sal   *(Univ 1945)*
That Night with You   *(Univ 1945)*

39

Mona Freeman

Most Hollywood actresses, especially in the cautious 1940s, believed that remaining perpetually young was absolutely necessary for the continuation of their careers. For that reason, biographical statistics vary quite often for some of these people. Mona Freeman was an exception. She was the girl who could not, and would not, grow up. Her baby face so stifled her career that she was stuck with teenager roles on-screen for years. She succeeded Diana Lynn as Paramount's perennial teenage brat; however, since Mona lacked Lynn's sophistication, it took her longer than the talented Diana to break the mold. Mona even described herself as "the female Andy Hardy," and was still playing bobby-soxers years after she herself became a mother. The petite (5' 3") actress was always playing the stars' daughter (that of Irene Dunne, Rosalind Russell, or Betty Grable) or sister (that of Faye Emerson, Peggy Ann Garner, Joan Caulfield, Veronica Lake).

When Paramount signed her to a long-term contract she was immediately cast as Barbara Stanwyck's teenage stepdaughter in Billy Wilder's *Double Indemnity* (1944), but after three days they realized that she photographed like a sub-teenager and she was replaced by Jean Heather. However, she still made her debut in the film because they gave her a one-line part as a secretary who tells Fred MacMurray that he is wanted in Edward G. Robinson's office. A few months later she was loaned out to MGM to play Elizabeth Taylor's older sister in *National Velvet*

(1945) and, once again, this time after only one day's work, was fired because it was decided that she did not look much older than Elizabeth. Contract player Angela Lansbury replaced her. Not a very auspicious beginning for the very pretty ash blonde with the variously changing gray-green-blue eyes. She did come into her own when she was cast as Joan Caulfield's bratty sister in *Dear Ruth* (1947). The comedy was quite popular, so she repeated her role in two less successful sequels, *Dear Wife* (1950) and *Dear Brat* (1951). In the latter film, of course, she had the title role and was twenty-four years old. "How old do you have to be to be grown up?" asked Mona, and, after eight years with Paramount, refused to re-sign with them.

Mr. and Mrs. Stuart Freeman's daughter, Monica Elizabeth (her real name), was born on June 9, 1926, in Baltimore, Maryland. She was born exactly one day before another small, blonde film actress, June Haver, whom she somewhat resembles. Of English, Irish, and French stock, Mona traveled about a good deal as a child because her father was a contractor. The family, including older brother Peter, finally settled down in Pelham, New York, where Mona attended high school. Her summers were spent at her aunt's home outside Baltimore.

Mona's brother was indirectly responsible for her show business career. He was a highly intelligent

252

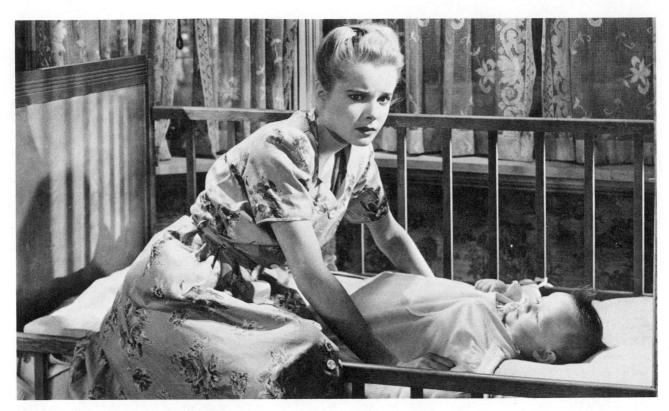

In That Brennan Girl *(Rep 1946)*

With Edward Arnold in Dear Ruth *(Par 1947)*

young man and his parents wanted to send him to Yale but could not afford to do so. Mona took it upon herself to help the family by getting a job. "Secretly I had decided I wanted to be a model, as certainly it must be easier work and better paid than being a mother's helper—my only alternative." She made an appointment with the John Robert Powers' modeling agency and in very short order became a successful teenage Powers' model in Manhattan. She was also the second of the "Miss Subway" girls.

Mona's discovery for films reads like a Lana Turner script without the more degenerate aspects of that star's films. Howard Hughes, the airplane and movie magnate, saw her photograph on a magazine cover and signed her to a personal two-year contract with the usual option rights. This agreement was made without his ever having met Mona in person. Since it was then wartime, Hughes was more interested in planes than he was in films, so Mona was notified that she did not have to go to Hollywood and could continue with modeling and school in New York. "I almost forgot about it," recalled the protege, "until the second year, when Mr. Hughes sent me four hundred dollars for a dramatic course. I enrolled dutifully at Finch Junior College, but went only once." Mona just was not interested in acting. She wanted to be an artist or a fashion designer and, instead, attended the Maryland Institue of Art. After a few weeks at the school, Hughes summoned her to Hollywood for a screen test.

She and her mother went and sat, and sat, and sat for three months twiddling their thumbs while Mona was doing nothing professionally. She attempted to contact her employer but Hughes, according to his office, was always out of town. Finally, she decided to seek him out personally, only to find that his actual office was in an airplane factory instead of a studio. "I was flabbergasted," said Mona, "And Mr. Hughes was still out of town." She then took matters into her own hands and wrangled an interview with Paramount Pictures through a friend from the Powers Agency. They were interested in signing her but would have to wait until her option with Hughes lapsed. "Then I was angry," said Mona. "I made his office get him on the phone and told him I didn't want my option lifted because I had other plans." Hughes then flew back to see Mona for the first time, and after two hours of heated discussion he told her he was extending the option and walked out the door. Paramount, however, simply bought her contract from Hughes and she signed with them at one hundred dollars a week, without ever having done a movie for the enigmatic Howard Hughes.

After a few small roles, which included two walk-ons in *Our Hearts Were Young and Gay* (1944), starring Diana Lynn and Gail Russell, and *Here Come the Waves* (1944), with Bing Crosby and Betty Hutton, Mona was farmed out to almost every major studio in Hollywood: *Together Again* (1944), with Irene Dunne, at Columbia; *Roughly Speaking* (1945), with Rosalind Russell and Jack Carson, and *Danger Signal* (1945), with Zachary Scott and Faye Emerson, at Warner Bros; *Junior Miss* (1945) and *Black Beauty* (1946) at Twentieth Century-Fox; and *That Brennan Girl* (1946), with James Dunn at Republic. Her home studio only used her once during the 1945–46 period and that was for a very small role at the closing of *Our Hearts Were Growing Up* (1946), even though she had already played a major supporting role as Peggy Ann Garner's sister in *Junior Miss* and was receiving first billing as *Black Beauty's* owner. In the Adela Rogers St. John story, *That Brennan Girl,* Mona had the title role, which required her to age from eleven years old to twenty-five. She also had to be hard and cynical in the first half of the picture. The *New York Times* said of her performance, "In her essaying a weighty dramatic role, Mona Freeman is defeated by some non-weighty lines and her appearance, which is closer to the pure junior miss type rather than the hard-bitten demi-mondaine's." A number of years passed before she tried another such dramatic role.

In 1945, Mona married wealthy Hollywood automobile dealer Pat Nerney. They had a daughter, Mona, Jr., called Monie, who was born in 1947, the same year Mona made a big hit as the thirteen-year-old letter-writing brat in *Dear Ruth,* a very funny film based on Norman Krasna's hit play. The *New York Herald-Tribune,* in reporting about this feature, said, "Mona Freeman makes much of few entrances as the kid sister who inspires all the antics." Mona was pregnant when she played the older daughter of Betty Grable and Dan Dailey in *Mother Wore Tights* (1947). The Technicolor musical was a big popular success and Mona did some pleasant singing in it. After Paramount put her in the poorly conceived song-and-dance film *Isn't It Romantic?* (1948), featuring a waning Veronica Lake, Mona confessed to a member of the press, "I'm not the type to play roles which win Academy Awards. I can't see myself in a big historical picture or in a difficult emotional role."

The closest she ever came to playing history was in some fictional Westerns and some war films. Her first sagebrush excursion was *Streets of Laredo* (1949), with William Holden, Macdonald Carey, and William Bendix. She gave a good account of herself as a tomboy who, in the end, saves Holden by gunning down villain Carey, whom she loved. It was a remake of *The Texas Rangers* (1936), with variations and the publicity for the film which read: "Three men and a blond bobcat! One for all and all for one."

In a surprising bit of casting, Mona played a very small role in William Wyler's superb production of *The Heiress* (1949). She was cast as a girl of her own age, for a change, who had a five-year-old child. This starring vehicle for Olivia de Havilland and Montgomery Clift was a prestigious production, Mona's first good film since *Double Indemnity,* and her last. At this time, director John Farrow showed Mona a story called *I Married a Dead Man,* a suspense yarn about a woman with an illegitimate child who passes herself off as the wife of a dead war hero. Mona coveted the role but was not even considered for it when it was finally filmed by Mitchell Leisen as *No Man of Her Own* (1950), with much more mature Barbara Stanwyck in the lead. Instead, Mona was loaned out again, this time to Universal, for the role of a wealthy kleptomaniac in *I Was a Shoplifter* (1950). It was by all accounts a routine program picture, which held interest primarily because of its documentary approach to the subject of shoplifting. Mona did two other films for Universal, *The Lady from Texas* (1951) with Howard Duff, and *Flesh and Fury* (1952) with Tony Curtis and a prominently billed Jan Ster-

ling. Because of her diminutive size, like Veronica Lake and Wanda Hendrix in the past, Mona was cast opposite Alan Ladd, this time in *Branded* (1951), which turned out to be just another western. After her role as Dean Martin's love interest in *Jumping Jacks* (1952), she made a fleeting appearance with her daughter Monie, as part of the audience, in Cecil B. DeMille's *The Greatest Show on Earth* (1952), and then terminated her Paramount association. When Mona left the Marathon Street lot, Paramount lost another personality of the prime 1940s.

She also terminated her marriage to Pat Nerney on September 26, 1952. She testified that he was so possessive that he hurt her film career. She was then twenty-six and he was thirty-two. "He criticized our marriage," claimed Mona. "He criticized the way I reared our daughter. During the last three years he interfered with my career by refusing to let me go on location or personal appearances unless he could go along." After her divorce, Mona suddenly began appearing on the social circuit with great frequency, dating Robert Wagner, lawyer Gregory Bautzer, Nicky Hilton, Vic Damone, and Frank Sinatra. She also saw a great deal of Bing Crosby, after his wife, actress Dixie Lee, had passed away. By November of

With J. M. Kerrigan in Black Beauty *(20th 1946)*

255

1953, most people expected Crosby and Mona to wed, but to Mona, and Crosby, both Catholics, it would have meant giving up their religion, because she was a divorcee and there was no reason for annulling her first marriage. Crosby later married Columbia starlet Kathryn Grant.

In 1952, Mona signed with pedestrian RKO and was again under contract to her discoverer, Howard Hughes. This time at least, she did one film for him: *Angel Face* (1953). Jean Simmons was the star of this drama, but Mona collected some nice reviews. The *New York Times* complimented her with, "Any paying customer out for sense and sensibility will have to hang on to the brief appearances of Mona Freeman as the spanky, realistic little nurse whom Mr. [Robert] Mitchum jilts." Mona was not on the screen again until 1955 when she received third billing, over other female cast members Nancy Olson, Dorothy Malone, and Anne Francis, in the CinemaScope filming of Leon Uris' novel *Battle Cry*. In this Marine Corps feature of World War II days, she was an ingenue again, this time quite a sappy one, as Tab Hunter's sweetheart back home. It was her last appearance in a big film. All the rest of her onscreen appearances were minor entries with *Huk* (1956) and *Dragoon Wells Massacre* (1957) being somewhat memorable because of their grittiness. Her final film to date was the routine courtroom drama, *The World Was His Jury* (1958) with Edmond O'Brien.

Earlier in her career Mona professed that she would be much too scared to tackle a stage role. However, in 1957, never having been before the footlights before, except in grammar school as Little Eva (she says she was awful), she did the national tour of *Middle of the Night* with Edward G. Robinson. She played the role originated on Broadway by Gena Rowlands and later played in the film by Kim Novak. Mona received first feature billing and *Variety* penned, "She gives a fine reading of the distraught young wife and adds an attractive physical presence."

Starting in 1955 and continuing to the early 1960s, Mona was one of television's most prominent actresses, having appeared in over eighty shows, both live and on film. She starred in all the major dramatic programs such as "Playhouse 90" (*Seidman and Son*), "Climax" (*Fear Strikes Out*), "Lux Video Theatre" Barbara Stanwyck's role in *Christmas in Connecticut*) and "U.S. Steel Hour" (*The Two Worlds of Charly Gordon*, playing the role Claire Bloom had assumed in the 1968 film version, *Charly*). By the mid-1960s, Mona had lost most of her desire to perform and only occasionally did a "Perry Mason" show or an "Alfred Hitchcock Presents," and then finally retired. Mona enjoyed working in television, especially in the live shows of the 1950s. She explained, "You have to forget all that silly nonsense you were taught in pictures. I mean about the importance of the star, the glamour stuff and all that. On a alive TV show, everybody works together on the same level. You can learn more about acting in five minutes of television than you can during an entire picture." She adds, "A nice thing about TV, it pays a lot of bills and lets you turn down pictures you really don't want to do."

Since June of 1961, she has been married to Los Angeles businessman H. Jack Ellis who adopted her daughter Monie. Monie Ellis is now an actress herself and won out over other contestants for the role of Gidget in *Gidget Gets Married* (1971) on the "ABC Movie of the Week." Mona came out of retirement—briefly—to do an original CBS television film, *Welcome Home, Johnny Bristol* (1972). However, her role was so minor that her presence almost was missed by any viewer. She played Martin Landau's mother, seen in a quick flashback sequence.

Mona still lives in Hollywood and spends much of her time painting portraits and landscapes, something she always wanted to do. Gail Russell, her Paramount contemporary, also had the same desire. It is hard to think of Mona as the mother of a daughter in her late twenties. Faithful fans still think of her as a teenager. Today, looking youthful does not bother her one bit, and she still seems years younger than she actually is.

MONA FREEMAN

Double Indemnity   *(Par 1944)*
Our Hearts Were Young and Gay   *(Par 1944)*
Till We Meet Again   *(Par 1944)*
Together Again   *(Col 1944)*
Here Come the Waves   *(Par 1944)*
Roughly Speaking   *(WB 1945)*
Junior Miss   *(20th 1945)*
Danger Signal   *(WB 1945)*
Our Hearts Were Growing Up   *(Par 1946)*
Black Beauty   *(20th 1946)*
That Brennan Girl   *(Rep 1946)*
Dear Ruth   *(Par 1947)*
Variety Girl   *(Par 1947)*
Mother Wore Tights   *(20th 1947)*
Isn't It Romantic?   *(Par 1948)*
Streets of Laredo   *(Par 1949)*
The Heiress   *(Par 1949)*
Dear Wife   *(Par 1950)*
I Was a Shoplifter   *(Univ 1950)*

Copper Canyon   *(Par 1950)*
Branded   *(Par 1951)*
Dear Brat   *(Par 1951)*
Darling, How Could You?   *(Par 1951)*
The Lady From Texas   *(Univ 1951)*
Flesh and Fury   *(Univ 1952)*
Jumping Jacks   *(Par 1952)*
The Greatest Show on Earth   *(Par 1952)* (Unbilled guest appearance)
Angle Face   *(RKO 1953)*
Battle Cry   *(WB 1955)*
The Road to Denver   *(Rep 1955)*
The Way Out   *(RKO 1956)*
Shadow of Fear   *(UA 1956)*
Hold Back the Night   *(AA 1956)*
Huk   *(UA 1956)*
Dragoon Wells Massacre   *(AA 1957)*
The World Was His Jury   *(Col 1958)*

40

Peggy Ann Garner

The 1930s spawned fantastically talented and cute child movie stars. The greatest was undoubtedly Shirley Temple, despite the claims of followers of Jackie Coogan, Jackie Cooper, and Jane Withers. Then came a flock of would-be successors, all precocious, many talented, and none as enduringly popular as the aforementioned Miss Temple, who in new guises still remains in the limelight. Among the crop of kiddie players who gained prominence in the early 1940s were Elizabeth Taylor, Roddy McDowall, Margaret O'Brien, Bobby Driscoll, Dwayne Hickman, Bobby Blake, Ted Donaldson, Dean Stockwell, and Peggy Ann Garner. Each of these tykes helped to provide war-weary Americans with cinematic distractions.

Virginia Jean Craig Garner was an unabashed stage mother of whom her daughter once admitted, "My mother had drive, ambition and aggressiveness—but no talent. I didn't have any drive, but I had talent." The daughter was Peggy Ann Garner, who was born on February 3, 1932, in Canton, Ohio. Her father was William George Huxley Warburton Garner, a lawyer then with the N.R.A. in Canton, who had emigrated to the United States from County Durham, England, in 1920. In 1936 the Garners transferred to Washington, D.C., where William G. H. W. Garner served as legal adviser to the British Embassy. Peggy Ann was sent to the Marion Venable Dancing School, and at the Olney Theatre she became the youngest member of their summer stock company in her first stage role in *Mrs. Wiggs of the Cabbage Patch.*

Virginia then took her talented daughter to New York City and enrolled her in the Alivene Dramatic School of the Theatre. Peggy Ann's first professional work was with the noted John Robert Powers modeling agency. After appearing as a fashion model in newsreels her ambitious mother was convinced Hollywood was ready for Peggy Ann.

Five weeks after arriving in the film capital, Peggy Ann was screen-tested by director John Farrow and given a five-day bit part in his Warner Bros. film, *Little Miss Thoroughbred* (1938), which starred Ann Sheridan. Months passed before Peggy secured another small, but more important part, in RKO's *In Name Only* (1939), John Cromwell's expertly directed feature adapted from Bessie Breuer's novel, *Memory of Love.* Peggy Ann played Ellen Eden, the daughter of commercial artist Carole Lombard. The latter is in love with Cary Grant, whose onscreen spouse (Kay Francis) is not about to divorce her husband's money. A small part in Columbia's *Blondie Brings up Baby* (1939) followed, as did a minor role in RKO's *Abe Lincoln in Illinois* (1940).

"After that," Mrs. Garner later related, "we had to wait two years for another picture. They kept telling me that they didn't want a little girl with straight hair; she must have curls and Peggy Ann's hair refused to curl and I thought she was too young for a perma-

With Barbara Whiting in Junior Miss *(20th 1945)*

nent.'' Another bit in Universal's *Eagle Squadron* (1942) led to a telling performance as Sheila in Twentieth Century-Fox's *The Pied Piper* (1942), where Monty Woolley rescued Roddy McDowall, Peggy Ann, and other English children from Nazi-invaded France.

Convinced her daughter was now en route to certain stardom, Mrs. Garner moved into the swank Garden of Allah bungalow hotel, once the home of the famous exotic actress Nazimova and well known residence of the Hollywood greats, near-greats, or once-greats. Their neighbor was awesome Orson Welles, who, in residence, was working on a projected screenplay. The towering actor was also blithely rewriting the Lord's Prayer in full conviction that his version was better. Welles studiously ignored little Miss Garner and only after she and mama had returned in desperation to New York did he decide Peggy Ann was perfect for the role of the young *Jane Eyre* (1944). Peggy Ann's winsomely appealing performance as the youngster Jane won her a term contract with Twentieth Century-Fox. Metro offered to purchase half of her Fox contract and star her in their screen version of *National Velvet,* but Darryl F. Zanuck refused the offer, keeping his juvenile talent for a larger, more demanding project after she completed a brief role as Nora in *Keys of the Kingdom* (1944).

Zanuck's larger project was the filming of Betty Smith's poignant novel, *A Tree Grows in Brooklyn* (1945). Zanuck assigned Elia Kazan to this film, his first directorial job in Hollywood, and the resultant production became one of the best films of the forties, made a fortune for Twentieth Century-Fox, and received glowing national reviews. James Agee (The *Nation*) wrote of Peggy Ann's charm in a role so well suited to her, and other critics lavished a plethora of adjectives on the deeply intuitive performance that caught the quick nuances of childhood that the plain-faced, lank-haired, little actress so ably portrayed. Peggy Ann brought Betty Smith's Francie Nolan to life and few performances by children on the screen can compare with it. Recently Peggy Ann revisited the *Tree* again. ''Every couple of years I'll call Twentieth Century-Fox publicity departments and they'll arrange for a projection room. Then I'll sit there alone in the dark and watch *A Tree Grows in Brooklyn* and cry. It's that beautiful.'' Her favorite scene is where James Dunn, as her father, boozy Johnny Nolan, takes her to a new neighborhood where both of them know they will never be able to afford to live, and he

With Dorothy McGuire and Ted Donaldson in A Tree Grows in Brooklyn *(20th 1945)*

points out a new school he says she will attend. Her Francie looks intently at the school and the high class neighborhood and says, "Poppy, bend down." She tells her father, "My cup runneth over."

Juvenile Academy Awards were initiated by the Academy's Board of Governors, rather than voted by the full active membership, and the first such award went to Shirley Temple in 1934. In 1945 Peggy Ann Garner received a similar Academy Award from the Board of Governors as the outstanding child actress of the year. James Dunn received a Best Supporting Actor Oscar for his work in *A Tree Grows in Brooklyn.* Peggy Ann, Dunn, and other cast members repeated their film roles on CBS radio on "Hollywood Star Time." From the accolades of *A Tree,* Peggy Ann was cast *a la* Margaret O'Brien as Irish immigrant Katie Flanagan in several reels of unadulterated corn worsened by George Raft's wooden acting and called *Nob Hill* (1945).

Max Gordon's hit Broadway play *Junior Miss* by Jerome Chodorov and Joseph Fields from the stories of Sally Benson was purchased by Fox for Peggy Ann. As Judy Graves, a teenager with a melodramatic imagination fed by too many movies, she was delightful, and her perfect comedy timing accelerated the laughter. Peggy Ann was always quick to learn and was never known to blow lines on the set. At the Fox studio school, with classmate Roddy McDowall, she was a straight A student and served as a reporter for the school newspaper, "Fox Fun." In contrast to the joy of *Junior Miss,* Peggy Ann played Dinah Carstairs, daughter of mystery story writer Lynn Bari, who tries to solve a murder with two other youngsters—Dean Stockwell and Connie Marshall. Peggy Ann's final picture for Twentieth was the Joan Crawford, Dana Andrews, Henry Fonda triangle tale, *Daisy Kenyon* (1947).

After the New Year of 1948, Peggy Ann started rehearsals in the part of Elizabeth Collins in Elsa Shelley's stirring stage play, *Pick-Up Girl* which was preparing for a national tour. The action of the drama was set in a juvenile court room and Peggy Ann's performance as the uninhibited adolescent being tried on a sex delinquency charge as a Times Square tart was tautly professional. She returned to the west coast following the road tour in *Pick-Up Girl,* to appear as Christine St. Aubyn, stepdaughter of a strong-willed, self-centered invalid Susan Peters in Columbia's vapid and overblown melodrama, *The Sign of the Ram* (1948). After appearing as Doris with her

With Allene Roberts, Phyllis Thaxter, Alexander Knox, and Paul Scardon in The Sign of the Ram *(Col 1948)*

friend Lon McCallister in *The Big Cat* (1949) for low-budget Eagle Lion, she was next seen in a routine role in *The Lovable Cheat* (1949). It was a far comedown for the one-time Oscar winner to become involved as the heroine of *Bomba, the Jungle Boy* (1950), the first entry in the Johnny Sheffield series.

During the summer of 1949 she toured in the play *Peg O' My Heart,* and on January 19, 1950, she made her Broadway debut giving a competent performance as Ruth, a brash teenager, with Dorothy Gish, in Mel Dinelli's drama, *The Man* at New York's Fulton Theatre. The show lasted for ninety-two performances. On television, Peggy Ann was seen on "Tele-Theatre" in "Once to Every Boy," and with Kay Francis and John Loder she appeared in the video version of the play, *Call It a Day.* She settled in New York, living with Ed Sullivan and his family, partly because his daughter was Peggy Ann's close friend. She began a Saturday noon television series called "Two Girls Named Smith" with Peggy French, Joseph Buloff and, as her beau, a young singer named Richard Hayes.

The "Two Girls Named Smith" series started in January, 1951 and on February 23, 1951, before some fifty guests in the banquet room of the Hotel Delmonico, Peggy Ann was given in marriage by television's "Toast of the Town" master of ceremonies and newspaperman, Ed Sullivan, to Richard Herbert Hayes. The marriage lasted two years. In the same year as her marriage, Peggy Ann did a film for Metro called *Teresa,* which starred Pier Angeli. Then at the New York City Center, Peggy Ann starred with Ruth Hussey, Ethel Griffies, John Emery, and J. Edward Bromberg in a revival of *The Royal Family.* With Isobel Elsom and Margalo Gillmore she was a 1920's flapper disillusioned with her father's morality in Booth Tarkington's *Claire Ambler* on TV's "Robert Montgomery Presents." During 1952, she continued working in television for "Video Theatre," "Studio One," and "Playhouse of Stars" and returned to the stage again at the New York City Center, starring with Helen Gahagan Douglas, Edna Best, and Ona Munson in a revival of *First Lady.* That summer she joined her former Twentieth Century-Fox colleague Roddy McDowall for a tour of the straw-hat theatres in Philip Barry's play, *The Youngest.*

On September 22, 1954, she was back on Broadway, starring with Walter Macken in *Home Is the Hero,* with Glenda Farrell and J. Pat O'Malley. Her persuasive performance as Josie added stature to her career although the play survived only thirty showings. Peggy Ann gave a commendable performance as Kaye Hamilton in Gore Vidal's TV adaptation of the play *Stage Door* in CBS's April 7, 1955 "Best of

262

Broadway" telecast in a cast that included Diana Lynn, Dennis Morgan, Victor Moore, and Rhonda Fleming. She was also seen as Nora Wallen on "Climax" in John Galsworthy's *The First and the Last,* as Jenny on *Strange Companion* on "Studio One," and on *Time of Day* for "Stage 7."

The outstanding success of William Inge's play *Bus Stop* on Broadway prompted the producers to form a national company for which they engaged Peggy Ann as the sex pot Cherie, played by Kim Stanley in New York and later on film by Marilyn Monroe. About *Bus Stop,* Peggy Ann recalls, "Albert Salmi and I first met when we were touring with the National Company pany in *Bus Stop.* Albert had been in the New York Company [as the shy cowboy Bo Decker]; he was from the Actor's Studio which, at time, was at the height of its fame. He was the toast of Broadway and was being hailed as the new Marlon Brando. When I heard he was to be my co-star, I was scared to death." By the time the show reached Los Angeles Peggy Ann and Salmi had discovered one another and were married. After three miscarriages Peggy Ann finally had her first baby, which she and Albert named Catherine Ann, but called, for short, "Cas."

There was no conflict of careers in the marriage, since Peggy Ann gave up roles that would have separated her from Salmi, settling for TV work on "Kraft Theatre," and "Show of the Month." On the television series "Naked City," she and Albert appeared as husband and wife, Len and Edie Baker, dodging a parole officer. But by this time, the second marriage for Peggy Ann was floundering.

After a two-year separation from Salmi, Peggy Ann received a divorce and custody of their daughter Cas. Later she wed Kenyon Foster Brown, a real estate broker. Before that marriage ended in divorce, she had learned enough about the real estate business to become a successful saleswoman. She continued her TV work throughout the 1960s and she appeared on most of the major network drama shows. On the summer stock circuit, she traveled with Mark Richman and Ethel Griffies in *Write Me a Murder* in 1962, and during the next summer, she joined Joan Blondell and Alan Alda in a meandering comedy, *Watch the Birdie.* By 1964, television offers declined to an appearance as William Shatner's wife Anne Donfield on "The Man from U.N.C.L.E." episode, *The Project Strigas Affair,* and one of her last TV appearances was as Betsy Boldface, friend of the Riddler (Frank Gorshin) on the "Batman" series.

Today, Peggy Ann Garner, in her mid-forties, is a successful business woman as sales manager for Speight Buick-Opel Automobile Dealers in Santa

Monica, California. Her last motion picture was *The Cat* (1966), but she still considers herself a member of the acting profession, saying, "I'm certainly not over the hill entertainment-wise, physically or mentally or whatever. I'm not through with show business. I have an agent scouting the right parts for me and I'm confident that something will come up." Meanwhile she is apparently content as a fleet car executive for a company whose slogan is: "Where the Stars Buy Their Cars."

PEGGY ANN GARNER

Little Miss Thoroughbred   *(WB 1938)*
Blondie Brings Up Baby   *(Col 1939)*
In Name Only   *(RKO 1939)*
Abe Lincoln in Illinois   *(RKO 1940)*
Eagle Squadron   *(Univ 1942)*
The Pied Piper   *(20th 1942)*
Jane Eyre   *(20th 1944)*
Keys of the Kingdom   *(20th 1944)*
A Tree Grows in Brooklyn   *(20th 1945)*
Nob Hill   *(20th 1945)*
Junior Miss   *(20th 1945)*

Home Sweet Homicide   *(20th 1946)*
Thunder in the Valley   *(20th 1947)*
Daisy Kenyon   *(20th 1947)*
The Sign of the Ram   *(Col 1948)*
The Big Cat   *(EL 1949)*
The Lovable Cheat   *(Film Classics 1949)*
Bomba, the Jungle Boy   *(Mon 1950)*
Teresa   *(MGM 1951)*
Black Widow   *(20th 1954)*
Black Forest   *(German 1954)*
The Cat   *(Emb 1966)*

41

Virginia Gilmore

For reasons precious to devoted film enthusiasts, Virginia Gilmore is better known as the ex-wife of Yul Brynner than as the very competent actress who greeted the 1940s with a studio contract jointly held by Twentieth Century-Fox and Samuel Goldwyn. Hopefully, the following career refresher will change that understated image.

She was born Sherman Virginia Poole on July 26, 1919, in El Monte, California, the daughter of Albion Winchester Poole, a retired English army officer, and his wife Lady May (Adams) Poole. When her parents were divorced, she dropped her first name, Sherman, took her middle name and her stepfather's last name and became Virginia Gilmore. After six years in Hollywood's Immaculate Heart Convent, she returned to her home in Burlingame near San Francisco and, as she entered her teens, made her stage debut at San Francisco's Green Hat Theatre as Winifred in *The Awakening of Spring.* At sixteen she played Curley's wife in the premiere of Steinbeck's *Of Mice and Men* at the John Steinbeck Theatre in Monterey. She spent a few seasons with the San Francisco Theatre group and thereafter signed a seven-year contract with Samuel Goldwyn starting at fifty dollars a week.

Immediate studio publicity releases lacked any comment on Virginia's acting ability but were enthusiastic about her legs, stating that they were the best seen in Hollywood since the arrival of Fraulein Die-

trich. In the mid-1960's, reflecting on her Hollywood career, she said, "I was the Queen of the B's for years. But I was never a movie actress. My original training was for the stage. The movies want a personality. I just never was that. I'm not interested in being that. The screen is the director's medium. The stage belongs to the actors. Once the curtain is up, the director is non-existent." Always a competent actress, her stage ventures were far better than any of the parts Hollywood tossed her way.

Walter Wanger produced a film set against the background of his alma mater, Dartmouth, called *Winter Carnival* (1939) that was beset with script problems. It began with Wanger hiring and firing F. Scott Fitzgerald as co-writer with a recently graduated Dartmouth man, Budd Schulberg. Schulberg completed his first screen script and Virginia Gilmore made her movie debut as Margie Stafford in this Ann Sheridan film.

Goldwyn cast Virginia in the remake of *Raffles* (1940) starring David Niven, but none of her scenes remained in the release print. Then, happily cast opposite Gary Cooper in Goldwyn's *The Westerner* (1940), she was suddenly replaced by Doris Davenport. At this juncture, Goldwyn negotiated a deal to share Virginia's contract with Twentieth Century-Fox and she was shipped over to the Pico Boulevard lot for *Manhattan Heartbeat* (1940), joining Robert Sterling and Joan Davis in this minor tale. She was then Tim Holt's love interest in the third version of *Laddie*

Publicity pose ca. 1941

(1940). Robert Young and Randolph Scott vied for the love of Sue Creighton (Gilmore) while stringing telegraph lines across the West in Fritz Lang's *Western Union* (1941), widely and wildly advertised as a Zane Grey adventure but actually written in Fox's script department two years after the novelist's death. Virginia received critical compliments as the "unobtrusive love interest."

Virginia's career hopes rose when Goldwyn promised her the meaty part of Bette Davis' daughter Alexandra in his scheduled production of Lillian Hellman's *The Little Foxes* (1941). But the Goldwyn hierarchy finally decided to give the role to new contractee Teresa Wright, and Virginia, taking over where Claire Trevor and Lynn Bari were leaving off as Fox's heroines in penny-ante B pictures, returned to that studio for *Tall, Dark and Handsome* (1941). She was Judy, a nightclub dancer in love with a timid racketeer (Cesar Romero), and managed to hold her own against such seasoned scene stealers as Charlotte Greenwood and Milton Berle. Her role as Mabel McKenzie in Twentieth Century-Fox's *Swamp Water* (1941), directed by Jean Renoir and with Anne Baxter in the lead female assignment, remains her favorite movie work. She recalls "It was the brilliant French

At the piano, with Joan Davis in Manhattan Heartbeat *(20th 1940)*

director who made the difference. That was the most interesting one because he was such a hell of a guy to work for. I don't think the picture made a dime." (The film was remade as *Lure of the Wilderness,* 1952, with Constance Smith inheriting Virginia's part.)

Virginia was fine in *Berlin Correspondent* (1942), as pro-Nazi Karen Hauen out to trap Dana Andrews, a newspaperman leaking Nazi information via radio broadcasts, only to discover her father was the source of the reporter's information. She was Elmira Roysten, the childhood sweetheart of the doomed poet (John Shepperd) in *The Loves of Edgar Allen Poe* (1942), but it was Linda Darnell who had the focal female role in this romanticized account. *Orchestra Wives* (1942) was blessed with the music of Glenn Miller and his Orchestra, a good cast that included Carole Landis, Jackie Gleason (in a bit part) and Virginia as the bitchy Elise, joining with two other wives in telling Ann Rutherford about husband George Montgomery's affair with Lynn Bari.

She was assigned to Tyrone Power's *Son of Fury* (1942), but a few weeks into production she was yanked out of the film. In *That Other Woman,* also at Fox, she played another girl whose Christian name began with "E," this time as Emily in a dreary secretary-chases-boss tale with James Ellison and Dan Duryea. She was wasted again as Natalie, in a substandard B movie called *Sundown Joe* (1942), whose reason for being was to highlight the supposed talents of Jim Kimbrough, an ex-Texas A & M fullback. In the summer of 1942, Virginia escaped Hollywood to renew her perspective and, undoubtedly, her artistic balance, by appearing in stock at Holyoke, Massachusetts. Her one highlight in the movies that year was appearing in *Pride of the Yankees* (1942) as Myra, the lisping coquette who embarrasses Gary Cooper's Lou Gehrig. Once again, it was Virginia's Goldwyn Studio rival, Teresa Wright, who had the distaff lead in this superior biographical film.

After a supporting role with Philip Dorn and Anna Sten in *Chetniks* (1943), the true war account of Draja Mihailovitch, a heroic Yugoslavian guerrilla, Virginia wisely returned to the stage.

Max Gordon, one of the theatre's most astute and successful producers, premiered Edward Chodorov's *These Endearing Young Charms* on April 4, 1943 in Philadelphia, with Peggy Conklin, Mabel Taliaferro, Zachary Scott, and Dean Harens. The performances were praised but the play was found lacking. Gordon withdrew the show, Chodorov revised the script, and Miss Taliaferro was replaced by Blanche Sweet. Harens and Scott were retained, and Virginia Gilmore was signed for the part of Helen Brandt. The show opened at the Booth Theatre in New York on June 15,

Advertisement for Laddie *(RKO 1940)*

1943 to less than enthusiastic reviews. This war romance was concerned with an unpleasant rake of an air corps lieutenant (Scott), and Virginia, whose patriotism and acute sexual attraction to the officer about to leave for the Pacific culminates in a rushed seduction and climaxes in a last-minute wedding at the airport.

Virginia's notices for *Young Charms* ranged from "engaging," "skillful in her playing" to "perfect casting" and she was applauded for convincingly delivering a long difficult speech with great artistry. Unfortunately the show folded after sixty-one performances. (When RKO made a film version of the play in 1945, Laraine Day had Virginia's part.)

Twentieth Century-Fox financed *The World's Full of Girls,* adapted by Nunnally Johnson from a Thomas Bell novel, and Jed Harris produced and directed the show. Virginia, in the role of Sally, had little to do in the proceedings, which opened on Broadway on December 6, 1943. Only Harry Bellaver as a tough Marine stood out in a cast that included Frances Heflin and Barry Kroeger. After nine performances the show closed.

Nineteen forty-four was to be Virginia's jackpot year. Early in that year she had met a fascinating, if mysterious, actor at a party in Los Angeles. He was a Swiss citizen beginning a career in the performing arts in America, and creating a legend that started in Elizabetsk, Outer Mongolia, Vladivostok, or the Island of Sakhalin off the coast of Siberia. First known as Taidje Khan, Jr., then Youl Bryner, and later as Yul Brynner, he would become an unusual sex symbol as the bald-pated King in *The King and I* on Broadway and in the movies. When Virginia married Yul on September 6, 1944, he was a television director. At that time he was inscrutably handsome and did have hair. The newlyweds returned to New York and Virginia won her best role (on stage or film) as Ruth Wilkins in Norman Krasna's hit comedy, *Dear Ruth* (December, 1944). Her performance was glowing, richly lovable, and comic, justifying her fine notices. (When Paramount instituted its *Dear* . . . series in 1947, Joan Caulfield inherited the Ruth part.)

After her great personal triumph in *Dear Ruth,* Virginia signed with the Theatre Guild for the part of Ferne Rainier in S. N. Behrman's *Dunnigan's Daughter.* She opened with the show in Washington, D.C. and played the show nine weeks on the road when it was withdrawn, rewritten, and recast. Only Dennis King and two minor actors remained of the original company when the comedy, turned drama, opened unsuccessfully in New York on December 26, 1945 for a brief run. June Havoc played Virginia's role of Ferne. All of Virginia's hopes of playing on Broadway

at the same time as her husband vanished. Brynner and Mary Martin arrived in February of 1946 in the hauntingly lovely *Lute Song* and Virginia was, by then, rehearsing another play, Maxwell Anderson's post-war problem drama, *Truckline Cafe,* which opened in Baltimore, Maryland the same month.

The Anderson play provided Virginia with a plum acting role as Anne Carruth, embracing alcohol and nymphomania after learning her husband is missing in the war. After an abortion she hides as a waitress in *Truckline Cafe* where her presumed dead husband finds her. Mutually confessing their multiple sins (he has fathered a French child whose mother died in childbirth), they determine to start a new life together. The high-powered cast included Irene Dailey, June Walker, David Manners, Kevin McCarthy, Karl Malden, and a promising young actor, Marlon Brando. The drama was slaughtered by the critics and closed only thirteen performances after it debuted at the Belasco Theatre on February 27, 1946.

While Yul Brynner was captivating Broadway in *Lute Song,* Mrs. Brynner gave birth in December, 1946 to a son, Yul Brynner, Jr., whom his parents nicknamed "Rocky." Six years later and long after her Goldwyn contract (which ended with her supporting role in Danny Kaye's *Wonder Boy* (1945) had been forgotten, Virginia returned to the screen in Columbia's *Walk East on Beacon* (1952), based on J. Edgar Hoover's revelations of the F.B.I.'s tracking of Communists. It was done in semi-documentary style and filmed on location in Boston and Washington, D.C.. George Murphy and Finlay Currie helped Virginia, playing the spy Millie, generate a good deal of suspense in this thriller.

Also in 1952 she appeared on television in *The Barker* and *The Night of January 16th,* and, as the year ended, she returned to the theatre as Alice Hart, Walter Matthau's wife, in *The Green-Eyed People,* a farce on suburban family life. "But after that I didn't do much theatre," she later explained about her semi-retirement. "It was just too demanding and besides I don't think two actors can manage together. The separations aren't good. Two careers can make for many problems. Someone has to give. So I quit. I really quit work. I even got over the desire to."

Eight years later the Brynners were divorced in Mexico. Virginia, explaining the adjustment, said, "Life takes some funny turns. I was broke so I got into soap opera, 'The Edge of Night' on television. It kept me alive." By December, 1960, she was back on Broadway as actress Ivy London who divorces her critic husband (Henry Fonda) after he pans one of her stage performances. Virginia was beguiling and sensual, and made the most of her lines in Ira Levin's

Critic's Choice, heavy-handedly directed by Otto Preminger. It ran for 189 performances until May, 1961. (In the 1963 Warner Bros. film version, Lucille Ball won Virginia's role.)

In 1962, Virginia appeared in a stock production of *Sweet Bird of Youth* at Paramus, New Jersey. Since that production and aside from infrequent television appearances, she has retired from acting.

After her divorce from Brynner, their son Yul Jr. or Jay Rockwell as he was frequently called, was sent to boarding school and to the International School in Geneva. Rocky then completed four years at Trinity College in Dublin. His godfather, Jean Cocteau, had once written a record of his own withdrawal agonies from opium and in 1969 Rocky adapted the searing study into play form. Using Roc Brynner for his professional name, the young man appeared in his one character play, *Opium Journal of a Cure* at the Edison Theatre in New York on October 5, 1970. The first-night audience included his mother, Sherman Virginia Poole Brynner.

Back in the 1950s, while Yul Brynner had been making films abroad, Virginia had become interested in zoology from courses at the University of California. She graduated from the University of Vienna as a qualified cytologist (a specialist in the branch of biology dealing with the study of cells). More recently she has turned into a successful drama coach in Manhattan, proving that she is also still a fine actress.

VIRGINIA GILMORE

Winter Carnival *(UA 1939)*
Raffles *(UA 1940)* *
Manhattan Heartbeat *(20th 1940)*
Laddie *(RKO 1940)*
Jennie *(20th 1940)*
Western Union *(20th 1941)*
Tall, Dark and Handsome *(20th 1941)*
Swamp Water *(20th 1941)*
Mr. District Attorney in the Carter Case *(Rep 1941)*
Berlin Correspondent *(20th 1942)*
*Scenes deleted

The Loves of Edgar Allan Poe *(20th 1942)*
Orchestra Wives *(20th 1942)*
That Other Woman *(20th 1942)*
Sundown Jim *(20th 1942)*
Son of Fury *(20th 1942)* *
Pride of the Yankees *(RKO 1942)*
Chetniks *(20th 1943)*
Wonder Man *(RKO 1945)*
Close-Up *(EL 1948)*
Walk East on Beacon *(Col 1952)*

42

Farley Granger

Farley Granger may or may not be one of the few actors ever to be discovered for films because he answered a want ad. The story goes that movie mogul Samuel Goldwyn was having difficulty finding a young actor to play a Russian youth in Lillian Hellman's *North Star* (1943), so he took out an ad in a Los Angeles newspaper. Seventeen-year-old Farley applied for the job and got it. Another, and somewhat more credible, story is that Bob McIntire, a Goldwyn casting director, spotted young Granger in a little theatre production of *The Wooly* at the Mary Stewart Playhouse in Hollywood, and, after a reading, the fledgling performer was signed to a seven-year Goldwyn contract. Whichever story is believed, Granger did become a Goldwyn commodity.

After delivering two fine, natural performances in his first two films, under director Lewis Milestone's guidance, his career was interrupted by the World War II draft. After the war he returned to moviemaking in *They Live by Night* (1949) and for the next few years was Hollywood's major poverty-stricken, disturbed young man or poor little rich boy. It was a hard way on which to build a maturing screen image. In neither of these two acting poses was he very successful. He came closest to solidifying his industry status as the pro tennis player accused of murder in Alfred Hitchcock's exciting *Strangers on a Train* (1951), but even in this film the "boy poet" look, which he has always had, kept him from being totally believable.

Granger was born in San Jose, California, on July 1, 1925, to Farley Earle, a civil service employee, and Eva Hopkins Granger, and was named Farley Earle II. He first appeared on the stage at the age of five playing an elf in a school Christmas pageant. While he was attending North Hollywood High School he was signed to the above-mentioned Goldwyn contract, which began at one hundred dollars weekly and escalated to five hundred dollars per week. His first feature *North Star* (later re-edited for television as *Armored Attack*), one of the best propaganda war films of the period, was originally to be directed by William Wyler. However, Wyler joined the Army and Lewis Milestone replaced him. That director handled the inexperienced actor quite well and bobby-soxers of the time took a strong liking to Farley. Convinced he had a future star on his hands, Goldwyn described Granger in press releases as the acting sensation of the film. Fine as he was, Farley was not quite that, not with such performers as Walter Huston, Walter Brennan, Ann Harding, and Erich von Stroheim also in the picture. Milestone then borrowed Farley from Goldwyn to appear as one of eight American fliers captured by the Japanese in Twentieth Century-Fox's *The Purple Heart* (1944) and he suffered very well oncamera in this other well-made World War II propaganda movie.

Farley was then off to war himself, spending much of his duty time in Hawaii in Special Services and as

With Joan Evans in Roseanna McCoy *(RKO 1949)*

part of Maurice Evans' actors unit, but at one point he was also stationed at Midway. In 1946, two years after he entered the Navy, he received his honorable discharge. Upon his return home he was greeted with a new Ford car, a gift from his studio and a role in Nicholas Ray's *They Live by Night,* which would not be released until 1949. (Howard Hughes's takeover of RKO was responsible for the film's long-time shelving.) This study of fugitives from justice had many pre-release problems, one of which was the title. It was variously known as *Your Red Wagon* and *The Twisted Road* before it was finally pushed into release by a hesitant RKO. The *New York Times* found Granger's performance as the soulful criminal "wistful and appealing" but the critics now seem to feel that Robert Altman's remake, *Thieves Like Us* (1974) with Keith Carradine, was more honest. Granger believes that *They Live by Night* was just too much ahead of its time to be popular in its day.

Next came Alfred Hitchcock's *Rope* (1948) starring James Stewart. Farley and John Dall were cast as the two murderers, who decide to commit the perfect homicide, much in the mold of the well-known Leopold and Loeb "thrill killing" case. Granger portrayed Dall's weak accomplice in this screen adaptation by Hume Cronyn and Arthur Laurents. The *New York Morning Telegraph* remarked on Farley's performance, that he "shakes and trembles at all appropriate moments." Farley has stated that working with Hitchcock was more like being a prop than anything else, "But," he hastens to add, "you just have to accept the way he·works." Because of his performance in *Rope,* the *Encyclopedia Britannica* named him, along with Montgomery Clift and Richard Basehart, the three most promising newcomers of the year.

Goldwyn then cast him in *Enchantment* (1948), a David Niven–Teresa Wright vehicle which was a moving history of an English family. His next film, *Roseanna McCoy* (1949), dealt with the hatred between the Hatfields and the McCoys in the manner of *Romeo and Juliet* and introduced to the screen Joan Evans, a Joan Crawford protegee and a very inferior actress, in the title role.

MGM borrowed both Farley and his *They Live by Night* co-lead, Cathy O'Donnell, for *Side Street* (1950). The critics did not take kindly to this Anthony Mann-directed picture. The *New York Herald-Tribune* thought that Granger gave a "nervous, vacuous, unsympathetic performance as a part-time postman who steals to help out his pregnant wife." Back under Goldwyn's aegis, he and Joan Evans were teamed in two 1950 releases: *Our Very Own* and *Edge of Doom.* The latter was slaughtered by the reviewers and rightfully so, being an unbelievably trite account

of a confused young man (Granger) baffled by the pressures of the cruel world about him. Dana Andrews was just as far off the mark as the priest on the scene. As for Farley, the *New York Herald-Tribune* insisted, "Granger, playing the part of a young man obsessed by love for his dead mother and resentment toward the Church, is not up to the task of sustaining a whole picture with studied monomania. Granger does not seethe; he's limited to varying degrees of unhappiness in a monotonous performance."

Farley was under consideration for two of the finest male roles of the early 1950s: the writer in *Sunset Boulevard* (1950) and the tragic Eastman boy in *A Place in the Sun* (1951). (William Holden played the former, and Montgomery Clift the latter.) Granger recently told an interviewer that it was Goldwyn who refused to release him for the assignments, a rationale that is difficult to concede.

Goldwyn did loan Farley to Alfred Hitchcock for Warner Bros.' *Strangers on a Train* (1951), which proved to be the actor's best film to date. "I deliberately picked that sane part in *Strangers on a Train* instead of the Bob Walker one—a good one," says Granger, "because I'd been a little wacky in *Rope* and *Edge of Doom.* . . . I needed that change, I felt." The critics were not so sure Farley had made the proper casting choice. Said Bosley Crowther (*New York Times*), he "plays the terrified catspaw (as he did in *Rope*) as though he were constantly swallowing his tongue."

It was decidedly offbeat casting to have Farley and Shelley Winters—at a similar point in each of their careers—thrown into the comedy, *Behave Yourself* (1951) in which they were the owners of a pooch wanted by a criminal gang because the dog knows the whereabouts of a cache of money. Granger looked more perplexed than engaging in his change-of pace role. His next film, *I Want You* (1951), was intended to be a Korean War version of *The Best Years of Our Lives* (1946), but Goldwyn almost fell flat on his face with this tearjerker.

The only good things about Granger's last Goldwyn production, *Hans Christian Andersen* (1952), starring Danny Kaye, were the score and the film's colorful production values. It was Farley's first musical and he even did some (amateur) dancing in it. "I'm a frustrated song and dance man," the actor has said. The *New York Times* said, "The less said about Farley Granger and Joey Walsh, in lesser roles, the better for health and digestion." Thereafter Goldwyn placed him on suspension for refusing to do publicity on *Hans,* but lifted it in order to lend him to Universal for the lead in *The Golden Blade* (1953), with Piper Laurie. Granger refused the part saying the script was

With Richard Conte, John Craven, Dana Andrews, Charles Russell, and Sam Levene in The Purple Heart (20th 1944)

With James Stewart and John Dall in Rope (WB 1948)

awful and was immediately put back on suspension. Rock Hudson replaced him in that sword and sand clinker. After being borrowed by MGM for roles in *The Story of Three Loves* (1953) and *Small Town Girl* (1953), he bought out his Goldwyn contract which still had two years to go. "I just had to," said Granger. Since Goldwyn did not make very many films, Granger's time was generally spent on loanout. "He charged a great deal of money for me."

Feeling confused about his position in the Hollywood firmament, Farley decided to try his luck elsewhere. "I didn't know what kind of an actor I was regarded as. That's why I wanted to get out. Everybody was saying one thing after another, and I realized that romantic leads were such a bore and that I really wanted to do character things. But that's difficult when you're young, especially if you're good looking."

His next film job was in the Italian *Senso* (1954) with Alida Valli and directed by Luchino Visconti. Marlon Brando and Ingrid Bergman had been the original choices for the production. Farley accepted this job because he needed the money. Buying out his Goldwyn contract had cost him a great deal and he was preparing to move to New York and study acting. *Senso* was to have had three months of filming in Italy but it finally crawled to a conclusion after nine months of work. *Senso* has since become an Italian classic. It was released to American television before it finally had its first real theatrical bookings here in 1968. The film has also been called *Summer Hurricane* and *The Wanton Contessa*.

Instead of settling in New York after his European filmmaking venture, Farley returned to Hollywood to accept film offers in *The Naked Street* (1955) and *The Girl in the Red Velvet Swing* (1955). The two scripts had him electrocuted in the former, and going crazy in the latter. *Red Velvet Swing* was a CinemaScope, color, fictionalized account of the life of Florodora girl Evelyn Nesbit (Joan Collins) and her headlined problems with architect Stanford White (Ray Milland) and millionaire Harry Thaw (Granger). Archer Winsten of the *New York Post* was not enthusiastic about Farley's interpretation, "Thaw, himself, played by Farley Granger, is a tempestuous lad and therefore quick to resort to the pistol when eaten by jealousy, but he never seems really deranged. To be truthful, Farley makes him so charming that you suspect he might really win the girl at any moment if the scenarists weren't stuck with that ancient, famous Thaw melodrama." At this point Granger quit the movies.

Farley was hopeful of developing in all directions as a performer, primarily intending to work on the stage. In New York he studied acting with Sanford

Meisner, Stella Adler, and Lee Strasberg. He also took singing and dancing lessons. During this training period he worked in stock and on television. His professional stage debut was in *John Loves Mary* in 1953 in Matunick, Rhode Island followed by a stint as Lachie in *The Hasty Heart*. Quite frequently theatre packagers, content to trade on his marquee value, miscast Farley. He played the title role in *Mister Roberts* and *The Rainmaker* and was even (!) Hal in *Picnic*. His Manhattan stage debut was as Actor--man in the Phoenix Theatre's 1955 production of *The Carefree Tree*. His co-star in the show was Janice Rule. For a brief time she and Granger were engaged to be married.

Farley's Broadway debut was in the short-lived but finely-mounted *First Impressions,* a musical version of Jane Austin's *Pride and Prejudice,* which opened at the Alvin Theatre on March 19, 1959. Farley was Darcy, and his co-stars were Polly Bergen and Hermione Gingold. The *Saturday Review* remarked that Bergen sang better than she acted and that Granger acted better than he sang. That same season he was back on Broadway in the equally unprofitable *The Warm Peninsula* with Julie Harris and June Havoc. His later stage appearances include Jeff in *Brigadoon,* the King in *The King and I,* done at New York's City Center, and the Broadway revival of *The Glass Menagerie,* in 1965, with Jo Van Fleet, Hal Holbrook, and Carol Rossen. Farley, of course, played the sensitive, tormented son. He also toured as Brigadier Anderson in the national company of *Advise and Consent.* Granger became a bit disappointed in Broadway saying, "A lot of things I thought wrong about Hollywood are also wrong in the theatre; the same type casting and expense of production is wildly out of proportion." Then, for very little money, he toured with Signe Hasso and Denholm Elliott as part of the National Repertory Company, appearing in *The Seagull, The Crucible,* and *Ring Round the Moon.* The first two plays had limited engagements on Broadway. Farley remained with this company for another season, playing the title role in *Liliom,* Lovberg in *Hedda Gabler,* and had a part in *She Stoops to Conquer.*

Farley's television roles were mostly that of disturbed young men and sons—not terribly different from his previous movie roles. His theatrical experiences did give him an added amount of stage presence, but his performances were not that much better than before. Television, however, occasionally gave him the opportunity to play varying parts such as the title role in *Arrowsmith,* Rupert in *The Prisoner of Zenda,* Apollodorus in *Caesar and Cleopatra,* and Freud in the "U.S. Steel Hour"'s *The Wound Within.*

As the famed psychiatrist, the *New York Times* found Granger "a strident healer whose excitable manner would drive a fairly normal patient to distraction." His performance as Morris Townsend in *The Heiress* (starring Julie Harris) on TV's "Family Classics" was a weak one.

In the late 1960s, wanting to return to films, Farley made *Rogue's Gallery* (1968), starring Roger Smith and Dennis Morgan, but the A.C. Lyles production was never released theatrically, finally having its "world premiere" on television in 1973. With the exceptions of the telefeature *The Challengers* (1969) about car racing, and *Arnold* (1973) in which he plays a lawyer, his other feature films to date have been foreign-made productions. In late 1974 he returned to Hollywood where he began dating actress Brett Sommers, the estranged wife of Jack Klugman.

Six-foot-one, brown-eyed Farley, who still has a youthful quality about him, is eagerly seeking character roles in the European filmmaking market, still trying to rid himself of his earlier screen image. "I'm really getting a whole other point of view as to what I can do now. Things are beginning to add up. As I get older, I don't think there is any way to go except to get better as an actor all the time."

FARLEY GRANGER

The North Star *(RKO 1943)*
The Purple Heart *(20th 1944)*
Rope *(WB 1948)*
Enchantment *(RKO 1948)*
Roseanna McCoy *(RKO 1949)*
They Live by Night *(RKO 1949)*
Side Street *(MGM 1950)*
Our Very Own *(RKO 1950)*
Edge of Doom *(RKO 1950)*
Strangers on a Train *(WB 1951)*
Behave Yourself *(RKO 1951)*
I Want You *(RKO 1951)*
O.Henry's Full House (episode: The Gift of the Magi) *(20th 1952)*
Hans Christian Andersen *(RKO 1952)*
The Story of Three Loves *(MGM 1953)*
Small Town Girl *(MGM 1953)*
Senso (a.k.a., The Wanton Contessa, Summer Hurricane) *(Italian 1954)*

The Naked Street *(UA 1955)*
The Girl in the Red Velvet Swing *(20th 1955)*
Rogue's Gallery *(Par 1968)*
Those Days in the Sun *(Italian 1968)*
Maharlika *(Italian 1969)*
Qualcosa Striscia Nel Buio (Shadows in the Dark) *(Italian 1970)*
Planet Venus *(Italian 1970)*
Alla Ricera Del Piacere (Hot Bed of Sex) *(Italian 1972)*
Rivelazione Di Un Maniaco Sessuale Al Capo Della Squadra Mobile (Confessions of a Sex Maniac Involving the Chief of Homicide) *(Italian 1972)*
Delitto Per Delitto (Violence) *(Italian 1972)*
A Man Called Noon *(National General 1973)*
White Fang *(Italian 1973)*
Arnold *(Cin 1973)*
The Serpent *(Avco Emb 1974)*
So Sweet, So Dead *(Italian 1975)*
Death Shall Have Your Eyes *(Spanish 1975)*
La Polizia Chiede Aiuto (The Police Want Help) *(Italian 1975)*

43

Sydney Greenstreet

One of the many phenomena peculiar to 1940s' Hollywood was the indulgence of excessively eccentric screen personalities. Could one imagine a Maria Montez, Turhan Bey, or Vera Ralston legitimately succeeding in today's film market? Equally bizarre were the onscreen likes of two literal heavyweights, Sydney Greenstreet and Laird Cregar, neither of whom, unfortunately, would survive in the cinema beyond the end of that decade.

Both could be said to follow in the physical tradition of John Bunny, Charles Laughton, Robert Morley, and Francis L. Sullivan. However, Greenstreet and Cregar were, in their way, freaks by cinema standards, who were exploited as much for their physical appearance as for their very considerable talents.

Cregar, some thirty years younger than Sydney Greenstreet, aspired to the ranks of silver screen leading men and in his determined efforts to reduce to a more comfortable size, died in 1944 of complications that resulted from a crash diet. On the other hand, Sydney, who could easily be termed a character star —in contrast to Claude Rains who swung back and forth between villainous or sympathetic leads and character roles—used his bulk to make an impressive dent in the movie world, 1940s style. His vast stage experience made his transfer in middle age to the movies easier, and once berthed at Warner Bros., he frequently teamed with small and sinister Peter Lorre. His girth never for a moment prevented him from maneuvering in front of the cameras with a maximum

of agility and sensitivity. Had not multiple illnesses curtailed his professional activities, he would have lasted well into succeeding decades.

Since 1066 there had been Greenstreets in Sandwich, Kent, England, holding a family crest given to them by William the Conqueror and, since the seventeenth century, following the family trade of leather-making. The house in which Sydney Hughes Greenstreet was born to John J. and Ann Baker Greenstreet on December 27, 1879, was steeped in four hundred years of family tradition. The high, ancient Roman walls that adjoined the Greenstreet property provided an enchanted playground for young Sydney and his seven brothers and sisters. The children were educated in the nearby town of Deal, and Sydney followed his three older brothers to Danehill College at Margate, a preparatory school for Oxford and Cambridge. He excelled in hockey, cricket, and soccer, and later claimed these sports to be his only distinction as a student.

Sydney departed from the family tradition and trade and at eighteen arrived in Ceylon as a "creeper" (trade name for a novice) in the tea business. He filled the lonely nights in Ceylon reading Shakespeare and, in his later years, could recite over 12,000 lines by the Bard from memory. A drought in Ceylon forced him to return to England, and, after a few meaningless jobs, he decided on an acting ca-

With Reginald Gardiner and S. Z. Sakall in Christmas in Connecticut *(WB 1945)*

reer. Financed by his mother, he entered the Ben Greet School of Acting and even before completing the course, Greet had him playing in several London productions. His first speaking part was in *Sherlock Holmes,* as Craigen, a murderer (virtually a forecast of his later film career).

In 1904, Ben Greet organized a company to tour America, which included Sybil Thorndike, Fritz Leiber, and Greenstreet who was hired for leading comedy roles. The tour lasted five years, during which Sydney later said, "I could be traced from coast to coast by the beds I broke down in hotels. I'd go down on the slats once every fifth hotel. Never knew it to fail." He made his Broadway debut as Good Fellowship in the morality play *Everyman,* and then played in eighteen Shakespeare productions, finally deciding that his theatrical future was in New York, not London. He spent a season with the Henry David stock company in Pittsburgh, Pennsylvania, and returned to Broadway as the American husband in the farce *Excuse Me,* produced by Henry W. Savage, for whom he worked two years. His following years comprise a lengthy and impressive column in *Who's Who in the Theatre* as Sydney acted with Julia Marlowe, Sir Herbert Beerbohm Tree (who claimed Greenstreet was the greatest unstarred star on the English speaking stage), Viola Allen, and for Lou Tellegen, playing Henry VIII in *The King from Nowhere.*

It amused Sydney to relate an experience while playing an outdoor performance with Margaret Anglin in *As You Like It,* when the three-foot-high stage caved in and he disappeared from sight. "They always blamed me for it," chuckled the massive actor, "But I climbed up out of the wreckage and shouted my next speech to a hysterical audience. 'True it is, we have seen better days.' The audience was roaring and I was hanging on to a stage prop for dear life while trying to get out my next line—'Sit you down in gentleness.' Well, sir, that ended the performance." Years later, while on tour with the Lunts in *The Taming of the Shrew,* he crashed through a locked door. That cost the Theatre Guild five hundred dollars in set damages. During his film career, he once became stuck in a telephone booth that Warner Bros. carpenters had to dismantle. His weight had at one time reached 325 pounds, but "normally" he was 280. Still a lot of bulk for a man five feet ten and a half inches tall.

Greenstreet's versatility as an actor was astounding. He spent several seasons in musical comedy playing an unctuous butler in *The Rainbow Girl,* Mitzi's benefactor in *The Magic Ring,* and then to Sigmund Romberg's *The Student Prince.* In 1933, he returned to the musical field as the friend of Aunt Minnie's (trade name "Roberta") Lord Henry Delves, in Jerome Kern's lovely *Roberta,* joining Bob Hope,

With Ida Lupino and William Prince in Pillow to Post *(WB 1945)*

278

Lyda Roberti, and Ray Middleton in the song, "Let's Begin." He dismissed his big move from Shakespeare and the classics to musical comedy by saying that "musical comedy pays better."

His most creative stage assignments came with many seasons with the Theatre Guild, especially in plays starring the Lunts, who considered Greenstreet the only actor capable of delivering their highly polished technique of overlapping lines. For what he called "the loveliest six years of my life," Greenstreet appeared with the famous Mr. and Mrs. Lunt as Peter Sorin in Chekhov's *The Sea Gull*, Baptista in *The Taming of the Shrew*, the Trumpeter in *Amphytrion '38*, and Dr. Waldersee in Robert Sherwood's *Idiot's Delight*.

As Uncle Waldemar Sederstrum in Sherwood's *There Shall Be No Night*, Sydney was superb. To make his physical appearance more than comparable to the Jan Sibelius-like part, he shaved his head to resemble the bald composer, and, during the course of the play, he performed parts of Sibelius' music on the piano. While he was playing Uncle Waldemar in Los Angeles, Greenstreet was signed by John Huston for the role of Kasper Gutman in his remake of Dashiell Hammett's thriller *The Maltese Falcon* (1941). Warner Bros. had made the original film in 1931 with Ricardo Cortez and Bebe Daniels, with Dudley Digges as Gutman, and again in 1936 as *Satan Met a*

Lady with Bette Davis and Warren William. Huston wrote the script for the remake and, as his first directorial assignment, produced a motion picture classic.

Greenstreet, at the age of sixty-one, started a film career as the master villain, the epicene Gutman. Reeking with gross self-indulgence and slyly chortling his lines from his opening gambit to private detective Sam Spade (Humphrey Bogart), "I am a man who likes to talk to a man who likes to talk," he oozed a malevolent charm while maintaining the appearance of a benevolent, if overdressed, Buddha. The precise shading of his characterization carefully underlined the homosexual overtones of his relationship with his protege/gunman Wilmer (Elisha Cook, Jr.), which made definitive dialogue unnecessary—other than his observation, after it has been agreed to use Cook as the fall guy for two murders, "If you lose a son it is possible to gain another. There is only one Maltese Falcon." He received his first and only nomination as Best Supporting Actor for his rich portrayal in *The Maltese Falcon*, but the Oscar went to Donald Crisp (*How Green Was My Valley*).

Taking advantage of Greenstreet's leave of absence from the Lunts, and acutely aware of the audience acclaim for his *Maltese Falcon* performance, Warner Bros. rushed him into the role of General Winfield Scott in *They Died with Their Boots On* (1941). One more of the Errol Flynn-Olivia de Havilland adven-

With John Emery, Eleanor Parker, and Matthew Boulton in The Woman in White *(WB 1948)*

With James Stewart and Spencer Tracy in Malaya *(MGM 1949)*

ture outings. Sydney's performance as the onion-loving commander was splendid and, having grown to like California, he signed a studio contract in spite of his many years of resisting and his own long standing rule not to be contractually tied to anyone. In *Across the Pacific* (1942), also directed by John Huston, he was cast as the coldly murderous white-suited Dr. Lorenz passing himself off as a sociologist but working for the Japanese and planning to blow up the Gatun Locks of the Panama Canal. He made a marvelous adversary to patriotic Humphrey Bogart and decorative Mary Astor.

He was the fly-swatting, fez-wearing Senor Ferrari, head of the black market and proprietor of the Blue Parrot Cafe, trying to coerce Rick's (Bogart) cafe piano player (Dooley Wilson) into working for him in *the* motion picture classic of the forties, *Casablanca* (1943). Howard Koch, co-author of the script, recently wrote that Greenstreet's role could have been played by no one else before or since. It would be difficult to imagine any of the early Greenstreet villains, expertly weaving their web of ultimate evil and speaking so eloquently in cultured tones, played by anyone other than Sydney Greenstreet.

In 1944, Greenstreet was featured in five pictures. He played himself working in the *Hollywood Canteen,* and then appeared as Major Duval, comman-

deering a ship carrying five convicts who escaped from Devil's Island to join the Free French, in *Passage to Marseille.* This role was followed by that of Reverend Frank Thompson, the Heavenly Examiner, who directs the destinations of a group of lost souls in a remake of Sutton Vane's *Outward Bound*—updated and retitled, *Between Two Worlds.* One of his better roles was as the sinister and mysterious Mr. Peters in an uneven production of Eric Ambler's *A Coffin for Dimitrios* retitled *The Mask of Dimitrios.* The film's story was told in confusing flashbacks and not helped by the ridiculous casting of Faye Emerson in a black wig as Zachary Scott's sluttish girl friend, but Greenstreet was substantial, especially his poise after killing Dimitrios and his chilling yet oddly comic reading of the line, "There's not enough kindness in the world." His final 1944 effort was a sudden switch to the right side of the law as Colonel Quintanilla, leading the underground movement in *The Conspirators.* It was not one of his better performances. Sydney excelled as no other "heavy" before him, however, in portraying the sinister, malicious, and often vicious villain with an air of almost charming, deceptive corruption. With its continuing program of well-mounted action pictures, Warner Bros. was just the studio to take advantage of Greenstreet's talents.

Occasionally, the studio indulged the actor and put

him into comedy, as in *Pillow to Post* (1945), a farce with Ida Lupino, and in another lightweight effort, *Christmas in Connecticut* (1945), in which he maneuvered events as Barbara Stanwyck's suspicious boss. He became involved in a fascinating battle of wits with a wife-killer (Bogart, again) as Dr. Mark Hamilton, a psychiatrist, in *Conflict* (1945). As Jerome K. Arbutny, a crooked barrister agonizingly unsuccessful in romancing wealthy widow Rosalind Ivan, whose fortune he has been stealing, he joins with two others in the purchase of a sweepstakes ticket on the eve of the Chinese New Year in the constantly tight and exciting movie written by John Huston, *Three Strangers* (1946). Again effectively cast with Peter Lorre, the bizarre adventure was heightened by a strong performance from Geraldine Fitzgerald as the "third" stranger who is killed by Greenstreet with the statue of Kwan-Yin, Goddess of fortune and destiny, of life and death.

Devotion (1946) was one of Warner Bros.' frequent (and often disastrous) excursions into history and had, as Greenstreet put it, "cast me as William Makepeace Thackeray, a perfectly lovely gentleman." Then, as Superintendent Grodman, he and Peter Lorre were teamed yet again in a rather pedestrian melodramatic Victorian story, *The Verdict* (1946), set in fog-bound, gas-lit London. The film was greatly enlivened by a beautiful performance from Rosalind Ivan. The effective contrast of teaming hearty, cultivated Greenstreet with the diminutive, obsequious, whining Lorre (both notorious scene-stealers) was smart boxoffice, and they have been described as an unholy Laurel and Hardy. A remake of George Arliss' *The Millionaire* (1931), called *That Way with Women* (1947), did nothing for Greenstreet and, for the first time oncamera, he seemed quite miscast. For MGM he supported Clark Gable in *The Hucksters* (1947), having a wonderful moment where, as the tyrannical soap company head, he spits on the executive board table

at the advertising agency. He was wasted in a thankless role in *Ruthless* (1948) at Eagle-Lion, but as the evil lecher, Count Fosco, plotting to murder his way into a family fortune, he milked every ounce of drama from his role in Warners' version of Wilkie Collins' 1860 Gothic novel, *The Woman in White* (1948).

For RKO, he returned to the right arm of the law as Captain Denbury, almost taken in by murderess-for-love Rosalind Russell in *The Velvet Touch* (1948). He almost met his screen match when he was pitted against Joan Crawford's ex-carnival dancer in *Flamingo Road* (1949), in which he was Titus Semple, a vicious southern sheriff, glibly corrupting political candidates while living high on public funds. In this film, Sydney was at his hammy best, even in the sequence in which he is shot down by a determined Miss Crawford. In his last film he was back in the black market, stealing supplies of rubber from the Japanese for America in MGM's *Malaya* (1949).

During his last years, Greenstreet suffered from diabetes and Bright's disease and he died on January 19, 1954. He was survived by his wife of thirty-six years, Dorothy Ogden Greenstreet, and a son, John.

Years before he entered motion pictures, while he was playing the role of Wang Lung's Uncle in the Theatre Guild's production of *The Good Earth,* he told a reporter, "The eyes are the spiritual part of your face, the mouth, the physical part. If you're playing a physical, brutal sort of person you subordinate the upper part of your face and emphasize the mouth and chin." He used this knowledge for his film portrayals, from the charming rogue Colonel Robinson in Raoul Walsh's *Background to Danger* (1943), through all his memorable Warner Bros. villainy—especially as Kaspar Gutman discovering the Maltese Falcon at hand to be a fake, or getting down to business with Bogart by saying in that same film, "You're the man for me, sir, no beating about the bush."

SYDNEY GREENSTREET

The Maltese Falcon *(WB 1941)*
They Died with Their Boots On *(WB 1941)*
In This Our Life *(WB 1942)* (Unbilled guest appearance)
Across the Pacific *(WB 1942)*
Casablanca *(WB 1942)*
Background to Danger *(WB 1943)*
Hollywood Canteen *(WB 1944)*
Passage to Marseille *(WB 1944)*
Between Two Worlds *(WB 1944)*
The Mask of Dimitrios *(WB 1944)*
The Conspirators *(WB 1944)*
Pillow to Post *(WB 1945)*
Christmas in Connecticut *(WB 1945)*

Conflict *(WB 1945)*
Three Strangers *(WB 1946)*
Devotion *(WB 1946)*
The Verdict *(WB 1946)*
That Way with Women *(WB 1947)*
The Hucksters *(MGM 1947)*
The Woman in White *(WB 1948)*
Ruthless *(EL 1948)*
The Velvet Touch *(RKO 1948)*
It's a Great Feeling *(WB 1949)*
Flamingo Road *(WB 1949)*
Malaya *(MGM 1949)*

44

Signe Hasso

For a country that until recent decades has been persistently chauvinistic about its homeland and has eschewed foreign involvement, the United States has always been exceedingly over-impressed with non-native talent in the creative arts. It has much more easily accepted a "foreigner" as an artistic leader on Broadway or in Hollywood than it would were a "native" concerned. The success of Pola Negri, Greta Garbo, Marlene Dietrich, and Ingrid Bergman, among others, was a natural inducement for movie producers to ferret out successors for these determined living legends. Two prize misfires in the 1930s were Samuel Goldwyn's import Anna Sten and the later arrival of Sigrid Gurie (who, it proved, actually hailed from Brooklyn). Along the way there was MGM's Luise Rainer, who won two successive Best Actress Oscars, but never became a true part of the Hollywood firmament and, of course, the gorgeous Hedy Lamarr whom Metro used and then rejected in the World War II years.

In the 1940s, when a great many European performers were leaving Europe to avoid the Third Reich, Hollywood was inundated with foreign talent. Among the new arrivals was Signe Hasso*. This Swedish-born actress never became the glamour figure some people predicted, but she did establish herself as a solid screen actress in dramas, with an occasional side excursion into comedy.

*Pronouncing her first name has created problems but the lady laughingly says, "You can pronounce it any old way—it means 'Bless You' in Swedish."

Signe Eleonora Cecilia Larsson was born in Sweden on August 15, 1918 to Helfrid Lindstron Larsson, artist-writer and businessman Kefas Larsson. Mr. Larsson died when Signe was four, and the family of three children, mother, and grandmother Elenora Henig Lindstrom (one of Europe's foremost woman painters) found themselves penniless, living in a six floor walkup in a Stockholm housing project. Wealthy relatives paid for Signe's education in expensive private schools. Her stage debut as Louisa in *The Imaginary Invalid* in 1928 at the Royal Dramatic Theatre in Stockholm led to a scholarship with the Royal Dramatic Academy where another fledgling actress had enrolled five years before; Greta Gustafsson, who became the unique Garbo.

With the Royal Dramatic Theatre company she appeared in plays by Schiller, Strindberg, Eugene O'Neill, and in numerous Shakespearean productions. For her performance as Manuela in *Maids in Uniform* she received the Anders de Wahl Award in 1934. Touring Scandinavia as Norah in *The Doll's House*, Hilda in *The Master Builder,* among other leading roles, she and the company once walked fifteen miles through deep snow to keep an engagement.

On October 12, 1936 she married Harry Hasso, a director-inventor-engineer, and in 1938 she received the first Swedish "Oscar" Award presented to a woman for her performance in a comedy based on the private lives of stage players. The film was *Karriar* (1938), directed by Schamyl Bauman. Her work in

With Felix Bressart and James Craig in Dangerous Partners *(MGM 1945)*

With Vladimir Sokoloff, Peter Chong, and Dick Powell in To the Ends of the Earth *(Col 1948)*

283

the picture was considered superior to a moving performance by Tollie Zellman who appeared as an aging actress. To underscore her standing as Sweden's leading actress she received the Gösta Ekman Scandinavian Award for Theatre in 1938. While continuing in the theatre, Signe made additional films, including *Den Ljusnande Framtid* (*The Bright Prospect*) (1941) with Swedish actor Alf Kjellin.

A son, Henry, was born to the Hassos, a year after their marriage, and the next year her husband directed her in the Swedish-German film, *Geld Fallt Vom Himmel* (1938) known in Sweden as *Pengar fran Skyn* (*Money from the Sky*). In 1941 Signe divorced Hasso and left Sweden for America, having negotiated a RKO film contract. She journeyed to the States via Moscow, Siberia, Japan, and Manila, recording her wartime travels for a Swedish newspaper.

The talented and lovely Swedish actress soon discovered that RKO was at a total loss, not knowing what to do with her. Unlike her country-woman Ingrid Bergman, who had arrived two years before with the inestimable advantage of career-guidance from David O. Selznick, or Garbo, backed by the prestigious MGM empire, Signe's unheralded arrival at the confused RKO lot culminated in a release from her unconsummated contract. She went to New York to make her American stage debut at the Cort Theatre on December 8, 1941 as Judith in *Golden Wings*. The play closed after six performances but her playing and personal notices won her a film contract with Metro and a bit part in *Journey for Margaret* (1942).

Her first featured role was Elise, a Nazi sympathizer, who betrays Jean Pierre Aumont to the Germans in *Assignment in Brittany* (1943), followed by a delightful performance as the mademoiselle who flirts outrageously with Don Ameche in Ernst Lubitsch's sparkling comedy, *Heaven Can Wait* (1943). From her job at Twentieth Century-Fox, Signe went to Paramount where Cecil B. DeMille directed her as Bettina, a Dutch nurse involved with Dr. Corydon M. Wassell (Gary Cooper), in *The Story of Dr. Wassell* (1944). She was overshadowed by the performances of Spencer Tracy and Hume Cronyn in MGM's story of escapees from Hitler's concentration camps, *The Seventh Cross* (1944).

Of the nearly two dozen American films Signe has made, she is best remembered today for her portrayal of couturiere Elsa Gebhardt, owner of *The House on 92nd Street* (1945), and the domineering head of a Nazi spy ring seeking the formula for Process 97 (the Atomic Bomb). Produced by Louis de Rochemont from F.B.I. records, and largely filmed in the actual locations in semi-documentary style by Henry Hathaway, this absorbing film was heightened by Signe's expert playing of the vicious Elsa, who in the course of the film removes her blonde up-swept wig to reveal close-cropped hair and admits she is the elusive Mr. Christopher. Then, unfortunately, MGM wasted her talents in a B film of complicated Nazi confusions called *Dangerous Partners* (1945).

Although neither a singer nor a dancer, Signe did both in Douglas Sirk's expertly maneuvered *A Scandal in Paris* (a.k.a., *Thieves Holiday,* 1946), bursting through a fiery hoop and singing a Dietrich-type song in a hoarse, throaty voice. She played the role of Therese, a woman trying to reform the real-life arch criminal Vidocqu (George Sanders) only to be killed by her jealous husband (Gene Lockhart). In *Where There's Life* (1947), a Ruritanian comedy with Bob Hope, which had smatterings of *Ninotchka,* she was General Katrina Grimovitch. One of her finest screen portrayals was in *A Double Life* (1948) as Brita, ex-wife and leading lady of obsessed actor Anthony John (Ronald Colman), playing Desdemona to his Othello. In *To the Ends of the Earth* (1948) she was Ann Grant, a mysterious woman chaperoning a Chinese girl while Dick Powell trails poppy seeds and opium. For Universal's *Outside the Wall* (1948) she was mobster Richard Basehart's ex-wife, defying him to go straight. As Isabel Farrago in *Crisis* (1950), holding American brain surgeon Cary Grant hostage to operate on her dictator husband (Jose Ferrer), she was excellently cast.

But Hollywood was not doing right by Signe and, like her compatriot from Sweden, Viveca Lindfors, her great talent for emoting was hardly being utilized. In 1950 she returned to Sweden to film *Sant Hander Inte Har* (*This Can't Happen Here*) with Alf Kjellin, and then she returned to the New York stage. En route to New York she played Rebecca West in an Ibsen Festival production of Ibsen's classic, *Rosmersholm,* in London and in the fall of 1950 she opened in Boston in *Edwina Black,* a show which lasted only fifteen performances after it debuted in New York on November 21, 1950.

On July 16, 1951, she opened the Princeton Summer Theatre with a new play called *Sacred and Profane* that became *Glad Tidings* when it opened at the Lyceum Theatre in New York on October 11, 1951. Signe was flamboyant and effervescent as Maud Abbott throughout one hundred performances with co-star Melvyn Douglas, with whom she starred in "Celanese Theatre"'s television production of *Reunion in Vienna.* In whatever medium she appeared, was always a working performer, and in 1952 she was on the airwaves in *Cries the String* ("Lights Out"), *Something to Celebrate* ("Lux Video Theatre") and *The Two Mrs. Carrolls* ("Television Theatre").

In 1953 she returned to her native Sweden to produce and star in the first American film to be made in that country. It was called *The True and the False.* Back in the States she toured the summer circuits in *Love from a Stranger,* went off-Broadway as Elena Andreevna with Franchot Tone in *Uncle Vanya,* giving a merciless portrayal of the timid, crushed woman. For Maurice Evans' successful revival of George Bernard Shaw's *The Apple Cart,* Signe was a devastatingly lovely Orinthia, the impetuous and frolicking mistress of mythical King Magnus. During the tour of *The Apple Cart* her son Henry was killed in an automobile accident. Trouper Signe continued working regardless of her personal loss, touring the strawhats as *Anastasia* with Gale Sondergaard, occasionally appearing on television, and returning to England's stage as Stella in *The Key of the Door,* touring the show throughout England and Scotland.

Because it provided an opportunity to see her aging mother and to be reunited with her family, she returned to the Stockholm stage in *The Final Moment.* Then this vibrant woman decided to use several of the lyrics she had set to music for a one-woman show at Stockholm's massive nightclub Berns. Following Harry Belafonte and Edith Piaf in this arena was nerve-wracking enough, but Hasso added, "This was

Publicity pose ca. 1943

With Wilton Graff and Ronald Colman in A Double Life *(Univ 1947)*

something I'd never done before—that is to sing. I have no singing voice but I can give the illusion of it. How do I belt out a song? That's something else. I just pray and belt!" Standing ovations at Club Berns reassured her.

"I can't understand actors hanging around Broadway, waiting and starving when the whole country enjoys good theatre," she said after returning to New York. "All kinds of people everywhere do enjoy the so-called classics, even when they're serious dramas. I say 'so-called' because what are the classics anyway except damned good plays that have survived the years." And to back her philosophy she struck out on a cross country tour in Tyrone Guthrie's production of Friedrich Schiller's *Mary Stuart* with Eva Le Gallienne as Elizabeth. The following year she repeated her *Mary Stuart* on the television "Play of the Week."

Her work was constant, ranging from various television shows such as *One Tiger to a Hill* on "Route 66" to *The Contenders* on "Alcoa Theatre" to another season with the National Repertory Theatre with Eva Le Gallienne, where she played the small role of Mrs. Muskat in *Liliom,* alternated by the lead in *Hedda Gabler.* Of *Hedda* she has said, "Acting is very painful to me, especially in a portrait like this. To play an evil part one has to dredge up all kinds of dark emotions which one has either grown beyond or learned how to cope with." Signe proved to be a very chillingly convincing Hedda.

In 1963 she returned to the West Coast for the part of Rina Givros with Chester Morris and Kay Medford in *The Tender Heel,* which had a brief run at the Curran Theatre in San Francisco (September 30th to October 3rd). She returned to Stockholm the following spring in Pirandello's last play *The Mountain Giants,* again captivating audiences in Sweden. Having written over forty songs in English, Swedish, and German, she wrote new lyrics for twelve folk songs sung by Alice Babs, a famous Swedish singer, and recorded by Philips Records. The 1965 album, "Scandinavian Folk Songs—Sung and Swung," won the most coveted prize in the European record industry, the Grand Priz Edison International Award. In Los Angeles, Signe played what has remained her favorite role in Edward Albee's *Tiny Alice.*

For television's "Bob Hope Chrysler Theatre" she played Lydia, the widow of spy Kurt Kasznar, running a clearinghouse for cold war secrets and dying a violent death. The two episodes of this 1967 show, *Code Name: Heraclitus,* were spliced together and released abroad as a feature film, whereas her last real film appearances to date have been a cameo part in *Picture Mommy Dead* (1966), a less than classic mystery filmed in the old Doheny mansion on Sunset Boulevard in Hollywood, and *The Black Bird* (1975), a follow-up to *The Maltese Falcon.*

Harold Prince's highly successful stage musical *Cabaret* received eight Tony Awards, including Best Musical, and for the national company he employed Signe Hasso to star as Fraulein Schneider (a part played on Broadway by Lotta Lenya). Her performance was an engaging portrayal of a lonely woman who runs a decadent boarding house in pre-Nazi Berlin and sacrifices love and decency for survival. She sang in a hoarse voice that was most appropriate. When the extensive tour of *Cabaret* concluded, Signe was back on television as Tasha, a mental patient refusing to communicate with anyone on "The Interns," and as Mrs. Eliscu, a medium conjuring up the ghost of a woman seeking her twin sister in death on "Ghost Story." In the two and a half million dollars filmed-for-television version of Leon Uris' *QB VII* (April, 1974), Signe appeared during the second and final part of the six hour film, in a showy but overplayed role of a Polish prostitute. In mid-July 1975, Signe was at the stockbridge, Mass. Playhouse, co-starring with June Havoc in *Come and Be Killed,* a would-be Broadway entry. Said *Variety* of Miss Hasso's performance. "[She] gives dignity to the absurd role of the lethal mint pudding purveyor."

Of her performance in the aforementioned *The Final Moment,* a Stockholm critic wrote, "The play offers Signe Hasso a five finger exercise. She turns it into a concerto." Miss Hasso has been augmenting and orchestrating minor roles into major memories for many years.

SIGNE HASSO

Tystnadens Hus (House of Silence)   *(Swedish 1933)*
Haxnatten (Witches Night)   *(Swedish 1937)*
Karriar   *(Swedish 1938)*
Geld Fallt Vom Himmel   *(Swedish-German 1938)*
Pengar Fran Skyn   *(Swedish 1939)*
Vi Iva   *(Swedish 1939)*
Emilie Hogqvist   *(Swedish 1939)*
Vildmarkens Sang (Song of the Wilds)   *(Swedish 1940)*
Stal (Steel)   *(Swedish 1940)*
Far Och Son   *(Swedish 1940)*
Stora Famnen (A Big Hug)   *(Swedish 1940)*
Vi Tre (The Three of Us)   *(Swedish 1940)*
Den Ljusnande Framtid   *(German 1941)*
Journey for Margaret   *(MGM 1942)*
Assignment in Brittany   *(MGM 1943)*
Heaven Can Wait   *(20th 1943)*
The Story of Dr. Wassell   *(Par 1944)*
The Seventh Cross   *(MGM 1944)*
The House on 92nd Street   *(20th 1945)*

Johnny Angel   *(RKO 1945)*
Dangerous Partners   *(MGM 1945)*
Strange Triangle   *(20th 1946)*
A Scandal in Paris (a.k.a., Thieves Holiday)   *(UA 1946)*
Where There's Life   *(Par 1947)*
A Double Life   *(Univ 1947)*
To the Ends of the Earth   *(Col 1948)*
Outside the Wall   *(Univ 1950)*
Crisis   *(MGM 1950)*
Sant Hander Inte Har (This Can't Happen Here)   *(Swedish 1950)*
Maria Johanna   *(Swedish 1953)*
Die Sonne Von St. Moritz   *(German 1954)*
Den Under Brara Lognen (The Wonderful Lies)   *(German 1954)*
Taxi 13   *(Swedish 1954)*
The True and False   *(Helen Davis Pictures 1955)*
Picture Mommy Dead   *(Emb 1966)*
Code Name: Hercalitus   *(Univ 1967)*
A Reflection of Fear   *(Col 1973)*
The Black Bird   *(Col 1975)*

45

June Havoc

When June Havoc entered the world of feature films in the early 1940s, she had three professional strikes against her. The average movie-goer of the day might well have been oblivious to these liabilities, but the hierarchy of studio-controlled Hollywood were very well aware of them, and they guaranteed from the start that June would never reach the pinnacle of stardom. The three things that would hold her back were: She had *once* been a very famous child performer in vaudeville; her sister Gypsy Rose Lee, a burlesque performer-actress-writer-celebrity, was by then far *more* famous; and June was too talented and energetic to be conventional celluloid kewpie doll.

June was born in Seattle, Washington on November 8, 1916, to Rose Thompson Hovick and John Olaf Hovick, an Oslo-born newspaperman. According to June's late sister, Gypsy Rose Lee, June's career started at the age of two. As a dubious accolade to their dominating, theatrically ambitious mother, whose story was related in the musical *Gypsy*, Gypsy added, "We never earned a dime until we could talk!" Baby June danced with the great Pavlova, made several short films with Harold Lloyd and, at the age of five, was a headliner in vaudeville in a thirty-two-minute act later known as "Dainty June and Her Newsboys." Reflecting on those years June has said, "I earned fifteen hundred dollars a week when I was six and I knew exactly how I got the laughs and the applause.

There were nine numbers in our act. I did seven of them." She also admitted, "My fathers were stagehands. They taught me everything. They even taught me it was naughty to wear lipstick at twelve." However, when she was thirteen, she eloped with a boy from the act and married him in North Platte, Nebraska, lying about her age and giving her name as Ellen Evangeline Hovick (her real name). *Variety* headlined their announcement of her elopement as "Meal Ticket Escapes." Before her teenage marriage collapsed along with vaudeville itself and the nation's economy, a daughter, April, was born on April 1, 1935.

Unable to find work in show business, June modeled dresses, posed for commercial artists, and danced some 2,600 hours in seven dance marathons that she described later in her autobiographical book, *Early Havoc* (1959), and in the play *Marathon '33* (1963) which she also directed.

Late in 1935, the ex-Baby June wed Donald S. Gibbs, a Manhattan advertising man, and, during the summer of 1936, she appeared in musicals at the St. Louis Municipal Opera. The five-foot-four blonde with Dresden-blue eyes was bent upon learning the acting trade and did "apprentice" work with the Borscht-circuit groups in the Catskill Mountains and appeared with second-string stock companies. One week before her twentieth birthday, on November 2, 1936, she made her Broadway debut as Rozsa in the musical *Forbidden Melody*.

In 1938 she shivered nightly in Chicago as Crystal

With Tom Tully in Intrigue *(UA 1947)*

With Jack Oakie in When My Baby Smiles at Me *(20th 1948)*

Allen taking an onstage bath in *The Women,* but her career took off when she opened on Christmas night, 1940, at the Ethel Barrymore Theatre as Gladys in Rodgers and Hart's ahead-of-the-times musical, *Pal Joey.* Of the three numbers she performed in the show one of them, "That Terrific Rainbow," sung and danced with an aspiring but unknown actor, Van Johnson, was nearly always a show-stopper. Three performers from the *Pal Joey* cast headed for Hollywood with contracts: June, Gene Kelly, and Van Johnson. Kelly and Johnson luckily berthed at MGM, while June not so luckily checked in at RKO, debuting as Opal opposite her *Pal Joey* partner, Jack Durant. Together they did some bright singing and cavorting with Ray Bolger and Desi Arnaz in *Four Jacks and a Jill* (1941). Her next two efforts for RKO were dreary B-grade productions, but at Columbia, in *My Sister Eileen* (1942) starring Rosalind Russell and Janet Blair, she finally was able to show her ability in her role as Effie Shelton, the former tenant of the Sherwood girls' flat in Greenwich Village.

June's early screen efforts were forced, and she extended too much of her personality in front of the cameras. While she was making *No Time for Love* (1943) at Paramount, star Claudette Colbert took her aside and said, "June, I've been watching you on the set and I think you're the kind of woman who can do it. The trouble with you is that you use too much of your talent. You overplay everything. Too much frosting can spoil the cake. Go home now and read your lines in front of a mirror, just as you've done today. Then read them again with one per cent of strength. I don't know you very well, but I'm willing to bet that that formula, one per cent of strength could be applied to everything about you—not just your acting." Havoc admitted that Miss Colbert was right: Her whispers were too low and her shouts too loud and she came on as strong as she could, just as she had been taught in vaudeville. Although her next film roles were not as strident as her first efforts, it was obvious her career was moving rapidly toward a repetition of virtually the same role with each new production. For this reason she returned to Broadway.

The combination of Cole Porter, the great clown Bobby Clark, and June Havoc as Montana, a female toreador, kept *Mexican Hayride* moving along from its opening (January 28, 1944) through 481 performances. But June left *Mexican Hayride* in September, 1944, when Ethel Merman relinquished the lead in Howard Dietz's and Rouben Mamoulian's proposed musical version of *Rain.* It fulfilled a long-standing dream of June's to some day play the character of Sadie Thompson. All the ingredients were there: Havoc dancing and singing the fine Vernon Duke score, sturdy direction by Mamoulian, good production values, and an erotic book. However, *Rain* survived only sixty performances after its Alvin Theatre opening on November 16, 1944.

June had completed *Brewster's Millions* (1945) at United Artists before leaving Hollywood for Broadway and was unhappy about her part as Trixie Summers helping Monty Brewster (Dennis O'Keefe) spend his money in sixty days. In fact, she was discouraged by all of her movie work. "Nobody ever found out what to do with me in Hollywood," she told reporters. "I run like mad from the pictures I've made. I know when I'm bad and I know when I'm good and I haven't been even passable in the dozen movies I've made."

Her Donaldson Theatre Award for *Mexican Hayride* was something to cherish, unlike her Hollywood fling. She also had a strong attachment to her Sadie Thompson part: "How I loved that show! Sadie had songs, but the acting was the important thing and it carried me along in the direction I wanted to go. Besides, the whole production was beautiful. When it closed I was heartsick. It was like being in love with a man who throws you over. He's gone, and yet you keep on caring." The latter remark had nothing to do with her announced marriage to Lieutenant Wil-

Publicity pose ca. 1947

liam O'Brien during the tryout of *Rain,* a wedding, that never reached final staging. However, her remark did refer to her intense desire to appear as a straight dramatic actress in Edmund Goulding's melodramatic *The Ryan Girl* (1945). She refused all offers other than personal appearances at New York's Capitol Theatre and picture houses featuring vaudeville acts until Goulding's script was finalized.

Goulding directed his own play with Havoc as Venetia (Vinney) Ryan, an ex-follies girl who kills her gangster lover (Edmund Lowe) to prevent his taking advantage of their hero-son, who has received the Congressional Medal of Honor. Although the play survived only forty-eight performances, it was a personal triumph for June. From *The Ryan Girl,* she replaced Virginia Gilmore as Ferne Rainer under Elia Kazan's direction in S. N. Behrman's short-lasting *Dunnigan's Daughter,* and then replaced Haila Stoddard as Georgina Allerton in *Dream Girl.*

George Raft had gone arty as his own producer and decided that for *Intrigue* (1947) he must have a name actress. He rejected the likes of RKO's Jane Greer, but did concede that June, now back in Hollywood, would be acceptable in the role of the exotic femme fatale of the picture. With this bread-and-butter assignment completed, June was available to accept one of her best screen assignments: Miss Wales, Gregory Peck's bigoted secretary in *Gentleman's Agreement* (1947). Later, as espionage agent Karanova out to trap defector Dana Andrews, her studies in acting and the application of Colbert's wise advice were evident in *The Iron Curtain* (1948).

For Universal, she starred in *The Story of Molly X* (1949), and later that year, played Betty Hutton's cynical roommate Sandra in *Red, Hot and Blue* and Alan Ladd's perplexed girl friend Leona in *Chicago Deadline,* both at Paramount. Also in that year she married William Spier, former director of *The March of Time* and innumerable television shows. To Louella O. Parsons, June declared she was the luckiest girl in the world to find perfect happiness with Bill Spier, and added, "I grabbed that grand guy quick. I knew he was for me." Apparently, her judgment was correct, for the William Spiers are still wed.

June forged ahead with a dramatic career playing summer stock everywhere. In June, 1951, she replaced Celeste Holm in *Affairs of State* as Irene Elliott, a mousey Minneapolis school marm who turns into a scintillating sexpot. Her expert playing plus the excellent original cast (Reginald Owen, Barbara O'Neill, and Sheppard Strudwick) carried the show through the summer and into the following season, and

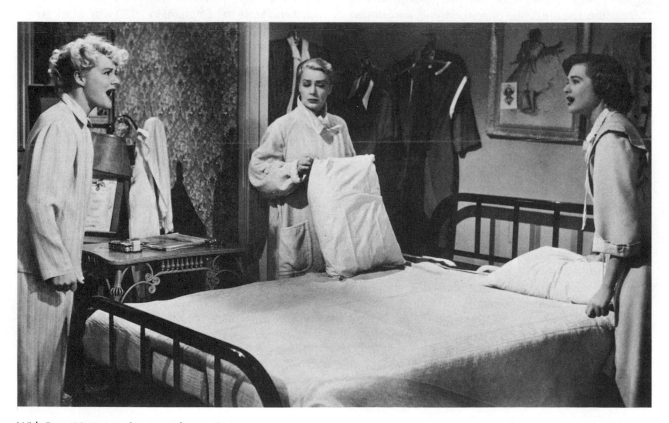

With Betty Hutton and Jane Nigh in Red Hot and Blue *(Par 1949)*

291

brought it equal success in Boston for six weeks and on tour.

June's mania for having pets (she refers to them as "animal people") started in her vaudeville days and continued through the years; she has had an impressive line of odd pets: There was the baritone-voiced canary Madame Zaza, Fanny-by-Gaslight, who was a six-toed cat, two turtles named Joseph and Brethren Wooly-Face, an aging mutt, and Boswell, the offspring of a romance between a Yorkshire terrier and a long-haired Chihuahua. Her friendship with the James Masons increased through their mutual love for animals, and June and the Masons were able to house a good number of cats around Hollywood.

In 1952, June left for England for the filming of *Lady Possessed*, produced by James Mason, directed by June's husband, William Spier, and based on a script by Mason's wife at the time, Pamela Kellino. That same year June played O'Neill's *Anna Christie* on television with Richard Burton as her co-star, was in *Daisy Mayme* on "Pulitzer Prize Playhouse," and, for "Robert Montgomery Presents," she played the publisher of a magazine in *Fairfield Lady*.

Television occupied her talents during most of 1953. She was on Spier's "Omnibus" in a one-act farce, "The Beat," with Michael Redgrave, in *Happy Birthday Aunt Sarah*, and, on the Spier-produced "Medallion Theatre", she played Helene, a frustrated wife trying to compete with her husband's mania for model railroads in *Mrs. Union Station*. On September 19, 1954, her television series "Willy" began. Originally called "The Artful Miss Dodger" the show cast June as a small town New Hampshire lawyer. The critics described this situation comedy as a pretty dismal situation for the artful Miss Havoc. The show deservedly died a quick death, but June continued in the medium with appearances on such programs as "Fireside Theatre."

London critics stumbled over their adjectives trying to describe June's sensational acting on BBC's production of the TV version of Somerset Maugham's *Theatre* in the mid-1950s. Her three-week booking at London's elegant Cafe de Paris was extended to five weeks and, again, the reviewers were ecstatic. Returning to New York, she was enthusiastic about her appearances in theatre: "Success in TV disappears as rapidly as failure. In the theatre, it's different. It stays with you in the theatre." Her return to the footlights had great promise which, unfortunately, was not reflected in her choice of a new play. She opened as Rose Stone in a tasteless, dull trifle called *One Foot in the Door* (1957), backed by Jack Benny and George Burns, which tried out in Philadelphia and closed in Boston.

Hit or flop, June continued working: As Queen Jocasta in *The Infernal Machine*, Titania in the American Shakespeare Festival production of *A Midsummer Night's Dream* in Stratford, Connecticut, Mistress Sullen in *The Beaux' Stragagem*, and Joanne de Lynn in *The Warm Peninsula* (1959). The latter play was on Broadway briefly with Julie Harris and Farley Granger. In the spring of 1961 she toured the European capitals and Israel for the U.S. State Department as Sabina in *The Skin of Our Teeth* and Kate in *The Miracle Worker*. When the State Department-sponsored tour reached South America, June received an award as Best Foreign Actress—and the repertory company included Helen Hayes! In the all-star cast of *Dinner at Eight* (1966) June was the hostess Millicent Jordan. When Broadway jobs were scarce she toured in *A Delicate Balance* and *Don Juan in Hell*. In 1970 she became the artistic director of the New Orleans Repertory Theatre, directing, among other shows, *The Threepenny Opera* in which she played Jenny, and *The Skin of Our Teeth* in which she was again Sabina.

For television's "World of Disney" she made *The Boy Who Stole the Elephant* in 1970 with Mark Lester and David Wayne, and the next year played a dizzy society matron whose prized Pekingese dog is kidnapped on an episode of "McMillan and Wife." Between acting and directing across the country, June wrote a play, *I Said the Fly*, which was produced by the Tyrone Guthrie Theatre in Minneapolis in September, 1973, with June as Fanny Brads, an ex-vaudevillian actress struggling through the twilight hours of the two-a-day shows. The play did not work, and *Variety* dismissed it with, "Vaudeville was seldom this bad."

In late 1974, June began preparing for another go at Broadway, this time in Arthur Whitney's new play, *The Lydia Lamont Club Will Please Come to Order*, which did not make it, nor did *Come and Be Killed*, in which she co-starred with Signe Hasso during mid-July, 1975.

Regarding her compulsive desire to work professionally, June once admitted, "The only time I ever stepped out of show business I got poked in the nose, so I stepped right back in."

JUNE HAVOC

Four Jacks and a Jill   *(RKO 1941)*
Powder Town   *(RKO 1942)*
Sing Your Worries Away   *(RKO 1942)*
My Sister Eileen   *(Col 1942)*
No Time for Love   *(Par 1943)*
Hello, Frisco, Hello!   *(20th 1943)*
Hi Diddle Diddle   *(UA 1943)*
Timber Queen   *(Par 1944)*
Casanova in Burlesque   *(Rep 1944)*
Sweet and Low Down   *(20th 1944)*
Brewster's Millions   *(UA 1945)*
Intrigue   *(UA 1947)*

Gentleman's Agreement   *(20th 1947)*
When My Baby Smiles at Me   *(20th 1948)*
The Iron Curtain   *(20th 1948)*
The Story of Molly X   *(Univ 1949)*
Red Hot and Blue   *(Par 1949)*
Chicago Deadline   *(Par 1949)*
Once a Thief   *(UA 1950)*
Mother Didn't Tell Me   *(20th 1950)*
Follow the Sun   *(20th 1951)*
Lady Possessed   *(Rep 1952)*
Three for Jamie Dawn   *(AA 1956)*

46

Sterling Hayden

Sterling Hayden was born in the wrong century. He would have thrived in the 1800s, sailing the seven seas. Other than his children, the only thing he has ever really cared about has been the deep waters. He could never come to terms with Hollywood, marriage, or himself. He was married three times and virtually had three film careers. When he first appeared on the Hollywood scene he was publicized as a "beautiful blond Viking God," and after only two films, *Virginia* (1941) and *Bahama Passage* (1941), he quit moviemaking, first to escape to the sea, then to join the Marine Corps. "I'm not criticizing Hollywood or its people," he said at the time. "They're all swell to me. No doubt I'd have made a lot of money, but I couldn't stand the place. It got on my nerves." Returning to films in the late 1940s, he became a leading man in mostly minor efforts, save for John Huston's *The Asphalt Jungle* (1950), where he proved that he was no longer a pretty boy, but had definite acting prowess. In recent years, with a now weather-beaten complexion, he is a character performer who only works, if he is lucky enough to get a role, when he desperately needs the money.

Six-foot-five Hayden was born in Upper Montclair, New Jersey, on March 20, 1916. His parents' ancestry was Dutch on his mother's side and English on his father's. His father, George Walter, who sold advertising for a New York newspaper, died when his only

son was nine years old. His mother, Frances, a classical pianist, remarried, and Sterling adopted his stepfather's name, Hayden. Sterling was called Buzz by his family and Chris by his friends. He and his family lived in many cities in New England, and he went to schools in Maine and Massachusetts.

When he was sixteen, he quit school and went to sea, obtaining a job aboard a schooner, and in three years he received his master's papers. By the time he was twenty-two, he was the captain of his own vessel. During this adventurous period he entered a fisherman's race and won by one hundred fathoms. A Boston reporter covered the story, which was printed with pictures of Sterling in the Boston *Post*. The news story insisted that Sterling "ought to be in pictures," for here was a sailor who looked like a movie idol. When Sterling later lost his ship in a storm, a friend of his, Tom Horgan, wrote a letter to a friend at the William Hawks theatrical agency in Hollywood, sending along pictures of Sterling. Through another friend, Boston artist Larry O'Toole, he got himself a New York agent—on his looks alone, for he had absolutely no theatrical experience.

While in Manhattan, Sterling earned some needed money by modeling, a fact that was hushed up once he arrived in Hollywood. West-coast publicists thought it better that he be known only as a sailor turned actor. The Los Angeles agent showed his portfolio of photographs to Edward H. Griffith, a director-producer under contract to Paramount, and Griffith

With Madeleine Carroll in Bahama Passage *(Par 1941)*

With Howard da Silva in Blaze of Noon *(Par 1947)*

made an appointment to see Hayden in New York. Their meeting went well, with Griffith acknowledging that the tall blue-eyed blond was definitely movie material. Hayden made his screen test in New Jersey in March, 1940, and was flown out to the west coast to make another test with Jeanne Cagney in a scene from *Anna Christie*.

After Paramount signed him to a seven-year contract (starting at $150 a week and escalating to $7,-500) Sterling made his residence in Laurel Canyon, California, where his mother then kept house for him. The studio changed the spelling of his first name to Stirling. Hayden went along with everything because he was only interested in making enough money to purchase his own schooner. He was given the second male lead in *Virginia,* which starred Madeleine Carroll and Fred MacMurray. Stirling's role originally had been intended for either Henry Fonda or Franchot Tone. Hayden only got the part after Miss Carroll, who had casting approval, met him. "It was the toughest job I ever had," said Hayden. "I lost eighteen pounds." In the picture he came across as awkward but charming, and his rugged masculinity and very handsome face enhanced his acting. Hayden recalls that at the first screening of *Virginia,* "I really expected the audience to rise up and boo me out of

the room." The *New York Herald-Tribune* insisted, "The new acting find, Hayden, takes to technicolor handsomely and is remarkably assured in his first screen role." The actor disagrees with that positive review of his performance, stating, "It should have been my last."

British-born Madeleine Carroll and Hayden soon became a "Hollywood item" and when he was cast opposite Dorothy Lamour in *Dildo Cay,* an island film, Miss Lamour was asked to relinquish her role so that Carroll could do it. The film, released as *Bahama Passage,* was inferior entertainment, but it gave Hayden the chance to display his beautifully sun-tanned figure. If it seemed virtually impossible for anyone to be more attractive oncamera than Miss Carroll, Hayden almost overcame this "impossibility" by his attention-getting presence. Still billed as "Stirling," he shared star status with his leading lady. One reviewer said that Sterling "couldn't have made his role less dull if he were the greatest, most accomplished actor in the world." Paramount was then planning to co-star Hayden with Virginia Dale in *Little Miss Muffett,* which would have been a sight for weary eyes, and in *Tomorrow's Admirals* (a follow-up film to the studio's successful *I Wanted Wings,* 1941), a film about Naval training with William Holden and Betty Field.

With Dewey Robinson, John Payne, John Hart, Reed Howes, and Henry Hull in El Paso *(Par 1949)*

Instead, Hayden informed the Paramount executive force that he was leaving films, that he had done the first two only to make a bankroll and that "I hate my guts for it." He was anxious to return to the sea and also to separate himself from Madeleine Carroll, with whom he had fallen in love. Paramount, eager to hold on to this virile commodity, threatened to sue him and vowed that he would never again work in films. These moves, however, did not worry the determined young man. The wily top brass then promised the "guileless" newcomer a new contract at a much higher salary and even suggested that he might well be given the part of Robert Jordan, the male lead in *For Whom the Bell Tolls* (1943), even though Gary Cooper had already been mentioned for the hero's part. Hayden said no and disappeared from the Hollywood scene. "I felt silly making pictures with a war going on," he explained.

One part of Hollywood he could not leave behind was Madeleine Carroll, though. He went east to find her and marry her, which he did. They were wed in 1942, a union which lasted for four years, during which time they were together perhaps only four months. They were, at best, completely mismatched. She was beautiful, effervescent, witty, and ten years older than he. He, rather humorless, was only inter-

ested in boats. He left her for the sea and later for the war effort, though they remained married until after the war, when he divorced her in Reno, Nevada, in 1946. At the time, she was residing in France. Remembering, Hayden recalls, "Oh, Christ, she was a beautiful woman."

While Paramount, in 1942, tried grooming James Brown to replace the wandering Sterling Hayden, he was running cargo in the West Indies. Soon, he enlisted in the Marines, then became a member of the O.S.S. as a second lieutenant and ended up a captain. To cut off his last ties with Hollywood Sterling even changed his name, legally, to John Hamilton (Madeleine Carroll did all the paper work for him). He went behind German lines as a U.S. secret agent, but it is very surprising that even a so-called professional actor, who could have been world famous, was given such a task. While gun-running in Albania he became involved with the Communist partisans and was quite taken with their bravery. At the end of the war Sterling received the Silver Star for his own bravery. Today, the actor insists that distinction was entirely undeserved.

After the war, all was forgiven at Paramount (where a new regime was in control), and he returned to a new contract starting at fifteen hundred dollars a week for the first year, two thousand dollars the second, with the months between June and September off each year, and the right to use the original spelling of his Christian name. Ironically, at this point, Paramount had no idea what to do with Hayden. He did guest-star service in *Variety Girl* (1947) and played, quite sympathetically, William Holden's brother in *Blaze of Noon* (1947), a barn-storming pilot drama directed by John Farrow. He then did not work for a year and collected $70,000 from the studio while living on his boat. The following season he made two films for Paramount, the western *El Paso* (1949) and *Manhandled* (1949), a timorous melodrama with Dorothy Lamour. Hayden properly calls these features "abortions," adding, "they were conceived and dead in less than three weeks." After these pictures Paramount dropped him.

For some reason, John Huston requested Sterling for his production of *The Asphalt Jungle* at Metro. That studio was totally against the choice, feeling that some better boxoffice choice should be cast. Hayden tested for the role of the thief with Jean Hagen. After the telling test, Huston exclaimed, "The next time somebody says you can't act, tell them to call Huston." The actor received excellent notices for his naturalistic characterization of Dix Handley, leading tough-to-please Bosley Crowther (*New York Times*) to rhapsodize that Sterling was "sure-fire as a brazen hoodlum who just wants to go back home." For the first time in his film career, Hayden cared. "But after that I never really took off," he said, "because I didn't know my craft." Sol Lesser offered Hayden the opportunity of being the new Tarzan, but he refused and the ape-man role went to Lex Barker.

While Hayden was filming *Skid Road,* released as *Journey into Light* (1951), he made headlines in newspapers across the country when he testified before the House Un-American Activities Committee that he had been a member of the Communist Party from June to December, 1946. He told the Congressmen that it "was the stupidest, most ignorant thing I've ever done." Hayden named other Hollywood figures who were also Party members, and after three hours of testimony was informed that he "deserved the commendation of the committee and the country for speaking out as an intensely loyal citizen." Sterling was luckier than many, especially Larry Parks, in that his career did not suffer too many ill effects from his confession. In fact, Hayden over-exposed himself by making thirty-two features between 1952 and 1958, but none of the pictures gave him a meaty role equal to the gem in *The Asphalt Jungle.* Hayden claims that the reason he never attained another great starring vehicle was that everyone seemed to know

he did not really care about the movie business, that he had only done one good film previously and that he was, perhaps, too "pink" for some people. Today, Hayden despises himself for having given the Committee for Un-American Activities names of other Hollywood people.

Two of his better features in the 1950s were *The Star* (1953), with Bette Davis, and *So Big* (1953), a second remake of the Edna Ferber novel, this time starring Jane Wyman as the downtrodden but unbeatable rural woman. Hayden says he was uncomfortable in both productions, but that he thoroughly enjoyed working with Davis, calling her "a lovely dame." The two players had a lot in common—their love for the Maine coast and their attraction to ships. Uncomfortable or not for Sterling, at least these motion pictures were well-made major productions and not the tripe in which he was generally cast, such as *Flaming Feather* (1952), *The Golden Hawk* (1952), *Arrow in the Dust* (1954), and *Timberjack* (1955)—the latter with Vera Ralston. The film in which he certainly did look uncomfortable was *Prince Valiant* (1954), where he was the comic-strip figure Sir Gawain. Republic's *Johnny Guitar* (1954), in Trucolor, was directed by Nicholas Ray, and has since become a very popular film in certain cinema circles. Hayden, in the title role, played a drifter, which he thinks is the reason for its popularity, "A pre-*Easy Rider,* I guess, with a horse instead of a motorcycle." Though he had the central role in the film, he merely supported flamboyant Joan Crawford, whom he refers to as a "bulldozer of a woman." The *New York Times* reported, "Mr. Hayden gallumps about morosely as though he'd rather play the guitar."

Hayden was not very pleased combatting Frank Sinatra's ego in *Suddenly* (1954), a presidential assassination melodrama. Occasionally, Hayden did make a good B film. Both *Flat Top* (1952) and *Fighter Attack* (1953) were interesting war films: the latter was quite reminiscent of *For Whom the Bell Tolls,* but, of course, on a much smaller scale. *Crime Wave* (1954) and *Naked Alibi* (1954) were better-than-average mysteries, and *The Last Command* (1955), with Anna Maria Alberghetti, was a better "remember the Alamo" film than John Wayne's tedious 1960 epic. Hayden received his best review notices in years as Admiral John M. Hoskins in Republic's *The Eternal Sea* (1955).

Sterling was originally set for the male lead in *Tension at Table Rock* (1956), just another RKO western, but at the last minute, inexplicably, the studio cast Richard Egan in the role and had to pay off an already contracted Hayden. It all happened for the best, however, because Hayden then was free to accept a role in one of the best gangster films of the 1950s, Stanley Kubrick's *The Killing* (1956). As Johnny Clay, the ex-convict who masterminds the two-million-dollar haul, Hayden was extremely effective, leading the *New York Times'* A. H. Weiler to exclaim that "[he] makes a restrained but hard and efficient leader." After many more insignificant films he was ready, again, to escape to sea on his big new sailing ship, but John Frankenheimer wanted him for *A Sound of Different Drummers* to be done live on CBS-TV's "Playhouse 90." Hayden had never appeared live before except for some film promotional work in the East. Frankenheimer had an excellent reputation as a director and Sterling accepted the challenge. However, after three days of rehearsal, he panicked and quit. He was talked into returning and it turned out to be one of his most memorable acting achievements. He went on to do a few more live TV shows, three others with Frankenheimer. In 1960, he co-starred with Julie Harris in the TV version of *Ethan Frome* on the "Dupont Show of the Month." Later he was offered the lead in the television version of Hemingway's short story "The Killers," but by that time he was out at sea again and refused to come back for it.

Hayden married Betty DeNoon on April 25, 1947.

The marriage was a "disaster," according to Hayden, "except that it produced four wonderful kids." The union also produced many headlines, beginning with the couple's 1955 divorce. Hayden was awarded custody of the children because, in the words of the court, Mrs. Hayden was not a fit mother. Four years later Hayden took his four children on a 4,600-mile voyage from Sausalito, California, on his vessel, *The Wanderer.* The purpose of the trek was to make films for television, that is, films dealing with the sea. When he was contacted in Tahiti, he claimed that he was on his way to Brazil to co-star with James Mason in a jungle film, *Mato Grosso.* The children's mother, though she had not been awarded custody, was entitled to have the children with her part of the time, and through her attorneys she moved to stop the voyage. The court agreed with her and Hayden defied them. The voyage was financed from money borrowed from Republic Pictures and he, in turn, would have to do a television series for them, or eight features. At the very least he had to pay the studio back. When he did neither, the studio sued him. Hayden hoped that making a documentary film about the sea would suffice, but he did not do that, either. Out of money, he sailed back home and apologized to the court.

With Morgan Farley and Art Smith in Manhandled *(Par 1949)*

299

During this famous voyage, Delmer Daves offered him a co-starring role in *A Summer Place* (1959) for $40,000 and six weeks' work. Hayden rejected the offer, explaining that he could not abandon the men and women on his crew who had given up jobs to join him to make pictures. Arthur Kennedy replaced him.

Hayden married for the third time in March, 1960. His new wife, Mrs. Catherine Devine McConnell, had a son from a previous marriage. She and Sterling later had a son of their own. The third Mrs. Hayden could not tolerate Sterling's unique lifestyle and, in 1969, she left him, taking the two boys with her.

Hayden's autobiography, *Wanderer,* was written during this time and published in 1963. The book holds far more interest for sea-worshippers than for film enthusiasts.

Stanley Kubrick sought him out again for a part in *Dr. Strangelove* (1964) as General Jack D. Ripper, commanding officer of the U.S. Air Force base at Burpelson, who launches an all-out atomic bomb attack on Russia. Having been away from the screen for a number of years he felt rusty and had a difficult time remembering his lines: One of his scenes required thirty-eight takes, and Kubrick ended up shooting it line by line. However, it was done and the terror in Hayden's eyes may not have been acting but it served the role perfectly. Hayden says, "It shows that perhaps the magic of film can be bigger than the actor." Sterling did not consider the film a come-back venture, because, he says wryly, "There was nothing to come back from." He did not appear in another film until the European-lensed *Hard Contract* in 1969.

After a good performance, as a Moses-like figure in *Loving* (1970), he appeared in two controversial features: The immensely popular Oscar-winner *The Godfather* (1972) and Robert Altman's travesty of Raymond Chandler's *The Long Goodbye* (1973). The latter picture had opened to such uniformly poor notices in Los Angeles that it was shelved for a while. Upon re-release, in a somewhat altered version, it received some unnatural raves. Hayden had replaced the late Dan Blocker in the role of the iconoclastic, mentally unstable novelist, a drunken variation of Ernest Hemingway. Physically, Sterling looked a mess in *The Long Goodbye,* which is exactly how he looks offscreen: Long straggling hair and a white beard reaching down to his chest.

One of Hayden's younger sons, Andrew, appeared with him in *Sweet Hunters* (1970) a film which also stars Stuart Whitman and Susan Strasberg, but which has had scant release in the United States. His oldest son, Christian, who was born in 1948, was sentenced to three and a half years in prison in 1969 because of two draft violations. Hayden supported his son's views against the Vietnam war and the Selective Service System.

In the early 1970s Sterling appeared in two French films and then in a British-produced one, *The Final Programme* (1973), directed by Robert Fuest and starring Jon Finch. In this picture, he plays the role of Major Wrongway Lindbergh, a character which seems to have strayed in from *Dr. Strangelove.* He considers Fuest, along with John Huston and John Frankenheimer, the best directors with whom he has worked. Recently, Sterling performed a cameo assignment in the Italian-lensed films *1900* (1975) and *Cry Onion!* (1975).

These days, Hayden lives on a covered barge on the Seine in Paris, often without any money. Every time he makes a few thousand dollars on film assignment it disappears quickly, due to debts or the purchase of a new boat. He also has back-tax problems. He made a rare television appearance in 1973 on the "Starlost" series and is presently writing another book. Along with Arthur Miller, Lillian Hellman, and Larry Parks, he was in the cast of Eric Bentley's play, *Are You Now or Have You Ever Been,* which deals with the investigation of Un-American Activities in the early 1950s. The drama was staged off-Broadway in New York in 1973.

"He was the handsomest man I'd ever seen," said Hedda Hopper of the early Hayden. But today there is hardly a trace of that "Viking god." He is now a weather-beaten veteran whose years of heavy drinking show visibly. Yet, he remains the adventurous rebel who turns to the sea as an escape. He never admitted he wanted to become a good actor because he was afraid that he would never become one. "You don't need talent to star in a motion picture," he once said. "All you need is some intelligence and the ability to work freely in front of the lens."

In 1960 he told columnist Earl Wilson, "If I had the dough, I'd buy up the negative of every movie I ever made and start a hell of a fire that would light up all of San Francisco Bay some night."

STERLING HAYDEN

Virginia   *(Par 1941)*
Bahama Passage   *(Par 1941)*
Variety Girl   *(Par 1947)*
Blaze of Noon   *(Par 1947)*
El Paso   *(Par 1949)*
Manhandled   *(Par 1949)*
The Asphalt Jungle   *(MGM 1950)*
Journey into Light   *(20th 1951)*
Flaming Feather   *(Par 1951)*
The Denver and Rio Grande   *(Par 1952)*
Hellgate   *(Lip 1952)*
The Golden Hawk   *(Col 1952)*
Flat Top   *(AA 1952)*
The Star   *(20th 1953)*
Take Me to Town   *(Univ 1953)*
Kansas Pacific   *(AA 1953)*
Fighter Attack   *(AA 1953)*
So Big   *(WB 1953)*
Crime Wave   *(WB 1954)*
Prince Valiant   *(20th 1954)*
Arrow in the Dust   *(AA 1954)*
Johnny Guitar   *(Rep 1954)*
Suddenly   *(UA 1954)*
Naked Alibi   *(Univ 1954)*
Battle Taxi   *(UA 1955)*
Timberjack   *(Rep 1955)*
Shotgun   *(AA 1955)*

The Eternal Sea   *(Rep 1955)*
The Last Command   *(Rep 1955)*
Top Gun   *(UA 1955)*
The Come On   *(AA 1956)*
The Killing   *(UA 1956)*
Five Steps to Danger   *(UA 1957)*
Crime of Passion   *(UA 1957)*
The Iron Sheriff   *(UA 1957)*
Valerie   *(UA 1957)*
Gun Battle at Monterey   *(AA 1957)*
Zero Hour   *(Par 1957)*
Terror in a Texas Town   *(UA 1958)*
Ten Days to Tulara   *(UA 1958)*
Dr. Strangelove Or: How I Learned to Stop Worrying
   and Love the Bomb   *(Col 1964)*
Hard Contract   *(20th 1969)*
Sweet Hunters   *(French 1970)*
Loving   *(Col 1970)*
The Godfather   *(Par 1972)*
Le Sant De L'Ange (a.k.a Cobra)   *(French 1972)*
Le Grand Depart   *(French 1972)*
The Long Goodbye   *(UA 1973)*
The Final Programme   *(MGM—British 1973)*
1900   *(Par 1975)*
Cry Onion!   *(Italian 1975)*

47

Dick Haymes

The big band era produced many popular singers who achieved fame and fortune. Some of the women were Doris Day, Jo Stafford, Margaret Whiting, Peggy Lee, and Dinah Shore. The big three male crooners of the 1940s, after Bing Crosby, were Frank Sinatra, Perry Como, and Dick Haymes. Doris Day and Sinatra went on to become top cinema personalities; Como and Dinah Shore made it big in the recording and television fields after brief and unsuccessful film appearances; the Misses Lee, Stafford, and Whiting kept primarily to club engagements and recordings.

For a few years, Dick Haymes, who was an antiseptic actor, was rather successful in a string of Hollywood musicals, as the farmboy in Twentieth Century-Fox's remake of *State Fair* (1945), and as Betty Grable's co-star in *Billy Rose's Diamond Horsehoe* (1945) and *The Shocking Miss Pilgrim* (1947). Haymes sang romantic ballads with feeling, with range, with voice control and power, making him the best popular ballad singer of the decade. In his heyday, Haymes lacked as much common sense in his choice of wives (including Joanne Dru and Rita Hayworth) as in the spending of his fabulous yearly income. He was known at the time as "Mr. Charm."

The six-foot, sandy-haired, blue-eyed singer was born Richard Benjamin Haymes on September 13, 1916, in Buenos Aires, Argentina. His mother, Marguerite, had run away from her home in Santa Bar-

bara, California, to sing in musical comedies in the United States and England. On tour in South America, she married Benjamin Haymes, a successful cattle rancher of Scottish and English descent. When Dick was two years old, his father's ranch was wiped out by drought and his parents separated soon after that. Marguerite took Dick and his younger brother, Robert, to Rio, where she opened a dress shop. Robert later became known as Bob Haymes or Bob Stanton, also a singer-actor, but never as popular as his older brother. Marguerite did most of her dress-shop purchases in Paris, and her two sons were educated in French and Swiss schools and lived in Paris and London for about twelve years. In 1936, Mrs. Haymes and her two sons moved to Connecticut and Dick attended schools in Tarrytown and Peekskill before entering Loyola University in Montreal. Marguerite taught each of her sons singing and later said that Dick, as a child, was "a little ham running around the house." Over the years Marguerite would continue teaching voice; she even coached Dick's eldest son, Dick Jr. (known as Skip), in her Carnegie Hall vocal studio in Manhattan.

Haymes made his professional singing debut in New Jersey and then joined the Johnnie Johnston and Bunny Berigan bands at a salary of twenty-five dollars a week. He later sang with the Freddie Martin, Orin Tucker, and Carl Hoff orchestras, before striking out with his own band, The Katzenjammers. Between band jobs he worked as a radio announcer. He mar-

Publicity pose (1944)

ried the first of his six wives, singer Edith Harper, whom he had met in Chicago, in 1939. The marriage was annulled a few weeks later in Little Rock, Arkansas.

Hoping to improve his professional standing, Dick went to Hollywood and began writing songs, while waiting for a show-business break. While he was there he found some extra work in westerns and obtained a bit part in MGM's *Dramatic School* (1938), starring Luise Rainer.

When nothing sensational developed for him in California, he returned to New York where he tried selling some of his songs to band leader Harry James. The trumpeter did not take the songs but he did hire the singer. In September, 1941, Dick married dancer Joanne Marshall, who later became actress Joanne Dru, and when Harry James went on the road again, Dick quit the band because Joanne was expecting their first son, Dick, Jr.

It was a nine-week job with Tommy Dorsey and his band that brought Dick back to California, and he appeared with the group in Metro's *Du Barry Was a Lady* (1943), camouflaged, during most of it in a powdered wig. It was agent Bill Burton who won Dick his first nightclub engagement at New York's La Martinique in 1942. *Variety* called him "a surefire nitery

bet. All signs indicate he'll become a strong favorite." This engagement led to record contract offers. After singing with Decca Records, he became one of their top-selling singers.

Haymes's most successful recording was "Little White Lies," which sold over 2.25 million copies and netted him $75,000. On the strength of his record sales, Darryl F. Zanuck signed him to a seven-year contract at Twentieth Century-Fox. At the same time, Dick negotiated a deal to be the singing star of "Something for the Boys" on NBC radio.

Dick's first feature for Fox was *Four Jills in a Jeep* (1944), the semi-autobiographical account of four movie celebrities (Kay Francis, Martha Raye, Mitzi Mayfair, and Carole Landis) on a U.S.O. tour to Africa. Haymes was the Army lieutenant who romances Mayfair and sings two songs. The *New York Herald-Tribune* complained that his "screen singing doesn't measure up to his past nightclub performances." As Irish composer Ernest R. Ball, he was completely overshadowed by the delightful June Haver and the sardonic Monty Woolley in *Irish Eyes Are Smiling* (1944). Bosley Crowther *(New York Times)* remarked, "Mr. Haymes is not a young man whose appearance or acting virtuosity exposes him to the danger of great success. He is plainly the sort of fellow who should

With William Gaxton and Phil Silvers in Billy Rose's Diamond Horseshoe *(20th 1945)*

With Jeanne Crain and Dana Andrews in State Fair *(20th 1945)*

A publicity pose with Deanna Durbin for Up in Central Park *(Univ 1948)*

be content to sing in front of a band." His screen appearances with Fox's top musical comedy star, Betty Grable, gave Haymes a good deal of exposure even though the films were mere cotton-candy trifles. But his Grable frolics did furnish him with two very popular songs: "The More I See You," from *Billy Rose's Diamond Horseshoe*, and "For You, For Me, For Ever More," part of the George and Ira Gershwin score from *The Shocking Miss Pilgrim*.

State Fair, with its Rodgers and Hammerstein score, remains one of the loveliest of film musicals. As the farmer's son who goes to an Iowa fair and falls in love with redheaded vocalist Vivian Blaine, Haymes sang "It's a Grand Night for Singing" and "That's for Me." Jeanne Crain, portraying his sister in the picture, mouthed a dubbed version of "It Might as Well Be Spring," but it was Haymes who made the 78 r.p.m. recording, and it is possibly his most famous disc. His acting was somewhat less dull in this film in the role that was played in the 1933 version by Norman Foster, and in the poor 1962 revamp by Pat Boone.

Dick was reunited with Harry James in *Do You Love Me?* (1946), originally titled *Kitten on the Keys*, and starring the beautiful Maureen O'Hara. In *Carnival in Costa Rica* (1947), a project that had been rejected by the top echelon of Fox musical comedy people, and was finally directed by Gregory Ratoff, Haymes received top billing for the first time. It was a strictly routine musical, with the silly plot revolving around newlyweds and their quarreling parents. Vera-Ellen was Haymes's co-lead, with Cesar Romero on hand to play his stock "other man" assignment. To be fair, the song "Mi Vida" was excellently sung by Haymes, who always seemed to come alive onscreen for his musical interludes.

Carnival in Costa Rica terminated his Fox contract, even though the seven years were not up. Universal then picked up his services to co-star him with the waning Deanna Durbin in a weak translation of *Up in Central Park* (1948), in which he was the vapid newspaperman. Then, Dick was relegated by that studio to a best-friend role in *One Touch of Venus* (1948), which featured Ava Gardner and Robert Walker. He did not appear on the screen again until *St. Benny the Dip* for United Artists in 1951, a small film which was somewhat of a sleeper and got quite respectable reviews. In this crook-saint yarn he sang the very popular tune, "I Believe." *Variety* claimed that "as the youngest of the con men, [he] surprises with a smooth performance."

By the late 1940s his film career was virtually at a standstill—the big bands and the crooners would be one of the post-World War II casualties—but his records continued to sell heavily, often beating out those of Crosby, Sinatra, and Como. Other hit songs of his were, "You'll Never Know," "It Happens Every Spring," "Maybe It's Because," and "The Girl that I Marry." He did some club and theatre work, such as an appearance in the stage show at the Roxy Theatre. He also had his own radio show. He made his musical comedy stage debut in Dallas in 1951 in *Miss Liberty*, playing the role Eddie Albert originated on the New York stage.

Joanne Dru, who would subsequently wed actor John Ireland, divorced Haymes in 1949 and received $350,000 in alimony over a period of seven years. They had had three children. In July of 1949, Dick married Nora Eddington, who had just divorced Errol Flynn, but the marriage was short-lived. His whirlwind romance with Rita Hayworth was widely publicized and the couple married on September 24, 1953. It seemed that the deeper he became involved in financial and legal difficulties the more persistent Rita became, in loyally sticking by "her man." Rita helped Haymes obtain a few film parts at her studio, Columbia. The films, *All Ashore* (1953), with Mickey Rooney and Peggy Ryan, and *Cruisin' down the River* (1953), with Audrey Totter, were poor ones that were vaguely elevated by Haymes' fine singing voice. Part of Rita's contract for Columbia's *Joseph and His Brethren*, which she never made, was the advance payment of $75,000 for her and a $50,000 loan for Haymes. Rita proved to be his most expensive indulgence. He once threw an all-nude surprise party in her honor.

Haymes's years with Rita led to the worst publicity of his entire career. During World War II, he had registered as a resident alien, avoiding the draft and waiving his right to become a citizen. He could live in this country but could not leave without a special re-entry permit. In 1953 he followed Rita to Hawaii (not yet a state), where she was filming the 3-D *Miss Sadie Thompson*, and re-entered the States illegally. He was ordered deported as an undesirable alien. Much was made of the fact that Rita would "stand by" him. The deportation case was later dismissed, but Haymes has never been able to become a United States citizen. The couple made more headlines when the furniture in their fourteen-room rented mansion in Connecticut was repossessed for nonpayment of rent. At this period—he was also being sued for back alimony and child support by his ex-wives—Haymes was on the edge of a nervous breakdown and had to be hospitalized. He said, "I don't know what to do. I'm going insane. My nerves are shot, I don't know where to turn. I want to work. I'm trying to work, but they won't let me." He was also drinking quite heavily and in one drunken rage punched Rita at a party. The marriage ended in 1954. Miss Hayworth was to receive one million dollars in alimony over a two-year period.

Dick's come-back attempts were not very successful. He was engaged for a stock production of *The Tender Trap* in 1956, but Actors Equity would not allow him to open in it, stating that aliens could not take jobs away from Americans in stock presentations. Johnny Desmond replaced him. Haymes's few club engagements at the time were still highly praised. Gene Knight in the *New York Journal-American* reported, "What I like about Dick Haymes is that he stands up straight and sings out straight. No gyrations. He just sings. And it's fine."

Dick's nightclub act with his new wife, singer Fran Jeffries, was picking up momentum, but it dissolved when the marriage did. She married director Richard Quine, one of Haymes's best friends. The Haymes-Jeffries marriage had lasted five years and had given him his fourth child, Stephanie. In the years following this break-up, Dick has had to declare bankruptcy twice. In 1960 his assets totaled less than one thousand dollars, and in 1971 his bank account was down to a minus figure.

His marriage to English model Wendy Smith seems to be working out well and he publically claims that he has not taken a drink since 1965. He has been rebuilding his career slowly in the last few years. After living in Spain, he and his present wife moved to Dublin, Ireland, where they now live with their two children, Sean and Samantha. Haymes became an Irish citizen in 1965. They also keep a small apartment in London. After testing his new nightclub act in England, Ireland, Australia, and Africa, Dick returned to this country and appeared at the St. Regis in New York, the Coconut Grove in Los Angeles, and at the Sahara Hotel in Las Vegas. *Variety*, reviewing him in

the gambling capital said, "He's an exceptional saloon singer despite the long layoff."

He had a very nostalgic reunion with Maureen O'Hara and Betty Grable on Tennesse Ernie Ford's 1972 television special, *The Fabulous Fordies*, in which he and Grable dueted "The More I See You." He has also performed some straight acting work on television recently, playing a businessman named Billy Calm on NBC's "McMillan & Wife" and giving an adequate account of himself on "Adam-12" and "Hec Ramsey."

On television's 1974 *Grammy Salutes Oscar*, Dick sang some Oscar-winning songs. In the fall of 1974, after an absence of twenty years, he returned to perform in Las Vegas as special guest with Dan Rowan and Dick Martin at the Sahara Hotel. He had such a solid reception that he whipped together an act, Dick Haymes & Company, that played in the lounge at the MGM Grand Hotel there in November. *Daily Variety* reported of the occasion, "First-nighters saluted Haymes and company with a standing ovation."

His hair is now streaked with silver, he looks tired, and is too thin. All those years of drinking and all those financial problems have taken their toll physically, but the warm baritone sound has hardly changed. Haymes, father of six and grandfather many times over, desperately wanted only one role in his acting career: The down-and-out sentimental Irish dreamer Johnny Nolan in *A Tree Grows in Brooklyn* (1945). But he was far too young for the part and did not have enough acting experience or talent either to get it or to play it. It won James Dunn a Best Supporting Actor Oscar.

"I'm a different person than I was in the Fifties," says Haymes of himself today. "When I see myself on the late show in an old musical, I think: That person is no longer—he's been reborn."

DICK HAYMES

Dramatic School   *(MGM 1938)*
Du Barry Was a Lady   *(MGM 1943)*
Four Jills in a Jeep   *(20th 1944)*
Irish Eyes Are Smiling   *(20th 1944)*
Billy Rose's Diamond Horseshoe   *(20th 1945)*
State Fair   *(20th 1945)*
Do You Love Me?   *(20th 1946)*

The Shocking Miss Pilgrim   *(20th 1947)*
Carnival in Costa Rica   *(20th 1947)*
Up in Central Park   *(Univ 1948)*
One Touch of Venus   *(Univ 1948)*
St. Benny the Dip   *(UA 1951)*
All Ashore   *(Col 1953)*
Cruisin' Down the River   *(Col 1953)*

48

Wanda Hendrix

Wholesome baby-faced ingenues were once considered a "must" for any self-respecting studio roster, and, in the 1940s, Paramount had the monopoly on the type with a trio of contractees: Diana Lynn, Mona Freeman, and Wanda Hendrix. Of the three, Wanda was the most astute in dramatic roles, while Diana Lynn was perfect in comedy parts. Wanda came to Hollywood when she was sixteen years old and within two years gave two outstanding performances: As the cockney servant girl in *Confidential Agent* (1945), her first film, and as Pila, the Mexican girl, in Robert Montgomery's *Ride the Pink Horse* (1947). Neither of these pictures were for her eventual home lot, Paramount, and interestingly enough, she never again won a good dramatic role. As she matured, her performances became more and more bland with the exception of the tomboy role she played opposite Joel McCrea in Universal's *Saddle Tramp* (1950).

Born as Dixie Wanda Hendrix in Jacksonville, Florida, on November 3, 1928, she later dropped the name Dixie because she felt it sounded too theatrical. Early publicity in Hollywood capitalized on the fact that she was born in a log cabin, with exaggerated publicity references to Abraham Lincoln and the fact that in America anyone could get ahead in the world. Actually, her father, Max Sylvester Hendrix, held down a very good job as a logging camp boss.

He later worked for Lockheed Aircraft. Wanda's first and only ambition from childhood on was to be an actress. After graduation from junior high school in Jacksonville, she joined the Jacksonville Little Theatre where she enjoyed leads in *Personal Appearance* and in *Junior Miss*. A Warner Bros. talent scout witnessed her performance in one of these productions and sent her to Hollywood for a screen test. When the Burbank studio signed her, she and her parents promptly moved to California.

In her Herman Shumlin-directed debut film, *Confidential Agent,* based on the Graham Green novel and starring Charles Boyer and Lauren Bacall, she is Else, the slavey in a cheap British hotel, who is eventually eliminated by Nazi agents Katina Paxinou and Peter Lorre. The *New York Times,* who had very unkind words for Miss Bacall's non-performance, found Wanda "touching," and the *New York Daily News,* in its two-and-a-half star review, termed the newcomer "impressive." One would have thought that Wanda's career at Warners would have accelerated after this glowing debut, but it was nearly two years before she was again seen on the screen, because of delayed-release patterns. In her next film, *Nora Prentiss* (1947), which starred Ann Sheridan, she had the non-crucial role of Kent Smith's and Rosemary DeCamp's daughter. Obviously, with contractees Joan Leslie, Joyce Reynolds, Martha Vickers, and Janis Paige on tap to handle the array of young ladies' roles in studio

With Macdonald Carey in Song of Surrender *(Par 1949)*

productions, there was little for Wanda to do but continue in her drama school courses on the lot, that is, until the company discharged her.

However, early in 1946, Paramount learned that Wanda was at liberty and signed her to a term contract. She had graduated from the studio's high school, excelling in literature, and appeared, briefly, in the all-star *Variety Girl* (1947) and as a young girl in Bing Crosby's *Welcome Stranger* (1947). Everyone in Hollywood, except Robert Montgomery, seemed to have forgotten her lovely performance in her initial feature. Montgomery asked for her to play a very important role in his *Ride the Pink Horse,* an excellent suspense account which he starred in and directed. The film, which she made on loanout to Universal, won her belated recognition as a fine actress. She missed out on being selected as one of the five nominees for supporting actress for the 1947 Oscars, but the *Film Daily* Poll ranked her as one of the year's best. (The year before, that same poll had named her as one of the five best juvenile actresses for her performance in *Welcome Stranger,* as well as naming her "Find of the Year.") Reviewing the taut *Ride the Pink Horse,* the *New York Times* noted that Montgomery "has given the heart of the story to Wanda Hendrix, a newcomer, who is fine. As a little Mexican

With Robert Montgomery in Ride the Pink Horse *(Univ 1947)*

moon-child who shadows the bruiser [Montgomery] through the night and finally is able to assist him in his last violent race with fate and death, Miss Hendrix is remarkably sensitive and reflective of sad and mystic moods."

As a result of her shining performance at Universal, Paramount decided to give her starring roles—but they were the wrong ones. In *Miss Tatlock's Millions* (1948), Paramount provided her with a very funny script and an exceptional cast, but Wanda was ill at ease in this comedy. (In the farce *The Admiral Was a Lady,* 1952, in which she would be courted by four gentlemen, she would be totally at sea.) The studio also starred her in two dismal domestic dramas: As Melvyn Douglas' daughter in *My Own True Love* (1948) and as the young wife of neurotic Claude Rains in *A Song of Surrender* (1949). Those two debilitating parts would have been enough to ruin anyone's budding career. She then went over to Twentieth Century-Fox to play the romantic lead to Tyrone Power in *Prince of Foxes* (1949), a meandering tale set in medieval Italy. At least she had the opportunity to wear expensive-looking brocaded costumes in this Henry King-directed feature. Because of her petite size (5'2"), she was an ideal choice to play opposite Paramount's diminutive leading man Alan Ladd, and in *Captain Carey, U.S.A.* (1950), which proved to be her final contract assignment, she had the role of the Italian countess who falls in love with ex-G.I. Ladd. As in *Prince of Foxes,* she seemed too young and emotionally inexperienced for the demands of the role. The *New York Herald-Tribune* complained, "Neither as Countess nor as heart throb does Miss Hendrix convey any more than a vague thought of a high school drama heroine." The most redeeming feature of *Captain Carey, U.S.A.* was its theme song, "Mona Lisa," which won an Academy Award.

Freed of studio contractual obligations, Wanda was already enmeshed in matrimonial commitments. On February 8, 1949, she wed Audie Murphy, World War II's most decorated soldier, who had turned into a popular Hollywood performer. Five years prior, Murphy had spotted Wanda's photograph on the cover of *Coronet* Magazine and had asked his mentor, James Cagney, to arrange an introduction for him with the young girl.

The day of the wedding augured a bad future for the handsome young couple. Having returned to the States ill after the Italian filming of *Prince of Foxes,* Wanda rose from a sick bed to be wed. Murphy went to the ceremony nursing an ulcer. As she remembers, "Standing at the altar, he rejected me. It was the moment when I lifted my veil for him to kiss me that I

With Frank Faylen and Bing Crosby in Welcome Stranger *(Par 1947)*

noticed the change. His eyes were those of a stranger." The subsequent weeks of their marriage was hellish. They separated seven months after the nuptials and were divorced in 1950 on the grounds of mental cruelty. Wanda was twenty-one years old at the time.

Murphy was understandably difficult to live with after his war experiences. He admitted he could not sleep at night unless he had a gun by his bed and generally experienced terrible nightmares. She recalls, "There were times he held me at gunpoint for no reason at all. Then he would turn around and put the gun in his own mouth. I finally told him one night to go ahead and shoot. He put the gun away and turned all white." Murphy wanted Wanda to give up her film career and move to Texas with him, but he eventually understood that the movie business meant too much to her. ("I didn't dare sacrifice what little security I had," Wanda once explained about clinging to her professional ties.) Murphy blamed the divorce on Hollywood gossips. "Those phonies in Hollywood," he said, "never left [us] alone." Regarding her marriage to Murphy, Wanda recently told gossip columnist Toni Holt, "The only thing I did know was that if I didn't wind up in the nut house, I'd wind up in the grave."

Meanwhile, Wanda's career was not exactly progressing in dynamic directions. At Universal, she made the homey western *Saddle Tramp,* in which she was ideally cast and showed more animation oncamera than she had in a long time. As the rugged young miss who blossoms into a charming young lady she seemed to have a much more natural look wearing dungarees or calico dresses than she had in wearing the sophisticated costumes in her two Italian-set features. By the time Universal's *Sierra* (1950) was released, its co-stars, Wanda and Audie Murphy, were on the path to matrimonial separation. In this color western, she played a lady lawyer. Besides the pleasing photography, the best elements of the picture were its supporting cast, including Dean Jagger, Burl Ives, Sara Allgood, and James Arness.

Her next eight motion pictures were all minor efforts for United Artists, Columbia, Republic and Allied Artists; four of them were westerns, and in two she co-starred with the almost excessively handsome John Derek: *The Last Posse* (1953) and *Sea of Lost Ships* (1953). She was the innkeeper's daughter who falls in love with the nobleman bandit (Philip Friend) in *The Highwayman* (1951), a mediocre cinemazation of the famous poem by Alfred Noyes, and the movie went ridin', ridin', ridin' into near oblivion.

In 1954, the year three of her features were released, Wanda married millionaire playboy and sportsman James L. Stack, Jr., brother of actor Robert Stack. She had appeared with performer Robert on-screen in *Miss Tatlock's Millions* and *My Outlaw Brother* (1951). She relinquished her career for this second marriage, which ended in divorce in 1958 when he charged her with the standard ploy of "extreme cruelty." Among other items, the divorce settlement provided Wanda with $1,100 monthly for ten years, *if* she had not married in this period. And she followed that provision precisely, for she did not wed again until 1969 when she married oil company executive Steve LaMonte in Las Vegas.

After her divorce from Stack, she returned to acting, performing some guest spots on television (in 1952 she had been on an episode of "Robert Montgomery Presents"), such as segments of "Wagon Train" (1958), "Bat Masterson" (1960), and "Deputy" (1961). She was also featured in a west-coast stage version of *Who Was That Lady I Saw You With?* in which the *Los Angeles Times* found her "very funny and always beautiful." Her come-back film was the little programmer, *The Boy Who Caught a Crook* (1961), and she received first billing. Her last two released films were the brutal gangster movie *James Cool* (1963), in which Elizabeth Montgomery had the top female role, and A.C. Lyles' inferior western *Stage to Thunder Rock* (1964), in which ex-MGM player Marilyn Maxwell was the most exploited performer. Wanda had small roles in both features and photographed rather poorly; age had given her former madonna-like looks an unattractive, hard veneer. In the early 1970s she tried for yet another movie return by making two pictures, *Mystic Mountain Massacre* with Ray Danton, and the Canadian-lensed *The Oval Portrait* with Gisele MacKenzie, neither of which have yet been released.

In late 1974, some months after the death of her one-time spouse Audie Murphy, Wanda announced that she was collaborating with author Douglas Warren on an autobiography, a good deal of which would deal with her union to the late Western star.

WANDA HENDRIX

Confidential Agent   *(WB 1945)*
Nora Prentiss   *(WB 1947)*
Welcome Stranger   *(Par 1947)*
Variety Girl   *(Par 1947)*
Ride the Pink Horse   *(Univ 1947)*
Miss Tatlock's Millions   *(Par 1948)*
My Own True Love   *(Par 1948)*
Prince of Foxes   *(20th 1949)*
Song of Surrender (a.k.a., The Sin of Abby Hunt)   *(Par 1949)*
Captain Carey, U.S.A.   *(Par 1950)*
Saddle Tramp   *(Univ 1950)*
Sierra   *(Univ 1950)*
The Admiral Was a Lady   *(UA 1950)*

My Outlaw Brother   *(UA 1951)*
The Highwayman   *(AA 1951)*
Montana Territory   *(Col 1952)*
The Last Posse   *(Col 1953)*
Sea of Lost Ships   *(Rep 1953)*
Highway Dragnet   *(AA 1954)*
The Golden Mask   *(UA 1954)*
The Black Dakotas   *(Col 1954)*
The Boy Who Caught a Crook   *(UA 1961)*
Johnny Cool   *(UA 1963)*
Stage to Thunder Rock   *(Par 1964)*
Mystic Mountain Massacre   *(unreleased 1974)*
The Oval Portrait   *(unreleased 1974)*

49

John Hodiak

The causes, course, and results of World War II created many strange repercussions, most of them devastating. One of the less horrendous aspects for filmdom was a situation in which, because many of Hollywood's leading men enlisted or were drafted into the armed forces, the studios were forced to sign on new faces. John Hodiak was one of the new faces. He had been rejected from active duty in the war because of hypertension. MGM perhaps thought that Hodiak could be built up to play Clark Gable roles while their biggest star was in the service. But although Hodiak could act, he did not have the necessary glamour, a prerequisite for MGM luminaries. However, other studios were feeling the pinch of an inadequate supply of established screen names, and Twentieth Century-Fox borrowed Hodiak from Metro for *Lifeboat* (1944) and *A Bell for Adano* (1945), the two films which consolidated his status in the movie colony and with the public.

John Hodiak was born in Pittsburgh, Pennsylvania, on April 16, 1914, and when he was eight years old he and his family moved to Hamtramck, Michigan, a large Polish community near Detroit. He was the eldest child of Walter Hodiak, born in the Ukraine, and Anna Pogorzelliec, of Poland. They had two other children, Walter Jr. and Ann, and later adopted a girl, Mary. As a child, Hodiak was enthralled with the movies. He once said, "I swore to myself that I would

be in pictures someday and I never lost the ambition." The Hodiaks did not have the money to give their son training in order to nurture his dramatic ambitions, but while he was in grammar school he appeared in plays given by the parish church. These plays were done in either Polish or Hungarian. He also joined the church choir and learned to play the clarinet. While attending Hamtramck High School, he played third base for the school's baseball team. He was such a good player that a scout from the St. Louis Cardinals offered to sign him for their farm league. Hodiak declined the offer because of his preference for acting.

At that time Hodiak considered himself "an awfully homely kid. I must have had plenty of ham in my system not to be discouraged by a mirror." In later years he described himself as looking "like a broken-down boxer."

When he was thirteen, he made a campaign speech for Wilbur M. Brucker, candidate for the governor of Michigan, and when Brucker won the post, he introduced John to radio director James Jewell. The latter auditioned him but thought John was too young to begin a radio career and closed their first meeting with the suggestion that he should do something about his diction. John's speech was filled with guttural sounds and he dropped "g" endings. From this time on, he diligently worked on his diction.

After high school school graduation, he got a job as a caddy at a local golf club and then as a stockroom

With Lloyd Nolan and Lucille Ball in Two Smart People *(MGM 1946)*

With Nancy Guild in Somewhere in the Night *(20th 1946)*

checker for Chevrolet. During this period he made a recording, modulating his voice in various ways, and took it to radio station WXYZ in Detroit where James Jewell was still in charge. Jewell noticed not only a big change in his voice but also in his appearance. John was now six feet tall, weighed 180 pounds, and was broad-shouldered. This, along with his hazel eyes and brown hair, had turned him into a very good-looking young man. Jewell hired him for twenty-six weeks, but without pay. John held on to his job at Chevrolet and played bits in a number of radio series. He soon graduated to larger roles and became a regular stock actor at thirty-five dollars a week. He then quit Chevrolet. His father was pleased for the boy but his mother considered radio a fly-by-night business.

When John tired of playing gangsters and old men on shows such as "The Green Hornet," he left Detroit for Chicago, where he found a radio job at a hundred ten dollars a week. When that job ended, in 1939, he was out of work for a spell until he heard about auditions for the title role in radio's "L'il Abner" serial. Hodiak described the incident: "I spent hours trying to create a voice, a sort of portrait of that naive, gangling hunk of hillbilly muscle. Well, I was lucky. There must have been fifty or sixty actors after the job. I got it." He worked exclusively on radio for the next three years, not only as the title figure in "L'il Abner," but also in such serials as "Ma Perkins" and "Wings of Destiny." L'il Abner was filmed in 1940 by RKO, but the lead role went to Granville Owen.

In Chicago, MGM talent scout Marvin Schenck met Hodiak and arranged a film test for him in New York. John made the test with actor Canada Lee, with whom he would work later in Lifeboat. The test was a success and he was signed by MGM. Studio head Louis B. Mayer wanted Hodiak to change his name because it was not "actor-sounding." Hodiak refused, insisting, "I look like a guy named Hodiak." He also asked Mayer if he thought Heflin, Bogart, Ameche, or Fonda were "actor-sounding" names. Mayer did not pursue the matter further.

Hodiak's first MGM film was a walk-on part, without dialog, in A Stranger in Town (1943), starring Frank Morgan. He was mentioned, along with Peter Lawford, as a replacement for the injured Van Johnson in A Guy Named Joe (1944), but Spencer Tracy, the film's star, refused to have anyone else take over the Van Johnson role. John then had one line in Swing Shift Maisie (1943), one of the Ann Sothern series. Years later, Hodiak said, "Even to this day I remember the whole part by heart. It was: 'Will those holding green cards please rise and follow me?'" The following year he would be Ann Sothern's token lead-ing man in yet another of the series, Maisie Goes to Reno (1944). He had a small role, as a peasant, in Song of Russia (1943), and did an agile job as an actor-saboteur in Red Skelton's silly I Dood It (1943), in which he received ninth billing. One of his scenes in this film was a brief telephone conversation in close-up with his conspirators, and it showed that he could convincingly project dramatic tension, strength, and charm. When he appeared as Lana Turner's soldier husband in Marriage Is a Private Affair (1944), he began getting fan magazine publicity. He and Turner dated at the time, but for publicity purposes only. A recent biography of Miss Turner states that John was one of the few MGM men who would not submit to Lana's charms and that it infuriated her.

Alfred Hitchcock viewed a screen test of Canada Lee, whom he was interested in for Lifeboat. He cast black performer Lee in the film, but also liked the other actor in the test. Hodiak was astounded when he found out that Hitchcock asked to borrow him from Metro to play Kovac, the torpedoed ship's crew member, in Lifeboat. "This was an important asset for me," said Hodiak, "because it projected me into a certain prominence in the moving picture colony and gave me the opportunity to work with Tallulah Bankhead and other great performers and, of course, it allowed me to work with Alfred Hitchcock." As for Bankhead, "Working with her was an education. What a trouper!" The New York Sun said, "A newcomer, and one to be watched, is John Hodiak, whose portrayal is one of the dominating performances."

Twentieth Century-Fox kept him on for two more film assignments and at a much higher salary, which, of course, was gratefully accepted by the MGM coffers. He co-starred with Anne Baxter in Sunday Dinner for A Soldier (1944) as the soldier of the title. It was nice comedy-drama, but his other casting, as Major Joppolo in the film version of John Hersey's A Bell for Adano, made him a star. The major, created on Broadway by Fredric March, brings happiness to a small Italian village by securing a much wanted town bell. It is a lovely picture dampened by the appearance of a much miscast Gene Tierney as a blonde Italian. This proved to be Hodiak's favorite film; he once recalled. "This one had warmth and it gave us the chance to show democracy in action under the American military government in Italy. Each of us felt a particular affinity for the picture and what it represented." The New York Times judged, "Hodiak is excellent, firm and unquestionably sincere, with just the right shade of emotion in his response to human problems." Hodiak never again repeated the screen stardom he achieved in Adano and Lifeboat.

316

Hodiak returned to radio to be heard on Cecil B. DeMille's "Lux Radio Theatre." He read *In Old Chicago* with Dorothy Lamour and Robert Young on October 9, 1944, and *Bride by Mistake* with Laraine Day and Marsha Hunt on January 22, 1945. In the summer of 1945, he mused that "marriage is about all I need now to round out a pretty full life." A few weeks later, at a party, be bumped into Anne Baxter, with whom he had played in *Sunday Dinner for a Soldier* and they began dating. They were married on July 6, 1946: He was thirty-two and she was twenty-three. Because of their divergent backgrounds (she was from the upper class, he was not), Hollywood gossip columnists kept insisting the marriage would not work. The couple would work together once on screen, when MGM borrowed Miss Baxter from Fox to co-star with Clark Gable, Lana Turner, and Hodiak in *Homecoming* (1948), a wartime love triangle.

In 1946, after John's consecutive hits for Fox, MGM wasted him in some B films with the exception of *The Harvey Girls* (1946), a very high-calibre Judy Garland color musical. Hal B. Wallis and Paramount borrowed Hodiak for *Desert Fury* (1947), in which he received top billing over Lizabeth Scott and Burt Lancaster. He was cast as a gangster and received generally unfavorable notices for his wooden, glassy-eyed performance. He was on the wrong side of the law again in his other 1947 loanout film, *Love from a Stranger,* which was filmed on the relative cheap in England, and co-starred Sylvia Sidney. *Variety* reported that Hodiak "plays the homicidal psychotic with a glowering sort of intensity that would tip off the most credulous wife and servant."

With all of its star talent back from the World War II battlefronts, MGM had much less need of John's on-screen services, and from 1948 through 1951, he appeared in twelve Metro films, mostly in support of the studio's top male talent: Clark Gable, Robert Taylor, Van Johnson, Spencer Tracy, James Stewart, Walter Pidgeon, and Paramount's loaned Ray Milland. He even supported the lofty Greer Garson in *The Miniver Story* (1950), a pitiful sequel to the superb *Mrs. Miniver* (1942), and Hedy Lamarr in the terrible *A Lady without Passport* (1950). During that period, however, he did appear in two fine war films. *Command Decision* (1948) and *Battleground* (1949), but most of his roles were rather thankless, such as the part of the white man who lived with Indians in *Across the Wide Missouri* (1951). Hodiak was offered either male lead in *Cause for Alarm* (1951) opposite Loretta Young. He

With Anne Baxter in Homecoming *(MGM 1948)*

turned down the role of Young's psychopathic husband, a good part, and did accept a lesser role in the film. He must have had second thoughts about it, because he never showed up for filming and was replaced by Bruce Cowling. Barry Sullivan played the husband. Hodiak's MGM contract expired with *The Sellout* (1951), which dealt with corrupt local law enforcement, and then he became a freelance actor. It was also in 1951 that the Hodiaks became the parents of Kristina Baxter.

Since he could only obtain parts in low-budget pictures like *Battle Zone* (1952) for Allied Artists, John turned to the New York stage, where he made his Broadway debut on April 15, 1952, as Sheriff Hawes in *The Chase*. The New York *Morning Telegraph* reported: "Mr. Hodiak plays this sheriff with uncommon perception and a loose-jointed naturalness that makes me think we of Broadway are suckers per se if we let him go back to the movies. This is a leading man in the tradition, and on top of that he is an excellent and skilled actor." He won a Donaldson Award for his performance in the part that would be played by Marlon Brando in the 1966 film version. As thrilled as Hodiak was with his Broadway success, his personal life was in bad shape. Anne Baxter and he divorced on January 27, 1953, with Anne charging, in a very mild way, cruelty. The actress later admitted, "I loved him very deeply, but two careers are murder, and two in the same profession is double murder." After the divorce, Hodiak lived with his parents and younger brother in Tarzana, California.

After appearing in another minor war film and two lower-case westerns in 1953—he had the title role in Columbia's *Conquest of Cochise*—he returned to the Broadway stage in the most satisfying role of his career: Lieutenant Maryk in *The Caine Mutiny Court Martial* (1954). It was a part he desperately wanted. He co-starred with Henry Fonda and received second billing. The play was originally directed by Dick Powell but was taken over by Charles Laughton. The New York *Morning Telegraph* noted that Hodiak played the part "with a big but not too bright football player's doggedness. It is the right interpretation for the Maryk character." When Stanley Kramer produced the film version of *The Caine Mutiny* novel and play, his excuse for not using Hodiak as Maryk was that he was "too much the type." The film role would have aided his waning Hollywood career, as it did with Van Johnson who played the part oncamera.

Once single, John occasionally dated Eva Gabor,

Betsy Von Furstenberg, and Janis Paige, but the relationships never lasted long. As confused and upset by his social life as he was, he was equally depressed by his waning film career. "The picture business was going stale for me and I was for it. I just wasn't cut out to play the star's brother all the time. I was getting second fiddle roles. It began to be obvious that I wasn't in line to be a Gary Cooper, a John Wayne, or a Bing Crosby. Oh, I had good parts, but not top star roles."

The Caine Mutiny Broadway success did put him in a better position so that he could be more selective about his next film roles. He chose to play the prosecuting attorney in *Trial* (1955), made at his old home lot, MGM. He then appeared as Lieutenant Colonel John Stapp in *On the Threshold of Space* (1956), starring Guy Madison, and in *The Last Spring*, a television segment of "The Loretta Young Show" which was televised October 16, 1955. His film career was picking up again, but on the morning of October 19, 1955, while shaving to prepare to go to the studio to complete last minute work on *On the Threshold of Space*, the forty-one-year-old actor suffered a coronary thrombosis and died instantly. He had no previous record of heart ailment.

When John Hodiak had begun filming *Lifeboat*, his first important role, he was understandably nervous. Hitchcock teased him, "What are you shaking for, Hodiak? This is just another picture on which your whole career depends." It was one of the few times that anyone ever saw Hodiak display outward tenseness and nervousness. He once told Ed Sullivan that he was never nervous about anything, but that was only a cover-up because he did believe that each role he portrayed was one on which his entire future career relied. Perhaps this was not visible onscreen, which was definitely important, but acting was a tremendous strain on him. He once stated, "I don't know whether I'm an actor or not because I've never been sure what acting is. I've played different types, but it seems to me they turn out to be just myself every time."

After his death, Anne Baxter said, "He took things hard inside. He was the most sensitive person and he suffered from a lack of confidence and never realized how damned good an actor he really was." He, himself, once admitted, "No part has even come easily to me. Every one has been a challenge. I've worked as hard as I could on them all." Perhaps he worked too hard.

JOHN HODIAK

A Stranger in Town   *(MGM 1943)*
Swing Shift Maisie   *(MGM 1943)*
I Dood It   *(MGM 1943)*
Song of Russia   *(MGM 1943)*
Maisie Goes to Reno   *(MGM 1944)*
Marriage is a Private Affair   *(MGM 1944)*
Lifeboat   *(20th 1944)*
Sunday Dinner for a Soldier   *(20th 1944)*
A Bell for Adano   *(20th 1945)*
The Harvey Girls   *(MGM 1946)*
Somewhere in the Night   *(20th 1946)*
Two Smart People   *(MGM 1946)*
The Arnelo Affair   *(MGM 1947)*
Desert Fury   *(Par 1947)*
Love from a Stranger   *(El 1947)*
Homecoming   *(MGM 1948)*
Command Decision   *(MGM 1948)*

The Bribe   *(MGM 1949)*
Battleground   *(MGM 1949)*
Ambush   *(MGM 1949)*
Malaya   *(MGM 1950)*
A Lady without Passport   *(MGM 1950)*
The Miniver Story   *(MGM 1950)*
Night Into Morning   *(MGM 1951)*
The People Against O'Hara   *(MGM 1951)*
Across the Wide Missouri   *(MGM 1951)*
The Sellout   *(MGM 1951)*
Battle Zone   *(AA 1952)*
Mission Over Korea   *(Col 1953)*
Conquest of Cochise   *(Col 1953)*
Ambush At Tomahawk Gap   *(Col 1953)*
Dragonfly Squadron   *(AA 1954)*
Trial   *(MGM 1955)*
On the Threshold of Space   *(20th 1956)*

50

Celeste Holm

Celeste Holm does not like to be referred to as "versatile." "I'm an actress," she says, and "not just a lady-like actress." But any performer who is at home in any medium must be classified as versatile. Celeste's range encompasses every branch of show business: films, theatre, radio, television, supper clubs, and even the lecture circuit. Oscar-nominated for Best Supporting Actress three times, she won on her first try for *Gentleman's Agreement* (1947), her third film. The award was for a role that was far-removed from her part as Ado Annie, the girl who "cain't say no" in the original production of *Oklahoma!* (1943), or her later performance as Karen, the playwright's wife and Margo Channing's loyal friend, in *All About Eve* (1950).

Celeste was born in New York City on April 29, 1919. Her father, Norwegian-born Theodor Holm, an insurance adjuster who represented Lloyds of London in the States, now resides on the family farm in northern New Jersey, where Celeste and her actor husband Wesley Addy spend weekends. Celeste's mother, Jean Parke Holm, was a portrait artist who passed away a few years ago. Celeste's parents encouraged her theatrical ambitions and even started her taking ballet classes when she was three. She received her early schooling in France and Holland and still speaks French fluently. High school was spent in Chi-

cago where she worked hard to graduate in three years so she could get on with her career.

While in high school she studied drama at the University of Chicago and upon graduation she moved back to New York to continue studying acting, dancing, and singing. Her first professional job was with a stock company in Deer Lake, Pennsylvania, in 1936, in a production of *Night of January 16th*. The following year she understudied Ophelia in the national tour of Leslie Howard's *Hamlet* and played Crystal in the national company of *The Women* for fifty dollars a week. Her first New York appearance was as Lady Mary in *Gloriana*, which played the Little Theatre in 1938, but it was the small part of Mary L. in *Time of Your Life* (1939) which brought her to the attention of the New York theatrical circle. She left this show to appear in *Another Sun*, the first of five successive flops in a row, including *Return of the Vagabond* with George M. Cohan, *Papa Is All* with Jessie Royce Landis, and *The Damask Cheek* with Flora Robson and Zachary Scott.

While appearing in the latter show, Celeste read that the Theatre Guild was preparing a musical version of Lynn Riggs' *Green Grows the Lilacs* and applied for an audition. She sang "Who Is Sylvia" for Rodgers and Hammerstein who praised her lovely voice but told her that they required someone who could sing both loud and funny. Well, she sang loud and funny enough to get the role of Ado Annie in

Publicity pose ca. 1946

Away We Go, the title of which was changed later to *Oklahoma!* When it opened on Broadway at the St. James Theatre on March 31, 1943, and made musical comedy history with its 2,212 performance run. The *New York World-Telegram's* review of *Oklahoma!* said, "Among the principals, Celeste Holm simply tucked the show under her arm and just let the others touch it. This is an astounding young woman. When you see and hear her sing the rather naughty song *I Can't Say No* you are in for a tickling thrill. Miss Holm, with her fresh beauty, has too much talent to be quite credible." While she was in *Oklahoma!* she also sang nightly at the La View Parisienne club.

Twentieth Century-Fox's Darryl F. Zanuck was enthusiastic about Celeste's screen potential and he offered her a role in *Where Do We Go From Here?* (1945), but she wisely rejected the part which went to June Haver. This was one of many offers she received after her *Oklahoma!* success. The Theatre Guild wanted her for *Romeo and Juliet* and another producer offered her the leading role in a musical version of *Rain* (which June Havoc eventually accepted). Celeste, however, did select *Bloomer Girl* (1944), with music and lyrics by Harold Arlen and E. Y. Harburg. It made her a full-fledged Broadway star despite the fact that the *New York Post* judged, "Just because Celeste Holm shouted a comedy song at the top of her lungs in *Oklahoma* is no reason for anybody to assume that she can carry a score like Arlen's for *Bloomer Girl,* and it's a pity, for she's a lovely person and a nice actress. For heaven's sake, Miss Holm, go back to the drama where you belong. You're killing us."

Darryl Zanuck kept after Celeste, and finally, during the run of *Bloomer Girl,* signed her to a long-term contract at Fox, but she would not make a film for them until she did a USO tour throughout Europe. In her first film, the musical *Three Little Girls in Blue* (1946), starring June Haver and Vivian Blaine, she sang the song "Always a Lady" so delightfully and showed so much spunk, that, even in her relatively minor role, she stole the entire film. The *New York Herald-Tribune* enthused, "It is Celeste Holm who gives distinction to the wisps of genuine acting." She was also the best thing in *Carnival in Costa Rica* (1947), another musical, which featured Dick Haymes. Then came her Oscar-winning role of Anne, the sophisticated fashion editor, in *Gentleman's Agreement.*

Celeste says she was forced to appear in *Road House* (1948), with Ida Lupino, Cornel Wilde, and Richard Widmark, "because I had been on suspension and was going broke." She claims it was the only

With Leonide Massine in Carnival in Costa Rica *(20th 1947)*

film she never wanted to do. Said the *New York Times*, "Celeste Holm is her customary witty self in the decidedly minor role of road house cashier." It was a part that seemed more suited for an actress of the caliber of Eve Arden. After her small but dramatic role as the hospital inmate who is friendly to Olivia de Havilland in *The Snake Pit* (1948), she was given her first female lead, playing Dan Dailey's long-suffering but loving wife in *Chicken Every Sunday* (1949), a turn-of-the-century comedy drama. *Come to the Stable* (1949), with Celeste as the tennis-playing French nun, co-starred her with Loretta Young and brought her a second Oscar nomination (but she lost to Mercedes McCambridge of *All the King's Men*). She did receive the Alliance Francaise award for *Come to the Stable*. If Oscars were awarded to best narration performances, Celeste surely should have received one for her recorded performance in *A Letter to Three Wives* (1949). As Addie, who pens the letter to three women saying she has run away with one of their husbands, Celeste never appears oncamera. It is to her great credit that she is equally as remembered in this film as onscreen leads Jeanne Crain, Linda Darnell and Ann Sothern.

Celeste demonstrated her adeptness for wacky comedy in *Everybody Does It* (1949), as the hysteri-cally funny wife of Paul Douglas who aspires to be an opera diva. She was loaned to United Artists to be Ronald Colman's *vis-a-vis* in *Champagne for Caesar* (1950). Then came *All About Eve*. Her performance in this film is unquestionably the finest of her career and one of the best non-bravura performances in cinematic history. Her Karen is a blend of sophistication, intelligence, warmth, and complete honesty, without any telltale histrionics. From the moment the viewer hears her narrating, "Lloyd always said that in the theatre a lifetime was a season, and a season a lifetime," every nuance of her character is seeming perfection. Obviously Celeste thoroughly understood her role of a woman whose only association with the world of theatre is through marriage (to playwright Hugh Marlowe): She was an alien in this strange world and had to be satisfied with a back seat. Her scene in the front seat of the car (with Bette Davis) after she has drained the gas tank is one of the most brilliantly acted moments in this scintillating motion picture. Quite naturally, Celeste was Oscar-nominated, but she lost the Best Supporting Actress Award to Josephine Hull of *Harvey*.

Well into 1949, Celeste realized she had to make a decision whether to stay in Hollywood or return to her first professional love, the theatre. She did hope

With Connie Gilchrist and Olivia de Havilland in The Snake Pit *(20th 1948)*

With Hugh Marlowe and Loretta Young in Come to the Stable *(20th 1949)*

for the Billie Dawn role in the film version of *Born Yesterday* (1950) but, of course, Columbia finally signed the play's original star, Judy Holliday, for the part. Paramount offered her a role, opposite Bing Crosby in *Mr. Music* (1950), that Celeste did not want (Ruth Hussey played it). She asked to be released from the Fox commitment, a decision which amazed Hollywood.

She returned to New York to co-star with Brian Aherne and Burl Ives in the City Center's revival of *She Stoops to Conquer* (December, 1949) and after losing the role of Nellie Forbush in the national company of *South Pacific* to Janet Blair, she was back on Broadway as the sole star of *Affairs of State,* a play written especially for her by Louis Verneuil. The *New York Journal-American* applauded, "Out of all the trickery and skullduggery [comes] Celeste Holm, flashing her teeth, twinkling her eyes, blonde, intelligent, appealing, triumphant, beautiful, charming, serene and supreme. Holm, sweet Holm!"

Other plays followed. She had the title role in *Anna Christie* at the City Center revival of 1952 and later that year she temporarily replaced Gertrude Lawrence in *The King and I,* as Mrs. Anna, the English school mistress at the Siamese court. Then came another Broadway engagement in *His and Hers* (January, 1954) with Robert Preston, and her ability as a comedienne was once more acknowledged. However, her wardrobe received the best reviews. When the show folded, she returned to Hollywood to star in her own television series, "Honestly, Celeste" (1954). She was convinced that national exposure was important to her career. The series, in which she played a journalism teacher, lasted a brief eight weeks on the air. Celeste was no stranger to the television medium, having appeared on programs since her debut on the "Chevy Show" in 1949.

She remained on the west coast to appear opposite Frank Sinatra in two films: *The Tender Trap* (1955) and *High Society* (1956). Dore Schary, head of MGM at the time, was not very thrilled with the idea of casting Celeste in *The Tender Trap,* but Sinatra knew how right she would be in the role of the cool bachelor girl, Sylvia, a role that was done on Broadway by Kim Hunter. Sinatra pushed for her and MGM executives were so pleased with her work that they immediately cast her as Liz Imbrie in *High Society,* a musical version of *The Philadelphia Story.* Celeste loses Sinatra to Debbie Reynolds in the final reel of *The Tender Trap,* but she traps him in *High Society* by being patient and witty. In fact, whenever she is oncamera (as in the "Who Wants to be a Millionaire?" number) the film's three stars, Bing Crosby, Grace Kelly, and Sinatra fade in importance. Ruth Hussey played Celeste's

role in the 1940 film version that was originated earlier on the Broadway stage by Shirley Booth.

In 1957 Celeste toured in *Back to Methuselah,* and the following season appeared on Broadway twice. The Theatre Guild starred her in *Third Best Sport* (1958) and she was in the psychological melodrama *Interlock* (1958) by Ira Levin, playing her entire role from a wheelchair. The play also featured Maximillian Schell and Rosemary Harris. The *New York Daily News* reported, "In *Oklahoma* Miss Holm sang a great song, 'I Cain't Say No!' She should have said that to the producers of *Interlock.*" When Shelly Winters withdrew from the Arthur Laurents play, *Invitation to a March* (1960), Celeste took over, both on Broadway and on tour.

Celeste has been married four times. Her first husband was director Ralph Nelson and they had a son, Ted, who is now in his thirties. She then married Francis Harding Emerson Davies of England in January, 1940. He worked for an accounting auditing firm, and, for this legal union, Celeste was baptized in the Catholic faith. The marriage, however, did not last and Celeste married again in 1946, this time to airline public relations executive A. Schuyler Dunning. They had a son, Daniel, born in November, 1946, and when they divorced Celeste received custody of the boy and the return of her maiden name. Her next spouse was, and is still, Wesley Addy, an actor whom she met during *Invitation to a March.* Addy, a fine actor, is tall, slim and has a handsome head of white hair. He is quiet, reserved, and a good contrast to the vivacious Celeste. He also epitomizes the word "gentleman," especially in the business of show. They work together whenever possible. In 1963 they did *A Month in the Country* in New York and have done stock productions of *Affairs of State, Finishing Touches,* and *Irregular Verb to Love,* among others. In 1970, they opened on Broadway in Shaw's *Candida,* with Celeste in the title role and Wesley as Morell, a role he had played opposite Katharine Cornell years before. The revival was unfortunate. She was charming and gracious in it, but seemed oddly miscast, which is not often said of Celeste.

Celeste has been a guest star on just about all the major television shows but her most popular appearance in the medium was probably as the fairy Godmother in Rodgers and Hammerstein's musical, *Cinderella* (1966), a special which is often repeated. Back in the mid-1950s she briefly filled in for host Hal March on "The $64,000 Question," and appeared more nervous and upset than the contestants. She played the mother in TV's second version of *Meet Me in St. Louis* (1966) and was seen earlier opposite Alfred Drake, of *Oklahoma!* fame, in *Yeoman of the*

Guard (1957). One of her strongest dramatic roles on television was as the lead in Arthur Laurents' *A Clearing in the Woods* on "Play of the Week" in 1960. In 1970 she did another weak video series called "Nancy" for NBC. In it she played the press secretary to a fictional president as well as chaperone to the president's daughter, Nancy. *Time* Magazine labeled the featherweight domestic comedy "the most contemptible show of the season." It was nostalgic to see Celeste on CBS's early 1970s tribute to Oscar Hammerstein II because she sang her very famous "I Cain't Say No." She has made two television features so far, *The Delphi Bureau* (1972) and *The Underground Man* (1974), the latter with Peter Graves. Despite her apprehensions about the powers of television, she continues to work in the medium, appearing as a guest in such shows as "Medical Center."

If there is one thing to regret about Celeste's career, it is the fact that she has appeared only in sixteen films to date. She was in two poor screen comedies in the 1960s. In *Bachelor Flat* (1961) she returned to Twentieth Century-Fox to give support to Terry-Thomas, Tuesday Weld, and Richard Beymer, while in *Doctor, You've Got to Be Kidding!* (1967) she was Sandra Dee's mother. In the latter she found ways of being both funny and moving without any help from the disastrous screenplay. Her most recent motion picture is the musical version of *Tom Sawyer* (1973), playing Aunt Polly, much in the manner of an updated Charlotte Greenwood. *Variety* thought her "just sensational," adding that "she returns to the screen in personal triumph. Her singing of the title song, first in happy exasperation, is delightful, and later in mournful soliloquy when [Johnny] Whitaker [in the title role] is feared drowned, is a high spot not only of the film but of her career."

Over the years, Celeste has been the recipient of a number of awards. In 1966 she was named performer of the year by the Variety Clubs of America, and in 1973 the Variety Club Women of New York named her Entertainer of the Year, a tribute to "her continuing artistry." She has the title of First Lady of the California State Theatre and won the Sarah Siddons Award for her role of *Mame* in Chicago. Ironically, the Sarah Siddons Award was invented by director Joseph L. Mankiewicz as a fictional award for his film *All About Eve.* Chicago made it a reality. Celeste had been a *Mame* replacement on Broadway and then took over the role from Susan Hayward in the Las Vegas production. Celeste was always charming as *Mame* but was not vocally suited to the difficult task.

Blue-eyed, ash blonde Celeste has been chairman of the National Association for Mental Health and is a member of the Board of Directors. She also works diligently for UNICEF and has been the "adopted" mother to seven youths who have lived with her for varying periods. Helping the young has taken much of the time of her private as well as public life.

Celeste is constantly involved in theatrical projects, whether on Broadway or on the road. She was in the out-of-town tryout of Truman Capote's musical *The Grass Harp,* but wisely left the production before it opened (and soon closed) on Broadway. She was replaced by Karen Morrow. Buffalo saw her and Wesley Addy in the musical version of *I Remember Mama.* When she left a tour of *Butterflies Are Free* to do the *Tom Sawyer* film, Ann Sothern took over her role. In early 1975 she was part of a tour package of *Light up the Sky* and continued with guest spots on TV shows and telefeatures.

Not only is Celeste Holm an intelligent witty lady, she is positive and completely sure of herself. "You need spunk, guts, and drive to live," she insists. She has a definite sense of presence and should not be confused with the women she has played onscreen (especially in the 1940s), even though the presence is always there. She is far stronger and much more determined in life. She can become quite pushy and is a great one for giving instructions. "It's a compulsion," she admits. "A compulsion to get results." Celeste, a grandmother, still hangs onto the star image. "Maintaining our image offscreen is the only way we can remain illusory onscreen," she explains. "As an actress I create illusions and I must be permitted to."

CELESTE HOLM

Three Little Girls in Blue   *(20th 1946)*
Carnival in Costa Rica   *(20th 1947)*
Gentleman's Agreement   *(20th 1947)*
Road House   *(20th 1948)*
The Snake Pit   *(20th 1948)*
Chicken Every Sunday   *(20th 1949)*
A Letter to Three Wives   *(20th 1949)* (Voice only)
Come to the Stable   *(20th 1949)*

Everybody Does It   *(20th 1949)*
Champagne for Caesar   *(UA 1950)*
All About Eve   *(20th 1950)*
The Tender Trap   *(MGM 1955)*
High Society   *(MGM 1956)*
Bachelor Flat   *(20th 1961)*
Doctor, You've Got to Be Kidding!   *(MGM 1967)*
Tom Sawyer   *(UA 1973)*

51

Tim Holt

Tim Holt broke the Hollywood rules in at least two categories. He was the son of a movie star who made good in the profession, and he was a western movie lead who demonstrated that he was quite capable in other celluloid genres.

He was born John Charles Holt, Jr. in Beverly Hills, California on Feburary 5, 1918, two years after the marriage of Margaret Woods to Virginian Jack Holt, who was then a comparative newcomer to the film medium. Young "Tim," as he was nicknamed, was to the saddle born, working on his father's Fresno ranch between classes in a private grammar school. Tim made his motion picture debut, quite naturally, in one of his father's films. It was *The Vanishing Pioneer* (1928), one of the last Zane Grey stories in which Jack Holt would appear prior to his rebellion against Paramount for keeping him in westerns. After making that film, he went to Columbia where he found more diversified roles.

After one year of public high school, Tim was sent to Culver Military Academy, where his roommate was Hal Roach, Jr. At Culver, Tim played polo, winning the Gold Spurs, the highest award in horsemanship, and graduating *cum laude*. While attending the University of Southern California, young Holt met Virginia Mae Ashcroft, the daughter of a New York manufacturer, at a sorority dance. They were married

on December 10, 1938, and Tim decided to pursue an acting career.

He became a member of the Westwood Theatre Guild, appearing in various stock productions. At Universal he waited five hours to see the casting director for a part in *The Road Back* (1937), a role that never materialized for him, but producer Walter Wanger, convinced of Tim's sincerity in pursuing a screen career, gave him a movie test—as a drunkard with Pat Paterson. That screen test led to a contract and a small role in *History Is Made at Night* (1937). As Richard Grosvenor (Douglas Fairbanks, Jr.'s part in the silent version) in *Stella Dallas* (1937), Tim received excellent reviews. He made a further impression in vying for acting honors with Claude Rains and Olivia de Havilland, as the latter's brother, Lance Ferris, in Warner Bros.' *Gold Is Where You Find It* (1938).

Obviously, he was establishing himself on the screen as Tim Holt and not as his father's son, and Tim was proud that his dad never asked a producer or director to give him a job. Because of his riding ability, RKO cast Tim (as The Tonto Kid) with veteran westerner Harry Carey in *The Law West of Tombstone* (1938). In John Ford's epic classic *Stagecoach* (1939), the first to be filmed in Monument Valley, Tim was splendid as the rigid code-book officer, Lieutenant Blanchard, and, thereafter appeared to advantage as Tim Borden with Ginger Rogers in *Fifth Avenue*

328

With Richard Martin in Indian Agent *(RKO 1948)*

Girl (1939). Holt then gave one of his best screen performances as Fritz, the eldest of four sons in *Swiss Family Robinson* (1940), with Thomas Mitchell and Edna Best as the beleaguered parents.

On January 15, 1940, Tim became the father of a son, Lance. In the same year he was seen onscreen in RKO's remake of *Laddie* (1940), based on the well-known Gene Stratton-Porter story. With his handsome, dimpled face, penetrating brown eyes inherited from his father, and brown, curly hair, Tim was an excellent choice for the picture. Universal borrowed Holt for the part of Charles Boyer's son Richard Saxel, in their remake of Fannie Hurst's weeper *Back Street* (1941), with Margaret Sullavan. Then his home lot, RKO, started a series of well-produced westerns with Tim and he found his true cinema forte.

His ability to wipe off the prairie dust and take on a prime role in a major production should have encouraged the RKO management to build him into a major star, but Tim enjoyed the western genre and did not rebel at his many assignments in the oaters. The RKO front office was aghast when Orson Welles announced his selection of Tim for *The Magnificent Ambersons* (1942). Welles himself originally had

With Dolores Costello in The Magnificent Ambersons *(RKO 1942)*

planned to play the role of George, the spoiled, despicable son who ruins both his life and his mother's (Dolores Costello), but seeing Tim on the RKO lot, he changed his mind. Explaining his unusual choice, Welles recalled, "I saw him first in *Stagecoach*. He had one close-up that made a tremendous impression on me—when, as a young cavalry officer, he saluted and rode away to his death. It was the way he did it, the way he rode, the poignant, dashing style of his performance that got me. I was so excited I saw practically every other picture he had made. Then I noticed him in his cowboy clothes on the RKO lot, and we soon met."

When *The Magnificent Ambersons* debuted in New York (August 13, 1942), there was a wide division of critical opinion over Welles's interpretation of the Booth Tarkington novel, but in evaluating the actors' performances, most critics agreed with the *New York Times's* evaluation: "Tim Holt draws out all of the meanness in George's character, which is precisely what the part demands."

"It wasn't an easy decision for me to make," Welles grandly explained after Tim had received praise for his acting, "It was a gamble, but I think he is wonderful in this picture. I was lucky to get him." Tim's response to Welles could also explain why he remained in the saddle in minor westerns most of his career, "Don't let him kid you. I'm not an actor. I'm a horse mechanic!"

Throughout 1942–43 Tim appeared in a series of RKO westerns with Cliff "Ukelele Ike" Edwards as his sidekick. Tim deserted the range only once during that period to give a good account of himself as a serious actor as the Gestapo-trained Karl in RKO's *Hitler's Children* (1942). The film's boxoffice take spiraled with the help of an innovative, exploitative radio advertising campaign.

The westerns with Tim were made during a two-month furlough, granted Holt by the government, from the Air Corps, in which he had enlisted as an aviation cadet. After pre-flight training at Victorville, California, Tim graduated as a second lieutenant. Toward the end of World War II he served as a bombardier on a B-29 named *The Reluctant Dragon*, making many air raids over Tokyo. When he returned to Hollywood he wore mementoes of his war service: The Distinguished Flying Cross, Air Medal (with three clusters), Pacific Defense Medal, Presidential Citation (two clusters), Victory Medal, and the Asiatic-Pacific Medal.

His marriage with Virginia Mae Ashcroft Holt dissolved and, in June 1944, before leaving for overseas duty he married Alice Harrison whom he had met at the officer's club in El Centro, California.

With Kenneth MacDonald and Frank Wilcox in The Mysterious Desperado *(RKO 1949)*

His first screen role after leaving the service was as Virgil Earp in *My Darling Clementine* (1946). This John Ford-directed film was a revamping of *Frontier Marshal* (1939), which would be remade again in 1957 as *Gunfight at the O.K. Corral.* For his home studio, RKO, he made two Zane Grey stories, *Under the Tonto Rim* (1947) and *Wild Horse Mesa* (1947). In the latter he played the role his father had had in Paramount's 1925 version. Then Warner Bros. borrowed him for a John Huston film that has become a classic and one of the hallmark films of the Forties.

On April 6, 1947, Tim, with Humphrey Bogart, Walter and John Huston, and two dozen technicians left for Mexico to start filming John Huston's adaptation of B. Traven's *The Treasure of the Sierra Madre* (1948). The part of Curtin, originally announced for John Garfield, was played sensitively by Holt against virtuoso performances from Bogart and, especially, sixty-three-year-old Walter Huston, who crowned a brilliant career with his portrayal of the toothless, greedy old prospector Howard. Huston *pere* garnered an Academy Award for Best Supporting Actor, while Huston *fils* earned Oscars for Best Director and Screenplay. If not for *The Magnificent Ambersons,* then for *Sierra Madre,* Tim has been remembered as a truly fine performer. Recalling his work for Huston, Holt later said, "I made a great picture like *The Treasure of the Sierra Madre* then went back to RKO for a hundred-thousand-dollar western. I couldn't see it. But I had a contract, so I did a lot of those westerns. Sure, I got some good pictures, but I had to get them myself. RKO, where I was under contract, did nothing for me. *Magnificent Ambersons* was virtually an independent picture."

Tim Holt continued riding the RKO range, usually with sidekick Richard Marton (as Chito Rafferty). He was delighted to have his father with him in *The Ari-* *zona Ranger* (1948) and proud of his father's World War II service record as a horse buyer for the U.S. calvary under General George Marshall. Father and son Holt remained close until Jack's death on January 18, 1951.

Throughout the forties, Tim made the top ten list of money-making cowboys at the boxoffice, but, by the early Fifties, he became disenchanted with the scripts that were merely rehashes of past years' westerns, now produced on lower budgets. In 1952, his last year as a cinema cowboy, he placed fifth on a poll of ten best western stars, coming in behind Roy Rogers, Gene Autry, Rex Allen, and Bill Elliott.

He continued to get film offers, including a request to star in the television series "Wyatt Earp," but he found contentment on his ranch in Hurrah, Oklahoma, with his wife and three children: Jack, Jay, and Bryanna. By then, he was quite satisfied with his post as sales manager for radio station KEBC-FM in Oklahoma City.

Early in 1973 he discovered he had terminal cancer, and a few hours before his death he appeared on Oklahoma City station KWTC, which, at Holt's suggestion, had programmed a TV documentary for detection of cancer. Holt told the video audience, "'I've had a good life. I don't regret anything. I'm not afraid to die." At the Shawnee Medical Clinic, Tim Holt died on February 15, 1973.

Years before, Orson Welles had summed up Tim's talent: "Tim is so different from the average leading man. In fact, he is not a leading man and never will be one. He has no vanity. There are no funny tricks to his personality, there's no nonsense about him. He is a real actor, has all the fine qualities of youth without its foolishness. He is a hard, conscientious worker and still he does everything with a certain natural ease."

TIM HOLT

The Vanishing Pioneer   *(Par 1928)*
History Is Made at Night   *(UA 1937)*
Stella Dallas   *(UA 1937)*
Gold Is Where you Find It   *(WB 1938)*
The Law West of Tombstone   *(RKO 1938)*
I Met My Love Again   *(UA 1938)*
Sons of the Legion   *(Univ 1938)*
The Renegade Ranger   *(RKO 1939)*
Spirit of Culver   *(Univ 1939)*
Stagecoach   *(UA 1939)*
Girl and the Gambler   *(RKO 1939)*
Fifth Avenue Girl   *(RKO 1939)*
The Rookie Cop   *(RKO 1939)*
Swiss Family Robinson   *(RKO 1940)*
Laddie   *(RKO 1940)*
Wagon Train   *(RKO 1940)*
The Fargo Kid   *(RKO 1940)*
Back Street   *(Univ 1941)*
The Bandit Trail   *(RKO 1941)*
Riding the Wind   *(RKO 1941)*
Dude Cowboy   *(RKO 1941)*
Robbers of the Range   *(RKO 1941)*
Along the Rio Grande   *(RKO 1941)*
Six-Gun Gold   *(RKO 1941)*
Land of the Open Range   *(RKO 1941)*
Come on, Danger!   *(RKO 1941)*
Cyclone on Horseback   *(RKO 1941)*
Thundering Hoofs   *(RKO 1941)*
The Magnificent Ambersons   *(RKO 1942)*
Pirates of the Prairie   *(RKO 1942)*
Bandit Ranger   *(RKO 1942)*
Hitler's Children   *(RKO 1942)*
The Avenging Rider   *(RKO 1943)*
Sagebrush Law   *(RKO 1943)*
Fighting Frontier   *(RKO 1943)*

Red River Robin Hood   *(RKO 1943)*
My Darling Clementine   *(20th 1946)*
Thunder Mountain   *(RKO 1947)*
Under the Tonto Rim   *(RKO 1947)*
Wild Horse Mesa   *(RKO 1947)*
Treasure of the Sierra Madre   *(WB 1948)*
Indian Agent   *(RKO 1948)*
The Arizona Ranger   *(RKO 1948)*
Western Heritage   *(RKO 1948)*
Gun Smugglers   *(RKO 1948)*
Guns of Hate   *(RKO 1948)*
Rustlers   *(RKO 1949)*
The Stagecoach Kid   *(RKO 1949)*
Brothers in the Saddle   *(RKO 1949)*
Masked Raiders   *(RKO 1949)*
Riders of the Range   *(RKO 1949)*
The Mysterious Desperado   *(RKO 1949)*
Border Treasure   *(RKO 1950)*
Dynamite Pass   *(RKO 1950)*
Storm Over Wyoming   *(RKO 1950)*
Rider from Tucson   *(RKO 1950)*
Law of the Badlands   *(RKO 1950)*
Rio Grande Patrol   *(RKO 1950)*
Gunplay   *(RKO 1951)*
Saddle Legion   *(RKO 1951)*
His Kind of Woman   *(RKO 1951)*
Pistol Harvest   *(RKO 1951)*
Hot Lead   *(RKO 1951)*
Overland Telegraph   *(RKO 1951)*
Target   *(RKO 1952)*
Trail Guide   *(RKO 1952)*
Road Agent   *(RKO 1952)*
Desert Passage   *(RKO 1952)*
The Monster That Challenged the World   *(UA 1957)*
This Stuff'll Kill Ya!   *(Ultima 1971)*

52

Robert Hutton

Every decade finds California filmmakers striving to locate, capture, and capitalize upon *the* quintessential boy-next-door type: A young male performer who is handsome but virile, wholesome but not bland, uniquely personable yet typical of Americana. One of the most successful finds of the 1940s was Robert Hutton.

He was born Robert Bruce Winne on June 12, 1920, at Kingston, New York. He later attended Blair Academy where he excelled in tennis and was a member of the track team. Six-foot-two Robert became interested in the theatre while he was at Blair, and during the summer vacations he joined the Woodstock Playhouse Stock Company. His slim, trim, honest looks later intrigued the studios, and he was signed by Twentieth Century-Fox, but he did nothing except collect a salary.

Released from this artistically unfulfilling bondage, Robert, who had now assumed the surname Hutton, moved into a long-term contract with Warner Bros. After a small bit in Errol Flynn's *Northern Pursuit* (1943), he made his "real" debut in Delmer Daves' imaginative, often implausible, but intense war film, *Destination Tokyo* (1943).

In this commendable drama, Hutton was among the crew on the submarine *Copperfin,* commanded by Cary Grant whose mission is to infiltrate Tokyo's harbor. As a member of the crew which included such actors as John Garfield, Dave Clark, and Alan

Hale, Hutton is Tommy the Kid, who, because he is the thinnest man aboard the vessel, has to dislodge a bomb caught in the deck of the submarine. Later in the film, he undergoes an emergency appendectomy by the ship's pharmacist's mate. The *New York Times* labeled Hutton's role as that of "the inevitable nervous kid," but audiences cottoned to his unaffected performance. Robert left the Warners' Navy only to be drafted into another uniform in *Hollywood Canteen* (1944), in which he played Slim, an Army corporal on sick leave dreaming of meeting young actress Joan Leslie. Around this thin premise, the studio wove their all-star musical directed by Delmar Daves. Hutton's Slim was the millionth G.I. to enter the famed Canteen, and in the story he wins the date with pert Joan Leslie. He exuded a good deal of boyish charm, as Bette Davis, the Canteen President, and John Garfield, its Vice-President, relate the history of the volunteer entertainment spot. During the film's 124 minutes the oncamera servicemen and the movie audiences are entertained by most of the Warners's star roster, plus the Andrews Sisters, Roy Rogers, Jack Benny, and even Trigger.

Warners put Hutton to work in their screen adaptation of a successful play by Josephine Bentham and Herschel V. Williams, Jr. called *Janie* (1944). The frivolous heroine was played by Joyce Reynolds, and Hutton was cast as Private First Class Dick Lawrence Van Brunt, with Ann Harding and Edward Arnold as Reynolds' bewildered parents, and Robert Benchley as Hutton's dad. The comedy was directed by Mi-

With Jack Carson and Janis Paige in Love and Learn *(WB 1947)*

With Joyce Reynolds and Clare Foley in Janie *(WB 1944)*

chael Curtiz, and a sequel (less popular with the public) was directed two years later by Vincent Sherman, using the same actors. But in the 1946 version, called *Janie Gets Married,* Joan Leslie played the bride. Robert was again teamed with the refreshing Miss Leslie in *Too Young to Know* (1945). That same year, he was in *Roughly Speaking* with Rosalind Russell and Jack Carson as one of their grown children.

If Robert seemed a bit too obliging oncamera, offscreen he was leading a rather hectic love life. In 1943 he married Natalie Thompson, but within two years the union had dissolved. The same day he was divorced, he met Cleatus Caldwell, who had just obtained a legal separation. She had been married since July 4, 1941, to performer Ken Murray, and was the mother of two bright-eyed, attractive sons, Kenneth Murray, Jr. and Cort. Though dazzled by Cleatus, Robert came under the spell of Lana Turner. MGM's sweater girl was then recovering from her romantic break-up with Turhan Bey, and Robert was very intrigued with the ubiquitous Lana,* However, he eventually returned to Cleatus, became a friend and pal to her two young sons and decided the ex-Mrs. Ken Murray was the girl for him. On October 20, 1946, Robert and Cleatus Caldwell Murray were married by Justice of the Peace Gene Ward in a cottage of the El Rancho Hotel in Las Vegas, with the Ritz Brothers, Mr. and Mrs. Jimmy Lydon, and Cleatus' mother in attendance.

They did not take a honeymoon, for Warners insisted Robert return to the home lot for a role with Jack Carson and Martha Vickers in *Love and Learn* (1947). (The picture did not warrant skipping the honeymoon.) Following the prophetic *Love and Learn,* Warners loaned the actor to Universal for *Time out of Mind* (1947), a film version of Rachel Field's fine novel. As the dilettante musician Christopher Fortune, a gentle misguided wastrel, Hutton was way out of his depth and the movie was just as uneven in all other departments.

Back at Warners, he again played the handsome, sly juvenile with Joyce Reynolds in *Always Together* (1947), a film relieved by the expert comedy acting of Cecil Kellaway and Ernest Truex. In 1948's *Wallflower,* adapted from a mildly successful Broadway play, Joyce Reynolds and Janis Paige were sisters battling for the affections of handsome Mr. Hutton, with more than able direction by Frederick de Cordova. After an inept bit of gab called *Smart Girls Don't Talk* (1948), in which Virginia Mayo and Bruce Bennett were the leads of this gangster melodrama, Robert was cast as Johnny Younger, one of the several of *The Younger Brothers* (1949). The film was a mediocre fictional-

*Walter Winchell's column proclaimed Hutton as "Lana's biggest thrill yet!"

ized tale of the western outlaws. The forties were over and so was Hutton's Warners' contract. He then began freelancing.

For Columbia he made *And Baby Makes Three* (1950), in which he was Herbert Fletcher, planning to marry a rather pregnant Barbara Hale who has divorced her husband Robert Young. He then moved to RKO to play weakling Bill Kirby in a cast of expert scene stealers (Charles Laughton, Franchot Tone, and Burgess Meredith), who were all upstaged by the city of Paris, in *The Man on the Eiffel Tower* (1950). At the same studio he was in *The Racket* (1951) as reporter Dave Ames following justice-seeking Robert Mitchum, who was out after mobster Robert Ryan.

As he approached his thirties, Hutton's face was taking on a more mature character, which gave his performances more depth. In the spring of 1951 he went on location to Gallup, New Mexico, to play the role of Lieutenant Vermont, who assists Lew Ayres to quell an Indian uprising, in the scenic Ansco color film, *New Mexico*. He played another Lieutenant—Morgan—in a dismal set of reels starring Brian Donlevy and Gig Young, and featuring more Indians on the rampage along RKO's *Slaughter Trail* (1951).

In 1952 Hutton began appearing on the nation's television screen for "Gruen Guild Playhouse" in *Al Haddon's Lamp,* with Bonita Granville in *Hit and Run,* and for the "Century Theatre" shows, *Cafe Berlin,* and *The Puppeteers* with Gale Storm. The following year on the screen he was Charlie Johnson in Columbia's unengaging yarn *Paris Model.* The four stories relating the disposition of an elegant evening gown in this film were not as inspired as the similar *Tales of Manhattan,* made eleven years before. Robert's role as Dr. Peter Kirk was lost in a tedious melodrama *The Big Bluff* (1955), and only J. Carrol Naish's performance saved *Yaqui Drums* (1956), one of his next features, from being an aimless western.

Hutton's TV spots were far better than his screen roles; he was a frequent guest star on "Fireside Theatre, "G.E. Theatre," and other similar anthology shows. On a 1955 episode of "Crossroads," called *The Gambler,* he was effective as a suicidal gaming man whom Dennis Morgan tries to help.

Most of his film work from the mid-fifties onward consisted of programmers or potboilers: Jerry Seabrook in *Outcasts of the City* (1958), Professor John Carrington in *The Colossus of New York* (1958), Dr. John Lamont in *Invisible Invaders* (1959), or as Tom in a small, feeble effort called *Jailbreakers* (1960). Occasionally, he returned to A films, but in *It Started with a Kiss* (1959), with Debbie Reynolds and Glenn Ford, he was only briefly oncamera in the small part of a millionaire.

After playing Rupert, Jerry Lewis' rival for Anna

Marie Alberghetti's hand in the abysmal *Cinderfella* (1960), Robert and Charles Baldour coproduced *The Secret Door* (1964), but his role as Joe Adams, a safe-cracker working for U.S. Naval Intelligence, was a thankless part and the film's story was implausible. As Dr. Curtis Templer, an astrophysicist, he ably portrayed the lead in a British-produced science fiction item called *They Came from Beyond Space* (1967). He remained in this genre for *The Vulture* (1967), a creepy picture featuring Akim Tamiroff and Broderick Crawford. He kept everything on an even keel as an American Army commander seeking an illusive mini-bomb during a Spanish fiesta in the British-packaged *Finders Keepers* (1967), and played a very minor role, the aide to the U.S. president (Alexander Knox), in the James Bond adventure adeptly written by Roald Dahl,

You Only Live Twice (1967). Hutton was Bruce Benton in a series of four short stories made by British-Amicus with Jack Palance, Peter Cushing, and Burgess Meredith called *Torture Garden* (1968), and he appeared on the bottom of the cast in Vincent Price's entanglement with brilliant German actress Elizabeth Bergner, *Cry of the Banshee* (1970). Robert was most recently seen in a tiny part on the six-hour April, 1974 telecast of Leon Uris' *QB VII*.

Once tagged "Adonis in Hollywood," and personifying the typical shy, well-mannered, well-bred young man next door during the forties, Hutton's career never regained momentum after the termination of his Warner Bros.' contract. Even the boy next door grows older—and the neighborhood changes drastically.

ROBERT HUTTON

Northern Pursuit *(WB 1943)*
Destination Tokyo *(WB 1943)*
Hollywood Canteen *(WB 1944)*
Janie *(WB 1944)*
Too Young to Know *(WB 1945)*
Roughly Speaking *(WB 1945)*
Janie Gets Married *(WB 1946)*
Love and Learn *(WB 1947)*
Time Out of Mind *(Univ 1947)*
Always Together *(WB 1947)*
Wallflower *(WB 1948)*
Smart Girls Don't Talk *(WB 1948)*
The Younger Brothers *(WB 1949)*
And Baby Makes Three *(Col 1950)*
The Man on the Eiffel Tower *(RKO 1950)*
Beauty on Parade *(Col 1950)*
The Steel Helmet *(Lip 1951)*
The Racket *(RKO 1951)*

New Mexico *(UA 1951)*
Slaughter Trail *(RKO 1951)*
Tropical Heat Wave *(Rep 1952)*
Gobs and Gals *(Rep 1952)*
Paris Model *(Col 1952)*
Casanova's Big Night *(Par 1954)*
Tales of Adventure *(Pathe 1954)*
The Big Bluff *(UA 1955)*
Scandal Incorporated *(Rep 1956)*
Yaqui Drums *(AA 1956)*
The Man Without a Body *(Eros 1957)*
Thunder over Tangier *(Rep 1957)*
Showdown at Boot Hill *20th 1958)*
Outcasts of the City *(Rep 1958)*
The Colossus of New York *(Rep 1958)*
Invisible Invaders *(UA 1959)*
It Started with a Kiss *(MGM 1959)*

Wild Youth *(Cinema Associates 1960)*
Jailbreakers *(AIP 1960)*
Cinderfella *(Par 1960)*
The Secret Door *(AA 1964)*
The Sicilians *(Buncher's 1964)*
The Slime People *(Hansen Enterprises 1964)*
Los Novios De Marisol *(Spanish 1965)*
Busqueme A Esa Chica *(Spanish 1965)*
Doctor in Clover *(Rank 1966)*
They Came from Beyond Space *(Emb 1967)*
The Vulture *(Par 1967)*
Finders Keepers *(UA 1967)*
You Only Live Twice *(UA 1967)*
Torture Garden *(Col 1968)*
Cry of the Banshee *(AIP 1970)*
Trog *(WB 1970)*
Tales from the Crypt *(Cin 1972)*

With Dolores Moran, Virginia Patton, Lynne Baggett, John Ridgely, Zachary Scott, Richard Whorf, and Robert Shayne in *Hollywood Canteen (WB 1944)*

53

Harry James

The fabulous big band era of the 1930s and 1940s produced such "hep" groups as those shepherded by Glenn Miller, Benny Goodman, Jimmy Dorsey, Tommy Dorsey, and, of course, Harry James. The suave trumpet-playing James explained his goal early in his career, "I want to have a band that really swings and that's easy to dance to all the time. Too many bands, in order to be sensational, hit tempos that you just can't dance to. We're emphasizing middle tempos. They can swing just as much and they're certainly more danceable."

With his band and its array of vocalists (Connie Haines, Frank Sinatra, Helen Forrest, Dick Haymes, *et al*), the clear, crisp Harry James sound was hep. On his own, angular Harry cut quite a trim figure, being renowned in the 1940s for his passion for the racetrack and his coup in winning the cinema Pin-Up Queen, Betty Grable, away from George Raft and marrying her. In conjunction with his swing band Harry had appeared in several movies, but unlike the other well-known bandleaders, he was pushed into two co-starring features of his own, through Grable's studio, Twentieth Century-Fox. These films gave him a special edge over his rivals among the big bands.

Harry Haag James was born in Albany, Georgia on March 15, 1916, in a run-down hotel next to the town's jail. His mother was a trapeze artist and his father, Everett, was the band director for the Mighty Haag Circus, one of the most widely known circuses in the South. When the James' son was born, the circus consisted of fifty-two wagons, 130 horses, three elephants, ten camels, and proudly owned one of the most beautiful and popular bandwagons in the circus world. Old time circus people vowed no one had really trouped until he had spent a season with the Mighty Haag Circus that pioneered the less traveled areas of the South through the hills of West Virginia, Georgia, Alabama, and Kentucky.

When Harry was four years old he became an active part of the circus, billed as "The Human Eel" in an act called "The Youngest and Oldest Contortionists in the World." His partner was seventy years old. His father taught him to play the trumpet and permitted him to sit in with the circus band. A mastoid operation ended Harry's career as "The Human Eel" and his father started him on playing both the drums and, in particular, the trumpet for Bessie, the beautiful high wire queen. The James family eventually settled in Beaumont, Texas, and Harry went to school and studied theory and harmony for the trumpet. Back in the circus he became leader of the number two circus band but soon left the Mighty Haag two-ringer to join Joe Gill's band in St. Louis. From this he then switched to Ben Pollack's great popular band. While James was with Pollack, Benny Goodman wired him in California, "Come on boy, meet us at the Pennsylvania." James' impact on the Goodman organization was immediate and impressive.

With Vivian Blaine, Phil Silvers, and Carmen Miranda in If I'm Lucky *(20th 1946)*

With Nancy Walker in Best Foot Forward *(MGM 1943)*

Benny Goodman's classic Carnegie Hall Concert on January 16, 1938, was revolutionary. It was the first time integrated musicians had appeared on a New York concert stage. With Teddy Wilson on piano and Lionel Hampton on the vibes, the Goodman contingent jiving the aristocratic hall included Bobby Hackett, Gene Krupa, and, in the trumpet section, Ziggie Elman, Chris Griffin and young Harry. James was so impressed with the band's performance in Carnegie Hall and the wildly enthusiastic audience response that he said, "I feel like a whore in church!" Krupa left Goodman to form his own band and in 1939 Harry decided to follow suit. Goodman, a good sport about the departure, advanced Harry $4,500 toward what he considered a successful investment. In 1942, Harry repaid Benny twenty thousand dollars for his original interest in Harry James and his Music Makers.

The new James band opened its first engagement at the Benjamin Franklin Hotel in Philadelphia on February 9, 1939 and started recording for Brunswick Records. Mary Louise Tobin, a vocalist with Goodman's band whom Harry had married, brought to his attention a young male vocalist singing at Englewood, New Jersey's Rustic Cabin. James hired the young singer, and in July, 1939, the new boy vocalist cut his first sides with the James group, "From the Bottom of My Heart" and "Melancholy Mood." Frank Sinatra became James's prime male vocalist, joining girl singer Connie Haines. The new James band toured the country, growing less financially secure with each engagement, and when they played the Sherman House in Chicago, Sinatra was offered a job with Tommy Dorsey and James gave him his release. Harry replaced Sinatra with a newcomer named Dick Haymes. The engagement at the Dancing Campus of the New York World's Fair in the summer of 1940 enhanced the band's growing national reputation as one of the best in the business. Haymes' vocals were brilliant but the organization prospered even more when Harry acquired the singing services of Helen Forrest, who had been with Benny Goodman and Artie Shaw in past band engagements. There developed a set of successful arrangements between Helen's well-paced vocals and Harry's virtuoso trumpeting, reflected in their hit recordings of "I Don't Want to Walk without You," "But Not for Me," "Skylark" and the classic "I Had the Craziest Dream." Awards, radio work, and the adulation of the country's jive set made the James name magic, and Hollywood beckoned.

Harry had appeared in Warner Bros.' 1937 Hollywood Hotel as a member of the Benny Goodman band, a film remembered for the singing of Frances Langford and Johnny "Scat" Davis in "Hooray for Hollywood." In 1942, Harry made Syncopation at RKO, then Private Buckaroo at Universal, featuring his band in the army with the Andrews Sisters and, for Twentieth Century-Fox, he and his musicians backed Betty Grable in Springtime in the Rockies (1942). During the course of this film's making, Harry and Betty furthered their once casual acquaintance. Grable was then dating steadily with George Raft and, during James' engagement in a Hollywood nightclub, Raft and Harry tore up the evening with a fist fight over the luscious Betty, whose divorce from ex-child star Jackie Cooper had become final in October, 1940. At this time Harry and his Music Makers were at work at Metro-Goldwyn-Mayer, filming the Broadway hit, Best Foot Forward (1943), featuring Lucille Ball. In this film, Harry did a comedy routine on the dance floor with comedienne Nancy Walker, who also sang "Alive and Kicking" with his band.

On April 21, 1943, Harry and his troupe opened at New York's Paramount Theatre and created pandemonium on Times Square. As early as five A.M. teenagers started queuing along Forty-Third Street until an estimated four thousand fans were standing in the rain from Broadway to Eighth Avenue. By noon the boxoffice had sold over ten thousand tickets. The following day the boxoffice opened at seven A.M. and the frenetic crowds continued for the rest of the first week, for which James and his band received $12,-500, did forty-three shows and the Paramount Theatre grossed a mighty $105,000. James and his gang were featured in the stage show that also included the Golden Gate Quartet, and Paramount's China, starring Alan Ladd and Loretta Young, was shown on the screen. Newspapers avidly reported that during James's engagement at the Paramount, the teenage "hepcats" were jitterbugging in the aisles when the band played "The Two O'Clock Jump." Also that spring, the James ensemble played on the Astor Roof in Manhattan where Miss Grable was a frequent nightly guest near the bandstand.

Harry's divorce from Louise Tobin was finalized on July 5, 1943, in which she received custody of their two sons and, according to Walter Winchell, "$1,000 per week for the lifetime of the James' Band." On the day following the Allied invasion of Sicily, July 11, 1943, Grable and Harry eloped to Las Vegas, Nevada, where at 4:15 A.M. they were married by Reverend Dr. C. H. Sloan, a Baptist minister, in the Little Church of the West. Mrs. Edith Wassermann, actress Betty Furness, and recording executive Emmanuel Sacks were witnesses. The newlyweds returned to Hollywood that morning for work. Betty went into Fox's Sweet Rosie O'Grady (1943) and Harry made a gag-guest appearance in MGM's *Swing Fever* (1943), which featured Kay Kyser and Lena Horne.

Metro continued its formula of combining class and popular musical entertainment with its *Two Girls and a Sailor* (1944), in which Van Johnson, June Allyson, Gloria De Haven and Jimmy Durante cavorted with Xavier Cugat and his Band and Harry James (with vocalist Helen Forrest) and his Music Makers. The James gang played "Flash," "Dardenella," and "Charmaine," were accompanied by Durante in "Inka, Dinka, Doo" and by Allyson's vocal of "Young Man with a Horn." James contributed a trumpet solo of "Estrellita." The public wholeheartedly endorsed the colossal musical. Harry and his musicians then supplied the music for Esther Williams' first starring film, *Bathing Beauty* (1944), also at MGM.

On March 4, 1944 the Armed Forces' favorite Pin-Up Girl presented Harry James with a daughter, Victoria Elizabeth, delivered by Caesarean birth. For the Seventh War Loan Drive, a screen short, *All Star Bond Rally,* was released in the spring of 1945 in which James and his orchestra appeared with Grable, Bing Crosby, Harpo Marx, Frank Sinatra, Bob Hope, Carmen Miranda, and others. Darryl F. Zanuck's Twentieth Century-Fox thought it a cool idea to hire Grable's husband for his own starring vehicle and perhaps turn him into a cinema leading man. The studio made *Kitten on the Keys* in 1945, and then virtually completely remade it and released it in 1946 as *Do You Love Me?* Harry played a hot trumpeter who loses the girl (Maureen O'Hara) at the end of the picture. Grable was reportedly incensed about the storyline and insisted on a final rewritten scene in which she was waiting for the rejected Harry outside in a car. Gimmick or publicity, it was a surprising finish. Between films, the James enjoyed their 103-acre ranch managed by Betty's father, and both Betty and Harry became avid devotees of the racetrack. This mutual interest led them to add a sixty-nine-acre horse breeding ranch to their spread. The *Racing Form* replaced *Variety* in their household. Then, Harry played Earl Gordon, a bandleader, in a dismal affair produced by Twentieth with Perry Como and Vivian Blaine called *If I'm Lucky* (1946), while Betty was at the same studio starring in *The Shocking Miss Pilgrim* (1947) with Harry's former vocalist Dick Haymes.

During Betty's second pregnancy, Harry appeared with Leopold Stokowski, Jascha Heifitz, Lily Pons, Rise Stevens, Walter Damrosch, Artur Rubinstein, and Vaughn Monroe in a musical fest hinged on a thin tale called *Carnegie Hall* (1947), which was released by United Artists. In July, 1947, James and his

With Betty Grable on their wedding day (July 6, 1943) in Las Vegas

crew appeared at Atlantic City's Steel Pier with *Carnegie Hall* as the Pier's feature screen attraction. On May 20, 1947, Betty gave birth to their second daughter, Jessica.

In the late 1940s, Harry, who had announced his retirement when public reaction to his group's performing had begun to turn sour, restructured his band. He streamlined his group and embarked on a series of one-night engagements, finding that there was still a viable market for his brand of jazz. Harry made a guest appearance in a United Artists' fiasco that started life as *A Miracle Can Happen* and eventually became *On Our Merry Way* (1948), neither title indicative of the picture's fortune. When Harry and his orchestra were doing one of their recording sessions, Grable, unable to make recordings under her Fox contract, joined the group for a rendition of "I Can't Begin to Tell You," using the name Ruth Haag.

Warner Bros. filmed *Young Man with a Horn* (1950), loosely based on the life of Bix Beiderbecke, with Kirk Douglas in the lead role. The ambitious perfectionist, Douglas, spent three months with Warner studio orchestra trumpeter Larry Sullivan learning to finger the valves of the instrument and to purse his lips properly. Harry James was hired for the actual trumpet playing. Back on the Twentieth Century-Fox lot, Harry played Harry James in a June Haver, Gloria De Haven musical *I'll Get By* (1950). Betty and Harry toured the top nightclubs in 1955 after her final films and then she retired from moviemaking. The Jameses had appeared on television in 1954's "Shower of Stars" with Danny Thomas, and Betty had been the initial star of the "Showers of Stars" debut on September 30, 1954. In February, 1955, Grable, Johnny Ray, and Larry Storch did a behind-the-scenes musical, *That's Life*, for "Shower of Stars," featuring a cavalcade of James's hit recordings.

With Gene Krupa, Lionel Hampton, Ben Pollock, Teddy Wilson, and Steve Allen, Harry played himself in Universal's *The Benny Goodman Story* (1955). The next year he was again cast as Harry James in MGM's *The Opposite Sex* (1956), a musical remake of *The Women* (1939). Betty played an unhappy engagement in Las Vegas in 1956 and the Jameses continued their passion for horse racing even to successfully running a few horses from their own stable. Harry indulged himself by playing the male lead in an inexpensive Western, *Outlaw Queen* (1957), and on February 3, 1958, Harry and Betty joined Lucille Ball and Desi Arnaz for a one-hour CBS-TV special whose plot revolved around race horses. Harry played his trumpet, and Betty and Desi created a new dance called The Bayamo. James's recordings were still selling despite the general failure and economic depression of the big band business. He made recordings with Doris Day ("The Very Thought of You" and "I May Be Wrong," plus others) and with Frank Sinatra ("Deep Night" and "Farewell to Love" among others).

Universal assembled a large cast of former greats in the music business, all playing themselves. They included The Four Aces, the Mills Brothers, George Shearing, Fats Domino, and Harry James, plus other notably once great jazz artists, and the picture was titled *The Big Beat* (1958). Betty opened a nightclub act in 1959 at New York's Latin Quarter and she and James played El Rancho in Las Vegas the following year. Harry's last film was a Jerry Lewis contrivance called *The Ladies' Man* (1961) in which Harry again played Harry James and his one-time rival for the charms of Mrs. James, George Raft, turned up as George Raft. Harry occasionally reorganized his band and his familiar theme, "Cìribiribin," would pop up over the years with new musicians and a resurgence

of past greatness. In December of 1962, Grable and Dan Dailey did a successful condensed version of *Guys and Dolls* at Las Vegas' Dunes Hotel. The show continued for other engagements into 1963.

After twenty-two years of marriage, there was no little amazement when the seemingly well-matched Jameses were divorced on October 7, 1965 in Las Vegas. Betty was then rehearsing for the role of Dolly Levi in *Hello, Dolly!* that ran ten months at the Riviera Hotel in Las Vegas and then went on a national tour before she assumed the starring role at New York's St. James Theatre on June 12, 1967. Meanwhile, Harry reorganized his band in 1966 with young musicians, but with veteran Corky Corcoran replacing Buddy Rich on drums, and the group did club and television dates. These engagements proved that the effervescence of James' trumpet playing had not diminished with the years.

Betty Grable had made her home in Las Vegas and her constant companion was Bob Remick who doubled as escort, secretary, and devoted companion. He maintained that Betty still carried a torch for Harry. On December 27, 1967, Harry James, age fifty-one, married a former Las Vegas showgirl, Joan Boyd, whose first marriage had been annulled in 1962. The twenty-seven-year-old Joan wore a white satin mini-skirt while Harry, the groom, donned a powder blue jacket, white turtleneck shirt, and black slacks for the ceremony.

Betty made several television commercials with her grandchildren (there were five) but her recurrent illness culminated in death from lung cancer on July 2, 1973, at St. John's Hospital in Santa Monica, California. The church funeral was overcrowded with old friends, ex-husbands and her daughters by James, Mrs. Victoria Bivens of Troy, Michigan, and Mrs. Jessica Yahner of Los Angeles. Following the funeral service, Harry James left by a side door and sped off in a waiting car. It was like the ending of an era, when all America seemed to have had "The Craziest Dream Last Night," and men in uniform were pinning up Grable's picture all over the world, and when a younger generation was jitterbugging down the aisles of New York's Paramount Theatre, driven to impulsive, frantic jive by a young man with a horn that he had learned to play years before in the Mighty Haag Circus.

HARRY JAMES

Hollywood Hotel   *(WB 1937)*
Syncopation   *(RKO 1942)*
Private Buckaroo   *(Univ 1942)*
Springtime in the Rockies   *(20th 1942)*
Best Foot Forward   *(MGM 1943)*
Two Sisters and a Sailor   *(MGM 1944)*
Bathing Beauty   *(MGM 1944)*
Do You Love Me?   *(20th 1946)*
If I'm Lucky   *(20th 1946)*
Carnegie Hall   *(UA 1947)*

On Our Merry Way (a.k.a. A Miracle Can Happen)   *(UA 1948)*
Young Man with a Horn   *(WB 1950)* (Soundtrack trumpet playing only)
I'll Get By   *(20th 1950)*
The Benny Goodman Story   *(Univ 1955)*
The Opposite Sex   *(MGM 1956)*
Outlaw Queen   *(Globe Releasing 1957)*
The Big Beat   *(Univ 1958)*
The Ladies' Man   *(Par 1961)*

54

Arthur Kennedy

When Arthur Kennedy burst upon the film scene in *City for Conquest* (1940) as the symphony-composing brother of James Cagney, there was every reason to believe that both Warner Bros. and the film-going public would soon make him a major, if not stellar, name on the motion picture scene. Until he was engulfed in World War II, Kennedy was kept busily at work in studio productions, consistently turning out finely-edged performances, whether the picture was a western, gangster yarn, or service drama. But as time would prove, he lacked the magical ingredient requisite for top-level stardom and had to content himself with leads in smaller projects or high echelon supporting roles in major films.

Thus, while Kennedy rarely starred in films, he had the capacity to frequently carry them, and that he did. There are several ingredients responsible for his healthy survival of almost forty years of acting. First of all, he is blessed with a face that is marvelously adaptable to any type of role, be it the disgusting rapist of *Peyton Place* (1957), or the cynically intellectual reporter in *Elmer Gantry* (1960). Secondly, his histrionic talent is exceptional, reaping him a large number of awards, including five Oscar nominations and a Broadway Tony Award. And lastly, he has never let the sophistication of his talent make him pompous or myopic in choosing work. The fact that he scored in such critically plaudited cinema productions as *Boomerang* (1947) and *Bright Victory* (1951), never prevented him from enjoying mindless excur-

sions such as *Bend of the River* (1952) and *Man from Laramie* (1955). Both he and the films were that much better for his presence.

John Arthur Kennedy was born on February 17, 1914 in Worcester, Massachusetts, the only child of Dr. and Mrs. John Timothy Kennedy. Theatrics at the Worcester Academy persuaded the youth that he did not want to take over his father's dental practice, and he matriculated at Pittsburgh's Carnegie Tech to study drama. After graduation in 1936, he set out for New York.

Rooming with seven other hopefuls, including David Wayne, he only had a brief starvation period before he found his way in the theatrical profession. His first job was with the Globe Theatre, a shirt-tail Shakespearean group that toured the mid-west fair circuit with abridged versions of the Bard, giving as many as nine shows daily. It was low pay but great experience, and it led to Kennedy's Broadway bow with Maurice Evans' Shakespearean company as Bushy in *Richard II* (September, 1937). The next three years saw the young actor continuing his apprenticeship with Shakespearean works, balanced by appearances in a number of contemporary Broadway shows, as well as work with the WPA theatrical group. With the latter organization he played Jerry Dorgan in *The Life and Death of an American* (May, 1939) which brought him to the attention of a Warner Bros. talent

With John Compton, Jane Wyman, Dennis Morgan, and John Ridgely in Cheyenne *(WB 1947)*

With Anthony Quinn and Cliff Edwards in Knockout *(WB 1941)*

scout. Offered a screen contract, he defected from Broadway to Hollywood, planning to return to New York "when possible."

Now using the professional name of Arthur Kennedy (Equity already had a John Kennedy registered), he arrived at Warners and won the role of James Cagney's brother, Eddie, in *City for Conquest,* directed by Anatole Litvak. The plot found rugged Cagney fighting his way to eventual blindness and misery in order to finance his brother's dream and to reconcile his broken romance with neighborhood girl friend Ann Sheridan. To Arthur's credit, he managed to instill the idealistic role with enough character and likeability to overcome the part's difficult facets, which could have produced audience resentment. The *New York Times* rated Kennedy "a pleasing newcomer."

A Warners' contract accompanied the performance, and Elia Kazan, who played a small part in *City of Conquest,* recalls, "Warner's plan was to have me replace George Raft when he got too old, and Arthur was going to be the next Cagney." Unfortunately, things never worked out that way. Along with Dennis Morgan, Ronald Reagan, Wayne Morris, and William Lundigan, Arthur was shuffled into top supporting roles in the A films, with leading roles in the double bill entries.

In his secondary lead capacity, Arthur performed in several top notch productions: *High Sierra* (1941), in which he played an inexperienced hood whose assistance to Humphrey Bogart in a last big heist ends in an exploding car; *They Died with Their Boots on* (1941), in which he gave Errol Flynn a rough time as a feuding fellow West Point graduate; and *Air Force* (1943) in which he played a bombardier in a straightforward chronicle of a flying fortress crew's adventures. Leading parts in such modest pictures as a Younger brother in *Bad Men of Missouri* (1941) and the cocky fighter of *Knockout* (1941) gave Kennedy audience exposure, if not the desired stardom.

As with many other Hollywood figures, the war cut into Kennedy's career. After playing the dissipated Bramwell Bronte of the celebrated Bronte clan in *Devotion* (shot in 1943, released in 1946), Kennedy entered the Air Force, became a private, and spent the majority of his time making training films. "Some of the films I was in, and others I narrated—I can't recall titles—are still being used, I'm told, as standard lecture material," he said recently. Upon his military discharge, he settled with the brothers Warner by appearing in *Cheyenne* (1947), his third film with director Raoul Walsh, portraying the infamous Sundance Kid. It was his last experience with a long-term contract and he has freelanced ever since.

After departing from Warners, Kennedy accepted an offer to appear in a film by his friend Elia Kazan (now a director), called *Boomerang.* Shot largely in Stamford, Connecticut, and White Plains, New York, and stocked mainly with players from New York's Group Theatre, the feature cast Arthur as an innocent ex-G.I., railroaded into a murder accusation by circumstantial evidence. It was quite a film, and one which James Agee (*The Nation*) lauded. It "never tries to get beyond the very good best that good journalistic artists can do, but on that level it is a triumph, a perfect job." As for Kennedy's handling of the pivotal fall guy assignment, the *New York Times* decided he is convincingly distraught as the suspect tagged for slaughter, especially the third-degree sequence." This film earned Kennedy a boost in critical attention and served as the background for his later meeting with playwright Arthur Miller.

"I think Miller thought, quite correctly, that 'Johnny' Kennedy was the very model of the all-American boy, an exceptionally honest, fine actor, and an exceptionally nice person," recalls Kazan. His opinion is supported by Miller's subsequent casting of Kennedy as Chris Keller, the veteran who discovers his father to be a war profiteer in *All My Sons,* which opened on Broadway on January 29, 1947. It was the beginning of a most rewarding relationship professionally between Kennedy and Miller. Other Miller characters that Kennedy has created on the Broadway stage are Biff in the classic *Death of a Salesman* (for which Kennedy won the 1949 Best Supporting Actor Tony Award) John Proctor, farmer turned defender at the Salem witch trials in *The Crucible* (January, 1953), and Walter Franz, the successful but bitter doctor of *The Price* (February, 1968). Ironically, although Kennedy has been a Miller favorite on Broadway, he has not appeared in any film versions of that playwright's works. When *Death of a Salesman* was filmed in 1951, Columbia selected Kevin McCarthy to play Biff.

Kennedy's subsequent film career has been expansive, and perhaps can be best summed up by the films for which he was Oscar-nominated.

Champion (1949) is perhaps the finest picture ever made about boxing. It made a star of Kirk Douglas, pushed Mark Robson to directorial prominence, and began the Robson-Kennedy professional relationship that resulted not only in this Oscar nomination for the actor, but the next three nominated films as well. Kennedy played Douglas' devoted, crippled brother, Connie Kelly, and served as the "conscience" of the film. He lost the Best Supporting Player's Oscar to Dean Jagger (*Twelve O'Clock High*).

With Lizabeth Scott in Too Late for Tears *(UA 1949)*

Bright Victory was a superb, powerful film that starred Arthur as a blinded war veteran attempting to readjust to civilian life. The film was shot at the Veterans Hospital at Valley Forge, Pennsylvania, where ten totally blind ex-GI.s were hired to teach the cast to play their blindness convincingly. In addition, Kennedy wore opaque contact lenses so that he was virtually blind when before the cameras. His beautiful interpretation won him the New York Film Critics' Award for Best Actor, and a Best Actor Oscar nomination. Humphrey Bogart of (*The African Queen*) was the Oscar winner that year.

Trial (1955) was MGM's complex but interesting story that found Kennedy as Barney, the Communist lawyer seeking to make a martyr of a young Mexican rapist-murderer (Rafael Campos) for the Red cause. It is a prime example of Kennedy's capacity to etch shrewd, unsympathetic characterizations. It won him a Golden Globe Award and another Oscar bid (he lost the Best Supporting Actor's award to Jack Lemmon of *Mr. Roberts*).

Peyton Place was described by the National Board of Review as "an example of how a fine motion picture can be made out of a cheap and dirty book." In this film version of the Grace Metalious best seller, Kennedy drew complete dislike from audiences as Lucas Cross, the leering, unshaven, drunken school janitor who rapes his stepdaughter (Hope Lange), and who is killed subsequently by her. Being Kennedy's fourth nomination in a Robson picture, it is obvious why Arthur dubbed the director his "walking rabbit's foot." Red Buttons *(Sayonara)* won the Best Supporting Academy Award this round.

Some Came Running (1958) the Vincente Minnelli-directed version of James Jones' novel, cast Kennedy in another unlikeable role, that of Frank Sinatra's selfish, social-climbing brother, who is not above indulging in a sordid romance with his jewelry store secretary (Nancy Gates). His last Oscar nomination to date (Burl Ives won the Best Supporting Actor's award for *The Big Country*), the film demonstrates once again how versatile Kennedy is at depicting different aspects of the contemporary man.

While the above array of motion pictures were and are quite prestigious, both in intent and, usually, in budget, Arthur was a workmanlike performer who hardly ever rejected an offer for less important chores. As a result, he gave enjoyable accountings of himself in films like *The Walking Hills* (1949), a Randolph Scott Western in which he sought buried treasure in Death Valley, *Red Mountain* (1951), an action tale in which Alan Ladd saves him from a lynch mob, and *Crashout* (1955), in which he joins William Bendix in a prison breakout. An unusual film he did was

Fritz Lang's *Rancho Notorious* (1952), one of the few films that Kennedy has made which has left him with concrete memories, due largely to his glamorous co-star, Marlene Dietrich. Kennedy recollects, "That woman ate like a Danish stevedore and drank champagne. She told me about her lovers. Hell, she went through the whole French cabinet, but she said Jean Gabin was her favorite."

Despite Arthur's capacity for versatility, moviemakers have often thrown him into stereotypes. When Sterling Hayden refused to leave his boating to make *A Summer Place* (1959) Delmer Daves hired Kennedy to portray Bart Hunter, the drunken father of Troy Donahue. It was a role with many parallels to his *Peyton Place* assignment. His part of Jim Lefferts in the Richard Brooks-directed *Elmer Gantry* was a direct foreshadowing of his similar reporter's role in David Lean's *Lawrence of Arabia* (1962). Since his experience in *Italiano Brava Gente* (1964), Kennedy has taken to working increasingly in Italy: *Kiss Thy Hand* (1973) and *Rico* (1974), *The Police Can't Move* (1975). Kennedy explains this preference because he feels the filmmakers there have the enthusiasm and capabilities no longer a part of Hollywood.

Kennedy has worked regularly on television, appearing as early as 1954 on "Ford Theatre," and since then has appeared on episodes of most of the dramatic series. He has made three telefeatures: *The Movie Murderer* (1970), *Crawlspace* (1972), and *The President's Plane Is Missing* (1973). In early 1974 he appeared on the special, *Portrait: The Man from Independence,* in which Robert Vaughan impersonated Harry Truman. *Variety* reported, "Most of the cast performed ably, with special credit to Arthur Kennedy, who looked and sounded exactly as a tough and corrupt political boss might." After so many years in the medium, Kennedy finally tackled a video series, when in the fall of 1974 he played the sheriff in the program "Nakia," starring Robert Forster.

Nor has Kennedy ever divorced himself from the stage. Aside from his work in Arthur Miller shows, he has appeared on Broadway in *Time Limit* (January 1956), concerning North Korean brain-washing of American P.O.W.s, and in 1961 he starred in *Becket* with Sir Laurence Olivier, replacing a departing Anthony Quinn. He later toured with Olivier in the Jean Anouilh historical drama, and followed the tour with a three week return engagement in New York. In November, 1973, Arthur starred with Eileen Heckart in *Veronica's Room,* a wild little chiller by Ira (*Rosemary's Baby*) Levin that incorporated into its tight script, ritual murder, incest, necrophilia, and insanity. One reviewer labeled the show "perversions for the whole family." The drama closed before the end of

1973, and Kennedy's experience with this stage venture led him to state, "You've got to get an author when he's young and start kicking his brains in. Once they've won a Pulitzer Prize, they're practically useless to you. I think all playwrights should be under 30."

Kennedy is tapering off gradually from strenuous work these days. "I don't like working six days a week. I miss my Saturdays. I'm getting a little fat and sassy from tv commercials. I do a few of them every year, voice off stuff mainly, and I can live from that money alone." Married since 1938 to his only wife, Mary Cheffey, with two grown children, the actor mainly divides his time between a Palm Beach apartment building that he owns and lives in, and a Nova Scotia farm.

Despite his many memorable film portrayals, he candidly admits, "Films don't hold any memories for me. I do know I enjoyed the westerns. And then there was a Mark Robson film—yes, *Trial*, that was it—and an Elia Kazan thing—*Boomerang*, wasn't it?" He no longer even tries to recall what fellow players were in what pictures with him ("I'm terrible at names"). While many of Kennedy's features were praised for their realism, Arthur attests today, "Perhaps I'm an old-fashioned romantic, but I believe movies should be fantasy." He adds that movies worked to create "fantastic images," reminiscing that if a director "wanted 10,000 Indians he could get them—if he wanted a white elephant, he could get one. The eye was constantly startled, and naturally we actors enjoyed every minute of it."

He sums up his craft: "Films were a magic box. All of life was in them. If you wanted heroes, there they were. If you wanted passion, or love, or tenderness, they were there too. Our job was to give people confidence that 'goodies' came out best in the end and 'baddies' don't—today's films give people more worries."

ARTHUR KENNEDY

City for Conquest   (WB 1940)
The Santa Fe Trail   (WB 1940)
High Sierra   (WB 1941)
Strange Alibi   (WB 1941)
Knockout   (WB 1941)
Highway West   (WB 1941)
Bad Men of Missouri   (WB 1941)
They Died with Their Boots on   (WB 1941)
Desperate Journey   (WB 1942)
Air Force   (WB 1943)
Devotion   (WB 1946)
Boomerang   (20th 1947)
Cheyenne   (WB 1947)
The Walking Hills   (Col 1949)
Champion   (UA 1949)
The Window   (RKO 1949)
Too Late for Tears   (UA 1949)
Chicago Deadline   (Par 1949)
The Glass Menagerie   (WB 1950)
Along the Great Divide   (WB 1951)
Bright Victory   (Univ 1951)
Red Mountain   (Par 1951)
Bend of the River   (Univ 1952)
Rancho Notorious   (RKO 1952)
The Girl in White   (MGM 1952)
The Lusty Men   (RKO 1952)
Crashout   (Filmakers 1955)
The Man from Laramie   (Col 1955)
Trial   (MGM 1955)
The Naked Dawn   (Univ 1955)
The Desperate Hours   (Par 1955)

The Rawhide Years   (Univ 1956)
Peyton Place   (20th 1957)
Twilight for the Gods   (Univ 1958)
Some Came Running   (MGM 1958)
A Summer Place   (WB 1959)
Elmer Gantry   (UA 1960)
Home is the Hero   (Showcorporation 1961)
Claudelle Inglish   (WB 1961)
Murder She Said   (MGM 1962)
Hemingway's Adventures of a Young Man   (20th 1962)
Barabbas   (Col 1962)
Lawrence of Arabia   (Col 1962)
Cheynne Autumn   (WB 1964)
Joy in the Morning   (MGM 1965)
Murieta   (WB 1965)
Italiano Brava Gente   (Emb 1966)
Nevada Smith   (Par 1966)
Fantastic Voyage   (20th 1966)
A Minute to Pray, A Second to Die   (Cin 1968)
Anzio   (Col 1968)
Day of the Evil Gun   (MGM 1968)
Monday's Child   (unreleased 1968)
Hail Hero   (National General 1969)
Shark   (Excelsior 1970)
Glory Boy (a.k.a. My Old Man's place)   (Cin 1971)
Kiss Thy Hand (a.k.a. Ferente)   (Italian 1973)
Rico   (Film Venture, International 1974)
Fin De Semana Para Los Muetos   (Spanish-Italian 1974)
The Antichrist   (Italian 1974)
The Police Can't Move   (Italian 1975)

55

Evelyn Keyes

With Rita Hayworth so consistently hugging the spot-light at Columbia Pictures throughout the 1940s, it was very difficult for other female players on the stu-dio's roster to claim much career attention, no matter how talented. Certainly, blonde, blue-eyed Evelyn Keyes had all the prerequisites for screen success: a shapely figure, poise, a talent for dancing, and a sense of timing that allowed her to excel (when given that rare chance) in comedy, drama, or musical.

She was born in Port Arthur, Texas on November 20, 1919 and when she was only a baby, her father, who was in the oil business, died. The family moved to Atlanta, Georgia, where she was educated and studied music and dancing. Hopes for a ballet career diminished to a chorus line job in a second-rate nightclub. However, in 1935 she won a beauty con-test sponsored by Universal Studios and, as a prize, accepted a free trip to Hollywood and a screen test. Nothing developed from her "break" and she re-turned to Atlanta and the chorus line. But then later, while visiting her sister in Los Angeles, she met Jeanie MacPherson, one-time silent screen actress and, for many years, Cecil B. DeMille's top scriptwriter. De-Mille signed Evelyn to a personal contract and pro-vided her with a small role, as Madeleine, in his epic *The Buccaneer* (1938). She appeared in four minor roles in Paramount pictures and returned to DeMille, playing Mrs. Calvin in his 1939 *Union Pacific*. She

then was Mary Patterson, the daughter of Charles Ruggles and Marjorie Rambeau in a dismal farce called *Sudden Money* (1939).

Margaret Mitchell, in her monumental novel *Gone with the Wind*, describes Suellen as "an annoying sis-ter with her whining and selfishness" and because Evelyn Keyes' acting in the 1939 MGM classic of Mrs. Mitchell's Civil War-set novel personified the des-cription of Scarlett O'Hara's (Vivien Leigh) sister Suel-len so aptly, she was signed to a long term contract by Columbia. About the pivotal role of Suellen, Miss Keyes has said, "I thought I was getting a wonderful break when Mr. Selznick agreed to let me play the role of Suellen in the year's biggest picture. But Suel-len, in spite of her importance in the novel, meant little in the finished movie. I worked on the picture for months and months—and wound up on the cutting room floor. But I was glad to be in it and work for Victor Fleming, who is a grand director."

Her first role for Columbia was Francois Morestan, Brian Aherne's daughter, in *Lady in Question* (1940), a film which featured Rita Hayworth and Glenn Ford. At Columbia her career continued, playing Boris Kar-loff's understanding daughter, Martha Garth, in *Be-fore I Hang* (1940) and then, a blind girl, Helen Williams, loved by disfigured Peter Lorre in *The Face Behind the Mask* (1941). But it was as Bette Logan in Alexander Hall's whimsical spoof of the hereafter and here-now, *Here Comes Mr. Jordan* (1941) that she was applauded critically for a beautiful performance

With Ann Savage, Lynn Merrick, Edmund Lowe, and Anita Louise in a publicity pose for Dangerous Blondes *(Col 1943)*

With Lee J. Cobb and Dick Powell in Johnny O'Clock *(Col 1947)*

in a highly professional and competitive comedy cast that included Robert Montgomery, Edward Everett Horton, and Claude Rains. Her progression as an actress was evident as Lucy, the maid who discovers mayhem in *Ladies in Retirement* (1941) and, although unflatteringly photographed, she was acceptable as Glenn Ford's love, Ruth Morley, in *The Adventures of Martin Eden.* For the next two years her assignments were less than exciting in Columbia B pictures.

While Evelyn's Columbia screen career was sedate, unspectacular, and only successful in a cumulative sense, her private life was far more spectacular. In 1938 she had wed Barton Leon Bainbridge, an architect and owner of a swimming pool corporation. One month following their separation, in the summer of 1940, Bainbridge sat in his car with a rifle between his knees, braced against his chest and pulled the trigger. Some thirty-three months later, on March 3, 1943, she married Charles Vidor, a handsome Hungarian (born on July 27, 1906) who, during the Forties, became Columbia's most serviceable director. He had helmed Evelyn's *Lady in Question.* Vidor had formerly been the husband of actress Karen Morley and, after his divorce from Keyes, would marry Harry Warner's daughter, Doris Warner LeRoy. Vidor also took Columbia's belligerent mogul, Harry Cohn, to court in 1946, trying to break his contract with the studio and charging Cohn with using multiple and colorful obscenities, and abusive language. The judge decided against Vidor, maintaining Cohn's normal conversation was composed of vulgar, superlative language.

By November, 1944, Evelyn Louise Keyes Bainbridge Vidor had separated from Vidor and returned to Columbia as an entrancing Genie in a nonsensical, color fantasy, *A Thousand and One Nights* (1945) with Cornel Wilde, Phil Silvers, and Rex Ingram (repeating his spirit's role from *The Thief of Bagdad,* 1940). And, in late June, 1946, she met the son of her good friend Walter Huston, with whom she had been on a bond-selling tour during the War when the elder Huston, proud of his actor-son's accomplishments as U.S. Signal Corps major John Huston, talked incessantly of his boy John. Three weeks after meeting John Huston the two dined at Romanoff's and John impulsively asked Evelyn to marry him. "When?" she asked. "Right now, tonight." Huston's directorial abilities were never more apparent than that July night in 1946 when he sent Mike Romanoff home to get a wedding band someone had lost in his pool, chartered a plane and, at 3:30 A.M., married Evelyn Keyes before Justice of the Peace Gene Ward with Paul Mantz, the chartered plane pilot, and a taxi-cab driver as witnesses.

Sidney Skolsky is credited with the idea of a film biography of Al Jolson, but it was Harry Cohn's reverence for the art of the star that turned the project into a reality. *The Jolson Story* (1946) accomplished several milestones. The film made an instant star (if of short endurance) of Larry Parks, showcased the talents of Evelyn Keyes, made a profit for Columbia of over eight million dollars on a cost of two million, eight hundred thousand, and re-established Al Jolson in show business so that he became one of the highest paid stars on radio's weekly "Kraft Music Hall," at $5,500 weekly.

Of the many films Evelyn made during the Forties and into the early Fifties she is remembered best today as Julie Benson (a thickly disguised portrayal of Ruby Keeler) in *The Jolson Story,* a role for which she spent long hours rehearsing dance routines with Columbia's dance authority, Audrienne Brie. *Photoplay* magazine lavished Gold Medal Awards on *The Jolson Story.* Producer Sidney Skolsky, Al Jolson, Larry Parks, Harry Cohn, and Evelyn Keyes, all received Gold Medals, as did, of course, the film itself. The typically unpleasant Bosley Crowther (*New York Times*) was one of the contra-opinions who insisted, "Nor is Evelyn Keyes any more than pretty in the eminently vapid role of a musical comedy actress who is married to Jolson and finds, for unconvincing reasons, that it won't work."

After her adequate performance in *The Jolson Story,* she was Nancy Hobson with Dick Powell in *Johnny O'Clock* (1947). Her performance was dominated by an eagerness to appear as an exceptionally good person, which resulted in a good deal of overacting, and her efforts as a super efficient Millie McGonigle turning into a chic chick with Glenn Ford in *The Mating of Millie* (1948) was dismissed as "run of the mill-ie."

On location in Mexico with her husband Huston, who was filming Warner Bros.' *The Treasure of the Sierra Madre* (1948), Evelyn and John adopted a Mexican boy, Pablo Albarran, but in the following year the marriage collapsed. Evelyn left the 480-acre Huston ranch in San Fernando Valley, telling the press, "John is the best director and the worst husband in Hollywood." She elaborated on her allergy to fur and the animals that abounded in Huston's menagerie in the valley, claiming she had to share her husband's time with wild horses, dogs, cats, monkeys that had not been housebroken, goats, pigs, and a burro named Socrates that her good friend Paulette Goddard had sent to her. The parting with Huston was amicable and they tossed a coin for a set of Incan figures rather than wrangle over their community property status. Evelyn won. On February 10, 1950,

Huston obtained a Mexican divorce from his allergy-ridden wife Evelyn, and the following day he married Enrica Soma.

As Kathy O'Fallon, a Boston-bred turn-of-the-century girl who is transported to the great Northwest as the bride of Royal Northwest Mounted Policeman Mike Flannigan (Dick Powell), Evelyn gave an honest, believable, dramatic performance in *Mrs. Mike* (1949). Louella O. Parsons was so excited about her performance that she gave her the Parsons' *Cosmopolitan* Award and gushed over an entire day's column when Evelyn returned from shooting scenes in Manhattan for *The Killer that Stalked New York* (1950), in which she portrayed a smallpox victim. Having left Columbia, Evelyn provided distaff decoration for yet another remake of Universal's *The Iron Man* (1951) with Jeff Chandler and newcomer Rock Hudson providing the oncamera masculinity. She then left for Acapulco and serious beachcombing, but an offer to co-star with Van Heflin ended her Mexican holiday. She returned to make United Artists' *The Prowler* (1951), directed by Joseph Losey from a well-developed, well-constructed script by one-time blacklisted Dalton Trumbo. Miss Keyes still considers *The Prowler,* in which Heflin, passionately in love with her, plans to kill her husband, the best thing she did onscreen. She was paid a nominal salary for the film but was given a percentage of the profits and as such made extensive personal appearances with the film to boost its boxoffice receipts. She spent the summer of 1953 touring in *I Am a Camera* and left for England to film *Rough Shoot* (released in the States as *Shoot First*) based on an Eric Ambler espionage caper, in which Joel McCrea was her co-star. And then she met the irrepressible Avrumele Goldbogen, better known to the world as Michael Todd.

Her long, intense friendship with Mr. Todd was mutually beneficial. Todd appreciated her liberal candor and had never known a woman like her. "Marriage?" she told Louella Parsons. "No. I'm not going to marry anyone. I've been married three times and struck out." Her love for Todd appeared unselfish and unconditional but she went to a psychiatrist for stabilization and to deal more effectively with Todd. Yet she told reporters, "It has been a lot of fun the last two years; I have enjoyed my freedom and I don't know as I would want to give it up." During the hectic filming of Todd's *Around the World in 80 Days* (1956) the producer engaged a yacht to film a Japanese sailing master, the Kawio Maru, under full sail. Among the guests invited for the sailing were Evelyn, Kevin McClory, Ketti Frings and husband, and Mi-

Publicity pose (1946)

353

chael Wilding and his then wife, Elizabeth Taylor. Everything about Todd was extravagant and his *80 Days* was his most colossal production. Evelyn's last role had been as Helen Sherman, Tom Ewell's wife in *The Seven Year Itch* (1955), and for Todd she played one of many cameo roles in his block-busting film, that of a pretty flirt in the Place Vendome in Paris. The following year she married again and the pundits and scribes were tagging the marriage a disaster.

In Paris she had met an old acquaintance from Hollywood. They fell in love and found peace and contentment for five years in Spain where they married, built a home, and confounded their detractors. The man was marathon-groom Artie Shaw, and Evelyn Keyes became his eighth wife. Shaw's marriages had lasted in varying years from one to four and included sprints from the altar with Lana Turner (3), Jerome Kern's daughter Betty (4), Ava Gardner (5), author of *Forever Amber* Kathleen Winsor (6) and, prior to Evelyn, Doris Dowling (7). Still married to Shaw, Evelyn says, "I am absolutely happy now, because we have a good marriage and, suddenly, in my middle age, I have a completely new career. At the end of last year [1971] my first novel was published. [*I Am a Billboard*] and I'm working on my second." She credits her lengthy separations from her husband as having added to the longevity of her marriage with Shaw, and cites a two year stint in London working on British television when she saw very little of her talented husband. Her TV appearances in the United States have been rare, from a guest shot on an early "Jack Carson Show" to ABC's "The Ugliest Girl in Town" in 1968, a title in no way referring to Mrs. Artie Shaw. More recently, on stage, Evelyn has been touring in the road company of *No, No, Nanette,* playing the role Ruby Keeler did in the Broadway revival. The show opened in Dallas on October 6, 1972 and closed in Woodbridge, New Jersey on August 4, 1973. Also with her in the company were Don Ameche and Ruth Donnelly. Currently she is completing her autobiography.

The candid Evelyn seldom looks back but has noted that her whole Hollywood career was in a bunch of junk—excluding *The Jolson Story* and *Gone with the Wind*—and adds: "That's the way it was for me. I never really got anything to do that was great. We're all ill-prepared for what we start out to do. We have to decide too early in our lives what we're going to do and we haven't had enough experience. Life forces you into something you know so little about. But you can't go on being a student. You have to pay for a living."

EVELYN KEYES

The Buccaneer   *(Par 1938)*
Men with Wings   *(Par 1938)*
Sons of the Legion   *(Par 1938)*
Dangerous to Know   *(Par 1938)*
Artists and Models Abroad   *(Par 1938)*
Union Pacific   *(Par 1939)*
Paris Honeymoon   *(Par 1939)*
Sudden Money   *(Par 1939)*
Slightly Honorable   *(UA 1939)*
Gone with the Wind   *(MGM 1939)*
Lady in Question   *(Col 1940)*
Before I Hang   *(Col 1940)*
Beyond the Sacramento   *(Col 1940)*
The Face behind the Mask   *(Col 1941)*
Here Comes Mr. Jordan   *(Col 1941)*
Ladies in Retirement   *(Col 1941)*
The Adventures of Martin Eden   *(Col 1942)*
Flight Lieutenant   *(Col 1942)*
Dangerous Blondes   *(Col 1943)*
The Desperadoes   *(Col 1943)*
There's Something about a Soldier   *(Col 1943)*
Nine Girls   *(Col 1944)*
Strange Affair   *(Col 1944)*

A Thousand and One Nights   *(Col 1945)*
The Thrill of Brazil   *(Col 1946)*
Renegades   *(Col 1946)*
The Jolson Story   *(Col 1946)*
Johnny O'Clock   *(Col 1947)*
The Mating of Millie   *(Col 1948)*
Enchantment   *(RKO 1948)*
Mr. Soft Touch   *(Col 1949)*
Mrs. Mike   *(UA 1949)*
The Killer that Stalked New York   *(Col 1950)*
Smuggler's Island   *(Univ 1951)*
The Iron Man   *(Univ 1951)*
The Prowler   *(UA 1951)*
One Big Affair   *(UA 1952)*
Rough Shoot (a.k.a. Shoot First)   *(UA 1953)*
99 River Street   *(UA 1953)*
Hell's Half Acre   *(Rep 1954)*
It Happened in Paris   *(French 1954)*
Top of the World   *(UA 1955)*
The Seven Year Itch   *(20th 1955)*
Around the World in 80 Days   *(UA 1956)*

56

Joan Leslie

At the American Film Institute's 1974 testimonial, Life Achievement award-winner James Cagney recalled how much the movies used "types"— "We had them, oh, how we did have them!" They certainly had them at Cagney's main studio, Warner Bros., where an entire fleet of familiar faces sacrificed repertorial challenges for weekly paychecks. There was George Brent, invariably successful and level-headed, zesty "oomph" girl Ann Sheridan, John Garfield, always sporting a chip on his shoulder, Olivia de Havilland, always in healthy and productive possession of her needs, and so forth.

A favorite Warners starlet of the 1940s was Joan Leslie, whose beauty was so fresh and wholesome that her name was a virtual synonym for the work ingenue. Reaching her popularity peak during the war years, she was a perfect symbol of the wide-eyed, good girl next door, even though few people were fortunate enough to have such gorgeous neighbors. The tens of thousands of G.I.s who sent for her studio photograph did not want or expect the heavy-panting glamour of Sex Goddess Rita Hayworth, or even the pure but sassy charm of a Betty Grable, but rather a girl who would be the ideal girl to bring home to mother.

Joan's face was radiant with a soft beauty that, with appropriate makeup, could be transformed into absolute glamour (though it rarely was). Her figure was slender but well enough endowed to please the most red-blooded male. Her acting was quiet enough nev-

er to interfere with the gentle ambiance of her looks, and since her Warners' chores were frequently more lightly decorative than heavily thespianic, it was rarely tested. In fact, whenever Joan did supply some histrionics, as in *The Hard Way* (1942), critics and audiences were so awed by this bonus touch that the actress received more accolades than she actually deserved.

She was born in Detroit, Michigan, on January 26, 1925, and christened Joan Agnes Theresa Sadie Brodel. The third of three sisters in a family kept close by a deep love of music, she made her stage debut at age two and a half, singing "Let a Smile Be Your Umbrella". The three sisters performed for local socials and events, accompanied on the piano by their mother. When Joan was nine, the girls, billed as "The Three Brodels," went on the road professionally, appearing in stage shows up and down the east coast. By this time, Joan had added movie star impersonations to her singing and dancing repertoire. When Mr. Brodel lost his job with a Detroit bank in the Depression, he joined his family on the road.

Joan recalls of those days: "We were a very unorthodox group. We weren't a family with any theatrical tradition. To the contrary, we were just a close clan that sang and danced together for sheer enjoyment, and we were thrilled when someone paid us to perform. It was a crazy-quilt kind of childhood, but

With Ronald Reagan in This Is the Army *(WB 1943)*

With Margaret Early and Robert Alda in Cinderella Jones *(WB 1946)*

357

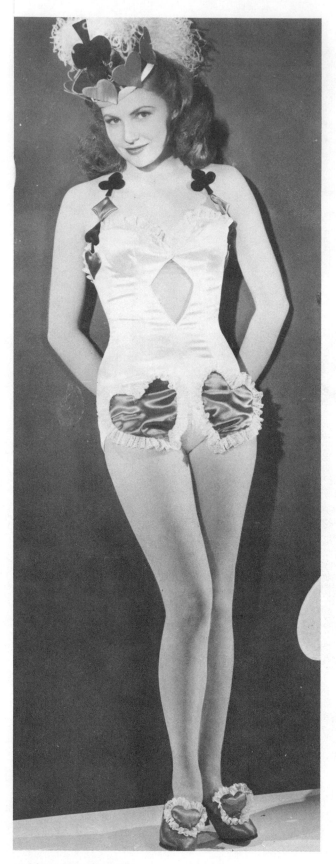

Publicity pose ca. 1944

thank goodness my parents were along to help keep us on an even keel.''

The young lady's exceptional looks reaped dividends early in her career, and in 1935, she became a model for John Robert Powers, earning the attractive fee of five dollars an hour. Eventually, the Brodels landed a Broadway engagement at the Paradise Club, where the eleven-year-old's juvenile sparkle won her a screen test for MGM.

Of that long-ago test, Joan remembers: ''It was a family affair. My mother wrote the script and my dog appeared in the scene with me. On the strength of the test, MGM signed me. We went to Hollywood and I was given a small role in *Camille* as Robert Taylor's little sister. I went to the studio school with Mickey Rooney, Freddie Bartholomew, and Deanna Durbin —that was right before she went to Universal.''

Joan's bit in Greta Garbo's *Camille* (1936) was hardly a showcase. Metro really did not have plans to launch any new child prodigies, and dropped Joan at the end of her first option. She returned to the family act in the East, but was barely back on the circuit before sister Mary was signed by Universal. This event prompted the family to return to Hollywood again, where Joan also tried to land a Universal contract, but to no avail. Nevertheless, Joan managed to make the rounds of casting offices and won bits in features at various studios, including three near walkons at Twentieth Century-Fox in 1940 and a part that year in Warner Bros.' short subject, *Alice in Movieland.*

It was Warners' who ultimately took note of her, signed her to a contract, and changed her name to Joan Leslie.

Looking quite mature for a girl of fifteen, Joan made her feature debut at Warners' in *High Sierra* (1941). She played the crippled daughter of migrating Henry Travers, and had the unique screen name of Velma Goodshoe. In the course of the Raoul Walsh-directed feature, Humphrey Bogart, as a hood freshly released from prison, meets her and is so impressed by her innocent beauty that he pays for an operation to correct her clubfoot. His fantasies of beginning life anew with this lovely, fresh creature are shattered when she takes up with a sharpie and rejects her benefactor. *High Sierra* was endorsed by most critics and by much of the film-going public.

After some assembly-line fare in *Thieves Fall Out* (1941), *The Great Mr. Nobody* (1941), and *The Wagons Roll at Night* (1941)—the latter a dismal reworking of the studio's 1937 *Kid Galahad*—Joan suddenly began receiving top treatment from Warner Bros. On her sixteenth birthday, Jack L. Warner, head of the studio, not only gave her a new Buick, but announced that she would play the role of Gary Cooper's bride in the upcoming *Sergeant York* (1941). The feature, with the real-life Alvin York supplying technical supervision, was Warners' epic of the year. It emerged as an intelligent movie, gradually and sensitively presenting its argument for the necessity of pacifism to sometimes give way to fighting. Cooper's Oscar-winning performance kept both the hillbilly antics and military heroics from ever getting out of hand. The front office requested director Howard Hawks to showcase Joan's role as much as possible. The result was stardom for her. Her comeliness, however, was far more impressive than her acting here and the *New York Times* was forced to note, "Joan Leslie plays a mountain beauty with little more than a bright smile, a phony accent, and a tight dress."

The studio followed up on Joan's newly won status by casting her in some of their more prestigious upcoming projects. In *The Male Animal* (1942) she played Olivia de Havilland's sister who has her own modern ideas. (The role had been played on Broadway by Gene Tierney.) The film was a big hit, despite, as Ted Sennett observes in his book, *Warner Brothers Presents* (Arlington House, 1971), being "flattened by Warners' pile-driving approach to comedy and a cast that included such dubious farceurs as Joan Leslie and Don DeFore." *Yankee Doodle Dandy* (1942) cast Joan as Mary, the prompter who finally weds James Cagney's George M. Cohan. She was fetching in the role and charming in the film's extravaganza numbers, and, like everyone else connected with that film, she found her professional status boosted by it. A chance to display some histrionics occurred in *The Hard Way*. Although it was basically Ida Lupino's picture—she won the New York Film Critics Award for Best Actress for her expert bitchiness as she pushed talented sister Joan to the heights of show business—it was Joan who was being pushed, and she got plenty of screen notice.

Whatever her degree of acting inadequacies, they washed away in the light of the response she received from the wartime audiences. Her hazel-eyed, freckle-faced loveliness not only appealed to the boys, but to mothers too, and her film following grew rapidly. She began making a formidable showing in exhibitors' popularity polls.

Offscreen, she lived in Beverly Hills with her parents and sisters. Much of her time was unselfishly donated not only to the Hollywood Canteen but also to personal appearances at Army bases and defense plants. Columnists at the time were continually surprised to discover, upon meeting Joan, that she was not the mature young lady she appeared to be on-screen. She wore braces on her slightly protruding teeth, talked of her school days on the Warners' lot, and was liable to gush unabashedly about her success, "Oh, it's all like a wonderful dream!" This lack of sophistication was very refreshing, if somewhat jarring, to some members of the fourth estate. As one fan magazine wrote of Joan's naturalness, "This shocks Hollywood, for Hollywood is accustomed to 17-year-olds who act like 25-year-olds."

Warners kept careful gauge of their contractee's appeal. They too saw her as a talisman of another inspiration that made G.I.s want to win and get home, and this image was reflected in a number of Joan's wartime releases. In *This Is the Army* (1943), an unabashed ode to the fighting man, she appeared prominently, and sang* "No You, No Me" with Dennis Morgan; in *Thank Your Lucky Stars* (1943), she was a song writer involved in producing a Calvacade of Stars benefit and dueted "I'm Riding for a Fall" with Dennis Morgan. And in *Hollywood Canteen* (1944), which found Joan at the height of her career, she not only received top billing in the all-star production and the accolade of playing herself, but her presence also inspired the plot: Soldier Robert Hutton's adventures in getting to meet his favorite star—Joan Leslie. Said the *New York Times*, "Miss Leslie plays herself with elaborate sweetness."

In the midst of this good cheer for the fighting men, Warners agreed to loan Joan out to RKO in 1943. The temporary sacrifice of her services seemed worthwhile, for RKO wanted her to be Fred Astaire's newest dance partner in *The Sky's the Limit*. It was an honor indeed to be so selected, and much fuss was made when she celebrated her eighteenth birthday on the set, becoming Astaire's youngest leading lady. However, the film itself, directed by Edward H. Griffith, was no earth-shaking affair, casting Fred as a serviceman who, for some inane reason, would rather allow his new acquaintance Joan think of him as a bum rather than as a flyer. Joan was simply not up to the par of her predecessors, even the more sophisticated but less agile Joan Fontaine of *A Damsel in Distress* (1937). The *New York Times* wrote: "Apparently they are having trouble finding more than dancing partners for Mr. Astaire. They are also having trouble finding stories. He has neither in this. The simple fact is that Miss Leslie, while a gracious and neatly attractive miss, is not a Ginger Rogers when she tries to make with her feet." Neither of the two dance numbers Joan performs with Astaire in the picture are remembered as favorites by his admirers.

Perhaps Warners was disappointed in the reception afforded Joan's RKO foray, for upon her return to the

---

*Sally Sweetland (nee Mueller) often dubbed for Joan's vocalizing.

With James Craig (on ground), Jack Oakie, Ray Bennett, and Chill Wills in Northwest Stampede *(EL 1948)*

home lot she was used mainly in program-type fare. There were exceptions: She was very presentable in *Rhapsody in Blue* (1945), the biography of George Gershwin (Robert Alda), in which she played one of the women in his life. The other woman was Alexis Smith, and it was clever of the studio to cast two such disparate types to condense the wide range of Gershwin's romances. On loan to Twentieth Century-Fox, she was in *Where Do We Go From Here?* (1945), along with Fred MacMurray and June Haver, encased in an offbeat musical about a man (MacMurray), who has 4-F draft status. He shuttles back and forth in time from Valley Forge to the Santa Maria to Manhattan Island before eventually landing in the Marine Corps in 1945. However, *Too Young to Know* (1945) was a maudlin story of a veteran who, on returning home, finds his wife has given up their baby. *Cinderella Jones* (1946) again teamed her with Robert Alda in a silly mess in which she played a dumb girl who has to marry a bright man in order to inherit an estate. *Janie Gets Married* (1946) reunited her with Robert Hutton in a perpetuation of *Janie* (1944) that had starred Joyce Reynolds and hardly merited a sequel. Finally, *Two Guys from Milwaukee* (1946) was memorable only for its closing scene featuring surprise appearances by Humphrey Bogart and Lauren Bacall.

Miss Leslie then made the mistake of her career. She decided to break away from Warners, and succeeded only after a lengthy court battle. It was a big error, for she never again received the loving care that the studio originally had provided her or had continued to give her in admittedly smaller doses.

Joan fared poorly on the freelance market. *Repeat Performance* (1947) at Eagle-Lion used as the plot device the fantasy that a woman, who has murdered her husband, could wish so hard for a chance to relive the past year that it actually happens. The actual presentation did nothing to help the insecure premise. *Northwest Stampede,* the next year for the same company, was not much better; it was standard western material handicapped by a particularly unfunny Jack Oakie. After a two-year absence, Joan returned to the screen in decorative assignments, such as playing straight lady to Robert Walker in MGM's *The Skipper Surprises His Wife* (1950), and then settled into a series of westerns for Republic Pictures. The most interesting of these, none of which was that bad, was *Jubilee Trail* (1954), a Trucolor epic decked out for the benefit of Vera Ralston (as a flashy New Orleans gal), in which Joan was a lovely, quiet widow. Joan's last picture to date was Twentieth Century-Fox's *The Revolt of Mamie Stover* (1956), a mecca for

Jane Russell worshippers, in which subordinated Miss Leslie played a very patient Honolulu heiress involved with egoistic writer Richard Egan.

Joan was active in television in the early 1950s—she appeared as early as December, 1951 on the "Bigelow-Sanford Theatre"—but she gradually tapered off her career as the decade progressed. The main reason was her family. On St. Patrick's Day of 1950 in Santa Barbara, California, she had married Dr. William Caldwell, then about to enter into private practice as an obstetrician and gynecologist. On January 5, 1951, Joan gave birth to identical twin girls, Patrice and Ellen. She explained her departure from filmmaking after the mid-1950s by saying: "My daughters were five years old. I felt that they had reached an age when they needed me, but I never retired officially. I didn't close any doors behind me. Bill has always said that as long as it wasn't hard for me, and that it was something I enjoyed, I should work if and when I wanted to."

When her moviemaking days ended, Joan did feel a need for other activity and became involved in dress designing. Today, the Joan Leslie line of fashions is a well-established brand name in the industry. Presently, Joan resides in the Los Feliz area of Hollywood, and is very active in charity work for the St. Anne Home for Unwed Mothers.

As for her past, a now matronly Joan reminisces: "I have wonderful memories of my years in Hollywood. But honestly, it's really a hard life. There are many pitfalls, particularly for young girls. You tend to become so self-centered, accustomed to being the center of things. It's difficult to retain your equilibrium." Recently, Joan, whose last acting credit was a 1965 episode of TV's "Branded," said, "I think it would be exciting to return to performing now. The world has never been in a greater need of people reaching out to others—in whatever way their talent allows—so perhaps one of these days, I'll be back onscreen again." Thus in January, 1975 she made a cameo appearance on a segment of "Police Story" as Howard Duff's matronly wife.

JOAN LESLIE

As JOAN BRODEL
Camille   (MGM 1936)
Men with Wings   (Par 1938)
Two Thoroughbreds   (RKO 1939)
Love Affair   (RKO 1939)
Winter Carnival   (UA 1939)
Nancy Drew, Reporter   (WB 1939)
Susan and God   (MGM 1940)
Foreign Correspondent   (UA 1940)
Young as You Feel   (20th 1940)
Star Dust   (20th 1940)
High School   (20th 1940)
Military Academy   (Col 1940)
Laddie   (RKO 1940)

As JOAN LESLIE
High Sierra   (WB 1941)
The Great Mr. Nobody   (WB 1941)
The Wagons Roll at Night   (WB 1941)
Thieves Fall Out   (WB 1941)
Sergeant York   (WB 1941)
The Male Animal   (WB 1942)

Yankee Doodle Dandy   (WB 1942)
The Hard Way   (WB 1942)
This Is the Army   (WB 1943)
The Sky's the Limit   (RKO 1943)
Thank Your Lucky Stars   (WB 1943)
Hollywood Canteen   (WB 1944)
Where Do We Go from Here?   (20th 1945)
Rhapsody in Blue   (WB 1945)
Too Young to Know   (WB 1945)
Cinderella Jones   (WB 1946)
Janie Gets Married   (WB 1946)
Two Guys from Milwaukee   (WB 1946)
Repeat Performance   (EL 1947)
Northwest Stampede   (EL 1948)
The Skipper Surprised his Wife   (MGM 1950)
Born to Be Bad   (RKO 1950)
Man in the Saddle   (Col 1951)
Hellgate   (Lip 1952)
Toughest Man in Arizona   (Rep 1952)
Woman They Almost Lynched   (Rep 1953)
Flight Nurse   (Rep 1953)
Jubilee Trail   (Rep 1954)
Hell's Outpost   (Rep 1954)
The Revolt of Mamie Stover   (20th 1956)

Oscar Levant

57

Someone once asked Oscar Levant if he actually believed in God. His speedy reply was negative, but he quickly added, "I hope I'm wrong about this one thing." Levant took few chances and went from this earth with more silence than had been associated with his quixotic lifetime. His funeral at Westwood Memorial Cemetery on August 18, 1972, was as much like him as if he had written the script. High on his list of hates was funerals or anything the least funereal, and the word "death" was *verboten* in his presence. At the cemetery, there were no flowers, no sad songs, no eulogies, no service, no rabbi, and no mourners other than his immediate family, and a long-time friend, Goddard Lieberson, president of Columbia Records. Levant had come to believe his oft-quoted remark, "Half of my friends dislike me, and the other half despise me."

Levant's caustic comments were quoted and recorded with all the passionate devotion given to Dorothy Parker's one-liners. Mrs. Parker and the late Oscar had much in common beyond their acerbic, if often scintillating remarks, which they both frequently lashed out to wither the most sophisticated bystanders. They were both suicidal as well—a trait about which Robert Benchley once warned Dorothy Parker—to the extent of permanently impairing their health. But for sheer, psychopathic, neurotic genius, Oscar far outdistanced Dorothy Parker Campbell. Once he ably described himself: "There is a thin line between genius and insanity. I have erased that line."

Levant's iconoclastic presence graced merely a few films, but this biting essence saturated these pictures with a tanginess that makes each one memorable. His was the same topsy-turvy but highly relevant view of life that so enhanced the madcap humor of the Marx Brothers.

Max and Annie Levant owned a jewelry store in Pittsburgh, Pennsylvania, and were the parents of three sons, Harry, Howard, and Benjamin when, on December 27, 1906, their youngest son was born. They named him Oscar. Oscar's talent for the piano exceeded his scholastic accomplishments and, after his fifteenth birthday, he migrated to New York City where he studied piano with Sigismond Stojowski, former pupil and disciple of Paderewski. His first important pianist job was at Ciro's, then one of New York's brighter nightclubs, where Clifton Webb danced nightly with his partner Mary Hay. Levant joined Ben Bernie's band, played with several theatre-pit orchestras, and later met George Gershwin.

In point of fact, Oscar Levant had more of a "Gershwin" career than George Gershwin himself. Oscar was the first (after Gershwin) to record the haunting "Rhapsody in Blue" and, over the years, he became the greatest exponent of Gershwin music. He played annual summer concerts at Lewisohn Stadium and whenever a Gershwin memorial arose, Oscar

With Dan Dailey in You Were Meant for Me *(20th 1948)*

With Alexis Smith in Rhapsody in Blue *(WB 1945)*

was found playing the "Rhapsody," "Concerto in F," or the "Preludes." He virtually became Gershwin's alter ego and later admitted, "I was often lightheartedly acrimonious or sarcastic with him, but my real feeling for him was undiluted idolatry." Idolatry could not still Levant's acid tongue, and when Gershwin wondered aloud if his music would be played a hundred years in the future, Oscar brightly observed, "It will, George, if you're around to play it." Gershwin rarely doubted his capabilities and musical genius and, once, after expounding his virtues to Levant, Oscar asked, "Tell me, George, if you had it to do all over again, would you still fall in love with yourself?" The friendship flourished despite Oscar's continual barbs and Gershwin gave him an inscribed wrist watch that Levant considered a good luck charm. He wore it for years, and would not play a concert without it.

In this vein, Oscar's superstitions grew to manic proportions throughout the years, and he would tolerate nothing connected with the number thirteen, glibly explaining, "I am not superstitious, but I won't sleep 13 in a bed." He dealt with his other superstitious fears rigidly by tapping water faucets, clothing, and other presumed malevolent objects eight times until he developed an almost holy ritual toward everyday, meaningless things. Hypochondria also became a religion. S. N. Behrman, who dedicated a volume of his published plays to Levant, said, "There's nothing the matter with Oscar that a good miracle couldn't cure." His battle with booze ("I tried to become an alcoholic. I drank steadily for one year but it didn't take"); pills that he hoped would bring him instant unconsciousness did not; and his frequent excursions to mental hospitals ("People saw Mozart operas every year at Salzburg with the same regularity as I was committed") are detailed in three autobiographical books, *A Smattering Of Ignorance* (1940), *The Memoirs of an Amnesiac* (1965), and *The Unimportance of Being Oscar* (1968). He dedicated *Amnesiac* to his second wife, June, "who picked up the pieces."

Oscar's first marriage on January 5, 1932, lasted less than a year, and when ex-wife Barbara Smith married Arthur Loew, Levant called long distance on her wedding night to ask, "What's playing at Loew's State, and what time does the feature go on?" He explained his first matrimonial failure: "Besides incompatibility, we hated each other." His next marriage, to June Gale, occurred on December 1, 1939. She was the youngest of two sets of twins known professionally as the Gale Quadruplets. She had made her Broadway debut with her three sisters in George White's *Flying High* (1930), received star bill-

ing in White's eleventh edition of his *Scandals,* and arrived in Hollywood in 1934 for Paramount's *Melody in Spring.* In addition, she made a series of B films in the later 1930s.

Levant's Broadway debut on September 1, 1927, was in the hit show *Burlesque,* starring the great Hal Skelly and the new toast-of-the-town, Barbara Stanwyck. Oscar played Jerry Evans, a song writer, for 372 performances on Broadway and then toured with the show. When Paramount made their film version of *Burlesque* in 1929, retitled *The Dance of Life,* Levant and Skelly repeated their roles with Nancy Carroll in the Stanwyck part. Oscar remained in Hollywood writing music for several minor RKO films: *Street Girl* (1929), *Half Marriage* (1929), *Jazz Heaven* (1929), *The Delightful Rogue* (1929), *Side Street* (1929), *Tanned Legs* (1929), *Love Comes Along* (1930), and *Leathernecking* (1930). (For Fox's *Charlie Chan at the Opera,* 1936, Oscar would compose a mini-opera, *Carnival.*) He joined ASCAP in 1930 and, with Edward Heyman, wrote the standard "Blame It on My Youth" and, with Irving Caesar, he composed the less than memorable score for Fred Stone's musical, *Ripples.* Later, he composed the theme song for Will Roger's last film, *Steamboat Round the Bend* (1935).

His studies with Arnold Schoenberg, the great Viennese composer now living in Hollywood, equipped him to compose more serious music that included a piano sonatina, two string quartets, a piano concerto, and the "Overture of 1912" that he had playfully subtitled, "A Polka for Oscar Homolka." Between his composing he found time to conduct orchestras for two Broadway shows, *The Fabulous Invalid* (1938) and *The American Way* (1939) for which he also composed incidental music.

Levant's musical prowess aside, his greatest recognition came in 1938 on the first, and most literate, of the radio talk shows, "Information Please," where his sharp wit and intelligent answers to questions on music and sports brought him national fame. During the six years he was on the network show, he earned tags of *"l'enfant terrible"* and "the Henny Youngman of the Intelligentsia."

After George Gershwin's untimely death on July 11, 1937, Levant became the leading interpreter of Gershwin's compositions. That year he played the composer's "Concerto in F" (which Oscar preferred over "Rhapsody in Blue") at a memorial concert in the Hollywood Bowl. Eventually, he recorded virtually all of Gershwin's piano works, until, as he later defined it, "I played Gershwin music until it exuded from my body like an excretion of a drug."

During the early forties Levant made two features for Paramount, although he once said of his feelings about being an actor, that he was even nervous reciting the Pledge of Allegiance. The first film was Bing Crosby's *Rhythm on the River* (1940), and the second, *Kiss the Boys Goodbye* (1941), starring Mary Martin and Don Ameche, had Oscar in the part of Dick Rayburn, a composer. About the latter role, he once said, "It's the kind of part you get when the studio wants to break your contract." Between pictures he appeared on many of the major radio shows and missed being drafted into the U.S. Army due to his medical records, which scarcely substantiated his being alive, and by telling a psychiatrist when asked if he could kill, "I don't know about strangers, but friends, yes!"

He started giving concerts in 1942 after spending a year perfecting his technique. Billed as "Oscar Levant, Composer-Pianist, in Person, in a program of Piano Music and Comments," he would open his program by informing the audience, 'I neither play nor speak particularly well, so my manager decided on two inadequate performances for the price of one." But his renditions of Bach, Chopin, and, of course, Gershwin, were brilliant. He played with most of the major symphony orchestras and his summer tours in the "Gershwin Concerts" drew large crowds. On December 14, 1943, he appeared at Carnegie Hall with Eugene Ormandy and the Philadel-phia Orchestra playing his own concerto and Gershwin's "Rhapsody in Blue."

In 1945, Warner Bros. released an alleged biography of George Gershwin, *Rhapsody in Blue,* that starred Robert Alda as the doomed composer and Levant as Oscar Levant. Oscar recorded the title composition and Alda did an excellent job faking its performance onscreen. The success of the film brought Levant the role of Sid Jeffers, the mediator between socialite Joan Crawford and lower eastside fiddle genius John Garfield in *Humoresque* (1946) at Warner Bros. It is Levant's biting dialog that gives the very mediocre story some substance, leading the *New York Times* to comment, "Whatever meagre resemblance it may have to reasonable life in the world of working musicians (aside from Oscar Levant) is merest luck." It is in this Jean Negulesco-directed feature that Levant says of Crawford, "She's as complex as a Bach fugue." For an additional fee, Oscar was also a technical adviser on *Humoresque.* Thereafter, he became a regular on Al Jolson's "Kraft Music Hall" radio show in 1947, and the following year he appeared in Doris Day's first onscreen acting assignment, *Romance on the High Seas* (1948). As Levant phrased it, this film was made before Doris became a virgin.

With Janis Paige, Doris Day, and S. Z. Sakall in Romance on the High Seas *(WB 1948)*

For Twentieth Century-Fox he made *You Were Meant for Me* (1948) with Jeanne Crain and Dan Dailey, a musical that was dismissed by James Agee in one of his shortest reviews, "That's what you think!" With Fred Astaire and Ginger Rogers in their last film as a team, Oscar was acerbic Ezra Miller in the MGM musical *The Barkleys of Broadway* (1949). He had to mouth some witless dialog, such as "I find you highly resistible—you are unfettered by the slavery of talent."

By 1949 Oscar was appearing regularly on television with John Cameron Swayze on "Who Said That?" and on his own shortlived General Electric "Guest House" television show from which he was fired for belting nasty cracks to members of the show and less than gentlemanly remarks to his guests. He was replaced by Durward Kirby.

For MGM he made one of his best films, *An American in Paris* (1951), where he played all the instruments, conducted the orchestra and applauded himself in an ego-fantasy of Gershwin's "Concerto in F," a scene he devised himself. With Gene Kelly he sang "Tra-la-la" and he and Kelly joined Mary Young, she as an aging ballerina, in Gershwin's delightful waltz, "By Strauss." All of the production had a touch of magic on celluloid. In Twentieth Century-Fox's *O'Henry's Full House* (1952), he appeared with Fred Allen in the comic segment, *The Ransom of Red Chief*, which, to shorten the feature, was cut from the release print in parts of the United States and in Europe.

By 1953 his addiction to pills and constant trips to a psychiatrist (which he explained with, "I go every day—it gives me something to do") were taking their toll, and, after cancelling several concerts, he was reprimanded by the American Federation of Musicians. Throughout this trauma he made another film, *The I Don't Care Girl* (1953), starring Mitzi Gaynor, and, as it turned out, neither did most of the audience care about the film. Then, six weeks after suffering a coronary occlusion, he returned to MGM for one of his best screen parts as Lester Marton, who, with his wife Lily (Nanette Fabray), writes a musical for a faded Hollywood star (Fred Astaire) in *The Band Wagon* (1953). Levant's motion picture career ended at MGM where, for his last picture, he wrote his own scenes for *The Cobweb* (1955), a study of romance and desperation among the staff and patients at a mental sanitarium.

Heart attacks, stepped-up medication, and a growing neurosis that included an attempted suicide ("I was only trying to be dramatic") complicated Levant's stormy second marriage. On several occasions, June left him with their three daughters, Marcia, Lorna, and Amanda. Finally, she filed for legal separation in 1947 and, then, filed for a divorce in 1958. But she returned and endured the relationship, seemingly proving Oscar's observation that "marriage is a triumph of habit over hate." When Ralph Edwards wanted Levant for a segment of "This Is Your Life," Oscar claimed he could not find one friend. His recommendation for the lead in a proposed movie based on his life was Rosalind Russell but then he decided she was too masculine. His barbs continued to mount and his health declined. Of Leonard Bernstein, later conductor of the New York Philharmonic, he said, "He uses music as an accompaniment to his conducting and has been disclosing musical secrets that have been well-known for over four hundred years."

He was constantly apologizing for his rudeness, admitting that he had a talent for opening his mouth and immediately insulting several million people, and called himself the verbal vampire of television. On late night talk shows he referred to ballet as "the fairies' baseball," described Debbie Reynolds as "about as wistful as an iron foundry," and nominated Elizabeth Taylor as "the other woman of the year." To avoid possible law suits his shows were generally taped in advance.

Levant died in his home in Beverly Hills on August 14, 1972, of an apparent heart attack. He summed up his life as: "In some situations, I was difficult, in odd moments impossible, in rare moments loathsome, at my best, unapproachably great."

OSCAR LEVANT

The Dance of Life   *(Par 1929)*
Rhythm on the River   *(Par 1940)*
Kiss the Boys Goodbye   *(Par 1940)*
Rhapsody in Blue   *(WB 1945)*
Humoresque   *(WB 1946)*
You Were Meant for Me   *(20th 1948)*
Romance on the High Seas   *(WB 1949)*

The Barkleys of Broadway   *(MGM 1949)*
An American in Paris   *(MGM 1951)*
O'Henry's Full House (episode: Ransom of Red Chief)   *(20th 1952)*
The I Don't Care Girl   *(20th 1953)*
The Band Wagon   *(MGM 1953)*
The Cobweb   *(MGM 1955)*

58

John Lund

Each decade had its idealized personification of male beauty: Francis X. Bushman (1910s), Rudolph Valentino (1920s), Tyrone Power (1930s), Rock Hudson (1950s), Paul Newman (1960s), and Robert Redford (1970s). In the 1940s, when the William Holdens, Alan Ladds, Guy Madisons, and others of the Hollywood scene were the mark of cinema good looks to be matched with "King" Clark Gable, Paramount offered John Lund as another possible candidate. Tall, handsome, blue-eyed, and blond, he had a clean-cut romantic appeal, but never came across as merely a pretty boy. His rough edges made him far more interesting. (His detractors said that his face in repose sometimes had a sneery, disagreeable, remote quality that turned off audiences.) His best cinematic portrayals were as young brash Americans, such as the World War I flying ace and his son in *To Each His Own* (1946), his first film, and the captain romantically involved with Jean Arthur and Marlene Dietrich in Billy Wilder's *A Foreign Affair* (1948).

John was born on February 6, 1913 in Rochester, New York, to a Norwegian father and Irish mother. His father was a glass blower; his mother was a busy housewife with six children to raise. John disliked school immensely and quit (or was expelled) from a number of public schools in his home town. "But," he says, "I spent four of the happiest years of my life in the freshman year in high school." When he

passed beyond the age of compulsory education, he left formal studying forever. Thereafter, he held various jobs, but none of them for very long. He dug ditches, worked at soda fountains, and was, at one time, a carpenter's helper. What he thought about most was how to get out of working too hard. He never gave the slightest thought to becoming an actor, even though as a child he was the "Spirit of Clean Teeth" in a grammar school extravaganza and later, by sheer force, played a role in *Waiting for Lefty* in a local stock company. In 1939 he went to New York City and found a job with an advertising agency. At the time, he shared a Greenwich Village apartment with Joe Bassett, who was then a stage manager for *Railroads on Parade,* an industrial show at the New York World's Fair at Flushing Meadows. Unhappy in his advertising job, John accepted Bassett's offer to join the show, which included such later names as Betty Garrett and Don DeFore. "My downfall had begun," Lund later said. "I was an actor in earnest." in the train tribute he played a number of characters, including a drunken prospector, a Swedish immigrant, and a mourner at Lincoln's funeral.

Lund made his Broadway debut in October, 1941, understudying Alfred Drake as Orlando, and playing some bit parts in *As You Like It.* The Shakespearean production collapsed after a one-week run. Lund found difficulty in obtaining other acting jobs, but he did attain some success as a writer. He was able to sell radio scripts which in turn led to acting on some

With Paulette Goddard in a publicity pose for Bride of Vengeance (Par 1949)

of the programs. He wrote for "The Billie Burke Show," and was employed as actor-writer on "Portia Faces Life," "The Story of Kate Hopkins," and "Lincoln Highway." In December, 1942, he opened at the Ritz Theatre in New York in Leonard Sillman's *New Faces of 1943*. Not only did he perform in the production, he also wrote the book and lyrics. Members of the cast included Alice Pearce, Doris Dowling, and an ex-model, Marie Charton, who earlier that year had become Mrs. Lund. When *New Faces* closed (the *New York Times* argued, "A mediocre revue requires a great deal more than cheerful enterprise to put it across") Lund went into the musical *Early to Bed*, which was a poor man's fairy tale for grown-ups. It opened at the Broadhurst Theatre on June 17, 1943, and featured Richard Kollmar, (who produced it), Muriel Angelus, and Jane Kean. (When the show tried out in Boston, censorship demands required the scripters to change the show's locale from a Martinique bordello to a gambling casino.) Most of the critical attention went to the Fats Waller songs, "Slightly Less than Wonderful" and "Hi-De-Ho High," and to Miss Kean's ebullient performance. John was scarcely acknowledged by the aisle sitters. After this venture, Lund decided to concentrate on writing for a while, knowing that if he never made it "big" as a performer, his writing of radio scripts, musical skits, and cabaret acts was, indeed, lucrative enough. John once stated that writers, partially at least, despise actors. "That accounts for drama critics, those most favored of mortals, able to express a peeve for pay."

Lund had to be talked into returning to stage acting. He accepted the role of Yank in John Patrick's *The Hasty Heart*, because he was convinced the play would be a critical success but a quick commercial flop. His scheme backfired because after it opened at the Hudson Theatre on January 3, 1945, it became a solid hit. Richard Basehart had the pivotal role as Lachie, the Scotsman who has only a short time to live. Lund, as the stuttering Yank from Georgia, had one especially telling scene in which he lambasts Basehart's character for his unyielding attitudes. The *New York Journal-American* thought Lund "superb" and the *New York Sun* penned, "There is also a compelling performance from John Lund, a young actor who has much of the quality that belonged to the late Lawrence Leslie, and in saying that I can pay Mr. Lund no greater tribute." At this juncture, Paramount offered John a seven-year contract, plus special "introducing" billing as the male lead in his first film. After some thought, John accepted. The thing he regretted leaving most was his job on the New York-based "The Ford Tuesday Night Radio Show."

Lund offered two splendid performances in his debut feature, *To Each His Own*, playing both father and son, opposite Olivia de Havilland in her first Oscar-winning performance. His masculine charm and devil-may-care attitude, along with his good looks, destined him for stardom. *Variety* confirmed that he had "the ability and personality to assure film success."

His film career had started off well, but might have been blighted permanently by his next assignment, *The Perils of Pauline* (1947), starring irrepressible Betty Hutton in a parody of the life of silent serial star Pearl White. As for Lund's hero role in this claptrap, the *New York Times* reported, "As the melancholy theatre 'ham' [he] is uncomfortably sober-sided and just a bit too heavy for support." John, who thrived on downgrading his work, later admitted, "I was the worst peril Betty encountered as Pauline."

Fortunately, the following year Lund had two fine films: *A Foreign Affair* and *Miss Tatlock's Millions*. He particularly enjoyed making the sophisticated *A Foreign Affair* in which, as Captain John Pringle, "I was a bit of a hero and a bit of a heel." He liked his pixilated role in *Miss Tatlock's Millions*. As Burke, the movie stunt man who poses as a dim-witted heir to a fortune, he got to chew bubble gum, inspect peoples' ears, dig up worms, and play with matches. His performance was daffy and funny, but he never again got another good comedy role in the cinema. In *Night Has a Thousand Eyes* (1948), he seemed visibly bored doing nothing but wooden leading-man duty while Edward G. Robinson gobbled up the vital moments of this E.S.P. tale. Many Paramount contract stars had rejected roles in *A Mask for Lucretia,* which Mitchell Leisen directed in a misguided moment. It emerged onscreen as *Bride of Vengeance* (1949), with John as the stodgy Alfonso D'este, the Duke of Ferrara, who weds Lucretia Borgia (none other than Paulette Goddard). The Renaissance costume story was a mess, but at least John looked more respectable in his period outfits than an out-of-whack Macdonald Carey as Cesare Borgia. Reviewing John in this movie, the *New York Times* admitted that he "gives a fair picture of a nice American prankster got up for a fancy-dress ball."

Why Paramount executives tossed away Lund as Al, Marie Wilson's bungling boy friend, in *My Friend Irma* (1949) and its sequel, *My Friend Irma Goes West* (1950), is almost beyond understanding. Producer Hal B. Wallis turned both slapstick fests into a showcase for his new property, the comedy team of Dean Martin and Jerry Lewis. The role of Al would have been much more suited to such an actor as William Bendix. One reviewer observed of John in these out-

With Wanda Hendrix, Monty Woolley, and Barry Fitzgerald in Miss Tatlock's Millions *(Par 1948)*

With Don DeFore, Diana Lynn, Jerry Lewis, Marie Wilson, and Dean Martin in a publicity pose for My Friend Irma (Par 1949)

ings that he offered "a painful demonstration of a dim-wit with gutter-snipe voice." While Lund's Paramount rival, William Holden, was emoting in *Sunset Boulevard* (1950), *Born Yesterday* (1950,—on loan-out to Columbia), and *The Turning Point* (1952), John faired less well on the home lot. His last three pictures for the studio were all directed by Mitchell Leisen, whose flair for entertaining the public seemed to diminish with each succeeding year. *No Man of Her Own* (1950) was a fairly decent drama in which Lund was left far behind after Barbara Stanwyck and Lyle Bettger finished chewing the scenery. Joan Fontaine and Lund were attractive enough in an updating of a Sir James Barrie's play retitled *Darling, How could You?* (1951), and *The Mating Season* (1951) was uplifted a great deal by Thelma Ritter's rich, wonderful performance as Lund's salty mother who comes to pay an unexpected visit.

By the 1950s Hollywood was adjusting to new industry practices and new faces. John's career began to go downhill at this time. MGM borrowed him for the second male lead in the Esther Williams' vehicle, *Duchess of Idaho* (1950), in which he is a playboy who loses the shapely swimmer to Van Johnson and has to settle for Paula Raymond. Metro used John again in *Latin Lovers* (1953), and this time around he

is jilted by Lana Turner who turns to Ricardo Montalban, which was fine for Lana because Lund played a stuffy tycoon. Poor John had another stuffy part in MGM's musical remake of *The Philadelphia Story* (1940), now called *High Society* (1956). He performed, with lackluster "perfection," the work-your-way-to-the-top role that John Howard handled in the earlier film production of the Philip Barry play.

In his forties in the 1950s, John made five features at Universal, two romantic comedies with the fading, ex-Warner Bros. "oomph" girl Ann Sheridan, and three westerns. He battled Cochise (Jeff Chandler) in *The Battle of Apache Pass* (1952) and was in contest against Victor Mature's *Chief Crazy Horse* (1955). In both cases, Lund's cavalry may have won the battle, but the once-Paramount star lost the status war. The best western in which Lund appeared was the intelligently made *White Feather* (1955) for Twentieth Century-Fox. John was again a stuffy soldier, Colonel Lindsay, in this CinemaScope entry, which spotlighted a trio of healthy Fox younger leads: Robert Wagner, Jeffrey Hunter (as Little Dog), and Debra Paget.

Time progressed and John moved further down the professional ladder. He was in a Linda Darnell B film, a fight-to-the-finish western entitled *Dakota Incident* (1956), and the next year he was a public relations man done in by a pseudo-bubbly Doris Singleton in Republic's very minor entry, *Affair in Reno* (1957). After these efforts, Lund concentrated—wisely—on television assignments, not returning to the big screen until 1961's *The Wackiest Ship in the Army*. In this film he was tight-lipped Lieutenant-Commander Wilbur Vandewater, and was submerged beneath the screen presence of the film's stars, Jack Lemmon and Ricky Nelson. In his last feature to date, John was Sandra Dee's staid Bostonian father in *If A Man Answers* (1962) at Universal.

John had made his final stage appearance back in 1953 in *An Evening with Will Shakespeare*, which played the Brooklyn Academy of Music and then went on tour with a cast that included Basil Rathbone, Viveca Lindfors, Faye Emerson, and Eva Le Gallienne.

For more than a decade, John, who always claimed he was lazy at heart, has preferred the anonymity of private life, remaining away from the spotlight of show business. He resides in the San Fernando Valley with Marie, his wife of thirty plus years.

JOHN LUND

To Each his Own   *(Par 1946)*
The Perils of Pauline   *(Par 1947)*
Variety Girl   *(Par 1947)*
A Foreign Affair   *(Par 1948)*
Night has a Thousand Eyes   *(Par 1948)*
Miss Tatlock's Millions   *(Par 1948)*
Bride of Vengeance   *(Par 1949)*
My Friend Irma   *(Par 1949)*
No Man of Her Own   *(Par 1950)*
My Friend Irma Goes West   *(Par 1950)*
Duchess of Idaho   *(MGM 1950)*
The Mating Season   *(Par 1951)*
Darling, How Could You?   *(Par 1951)*
Steel Town   *(Univ 1952)*

The Battle of Apache Pass   *(Univ 1952)*
Bronco Buster   *(Univ 1952)*
Just Across the Street   *(Univ 1952)*
Woman they Almost Lynched   *(Rep 1953)*
Latin Lovers   *(MGM 1953)*
Chief Crazy Horse   *(Univ 1955)*
White Feather   *(20th 1955)*
Five Guns West   *(American Releasing Company 1955)*
Battle Stations   *(Col 1956)*
High Society   *(MGM 1956)*
Dakota Incident   *(Rep 1956)*
Affair in Reno   *(Rep 1957)*
The Wackiest Ship in the Army   *(Col 1961)*
If a Man Answers   *(Univ 1962)*

59

Lon McCallister

While American servicemen were engaged in foreign theatres of war fighting for democracy, Hollywood was industriously inculcating movie-goers with prefabricated notions of just what wholesome Americana was all about, a none too easy propaganda task. To populate these supposedly elevating features, filmmakers busily recruited candidate after candidate to portray the milk-and-cracker set onscreen: Eddie Bracken, Diana Lynn, June Haver, William Eythe, Guy Madison, Dale Evans, Gale Storm, and Sonny Tufts were some of the more successful practitioners of this special sterotype. Producer Sol Lesser took a chance on another hopeful, yanked from the rank and file of bit players, when he signed Lon McCallister to the important role of the G.I. named California in United Artists' *Stage Door Canteen* (1943). From this film on, Lon was Hollywood's innocent young farm boy. Short (5' 6"), gentle, shy but friendly, his most appealing physical attributes were his gray eyes with a touch of brown in one, and his off-center smile.

Born Herbert Alonzo McCallister, Jr. on April 17, 1923, in Los Angeles, he always was and still is called "Bud" by his family and friends. (He would even be billed as Bud McCallister onscreen in 1942's *Over My Dead Body*.) His parents, Herbert Alonzo McCallister, Sr. and Madeline Hocking, were divorced in 1928 and Lon remained with his mother, who never remarried. His father did remarry and later moved to

Arkansas. Lon's interest in movies began through his maternal grandparents. His grandmother appeared in many feature films as an extra, and his grandfather was a nightwatchman at Universal and, later, the gateman at RKO.

Lon studied singing, dancing, acting, and even horseback riding, and hoped for a career in the movies. He took dancing class at the Ernest Belcher School along with Belcher's daughter Marge (Champion) and Gene Nelson. It was Lon's singing, though, that earned him his first film job. As a member of the Maxwell Choristers, he was among the background figures singing in George Cukor's *Romeo and Juliet* (1936) at MGM. Cukor and Lon have remained very close friends to this day. Years after Lon left films he would occasionally work for Cukor as his man Friday.

More small film roles followed. He himself cannot remember many of the early films in which he worked as an extra. Lon's big chance *almost* came in 1938's *Adventures of Tom Sawyer,* made by producer David O. Selznick and director Norman Taurog. Both Lon and Gloria De Haven were being considered for the juvenile leads, but the film's preparations took so long that they both outgrew the roles. Tommy Kelly and Ann Gillis won the top roles instead, while Lon settled for a near bit assignment. His first weekly contract was at Universal in Deanna Durbin's *That Certain Age* (1938). Two years later he won his first speaking part oncamera in *Joe and Ethel Turp Call on the President* (1940) at Metro. He had one scene with

With Ward Bond, Willie Best, and June Haver in Home in Indiana *(20th 1944)*

With Judith Anderson and Allene Roberts in The Red House *(UA 1947)*

Walter Brennan, in which he played Tom Neal as a boy. Besides doing bits and extras in motion pictures, Lon worked on the radio a good deal. He was heard on "Lux Radio Theatre," "The Jack Benny Show," and "Amos 'n Andy." He was also on "A Date with Judy" for one season as Joan Lorring's boyfriend.

While attending Chapman College in 1941, Lon made a test for Republic Pictures, who were looking for a young soldier type. He failed to win the job because they considered him wrong for the role. More thankless assignments followed, until the moment when, during an interview for a part in *Stage Door Canteen,* the film's director, Frank Borzage, saw Lon and insisted that he be given a reading. He got the movie job and played a nine-minute scene on-screen with Katharine Cornell. For his performance as California, he received so much fan mail that the film's producer, Sol Lesser, signed him to a personal contract and Lon never returned to college. The *New York World-Telegram* rated his *Stage Door Canteen* job with: "An immense charm, boyish and gentle, is brought into the picture by the shy boy played by Lon McCallister." It set the tone for his future film career.

Lon's contract with Lesser was very much on his own terms. He made $750 a week with a five-thousand-dollar yearly bonus and six months off every five years. He only had to appear in stories of which

he approved, and he had permission to ignore studio publicity departments. He also had the privilege to accept any radio work he wanted. This was an extremely free and gracious contract for a fledgling. But soon he was making only fifty dollars a month, rookie pay for initiates into the Signal Corps, which he joined in February, 1944.

Before entering the service, though, Lon had his first starring role at Twentieth Century-Fox in *Home in Indiana* (1944). He received introductory billing in the picture, along with June Haver and Jeanne Crain. It was to be his first celluloid farmboy role. Contrary to general belief, Lon was not a Fox contract player. He was always loaned out to them by Sol Lesser. The *New York World-Telegram,* reviewing *Home in Indiana,* noted, "The fledgling wiles of Lon McCallister, playing his first full-sized role, betray him into simpering sweetness at intervals, but basically his performance is sound and mellow." Other critics were encouraging on the same level: "Shyly agreeable" (*New York Times*), "pleasing and diffident" (*PM*), "imbues his role with a youthful enthusiasm" (*New York Post*). For most moviegoers of the decade, Lon's performance in this piece of Technicolor sentimentality would be his most identifiable piece of acting: A film in which he portrays the shy sulky-riding Hoosier nephew of Walter Brennan and must endure the rivalry of Misses Crain and Haver for his romantic attention.

Lon's next movie was the Air Force's *Winged Victory* (1944), which was released by Twentieth Century-Fox. It was directed by his friend George Cukor. "It's a funny thing about my being in *Winged Victory,*" said Lon. "At the time it was being prepared for the stage I was offered a part in it with the stipulation that I join the Air Force sooner. But I took the role in *Home in Indiana* because I wanted to establish myself a little in pictures first." Private Lon McCallister received first billing in *Winged Victory* appearing with Sergeants Edmond O'Brien, Mark Daniels, Peter Lind Hayes, and George Reeves, Corporals Don Taylor, Lee J. Cobb, Red Buttons, Barry Nelson, Gary Merrill, Karl Malden, Alan Baxter, and PFC Alfred Ryder. Jeanne Crain and Judy Holliday were inserted into the plotline for decoration. Most of the Broadway cast had been retained for the film version, with Lon and Jeanne Crain among the exceptions. One of the most memorable moments in the film occurs when Lon dies in a crash on his first solo night flight. After the film, Lon toured with the stage version for nine months and completed his war duty in Alaska.

He returned to films in *The Red House* (1947), a turgid melodrama which some consider his best acting assignment. The strong cast included Edward G.

Advertisement for Winged Victory *(20th 1944)*

Robinson and Judith Anderson, and the *New York Herald-Tribune* said that Lon "works with ease and assurance as the young farm hand." The song refrain, "How Are You Going to Keep Them Down on the Farm" obviously had no bearing for Lon's career, for in his next pictures he remained a representative of agrarian society. He appeared with Peggy Ann Garner in *Thunder in the Valley* (1947—original title, *Bob, Son of Battle*) and *The Big Cat* (1949). He was re-teamed with a wasted June Haver in *Scudda Hoo, Scudda Hay* (1948), and worked with a maturing Shirley Temple in *The Story of Seabiscuit* (1949). A role which Lon desperately wanted was that of the killer in Republic's *Moonrise* (1949). The picture was being directed by his *Stage Door Canteen* director, Frank Borzage, but he lost the role to Warner Bros.' Dane Clark, a better actor and a person better suited to the part. There was talk that he would star in the remake of Harold Lloyd's *Girl Shy*, but that never came about.

After Sol Lesser suffered a heart attack and closed down his producing company, he retained Lon on salary for another year. Lon's last films were even worse than the farmyard pictures he had done previously. His last rural excursion was Eagle-Lion's *The Boy from Indiana* (1950), which co-starred the cute Lois Butler. That film, as a matter of fact, ended her very unspectacular movie career. Lon then made two

low-budget war films and his only western *Montana Territory* (1952), and then retired from the screen at the age of thirty. He made a few stage appearances in the early 1950s in summer stock and played the role of Lachie, the doomed Scot, in *The Hasty Heart* (1951) in St. Louis.

Lon's biggest ambition in life was to sail around the world. If he did not do precisely that, he came pretty close. He traveled a good deal, spending time in Europe, Africa, and South America. Many of his trips were taken with his closest friend and housemate, William Eythe. They had become great pals while both were working for Twentieth Century-Fox. In 1956, he and Eythe produced *Joy Ride*, a musical revue, but the show collapsed in Chicago. They even made some travel films together. When Eythe died in 1957, Lon visited with friends in France and then moved to London where he lived for three years. These days, a much plumper, balding Lon resides in Malibu, California, where he has his beach house, the one he purchased in the early 1940s. He has worked in real estate and owns his own apartment building, which is managed by his mother, who has worked in the field for years.

Lon found pleasure being in the celebrity limelight in the 1940s but today, he says, he prefers "the anonymity of the has-been."

LON McCALLISTER

Romeo and Juliet   *(MGM 1936)*
Let's Sing Again   *(RKO 1936)*
Internes Can't Take Money   *(RKO 1937)*
Souls at Sea   *(Par 1937)*
Stella Dallas   *(UA 1937)*
Make a Wish   *(RKO 1937)*
Adventures of Tom Sawyer   *(UA 1938)*
Judge Hardy's Children   *(MGM 1938)*
Lord Jeff   *(MGM 1938)*
That Certain Age   *(Univ 1938)*
Little Tough Guys in Society   *(Univ 1938)*
Spirit of Culver   *(Univ 1939)*
Confessions of a Nazi Spy   *(WB 1939)*
Angels Wash Their Faces   *(WB 1939)*
Babes in Arms   *(MGM 1939)*
First Love   *(Univ 1939)*
Joe and Ethel Turp call on the President   *(MGM 1940)*
High School   *(20th 1940)*
Susan and God   *(MGM 1940)*
Henry Aldrich for President   *(Par 1941)*

Always in My Heart   *(WB 1942)*
Yankee Doodle Dandy   *(WB 1942)*
The Hard Way   *(WB 1942)*
Gentleman Jim   *(WB 1942)*
Quiet Please, Murder   *(20th 1942)*
Over My Dead Body   *(20th 1942)*
The Meanest Man in the World   *(20th 1943)*
Stage Door Canteen   *(UA 1943)*
Home in Indiana   *(20th 1944)*
Winged Victory   *(20th 1944)*
The Red House   *(UA 1947)*
Thunder in the Valley   *(20th 1947)*
Scudda Hoo! Scudda Hay!   *(20th 1948)*
The Big Cat   *(EL 1949)*
The Story of Seabiscuit   *(WB 1949)*
The Boy From Indiana   *(EL 1950)*
A Yank in Korea   *(Col 1951)*
Montana Territory   *(Col 1952)*
Combat Squad   *(Col 1953)*

60

Dorothy Malone

On the metaphorical Hollywood see-saw, few well-known, top-name talents have had so many ups and downs both in her career and personal life as Dorothy Malone. She graduated from RKO starlet status to contract player at Warner Bros. (Remember her as the bookshop girl in *The Big Sleep,* 1946?) From there, she rose to Academy-Award status for *Written on the Wind* (1956) and tremendous popularity as Constance MacKenzie on the nighttime TV soap opera "Peyton Place." Along the way she developed a throbbing delivery and a hypnotic stare as well as acquiring long, honey-blonde hair to cover one eye, reminiscent of early Lauren Bacall, Veronica Lake, and Lizabeth Scott; she used these new qualities to great advantage oncamera. The gaps between her career peaks make her life story intriguing and her resiliency to re-emerge appealing to film fans. Truly, she is a testament to the gutsiness of the film gals of the forties.

A devout Catholic, Dorothy was born Dorothy Eloise Maloney on January 30, 1925, to Robert and Esther Maloney in Chicago, Illinois. She is the oldest of three children. One brother, Robert, is a Dallas lawyer and her youngest brother, Will, died at the age of sixteen, in 1955, when he was struck by lightning. Her father, an auditor for American Telephone and Telegraph, was transferred to Dallas when Dorothy was six months old. There, he became an auditor for

Southern Bell Telephone. In Dallas, Dorothy attended public school, Ursuline Convent, Highland Park High School, and the Hockaday School for Girls. She was president of her high school class and was named Queen of ROTC as well as captain of the girls' basketball team. She also has medals proving that she is an expert diver. Dorothy studied dancing as a child and, while in school, modeled for Neiman-Marcus. She appeared in many school plays and received awards as best actress for two consecutive years, which in turn, earned her a scholarship at Southern Methodist University. While there she majored in both drama and languages. She speaks French and Spanish fluently.

It was RKO talent scout Edward Rubin who spotted Dorothy for movies. He saw a University production of *Starboard* in which she played a star-struck girl living in a studio club for women while awaiting her big break. Just like the play's heroine, Dorothy ended up doing the same thing. She was screen-tested in her own living room in Dallas then went to Hollywood, accompanied by her mother, where RKO signed her to a term contract. She later moved into the Hollywood Studio Club.

She sat around on the studio's warm-up bench, waiting for screen work. She had a few unbilled bits in films such as *The Falcon and the Co-Eds* (1943) and *Show Business* (1944). She was billed for the first time in Columbia's Boston Blackie entry, *One Mysterious Night* (1944), which starred Chester Morris. For

Publicity pose ca. 1949

the occasion she used her real name, Dorothy Maloney.

The studio club presented a showcase production of *Ladies Unmasked,* with Dorothy playing a Spanish dancer. Many scouts and casting directors attended, and when RKO released her from her contract, Warners picked her up. Still using the surname Maloney, she flashed across the screen briefly in *Hollywood Canteen* (1944), and then changed her name to Malone for *Too Young to Know* (1945), featuring such studio peers as Joan Leslie, Robert Hutton, and Dolores Moran.

After appearing in the inconspicuous part of Cary Grant's sister in *Night and Day* (1946), Dorothy got her chance as the proprietress of the Acme Book Shop, the academic girl in *The Big Sleep* who sheds her eye glasses and enjoys an afternoon fling with Humphrey Bogart's Philip Marlowe. It was a small role, but a good one, and her five-foot-seven brunette loveliness and sweetness held viewers' attention. At this point Warners started giving her larger roles. She was a foil for some of the antics of Dennis Morgan and Jack Carson in *Two Guys from Texas* (1948), and then co-starred with Morgan in *One Sunday Afternoon* (1948), a musical remake of *Strawberry Blonde* (1941)—itself a remake of a 1933 film—with Dorothy in Olivia de Havilland's old role. Before her five-year contract at Warners expired in 1949, she was seen in three good-girl roles: *Flaxy Martin* (1949), with Virginia Mayo, *Colorado Territory* (1949), with Mayo and Joel McCrea, and *South of St. Louis* (1949), with McCrea, again, and Alexis Smith in the more colorful female role. In the latter film, Dorothy won McCrea by the fade-out.

Unlike many performers who faltered hopelessly once they were forced to freelance, Dorothy seemed to thrive, and if she populated less prestigious productions, she still gave each assignment a competent approach. From 1950 to 1954 she was mostly in such minor films as *The Bushwackers* (1952) and *Law and Order* (1953), playing the female lead. But in bigger-budgeted affairs she was back to second female or, in the case of *Scared Stiff* (1953) with Dean Martin and Jerry Lewis, she was third.

In 1954 she appeared in seven feature films, and whether the picture was major or minor, she gave fine performances in each of them. Thus, 1954 was the beginning of Dorothy Malone, actress, and the end of Dorothy Malone, starlet. Columbia's *Pushover* (1954) was the first of three co-starring roles with Fred Mac-Murray, whom she greatly admires, both as an actor and a family man. In this corrupt policeman story, Dorothy should have given newcomer Kim Novak some acting lessons. Dorothy's last release of the year

was *Young at Heart,* back at her old studio, Warner Bros. It was a musical remake of *Four Daughters* (1938) and starred Doris Day and Frank Sinatra. In the economized update there were only three daughters: Day, Dorothy, and Elizabeth Fraser. Day and Sinatra were the charismatic boxoffice attractions, but Gig Young, Ethel Barrymore, and Dorothy provided the acting balance. A new quality was beginning to form in Dorothy with this film. Not only was she more beautiful, but there was a sadness in her usually twinkling blue-green eyes and her dramatic scenes were played with greater depth and believability. Even when she was not in the main focus of a sequence she was so totally involved that viewers could not help but watch her. Warners held on to her for a few more features, though they wasted her in *Tall Man Riding* (1955), with Randolph Scott, and in Liberace's *Sincerely Yours* (1955), and gave her one of the smaller women's roles in the star-clustered *Battle Cry* (1955).

The film version of Leon Uris's *Battle Cry* was the turning point in her film career. As Elaine, the married woman who has a brief affair with younger Tab Hunter in San Diego, she proved that she could project sexiness without vitiating her dramatic level. Critics never failed to mention her scenes with Hunter, and she personally received the best reviews in the film and of her early career.

Both her performance and appearance in *Written on the Wind* shocked Hollywood and audiences alike. As Marylee Hadley, the nymphomaniac oil heiress, hopelessly in love with Rock Hudson, Dorothy broke away from anything she had played onscreen before. She was blonde, sexy, and tortured, and did one of the best (suggested) strips, to a mambo record, that the screen has ever seen. Dorothy says that if the film were being done today she probably would have been asked to play it in the nude. Her performance in *Battle Cry* had earned her the part in *Written,* but few thought her capable of portraying a character like Marylee, because Dorothy has always had an extremely upright personal reputation. The exploitative but well-mounted feature received critical pans because of its Hollywood slickness, but it had a strong story and two superb performances by Dorothy and Robert Stack. (He was her bitterly jealous brother.) Dorothy's competition for the Oscar race—she was nominated in the Best Supporting Actress Division—were: Mildred Dunnock (*Baby Doll*), Mercedes McCambridge (*Giant*), Patty McCormack, and Eileen Heckart (the latter two for *The Bad Seed*). It was ironic that Dorothy's four competitors for the Actress Oscar were all in Warners' features and that Dorothy's victory was, in a way, a nice slap in the face to her one-time employers.

With Tom D'Andrea and Joseph Buloff in To the Victor *(WB 1948)*

Some say that the Oscar went to Dorothy's head, that she lost control of her acting skills, became agog with a "star" complex. If this was the case, it was not immediately noticeable, certainly not in her performance as the mentally disturbed Mrs. Lon Chaney in *Man of a Thousand Faces* (1957). She gave a moving portrayal in this rather tawdry assignment. Universal thought it commercially sound to reunite Dorothy with her *Written* players (except for Bacall) in *Tarnished Angels* (1957), based on William Faulkner's novel, *Pylon*. In this over-keyed melodrama she was Laverne Shumann, wife of World War I flying ace Roger Shumann, played by Robert Stack. *The Tarnished Angels* did not live up to the boxoffice success of *Written,* even though both were directed by Douglas Sirk.

Warner Bros. then came calling again, giving her the Diana Barrymore role in the lurid filmed biography *Too Much Too Soon* (1958), with Errol Flynn playing John Barrymore. (Carroll Baker had been the first choice for the lead.) She received billing over Flynn, making it the first time she was top starred in a feature. She was onscreen for almost every frame of the 121-minute picture, but she could not overcome the banality of the script or the wretchedness of Art Napoleon's direction. Besides, Flynn stole every

scene he was in. One New York reviewer said that Dorothy was "a winsome, earnest protagonist—but no Susan Hayward." As star of the film, she took the brunt of the movie's failure. Industry observers began claiming that she was incapable of carrying a film at the boxoffice and that her few good performances were flukes.

At Fox, she and Richard Widmark did not get along during the making of *Warlock* (1959). He considered her unprofessional, one of the few derogatory remarks ever uttered about Dorothy. (She had long had a reputation for hiding from the world behind a pair of prescription dark glasses and for pampering a tendency to be vague.) In Andrew Stone's *The Last Voyage* (1960), she and her screen husband (Robert Stack again) are aboard a luxury liner that goes down on the high seas. The *New York Times* said that of all the cast, Dorothy, "got a moving reflection of frenzy, futility and fear." In the western *The Last Sunset* (1961), she is married to older man Joseph Cotten and pursued by Rock Hudson and Kirk Douglas. It proved to be her last major role in a major film, because thereafter nobody offered her anything worthwhile. She wanted to work, but she should never have accepted the demeaning "adult" co-lead (with Robert Cummings) in *Beach Party* (1963), the first of American

381

International's Frankie Avalon-Annette Funicello musical outings. Later in the year, as a favor to producer Aaron Rosenberg, she accepted an unbilled cameo assignement in *Fate Is the Hunter* (1964).

In 1964, television proved to be Dorothy's career salvation. She was handed the lead role in "Peyton Place" on ABC-TV, and she remained with the continuing story for four years, at a salary of $250,000 a year. Almost a year to the day that "Peyton Place" first aired, Dorothy was rushed to the hospital fighting for her life. Newspaper headlines kept the public informed as to her condition. (She underwent seven and a half hours of surgery to remove clots from blood vessels leading to her lungs and narrowly escaped death, as her heart had stopped.)

Always a fighter, Dorothy survived. During her protracted illness, Lola Albright replaced her as Constance. By the series' third season, Dorothy had become dissatisfied with the part because Constance "never does anything." She was bored with the assignment and hinted that she wanted her contractual release. Her last scenes were shown in May, 1968, and found her being written out of the show as her character prepared to leave Peyton Place for an extended trip (at least she was not killed off in the story). After her departure from "Peyton Place," she announced her intention to sue the show's producing company, claiming that her part had been diminished because it was hoped she would quit. An out-of-court settlement was reached.

During her Hollywood years, Dorothy had been linked in particular with Scott Brady, to whom she was officially engaged in 1952. Everyone was convinced the handsome couple would wed, but in 1957 they ended their romantic relationship. She was also involved with Sidney Chaplin, with whom she had worked in *Pillars of the Sky* (1956) and *Quantez* (1957), and with actor Richard Egan. Then she surprised nearly everyone by marrying ladies' man Jacques Bergerac, ex-husband of Ginger Rogers. The wedding took place on June 28, 1959, in Hong Kong, while she was on location for *The Last Voyage*. It was the beginning of a very stormy four-year marriage, but it did result in their having two daughters, Mimi (born April 3, 1960) and Diane (born February 20, 1962). Claiming mental cruelty, Dorothy sued for divorce and it was granted on December 8, 1964, giving her custody of their two girls. During subsequent years, there were bitter court battles about visitation rights and other matters, but none of this was publicized. Dorothy claimed that Bergerac had lived off her earnings; Bergerac has stated that "Dorothy and her mother disparage men, me in particular." One court order even forbade her to publicly discuss her years of problems with Bergerac.

In 1968, Dorothy quit Hollywood and returned to Dallas to live, claiming her family and friends were there and that she found it less expensive to manage a household in Texas. For a time she studied real estate and worked in the profession for a short while. "It'd be nice to never have to work again," she said, "but I'm not financially secure enough to stop working forever." (One time, during a slack period in films, she had taken a public relations job on behalf of an insurance company and had toured thirty-six cities.) "Between the doctors and the attorneys, I've paid almost everything I'm worth as an actress just trying to buy peace and quiet." While in Dallas, she was featured with Harvey Korman in *Little Me* at the Dallas State Fair but seemed, from all reports, uncomfort-

With Zachary Scott and Tom D'Andrea in Flaxy Martin *(WB 1949)*

able on stage. (She had made her professional stage debut with Bergerac in a 1959 production of *Once More with Feeling* done at the Pheasant Run Playhouse in Chicago.)

In April, 1969, Dorothy wed New York businessman Robert Tomarkin. The ceremony took place in Las Vegas. Four weeks later the union was annulled when she claimed that he had married her for her money and that he had tried to swindle her out of her savings.* In 1971 she married motel chain executive Charles Huston Bell of Dallas.

She returns to Hollywood on occasion for work, saying Dallas "is really only a phone call away." She starred with Sammy Davis, Jr., Ricardo Montalban, and Pat Boone in *The Pigeon,* a made-for-television movie in 1969, has been seen on "The Bold Ones" (1972), and was special guest star on "Ironsides" in the first episode of the 1973–74 season. Her friend, Raymond Burr, star of the series, personally asked her to do it. She portrayed a spinster nurse who was once a lady of the evening. She wore hardly any makeup and looked older (of course, it was a character part), but she performed well. On the segment, Dorothy's character describes herself as "the leftover garbage from somebody else's picnic." Dorothy made the entire character ring true. Earlier in her career she had done a number of guest spots on such television se-

*He would later be involved in a plan to cheat the Franklin National Bank (of New York) in a two-million-dollar swindle "trying to beat Wall Street."

ries as "The Greatest Show on Earth" and "The Untouchables." On the latter she was a guest with Scott Brady and series regular Robert Stack, each of whom has had a lot of influence in her life.

Dorothy's recent feature film assignments have been a sad lot. In 1970 she flew to Rome to film *The Unsatiables* with John Ireland and Luciana Paluzzi, a picture which got scant release in the U.S. in 1974. *Target in the Sun* (1974) with Aldo Ray and Keenan Wynn and *Abduction* (1975) are her last films to date.

Still blonde—though occasionally brunette—Dorothy exists in Dallas today, in a nether world much like her former Constance MacKenzie role in "Peyton Place." Occasionally she returns to Hollywood, as for her role in the multi-part telefeature, *Rich Man, Poor Man* (1976). In a candid interview with Rex Reed, she admitted: "People think if you win an Oscar you're set for life on Easy Street. Forget it. Winning an Oscar can be a jinx. After I won it, I could sense it in people's faces. It was a look that said, 'Why did I vote for her?' There aren't many plum juicy roles in the first place, but after you win an Oscar you have a choice. You can either sit back and wait until the good roles come along or you can work constantly so people won't think you were a one-time joke. Instead of sitting around waiting, I tried to keep working, instead of better roles, they got worse and worse. The same thing has happened to others." It certainly did to Dorothy Malone who once said, "Fame is a kick and it's fleeting."

DOROTHY MALONE

As DOROTHY MALONEY
The Falcon and the Co-Eds *(RKO 1943)*
Show Business *(RKO 1944)*
Seven Days Ashore *(RKO 1944)*
Youth Runs Wild *(RKO 1944)*
One Mysterious Night *(Col 1944)*
Hollywood Canteen *(WB 1944)*
As DOROTHY MALONE
Too Young to Know *(WB 1945)*
Janie Gets Married *(WB 1946)*
Night and Day *(WB 1946)*
The Big Sleep *(WB 1946)*
To the Victor *(WB 1948)*
Two Guys from Texas *(WB 1948)*
One Sunday Afternoon *(WB 1948)*
Flaxy Martin *(WB 1949)*
South of St. Louis *(WB 1949)*
Colorado Territory *(WB 1949)*
The Nevadan *(Col 1950)*
Convicted *(Col 1950)*
Mrs. O'Malley and Mr. Malone *(MGM 1950)*
The Killer that Stalked New York *(Col 1950)*
Saddle Legion *(RKO 1951)*
The Bushwackers *(Realart 1952)*
Torpedo Alley *(AA 1953)*
Scared Stiff *(Par 1953)*
Law and Order *(Univ 1953)*
Jack Slade *(AA 1953)*
Loophole *(AA 1954)*

The Lone Gun *(UA 1954)*
Pushover *(Col 1954)*
Security Risk *(AA 1954)*
Private Hell 36 *(Filmakers 1954)*
The Fast and the Furious *(American Releasing 1954)*
Young at Heart *(WB 1954)*
Five Guns West *(American Releasing 1955)*
Battle Cry *(WB 1955)*
Tall Man Riding *(WB 1955)*
Sincerely Yours *(WB 1955)*
Artists and Models *(Par 1955)*
At Gunpoint *(Rep 1955)*
Pillars of the Sky *(Univ 1956)*
Written on the Wind *(Univ 1956)*
Tension at Table Rock *(RKO 1956)*
Man of a Thousand Faces *(Univ 1957)*
Tip on a Dead Jockey *(MGM 1957)*
Quantez *(Univ 1957)*
The Tarnished Angels *(Univ 1957)*
Too Much, Too Soon *(WB 1958)*
Warlock *(20th 1959)*
The Last Voyage *(MGM 1960)*
The Last Sunset *(Univ 1961)*
Beach Party *(AIP 1963)*
Fate Is the Hunter *(20th 1964)* (Unbilled guest appearance)
Carnal Circuit (a.k.a., The Insatiables *(Times Film 1974)*
Target in the Sun (a.k.a., The Man Who Would Not Die)
   (Suntarget 1974)
Abduction *(Independent 1975)*

61

George Montgomery

George Montgomery's current claims to fame, as Johnson's Wax TV spokesman and ex-husband of the ever popular Dinah Shore, obscure the fact that he had quite a film following during the World War II years. He began his great movie years as a beefcake boy at Twentieth Century-Fox, where he was equally at ease fighting Indians (*Ten Gentlemen from West Point,* 1942) as he was romancing fidgety Betty Grable (*Coney Island,* 1943). Later he became so expert in unpretentious but rugged western movies that the *New York Times* decided in 1953 he was "probably the most authentic and unintriguing buckaroo on the screen today."

He was born George Montgomery Letz on August 29, 1916, the son of Russian immigrants. He was reared on various ranches in remote areas of Montana, along with his seven brothers and six sisters. "Where I lived," he recalls, "you could hear a horse a quarter of a mile off." The first twelve years of his life were spent almost exclusively in the wilds, where young George could find little to do. "The rest of the kids did all the work. I had time to do other things, such as raising pigeons and chickens for 4-H contests, to sell, and even as food for the family. I suppose that's how I learned about woodworking. I built all my own coops. I did some wood carving and whittling, too."

The Depression was as difficult for farmers as for anybody else, and the Letz clan, unusually close for such a large brood, moved from farm to farm, hoping somewhere to find relief from their financial plight. Fortunately for George, they moved near Great Falls at the time he was ready for high school, so public education was available. He starred in football and baseball at school, and after graduation he attended the University of Montana for two years, specializing in interior decorating.

Montgomery managed to escape the effeminate labels then applied to most male decorating students by excelling in sports. He became a collegiate heavyweight boxing champion for the areas of Montana, Idaho, Washington, and Oregon. Staying in college was not easy financially, however, and he withdrew after his sophomore year to visit a brother who was by then an engineer in Los Angeles. George found a decorating job, overhauling a grimy cafe's walls for ten dollars a week. The thrill in this unaesthetic effort was minimal, and the combination of his physique and looks persuaded him that maybe the movies might hold a better future for him.

Unfortunately, George was more sold on his screen career idea than the studios were on him. The lots in general had no work for George, and he finally went to Republic to try to crash into the field of serials. This studio, who had given him a bit in Gene Autry's *The Singing Vagabond* (1935), hired him as a stunt man for *The Lone Ranger* (1938) serial, with Lee Powell, Herman Brix, and Lane Chandler. George kept asking

Publicity pose for Bomber's Moon *(20th 1943)*

for a bit in the film, and finally he was rewarded with one. He said, "Here come the rustlers!" from behind a mask before being killed off in the fifth episode. Subsequently, the Republic office was surprised when a slew of fan mail (written by his obliging family) came in for the masked man who yelled "Here comes the rustlers!" in the fifth segment of The Lone Ranger serial. They were further surprised that all such mail was postmarked from Montana and Los Angeles, a puzzle solved by looking up the young actor's home town. Republic was not impressed by George's gambit.

In late 1939, George's agent, Benny Medford, suggested that his hopeful client stay clear of the casting office rounds until something more fruitful could be arranged. George filled in the time gap by bartending. Then Medford wrangled an appointment with Fox's casting official, Lou Schreiber, and presented his six-foot-two, hundred-ninety-five-pound client. Schreiber thought George ideal for cowboy roles, a niche not very crowded on the studio's contract roster. Montgomery was taken to see Darryl F. Zanuck. The studio chief agreed that the husky Montanan might lend himself well to western bills and signed him to a contract.

Fox first cast George in The Cisco Kid and the Lady (1940), another of the series that starred Cesar Romero. By now, George was using Montgomery for his professional surname. The studio had heard about the Republic fan mail episode, and hence had a big laugh when Montana-postmarked mail began flowing in, extolling the young man in the small role in the Cisco Kid picture. But it was not long before Montgomery's family could rest their pencils and leave the fan letter writing to unrelated fans. George was given roles of interesting size in Star Dust (1940), a behind-the-scenes Hollywood story starring Linda Darnell, and in Young People (1940), a Shirley Temple sudsy story. When female film-goers began taking more notice of George, he was assigned a lead in Cadet Girl (1941), wholesale pre-World War II propaganda in which Montgomery had to decide onscreen between wedding Carole Landis or training at West Point. After an early screening of the film in Los Angeles, it was reported that two teenage girls left the theatre, went up to the billboard outside and kissed Montgomery's picture. It was all he needed for the big career push. As soon as Fox ascertained that the kissers were not related to the player, the studio publicized the incident and Montgomery began winning top attention from the company's promotional department.

To accelerate his stardom potential, Twentieth next cast George opposite Ginger Rogers in Roxie Hart (1942), a broadly played burlesque of the 1920s Chi-

cago. Miss Rogers, in pretty racy costumes and make-up, portrayed a gum-chewing swivel-hipped flapper who innocently becomes involved in a murder, and then uses the trial to gain attention. Adolphe Menjou was her actual onscreen co-star as the flamboyant lawyer, but George was the love interest. During filming, Ginger, still fresh from her Kitty Foyle Oscar and a divorce from second husband Lew Ayres, began dating Montgomery. Photoplay Magazine insisted that a wedding would be announced soon. The courtship supposedly ended one evening when the actress cracked to a yawning George (unused to her night life hours), "Go on home and get your sleep. You look like Karloff."

When George began his next home lot film, Ten Gentlemen from West Point, he was considered a big enough draw to win top billing over Maureen O'Hara. He was firm as a backwoodsman whose unsophisticated ways earns him a parcel of trouble at the Academy from by-the-book commandant Laird Cregar. John Sutton, another Fox contractee, was given the part of a dandified foil for Montgomery, and the two competed oncamera for the fair hand of Miss O'Hara. The film had a strangely balanced ending in which George injures his leg while rescuing Cregar from the Indians, then subsequently refuses to graduate from West Point because he does not want the first graduating class marred by a cripple. He wins Maureen as a consolation prize. Only the closing of the film makes it obvious how hard the producers were trying to tie in the historical account with the World War II problems. In the finale, as portraits of West Point heroes fill the screen and "The Caissons Go Rolling Along" reaches a musical crescendo, a picture of Douglas MacArthur appears, reminding viewers that the year was very much 1942.

From this rousing action tale, Montgomery went into Orchestra Wives (1943), a hep-cat melange that surrounded Glenn Miller and his Band with such familiar Fox faces as Carole Landis, Lynn Bari, Cesar Romero, Virginia Gilmore, and Mary Beth Hughes. Then followed Coney Island, the Technicolor musical that pitted George against Cesar Romero as rival carnival men and competitors for Betty Grable's affections. Besides Grable's legs, the film boasted tunes like "Everybody Loves a Baby," and "Cuddle up a Little Closer," as well as the comedy routines of Phil Silvers. After Bomber's Moon (1943), in which George and Annabella escape a POW camp, Montgomery himself went into the Army.

During his pre-Army service, George's romantic pursuits had become favorite reading material of the pulp magazine fans. He became seriously involved with MGM's Hedy Lamarr, and at one point the cou-

With Oscar O'Shea and Mary Howard in Riders of the Purple Sage *(20th 1941)*

With Spec O'Donnell and John Shepperd (Shepperd Strudwick) in Cadet Girl *(20th 1941)*

With Nancy Guild in The Brasher Doubloon *(20th 1947)*

ple announced their engagement, but the fickle European actress broke the engagement shortly afterward. Reasons offered for the break were Montgomery's purchase of a Montana ranch miles from nowhere, which did not appeal to the cosmopolitan Lamarr, and the actress' reluctance to marry into such a close-knit family. Shortly after this emotional upset, George met up-and-coming songstress Dinah Shore at the Hollywood Canteen. Dinah would recall, "In 1942, when I was singing at the Atlantic City Steel Pier, I would hurry from my dismal dressing room after each show to the nearest movie, where I'd watch George Montgomery make screen love five or six times a week." After their Canteen introduction, George was shipped to Alaska, but the two performers began a correspondence. When Dinah admitted in her epistles that she was dating other actors, she remembers, "I got the fastest proposal by return mail that any girl ever received." The couple were married in December, 1943.

After his discharge from military service, George returned to his Fox contract. His first film was *Three Little Girls in Blue* (1946), a musical in which he had little impressive work to do. A change of pace followed when the studio cast him as rugged detective Philip Marlowe in *The Brasher Doubloon* (1947). The *New York Times* reported that while there was nothing much wrong with Montgomery's acting, "he just doesn't look the part. Like Robert Montgomery, who played Marlowe in *Lady in the Lake* (1946), George Montgomery just looks too respectable and intelligent and lacks the ruggedness and borderline honesty of the Marlowes created by Dick Powell in *Murder My Sweet* (1944) and Humphrey Bogart in *The Big Sleep* (1946)." George then went over to Columbia, where he was done dirty, but always loved, by Dorothy Lamour in *Lulu Belle* (1948), which changed the Lulu of the famous stage play to a mixed-up chanteuse.

Belle Starr's Daughter (1948), starring Ruth Roman in the title role, was George's last film on the Fox lot. By the early 1950s he was a member of the Columbia actor roster where he continued in the western genre, except for a brief excursion to a historical swashbuckling tale in *The Sword of Monte Cristo* (1951). Even devout George Montgomery fans were disappointed when they went to see *Davy Crockett, Indian Scout* (1950) and found that their movie hero was not portraying the famed American, but rather the frontiersman's cousin. George continued in program films throughout the 1950s, later changing his home base to Allied Artists. Not only did he ride the sagebrush territories on the big screen, but on television as well. He starred in an frontier television series, "Cimarron

City," which had begun its twenty-six episode run on NBC on October 11, 1958.

During the series' year on television, George made a few pointed remarks about the film genre that was supplying his principal income:

"For expediency, you have to sit there and let a horse gallop right up behind you and you're not supposed to hear him until the director gives you the nod. Then you're supposed to turn around and say 'Oh! You here?' A guy is shot in the shoulder at close range with a .45, and all he gets is a flesh wound. In real life, his arm would be torn off. And sometimes you have somebody shooting at somebody else twenty times and missing. Nobody who had to shoot that many times would ever have reached manhood in the old days. But it all makes for good action on the screen. And even the most knowledgable audiences go along with it."

The Montgomery-Shore marriage ended in divorce in 1960. Many said it was expected since Dinah, a many-time Emmy Award-winner, had a soaring career as star of her Sunday night video show, while her husband's career had never really picked up after the war. They had a son and daughter (now married and a mother). Their parting, once it was announced, was rather amiable, or so the couple insisted. "Dinah and I are very close." George insists. "Our marriage ended on a friendly note, but almost immediately I was off, doing my own thing. I signed a four-way contract with Warner Bros. and went off as a writer-producer-star-hairdresser-make-up-man—you name it."

The first of these films, to be shot in the Philippines, was *The Steel Claw* (1961) in which George stars as a captain of World War II Filipino guerillas, and loses his hand in combat—hence, the film's title. It was not bad for its type of movie, but it suffered in distribution by being billed mainly on the lower half of action double bills. *Samar* (1962) followed, for which Montgomery was again producer-director-writer-star, in a basic story about a penal colony fighting against 1870 Spanish colonization. The *New York Times* noted: "It pivots in a kind of sweaty muscularity. This is Mr. Montgomery's limber direction, above and beyond his rather bare-chested performance as an American physician. In addition to having a directorial knack for crowd scenes, he is also blessed with a first-rate color photographer, Emmanuel Rojas. The picture looks genuine Philippine made, down to the last headhunter and palm, and the Montgomery-Rojas team really go to town in 2 battle sequences." Regarding George's scripting, the *Times* judged, "If the script substitutes briskness for depth, we'll buy it."

Over the past decade, George has made a number

of low-budget films: *Strangers at Sunrise* (1968), set in Africa, *Ride the Tiger* (1970), filmed in Manila, and *Hostile Guns* (1967), one of the A. C. Lyles ten-day quickies for Paramount, shot in Hollywood. But Montgomery's primary claim to fame during recent years is as a decorator-designer-craftsman. He had designed and supervised the construction of the luxurious home he and Dinah shared during their marriage, as well as his current elegant bachelor home. Over the years he has done similar work for Alan Ladd, Jack Webb, Debbie Reynolds' one-time husband Harry Karl, and for Warner Bros.' musical director, Ray Heindorf. Some of his work has increased in value over the years by four hundred percent.

It was with this craftsman's talent in mind that Johnson's Wax contracted George to be their video salesman. Besides this lucrative commercial work, he also does tours for the company. "They keep me jumping. I did a tour April, May, and June, then had about two and a half months to myself. I was preparing to go to the Philippines to do a picture, and Johnson's called—just as I had got my passport renewed—to say they'd like me to do another tour for them, twenty cities in thirty days. I'd no sooner said OK to that when they stretched it to 40 days so I could make the veterans hospital in each city."

George has never remarried. He says, "Marry again? As we used to say on the ranch, who buys the cow when you can get the milk for free? I'm really a loner, but I have all the companionship I want, when I want it. His frequent companion in early 1975 was twenty-one-year-old Rochelle Hayes. "She's getting to be a helluva good cook, too,"he said of the young lady, "and she didn't even read the Dinah Shore cookbook."

He is often asked about actor Burt Reynolds, Dinah's once publicized on-again, off-again flame. He has replied when asked about their relationship, "Reynolds has to be the top personality in the business, and I say, 'Hallelujah, it's great.' " George himself was asked to do a nude fold-out for *Playgirl* magazine. "I told the *Playgirl* editors I'd love to do it as a gag, but I knew the Johnson people wouldn't appreciate that. When we were shooting the first commercial, they noticed in the long shots that my shirt was open, went into a huddle before the close-ups, and suggested we button up."

Having completed a tri-level home near Trousdale, a project he did almost single-handedly (complete with a big-sized waterfall), he embarked to Manila and Bangkok to set up location sites for his independent production, *Ho Chi Minh Trail*. One project he would like to film is *The Boundary*, to be shot in his native Montana and using members of the Blackfoot tribe. A very with-it person, he is realistic and honest about the acting profession. "The business has changed. It's really hard to accept for actors and actresses who all of a sudden were on top in the profession and later they're nowhere. I've had forty years of it."

GEORGE MONTGOMERY

As GEORGE LETZ
The Singing Vagabond   *(Rep 1935)*
Springtime in the Rockies   *(Rep 1937)*
Conquest   *(MGM 1937)*
Gold Mine in the Sky   *(Rep 1938)*
The Lone Ranger   *(Rep serial 1938)* (released as feature *Hi-Yo Silver,* 1940)
Billy the Kid Returns   *(Rep 1938)*
Come on Rangers   *(Rep 1938)*
Shine on Harvest Moon   *(Rep 1938)*
Hawk of the Wilderness   *(Rep serial 1938)*
Rough Riders Round-Up   *(Rep 1939)*
Wall Street Cowboy   *(Rep 1939)*
Frontier Pony Express   *(Rep 1939)*

As GEORGE MONTGOMERY
Cisco Kid and the Lady   *(20th 1940)*
Jennie   *(20th 1940)*
Star Dust   *(20th 1940)*

Young People   *(20th 1940)*
Charter Pilot   *(20th 1940)*
The Cowboy and the Blonde   *(20th 1941)*
Accent on Love   *(20th 1941)*
Riders of the Purple Sage   *(20th 1941)*
Last of the Duanes   *(20th 1941)*
Cadet Girl   *(20th 1941)*
Roxie Hart   *(20th 1942)*
Orchestra Wives   *(20th 1942)*
Ten Gentlemen from West Point   *(20th 1942)*
China Girl   *(20th 1942)*
Coney Island   *(20th 1943)*
Bomber's Moon   *(20th 1943)*
Three Little Girls in Blue   *(20th 1946)*
The Brasher Doubloon (a.k.a., The High Window)   *(20th 1947)*
Lulu Belle   *(Col 1948)*
The Girl from Manhattan   *(UA 1948)*
Belle Starr's Daughter   *(20th 1948)*
Dakota Lil   *(20th 1950)*

Davy Crockett, Indian Scout   *(UA 1950)*
The Iroquois Trail   *(UA 1950)*
The Sword of Monte Cristo   *(20th 1951)*
Texas Rangers   *(Col 1951)*
Indian Uprising   *(Col 1952)*
Cripple Creek   *(Col 1952)*
The Pathfinder   *(Col 1953)*
Jack McCall, Desperado   *(Col 1953)*
Fort Ti   *(Col 1953)*
Gun Belt   *(UA 1953)*
The Battle of Rogue River   *(Col 1954)*
The Lone Gun   *(UA 1954)*
Masterson of Kansas   *(Col 1955)*
Seminole Uprising   *(Col 1955)*
Robber's Roost   *(UA 1955)*
Huk   *(UA 1956)*
Canyon River   *(AA 1956)*
Last of the Badmen   *(AA 1957)*
New Day at Sundown   *(AA 1957)*
Gun Duel in Durango   *(UA 1957)*
Street of Sinners   *(UA1957)*

Pawnee   *(Rep 1957)*
Man from God's Country   *(AA 1958)*
Toughest Gun in Tombstone   *(UA 1958)*
Badman's Country   *(WB 1958)*
Black Patch   *(WB 1958)*
Watusi   *(MGM 1959)*
King of the Wild Stallions   *(AA 1959)*
The Steel Claw   *(WB 1961)*
Samar   *(WB 1962)*
From Hell to Borneo   *(Commonwealth United 1946)*
Guerillas in Pink Lace   *(Commonwealth United 1964)*
Battle of the Bulge   *(WB 1965)*
Bomb at 10:10   *(Yugoslavia 1966)*
Outlaw of Red River   *(Spanish 1966)*
Hostile Guns   *(Par 1967)*
Hallucination Generation   *(Trans-American 1968)*
Warkill   *(Univ 1968)*
Strangers at Sunrise   *(Commwealth United 1968)*
Ride the Tiger   *(Balut/CBS 1970)*
Devil's Harvest   *(Independent 1971)*
The Daredevil   *(Trans-International 1972)*

62

Patricia Morison

Over the decades, Hollywood's crimes, public or private, have been many. One of its more unself-serving ones in the 1940s was its rape of talent. The careers of Patricia Morison, June Havoc, Eve Arden, Anne Jeffreys, and scores of others are testimonies to this fact. They were shuttled into minor and secondary leads in the studios' factory-like, mindless films that flourished during the decade, and then attained great success in other entertainment media. Patricia was to find her special niche in show business history in the Cole Porter-Sam and Bella Spewack musical *Kiss Me, Kate* (1948) as the tempestuous actress Lilli Vanessi, alternating in the play within the play as the shrew Kate.

Miss Morison was born on March 19, 1914 (some sources say 1915), to Selena Carson Morison and her husband William, a playwright and actor in New York City. (Mr. Morison appeared in unbilled film roles under the name Norman Rainey; during World War I, Mrs. Morison served with British Intelligence.) After Patricia graduated from Washington Irving High School, she took acting courses at the Neighborhood Playhouse School of the Theatre in New York City. She also studied dancing with Martha Graham, and while waiting for her acting break, worked as a dress designer at Russek's, a Fifth Avenue shop.

Her Broadway stage debut was in a show that had originally opened in San Francisco and ventured into New York's Ambassador Theatre on November 23,

1933. It was called *Growing Pains,* starred Junior Durkin, and featured a very young Johnny Downs. Patricia had the small part of Helen. The show lasted only twenty-nine performances. After understudying Helen Hayes in *Victoria Regina,* she was eventually cast as Laura Rivers in *The Two Bouquets,* a schmaltzy musical with Alfred Drake, which opened at the Windsor Theatre in New York on May 31, 1938. Brooks Atkinson (*New York Times*) said, "[The] two damsels in artificial distress are Marcy Westcott and Patricia Morison, who can sing with uncommon skill, who appreciate their music, and can act with the willowy elegance of counterfeit Victorian ladies." Three days after the show opened, Paramount, seeking a backstop performer to potentially temperamental Dorothy Lamour, tested Patricia, and after the play closed, signed her to a term contract.

Besides exotic Dorothy Lamour, the Marathon Street film lot already had Claudette Colbert to pepper their celluloid products, and would soon add Paulette Goddard and Veronica Lake to a roster that included an array of star(let)s, ranging from Marsha Hunt and Frances Farmer to Ellen Drew (then known as Terry Ray). However, Patricia managed to make an impressive debut in the studio's film version of J. Edgar Hoover's book *Persons in Hiding* (1939). She was soon being touted as the company's new "white hope," but strangely, she was thereafter relegated to secondary roles in her next two B films.

Then, the studio gave her a chance in its remake of

Publicity pose

With Jerome Cowan in The Song of Bernadette *(20th 1943)*

Sinclair Lewis' *Mantrap,* which had served as a 1926 vehicle for Clara Bow and Ernest Torrence. The new edition, titled *Untamed* (1940), provided Patricia with Bow's original role of Alverna Easter married to a rustic French Canadian guide (Akim Tamiroff). In the course of the George Archainbaud-directed feature she falls in love with a society doctor (Ray Milland). The movie was ostensibly set in the great Northwest and was filmed in Technicolor, which emphasized Patricia's photogenic beauty. (At times she bore an uncanny resemblance to the early Dorothy Lamour.) Whereas the 1926 silent version was designed to display the ebullient talents of Miss Bow, the remake gave preference to Mr. Milland as the New York physician. Patricia did her best to give her thin role some dimension, but she was saddled with some ludicrous dialog, such as the moment when she and Milland are lost in a snowstorm. She turns to Milland, and with tears in her eyes sighs, "Oh, Bill. I'm afraid we're lost."

She did two Westerns: *Rangers of Fortune* (1940), with Fred MacMurray and Albert Dekker, then *The Roundup* (1941), an account of a rancher attempting to get his cattle to market, in which she was Richard Dix's wife, Janet. The film version of the play *There's Always Juliet* suffered in the translation as *One Night in Lisbon* (1941), despite the cast which featured Fred

394

MacMurray, Madeleine Carroll, and Patricia. In mid-1941, Pat joined a large group of Hollywood stars, including her friend and admirer, Norma Shearer, as well as Joe E. Brown, Kay Francis, Wallace Beery, Laurel and Hardy, Sabu, and others, on a jaunt to the Mexico City Film Festival. (Patricia would develop a strong partiality for Mexico, and make frequent excursions there. At one point, her brother Alex, had a nightclub in Mexico City, and it has been rumored frequently over the years that the actress would settle there permanently.)

Paramount casually loaned Patricia to Twentieth Century-Fox for the part of Rosita in *Romance of the Rio Grande* (1941), with Cesar Romero as the Cisco Kid, and then she was Ethel Abbott in a stupendous flop for another of Paramount's Nights, this one *A Night in New Orleans* (1942). After a secondary lead in an unintentional burlesque called *Beyond the Blue Horizons* (1942), starring Dorothy "Sarong" Lamour, Patricia concluded her Paramount agreement with a not-too-successful adaptation of the delightful *New Yorker* Magazine Mr. and Mrs. Cugat stories called *Are Husbands Necessary?* (1942). Betty Field was the female lead in that entry.

With her shining blue-eyed beauty topped with waist-length hair often worn parted in the middle and severely tightened into a bun, Patricia should have been a screen name on looks alone. The fact that she had a disciplined talent to offer as well, made her Hollywood meanderings on the mere outskirts of stardom even more strange. She was excellent as Claire, the owner of an ice show, beloved of Kenny Baker, in Monogram's first attempt at a class A film, *Silver Skates* (1943). And she was lovely indeed as the Empress Eugenie in Twentieth Century-Fox's *The Song of Bernadette* (1943), which won an Oscar for Jennifer Jones. Hollywood's fascination with Adolf Hitler and his henchmen filled many cans of films in the mid-1940s; in 1943 Patricia was Jarmilla in Metro's version of the siege of Lidice for the murder of Hitler's hangman Heydrich (played to the hilt by John Carradine) in *Hitler's Madman.* (The same year United Artists released a similar story in their *Hangmen Also Die.*)

Secondary roles as Barby Taviton in RKO's *The Fallen Sparrow* (1943) and as Edwina Collins in MGM's classy Hepburn-Tracy outing *Without Love* did not advance Patricia's career, despite her energetic portrayals of not-so-nice women. One could not expect much professional advancement from playing Tanya, supporting Johnny Weissmuller, who struggled against hunters seeking animals for war-depleted zoos in *Tarzan and the Huntress* (1947), or as one of three singers complicating William Powell's investigation of a murdered musician in *Song of the Thin Man* (1947). However, one might have thought that her arch-villainess role as Hilda Courtney, a woman of many disguises, in the Sherlock Holmes entry, *Dressed to Kill* (1946) would have perked up critical and public interest in her. But Patricia made it all look so easy and smooth that everyone seemed to take her for granted.

Then it appeared that Patricia had won her big break when Twentieth Century-Fox cast her in the role of Victor Mature's suicidal wife in *Kiss of Death* (1947). Hollywood gossip at the time insisted she would win an Academy Award for her tremendous acting in the film, but when *Kiss of Death* was released, Miss Morison's predicted Academy role was almost entirely cut from the picture. However, the trivial *Queen of the Amazons* (1947), in which she had to cope with spotty dialog and even spottier sets, was released with her role intact. Patricia just did not seem to have luck.

Early in 1944 she left Hollywood to replace Shirley Ross (another Paramount outcast) as Marcia Mason Moore in the musical *Allah Be Praised!* The expensive flop opened on April 20, 1944, for twenty performances at New York's Adelphi Theatre, and, if it provided Miss Morison with the knowledge that she was equipped for something other than the Hollywood treadmill, *Allah* was scarcely worth the journey. For the 1948 film *Sofia,* with Gene Raymond and Sigrid Gurie, Patricia, as a nightclub chanteuse, was finally permitted to sing three songs on the screen.

Then came *Kiss Me, Kate,* which changed her career. When Cole Porter played his enchanting score for her, one high note was beyond her range and she told the surprised composer, "Oh, I sang it but that note is so high only a dog could hear it." With that remark, she was Porter's Kate!

Originally produced for $180,000, the show, which opened at Manhattan's New Century Theatre on December 30, 1948, eventually grossed over eight million dollars. Perhaps the most surprising accomplishment in the show was Patricia's performance. From her first number, "Another Op'nin, Another Show," with Alfred Drake, Lisa Kirk, and Harold Lang, she was perfection, alternating her sweet play-within-the-play characterization with her venom-dripped asides to her stage husband (Drake). The critics ran rampant with their enthusiasm for Patricia: "As a greasepaint hussy, Miss Morison is an agile and humorous actress who is not afraid of slapstick and who can sing enchantingly. She has captured perfectly the improvised tone of the comedy, and she plays it with spirit and drollery" (*New York Times*). "Having seen this stunning young woman playing an endless

With Robert Lowery in Queen of the Amazons *(Screen Guild 1947)*

series of baffled menaces in dubious movies and having long suspected that this was one of the signs of Hollywood's idiocy, I found gratification in noting that she looks beautiful, sings charmingly, acts with fire, spirit, and a sparkling sense of comedy, and in general, proves herself a performer of genuine personal distinction. No wonder Hollywood is in such a sorry state" (*New York Post*).

In June, 1950, Anne Jeffreys took over the role of Lilli Vanessi, and on March 8, 1951, Patricia opened in *Kiss Me, Kate* at the Coliseum in London to enthusiastic audiences who applauded her singing of the show's score, including "Wunderbar" and "So in Love."

The years of waste in the Hollywood factories were over; in 1948, aside from her success in *Kiss Me, Kate,* Miss Morison was nominated for the first Annual Emmy Award as the Most Outstanding TV Personality, losing it to a puppet, Judy Splinters and her Svengali, Shirley Dinsdale. On April 16, 1950, Patricia was on TV's "This Is Show Business" with Bea Lillie and Skitch Henderson, and in November, she did the television versions of *Rio Rita* and *Trial by Jury.* Before going to London with *Kate* she greatly enlivened a telecast of Moss Hart's *Light up the Sky* on "Pulitzer Prize Playhouse." She even was seen in

With Ruth Donnelly, Don Wilson, and Betty Brewer in The Roundup *(Par 1941)*

a television series (made in 1948, but released in 1952) as psychiatrist Dr. Karen Gayle in NBC's "The Cases of Eddie Drake" (Don Haggerty). Then, in 1952, with the assistance of Benita Hume, she helped to distract another psychiatrist, Ronald Colman, from retaining his usual detachment in his treatment of beautiful women on CBS's *The Ladies on His Mind.* Later, on "The Colgate Comedy Hour" the talented Pat did a commendable buck and wing with Donald O'Connor.

On February 22, 1954, a radiant Patricia replaced the replacement (Annamary Dickey) of the replacement (Constance Carpenter) of the late Gertrude Lawrence in the long-running Rodgers and Hammerstein success, *The King and I.* For the composers' television special on March 28, 1954, Yul Brynner sang "It's a Puzzlement" from the show, Patricia performed the lilting "Getting to Know You," and the two stars dueted "Shall We Dance?" With star billing, she toured in *The King and I,* opening March 22, 1954, in Hershey, Pennsylvania, and she continued playing the Welsh school marm Anna for almost two years.

On May 16, 1956, she returned to television on "Screen Director's Playhouse" starring with George Sanders and Sal Mineo in the thriller, *The Dream,* directed by actor-writer-director Hugo Haas. For

"Schlitz Playhouse of Stars" she played Jennifer Mauldon, constantly humiliated by her crude, rough-and-tumble newly rich husband (Jack Carson) in *The Trophy.* On "Hallmark Hall of Fame" she reprised her role in *Kiss Me, Kate* and for TV's "Voice of Firestone" she sang "All the Things You Are" in *Music of Jerome Kern,* and sang with Robert Merrill in the duet, "Why Do I Love You," from *Show Boat.* She became an exotic Maharani of Bwanipur enlisting aid from the Bengal Lancers on the January 6, 1957 segment of "Hallmark," and, in March, 1963, appeared as Angela Grecor, an opera singer, on the "U.S. Steel Hour" for its TV version of Booth Tarkington's story, *The Secrets of Stella Crozier.*

New York's City Center revived *Kiss Me, Kate* in 1965 with Bob Wright in Drake's original role and Patricia Morison on the job romping through her famed role, including a rendition of the show-stopping "I Hate Men," a song that almost had been cut from the original production. In the fall of 1965 Patricia was reunited with her *Kate* co-star Alfred Drake in a tour of *Kismet* in which she played the role of Lalume with seductive abandon.

Her last foray before the Hollywood cameras was as a trousered George Sand opposite Dirk Bogarde (as Franz Liszt) in Columbia's *Song without End* (1960). Her part consisted only of a few scenes and reduced the famed character, played as a lead part by Merle Oberon in *A Song to Remember* (1945), to a mere caricature. As a matter of fact, the Bogarde version of the Liszt story was filled with hollow pretension and Hollywood sham. It had been completed by George Cukor after Charles Vidor died during the production.

If Patricia (Eileen) Morison has not accepted a march down the aisle of matrimony and remains single, she is still singing, whether it be as Kate, or Anna, or, as in August, 1973, a new creation of scintillating aging, if ageless, sexpot called Vera, the sponsor of Dean Jones' *Pal Joey* in San Diego.

Outside of Hollywood, Patricia Morison became a star, but within the studio gates her considerable talents were totally wasted. (Allegedly, it was because of her Paramount contract that her engagement to a European nobleman was broken. In the early 1940s she was escorted about Hollywood by Cesar Romero, and in the 1960s, John Vivyan of "Mr. Lucky" was her suitor and onstage co-star in such properties as a stock tour of *Beekman Place*.)

About her departure from Paramount, Patricia recalls, "I was fitted for costumes in *The Glass Key* with Alan Ladd when I was told by the studio boss, Buddy De Sylva, that Veronica Lake would do the part. He said I could stick around and play heavies. I said no! I over-ate my way out of the Paramount contract."

PATRICIA MORISON

Persons in Hiding   *(Par 1939)*
I'm From Missouri   *(Par 1939)*
The Magnificent Fraud   *(Par 1939)*
Rangers of Fortune   *(Par 1940)*
Untamed   *(Par 1940)*
The Roundup   *(Par 1941)*
Romance of the Rio Grande   *(20th 1941)*
One Night in Lisbon   *(Par 1941)*
A Night in New Orleans   *(Par 1942)*
Beyond the Blue Horizon   *(Par 1942)*
Are Husbands Necessary?   *(Par 1942)*
Silver Skates   *(Mon 1943)*
The Song of Bernadette   *(20th 1943)*
Where Are Your Children?   *(Mon 1943)*
Hitler's Madman   *(MGM 1943)*
Calling Dr. Death   *(Univ 1943)*

The Fallen Sparrow   *(RKO 1943)*
Lady on a Train   *(Univ 1945)*
Without Love   *(MGM 1945)*
Danger Woman   *(Univ 1946)*
Dressed to Kill   *(Univ 1946)*
Tarzan and the Huntress   *(RKO 1947)*
Kiss of Death   *(20th 1947)**
Song of the Thin Man   *(MGM 1947)*
Queen of the Amazons   *(Screen Guild 1947)*
Sofia   *(Film Classics 1948)*
The Return of Wildfire   *(Screen Guild 1948)*
The Prince of Thieves   *(Col 1948)*
Song Without End   *(Col 1960)*

*Almost all her scenes were deleted from the release print

63

Tom Neal

Nothing Tom Neal portrayed on stage or screen could equal the drama of his own life —a life that ran like a wayward juggernaut across his path and, eventually, crushed him. His personal scenario included a lustily belligerent career as a lover to the ex-mistress of racketeer Arnold Rothstein, three unsuccessful marriages, headlined love affairs, and a denouement of murder.

New York gambler Arnold Rothstein was mysteriously shot to death in Room 349 of the Park Central Hotel on November 4, 1928. The murder investigation and ensuing trial provided the country with steamy headlines for some time. Prominent in the Rothstein case was his mistress Inez Martin, a buxom ex-Follies girl with a deep southern accent, who emerged from the fracas with Rothstein's life insurance of over one hundred thousand dollars, plus an additional windfall of $50,000 after contesting his will. In the fall of 1934, Miss Martin met Tom Neal who, after a career at Northwestern University that ran the gamut from varsity football, basketball, boxing, and swimming, to playing leads for the Dramatic Club, had arrived in New York to establish himself in the theatre.

Neal, reputedly the heir to nearly a million-dollar fortune, divided his time between Miss Martin and the New York Public Library, where he read well-known stock plays in which he later professed to have played when making the rounds of New York produ-

cers. Richard Whorf and Robert Ross hired him for a season of summer stock at West Falmouth, Massachusetts, and armed with this brief experience and a major ego, he stormed Broadway.

Tom's theatrical ambitions did not interfere with romancing the late Rothstein's mistress. An announcement to the press that he and Miss Martin would be married at the Little Church Around the Corner brought his father, a wealthy, retired banker from Evanston, Illinois (where Tom had been born January 28, 1914), flying to New York. Inez was nearly twice Neal's age, but the young man contended that "it was love at first sight." Father Neal provided second sight and Tom issued another explanation to the press:

"My father and I talked it over and decided I ought to get a job first and show I was able to get along in the world. We decided to postpone the wedding. That is, Dad decided it." Threats of disinheritance, along with Miss Martin's sudden departure for Bermuda, ended the actor's first round in his long and losing battle of the sexes.

Neal made his Broadway stage debut in *If This Be Treason,* which opened at the Music Box Theatre on September 23, 1935. He had the small part of Jarvis in this Theatre Guild production of a lively, if trite anti-war melodrama which dealt with the then unlikely prospect of war with Japan. The show ran only forty performances. Next, Tom was Doc Boyd in an unsuccessful play by Eleanor Golden and Eloise Bar-

With Ann Savage in Detour *(PRC 1945)*

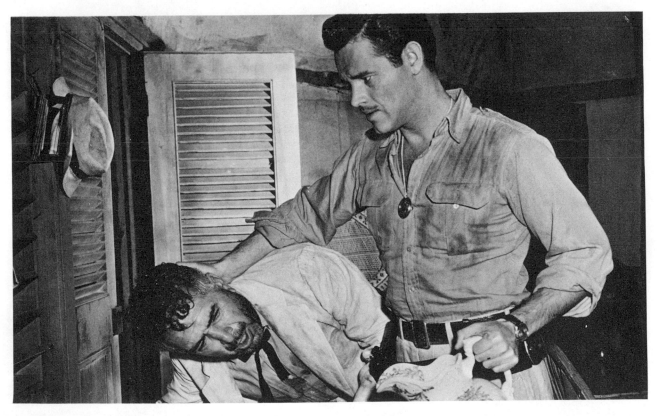

With J. Carrol Naish in Two-Man Submarine *(Col 1944)*

rangan that remained impressively unsuccessful in its rewritten version by Philip Barry as *Spring Dance* (1936). Relieved only by Jose Ferrer's performance, the revised play lasted twenty-four performances at the Empire Theatre. The next month, Tom started rehearsing one of the year's finer failures, selected as one of the season's ten best plays and notable for the brilliant acting of Maria Ouspenskaya. With Neal (as Hippolytos) in *Daughters of Atreus* were two eager young actors seeking a foothold in the theatre, Edmond O'Brien and Cornel Wilde. The play folded after two weeks.

Undaunted by his failure to capture Broadway, Tom descended on Hollywood with a Metro-Goldwyn-Mayer studio contract and made his film debut in 1938 as Aldrich Brown in *Out West with the Hardys.* He played a spate of minor roles during 1939, the best of which was in *They All Came Out,* a film that started as a short subject. But the exciting tale of two, tough gang kids (Neal and Rita Johnson) regenerated by federal prison was expanded into a feature film. As a result of his good work in this film, MGM gave him the juvenile lead in their uninspired remake of Bayard Veiller's *Within the Law* (1939), with Ruth Hussey in the role of Mary Turner (a part played by Joan Crawford in *Paid,* a 1931 film).

After a stock part in MGM's *Sky Murder* (1940), a Nick Carter mystery starring Walter Pidgeon, Tom left the studio. Aside from a couple of minor parts for Twentieth Century-Fox that included playing flyer Haynes in *China Girl* (1942)—a melee of foreign spies, Victor McLaglen, Gene Tierney, and Mandalay —plus three excellent roles for RKO, the rest of Neal's film career was spent with the independents along Poverty Row. He struggled through fifteen chapters of rescuing Frances Gifford as Nyoka in Republic's serial, *Jungle Girl* (1941), and at the same action studio was with John Wayne and John Carroll as Reardon in the above-average *Flying Tigers* (1942).

Given a meaty part, Neal could meet the challenge, as he proved in his role as squatter Dave Williams in the second, and one of the best of RKO's series with Jean Hersholt, *The Courageous Dr. Christian* (1940). That studio did not always use Tom effectively, and in the Samuel Goldwyn production, *The Pride of the Yankees* (1942) Neal, along with Dane Clark were just fraternity boys. National recognition did come to Neal when he played Taro Seki, a Cornell-educated Japanese transformed into a military tyrant in his own country, in the routine, but exploitative thriller, *Behind the Rising Sun* (1943). This film, directed by Edward Dmytryk, from a script

With John Carroll, Gordon Jones, Jimmie Dodd, John James, and Gregg Barton in Flying Tigers *(Rep 1942)*

With Martha Tilton and Leo Carrillo in a publicity pose for Crime, Inc. *(PRC 1945)*

by Emmet Lavery adapted from James Young's book, became a surprise hit and the "sleeper" of the year. Neal's performance matched his creative makeup as the young Japanese with an amazingly good performance.

Two years later, RKO hired Tom at $2,500 a week to play Major Ross, an American proficient in Japanese, who was made to look Oriental after undergoing plastic surgery. He was sent behind enemy lines to seek information on the atomic bomb in *First Yank in Tokyo* (1945). The critics lashed into the film —"A highly colored little thriller"—and deplored Neal's non-performance: "he is given a plastic-surgery job which necessitates a minimum of facial expression. Before the work is over he resembles nothing so much as one of the characters in a crime comic strip serial." Nevertheless, the topically coy feature did very nicely at the boxoffice.

From the point of view of his career, 1945 proved to be the start of a downward trend for Neal, although advocates of low-budget features have kind words for two of his entries at corner-cutting Producers Releasing Corp.: *Detour* (1945) and *Club Havana* (1945), the latter directed by Edgar G. Ulmer. In 1949 Columbia gave him the lead in *Bruce Gentry, Daredevil of the Skies,* but for fifteen chapters he was overly heroic apprehending inventors of a deadly secret weapon.

During these unspectacular filmmaking years, his lifestyle seemed to be improving, particularly after he married actress Vicky Lane and progressed to a Bel Air home. But, by the turn of the new decade, his wife divorced him, charging insane jealousy, and his personal life became more melodramatic than the string of B and C films he continued making until 1952.

Barbara Payton, a minor actress whose physical attributes far exceeded her talent, abruptly ended her affair with suave Franchot Tone by announcing her engagement to Neal in 1951, a few days after meeting him at a Hollywood party. She offered a gem of self-revelation: "It was love at first sight. I saw him in a swimming pool. He looked so wonderful in his trunks that I knew he was the only man in my life." When Tone returned to Hollywood from New York, Barbara rebounded, explaining she would marry Tone after all. In a few days she had again renounced the aristocratic actor and was planning a march down the aisle with Neal on September 14, 1951, in San Francisco. But she spent most of September 13th with the charming Mr. Tone, without knowing that a perplexed and furiously jealous Neal was trailing them, and would be waiting with increased fury in her home for their return from a night's revels in clubs.

When Tone and the mercurial Miss Payton returned at 1:30 A.M., the confrontation of screaming

401

invectives turned into an outright challenge by Tone; "Let's settle this thing outside." Ex-amateur boxer and all-around athlete Neal, who maintained his form by practicing every morning with bar bells, tried to dissuade the infuriated, much older Tone (whose physical training was apparently confined to legal battles with ex-wife Jean Wallace, party-go-rounds, nightclubbing, and Miss Payton's fancy footwork) but finally accepted the challenge by knocking Tone a distance of twelve feet and then battered him. Tom was interrupted from his combat by the shrieking Barbara, but he soon discouraged her intervention by a direct hook to her chin which sent her sprawling into the nearby rhododendron.

Tone was rushed unconscious to the hospital with a fractured cheekbone, broken nose, and brain concussion. During Tone's hospitalization, Neal made one of his rare television appearances in *Skin Game*, on the "Racket Squad" series. On recovering from surgery, Tone married Miss Payton at her home in Minnesota, but the marriage collapsed in a month's time and Barbara was back with Neal despite his observation that "Oh well, women come and go like trolley cars."

Neal's career collapsed, and what little existed of Payton's film career met its end in an effort to capitalize on some of the sleazy publicity surrounding the Tone affair. Lippert made a film, *The Great Jesse James Raid* (1952), featuring the embattled lovers: Neal appeared weary with a heavy beard and Barbara's acting consisted of trying to encase her voluptuous charms in a too tight, too small blouse. By 1962 Barbara was headlined again as a drunk. She was arrested a year later on the charge of prostitution and she died in 1967 at the age of thirty-eight.

With all his public notoriety, Neal's career was finished. He left Hollywood for Palm Springs, where he worked as the night manager of a restaurant, eked out a living as a gardener and eventually established his own landscaping business. He married a local girl, Patricia Fenton, by whom he had a son. Patricia died of cancer in 1958 and two years later Tom married Gale Bennett. The marriage was stormy. While Tom continued expanding his landscaping business, Gale worked as a receptionist at the fashionable Palm Springs Racquet Club. Then Neal's business failed and he went into bankruptcy. Gale decided to remain in Palm Springs when Neal went to Evanston, Illinois, to see his eight-year-old son who was living with Tom's sister. During his absence, Gale filed for divorce, charging extreme cruelty. When he returned from his ten-week stay in Evanston, Gale told him she had been followed home by a man, so Neal gave her instructions on the loading and firing of his .45 caliber pistol.

He left it on the coffee table.

On April 3, 1965, headlines across the country stated, "EX-ACTOR TOM NEAL HELD IN WIFE SLAYING." Shortly after midnight on the morning of April 2nd, Neal called James Cantillon, a top criminal attorney, in Los Angeles. "My wife's been shot. Can you come here immediately?" Neal was charged with murder, and the prosecution was asking for the death penalty, charging that he shot his wife as she was napping. Tom contended that they were sitting on a couch in the living room of their apartment on Cardillo Road when, after he had accused his wife of infidelity, she grabbed the pistol from the coffee table and while he struggled with her for the gun, Gale was killed by a bullet fired into the back of her head. The jury at the soul-bearing trial concluded in November that Tom was guilty of involuntary manslaughter. The jury pondered the verdict for two days and then sentenced him to ten years in prison. Six years to the day (December 7, 1965) he was paroled. Newspapers released two photographs of Neal: One taken during the Tone-Payton affair, and the second as he was leaving the prison. The latter photo looked like a younger Tom Neal made up for a horror movie. Only this was the real-life scenario playing its deadly course.

On August 7, 1972, eight months after his release from prison, Tom was found dead in bed at his North Hollywood home. The coroner's verdict was that he had died of natural causes.

Shortly after his release from prison, Tom had told reporters, "Women in my life brought me nothing but unhappiness." In turn, he obviously brought little happiness to them.

TOM NEAL

Out West with the Hardys   *(MGM 1938)*
Burn 'Em up O'Connor   *(MGM 1939)*
Honolulu   *(MGM 1939)*
Stronger than Desire   *(MGM 1939)*
Four Girls inWhite   *(MGM 1939)*
Another Thin Man   *(MGM 1939)*
6,000 Enemies   *(MGM 1939)*
Joe and Ethel Turp Call on the President   *(MGM 1939)*
They All Came Out   *(MGM 1939)*
Within the Law   *(MGM 1939)*
Sky Murder   *(MGM 1940)*
The Courageous Dr. Christian   *(RKO 1940)*
Jungle Girl   *(Rep 1941)* (Serial)
Under Age   *(Col 1941)*
Top Sergeant Mulligan   *(Mon 1941)*
The Miracle Kid   *(PRC 1941)*
Bowery at Midnight   *(Mon 1942)*
Flying Tigers   *(Rep 1942)*
Pride of the Yankees   *(RKO 1942)*
China Girl   *(20th 1942)*
Ten Gentlemen from West Point   *(20th 1942)*
One Thrilling Night   *(Mon 1942)*
Behind the Rising Sun   *(RKO 1943)*
Klondike Kate   *(Col 1943)*
Air Force   *(WB 1943)*
No Time for Love   *(Par 1943)*
She Has What It Takes   *(Col 1943)*
Good Luck, Mr. Yates   *(Col 1943)*
Two-Man Submarine   *(Col 1944)*

The Racket Man   *(Col 1944)*
The Unwritten Code   *(Univ 1944)*
Thoroughbreds   *(Rep 1944)*
Crime, Inc.   *(PRC 1945)*
First Yank into Tokyo   *(RKO 1945)*
Detour   *(PRC 1945)*
Club Havana   *(PRC 1945)*
Blonde Alibi   *(Univ 1946)*
The Hat Box Mystery   *(Screen Guild 1947)*
Beyond Glory   *(Par 1948)*
Amazon Quest   *(Film Classics 1949)*
Bruce Gentry, Daredevil of the Skies   *(Col 1949)* (Serial)
Radar Secret Service   *(Lip 1950)*
Joe Palooka in Humphrey Takes a Chance   *(Mon 1950)*
King of the Bullwhip   *(Realart 1950)*
Call of the Klondike   *(Mon 1950)*
Everybody's Dancing   *(Lip 1950)*
Train to Tombstone   *(Lip 1950)*
Danger Zone   *(Lip 1951)*
Stop that Cab!   *(Lip 1951)*
Varieties on Parade   *(Lip 1951)*
Fingerprints Don't Lie   *(Lip 1951)*
Navy Bound   *(Mon 1951)*
G.I. Jane   *(Lip 1951)*
Let's Go Navy!   *(Mon 1951)*
The Dupont Story   *(Modern Talking Pictures 1952)*
The Daltons' Women   *(Realart 1952)*
The Great Jesse James Raid   *(Lip 1952)*

64

Donald O'Connor

Donald David Dixon Ronald O'Connor, like June Havoc, never earned a dime until he could walk, but he has spent his entire life in show business and has the dubious distinction of being the only performer in the business whose career was salvaged by a jackass. He was literally born in the old theatrical tradition: but instead of "in the trunk," he was born at St. Elizabeth's Hospital in Chicago on August 28, 1925.

John Edward "Chuck" O'Connor of County Cork, Ireland, was an agile acrobat featured with Ringling Brothers-Barnum and Bailey Circus as a "leaper," running up a ramp and then hurling himself over four elephants. He also did a trampoline turn, some trapeze flying, and moonlighted as a boxer with the side shows to earn extra money for his growing family. While working a show in Washington, Pennsylvania, John met a fourteen-year-old circus bareback rider and dancer, Effie Irene Crane. They married three days later, formed their own vaudeville act, "The Nelson Comiques," and became the parents of seven children. Three children died in infancy but as the others arrived the "O'Connor Family" vaudeville act increased. Three days after Donald's birth, Effie was back in the act and, at thirteen months, her precocious baby Donald made his stage debut doing the "black bottom."

Shortly after Donald's entrance into the act, his five-year-old sister Arlene was killed by a hit-and-run driver in an alley behind an Hartford, Connecticut theatre where the family was then playing. Thirteen weeks later, John O'Connor, consumed with grief and exhaustion, died backstage of a heart attack. Nevertheless, mother Effie kept the act going. Soon Donald, at three-and-a-half, was a permanent member of the troupe, tap dancing and singing "Keep Your Sunny Side Up." The family act survived the Depression and the gradual collapse of vaudeville by living with Effie's brother in Illinois between bookings.

Donald's only formal education came via lessons sent by a Chicago professional school and his classrooms were theatre dressing rooms and dingy hotel bedrooms. But he was learning his trade from performers sharing the bill with the family act. "My learning may have been a bit irregular—but solid," he now reminisces. "I learned how to ride when we worked circus acts, bareback, western saddle and on my head. My brothers taught me hand-balancing and Mom put me through dance routines. A roller-skating act taught me to skate and from the age of nine months I rode in parades at fairs and carnivals." And in a full dress suit, spats, top hat and cane he sprinted into the footlights singing "Hail, Hail, the Gang's All Here."

While playing the west coast in 1936 Donald made his film debut with brothers Jack and Billy, doing a specialty routine in a quickly made and more quickly forgotten Warners musical, *Melody for Two,* featuring

With Patricia Medina in Francis *(Univ 1949)*

With Martha Stewart and George O'Hanlon in Are You with It? *(Univ 1948)*

James Melton. For the Motion Picture Relief Fund at the Biltmore Hotel in Los Angeles, in late 1937, Donald and brother Billy did a spot in the benefit. After the show, a Paramount movie scout asked Donald to test for the role of the kid brother of Bing Crosby and Fred MacMurray in Wesley Ruggles' *Sing You Sinners* (1938). The musical was successful and its highlight featured Donald and Crosby harmonizing Hoagy Carmichael-Frank Loesser's song, "Small Fry." Impressed with young O'Connor's work as Mike Beebe in *Sing You Sinners,* Paramount signed him to a standard contract.

His second film at that studio, *Sons of the Legion* (1938), concerned the efforts of offsprings of American Legionaries to reform bad-boy Butch Baker (O'Connor), and then he was Fred MacMurray as a youngster in Paramount's cavalcade of aviation, *Men with Wings* (1938). Donald made a good Huckleberry Finn in *Tom Sawyer, Detective* (1938). Paramount rushed him into something called *Unmarried* (1939), with out-of-the-saddle Buck Jones and Helen Twelvetrees, their *Million Dollar Legs* (1939), with Betty Grable, and finally, he was situated as Butch, an orphan hoping to get adopted by Charles Ruggles and Mary Boland in *Night Work* (1939).

The O'Connor family act without Donald suffered a further loss when his brother Billy died three days after contracting a severe case of scarlet fever. But Donald continued with his movie career. William Wellman's 1939 remake of *Beau Geste* lacked much of the intense excitement of Herbert Brenon's 1926 silent version with Ronald Colman as Beau and Maurice Murphy as Beau as a boy, the latter role played by O'Connor in Wellman's film. On loan to Warner Bros., Donald played Phil Dolan, Jr. as a boy who became—later in the film—Eddie Albert romancing Vera Zorina in a deplorable screen version of Rodgers and Hart's *On Your Toes* (1939). One critic wisely noted that the film suffered from fallen arches. When O'Connor returned to Paramount he had sprouted in height and was no longer the cute juvenile to be passed off as a pre-teenager. He was fourteen and looked it. When his option came up, Paramount brushed him off with, "You've come into that awkward age. It's tough on kid stars. Some can hold on but not many, and there just aren't any parts around here for you."

So dismissed from his nine-hundred-dollar-a-week job at Paramount, Donald hit the road again with the family act, doubling Billy's part of the act with his own. With his mother, brother, sister-in-law and niece he played what remained of vaudeville bookings for the next two years, including an extensive tour of Australia.

In 1941, Effie decided to retire, and the family act was finally disbanded. Brother Jack became a dance director for Warner Bros., and Donald's agent got him a contract with Universal where for the next two hectic years he appeared in minor, mindless—but fun—musicals usually teamed with the exhaustively exuberant Peggy Ryan, or with Universal's growing teenage population that included Gloria Jean, Ann Blyth, and Susanna Foster.

Most of Universal's meat-and-potato pseudo-musicals were pure escapist fare composed of a slim story line barely held together by the songs, jitterbug dancing, and the often featured big bands. The war years had produced a demand for quick celluloid entertainment, and Hollywood responded by mass-producing a good deal of hastily constructed trash. If the O'Connor-Ryan-Jean-Blyth-Foster musicals remain forgotten by some film-goers today, they did fulfill the need that had originally created them—instant diversion, one step removed from live variety turns. O'Connor received excellent notices for his energetic performances in many of these lower-case efforts. After *Mister Big* and *Top Man*—both in 1943—he was selected as one of the "Stars of Tomorrow," called Hollywood's most versatile teenage performer, and his gifts as a comic were applauded in films where his talent was the sole attraction. He was Universal's answer to the slightly older Mickey Rooney and there were more than a few movie-goers who felt he was superior in many areas of show business proficiency.

After he and Peggy Ryan performed a jitterbug dance routine in Universal's all-star victory campaign musical, *Follow the Boys* (1944), the duo again appeared as themselves in *Bowery to Broadway* (1944), singing "He Took Her for a Sleigh Ride in the Good Old Summertime." As Jimmy Monahan, in a vaudeville-oriented musical *The Merry Monahans* (1944), Donald put aside much of his strident, smart-alecky brashness that had been exposed in many of his previous films, and gave a solid performance in this picture, which featured Jack Oakie as his drunken vaudevillian father, Peggy Ryan (again) as his sister, and had Ann Blyth for the romantic touch.

On February 6, 1944, Donald eloped to Tijuana, Mexico, with pert, red-haired Gwendolyn Carter whom he had known back in his Paramount days. The following day O'Connor joined the U.S. Army Air Force Special Services and, during the next two years, did more than three thousand shows for the troops, several times being hospitalized for exhaustion. During his tour of duty across America with his wife, he became the father of a daughter, Donna.

Back in mufti and at Universal, O'Connor was fortunate enough to be given a chance to resume his

With Peggy Ryan and Gloria Jean in Mister Big (Univ 1943)

career. He supported Deanna Durbin in *Something in the Wind* (1947) and received good notices for his efforts. But his leading role in Universal's screen version of a not-very-good Broadway musical, *Are You With It?* (1948) was a setback, as was his frenetic and unnecessary presence in a stupid hillbilly comedy with Marjorie Main and Percy Kilbride, *Feudin', Fussin' and A-Fightin'* (1948) (The latter film title could have more accurately described Donald's marriage.) Then *Francis* arrived.

O'Connor refers to the appearance of Francis as "my mule-and-me era," but the talking mule series, which began with *Francis* (1949), was the needed straw to save not only Donald's sagging film career but to keep struggling Universal-International from bankruptcy. Based on David Stern's 1946 novel of an intelligent, highly articulate Army mule who seemingly possesses more common sense than most of the Army, the *Francis* series delighted audiences and was very successful at the boxoffice. Of the seven jackass adventures made, O'Connor was straight man for the

animal in six of them, with homespun Chill Wills providing the offcamera voice for the mule. The series also served as a showcase for Universal's promising female talent and male contract players. Tony Curtis was in the first of the series, and then, with *Francis in the Navy* (1955), there were such players as Clint Eastwood, Paul Burke, David Janssen, and Martha Hyer. Breaking up his Lieutenant Peter Stirling role in the *Francis* segments, O'Connor appeared in a hilarious satire on theatrical touring on the early frontier circuit, *Curtain Call at Cactus Creek* (1950). Donald also plunged into television work by alternating with Dean Martin and Jerry Lewis, Eddie Cantor, and Jimmy Durante, as hosts of the "Colgate Comedy Hour." Guests on his first show in November, 1951, were Harpo Marx, Yvonne De Carlo, and Reginald Gardiner.

Donald escaped from the mule teaming for one of the high points in his career as Cosmo Brown in *Singin' in the Rain* (1952), a film considered one of the best musicals ever made. In this Betty Comden-

With Susanna Foster in This Is the Life *(Univ 1944)*

Adolph Green spoof of the early talkies, Donald offered acrobatic dancing and propelled delivery of a song, "Moses Supposes" (unequalled for marathon high speed since Danny Kaye's composer's ditty in *Lady in the Dark*). O'Connor's amusing acting created a standout performance, even swamping his co-stars, Gene Kelly and Debbie Reynolds. He was cast again with the irrepressible Miss Reynolds in her first MGM starring picture, the better forgotten, if recalled at all, *I Love Melvin* (1953).

In early May, 1953, Donald was passing out cigars in celebration of becoming a "father" again. His mother, Effie, after twenty-five years of widowhood, had just married Earl C. "Bud" Kincaid, a Los Angeles vending machine wholesaler. Meanwhile, back on his home lot, Donald played the part of bandleader Jigger Millard in Universal's tepid musical, *Walkin' My Baby Back Home* (1953), with Janet Leigh and Buddy Hackett, and he joined Patsy-winner Francis again in *Francis Covers the Big Town* (1953).

Life for Donald with Gwen O'Connor was a series of arrivals and departures. Periodically Gwen would leave home and Donald claimed that fan magazines' reports of the O'Connors' feudin' and their editorializing of reasons for recapturing the marriage, saved his home life for several years. But in 1953, Gwen departed permanently and on June 16, 1953, he won an uncontested divorce.

At the sixth annual Emmy Awards in 1953, Donald was awarded an Emmy as the Best Male Star of a Regular Series for his "Colgate Comedy Hour." (He lost the nomination the previous year as TV's Most Outstanding Personality to Bishop Fulton J. Sheen.) O'Connor also received the 1953 Sylvania Award.

Donald always fared better away from the unimaginative Universal hierarchy; and for Twentieth Century-Fox he appeared as Kenneth, Ethel Merman's press attache in the film version of her Broadway smash, *Call Me Madam* (1953). The part was enlarged from the stage role played by Russell Nype, giving Donald dancing sequences onscreen, a new Irving Berlin song, "What Chance Have I with Love," a duet with Vera-Ellen, "It's a Lovely Day Today," and the show-stopping offbeat duet with Merman, "You're Just in Love." Thereafter, Paramount offered him the co-starring role with Bing Crosby in Berlin's *White Christmas* (1954), but Dr. Irving Lasky checked Donald into Cedars of Lebanon Hospital to treat his pneumonia. He was replaced in the VistaVision color musical by Danny Kaye.

In 1954, he helped in *Francis Joins the WACS* and began alternating with Jimmy Durante on the televised "Texaco Star Theatre" with his own show, "The Donald O'Connor Show." The program debuted on October 9, 1954, with guests Jimmy Durante, Mitzi Gaynor, and Donald's close friend Sid Miller, with whom he introduced a skit entitled "The Songwriters." He was reteamed with effulgent Miss Ethel Merman in Twentieth Century-Fox's *There's No Business Like Show Business* (1954), a film that contains over two dozen Berlin songs. One of them, written especially for the film, was Donald's big solo song-and-dance number, "A Boy Chases a Girl." The CinemaScope movie co-starred Marilyn Monroe, Johnny Ray, and, playing Donald's oncamera father, Dan Dailey, who, prior to production on the picture, had wed Gwen, the ex-Mrs. Donald O'Connor.

In August, 1955, Texaco dropped their "Star Theatre," and following the September tenth telecast O'Connor announced his retirement from television. The last picture on his Universal contract was in a dual role as sailor Slick Donovan and Lieutenant Peter Stirling, quelling Francis' fear he will be auctioned off as surplus material in *Francis in the Navy* (1955). O'Connor rebelled at a seventh *Francis* saga and Universal substituted Mickey Rooney for the final tale with Paul Frees supplying the animal's voice. The Rooney-Frees-Francis fantasy, *Francis in the Haunted House* (1956), was a disaster and the series died. (The series' director, however, was not through with his gimmick, and he went on to create television's "Mr. Ed, the Talking Horse".)

With diminished demands on him from the film or television studios, Donald concentrated on composing, and with the Los Angeles Philharmonic Orchestra he conducted his first symphony, "Reflections d'un Comique." Five years later the composition would be included in an album recorded by the Brussels Symphony Orchestra as "The Music of Donald O'Connor." In 1956, Donald's only screen appearance was with Bing Crosby in *Anything Goes,* a movie that had little reference to the original Cole Porter show other than a few of his songs, augmented by a few new ones by Sammy Cahn and Jimmy Van Heusen. On October 11, 1956, Donald married Gloria Noble. In 1957 they became the parents of Alicia; in 1960 of Donald Frederick; and of Kevin in 1961.

The life story of the great comedian Buster Keaton would have seemed a natural for a successful cinema biography. The Paramount brass selected Donald to play the leading role and, for added assurance, signed Buster as technical adviser. Keaton thought it was a strange yet wonderful experience working with O'Connor on the film and praised Donald's work, teaching the young actor many of his old tricks and sight gags. About the movie, O'Connor has said, "To me, the film was damned dishonest. It wasn't Buster's life. They called him a technical adviser but they never listened to him. I remember talking to him right after we'd shot a scene of him as a boy in the circus going on for his father who had just died. I asked Buster, 'What kind of circus was it?' He kind of looked at me and said, 'I never was in a circus.' So I asked him, 'Well, how old were you when your father died?' 'Forty-five,' he said." There was little O'Connor or Keaton could do with the highly fictionalized, one-dimensional script.

For the next four years Donald concentrated on TV specials, appearing on "Playhouse 90" as Robert Harrison in *The Jet Propelled Couch* with Peter Lorre, David Wayne, and Gale Gordon, and, on April 19, 1958, he starred with Shirley Jones, Elaine Stritch, Elaine May, and Mike Nichols in an updated TV version of Victor Herbert's ancient musical, *The Red Mill.* Delbert Mann paced the cast, helped by silent narrator Harpo Marx and the precocious child actress Evelyn Rudie, who explained to the home viewers what the harp was saying.

O'Connor returned to the screen in a slapstick *Sayonara* filmed in Japan, *Cry for Happy* (1961), as U.S. Sailor Murray Prince helping Glenn Ford (who was in *The Teahouse of the August Moon,* 1956) and James Shigeta turn a geisha house into an orphanage. If Donald's acting in a straight role came off well, the film was hardly worth the Japanese journey. But he followed the geisha number with a tour of Tunisia in a ninety-three-minute mirthless batch of hokum for Joseph E. Levine entitled *The Wonders of Aladdin* (1961), complete with dubbed English soundtrack.

Donald was Aladdin and Vittorio DeSica was the Genie, and the whole affair was an embarrassing squandering of fine talents.

After these two cinematic disasters, Donald returned to vaudeville, playing the Steel Pier in Atlantic City and top nightclubs in New York (receiving $12,000 a week) and Las Vegas. In 1964 he opened in Dallas with a road company of the Broadway musical *Little Me,* playing Sid Caesar's five-role part. If seemed that Joseph E. Levine had purchased the screen rights to the faltering stage musical and planned to star Donald in the movie version if he proved adept on stage. The movie was never made. O'Connor returned to Universal for the last time, supporting the likes of Sandra Dee and Bobby Darin in *That Funny Feeling* (1965), which arrived and departed with no noticeable boxoffice profits.

Turning his talents back to television he was seen on "Chrysler Theatre" in *The Brilliant Benjamin Boggs,* CBS's *The Hoofer,* and for ABC's "Stage 67," he starred as the Greek God Pan, teaching a football team dancing to improve their gridiron playing in a less-than-amusing original TV musical, *Olympus 7–000.*

Today, Donald continues at a slower pace after having suffered a heart attack in 1971, but he is still appearing in Las Vegas, has completed an eight-week tour in the hit musical, *Promises, Promises,* and, looking middle-aged and overweight, pops up as a frequent guest star on such shows as Dean Martin's or co-hosting on "The Mike Douglas Show."

DONALD O'CONNOR

Melody for Two   *(WB 1937)*
Sing You Sinners   *(Par 1938)*
Sons of the Legion   *(Par 1938)*
Men with Wings   *(Par 1938)*
Tom Sawyer, Detective   *(Par 1938)*
Unmarried   *(Par 1939)*
Death of a Champion   *(Par 1939)*
Night Work   *(Par 1939)*
Boy Trouble   *(Par 1939)*
Million Dollar Legs   *(Par 1939)*
Beau Geste   *(Par 1939)*
On Your Toes   *(WB 1939)*
Private Buckaroo   *(Univ 1942)*
What's Cookin'?   *(Univ 1942)*
Get Hep to Love   *(Univ 1942)*
Give Out, Sisters   *(Univ 1942)*
When Johnny Comes Marching Home   *(Univ 1942)*
It Comes Up Love   *(Univ 1943)*
Strictly in the Groove   *(Univ 1943)*
Mister Big   *(Univ 1943)*
Top Man   *(Univ 1943)*
This Is the Life   *(Univ 1944)*
Chip Off the Old Block   *(Univ 1944)*
Follow the Boys   *(Univ 1944)*
Bowery to Broadway   *(Univ 1944)*

The Merry Monahans   *(Univ 1944)*
Patrick the Great   *(Univ 1945)*
Something in the Wind   *(Univ 1947)*
Are You With It?   *(Univ 1948)*
Feudin', Fussin' and A-Fightin'   *(Univ 1948)*
Yes Sir, That's My Baby   *(Univ 1949)*
Francis   *(Univ 1949)*
The Milkman   *(Univ 1950)*
Curtain Call at Cactus Creek   *(Univ 1950)*
Double Crossbones   *(Univ 1951)*
Francis Goes to the Races   *(Univ 1951)*
Singin' in the Rain   *(MGM 1952)*
Francis Goes to West Point   *(Univ 1952)*
Call Me Madam   *(20th 1953)*
I Love Melvin   *(MGM 1953)*
Walking My Baby Back Home   *(Univ 1953)*
Francis Covers the Big Town   *(Univ 1953)*
Francis Joins the WACS   *(Univ 1954)*
There's No Business Like Show Business   *(20th 1954)*
Francis in the Navy   *(Univ 1955)*
Anything Goes   *(Par 1956)*
The Buster Keaton Story   *(Par 1957)*
Cry for Happy   *(Col 1961)*
The Wonders of Aladdin   *(MGM 1961)*
That Funny Feeling   *(Univ 1965)*

65

Dennis O'Keefe

Central Casting Corporation was founded on January 19, 1926, and started business on March 27, 1926, with Dave Allen as general manager and chief casting director. From the beginning to the eventual collapse of the major Hollywood studios, Central Casting was besieged by too many people for too few jobs. If the average actor's livelihood is tenuous, that of the extra has always been extremely precarious. The average daily income for an extra in the early days was $3.20 plus a box lunch, and, over the years, it has increased, if not always in proportion to the national cost of living, to $9.45 for general atmosphere people to $22.23 for "dress" extras. Of the seventy or more thousand people who have used the services of Central Casting since 1926, only a very few have risen from the extra ranks to film stardom. Among the exceptions were Jean Arthur, Richard Arlen, Gilbert Roland, Charles Farrell, Janet Gaynor, Jean Harlow—and Edward "Bud" Flanagan, who later became known as Dennis O'Keefe.

O'Keefe was born Edward Vanes Flanagan, Jr. on March 29, 1908, in Fort Madison, Iowa, to a vaudeville team known as The Rollicking Twosome, Flanagan and Edwards. The Flanagans arrived in Hollywood in 1918 and when Edward, Jr. was sixteen, he was reportedly writing scripts for Hal Roach's *Our Gang* comedies. He later dropped out of the University of Southern California to try vaude-

ville, but the two-a-day career was brief and he returned to Hollywood and joined Central Casting. Two of his earliest assignments from Central was in Douglas Fairbanks' *Reaching for the Moon* (1931) and RKO's *Cimarron* (1931). His employment as an extra was frequent and he fluctuated within the Casting Bureau's pay scale, from atmospheric extra of a drunk sleeping it off on a table in Paramount's *Night After Night* (1932) to higher scale employment in a brief speaking part in First National's *Crooner* (1932). He was a reporter in Mae West's *I'm No Angel* (1933) and for Columbia's *Mr. Deeds Goes to Town* (1936). He was a higher scale dress extra as the best man at a wedding in Metro's *Anna Karenina* (1935), and a cafe patron in *Anything Goes* (1936). With the number of film appearances he made in the early 1930s, it often seemed as if he were in perpetual motion, walking from one studio set to another, pausing just long enough to be caught in the background of some new-shooting film. His first screen credit as Edward "Bud" Flanagan was in Paramount's *Swing High, Swing Low* (1937) as a purser, and in *The Firefly* (1937) he was a French soldier to whom Jeanette MacDonald is singing.

From the start of filming on April 22, 1937, MGM director Jack Conway was beset with problems finishing *Saratoga* (1937) within its alloted thirty day shooting schedule. Production was delayed by Jean Harlow's illness, which ended with her untimely death on June 7th. The picture was completed using

412

With Edward Everett Horton in Week-End For Three *(RKO 1941)*

With Wallace Ford in T-Men *(EL 1947)*

Geraldine Dvorak for distance shots of Harlow and Mary Dees doubling in long full-face shots. Harlow's last film was not one of her best, but it was the turning point in Bud Flanagan's extra career. Clark Gable, noticing the personable extra on the set, arranged for a prime screen test for him that resulted in a MGM contract.

His first featured role—and by then he was using the professional name Dennis O'Keefe—was the juvenile lead as the rival (and long lost son) of Wallace Beery in *Bad Man of Brimstone* (1938). Then the studio featured him as Tommy Bradford, lying about his wealth and social position to Maureen O'Sullivan while Mickey Rooney walked away with *Hold That Kiss* (1938). MGM kept him busy in B films; as William Quincy Malone, a cowboy with a yen for polo in *The Kid from Texas* (1939) and as Jerry O'Connor, an egotistical hayseed racing midget cars in *Burn 'Em Up O'Connor* (1939). Louis B. Mayer's boast that all Metro-Goldwyn-Mayer pictures were good, could only indicate he saw only the studio's major products and not many of their quickies.

At the end of 1939 O'Keefe and Metro called it quits and Dennis started freelancing for Universal, RKO, and Republic. In Claudette Colbert's favorite

Publicity pose for Hi Diddle Diddle *(UA 1943)*

film for Paramount, *Arise, My Love* (1940), set against a background of the Spanish Civil War, he was Shep, one of Ray Milland's pals.

Dennis had married and divorced Louise Stanley and, in 1940, his friend, actor Richard Greene, invited him on a blind date with a friend of Greene's fiancée, Virginia Field. The blind date was Steffi Duna who, as Stefanie Berindey, had been discovered by Noël Coward dancing in a Berlin show. Later, in Hollywood, she made several films, wed screen player John Carroll and when she divorced him, attained custody of their daughter Julianna. O'Keefe was enchanted with the sparkling Hungarian actress who reminded him of his early screen idol, Renee Adoree. O'Keefe and Steffi were wed in the Spanish quarter of Phoenix, Arizona on October 18, 1940 and spent their honeymoon touring the state. The O'Keefes were an unusual Hollywood couple, devoted to their home and two children, Jimmy and Julie, and for Republic, in 1940, they were teamed in *The Girl from Havana*.

With persistence, Dennis' screen career grew to lead roles in B films and fluctuated between drama and comedy, ranging from routine racketeer stories, such as Tom O'Hara in *Bowery Boy* (1940), and harassed Lieutenant Mason confronting, of all people, Dame Judith Anderson as *Lady Scarface* (1941), to a romantic lead opposite Carole Landis in Hal Roach's *Topper Returns* (1941). As music publisher David Burton, he was in a not very hilarious farce *Good Morning, Judge* (1943), and then, in contrast, he had a dramatic role as Jan Horok withstanding Nazi revenge for the death of Hangman Heydrich in *Hangmen Also Die* (1943). Finally, in RKO's minor classic, *The Leopard Man* (1943), he was Jerry Manning tackling a "black cat", with Margo and her castanets featured in this Val Lewton production.

Hi Diddle Diddle (1943) was a breezy, bubbly, senseless farce made by Andrew Stone in which Pola Negri made a gossamer comeback as the giddy opera singer wife of Adolphe Menjou with a Wagnerian complex. Dennis played Sonny Phyffe, the sailor-bridegroom of Martha Scott. His talent for comedy was evident playing Gary Ainsworth in the aged farce *Up in Mabel's Room* (1944), in which he spent most of the footage trying to retrieve a compromising silk slip whimsically given to Mabel (Gail Patrick). Said the *New York Herald-Tribune*, "Dennis O'Keefe works valiantly in the leading role, and his talents deserve better material." If O'Keefe was developing into a fine light comedian, he was also effective as over-disciplined Navy officer Lieutenant Commander Yarrow teaching hot-headed John Wayne the Navy way in *The Fighting Seebees* (1944).

Cecil B. DeMille received the Order of Orange-Nassau from Queen Wilhelmina of the Netherlands for his film of Dutch heroism in Java called *The Story of Dr. Wassell* (1944). There were no such awards from the critics, all of whom, virtually unanimously, attacked the feature as more fiction than fact and also, nearly to the man, praised the highly dramatic, sincere performance of Dennis O'Keefe as Benjamin Hopkins, seaman first class. The 140-minute color film left O'Keefe making a last, desperate stand against the Japanese. However, before the Paramount picture was released, DeMille discovered that the seaman had not been killed but was a prisoner of war, and attached a soundtrack to the end of the motion picture with DeMille telling the audience that Hoppy was still alive. DeMille called O'Keefe's playing of Hoppy a moving performance. As the heroic Benjamin "Hoppy" Hopkins, Dennis came into his own as an actor and gave great impetus to his career. Sadly, in the years ahead, Dennis would never have such a showcasing assignment again.

Dennis and burly William Bendix were well matched as two Marines in Australia in *Abroad with Two Yanks* (1944) and, as Montgomery Brewster, Dennis' astute sense of timing added lustre to another remake of Winchell Smith's farce *Brewster's Millions* (1945), which at one time or another had served as starring vehicles for Edward Abeles, Roscoe "Fatty" Arbuckle and, in England, Jack Buchanan. United Artists' continued the resurrection of old farces with Avery Hopwood's creaking comedy, *Getting Gertie's Garter* (1945). Between the ancient farces, Dennis' talent was wasted on such fare as Twentieth Century-Fox's dreary *Doll Face* (1945) in which he played Mike Hannegan, publicity manager for burlesque queen Vivian Blaine. He was also Dr. Cousins, in Hedy Lamarr's highly unbelievable *Dishonored Lady* (1947). He helped to write and also starred in *T-Men* (1948) for Eagle Lion, appearing as government agent Dennis O'Brien. In *Raw Deal* (1948), he was exceptionally effective as Joe Sullivan, an escaped convict caught between Claire Trevor and Marsha Hunt while menaced by gangster Raymond Burr.

In 1949, O'Keefe, Mickey Rooney, and Jack Oakie played three clowns in a sketch that was a highlight of the Friars Frolics and attended by some six thousand patrons; this Frolics production brought in three hundred thousand dollars for the Motion Picture Relief Fund. On the screen he was seen as Jean Morhange with Maria Montez and Jean Pierre Aumont in *Siren of Atlantis* (1948), which sunk lower than the fabled lost continent. As an extra, Dennis had worked in Paramount's 1933 *The Eagle and the Hawk*. In 1950, Paramount used the story but a different title, *A Mission to General Houston,* in which O'Keefe played Whitney Randolph.

The new and challenging media of television caught Dennis' attention in 1951 and, with Edward Arnold, he appeared on the Ken Murray program in a playlet, *Town Wanted.* For "Video Theatre" he supported Charlton Heston and Vanessa Brown in *Route Nineteen.* Meanwhile, Hollywood studios offered him unchallenging roles that were mainly secondary: *Follow the Sun* (1951), a golfing story, *Passage West* (1951), a western with John Payne, and a backup role as Alec Takabury in Gower and Marge Champion's *Everything I Have Is Yours* (1952).

Fortunately, television provided Dennis with more versatile and showier assignments. In *Double By-Line* he was wed to Nina Foch and they were rival reporters. For the "Climax" telecast of Bayard Veiller's thriller, *The Thirteenth Chair,* O'Keefe helped Ethel Barrymore discover a murderer through a seance. On "Producer's Showcase," Dennis maintained his professional stature in *Yellow Jack,* with a cast that included Broderick Crawford, Raymond Massey, Rod Steiger, Eva Marie Saint, Jackie Cooper, Dane Clark, and E. G. Marshall.

Under his pen name, Jonathan Ricks, Dennis wrote several screenplays, including *T-Men, The Diamond Wizard* (1953) (in which he starred and directed), and the Italian-made Patria film released by Twentieth Century-Fox, *Angela* (1955). In the mid-fifties he starred in a series of exposé movies: *Las Vegas Shakedown* (1955), *Chicago Syndicate* (1955) and *Inside Detroit* (1955). He later described a film he made in England, *Sail into Danger* (1957) as being "perfectly terrible."

In 1958, O'Keefe and Les Hafner, for CBS and Cypress Productions (named for Dennis' favorite golf course) started producing "The Dennis O'Keefe Show" for television, a situation comedy set in a penthouse, where New York columnist Hal Towne (O'Keefe) lives with his young son and a burly housekeeper (Hope Emerson) named Sarge. The show lasted one season. After that he was seen on television on the "Joey Bishop Show" then as Hogan with Yvonne De Carlo in *The Longest Crap Game in History* (played during the Pearl Harbor attack), and in *Open Season,* he was Pete Flannery, involved in a Mexican divorce with Dick Powell and Dorothy Malone.

O'Keefe's last major film (he was also in *The Naked Flame,* 1965) was Twentieth Century-Fox's *All Hands on Deck* (1961), which showcased the talents of Pat Boone and Buddy Hackett, with Dennis as a very funny, bewildered Lieutenant Commander O'Gara. After playing Dan Muldoon, a prizefighter promoter on a "Riverboat" segment and a bartender on

With Susan Hayward in The Fighting Seabees *(Rep 1944)*

"Follow the Sun", Dennis looked for a new field to conquer —the legitimate stage.

His first outing in the legitimate theatre would have delighted any seasoned theatre man; the lead oppposite Mary Martin in a Howard-Dietz-Arthur Schwartz musical, *Jennie,* based on the early life of Laurette Taylor. The arduous rehearsals and new medium took their toll of O'Keefe. After the Boston opening (July, 1963) of *Jennie,* he was applauded for his vigorous playing of Martin's impractical first husband, James O'Connor, and commended for singing and dancing an acceptable soft shoe routine with Mary Martin in the "Waitin' for the Evening Train" number, but he resigned from the show and George Wallace replaced him. *Variety,* reviewing the Boston opening, reported, "Dennis O'Keefe, as the wild, reckless, boozing hubby, brings vigor to the role and does an OK acting job but was evidently suffering from laryngitis."

Dennis' determination to reach Broadway was realized on March 28, 1964 when he starred as Robert Miller in a pseudo-comedy, *Never Live Over a Pretzel Factory.* Although O'Keefe provided a colorful performance as a movie star on a gigantic binge while hiding from his producer, the show was merely a series of sight gags adding up to an "improbable demented bacchanalia," and the show closed on April 4th. By June, Dennis was back in the theatre, having replaced Paul Ford as the embarrassingly perplexed father-to-be in the comedy hit, *Never too Late.*

After a tour in the play *The Subject Was Roses,* Dennis went into rehearsal for a new comedy by Michael V. Gazzo called *What Do You Really Know about Your Husband?,* in which he starred with Kate Reid. O'Keefe's hope of returning to Broadway in a genuine hit died quickly after the opening in New Haven, Connecticut on March 9, 1967, and two days later the show was closed. From the Gazzo flop, O'Keefe jaunted to Florida for a tour as Oscar in *The Odd Couple,* with E. G. Marshall, Loretta Swit, and Huntz Hall.

In October, 1967, Dennis underwent surgery for lung cancer in Rochester, Minnesota. On August 31, 1968, the breezy, fast-talking, charming Irishman died at St. John's Hospital in Santa Monica, California. His wife Steffi, son James, daughter Julie Benito, and three grandchildren attended the funeral services at Forest Lawn Memorial Park's Wee Kirk O' the Heather.

416

DENNIS O'KEEFE

As: BUD FLANAGAN
Reaching for the Moon   *(UA 1931)*
Cimarron   *(RKO 1931)*
Crooner   *(FN 1932)*
Two Against the World   *(WB 1932)*
Cabin in the Cotton   *(FN 1932)*
I Am A Fugitive from a Chain Gang   *(WB 1932)*
Big City Blues   *(WB 1932)*
A Bill of Divorcement   *(RKO 1932)*
The Man from Yesterday   *(Par 1932)*
Merrily We Go to Hell   *(Par 1932)*
Night after Night   *(Par 1932)*
Central Park   *(FN 1932)*
Hello Everybody!   *(Par 1933)*
Blood Money   *(UA 1933)*
Broadway thru a Keyhole   *(UA 1933)*
Girl Missing   *(WB 1933)*
From Hell to Heaven   *(Par 1933)*
The Eagle and the Hawk   *(Par 1933)*
Gold Diggers of 1933   *(WB 1933)*
Too Much Harmony   *(Par 1933)*
I'm No Angel   *(Par 1933)*
Duck Soup   *(Par 1933)*
The House on 56th Street   *(WB 1933)*
Lady Killer   *(WB 1933)*
Torch Singer   *(Par 1933)*
Upper World   *(WB 1934)*
Wonder Bar   *(FN 1934)*
Jimmy the Gent   *(WB 1934)*
Smarty   *(WB 1934)*
The Meanest Gal in Town   *(RKO 1934)*
He Was Her Man   *(WB 1934)*
Desirable   *(WB 1934)*
Coming Out Party   *(Fox 1934)*
Girl from Missouri   *(MGM 1934)*
Death on the Diamond   *(MGM 1934)*
Registered Nurse   *(FN 1934)*
Fog over Frisco   *(FN 1934)*
Man with Two Faces   *(FN 1934)*
Madame Du Barry   *(WB 1934)*
Lady by Choice   *(Col 1934)*
College Rhythm   *(Par 1934)*
Transatlantic Merry-Go-Round   *(UA 1934)*
Imitation of Life   *(Univ 1934)*
Devil Dogs of the Air   *(WB 1935)*
Doubting Thomas   *(Fox 1935)*
Dante's Infero   *(Fox 1935)*
Rumba   *(Par 1935)*
The Daring Young Man   *(Fox 1935)*
The Man Who Broke the Bank at Monte Carlo
  (20th 1935)
Top Hat   *(RKO 1935)*
Mary Burns, Fugitive   *(Par 1935)*
Burning Gold   *(Rep 1935)*
Biography of a Bachelor Girl   *(MGM 1935)*
Gold Diggers of 1935   *(FN 1935)*
Mississippi   *(Par 1935)*

Let 'em Have It   *(UA 1935)*
Every Night at Eight   *(Par 1935)*
Anna Karenina   *(MGM 1935)*
Personal Maid's Secret   *(FN 1935)*
It's in the Air   *(MGM 1935)*
Shipmates Forever   *(FN 1935)*
Broadway Hostess   *(FN 1935)*
Anything Goes   *(Par 1936)*
Hats Off   *(Grand National 1936)*
Love Before Breakfast   *(Univ 1936)*
San Francisco   *(MGM 1936)*
Till We Meet Again   *(Par 1936)*
The Last Outlaw   *(RKO 1936)*
Three Smart Girls   *(Univ 1936)*
Mr. Deeds Goes to Town   *(Col 1936)*
13 Hours by Air   *(Par 1936)*
And So They Were Married   *(Col 1936)*
Nobody's Fool   *(Univ 1936)*
Sworn Enemy   *(MGM 1936)*
Rhythm on the Range   *(Par 1936)*
Yours for the Asking   *(Par 1936)*
Libeled Lady   *(MGM 1936)*
Theodora Goes Wild   *(Col 1936)*
The Accusing Finger   *(Par 1936)*
Born to Dance   *(MGM 1936)*
The Plainsman   *(Par 1936)*
Great Guy   *(Grand National 1936)*
Married Before Breakfast   *(MGM 1937)*
The Big City   *(MGM 1937)*
The Great Gambini   *(Par 1937)*
The Lady Escapes   *(20th 1937)*
One Mile from Heaven   *(20th 1937)*
Top of the Town   *(Univ 1937)*
When's Your Birthday?   *(RKO 1937)*
Parole Racket   *(Col 1937)*
Swing High, Swing Low   *(Par 1937)*
Captains Courageous   *(MGM 1937)*
A Star is Born   *(UA 1937)*
Riding on Air   *(RKO 1937)*
The Girl from Scotland Yard   *(Par 1937)*
Easy Living   *(Par 1937)*
The Firefly   *(MGM 1937)*
Blazing Barriers   *(Mon 1937)*

As: DENNIS O'KEEFE
Saratoga   *(MGM 1937)*
Bad Man of Brimstone   *(MGM 1938)*
Hold that Kiss   *(MGM 1938)*
The Chaser   *(MGM 1938)*
Vacation from Love   *(MGM 1938)*
The Kid from Texas   *(MGM 1939)*
Burn 'em Up O'Connor   *(MGM 1939)*
Unexpected Father   *(Univ 1939)*
That's Right—You're Wrong   *(RKO 1939)*
La Conga Nights   *(Univ 1940)*
Alias the Deacon   *(Univ 1940)*
Pop Always Pays   *(RKO 1940)*

I'm Nobody's Sweetheart Now   *(Univ 1940)*
Girl from Havana   *(Rep 1940)*
Arise, My Love   *(Par 1940)*
You'll Find Out   *(RKO 1940)*
Bowery Boy   *(Rep 1940)*
Mr. District Attorney   *(Rep 1941)*
Topper Returns   *(UA 1941)*
Broadway Limited   *(UA 1941)*
Lady Scarface   *(RKO 1941)*
Week-End for Three   *(RKO 1941)*
The Affairs of Jimmy Valentine   *(Rep 1942)*
Moonlight Masquerade   *(Rep 1942)*
Hangmen Also Die   *(UA 1943)*
Tahiti Honey   *(Rep 1943)*
Good Morning, Judge   *(Univ 1943)*
The Leopard Man   *(RKO 1943)*
Hi Diddle Diddle   *(UA 1943)*
Up in Mabel's Room   *(UA 1944)*
The Fighting Seabees   *(Rep 1944)*
The Story of Dr. Wassell   *(Par 1944)*
Sensations of 1945   *(UA 1944)*
Abroad with Two Yanks   *(UA 1944)*
Earl Carroll Vanities   *(Rep 1945)*
Brewster's Millions   *(UA 1945)*
The Affairs of Susan   *(Par 1945)*
Getting Gertie's Garter   *(UA 1945)*
Doll Face   *(20th 1945)*
Her Adventurous Night   *(Univ 1946)*
Mr. District Attorney   *(Col 1947)*
Dishonored Lady   *(UA 1947)*
T-Men   *(El 1947)*
Raw Deal   *(EL 1948)*
Walk a Crooked Mile   *(Col 1948)*
Siren of Atlantis   *(UA 1948)*
Cover Up   *(UA 1949)*
The Great Dan Patch   *(UA 1949)*
Abandoned   *(Univ 1949)*
The Eagle and the Hawk   *(Par 1950)*
Woman on the Run   *(Univ 1950)*
The Company She Keeps   *(RKO 1950)*
Follow the Sun   *(20th 1951)*
Passage West   *(Par 1951)*
One Big Affair   *(UA 1952)*
Everything I Have is Yours   *(MGM 1952)*
The Lady Wants Mink   *(Rep 1953)*
The Fake   *(UA 1953)*
The Diamond Wizard   *(UA 1953)*
Drums of Tahiti   *(Col 1954)*
Angela   *(20th 1955)*
Las Vegas Shakesdown   *(AA 1955)*
Chicago Syndicate   *(Col 1955)*
Inside Detroit   *(Col 1955)*
Dragoon Wells Massacre   *(AA 1957)*
Sail Into Danger   *(Patria 1957)*
Lady of Vengeance   *(UA 1957)*
All Hands on Deck   *(20th 1961)*
The Naked Flame   *(Corona 1965)*

66

Janis Paige

When Janis Paige—who had made something of a name for herself in the stage comedy *Remains To Be Seen* (1951)—walked onto the stage of the St. James Theatre on May 13, 1954, and sewed up Broadway as Babe in the instantaneous hit musical, *The Pajama Game,* most people could quite sincerely ask, "Where had the thirty-year-old performer been all these years?" For seven years in the 1940s she had been salted away at Warner Bros., mostly in dreary dramas and comedies, and generally as Jack Carson's on-screen girlfriend. Despite her early operatic training and her natural comic knack, the red-haired, vivacious Janis was too infrequently cast in a studio musical film or a dizzy comedy. She was too often stuffed into a restraining mold to perform roles similar to those of gentle Joan Leslie or Joyce Reynolds. Only after Janis was unceremoniously dumped from the studio's roster in the late 1940s did she key up her natural talents and reveal her best professional side: a frank, brassy dame, who possessed wide vocal range with a straightforward sound.

Janis's real name is Donna Mae Tjaden and she was born on September 16, 1923, in Tacoma, Washington. Her parents separated when she was four years old and she did not see her father again until thirty years later. "I like him," she admitted. "We look alike." Janis suspects her name is Norwegian, but she is not sure. She has a younger sister who is

now Mrs. R. L. Finney and also resides in California. Money was tight while she was growing up, and when her mother, Hazel, was forced to take on employment as a switchboard operator, Janis and her sisters went to live with their grandparents. Janis studied typing and shorthand while attending Stadium High School in Tacoma. She was generally a poor student, although she did excel in Spanish and American history. She studied opera, sang with the Tacoma Opera Company and had high school leads in *The Desert Song* and *The Merry Widow.* Her mother, to whom Janis was closely attached for years, thought her daughter the next Lily Pons or Gladys Swarthout. However, after Janis graduated from high school, she needed money immediately and accepted a secretarial job at a plumbing supply store in Seattle for fifteen dollars weekly.

But Mrs. Tjaden was determined that Janis should have a chance at a professional career. She bought a second-hand car and moved to Los Angeles with Janis in tow. Plans were that Janis should somehow be given voice lessons and then, perhaps, find a way to be accepted at the Juilliard School of Music in New York. Meanwhile, Janis took another secretarial position and, through an associate of her mother's, worked evenings at the Hollywood Canteen serving sandwiches and coffee. One night at the Canteen, when an entertainer failed to appear, Janis speedily replaced her and sang "Un Bel Di" from *Madame Butterfly* and, as a change of pace, the more contem-

With Jack Carson, Martha Vickers, and Dennis Morgan in The Time, The Place and The Girl *(WB 1946)*

Esther Williams, Jean Porter (on steps, head tilted) and Janis Paige (on steps, looking at camera) in Bathing Beauty *(MGM 1944)*

porary number, "The Man I Love." She was overwhelmed by the very enthusiastic response. At the Canteen that evening was Ida Koverman, girl Friday for MGM's mogul, Louis B. Mayer. Through the talent-perceptive Miss Koverman, Janis was offered a six-month contract at Metro at $150 weekly. During that period, when Janis' expectations ran so high, she was cast in only one film at the studio playing a schoolgirl who sings and dances in a few numbers of the Esther Williams-Red Skelton comedy; *Bathing Beauty* (1944). Janis recollects; "I was the clumsiest thing you ever saw." She had an inferiority complex and was extremely aware of how unglamorous she was, especially in the midst of the luminous beauties on that lot. She says she felt quite ugly compared to Ava Gardner, Esther Williams, and the other MGM women. At the end of the six-month option period, Janis was discharged from the Culver City studio.

But Warner Bros. talent scout Solly Biano got Janis a screen test at his studio and she was soon signed to a hundred-fifty-dollar-a-week contract which had escalation clauses to bring the salary to one thousand dollars a week. Ironically, Janis' first feature film for Warners was *Hollywood Canteen* (1944), playing a pigtailed Warner Bros. messenger girl. The feature

was jammed with guest appearances by most of the studio's stars and featured players, but Janis, as Angela, had one of the main storyline roles, along with Joan Leslie, Dane Clark, and Robert Hutton. It was also at this time that her name was changed professionally to Janis Paige. The surname was her maternal grandfather's and "Janis," so the publicity story goes, came from the popular World War I era personality, Elsie Janis.

During her first year as a starlet on the lot, she worked in short subjects such as *I Won't Play* (1945), and, for publicity purposes, was dubbed "Miss Airmail Parcel Post," "Miss Grapefruit," "Miss Delicious Apple," among others. Possibly the weirdest of all was "Miss Damsite," when she helped to inaugurate Oregon's McNary Dam.

Janis was wearing her messenger girl's costume for *Hollywood Canteen* when director Edmund Goulding spotted her on the lot. He was very impressed with her excellent figure and her striking blue eyes. He took for granted that she was actually a messenger girl at the studio and was elated that he had personally discovered a real "looker." When he was informed that she was already under contract, he arranged to use her for his remake of *Of Human Bondage*, made in 1944 but not released until July, 1946.* As Sally the daughter of kindly Mr. Anthelney (Edmund Gwenn), Janis played the role Frances Dee had had in the far superior 1934 version: The girl who reaffirms a belief in female kindness in clubfooted physician Philip Carey (Paul Henreid), the latter having suffered emotional torment at the hands of Cockney waitress Mildred Rogers (Eleanor Parker). This elaborate but thin rendition of the famed Somerset Maugham novel did nothing for anyone in the cast.

Chesty Janis had the occasion to torch a few songs (including "Something to Remember You By," and "Speak to Me of Love") as Georgia King, the gangster's moll in *Her Kind of Man* (1946), made after *Of Human Bondage,* but released before it. Janis seemed terribly young as the cafe singer in love with unscrupulous Zachary Scott. The *New York Sun,* however, found Janis "a newcomer with a pretty face and a pretty way." When Warner Bros'. contractee Jane Wyman got dramatic and went on to bigger and better projects, Janis took over for her in her usual roles in the studio's dizzy comedy parts. *Two Guys from Milwaukee* (1946) was the first of five times that she

*Due to the Kim Novak-MGM remake of *Of Human Bondage,* in which Nanette Newman had Janet's role, the 1946 version is not available for television, although, oddly, the 1934 edition is available for revival in art house showing.

appeared onscreen with Dennis Morgan and and the first of her six film pairings with Jack Carson. The three of them co-starred in *The Time, the Place, and the Girl* (1946) a remake of a 1929 musical, and even appeared together briefly in *Always Together* (1947), a lesser, if that was possible, Robert Hutton-Joyce Reynolds vehicle. When Morgan and Carson got together again to do *Two Guys from Texas* (1948), Janis was so busy in a host of other films that she was replaced by Penny Edwards. The Western *Cheyenne* (1947) was also with Morgan as was the limited-budget musical remake of *One Sunday Afternoon* (1948). In case Carson was feeling professionally slighted, Janis joined with him in *Love and Learn* (1947) and in *Romance on the High Seas* (1948). The latter picture introduced Doris Day to the medium. But nowhere along the line did the studio give plucky Janis the proper promotion or showcasing her talents deserved. She had the dubious honor of having appeared in Bette Davis' worst 1940s Warners feature, *Winter Meeting* (1948), and then she was tumbled into such minor fodder as *This Side of the Law* (1950), which featured Kent Smith and Viveca Lindfors.

In 1949, the studio dropped Janis. "They didn't know where I belonged," she said, "any better than I did." Whatever her professional mistreatment at the Burbank lot, it was a home base, financial security,

With Dennis Morgan in Cheyenne *(WB 1947)*

421

With Wayne Morris in The House Across the Street *(WB 1949)*

and, more importantly, it gave the emotionally tenuous Janis a point of reference for her life.

From a career point of view, Janis almost sank to oblivion after leaving Warners. She joined with another Warners alumnus, Jack Carson, in United Artists' *Mr. Universe* (1951), and they toured in a nightclub act together. (During her Warners years she had constantly performed at theatres that had vaudeville shows along with the Warner Bros. product, such as the Strand in New York.) Then, with Robert Alda, also ousted from Warners' factory, she made *Two Gals and a Guy* (1951) at United Artists, a minor yarn about this trials and tribulations of a performing couple involved in the pioneer days of commercial television. As for *Fugitive Lady* (1951) made at Republic, Janis has only two words to say: "Not good."

The lowest point of her career occurred between April and August of 1950. "I was as cold as last year's turkey," she recalls. She could not get any film offers, she was broke and eventually became ill. "I was scared stiff," she confesses. "Movies were all I knew. All of a sudden I had to find another way to make a living." When she was forced to sell her Cadillac she realized her salad days in movies were over. Her physical collapse occurred soon after her emotionally debilitating tour of low-class one-night stands in grubby clubs. Thereafter, with the help of her agent Ruth Aarons, she managed to pull herself together and evolved a slick club act that was suitable for the big-time.

Janis now refers to 1950 as the year she was born, because she divorced her husband, Frank Martinelli, whom she had married in 1947, and broke away from an overly dependent relationship with her mother. She had met Martinelli in San Francisco where he and his father operated the Bal Tabarin Cafe.

While appearing in the stage show at the Paramount Theatre in New York she was cast as Jody, the band singer in the stage play by Howard Lindsay and Russel Crouse, *Remains to Be Seen,* which opened at the Morosco Theatre on October 3, 1951. The comedy-melodrama co-starred her with Jackie Cooper, with whom she became romantically involved off-stage, but she was then not ready for another marriage. Janis found it exceedingly difficult to adapt her style to the new medium. "I was a novice who didn't know upstage from downstage; who never had memorized pages of lines and directions." The show was moderately successful, even though Brooks Atkinson wrote in the *New York Times:* "Janis Paige plays the part of the middle western singer with a lot of energetic clowning, but with no apparent talent." Janis found that she enjoyed working on the stage: "I was part

and parcel of it, not an outsider, not a girl coming in for a few scenes. It was wonderful."

When *Remains to Be Seen* closed (June Allyson played Janis' role opposite Van Johnson in the 1953 MGM film version), Janis went on to play the leading role in *Annie Get Your Gun* in Kansas City and then fulfilled an engagement at the Copacabana in Manhattan. At this time she also began appearing on television variety show such as the Jack Benny, Garry Moore, and Bob Hope programs. She has been a guest on Hope's video outings some ten times and also co-starred with him in the 1958 television play, *Roberta.* Moreover, she had joined the "Great Ski Nose" in entertaining the armed forces in both Korea and Cuba.

It was producer Hal Prince who caught Janis' act at the Copacabana and had her audition for the new musical he was co-producing with Frederick Brisson and Richard Griffith. Janis was signed for the leading role of Babe Williams, the factory worker and the head of the grievance committee in *The Pajama Game.* She had trouble doing the role at first and knew that director George Abbott was not very pleased with her, but she was determined to succeed. And succeed she did with this 1954 Broadway musical. This time, Brooks Atkinson of the *Times* described her performance as "exhilarating." With this show, Janis became the brassiest babe on Broadway and was in competition with Ethel Merman as the loudest singer in the world. Despite the attraction of John Raitt singing "Hey There," the dancing and singing of "new find" Carol Haney, and the comedy relief of Eddie Foy, Jr. and Reta Shaw, Janis made a fine showing in her part. (There are some who feel she delivered to a tough performance.) Her belted renditions of "There Once Was a Man" (with Raitt) and "I'm Not at All in Love" were excellently rendered. When the film version of the musical was cast, nearly all the original performers repeated their roles—except for Janis. The property was purchased for Doris Day at Warner Bros. Janis admits she did "get a twinge" when she was not picked for the 1957 film version, "but I really didn't care too much. I didn't worry over it. After all, it's still the role I created so I'll always feel it's mine." It was Janis' biggest show business success.

Losing out on the filmed *The Pajama Game* did get her the caricatured movie-queen role in the film version of the Broadway musical *Silk Stockings* (1957). Janis had originally been offered the role in the stage version (1955), but she turned it down and Gretchen Wyler had played it. The MGM movie starred Fred Astaire and Cyd Charisse in this musical revamp of

423

Ninotchka (1939), but the critics favored Janis, and it is her most popular film role. Her duet with Astaire, "Stereophonic Sound," was the best thing in the Rouben Mamoulian-directed feature. The *New York World-Telegram and Sun* declared, "A big share of the bountiful mirth is in charge of Janis Paige with her hilarious travesty of a fancy, flouncing movie star. Even Fred himself loses the attention when this girl is allowed on the screen.

Just as Janis had found it difficult to click on the big screen, she had her problems with television. After the huge success of *The Pajama Game,* she returned to Hollywood for her own half hour filmed series, "It's Always Jan" (1955–56). In the CBS comedy series, Janis played a widowed nightclub singer with a daughter, who shares an apartment with both a model and a cynical secretary. The lives and loves of three roommates were occasionally and happily, interrupted by a few songs sung by Janis, and by comedy patter between Jan and her agent (Sid Melton). The show could not survive the rating race, mainly because it was pitted against the voguish Lawrence Welk Show. TV producer-writer Arthur Stander, who created the series for Janis, became her second husband on January 18, 1956, when they were wed in Las Vegas. She divorced him the following year because he was "uncontrollably jealous" and had an "uncontrollable temper." Janis waived alimony.

MGM, the first studio she had ever worked for and who brought her back to pictures via *Silk Stockings,* signed her for the title role in the proposed "Maisie" series for television, based on the very successful motion picture property that had once featured Ann Sothern. Nobody bought the video rehash. Then, after Janis lost the leading role in the Broadway musical *Destry* to Dolores Gray, MGM used her talents to support Doris Day and David Niven in the pixilated *Please Don't Eat the Daisies* (1960) and Bob Hope and Lana Turner in *Bachelor in Paradise* (1961). Nobody, let alone Janis, could support anything in the Connie Francis mini-vehicle, *Follow the Boys* (1963), Janis' next film. It was also in that year, 1963, that Janis finally found vent for her dramatic prowess on-screen; she was cast as a prostitute in a hospital ward in *The Caretakers.* Her role was heavily stark, at times funny, and always very moving. Had the film been critically acclaimed, which it was not, she would have undoubedly received an Oscar nomination for Best Supporting Actress. The film's producers, aware of her chances for an Oscar bid, deliberately, and with Janis' consent, lowered her billing in the ads for the picture from equal starring to also-starring. Her last feature film appearance was in Metro's *Welcome to Hard Times* (1967), again playing a prostitute, only this time in the old West.

The 1960s were not diamond-studded years for Janis. In 1961 she was seen in an original musical comedy on television called *Happiest Day,* top-billing her with Craig Stevens and her old Warners buddy, Jack Carson. Two years later, on October 3, she opened on Broadway opposite Craig Stevens in *Here's Love,* Meredith Willson's saccharine, prefabricated musical* based on the charming movie, *Miracle on 34th Street* (1947), Janis played the role which Maureen O'Hara had had in the feature version, and the show lasted for 334 performances. Janis did not appear on Broadway again until 1968, when she replaced Angela Lansbury in *Mame* at the Winter Garden Theatre. (Job-desperate Judy Garland had been the other choice for the replacement role.) "She looks glowingly well," reported the *New York Times* of Janis, "and sings, dances and acts with a sweet enthusiasm, but not perhaps the bitter-sweet enthusiasm Miss Lansbury presented. She is less of a character but, as some compensation, perhaps more of a performer."

Janis has been married to Ray Gilbert, the Hollywood composer and music publisher, since August 30, 1962. Both had been married twice before and have no children. (Gilbert won an Oscar in 1947 for his song, "Zip-a-Dee-Doo-Dah" from the movie, *Song of the South.*) The Gilberts live in California but have spent much time in Brazil, where Janis studied Portuguese. Janis still takes daily jazz or ballet classes and continues her exercise routines. She also cooks every night for her husband: "I love to do that." In the past few years she has done *Guys and Dolls* and *Gypsy* at various music tents and starred in the South African production of *Applause.* On the dinner theatre circuit, she has played in *Born Yesterday* and *Desk Set.*

Looking back on her early movie career, Janis says, "I knew absolutely nothing about acting. I guess I had no right to be a star. I just did what the directors told me to do. The directors and the cameraman did the work. I guess I looked attractive on a screen." She is very well aware that she did not have the opportunity to work with good film scripts and that Warners persistently sidetracked her with many poor roles. But they also gave her lessons and did build up her name. "I'll always be grateful to Warner Brothers for the chance."

---

*It must be admitted that the stage version is superior to the assorted newly tuned video versions of the classic 1947 feature.

JANIS PAIGE

Hollywood Canteen   *(WB 1944)*
Her Kind of Man   *(WB 1946)*
Of Human Bondage   *(WB 1946)*
Two Guys from Milwaukee   *(WB 1946)*
The Time, the Place, and the Girl   *(WB 1946)*
Love and Learn   *(WB 1947)*
Cheyenne   *(WB 1947)*
Always Together   *(WB 1947)*
Winter Meeting   *(WB 1948)*
Wallflower   *(WB 1948)*
Romance on the High Seas   *(WB 1948)*
One Sunday Afternoon   *(WB 1948)*

The Younger Brothers   *(WB 1949)*
The House Across the Street   *(WB 1949)*
This Side of the Law   *(WB 1950)*
Mr. Universe   *(UA 1951)*
Fugitive Lady   *(Rep 1951)*
Two Gals and a Guy   *(UA 1951)*
Silk Stockings   *(MGM 1957)*
Please Don't Eat the Daisies   *(MGM 1960)*
Bachelor in Paradise   *(MGM 1961)*
Follow the Boys   *(MGM 1963)*
The Caretakers   *(UA 1963)*
Welcome to Hard Times   *(MGM 1967)*

67

Robert Paige

The multi-talented Robert Paige was Universal's resident leading man during the forties. The studio used his talents (some insist he had none) far better and more often than other studios used their similar, dependable boys.

Born John Arthur Paige in Indianapolis, Indiana, on December 2, 1910, Paige attended West Point but left the Academy to concentrate on a radio career. Arriving on the west coast he became an usher for the Fox West Coast Theatres. He then landed a job singing on a Long Beach, California radio station KGER and eventually moved to Hollywood as an announcer-program director for station KMTR.

Under the name David Carlyle, he began in motion pictures as early as 1931 in short subjects. By 1935 he had graduated to features, with tiny roles in *Annapolis Farewell* (1935) at Paramount, *Hearts in Bondage* (1936) at Republic, and *Smart Blonde* (1936) at Warner Bros. For the latter studio he sang "I'll Sing You a Thousand Love Songs" to Marion Davies in *Cain and Mabel* (1936), but the following year he was back making short subjects, such as *Murder in Swingtime* (1937) at Columbia. At Columbia he changed his screen name to Robert Paige. There, he had secondary leads, such as Swing Traynor in 1938's *Who Killed Gail Preston?*, to which one critic replied, "Who cares?" Paige graduated to such innocuous leads as William Rolph in *Highway Patrol* (1938), and

detective Mac Richards in *The Main Event* (1938). In Columbia's fifteen-chapter serial *Flying G-Men* (1939), he was Hal Andrews, alias *The Black Falcon*, who uncovers a widespread spy ring. After another substandard dud with Rita Hayworth at Columbia, titled *Homicide Bureau* (1939), he transferred to Paramount. If he had hoped for better projects at that more sophisticated studio, he was soon disillusioned. He sustained leads in films such as *Emergency Squad* (1940); he was Fred MacNeil with Ellen Drew in *Women without Names* (1940), Steve Eddson in *Parole Fixer* (1940), Wally Matson in *Golden Gloves* (1940), and was Larry Reed in a horror fracas, in which a man's mind is transferred to a gorilla, called *The Monster and the Girl* (1941). Of this latter picture, the *New York Times* rhetorically queried, "This corner has wondered how many dyspeptic dramas might be spared the public if only a scenarist had taken bicarbonate of soda before sitting down to the typewriter." Robert played his first feature film musical lead in *Dancing on a Dime* (1941) as Ted Brooks in a tale of a WPA, with music by Frank Loesser and Victor Young and featuring Grace McDonald, Peter Lind Hayes, and the song "I Hear Music."

For the next seven years Paige became Universal's "old reliable," fluctuating between minor musicals, infrequently amusing comedies, and any roles when Universal required a presentable, dependable leading man—that is, if Robert Stack, Robert Cummings, or Franchot Tone had not already taken the assignment.

426

With Ole Olsen, Chic Johnson, and Jane Frazee in Hellzapoppin! *(Univ 1941)*

With Billy Green and Sabu in Tangier *(Univ 1946)*

In 1940, Paige married Betty Henning and started providing the romantic interest in Universal's quickly made, quickly released, and quickly forgotten musicals. He appeared as Con Conway in *San Antonio Rose* (1941) with the Merry Macs and his frequent screen partner, Jane Frazee, with whom he also was teamed in *Hellzapoppin* (1941), *Don't Get Personal* (1942), and *What's Cookin'?* (1942). Paige had a good singing voice and his acting was more often than not creditable, despite the repetitive, one-dimensional romantic leads the studio tossed his way, such as James Manning II in *Almost Married* (1942) and Tommy Layton romancing Virginia Bruce in Bud Abbott and Lou Costello's *Pardon My Sarong* (1942).

Paige was teamed with the brittle Louise Allbritton in a better-than-average comedy, *Fired Wife* (1942). Allbritton and Paige made an extensive personal-appearance tour with the film, and although their expert handling of comedy as a team was very evident, Universal did not reunite them in a comedy until two years later. In the screwball comedy *Her Primitive Man* (1944). Paige writes a wildly exaggerated travel book and must pose as one of the aborigines he has invented. Between the two comedies, Robert and Allbritton were together in Universal's *Son of Dracula*

(1943), but Lon Chaney, Jr. had the showy title role as Count Alucard.

Generally, Paige was consigned to such dull affairs as Universal's version of the over-crowded Washington, D.C. farce situation, *Get Going* (1943), in which he was cast as F.B.I. agent Bob Carlton. Actually, he could be a most convincing hero, as when he was Steve, in a better-than-average western *Frontier Badmen* (1943). He was Johnny Blake, a crooner with an all-girl orchestra in *Hi, Buddy!* (1943), with Dick Foran (who could also sing) and Harriet Hilliard, and then turned to songwriting as George Selby in *How's About It?* (1943), with the Andrews Sisters. *Cowboy in Manhattan* (1943) got him involved, as Bob Allen, in a Texas-sponsored Broadway musical; as Professor Hanley, the romantic lead with Elyse Knox, he provided background for the jivings and raucous goings-on of Donald O'Connor and Peggy Ryan trying to put on yet another musical over the objections of a stuffy faculty in *Mr. Big* (1943). Paige remained the romantic interest mannequin again with Jane Frazee in the Ritz Brothers' frantic *Hi Ya, Chum!* (1943).

Universal's quickly made, mindless, but often infectiously entertaining musicals tried for the A class when the production involved their reigning queen of

With Robert Benchley and Edward Everett Horton in Her Primitive Man *(Univ 1944)*

With Marguerite Chapman and Milburn Stone in The Green Promise *(RKO 1949)*

song, Deanna Durbin. The Durbin musicals were usually well produced and engaging, and, in 1944, the studio persuaded Jerome Kern to write a score for their prize soprano's next film. The score was not top-drawer Kern, but it did provide Robert Paige with songs worth singing and he did extremely well* dueting with Durbin on the title song and "Californ-i-ay," and singing solo "Elbow Room" Unfortunately, the color production *Can't Help Singing* tried too hard to cash in on some of the popularity and flavor of Broadway's *Oklahoma!* in its covering of a haphazard jaunt across North America in 1849 that was far less solid than it could have been.

In 1945 Robert made one film that was entirely dominated by a sly scene stealer and expert performer, Charles Coburn, in a production unreasonably named *Shady Lady*. Robert was Bob Wendell, supplying the usual hearts and flowers to Ginny Simms. After being wasted in *Tangier* (1946), as was a soon-to-be-ousted Maria Montez, Robert moved to lower-class Eagle-Lion as Andy McBride in *Red Stallion* (1947) and then played the role of Barry McAllister in a Republic disaster geared to the not-very-extensive talents of Vera Hruba Ralston, *The Flame* (1947).

In July, 1948, Paige flew some 24,000 miles in a Glen McCarthy aircraft interviewing some forty-eight young 4-H Club girls for four prospective parts in *The Green Promise* (1949), which he produced for RKO release with Monty F. Collins, who wrote the story and the screenplay. Backed by the McCarthy firm, the Paige-Collins film cast, quite naturally, Paige as David Barkley, helping the impoverished Matthews farm family. In this film, he encourages pig-tailed Susan (Natalie Wood) to join the 4-H Club and raise a pair of lambs, to the delight of farmer Matthews (Walter Brennan) and his oldest daughter, the lovely Marguerite Chapman.

With Miss Chapman, Paige made his first television appearance (in 1951) on "Bigelow Theatre" in *The Lady's Companion*. Paige's TV appearances continued through 1952 and 1953. In the latter year he returned to Universal for a very supporting role in *Abbott and Costello Go to Mars*. Along with the love-restless wife role played by Alexis Smith, Paige gave a substantial performance as Arthur Ashton, one of several people trapped in a ghost town to be used as a target for an A-bomb test in Dick Powell's first, and successful, directorial job for RKO called *Split Second* (1953).

After *Split Second*, Paige, now called Bob, geared his talents to television. On "Cavalcade of America" he supported Gertrude Michael as *Major Pauline* (Cushman), spying behind rebel lines for the Union. With Frances Rafferty and Robert Hutton, Bob appeared in *Vacation Wife*, and he was well cast as Paul, the other man in Lilli Palmer's life in *Lady of the Orchids*, the latter for "Four Star Playhouse." In 1955 Paige won the Los Angeles area TV Award as the Most Outstanding Male Personality. On the "Crossroads" telecast, *Coney Island Wedding*, he appeared as Charlie, a press agent helping priest Dick Foran establish a church. By 1957, Paige was co-hosting the afternoon TV show "Bride and Groom," where couples actually married on television. His co-host, Byron Palmer, was eventually replaced by Frank Parker.

The next year Bob replaced Randy Merriman on another of television's many give-away shows, "The Big Pay-Off," co-starring with Bess Myerson, Miss America of 1945. Bob appeared as himself with other guest stars (Jayne Meadows, Garry Moore, Betsy Palmer, and Dave Garroway) in Columbia's 1959 Doris Day theatrical feature, *It Happened to Jane*.

Although the Leslie Stevens play was better on the stage, especially with Claudette Colbert and Charles Boyer in the leads, than the author's screen treatment of it, *The Marriage-Go-Round* (1960) provided Paige with an amusing role as Dr. Ross Barnett. He gave a good performance advising faithful, if frustrated, anthropology Professor James Mason to desert his egghead wife (Susan Hayworth) and run off to Bermuda for a relaxed, uninhibited affair with sexy Swede Julie Newmar.

Paige returned to television on January 20, 1960, on one of the "The Millionaire" episodes as a magazine editor who finally marries his fashion consultant after receiving a million dollars. In 1961 he supported Barbara Stanwyck on her video show in *Size Ten*. Bob's last theatrical feature-film appearance to date was a brief foray in the screen version of the Broadway musical hit, *Bye, Bye Birdie* (1963). In March, 1964, he became the father of a daughter.

Now in his sixties, Bob Paige has returned to his first career, radio, and, now, television. In 1966, he became a newscaster for KABC, channel 7, in Los Angeles.

---

*Regarding Paige as Durbin's leading man in this peaches-and-cream story, Bosley Crowther (*New York Times*) wrote, "Robert Paige, an outworn juvenile, is the incomprehensible gentleman of her choice."

ROBERT PAIGE

As DAVID CARLYLE
Annapolis Farewell   *(Par 1935)*
Hearts in Bondage   *(Rep 1936)*
Smart Blonde   *(WB 1936)*
Cain and Mabel   *(WB 1936)*
Melody for Two   *(WB 1937)*
Marry the Girl   *(WB 1937)*
Once a Doctor   *(FN 1937)*
Cherokee Strip   *(WB 1937)*
Meet the Boy Friend   *(Rep 1937)*

As ROBERT PAIGE
There's Always a Woman   *(Col 1938)*
The Little Adventuress   *(Col 1938)*
The Lady Objects   *(Col 1938)*
Who Killed Gail Preston?   *(Col 1938)*
When G-Men Step in   *(Col 1938)*
Highway Patrol   *(Col 1938)*
The Main Event   *(Col 1938)*
I Stand Accused   *(Rep 1938)*
The Last Warning   *(Univ 1938)*
Flying G-Men   *(Col serial 1939)*
Homicide Bureau   *(Col 1939)*
Death of a Champion   *(Par 1939)*
Emergency Squad   *(Par 1940)*
Women Without Names   *(Par 1940)*
Parole Fixer   *(Par 1940)*
Opened by Mistake   *(Par 1940)*
Golden Gloves   *(Par 1940)*
The Monster and the Girl   *(Par 1941)*
Dancing on a Dime   *(Par 1941)*
San Antonio Rose   *(Univ 1941)*
Hellzapoppin!   *(Univ 1941)*

Melody Lane   *(Univ 1941)*
You're Telling Me   *(Univ 1942)*
Don't Get Personal   *(Univ 1942)*
What's Cookin'?   *(Univ 1942)*
Jailhouse Blues   *(Univ 1942)*
Almost Married   *(Univ 1942)*
Pardon My Sarong   *(Univ 1942)*
Get Hep to Love   *(Univ 1942)*
Fired Wife   *(Univ 1943)*
Get Going   *(Univ 1943)*
Frontier Badmen   *(Univ 1943)*
Hi Buddy!   *(Univ 1943)*
Crazy House   *(Univ 1943)*
How's About It?   *(Univ 1943)*
Cowboy in Manhattan   *(Univ 1943)*
Mr. Big   *(Univ 1943)*
Son of Dracula   *(Univ 1943)*
Sherlock Holmes in Washington   *(Univ 1943)*
Hi Ya, Chum!   *(Univ 1943)*
Follow the Boys   *(Univ 1944)*
Can't Help Singing   *(Univ 1944)*
Her Primitive Man   *(Univ 1944)*
Shady Lady   *(Univ 1945)*
Tangier   *(Univ 1946)*
Red Stallion   *(EL 1947)*
The Flame   *(Rep 1947)*
Blonde Ice   *(Film Classics 1948)*
The Green Promise   *(RKO 1949)*
Abbott and Costello Go to Mars   *(Univ 1953)*
Split Second   *(RKO 1953)*
It Happened to Jane   *(Col 1959)*
The Marriage-Go-Round   *(20th 1960)*
Bye Bye Birdie   *(Col 1963)*

68

Larry Parks

When Larry Parks burst onto the screen doing an imitation of Al Jolson in *The Jolson Story* (1946), he was considered an overnight success. That was far from the truth, for he had apprenticed and appeared in thirty-odd previous features—and many of them were very odd releases indeed. Playing in mostly B and C motion pictures, Parks had an assortment of small roles: Soldiers, sailors, reporters, students, Indians, football players, jailbirds, etc. He appeared in such movies as *Harmon of Michigan* (1941), *Sing for Your Supper* (1941), *The Boogie Man Will Get You* (1942), and *Redhead from Manhattan* (1943). He would occasionally have a smaller role in more important products such as *You Belong to Me* (1941), *They All Kissed the Bride* (1942), and *You Were Never Lovelier* (1942). In 1942 alone he worked in thirteen films.

From 1941 to 1950, while under contract to Columbia Pictures, Parks made only one outside film and that was *The Deerslayer* (1943) for Republic. *The Jolson Story* turned him into a big star, but his marquee lure was short-lived. In 1951 he testified before the House Un-American Activities Committee that he had been a member of the Communist Party from 1941 through 1945, and his career was dealt such a severe blow that he was never able to professionally recover. He could not get show business work, and, for a time, his HUAC testimony also affected the acting career of his wife (Betty Garrett).

He was born Samuel Klausman Lawrence Parks on December 13, 1914, in Olathe, Kansas, and is of German-Irish descent. When he was a baby, his parents, Frank and Leona (Klausman) Parks, moved the family to Joliet, Illinois. During his childhood, Klaus—as Larry was then known—suffered from a number of illnesses. An attack of rheumatic fever left him with a weakened heart and another illness temporarily paralyzed him—leaving him with one leg slightly shorter than the other. Exercise and willpower corrected his damaged leg in time. Whenever his health permitted, he participated in Boy Scouts' activites and attended Farragut Grammar School in Joliet. Later, he was graduated from the University of Illinois with a Bachelor of Science degree. Originally, Larry planned to become a doctor, but while he was in school he became involved in campus dramatics, and by the time of graduation his aim had switched to a theatre career. Over his parents' objections, he joined an amateur drama group and toured Illinois in shows.

His greasepaint ambitions took him to New York with hopes of somehow landing a part in a Broadway show. Instead, he paid the rent on his furnished room by ushering at Carnegie Hall and being a tour guide at Radio City. He made friends with another tour guide and would-be actor, Gregory Peck. In 1936, Larry began getting work in summer stock, and the following year he made his Broadway debut in a miniscule role in the Group Theatre's production of *Golden Boy*

With Peter Lorre and Jeff Donnell in The Boogie Man Will Get You *(Col 1942)*

In Jolson Sings Again *(Col 1949)*

(November, 1937). He continued working with the Group Theatre for the next few years, and other small roles in Broadway shows followed. He was in *All the Living, My Heart's in the Highlands,* and *Pure in Heart.* Just as his career was beginning to develop, his father died and he returned home. He also decided to give up acting for a time and went to Chicago and became a Pullman inspector on the New York Central Railroad. He disliked the job intensely but stuck with it, until one day he received a wire from John Garfield, a friend from the Group Theatre, telling him to come to Hollywood to do a small role in one of his films at Warner Bros. The picture was called *Mama Ravioli.* Larry took a bus out west, but thirty-six hours before the film was to start shooting, it was cancelled.

Broke again, Larry moved in with two friends. One of them, an architect, owned a bit of land, and, between the three of them and some borrowed money, they built a bungalow on the property and sold it. Larry's share of the sale was $133. It was also the beginnings of Larry Parks, construction businessman. At about this time, Larry was granted an interview at Columbia Pictures. They did not give him a personal screen test but used him in Barry Fitzgerald's test for the role of Messenger 7013 in *Here Comes Mr. Jordan* (1941), with Larry playing the role Robert Montgomery did on the screen. Fitzgerald did not get the part (it was eventually played by Edward Everett Horton), but Larry was signed to a contract.

Larry made his film debut as Tommy Baker, a government agent in *Mystery Ship* (1941), featuring Paul Kelly and Lola Lane. For the next few years, few actors worked as often as he did, except that he was in more wretched movies than most, including *Reveille with Beverly* (1943), in which gangling Frank Sinatra crooned "Night and Day." If graduating to co-leads meant taking assignments like the soundstagebound *The Deerslayer,* then Parks might have been better off remaining in secondary roles in more distinguished productions. In this poor man's version of the James Fenimore Cooper novel, Larry was cast as an Indian called Jingo-Good, who was betrothed to Wah-Tah (Yvonne De Carlo). He received top billing in *The Black Parachute* (1944) as an American soldier behind enemy lines, combatting Nazi general John Carradine, and he was also top-billed in *Sergeant Mike* (1944) and *She's a Sweetheart* (1944).

Larry had first met Betty Garrett in New York when he was with the Group Theatre and she was studying at the Neighborhood Playhouse. Their paths crossed again when he was staging a revue at the Actors' Lab in Hollywood and she was performing at the Clover Club on Sunset Strip. They married on September 8, 1944, but spent most of their early married life sepa-

With Michael Duane and Nan Wynn in Is Everybody Happy? *(Col 1943)*

rated from each other due to their careers. She was beginning to make a name for herself on Broadway due to the Cole Porter show, *Something for the Boys* and was soon to begin rehearsals for the Olsen and Johnson comedy, *Laughing Room Only*. Larry's film career was also improving with a good supporting role as Kirchenko in the A feature, *Counter-Attack* (1945), starring Paul Muni. Whenever it was possible, they traveled coast to coast to be with one another. Betty became a star in *Call Me Mister* in 1946, stopping the show with her number "South America, Take it Away!" MGM promptly signed her to a contract and she made her film debut in *Big City* (1948). She and Larry were finally able to settle down in California where they bought a home. The Parkses have two sons, Garrett and Andrew, born in 1950 and 1951 respectively. Andrew has recently appeared in a number of television shows as an actor.

Larry's big break came, at long last, when Columbia cast him in the musical biography, *The Jolson Story* which grossed domestic rentals of over eight million dollars. This followed his third-billed outlaw role in the Technicolor western, *Renegades* (1946), with Evelyn Keyes and Willard Parker. The songs in *The Jolson Story* were dubbed by Jolson himself, but Parks did an excellent mouthing job and gave a clever imitation of the famous performer. However, Larry had not been the first choice for the stellar role. Harry Cohn, head of Columbia, had wanted James Cagney, who had had great success portraying George M. Cohan in *Yankee Doddle Dandy* (1942). But Cagney had not been interested in playing another showbusiness immortal. Danny Thomas, then a rising comedian, also had been offered the role, on the condition that he have plastic surgery to reconstruct his too-prominent nose. Thomas refused. Jose Ferrer and Richard Conte, too, had been under consideration for the role. Larry had tested for the film ten times, having studied Jolson films and recordings to perfect his imitation. Parks received a best-actor Oscar nomination, but lost the Award to Fredric March (*The Best Years of Our Lives*).

As good as Larry was in *The Jolson Story*, his performance was dimmed by the marvelous Jolson soundtrack. The *New York Times* complained: "Mr. Parks struts and mugs in the manner of Jolson, as a bright impersonator might do. Unfortunately, his speaking voice is silken while the singing voice of Mr. Jolson is full of sand, which calls unavoidable attention to another synthetic feature of the film." The film's sequel, *Jolson Sings Again* (1949), was not, as might have been anticipated, as good as the original, but it did gross several million dollars' profit. In this case, the *New York Herald-Tribune* went on record

with, "Parks' performance is something to admire objectively and he 'sells' songs so beautifully in a pantomime which is more than a mere Jolson imitation, that one wishes he had a voice of his own." Larry actually had a decent singing voice, but he was generally dubbed when performing in a musical film, as when he joined Rita Hayworth in *Down to Earth* (1947).

After starring in two Columbia swashbucklers, *The Swordsman* (1947) and *The Gallant Blade* (1948), and the Jolson followup, Larry sued the studio for release from his contract. He was now a star and was dissatisfied with his assignments. However, he did not win his professional freedom and, perhaps, as punishment, the studio teamed him with his *Jolson Sings Again* teammate, Barbara Hale, in the dreary *Emergency Wedding* (1950), a feeble remake of the Barbara Stanwyck-Henry Fonda *You Belong to Me* (1941). Columbia did allow Larry to do some summer stock, and he appeared with Joan Lorring and Cameron Mitchell in *A Free Hand* at the Lake Whalom Playhouse in Fitchburg, Massachusetts, where he had worked a decade earlier. He also appeared, for the first time professionally, with his wife, in vaudeville in 1949 and then took the show to London's Palladium. Larry was then scheduled to join Ann Sheridan in *Two of a Kind* (1951), but when she proved unavailable, it was recast with Lizabeth Scott and Edmond O'Brien.

Larry had just finished a romantic comedy with Elizabeth Taylor at MGM titled *Love Is Better Than Ever* (1952) when Parks' professional roof caved in—almost permanently. On March 21, 1951, Larry was ushered in front of the House Un-American Activities Committee. Under pressure he told the committee that he had been a member of the Communist Party for four years in the early 1940s. He said he had joined the Party because it was "the most liberal of the parties," and drifted out of it in 1945 from a "lack of interest—of not finding the things I thought I would find." Larry was the first Hollywood witness to admit Party membership in the latest Hollywood witch-hunt since the well-known "Hollywood Ten" catastrophe of 1947. Larry claimed that he was never very active in circles, and that he had a only limited amount of information on such political activities. He refused to take the Fifth Amendment as so many had before him, but he also refused to name names. In an emotional statement, he said, "The only loyalty I know is to America," and begged the Washington group, "Don't make me crawl in the mud." The hearings were then closed to the public and word spread that he had provided names, some big ones, in closed session. The committee praised Larry as a "loyal true American"

435

With Larry Thompson and Selmer Jackson in Hey, Rookie *(Col 1944)*

for being the first in his profession to make known his past Red affiliations. John Wayne, superstar and strong supporter of the committee, asked that Hollywood forgive Larry his mistake. "Duke" Wayne said, "The public will forgive Parks. I find his courage [in not taking the Fifth] commendable." However, the public was not really given a chance either way, for he could no longer find work in Hollywood. His MGM film with Elizabeth Taylor was held up from release for well over a year. Parks was never officially blacklisted, but what happened to him in Hollywood amounted to the same thing. Other stars, such as Sterling Hayden, followed him in front of the committee, and they continued to work. Larry said it was "because I was the first to testify. The first one always reaps the biggest headlines." In 1973, a play called *Are You Now or Have You Ever Been,* by Eric Bentley, was presented in New York, after premiering at Yale University. It dealt with the committee hearings of the 1950s and included such onstage characters as Parks, Haydn, choreographer Jerome Robbins, and director Elia Kazan. Clive Barnes in the *New York Times* said actor "Peter Thompson has great compassion as the baffled but doomed Larry Parks."

After Parks's fracas in the headlined hearings, Columbia cancelled his next film, which was to have been a comedy, *Small Wonder,* and they found enough loopholes in his employment contract to avoid paying his salary. "There was no alternative but to end the contract," said Larry. He and Betty were then obliged to find work overseas, and they toured Europe with their act. They returned to tour the States in the play *Anonymous Lover* (1952). By 1954, feelings had somewhat eased up and Betty obtained the best film job of her career as Ruth in Columbia's musical version of *My Sister Eileen.* (Judy Holliday had turned down the role.) Larry's first Hollywood outing after the hearings was on television's "Ford Theatre" in *The Happiest Day* (1954) with Teresa Wright. Larry and Betty later did some video programs together, and in 1957 they were called upon to replace Miss Holliday and Sidney Chaplin on Broadway in *Bells Are Ringing. Variety* reported, "Parks is an adept musical comedy performer, more skillful as both singer and hoofer than the previously inexperienced Chaplin, and a more pliable comedian."

Larry also played Sakini in the national touring company's production of *The Teahouse of the August Moon* on a year's jaunt, and then replaced Johnny Carson as Augie Poole in *Tunnel of Love* on Broadway. His other two Broadway ventures, the musical *Beg, Borrow or Steal* (1960) and the comedy *Love* and Kisses (1963), were flops. Meanwhile, Betty had her most rewarding Broadway part in the dramatic offering, *Spoon River Anthology* (1963).

Larry regards himself as "not a stingy man, but I am known as a close man with a dollar." It was very wise of him to save his money while he was under contract to Columbia. He bought up parcels of land and built apartment buildings. He is now a quite successful housing constructor. He is co-owner of nearly twenty apartment buildings in Los Angeles, and occasionally he dabbles in theatre, preferably working with his wife. They were in the Chicago company of *Cactus Flower,* and he then replaced Forrest Tucker on the road in *Plaza Suite,* opposite Betty. Though he does not work that often anymore, Larry remains a thoroughly professional performer.

Since the delayed released of *Love Is Better Than Ever,* Parks would only appear in two more theatrical features. He made a British film titled *Tiger by the Tail* (1955), which was released three years later in the States as *Cross-Up.* He was the only American in the cast, playing a reporter kidnapped by counterfeiters out to obtain a dead girl's diary. *Variety* claimed, "Parks vacillates between straight drama and out-of-place coyness." A few years later, John Huston cast a mature, graying Larry as Dr. Joseph Breuer in contrast to Montgomery Clift's *Freud* (1962), an unsatisfying melodrama that did no better when redistributed as *The Secret Passion.* On reporting about his feature, in which Larry received third star billing, *Variety* offered, "Larry Parks, in his return to the screen, etched a warm and appealing portrait of Freud's friend, colleague, and associate."

In the Seventies, Larry and Betty resided in the Nichols Canyon section of Hollywood. He no longer had an agent. Then on April 13, 1975 he died of a heart attack at his home. He left an estate consisting of $10,000 in cash, $10,000 in stocks and $75,000 in other personal property. In mid-1975, Betty Garrett returned to New York with plans to do her one-women show on the caberet circuits. Son Andy has just played the part of young W.C. in the W.C. Fields film biography, starring Rod Steiger.

Not long before he died, he had occasion to speak of his two-decade-old emotional wounds, which understandably, had not totally healed. He said, "A man could eat himself up with bitterness. But you can't live like that."

LARRY PARKS

Mystery Ship   *(Col 1941)*
Harmon of Michigan   *(Col 1941)*
Honolulu Lu   *(Col 1941)*
Three Girls About Town   *(Col 1941)*
You Belong to Me   *(Col 1941)*
Sing For Your Supper   *(Col 1941)*
North of the Rockies   *(Col 1942)*
Canal Zone   *(Col 1942)*
Alias Boston Blackie   *(Col 1942)*
The Boogie Man Will Get You   *(Col 1942)*
Blondie Goes to College   *(Col 1942)*
Harvard, Here I Come   *(Col 1942)*
A Man's World   *(Col 1942)*
Hello, Annapolis   *(Col 1942)*
Flight Lieutenant   *(Col 1942)*
They All Kissed the Bride   *(Col 1942)*
Atlantic Convoy   *(Col 1942)*
Submarine Raider   *(Col 1942)*
You Were Never Lovelier   *(Col 1942)*
Redhead from Manhattan   *(Col 1943)*
Power of the Press   *(Col 1943)*
Is Everybody Happy?   *(Col 1943)*

Reveille with Beverly   *(Col 1943)*
Destroyer   *(Col 1943)*
First Comes Courage   *(Col 1943)*
The Deerslayer   *(Rep 1943)*
The Racket Man   *(Col 1944)*
Hey, Rookie   *(Col 1944)*
Stars on Parade (a.k.a., Calling All Stars)   *(Col 1944)*
The Black Parachute   *(Col 1944)*
Sergeant Mike   *(Col 1944)*
She's a Sweetheart   *(Col 1944)*
Counter-Attack   *(Col 1945)*
Renegades   *(Col 1946)*
The Jolson Story   *(Col 1946)*
Her Husband's Affairs   *(Col 1947)* (Unbilled guest role)
Down to Earth   *(Col 1947)*
The Swordsman   *(Col 1947)*
The Gallant Blade   *(Col 1948)*
Jolson Sings Again   *(Col 1949)*
Emergency Wedding   *(Col 1950)*
Love Is Better Than Ever   *(MGM 1952)*
Tiger by the Tail (a.k.a., Cross-Up)   *(Eros 1955)*
Freud (a.k.a., The Secret Passion)   *(Univ 1962)*

69

Robert Preston

Anyone who has ever seen Robert Preston perform the role of Professor Harold Hill, *The Music Man,* onstage or onscreen would find it difficult to believe for an instant that this dynamic performer was ever considered just a run-of-the-mill leading man for B pictures during the 1940s. Most people would find it equally hard to believe that he was generally confused with another actor named Preston: Preston Foster.

Preston was born Robert Preston Meservey in Newton Highlands, Massachusetts, on June 8, 1917. (To this day he still uses his full real name to sign checks.) He was two years old when his parents moved to the Lincoln Heights section of Los Angeles, where his younger brother, Frank, Jr. was born. His father worked for a garment manufacturer and his mother, Ruth, sold records over a counter.

Lincoln Heights was a rough part of town and Robert had to put up with a lot of teasing from the neighborhood toughs, because his mother made him study piano, guitar, and trumpet. He became interested in acting while attending Lincoln High School and received help and guidance from the school's drama teacher, E. J. Wenig. Wenig even cast Preston as *Hamlet* when the boy was only fifteen years old.

Robert left school to join a Shakespearean company managed by Tyrone Power's mother, Patia, and, when he was eighteen, he entered the Pasadena Play-house Theatre School along with fellow students William Holden, Dana Andrews, and Victor Mature. For a while, he studied nights at the Playhouse and worked days as a parking attendant at the Santa Anita Racetrack.

He was playing Harry Van, the down-at-the-heels song-and-dance man, in *Idiot's Delight,* his forty-second Playhouse production, when he was spotted by a Paramount studio talent scout. For his screen test he played Killer Mears in *The Last Mile,* a role that had "star" written into it. Paramount signed Preston to a contract with a starting salary of one hundred dollars a week. At this time he dropped the name Meservey.

Even though Paramount's casting director thought Preston looked too much like a truck driver (he was 6'1", well-built, had green eyes, and wavy brown hair), he was nevertheless cast in three of the studio's crime series program pictures: *King of Alcatraz* (1938), *Illegal Traffic* (1938), and *Disbarred* (1939). In *Illegal Traffic,* with Mary Carlisle and J. Carrol Naish, he had the pivotal role which was, concidentally, that of a truck driver. These were good minor films which more closely resembled Warner Bros. products than the glossy efforts of Paramount.

Preston's first major film was Cecil B. DeMille's *Union Pacific* (1939). As Dick Allen, the railroad saboteur, he received fourth billing, following Barbara Stanwyck, Joel McCrea, and Akim Tamiroff. Preston adores Stanwyck, as most actors do. "Bill Holden was one newcomer she helped a great deal, and she

With Pedro Armendariz and Susan Hayward in Tulsa *(EL 1949)*

With Buddy Ebsen and Edmond O'Brien in Parachute Batallion *(RKO 1941)*

helped me," said Preston. "She was the first big star with whom I worked, and later, when I got involved with others who were selfish or put on the big star act, I didn't get bugged because Missy [as friends call her] had shown me that all stars aren't like that. Nobody else was quite like her." Stanwyck gave him a St. Genesius medal which he has always worn. He never goes onstage or in front of a camera without it. (Ten years later Preston and Stanwyck would co-star in *The Lady Gambles,* 1949).

Preston had no such friendly relationship with the lordly Cecil B. DeMille: "He was a big fraud as far as I'm concerned." Preston thought him good at handling big spectacular scenes but said he had no patience with the smaller ones. "Nobody argued with DeMille, demon that he was. He took me under his wing, and when DeMille did that you were putty in his authoritative hands. You became as much his property as his puttees or his megaphone, to be done with as he saw fit. DeMille typified much that was bad about those years. A dictator on the set, he made pictures by formula, a formula composed of bits and pieces of other people's formulas. I can't recall a single original contribution he ever made to films. But he was the most sacred of all the sacred cows at Paramount."

Even though Robert had already appeared in three prior films, DeMille demanded that history be changed: "*Union Pacific* will be your first film. We will announce to the public that I have discovered a new talent." He also told Preston that he looked too young and ordered him to grow a moustache. He did. Preston appeared in two other DeMille outdoors sagas: *North West Mounted Police* (1940), in which he was billed directly below Preston Foster, and in *Reap the Wild Wind* (1942), a very entertaining and lavishly Technicolored sea spectacle. Preston disliked the script for the former film and told DeMille that he did. The famed director replied, "What's the matter? It's the same part you had in *Union Pacific,* isn't it?" DeMille offered him roles in both *Unconquered* (1947) and *The Greatest Show on Earth* (1952), but Preston did not wish to work with the maestro again.

Actually, Preston's best performance in his early film years was as the younger brother in Paramount's remake of *Beau Geste* (1939), starring Gary Cooper and Ray Milland. Ralph Forbes had played John the younger brother in the 1926 silent version with Ronald Colman. In the 1939 edition, Preston was called Digby, while Ray Milland, as the middle brother, was John. The *New York Times* found Robert "capable but curiously un-anglican." Preston then took over where Ray Milland had left off, as Dorothy Lamour's leading man, in a South Seas tale called *Typhoon*

(1940). Preston remarked, "They gave me the part because Jon Hall got sick. I wore the male version of the sarong, and they had to design a special one so it would cover my navel, which was taboo in those days." That same year, he and Preston Foster did duty in another Lamour tropicana, *Moon over Burma.*

On November 9, 1940, Robert wed actress Catherine Craig (real name Kay Feltus). They had met as students at the Pasadena Playhouse. "Later we both were signed by Paramount," said Preston," and the romance flourished during the making of many B pictures." They never acted together in a film, but he did play opposite her in her screen test. She consequently gave up her career on the grounds that it absorbed her less than being Preston's wife. The Prestons had no children.

The only thing in Preston's career that really took an upswing in 1941 was his hairline. Some Paramount executives had the notion that he should have a higher forehead. His new hairline was visible in *New York Town* (1941), the film in which he loses Mary Martin to Fred MacMurray. However, for *The Lady from Cheyenne* (1941), made on loanout to Universal, his own hairline made a fast reappearance, because that picture's director, Frank Lloyd, informed him a high forehead changed his looks too drastically." He was able to let his hair question grow back because, luckily, electrolysis had not been used to change it. He never changed it again. *The Lady from Cheyenne,* a rather too gentle western, was originally called *Cheyenne,* but Loretta Young had it in her contract that she had to have the title role.

After *Reap the Wild Wind,* Robert's salary was eight hundred dollars a week, and he made two good features. *This Gun for Hire* (1942) was his first of three films with Alan Ladd. Although Preston had top billing, the film belonged to Ladd and Veronica Lake. It was the movie which turned Ladd, as the contracted killer, into a major film star. Preston's detective role was sturdy but not flashy. *Wake Island* (1942) was one of the superior war films of the era, and Bosley Crowther (*New York Times*) reported, "William Bendix and Robert Preston will snag the plaudits for their performances as tough marines. A more respectable pair of leathernecks has not come along since Flagg and Quirt." Bendix, the film, and director John Farrow were nominated for Academy Awards.

Preston's last film before he went into military service was *Night Plane from Chungking* (1943) with Ellen Drew, with whom he had previously co-starred in *Night of January 16th* (1941). Between the years 1940–42, Preston was still somewhat under Cecil B. DeMille's thumb, and the producer-director overused the actor's services on his own "Lux Radio

With Dorothy Lamour and Preston Foster in a publicity pose for Moon over Burma *(Par 1940)*

Theatre." He recreated his roles in *The Lady from Cheyenne* and *Wake Island,* and played the Don Ameche role in *Alexander's Ragtime Band,* with Alice Faye and Ray Milland, the Spencer Tracy role in *Test Pilot* with Robert Taylor and Rita Hayworth, and two James Cagney roles in *City for Conquest* and *The Fighting 69th.*

He spent three years with the Army Air Force, starting out as a G.I. physical instructor in Florida and working his way up to captain in Combat Intelligence for the Ninth Air Force. He coached fliers on what to expect from the Nazis in the way of opposition, spending most of his time stationed in England. At the same time, Preston's father was a fireman first class in the Navy Seabees. After his discharge, Preston returned to Hollywyood to try to rebuild the momentum of his film career.

Paramount loaned him to United Artists for *The Macomber Affair* (1947), participating with Joan Bennett and Gregory Peck in this love-triangle adventure based on an Ernest Hemingway story. Preston measured up strongly as Bennett's husband, who proves at long last he is no coward, only to be killed the very next instant. His part as the rich game hunter gave him a sense of status in the industry, something the executives back at Paramount constantly overlooked. After a guest bit in Paramount's *Variety Girl* (1947),

he supported Alan Ladd, now a huge boxoffice attraction, and Dorothy Lamour in *Wild Harvest* (1947).

Diplomatic but outspoken Robert once explained his fate on the home lot: "Once in a while I was given the lead in a movie nobody else wanted. It worked like this: A producer with a script would look over the Paramount list of leading men. Then he'd submit it to, say Fred MacMurray. It wasn't for Fred, so he'd pass it along to Ray Milland. Down the line it would come. Alan Ladd was next. He'd dump it in my lap. I would turn to get rid of it, but there was never anyone behind me. I lived in all the B pictures and died in all the A's. I got the girl in the B's and the fella in the A's." He vividly recalls one conversation he had with a Paramount official: "I'd said no to a couple of parts that they offered me and the guy told me, 'Next time you turn down a script we'll drop your option.' 'If you do,' I answered him, 'I'll buy you a suit.'" Preston also felt guilty because he was in a comfortable, but not very satisfying, economic rut. Other actors who felt the same were Edmond O'Brien, Barry Sullivan, Macdonald Carey, and Wendell Corey. "Each of us," Robert recalled, "was certain he was a better actor than the star he supported. Some actually were. Many of those personalities had to be surrounded with actors who could really act. Lloyd Nolan was a fine example of that. But some of those stars were more

441

With Barbara Stanwyck in The Lady Gambles *(Univ 1949)*

than mere personalities. Gary Cooper, for example. He never made a wrong move, never did anything that wasn't right in terms of the part he was playing. He was something special."

Preston's last film under his Paramount contract was, as fate would have it, another Ladd vehicle, *Whispering Smith* (1949), with Preston as the bad guy. There were problems during the filming because Sue Carol, Ladd's imposing wife and agent, demanded that the planned ending be altered to suit Ladd better. However, Preston protested loud enough so it was left as it was. Robert was so discouraged by his status at Paramount that he would do almost anything to be freed of the agreement. He told Louella Parsons about his plight "and the next day she had a headline about Paramount being mean to a returned war hero. The front office got the shakes over that kind of publicity and I got out."

Preston did find some professional satisfaction as a member of the "18 actors," a group of Pasadena Playhouse veterans and their wives, who staged and performed serious dramatic works. The Pasadena group included Dana Andrews, Victor Jory, Don Porter, and their wives. It was here that Robert and his wife acted together professionally for the first time in *The Play's the Thing* and *Girl of the Golden West.* The actors received forty dollars a week, the Equity

minimum, but each returned the money to the organization. It was at this juncture that Preston realized the stage was the proper medium for him, even if financial necessity required him to plod along in more films.

As a freelance actor, with a salary of $3,500 a week when he was making a film, he appeared with Margaret O'Brien in *The Big City* (1948) for MGM, he was in a good RKO western, *Blood on the Moon* (1948) starring Robert Mitchum, and he did three pictures for Eagle-Lion: *Tulsa* (1949), with Susan Hayward, *The Sundowners* (1950), the best of the lot, and *When I Grow Up* (1951). He then went off to England to make *Cloudburst* (1952). "I knew what the producer was after," said Preston, "a second-rate Hollywood name to strengthen the boxoffice appeal." He did it anyway and on the way home, stopped off in New York.

He learned that Jose Ferrer was looking for someone to replace him in the Broadway play, *Twentieth Century* (1951). Preston jumped at the opportunity and got the role. Even though the show only lasted another two weeks, he was determined to stay in New York "for my life, my career and self respect. I could have gone on at the same salary, making the same pictures, but money was never that important to me. I had a choice and I made it." He added: "I knew

442

that everyone expected me to be lousy in my first stage appearance on Broadway. People were saying, 'Who does Preston think he is? Just another B-picture leading man trying to rejuvenate a sagging career.' Well, the critics came and reviewed the show, and I got good notices."

The Prestons moved to Rye, New York, and he became a very serviceable actor on the New York stage. He starred in a popular revival of *The Male Animal* (1952), with Martha Scott and Elliott Nugent. The *New York Times* noted, "As the ex-football hero, long on brawn and short on brain, Robert Preston gives an exhilarating performance that represents velocity and assurance but also contains fine points of character." He also appeared in *Men of Distinction* (1953), *His and Hers* (1954), with Celeste Holm, *Magic and the Loss* (1954), with Uta Hagen, and played Joe McCall in *The Tender Trap,* which opened at the Longacre Theatre on October 12, 1954. Of his performance in this comedy, Walter Kerr (*New York Herald-Tribune*) tabulated, "Preston is his usual forthright self—why doesn't someone write a good play for his forthright self? At all times he is efficient, inventive and a help to the authors."

Other plays in which he starred were *Janus* (1955) opposite Margaret Sullavan and *The Hidden River* (1957), a serious drama with Dennis King and Lili Darvas, in which he was a veteran of the French resistance. He made only one film during this period, *The Last Frontier* (1955) for Columbia. "Columbia sent me the script and I wasn't interested," said Bob. "It was just the sort of thing I had gone to Broadway to get away from. They kept talking to me about it, so I named a salary that I knew would be impossible. They gave up. Then came the day before the company was to leave on location, and the role still wasn't cast. Harry Cohn, God rest his soul, said, 'pay the blankety-blank what he wants.' I did the role but I wouldn't even go see the picture afterward."

On December 19, 1957, at the Majestic Theatre in New York, Preston emerged as the season's number one male performer. As *The Music Man,* he stayed with the show for two years and two months and won the Tony Award for his stellar, non-stop performance of the con-artist salesman. Before that musical, he had never sung a note or danced in public. Milton Berle had desperately wanted the part and both Art Carney and Ray Bolger had been considered for it. Berle and Bolger both had wanted a spot in the show to do a personal routine which, of course, was out of the question. Morton DaCosta, the show's director, felt that Robert was "an actor who can project himself larger than life." *Time* Magazine offered, "His portrayal of a likable cad is a fine job of acting, but he

does more than act and sing. He kicks a mean one-step, dances the Castle Walk, and in an inspired number joins the dancing company in a soft-shoe, tippy-toe library ballet that is a triumph of precision and gaiety." After *The Music Man* had made him a name, Preston told one interviewer, "Not long ago I was just another unimportant actor. Oh, I did all right. There were always things for me to do, movies and plays, before *The Music Man* came along. But, of course, that was the big one, the role that put me over the top. It gave me a control over my career that an actor in a lesser position cannot exercise. I enjoy success and all it means."

After his *Music Man* success, he received a deluge of movie offers. He took an offer from Warner Bros. for three films, "because the deal gave me good money and plenty of freedom, and because I had a notion they were going to buy *The Music Man.*" The studio did buy the show for a million dollars, but it was not certain whether Preston would re-enact his original role. There were bigger Hollywood names who could play it and who wanted it, but the show's composer, Meredith Willson, was on Preston's side. Considered for the role in the picture version were Bing Crosby, Burt Lancaster, Frank Sinatra, Kirk Douglas, Dean Martin, and Cary Grant. Jack Warner offered the plum tree role to Cary Grant, who had seen the show twelve times. Grant told Warner, "Not only will I not play it, but if Preston doesn't do it, I won't even come to see the picture." Reviewing Preston's performance in the 1962 film version of *The Music Man*, *Variety* concluded, "Warners might have secured bigger screen names but it is impossible to imagine any of them matching Preston's authority backed by 883 stage performances. His know-how in this film is as close to a tour-de-force as is likely to be seen during the calendar year. Not only does he project verve, singing and dancing with a beguiling style of his own creation, but his acting has remarkable plausibility."

Prior to doing *The Music Man* film, Robert starred in the movie version of William Inge's play, *The Dark at the Top of the Stairs* (1960), portraying the husband role Pat Hingle had originated on the stage. Robert shouted his way through the film as the troubled head of the family who not only must find a new livelihood but must re-evaluate his domestic relationships. It was ironic that the star who had said upon his return to Hollywood, "I defy them to categorize me now," should begin to typecast himself, not because of the roles he selected (they were diverse enough), but because of the sameness of his high-pitched performances. It always seemed to be Professor Harold Hill in new guises, whether as the husband in the film *All the Way Home* (1963), onstage as Henry II in *The Lion in*

Winter (1966), or as Mary Martin's husband in Broadway's musical, *I Do, I Do* (1966) (for which he received his second Tony). One occasional bit of variant, mood-changing acting by Preston was his role as the wagonmaster in *How the West Was Won* (1963). Also during this period, Robert was before the footlight in *We Take the Town,* a musical based on Pancho Villa's escapades, but the show folded out of town. He was the burglar in *Too True to Be Good* (1963), a TV writer in *Nobody Loves an Albatross* (1963), and the famed baldheaded title role in the musical, *Ben Franklin in Paris* (1964).

Preston had made his video debut in 1951 on the "Blockade" series, and did a good deal of TV work through the fifties, highlighted by his interpretation of the priest in *The Bells of St. Mary's* (1959) opposite Claudette Colbert. But Preston dislikes most TV work. "In 1951," he explains, "CBS had a series called 'Man against Crime,' Ralph Bellamy played the leading character—Mike Barnett. I took over for him for six weeks as his brother Pat, and in that short period I learned enough to keep away from TV—for all of a sudden people started calling me 'Pat.' I was no longer Bob. In that short time I'd lost my identity." In 1963 Robert was a guest on the Carol Burnett special, *Carol and Co.,* and was host for six DuPont specials about America called *This Proud Land* (1966).

Early in the 1960s Preston had rejected two film offers. He turned down the part of Senator Van Ackerman in *Advise and Consent* (1962) to do *How the West Was Won* instead. (George Grizzard was cast as Van Ackerman.) The other part was the lead in the English filmed *The Third Secret* (1964), which eventually starred Stephen Boyd. But Preston was wise enough to accept the part of Steve McQueen's wandering father in *Junior Bonner* (1972), directed by Sam Peckinpah. The role was geared completely to his talent: Bigger than life, vital, boisterous, flamboyant, and gentle when need be. It is the film performance of his career. Had the film, which sat on the distribution shelf for some time, been a boxoffice success, Preston, along with Ida Lupino (who played his wife), would have been nominated for Oscars.

Preston's other 1972 film was also a boxoffice dud, David Merrick's screen version of *Child's Play.* Preston replaced Marlon Brando, who had been cast as the English teacher in a parochial boys' school, but Merrick found that he could not work with Brando. Preston was merely adequate in the part, depending too much on his natural enthusiasm instead of finding any new interpretation to offer. James Mason, as the harassed and self-tormented Latin teacher, walked off with the film's few acting honors. Preston was then

cast as Beauregard Jackson Pickett Burnside in the film musical *Mame* (1974), starring Lucille Ball, and reports were that by the end of production time Robert was not saying "I love Lucy." When the film debuted at Radio City Music Hall in early 1974, many critics wondered how the many pleasing qualities from the stage version could have evaporated so easily when transferred to the screen. Unlike Miss Ball, Preston, in his really small role, was not lambasted for his work in this unsavory cinema musical.

During the 1960s, the Prestons' married life could best be described as unstable. He and his wife separated on a few occasions, and, at one point, he became the constant companion of Glynis Johns, his *Too Good to Be True* co-star. In 1965, the rumor mills insisted the Prestons would divorce and that he would wed Ulla Sallert, the leading lady in *Ben Franklin in Paris.* But Preston, once again, returned to his wife.

Just when it seemed that Preston's stage laurels, once and for all, would have to rest with his *The Music Man* performance, David Merrick hired him for *Mack and Mabel,* a Broadway musical focusing on the lives and loves of moviemakers Mack Sennett and Mabel Normand. Directed by Gower Champion, with book by Michael Stewart and music-lyrics by Jerry Herman, it was geared for a late fall 1974 Broadway bow. Expectations were high for this expensively-mounted show. But it proved a vast disappointment As *Newsweek* analyzed it, it was " . . . a sad waste like half-baked pie. . . . the juicy reality has been distilled to dry cornballs. . . . As Sennett, Robert Preston has to tell the whole story in flashback, sometimes on an empty stage, and even his heroic professionalism cannot flesh out the proceedings." The show dragged on for some weeks, then closed, a financial disaster, ironically, in one of Broadway's best and most lucrative seasons of recent years.

Much more potent was his performance in the telefeature *My Father's House* (1975), in which he played Cliff Robertson's dad. In this stark, explicit drama, Preston offered a telling performance. *Daily Variety* reported, his "magnetism is irresistible" congratulating him on his display of "verve, the love-of-life bounce, the eventual recognition of defeat and despair."

"You're a blessed man if you are working and can do the things you like," says Preston. "I have fun. This is the joy. This is the hobby. I live in a dimension of imagination. Sherwood Forest means something to me. I've worn the green. I've lived in old Budapest through Molnar plays. I've lived through Lexington and Concord. I go back to Montezuma!"

ROBERT PRESTON

King of Alcatraz   *(Par 1938)*
Illegal Traffic   *(Par 1938)*
Disbarred   *(Par 1939)*
Union Pacific   *(Par 1939)*
Beau Geste   *(Par 1939)*
Typhoon   *(Par 1940)*
North West Mounted Police   *(Par 1940)*
Moon Over Burma   *(Par 1940)*
The Lady from Cheyenne   *(Univ 1941)*
New York Town   *(Par 1941)*
Parachute Battalion   *(RKO 1941)*
Night of January 16th   *(Par 1941)*
Pacific Blackout (a.k.a., Midnight Angel)   *(Par 1942)*
Reap the Wild Wind   *(Par 1942)*
This Gun for Hire   *(Par 1942)*
Wake Island   *(Par 1942)*
Star Spangled Rhythm   *(Par 1942)*
Night Plane from Chungking   *(Par 1943)*
The Macomber Affair   *(UA 1947)*
Variety Girl   *(Par 1947)*
Wild Harvest   *(Par 1947)*

The Big City   *(MGM 1948)*
Blood on the Moon   *(RKO 1948)*
Whispering Smith   *(Par 1949)*
Tulsa   *(EL 1949)*
The Lady Gambles   *(Univ 1949)*
The Sundowners   *(EL 1950)*
My Outlaw Brother   *(UA 1951)*
When I Grow Up   *(EL 1951)*
Best of the Badmen   *(RKO 1951)*
Cloudburst   *(UA 1952)*
Face to Face (Episode, The Bride Comes to Yellow Sky)   *(RKO 1952)*
The Last Frontier   *(Col 1955)*
The Dark at the Top of the Stairs   *(WB 1960)*
The Music Man   *(WB 1962)*
How the West was Won   *(MGM 1962)*
Island of Love   *(WB 1963)*
All the Way Home   *(Par 1963)*
Junior Bonner   *(Cin 1972)*
Child Play   *(Par 1972)*
Mame   *(WB 1974)*

70

Ella Raines

Not many actresses begin their Hollywood careers as the sole asset of a million-dollar film production corporation. Ella Raines did. Her green-eyed, auburn-tinged beauty so captivated Charles Boyer and Howard Hawks that, despite her having no professional experience, she became the first and only star showcased by their B-H Productions. It paid off, for Ella had acting ability as well as the "right" cinema look, and for a time she reaped a healthy fan following. Unfortunately, a long line of less than grade A pictures convinced her to embrace an early retirement.

She was born Ella Wallace Raubes on August 6, 1921, in Snoqualmie Falls, Washington, population 752 ("I presume they've been doing something about that," she says). The daughter of a dynamite engineer, she became a bright young lady, adept at both scholastics and athletics. Her skills in swimming, fishing, skiing, archery, mountain climbing, and riding later earned her the gratitude of Hollywood press agents anxious for outdoor shots of the new starlet.

Entering the University of Washington after high school, Ella majored in psychology and drama. She pursued her studies seriously, in particular her theatre work on campus. She even surmounted a near tragedy in 1941 when a stove exploded in her face, singeing her hair and eyebrows but leaving no permanent damage. Despite her career drive, her college graduation was prevented by a wartime romance which re-

sulted in her elopement to Florida in 1942 to marry Army captain Kenneth Trout. He shipped out eleven days after their vows.

Too late to return to college, Ella arranged to fulfill her scholastic requirements by writing a thesis, *How to Get into the Theatre,* and set out to New York City in the summer of 1942 to obtain first-hand experience.

Ella made the usual casting rounds, and was offered a small spot in the cast of *Away We Go!* (which later became *Oklahoma!*), but she turned it down when production was delayed. An enterprising agent decided her looks promised bigger jobs than Broadway chorus work, so he provided her with letters of introduction and a becoming wardrobe, and sent her to Hollywood. It was not too long before Boyer and Hawks signed her to the unique acting contract that earned her the title "the million-dollar actress."

The B-H corporation became a popular subject of gossip in industry circles, and scoffers waited anxiously to see if the newcomer would fall on her lovely face. She disappointed them. Her debut in *Corvette K-225* (1943), a pleasant naval action tale that Hawks produced through Universal, placed her as Randolph Scott's girl back home. Her work in the film's earlier sequences was all it should have been. Bosley Crowther wrote in the *New York Times* that she acquitted herself "prettily," which nobody could deny. MGM took notice, and promptly borrowed her for *Cry Havoc* (1943). Ella joined a half-dozen female

With Dan Duryea in a publicity pose for White Tie and Tails *(Univ 1946)*

stars elaborately suffering through this wartime ode to nurses, made in the style of Paramount's *So Proudly We Hail,* which had been produced earlier that year. Like most war films of the period, it met with a popular reception, and Ella gained more ground in Hollywood.

On February 28, 1944, Ella appeared on the cover of *Life* Magazine. The reason for this honor was a top performance in a nice little thriller from Universal entitled *Phantom Lady* (1944). The film was the brainchild of Alfred Hitchcock's frequent associate, Joan Harrison, and of German "horror" expert Robert Siodmak. The eighty-seven-minute picture cast Ella as the secretary of a man wrongly convicted of murder (Alan Curtis). She sets out to clear him, admiringly surmounting such jarring events as strangulations, blood-spilling street fights, her own near rape, and the presence in the story of Aurora Miranda (the equally "hotcha" sister of South American star Carmen Miranda). The film received its most attention for the telling scene in which Ella poses as a tart, to seduce drummer Elisha Cook, Jr. into spilling some helpful information. Clad in a black satin dress, an overly glamorous coiffure, and 1944's most provocative style of ankle-strap high heels, she sat on Cook's lap, fed him gin drinks, and generally increased his breathing before her guise was uncovered. Ella

played this racy scene to the hilt, gaining increased attention from the ever wide-eyed G.I.s and from the critics. ("Checking in an excellent performance," said the *New York Journal-American.*) Her follow-up performances that year, in Paramount's *Hail the Conquering Hero* (1944), the Preston Sturges-directed comedy hit in which she played Eddie Bracken's all-American girl friend, and in RKO's *Tall in the Saddle* (1944), a John Wayne outing in which she supplied the romance, consolidated her star status.

Anxious to market the garden variety glamour image, B-H Productions at first requested Ella to keep her marriage to Captain Trout a secret. For a time she complied, but soon the eligible and not-so-eligible began pestering her for dates. The actress was soon swamped with invitations, all of which she rejected, save such professional engagements as premieres. Soon, Ella's apparent apathy to the Hollywood males was causing whispers hinting at things far worse than publicity of her marriage would have meant for her, and the rumors were becoming public knowledge. Her publicity men started to change her image as a consequence of the rumors by switching their copy extolling "oomphy Ella" to vowing "she spends her evenings pitching baseball with the kids in the street."

With Boyer and Hawks involved with other pro-

With George Sanders in The Strange Affair of Uncle Harry *(Univ 1945)*

448

With Arleen Whelan and Peter Lind Hayes in The Senator Was Indiscreet *(Univ 1947)*

With Anna May Wong and Charles Coburn in Impact *(UA 1949)*

jects, the amount of time they could devote to promoting Ella's career was limited, so they eventually arranged to have Universal acquire her acting contract. She was at an advantage there, having little top-flight competition, save perhaps for Deanna Durbin; types such as Evelyn Ankers, Diana Barrymore, and Anne Gwynne certainly were not nearly as highly touted. However, the studio lacked the producing finesse to keep Ella in top-flight pictures. Universal gave her the romantic tasks in *Enter Arsene Lupin* (1944), that chestnut about jewel heisting which once had been a vehicle for John and Lionel Barrymore, and now a programmer for Charles Korvin and J. Carrol Naish. *The Suspect* (1945) had her wholesome loveliness inspire bulbous Charles Laughton to murder his nagging wife (Rosalind Ivan). In her role here, Ella seemed rather stiff and amateurish, perhaps uncomfortable in such a decidedly British milieu. (Evelyn Ankers, then under contract to Universal, would have been a much sounder choice for the role.) Finally, *The Strange Affair of Uncle Harry* (1945) showcased her refreshing beauty as a character who inspires George Sanders to murder his nagging sisters (Geraldine Fitzgerald and Moyna MacGill). Lots of celluloid drivel followed, including *White Tie and Tails* (1946) and *Time Out of Mind* (1947). When the studio did manage to cast her in a good motion picture, the laurels were usually cornered by someone else: By William Powell, for example, in the comedy, *The Senator Was Indiscreet* (1947), or Hume Cronyn in the prison drama, *Brute Force* (1947).

Meanwhile, in private life, Ella, who had been living in an apartment with her mother and sister-in-law, separated from husband Trout in 1945. They originally hoped for a reconciliation—after all, they were "childhood sweethearts"—but none developed and they divorced later that year. On February 6, 1947, she married another military man, Major Robin Olds, who had twenty-nine aerial victories to his wartime credit, and was then working as a jet aircraft test pilot. The marriage produced two children, Christina (recently involved with drama at Vassar) and Susan.

In 1947, Ella's Universal contract lapsed and she was offscreen throughout 1948. She returned to films in 1949 in United Artists *Impact,* an overly low-key story in which frigid wife Helen Walker tries to murder trusting husband Brian Donlevy, whose bitterness is soothed by nice girl Ella. Bosley Crowther (*New York Times*) jibed, "Ella Raines' performance as the Idaho small town girl reminds one of that state's most famous crop." Equally dull mashed potato roles in dull fodder followed, and Ella soon signed with Republic, Pictures, the domain of Vera Hruba Ralston, protegée of studio chief Herbert J. Yates. There, Ella

was relegated to a brigade of pot-boilers like *Singing Guns* (1950), *The Fighting Coast Guard* (1951), and *Ride the Man Down* (1952), and she was accompanied on her road to career ignominy by leading men such as Vaughn Monroe, Forrest Tucker, and Rod Cameron.

With her film career in such a slump, Ella turned to television. She reprised her best-received film performance (*The Phantom Lady*) on "Robert Montgomery Presents" in April, 1950, and later that year, appeared in the "Lights Out" episode, *Ides of April,* and on the "Pulitzer Prize Playhouse" adaptation of *You Can't Take It with You.*

In late 1953, Ella, then living with her family in Cornwall-on-Hudson in New York, formed Cornwall Productions. Her partner was William Dozier, then supervising producer in charge of all CBS-TV dramatic fare. The result was the series "Janet Dean, Registered Nurse," which starred Ella in the title role of a weekly series which debuted on March 23, 1954. She also wrote several of the episodes. The series was shot at Parsonnet Studios in Long Island City as a result of Ella's dictates: "Bill [Dozier] is here and because my husband is stationed in the East." The program received considerable attention, being the first video show principally about a nurse, and concerning itself with quite mature stories on social problems, including the touchy subject of anti-Semitism.

After "Janet Dean" left the air, Ella appeared in but one film, *The Man in the Road,* produced in England in 1956 and released in the United States the following year by Republic. It concerned Communist espionage. Ella then retired and has shown no signs of any come-back ambitions since. She and her family now make their home in Washington.

Actually, Hollywood rarely employed Ella in an acting area in which she possibly could have excelled. She had the sleek, well-bred appearance that could have lent itself splendidly to bitchy roles. (Her performance in *The Suspect,* in which she encourages Charles Laughton to beat his wife to death with a club, then leaves him, is a good example of this potential.) She herself commented late in her movie career, "I'm so tired of being sweet and pure all the time," and she resented the rash of publicity that ran parallel to her buttery image. She once attacked a projected story on her in a woman's magazine, stating, "What do they mean in this thing, calling me a suburban housewife? I wear Travis Banton dresses that cost me six hundred to seven hundred dollars apiece and drive my own Jaguar—and they call me a suburban housewife?" She also occasionally hinted at a temperament that must have been truly stifled in nice girl screen parts. She admitted that her rule is to "stay away from anything that bores you. I never try to take ice cubes out of a tray, or to sew on a button." In addition, "I have my maid trained now to tiptoe in with breakfast. If anybody says a word to me before I have that first cup of coffee—look out!"

Finally, Ella made news a few years back in Colorado when she encouraged a prowler to vacate her estate by firing at him with a gun. Luckily, she missed.

Since her husband's retirement in May, 1975, as Brigadier General at Norton Air Force Base, Ella and Olds have made plans to retire to a cozy mountain chalet in Colorado to "enjoy the good life."

ELLA RAINES

Corvette K-225 *(Univ 1943)*
Cry Havoc *(MGM 1943)*
Phantom Lady *(Univ 1944)*
Hail the Conquering Hero *(Par 1944)*
Tall in the Saddle *(RKO 1944)*
Enter Arsene Lupin *(Univ 1944)*
The Suspect *(Univ 1945)*
The Strange Affair of Uncle Harry *(Univ 1945)*
The Runaround (a.k.a., Deadly Enemies) *(Univ 1946)*
White Tie and Tails *(Univ 1946)*
Time Out of Mind *(Univ 1947)*

The Web *(Univ 1947)*
Brute Force *(Univ 1947)*
The Senator Was Indiscreet *(Univ 1947)*
The Walking Hills *(Col 1949)*
Impact *(UA 1949)*
A Dangerous Profession *(RKO 1949)*
Singing Guns *(Rep 1950)*
The Second Face *(UA 1950)*
Fighting Coast Guard *(Rep 1951)*
Ride the Man Down *(Rep 1952)*
The Man in the Road *(Grand National 1956)*

Hauntingly beautiful Gail Russell began her screen career, some might think, as a sort of Alice in Wonderland, or better yet, a Cinderella. She was discovered, groomed, and reached stardom in her third film, *The Uninvited* (1944). This Cinderella of the 1940s, an era in which Hollywood gobbled up new talent with a ferocity, knew no happy ending. Actually, this Cinderella had an unhappy life. Just existing in an ordinary life was terrifying to Gail and she never learned to cope properly with her emotional problems. She was painfully shy and self-conscious. Thrust into a film career that she never really wanted, her life became a hideous nightmare. She was afraid of the camera and equally distraught with the fear that she would never remember her lines. "I'm frightened," she exclaimed painfully. "Did you ever stand up on a set with everyone looking at you? All those electricians and grips and everyone? It's terrifying." She was also very much aware of the fact that she had no "natural" talent and no acting training to support her assignments. She had appeared onstage only once in her life—in grammar school. It was a play about the Pilgrims and she had only four lines to deliver. She could not say them and they were finally omitted. She ended up playing a part of the scenic background, sitting in a corner knitting and unable to even glance at the audience. This fear followed Gail into her Hollywood world and led her into the world of alcoholism.

Gail was born in Chicago on September 21, 1924, to Gladys and George Russell. Gail was their second child. Her older brother, George, later became a musician. As a youngster, Gail was very much a loner and spent most of her free time all alone in her room. She had few friends and always disappeared when company arrived at the hourse. She loved to paint and to go to the movies, both apparent escapes from the real world. Gail always wanted to be an artist, not an actress. When her family moved to Santa Monica, California, she was in her early teens and was a top art student at Santa Monica High School. One day, as the publicized story goes, Paramount executive William Meiklejohn gave two teenage boys a lift in his car and must have mentioned to them that he worked for Paramount Pictures. They began to rave about a classmate of theirs, comparing her beauty to Hedy Lamarr's. Meiklejohn played out a hunch and contacted Gail through the school, asking her to arrange an appointment with him at the studio. Gail thought the suggestion ridiculous, but her mother had different ideas. Gail was only seventeen at the time, and her mother took matters into her own hands.

Mrs. Russell had always hoped to be an actress herself and thought this was the vicarious chance of her life. "She practically dragged me there," Gail once ruefully admitted. The Paramount people were very impressed by Gail's dark beauty with her black hair and blue eyes. They offered her a screen test and

In The Unseen *(Par 1945)*

453

five days later she was at work in her first film, *Henry Aldrich Gets Glamour* (1943). Paramount knew full well that she had no experience and very little instinctual talent, but concluded she was worth the risk, believing she could be developed into a major personality. William Russell (no relation), the Paramount drama coach, helped Gail a great deal. He and others groomed her for stardom and began by teaching her how to walk correctly. Gail had always walked pigeon-toed with hunched shoulders and head hung forward. Her voice, pre-Paramount, had been too high and she possessed faulty diction. In a very short time she developed her rich, warm, velvety, though soft voice.

In her first acting assignment, *Henry Aldrich Gets Glamour,* she played a high-school beauty who steals Henry Aldrich (Jimmy Lydon) from his steady girl (Diana Lynn). Nevertheless, Diana wins him back by the end of the film. On the set, Diana took a shine to Gail and, with her extroverted, fun-loving personality, did her best to bring Gail out of her emotional shell.

Years later, Gail discussed her first film role, "I can hardly remember it. When I went over it with Mr. Russell, it seemed possible—well, almost possible. But, on the set, with the director [Hugh Bennett] shouting and the lights blazing, and the cameras threatening, I'd go deaf. Really. They'd tell me what to do and I simply couldn't hear. I'd try desperately to listen and all I did was wish I were dead."

Gail's second film was in the undernourished screen adaptation of *Lady in the Dark* (1944). She had a small role in this almost music-less Ginger Rogers vehicle, but it proved to be very exciting for the newcomer who had always idolized Miss Rogers. It was *The Uninvited* that paved the way for Gail's stardom. For the lead role of Stella, she had to master a British accent, which she did by constantly re-screening *Pygmalion* and *The Young Mr. Pitt.* The film proved a critical success, and to this day is still regarded as one of the best ghost tales ever produced on celluloid. The special effects were as superb as was the Victor Young score, which included "Stella by Starlight." If only for this film, Gail will be remembered as one of the most beautiful starlets that Hollywood in the 1940s produced. On the set of *The Uninvited,* Gail was befriended by star Ray Milland. Sensing her nervousness, he would deliberately fluff lines and flub scenes whenever she began losing her control of a scene. It was he who taught her to keep her face in the camera, for she would always shy away from the lens. Archer Winsten (*New York Post*) said of Gail's performance in this picture, "Any man who would not fight a couple of ghosts for Gail Russell, and thank her for the privilege, is missing something." Cornelia Otis Skinner was also in *The Uninvited,* and, coincidentally, Gal got to play the young Miss Skinner in her fourth film, *Our Hearts Were Young and Gay* (1944). The comedy was based on the well-known book written by Miss Skinner and Emily Kimbrough, an autobiography of their early years sailing to Europe together. Gail's good friend, Diana Lynn, played Emily in this nostalgia trip and also carried all the comedy scenes. Oncamera, Gail could be sweet and charming, but comedy was simply not the serious girl's forte. "I find comedy harder to play," Gail once said, "There's less involvement in what you're doing. I'm not sure enough of myself to find fun in it yet." Diana and Gail were also starred in the sequel, *Our Hearts Were Growing Up* (1946)—set in Princeton and with Brian Donlevy co-featured—but it was a cloying, self-conscious exercise. In 1945, clinging to the success of *The Uninvited,* Paramount starred Gail opposite Joel McCrea in *The Unseen,* an exciting melodrama about a girl who comes to a mysterious house to replace a murdered governess. This film established Gail as "Hollywood's Haunted Heroine."

With her sudden rise to eminence, Gail felt unable to cope with the rash of professional and social demands. She needed a crutch for her fears and inferiorities. She began by taking her scene breaks at a little cafe across the street from the studio in order to have just one or two drinks to steady her nerves for the camera or for an interview. Paramount was very understanding toward Gail through these difficult times. Sets would be closed to outsiders upon request and interviews were handled discreetly and sparingly. Before long, however, a bottle could be found in her dressing room.

Gail played opposite tough-guy Alan Ladd in two features. They would have made a very good film team had the properties been right for both of them. The Alan Ladd-Veronica Lake screen pairing was dwindling and Gail's soft, dark looks were appealing next to Ladd's blue-eyed blondness. Their first film together, *Salty O'Rourke* (1945), a horse racing story, gave Gail little opportunity to do anything other than look pretty. Their second, *Calcutta* (1947), directed by John Farrow, had a typically good Ladd plot line, but Gail was cast as a villainess (!) and it just did not ring true. She simply was not a good enough actress to supplant her ordinary personality behind the lens and project strength and cunning. *Cue* Magazine, reviewing the "cruel and ruthless killer" in the picture, stated, "And who do you think it turns out to be, but pretty, baby-faced apple-cheeked, lisping, teenage Gail Russell. It's quite a job trying to palm off this wide-eyed bobby soxer as a cold-blooded killer and

With Jean Heather in Our Hearts Were Young and Gay *(Par 1944)*

brains of a giant international jewel smuggling ring and Paramount doesn't quite manage it.''

Gail's first films away from her home studio were *The Bachelor's Daughter* (1946) at United Artists and *Angel and the Badman* (1947) for Republic. In the former, she was starred over veteran Claire Trevor. In the latter, co-starring with John Wayne, she played Prudence, a Quaker who falls in love with a man (Wayne) with a gun.

She returned to Paramount to provide the eerie ambiance in *Night Has a Thousand Eyes* (1948), starring her with Edward G. Robinson, as an ESP vaudevillian; a moustached John Lund played her love interest. This was her last screen association with ''the other world,'' and she confessed, ''I'm a refugee from the ghost gang. But I like to play in these spooky stories and it was the ghosties that gave me my break. I've analyzed it this way, maybe to bolster my inferiority complex: I'm still scared every time I face the camera and that helps the characterization. If I'm nervous, no one scolds me. I get away with it because they think I'm acting.''

Gail dated infrequently, but was pursued by many suitors. She did get to meet Guy Madison, a very handsome, young new actor and liked him very much. Their first date was a group occasion, with Diana Lynn and Guy's agent, Henry Willson, the oth-

With Dennis O'Keefe in The Great Dan Patch *(UA 1949)*

455

With John Payne in Captain China *(Par 1949)*

er parties to the quartet. Publicity agents soon started terming Gail and Guy "the beautiful couple" and building their casual friendship out of proportion. They began going steady, but had no immediate plans to wed. Guy, in particular, was anxious to build his career. Whether it was all the ballyhoo, or the proddings from anxious studio executives, or, perhaps, even true love, they married on August 31, 1949. Gail did not take kindly to married life and by January, 1950 she separated from her husband. When queried by reporters she replied that yes, it was true, they were separated, and they would add nothing further. She and Guy later reconciled.

Republic borrowed Gail again for *Wake of the Red Witch,* again as John Wayne's co-star. Gail was at her loveliest in this South Sea saga, but in *Moonrise* (1948), also at Republic, with Ethel Barrymore and Dane Clark, she was stuck in a moody tale of the backwoods country. Gail's final film at Paramount, *The Lawless* (1950), proved to be a "sleeper" of its day. It was directed by Joseph Losey and dealt with mob violence in a small California town. She was a Mexican-American reporter who attempts to aid a young Mexican immigrant wrongly accused of a crime. It was a powerful story excellently executed, and Gail garnered some of her best film reviews. *Vari-*

ety said she did "a fine piece of work," with Bosley Crowther (*New York Times*) one of the few qualifying reviewers, stating that she was "slightly languid." This movie should have propelled Gail forward on the path to solid dramatic work, but word was already running loose in Hollywood that she was a confirmed drinker. It began to show in her looks. She was getting very thin and beginning to look haggard, and she was only in her late twenties.

The following year, 1951, she appeared in a Universal economy feature, *Air Cadet,* as Stephen McNally's estranged wife. She preferred a flat, dull performance. Paramount then put her on suspension for refusing the female lead in their western, *Flaming Feather* (1951), and Barbara Rush replaced her in this Sterling Hayden film. Finally, Paramount terminated her contract because of her alcoholism. She was also mentioned for roles in *Loan Shark* (1952), with George Raft, and Republic's *Fair Wind to Java* (1953), with John Wayne again. Dorothy Hart got the Raft co-lead, and Vera Ralston and Fred MacMurray starred in the *Java* outing. Gail was then off the screen until 1956.

By 1953 Gail was too well known as an alcoholic to obtain film parts. She became labeled as the "hard luck girl" because that was only the beginning of her troubles. Gail and Guy separated again and, in October, 1953, her name was splashed in the headlines when John Wayne's wife, Esperanza, accused her of having spent a night with the actor a number of years before. In her divorce suit, Mrs. Wayne also claimed Wayne had given Gail a car for services rendered. Both Gail and Wayne denied the charge. He claimed that he had given her the down payment for a car when he had found out that his co-star was making an appallingly low salary on loanout from Paramount. The strain of the scandal was too much for Gail, and she entered a sanitarium in Seattle, Washington. In November, 1953, Gail was arrested for drunken driving and her estranged husband had to bail her out of jail. In the years following, she would be arrested two other times on the same charge.

In 1954, Gail filed for divorce, charging acts of cruelty that caused her mental suffering. Guy, under his real name, Robert O. Moseley, counter-charged mental cruelty, claiming that she had no interest in keeping up her home, would not allow servants, and showed no interest in his work. Gail dropped her charge and Madison was granted his divorce. He agreed to give Gail $12,000 in cash, two cars, and $2,400 to $6,000 a year alimony (depending on his earnings) for ten years or until she remarried. Madison married actress Sheila Connolly a few years later, but Gail never married again. In 1955 Gail publicly confessed, "I'll have to use the word alcoholic because that's what I am."

John Wayne was producing a western for Warner Bros. called *Seven Men from Now* (1956) and Gail heard of it. She tried to pull herself together and found the courage to contact an agent, who in turn called Wayne, to relay her message, "I'd like that help he promised me once." John was more than happy to assist and she was cast opposite Randolph Scott in this vengeance drama. She did a competent job in this Old West tale. Although her exceptional beauty was gone, her gentleness was still there. There was also more character and more dimension to her performing. She definitely proved she was a fine actress in her next film, Universal's *The Tattered Dress* (1957), starring Jeff Chandler, Jeanne Crain, and Jack Carson. It was a courtroom drama with Gail as a woman who lies under oath to protect her lover (Carson). When he later rejects her, she shoots him. It was not a large part, but she made every scene viable, especially the sequence in which she becomes hysterical on the witness stand.

At this point, Gail had a new career looming in front of her, but she did not have the strength to combat her alcoholism. She made headlines again when her car crashed through the window of a cafe, pinning a man under the wheels. Thereafter, producers were afraid to take a chance on her. She did a few television guest appearances (all unmemorable) and made a low-budget film for Republic, *No Place to Land* (1958). She did not work again until 1960 when she signed to do a "Manhunt" segment on television and a film for Twentieth Century-Fox, *The Silent Call* (1961). Gail was hopeful. "The future looks pretty good," she admitted. Gail received top billing in *The Silent Call,* but the film, about a boy and his dog, got few bookings. Gail played the boy's mother.

Gail died on August 27, 1961, at the age of thirty-six. She was found lying on the floor of her hundred-thirty-dollar-a month apartment. She lived alone under the name of Mrs. Robert Moseley (Guy Madison's real name). Police reported that she had apparently died of natural causes. Her body was discovered by two neighbors who had peeked in the window. There was an empty vodka bottle found next to the body and several other empties about the room. The neighbors claimed she saw no friends, but that a man from Alcoholics Anonymous would visit with her occasionally. They also remembered that she had started painting again and hoped to make a go of her art work. Her apartment was decorated with her paintings, mostly of animals and landscapes.

Gail once analyzed the pressures of her career. "There was this terrific amount of work and there was no time to catch up with myself. It was that way for ten years. Always a sense of pressure, no time to think, to relax, to take stock. Getting into this business at such an early age contributed to my problems. I was pushed into it and was playing opposite Ray Milland for fifty dollars a week."

GAIL RUSSELL

Henry Aldrich Gets Glamour   *(Par 1943)*
Lady in the Dark   *(Par 1944)*
The Uninvited   *(Par 1944)*
Our Hearts Were Young and Gay   *(Par 1944)*
The Unseen   *(Par 1945)*
Salty O'Rourke   *(Par 1945)*
Duffy's Tavern   *(Par 1945)*
Our Hearts Were Growing Up   *(Par 1946)*
The Bachelor's Daughters   *(UA 1946)*
Angel and the Badman   *(Rep 1947)*
Calcutta   *(Par 1947)*
Variety Girl   *(Par 1947)*
Night has a Thousand Eyes   *(Par 1948)*

Wake of the Red Witch   *(Rep 1948)*
Moonrise   *(Rep 1948)*
El Paso   *(Par 1949)*
The Song of India   *(Col 1949)*
The Great Dan Patch   *(UA 1949)*
Captain China   *(Par 1949)*
The Lawless   *(Par 1950)*
Air Cadet   *(Univ 1951)*
Seven Men from Now   *(WB 1956)*
The Tattered Dress   *(Univ 1957)*
No Place to Land   *(Rep 1958)*
The Silent Call   *(20th 1961)*

72

Peggy Ryan

Present-day sociologists may complain that society is too youth-fixated, but Hollywood in the forties was perhaps more so, and Universal Pictures in particular had a field day with its rash of inconsequential, diverting minor musicals, buoyed by such juvenile talent as Donald O'Connor, Gloria Jean, and Peggy Ryan. Miss Ryan was a particularly engaging addition to the studio's roster; her buoyant young personality, pleasant singing voice, and more than adequate hoofing was a welcome addition to the celluloid trivia being foisted on the public of the World War II era (with not many complaints, except from the critics).

Peggy's background was not dissimilar to that of her equally hard-working co-star, Donald O'Connor. Both came from vaudeville families and both were pros before losing their baby teeth.

Vaudeville's "Merry Dancing Ryans" became three when, on August 28, 1924, daughter Margaret O'Rene Ryan joined the act. Peggy soon learned the fundamentals of show business and, at an early age, could dance up a storm. At two she was doing a butterfly dance for the Elks Lodge in San Diego. Six years later the Ryans decided to try Hollywood and Papa Ryan resigned from his job as superintendent of service at San Diego's El Cortez Hotel to bolster the tryouts of Peggy's advance to movieland, where she was enrolled at the Hollywood Professional School. Her dancing was great, but her thin, pipe-stem legs

were slightly bowed and supported a thin, shapeless body. Her figure did not excite casting directors, but she did land a job at a Actor's Fund Benefit, and George Murphy, recalling the splendid dancing of the Ryan kid at the Benefit, recommended her for a part in his forthcoming Universal musical, *Top of the Town* (1937). (As a small child, Peggy had appeared in the short subject *The Wedding of Jack and Jill*.) For her feature-film bow, Peggy trained daily with Gene Snyder, dance director for Radio City, and did a zestful dance routine with Murphy in the picture that *Photoplay* Magazine selected as one of the month's six best movies, calling Peggy "a youthful dancing sensation." Thereafter, jobs were a little easier for Peggy to obtain. She cried her way through MGM's *The Women Men Marry* (1937) and performed similarly in *The Flying Irishman* (1939), with Wrong-Way Corrigan. In addition, she was tearful in the Virginia Weidler tradition as the Hungry Girl in John Ford's memorable *The Grapes of Wrath* (1940).

An abundance of talent was wasting away in Hollywood in 1939. A group known as the Hollywood Theatre Alliance determined to utilize some of this talent and put together a revue staged by Danny Dare, with music and lyrics by Jay Gorney and Henry Myers, and sketches directed by Mortimer Offner and Edward Eliscu. After a brief Santa Barbara tryout, *Meet the People* opened December 25, 1939, at the small Assistants League Playhouse. By February, 1940, the astonishingly successful revue moved to

With Donald O'Connor, David Holt, and Susanna Foster in Top Man *(Univ 1943)*

In Patrick the Great *(Univ 1945)*

the larger Hollywood Playhouse and ran for forty weeks. During the run William T. Orr was signed by Warner Bros., and a deadpan singer, Virginia O'Brien, was contractually tied to Metro. The other talented hopefuls included Jack Gilford, Nanette Fabares (later known as Nanette Fabray), Jack Albertson, Faye McKenzie, and a bubbling flash of Irish charm and lightning feet, Peggy Ryan.

Meet the People spent eight weeks at San Francisco's Geary Theatre, twelve weeks at Chicago's Grand Opera House, and opened on Broadway at the Mansfield Theatre on December 25, 1940, a year after its optimistic debut. The New York run continued for a healthy 160 performances and then the revue took to the road en route to California. When *Meet the People* played Detroit's Cass Theatre, Peggy Ryan's picture was on the cover of the program.

Peggy's success in *Meet the People* was not reflected in her private life. Her engagement to Johnny Peterson was broken when the show opened in New York City and she announced her engagement to Charles Peck III. That relationship ended when the revue began its cross-country tour.

Back in Hollywood, Universal, who had had such luck with Deanna Durbin, determined to continue its

With Ray McDonald in a publicity pose for Shamrock Hill *(EL 1949)*

460

youth-oriented song and dance features, and was signing up new talent. Peggy was committed to a term contract with the studio. With such pictures as *What's Cookin'?* (1942), she and equally vivacious Donald O'Connor became a screen team, in a lesser tradition, of course, than, say, MGM's Judy Garland and Mickey Rooney. Ryan and O'Connor were well matched in energy, clowning, and expert dancing synchronization. With variations on the usual teenage musical theme that generally found the young leads fighting to put on the big show, Peggy and Donald sparked many of the Universal youth-aimed jitterbugging movies with their energetic, talented presence. On the home lot Peggy and O'Connor romped through many flighty reels of hokum in *Private Buckaroo* (1942), *Give Out, Sisters!* (1942), and *Get Hep to Love* (1942). Peggy gave a well-modulated performance as Myrtle, Shirley Temple's pal in United Artists' *Miss Annie Rooney* (1942). Back on the home lot, *Mr. Big* (1943) continued the Ryan-O'Connor tandem, and, in *Top Man* (1943), Peggy was Jane Warren, O'Connor's sister, with Lillian Gish and Richard Dix as their unlikely parents.

In 1944, O'Connor eloped to Mexico with Gwendolyn Carter and Peggy was (again) engaged, this time to Marine sergeant Raymond Hirsch. Oncamera, in *The Merry Monahans* (1944), both Peggy and O'Connor played relatively straight roles as brother and sister carrying on a family vaudeville act despite the frequent jail terms of their drunken father (Jack Oakie). Mugging, rugging, and slugging, Peggy made *Chip off the Old Block* (1944) with Donald, and the pair did a fast routine in Universal's star-cast *Follow the Boys* (1944), which was followed by dancing and singing "He Took Her for a Sleigh Ride in the Good Old Summertime" in *Bowery to Broadway* (1944).

After O'Connor entered military service, Peggy was cast as Trudy Costello with Ann Blyth and June Preisser in Universal's *Babes on Swing Street,* in which she spent her considerable energies operating a settlement house and hoping to obtain scholarships for her talented residents. *That's the Spirit* (1945) had Jack Oakie as the ghost of a former vaudevillian returning to earth to get his daughter (Peggy) successfully launched on the stage and away from the cantankerous influence of her grandfather Gene Lockhart. Peggy's buoyancy as Patty helped Bud Abbott and Lou Costello garner much laughter as caretakers of a girls' school in *Here Come the Coeds* (1945).

In *On Stage, Everybody* (1945) Peggy was reunited with Jack Oakie, again as his daughter, and in a vaudeville-based background which allowed Peggy to do some fancy stepping with a bright young dancer, Johnny Coy. Following *Men in Her Diary* (1945),

With Jack Oakie and Donald O'Connor in The Merry Monahans *(Univ 1944)*

in which she played an imaginative secretary recording fictional affairs in a diary, Peggy married James Cross and had a son, James Michael Cross. By the time she was ready to return to the screen, Universal had changed executive regimes, new trends were in style, and Peggy had to find employment elsewhere. She was hired by Eagle-Lion to join Ray McDonald and others in *Shamrock Hill* (1949). In 1952 she divorced Cross and the next year her last film to date, Columbia's *All Ashore* (1953), was released. She played Gay Night, with Mickey Rooney, Dick Haymes, and Ray McDonald as her co-stars. She married the latter and toured with him across the country in a nightclub act.

Ray McDonald was a handsome, talented young dancer, who, with his equally talented sister Grace, had made his Broadway bow in *Babes in Arms* (1937), had been with the Army stage production of *Winged Victory* (1943), and then had made the film of that show in Hollywood. For Metro, he made *Life Begins for Andy Hardy* (1941), showed great promise in *Babes on Broadway* (1941), and continued with the Culver City musical in *Born to Sing* (1942). He then was to be seen smiling through *Presenting Lily Mars* (1943), and after the war was in *Good News* (1947). McDonald was an astute dancer and his career should have gone beyond its restrictive perimeters. Peggy and Ray became the parents of a daughter, Kerry McDonald, and continued their talented partnership dancing across America. But the marriage floundered and collapsed in divorce. On February 20, 1959, nine months after Peggy had married Eddie Sherman in Hawaii, Ray McDonald was found dead in his room at the Hotel Prescott in New York City from an overdose of barbiturates. He was thirty-eight years old.

Peggy had met Eddie Sherman in Hawaii when she was vacationing there in 1958, and he interviewed her. Five days later, on the condition that she hang up her dance shoes, she and Sherman were married aboard the Matson liner, *Lurline*, in port on June 11th. She later enthused, "All the beautiful girls in Hawaii wore black bands that day. Nobody could figure out how a skinny Irish girl could catch the most eligible Jewish bachelor in Hawaii. I couldn't figure it out myself. But here we are, just like the happy ending of *Abie's Irish Rose!*" (Sherman had been in Hawaii since 1945, as an announcer on a Honolulu radio station, a nightclub emcee, and, for the Honolulu *Advertiser,* he started writing a show-business column in 1945). Thereafter, Mrs. Sherman continued to

skirmish the outer edges of theatre by choreographing community shows like *The Music Man* and *Funny Girl.* Her inexhaustible energies found time for a wide range of charity work, to become a partner in one of the Islands' best boutiques and to fulfill very successfully her first duty as Mrs. Eddie Sherman, who, according to her husband, "makes the best cheese blintzes in Hawaii." Peggy and Sherman adopted a young son whom they named Shawn Edward Arthur Kim Kalaai Sherman, encompassing his ancestry of part Hawaiian, Chinese, and Caucasian.

Sherman relented once on her promise to store her dancing shoes when her old movie partner, and still best pal, Donald O'Connor, asked her to fly to the mainland and do a "surprise" fifteen-minute spot with him in a one-week musical variety show that O'Connor was doing at Hollywood's Greek Theatre. It was the 1940s all over again when O'Connor and Ryan were sizzling the nation's screens with exhaustive, hyper-energetic clowning and dancing. Peggy had virtually returned home.

Television's "Hawaii Five-O" debuted on September 20, 1968, and as the series progressed, it became obvious that McGarrett (Jack Lord), the show's guardian of justice in the Islands, would need an oncamera secretary. Leonard Freeman, the program's executive producer, finally persuaded a mid-fortyish woman with reddish-brown, page-boy cut hair that the small series role of Lord's helper, Jenny, would not interfere with her teaching tap dancing at the University of Hawaii, or with directing shows at the Honolulu Community Theatre, or with teaching dance to retarded youngsters on the Island and providing free dance lessons for the Blind and Deaf pupils at the Diamond Head school. Nor, he said, would it interfere with her long-time volunteer work with seriously disturbed patients at Honolulu's Puu (psychiatric) ward of Queen's Hospital. So, Mrs. Eddie Sherman accepted.

Peggy is now the grandmother of Chris Cross, her son James Michael Cross's boy. James Michael is now a successful songwriter, and stepfather Eddie Sherman still nurtures plans of producing a low-budget movie musical in Hawaii written by Peggy's first born. And if Peggy has hung up her dancing shoes, she is still teaching others, rationalizing, "Not many people know how to tap dance—there aren't many of us around anymore—so I figured I'd better teach some of the fundamentals to a few young people." Peggy Ryan's tap dancing could easily replace the hula as Hawaii's national dance.

PEGGY RYAN

Top of the Town   *(Univ 1937)*
The Women Men Marry   *(MGM 1937)*
She Married a Cop   *(Rep 1939)*
The Flying Irishman   *(RKO 1939)*
The Grapes of Wrath   *(20th 1940)*
Sailor's Lady   *(20th 1942)*
What's Cookin'?   *(Univ 1942)*
Miss Annie Rooney   *(UA 1942)*
Private Buckaroo   *(Univ 1942)*
Give Out, Sisters!   *(Univ 1942)*
Get Hep to Love   *(Univ 1942)*
Girls Town   *(PRC 1942)*
When Johnny Comes Marching Home   *(Univ 1942)*
Mr. Big   *(Univ 1943)*
Top Man   *(Univ 1943)*

The Merry Monahans   *(Univ 1944)*
Chip Off the Old Block   *(Univ 1944)*
Follow the Boys   *(Univ 1944)*
This Is the Life   *(Univ 1944)*
Bowery to Broadway   *(Univ 1944)*
Babes on Swing Street   *(Univ 1944)*
That's the Spirit   *(Univ 1945)*
Patrick the Great   *(Univ 1945)*
Here Come the Coeds   *(Univ 1945)*
On Stage, Everybody!   *(Univ 1945)*
Men in Her Diary   *(Univ 1945)*
Shamrock Hill   *(EL 1949)*
There's a Girl in My Heart   *(AA 1949)*
All Ashore   *(Col 1953)*

73

Sabu

The 1970s have Alice Cooper and David Bowie on the rock scene; in the 1940s the movies made a specialty of exotic oddities. It is hardly conceivable that any other decade could bear the responsibilities of nurturing the likes of Sabu, Carmen Miranda, Vera Hruba Ralston, Turhan Bey, and Maria Montez. Each of these figures flourished in the limelight for a while. Most of these unique creatures—real or manufactured—were more camp figures than authentic performers, but among them, Sabu was always ingenuous and earnest from his first film onward. His special qualities quickly captivated movie-goers and gave him an enduring profession to practice. On-screen, he was hardly ever allowed to be anything but boyish and asexual; a situation not so tough to accept when he was thirteen in *Elephant Boy* (1937), but very difficult for him and audiences to endure when he made *A Tiger Walks* (1964) at the age of forty.

Within the jungle called Karapur, stretching to a ridge of mountains in wild elephant country, is the town of Mysore, India. Here on January 27, 1924, Sabu Dastagir was born, the son of Shaik Ibrahim, a fourth-generation *Mahout* ("elephant driver") in the service of the Maharajah of Mysore. When the boy was nine, his father died and be became a ward of the royal elephant stables. Three years later the town was agog with the exciting news of the arrival of white sahibs planning a great *Keddah,* or "elephant drive."

The white sahibs were from Denham, England, taking location shots for a new Technicolor film based on Rudyard Kipling's story, "Toomai of the Elephants." Heading the group were Zoltan Korda, chief cameraman Osmond Borrodaile, and Robert Flaherty, famous for his documentaries and the silent films *Nanook of the North (1922) and Moana* (1926).

An exhaustive search for a native lad to play the leading character ended when Sabu was found by Borrodaile on the many sacred grounds of the Maharajah's palace. Robert Flaherty later related, "Osmond Borrodaile brought in a lad from the Mysore stables. This child was a twelve-year-old orphan, pathetic and shy. His name was Sabu." They took the young boy to Kakankote and, Flaherty continued, "It was not long before we fully realized what a great find we had in this smiling, engaging native lad. We put him into a jungle costume of breech-cloth and turban and made some tests of him. He was as natural and free that first time before the camera as any actor I have ever seen."

When the final location shooting of *Elephant Boy* (1937) was completed, Sabu, with his older brother Shaik (who remained his constant companion until he was killed by a robber in 1960 in a Van Nuys, California furniture store they jointly owned) were sent to England. Sabu became the ward of the British government and attended the best schools. *Elephant Boy* was completed in England and Flaherty succeeded in pulling a fine performance from the young *ma-*

In Rudyard Kipling's Jungle Book *(UA 1942)*

With Lon Chaney, Jr. in The Cobra Woman *(Univ 1943)*

hout, highlighted by the youngster's uncanny ability to handle the huge pachyderm Irawatha (called Kala Nag in the film), but the mutual love between beast and boy could not be directed, it was a natural respect cultivated and nourished in the stables of Mysore.

The film was a huge success in England and abroad, and Sabu, quickly learning English, was cast by Alexander Korda, who had placed him under personal contract, as Prince Azim in his elaborate Technicolor production of A.E.W. Mason's *Drums* (1938). Mason's tale of royal intrigue and war on India's northwestern frontier was filmed in the Welsh mountains at Cwm Bychanm a thousand feet above the village of Llanbedr. Here, Sabu learned to ride a white Arabian stallion, play soccer, and, with Desmond Tester, an English child actor who played a mischievous drummer boy in the picture, became fascinated with fishing in the Welsh lakes.

The natural charm and poise Sabu displayed in *Elephant Boy* remained in *Drums,* in which he played his part with authority, ease, and grace, holding his own among a seasoned cast of adult actors that included Raymond Massey, Valerie Hobson, and Francis L. Sullivan. All apprehension that his impressive initial film appearance was a mere stroke of luck

geared to time and place, his native habitat, and Flaherty's sensitive direction was dispelled with the release of *Drums.* Sabu's first visit to the United States was for a publicity tour for *Drums.* He captivated everyone from Hollywood stars to First Lady Eleanor Roosevelt with his boyish charm, dressed as a typically English school boy but wearing a bright red turban and constantly attended by two bearded, ancient Sikh bodyguards.

On October 24, 1940, Louella Parsons opened at New York's Loew's State Theatre on Broadway with a Hollywood-inspired-and-gathered vaudeville show in which she headed a company of young film personalities that included Ilona Massey, William Orr, Robert Stack, Brenda Joyce, Binnie Barnes, Mike Frankovich, and Sabu. The young Indian was highly presentable and composed, and in a "creditable light baritone" he sang "I Want to Be a Sailor." He continued on tour with Parsons and Company until United Artists sent him on a personal appearance with the opening in various major cities of Korda's *The Thief of Bagdad* (1940).

The Thief of Bagdad, his third Korda film, had started shooting in England with sea shots taken at Cornwall, but, halted by the London blitz, had shifted to Hollywood where distinguished designer William

In The End of the River *(Univ 1948)*

Cameron Menzies exceeded his past masterpiece (the 1924 Douglas Fairbanks, Sr., *The Thief of Bagdad*) with designs for the remake in the Korda production. His contributions included a spirited white-winged horse, a magic carpet, the fantastic all-seeing eye, a monstrous spider and web, and, aided by the special effects of Lawrence Butler, the outsized filming of the giant Djinni (Rex Ingram). It was sheer magic in Technicolor, filled with camera illusions, a beautiful princess (June Duprez), and a superb portrayal of the wicked Grand Vizier Jaffar by that master artist Conrad Veidt.

The Korda remake split the Fairbanks role between Abu the Thief (Sabu) and Prince Ahmad of Bagdad (John Justin). Subtitled "An Arabian Fantasy," it was directed by Ludwig Berger, Michael Powell, and Tim Whelan: Berger for the love scenes, Whelan for action scenes, and the rest of the film by Powell. It was all beautifully photographed by Georges Perinal. Sabu developed a strong case of star-temperament during filming, but Michael Powell took the *enfant terrible* aside and after a lecture on professional ethics, the two developed a lasting friendship. Sabu settled down and gave a sterling performance as Abu the Thief and the picture was finally completed in Arizona's Grand Canyon.

In mid-April, 1941, Sabu was part of a large Hollywood contingent at the Mexico City Motion Picture Festival which included such stars as Norma Shearer, Wallace Beery, Laurel and Hardy, Patricia Morison, and many others. The youngster's charm and poise fascinated the Mexican audiences.

Sabu's forth and final film under his Korda agreement was *Rudyard Kipling's Jungle Book* (1942), in which he was Mowgli, reared by a wolf pack but returned to his mother (Rosemary De Camp) who teaches him the ways of man. This "pageantry of primitive beauty" was filmed in Sherwood Forest some forty miles from Hollywood. Sabu then signed a contract with Universal, the home of ersatz luminaries, and appeared with Jon Hall and Maria Montez in three frantic fantasies: *The Arabian Nights* (1942), as the sly and amusing Orano, in *White Savage* (1943), and as Kado who helps friend Hall rescue his bride from her evil twin sister in *The Cobra Woman* (1943) with Montez playing both twins. The trio of films were all in Technicolor, which did much to relieve the exotic nonsense.

On January 4, 1944, Sabu became an United States citizen and enlisted in the U.S. Army Air Force. He distinguished himself in World War II as Staff Sergeant Dastagir, a tail gunner on B-29s during forty-

467

two Pacific combat missions, for which he received the Distinguished Service Cross, the Air Medal, four battle stars, and three clusters. Returning to Universal after his service with the Air Force, he made *Tangier* (1946), with declining Maria Montez, and was Narsin, whose wife is attacked by a tiger wounded by Wendell Corey in *The Man-Eater of Kumaon* (1948). One of his better film parts was for his friend Michael Powell and Emeric Pressburger in the movie version of Rumner Golden's novel, *Black Narcissus* (1947), in which he was the young native general observing the disenchantment of a group of nuns led by Deborah Kerr and Flora Robson in their Himalayan convent which had once been a harem. The story was filmed in superlative color with frequent spurts of fine acting.

With Gail Russell in Song of India *(Col 1949)*

However, the basic tale of the temptation of a group of nuns in the wind-swept Himalayas was often pretentiously arty. In 1948, Sabu married a young actress, Marilyn Cooper, eventually becoming the father of a son, Paul, and a daughter, Jasmine.

His fading movie career was not encouraged by a paternity suit brought against him in 1950 by a minor British actress, Brenda Marian Juleir, claiming he was the father of her daughter. The case continued for two years and the jury ruled that Sabu was not the father. Following the trial, Sabu went to Italy to make *Biongiorno Elefante* (*Hello Elephant*) (1952), directed by Franciolini, and with Vittoria De Sica in the cast.

In January of 1953, Sabu was back in the Los Angeles courts in a civil suit filed by the Fireman's Fund Insurance Company, accusing him of maliciously starting a fire that destroyed the second floor of his home two years before, for which he had received $9,700 in damages. His film career was virtually ended and he made a couple of television films for an unsold series that were later re-edited and released as a movie feature, *Sabu and the Magic Ring* (1957). In Europe he made *Il Tesoro del Bengala,* released in the United States as *Jungle Hell* (1956), and appeared with Martha Hyer and Micheline Presle in William Dieterle's German-made *Mistress of the World.*

Looking middle-aged and a bit frowsy, he was Talib in Warner Bros.' *Rampage* (1963), with Robert Mitchum and Jack Hawkins. This is the film in which he tries to divert Mitchum from his endless tracking of a tiger called "The Enchantress" by offering the hunter his woman (Cely Carriloo), explaining "Plenty for two. Is custom." The film, made in the San Diego Zoo with location shots in Hawaii, was filled with tired cliches that would have embarrassed child admirers of Johnny Weissmuller's acting. His last acting job was for Walt Disney's pedestrian *A Tiger Walks* as Ram Singh, a circus assistant helping Brian Keith capture a circus tiger. One wag noted that *A Tiger Walks* was a step in the wrong direction. It was.

On December 2, 1963, Sabu died of a heart attack at his home in Chatsworth, California. He was only thirty-nine.

SABU

Elephant Boy   *(UA—British 1937)*
Drums   *(UA—British 1938)*
The Thief of Bagdad   *(UA 1940)*
Rudyard Kipling's Jungle Book   *(UA 1942)*
The Arabian Nights   *(Univ 1942)*
White Savage   *(Univ 1943)*
The Cobra Woman   *(Univ 1943)*
Tangier   *(Univ 1946)*
Black Narcissus   *(Rank 1947)*
The Man-Eater of Kumaon   *(Univ 1948)*

The End of the River   *(Univ 1948)*
Song of India   *(Col 1949)*
Savage Drums   *(Lip 1951)*
Biongiorno Elefante (Hello Elephant)   *(Italian 1952)*
Il Tesora Del Bengala (a.k.a., Jungle Hell)   *(Italian 1956)*
Jaguar   *(Rep 1956)*
Sabu and the Magic Ring   *(AA 1957)*
Mistress of the World   *(German 1959)*
Rampage   *(WB 1963)*
A Tiger Walks   *(BV 1964)*

74

Martha Scott

When Martha Scott made her motion picture debut as Emily in *Our Town* (1940), it appeared that a major career had begun in Hollywood. Follow-up performances in *Cheers for Miss Bishop* (1941) and *One Foot in Heaven* (1941) supported this initial belief. Then, suddenly, the meteoric rise to stardom burned out as quickly as it had begun. Miss Scott has had a consistently active career since then—she has done much television and extensive theatre work—but only a dozen film roles followed her early successes, only half of which were worthy of interest and none of which have been produced in the past fifteen years. When the actress recently returned to feature films in *Airport '75* (1974), little notice was given to the fact that it was a virtual movie "comeback," because she has remained so familiar a name through television and the theatre.

She was born in Jamesport, Missouri, on September 22 of some year around 1914 ("Don't ask me my age because I won't tell the truth. In fact I've lied so much about it that the last time I saw my mother I had to ask her how old I was!"). She was the daughter of a farmer-maintenance engineer. Her father boasted descent from Sir Walter Scott, and her mother was a cousin of President McKinley. When Martha was twelve, the family moved for occupational reasons to Kansas City. Martha showed such promise as a student that an aunt of hers financed her higher education. As

such, she graduated from the University of Michigan in 1934 with a Bachelor of Arts degree. The family had assumed all along that the girl would use her degree to good advantage by becoming a teacher, and was more than a bit apprehensive when Martha decided to venture into the precarious world of the theatre. In her fledgling days, she played stock in Detroit and then joined the Shakespearean company in the Globe Theatre at the Chicago World's Fair. "We put on seven shows a day," she once recalled, "and I found it to be the most wonderful experience in the world."

After some additional stock work, this time in upper New York state and in New England, the actress came to Manhattan. "I made the rounds," she said, "and until I landed on Broadway, radio serials were my bread and butter." She first appeared over the airwaves as a "ten-dollar scream" on a CBS show with Orson Welles (she cannot recall the series). "I was in 'John's Other Wife,' 'Pepper Young's Family,' and many others. Finally, I managed to get a part in a Kenyon Nicholson play. After we had been in rehearsal a week, I got a call from my agent, who told me that Jed Harris had a drama called *Our Town* in rehearsal but wouldn't go on unless he could find a new ingenue. So I went to the Harris office for an audition, read a brief scene, and then told Jed I already had another job. He pushed back my hat, looked at my bangs, and said, 'Sign the contract.' But I remarked I was keeping Mr. Nicholson waiting. Jed

With Beulah Bondi in Our Town *(UA 1940)*

With John Wayne in a publicity pose for In Old Oklahoma *(Rep 1943)*

answered: 'Tell him you're quitting and be back at four o'clock.'"

Our Town opened on February 4, 1938, at the Henry Miller Theatre and was an immediate hit. Playwright Thornton Wilder wrote a basic Americana story as weepy as they come, but powerful enough to discourage scoffers. Miss Scott's New York stage debut as a smalltown girl, who marries after high school and a few years later dies in childbirth, made her a star. Frank Craven, as the "stage manager"-narrator, was the show's major star. The *New York Times* reported, "As the boy and girl, John Craven, who is Frank Craven's son, and Martha Scott turn youth into a tremulous idealization, some of their scenes are lovely past all enduring." The show ran for 336 performances and Martha won sufficient notice to be invited to Hollywood.

Idealistic Martha was quickly disenchanted by the world of films after taking a screen test for the role of Melanie in *Gone with the Wind* (1939). Producer David O. Selznick bluntly informed her, "You just don't photograph." She promptly returned East. Nevertheless, a film agent named Nell Gurney had taken note of her, and when United Artists scheduled *Our Town* for film production, he pestered producer Sol Lesser to heed Martha's talents. The producer did so,

In Cheers for Miss Bishop *(UA 1941)*

472

and she returned to California to recreate her telling role of Emily.

With Frank Craven repeating his role as narrator and William Holden added as Martha's love interest, *Our Town* fared almost as well as a motion picture as it had done on the Broadway boards. The *New York Times* was again abundant in its praise of the property, "There is reason to take hope this morning, to find renewed faith and confidence in mankind—and inadvertently, in the artistry of the screen. A more tonic and reassuring avowal of the nobility which resides in just plain folks—and the capacity for expression possessed by the screen—has not come this way in longer than we care to remember." As for the film's ingenue, the *Times* declared, "Martha Scott, as the young girl, is lovely and vibrant with emotion."

It was quite an introduction to movie audiences for Martha. For her first film, she was Oscar-nominated for Best Actress of the Year, but lost the Academy Award to Ginger Rogers of *Kitty Foyle*.

With such a promising debut behind her, Martha quite naturally anticipated other challenging assignments in her film future. One came when Joan Fontaine fell ill and a replacement was needed for *The Howards of Virginia* (1940), produced at Columbia. Director Frank Lloyd took advantage of the newly restored colonial Williamsburg in filming his account of 1770s Virginia. The star of the historical affair was Cary Grant, who was, unfortunately, as ill at ease in this dramatic role, as he was in his period costumes. But Sir Cedric Hardwicke as a hateful Tory and Martha as an aristocratic but tender love interest carried the film with their imposing characterizations.

A strong showcase role for the actress followed in *Cheers for Miss Bishop,* which proved to be a female version of *Goodbye, Mr. Chips* (1941). The film starred Martha as a school teacher, and in the course of the ninety-five-minute chronicle she ages from a nervous novice to a contented old lady. The film won her considerable publicity, was well-mounted, and opened at Radio City Music Hall. The *New York Times* judged her "charming as the young woman but very feeble when bowed down with the years." Nevertheless, it was the sort of picture that made most movie-goers look upon Martha as a great actress, and for a time her publicity took this tack in order to promote her cinema career.

She next appeared onscreen in Columbia's *They Dare Not Love* (1941). The trivial film concerned a dethroned Austrian prince (George Brent) and his adventures with an unroyal maid (Miss Scott) during the Nazi invasion. Director James Whale, famed for having directed *Frankenstein* (1931) and *The Invisible Man* (1933), among other films, was not at his best or

With Henry O'Neill and Jeffrey Lynn in Strange Bargain *(RKO 1949)*

even particularly interested in romances, and the film dragged noticeably. Fortunately, it did not receive enough critical or audience attention to be a serious detriment to the actress' career at this juncture.

There followed a film that matched *Our Town* in poignancy and audience appeal. It was Warner Bros.' *One Foot in Heaven.* Based on Hortzell Spence's biography of his father, minister William Spence, it cast Fredric March in the pivotal role and Martha as his patient, understanding wife. It was another of those "aging" roles for her. The *New York Times* applauded, "Mr. March is truly excellent. Miss Scott abets him magnificently as his loyal and loving mate—a woman of fine sensibilities and endures the humiliations of a poor parson's wife and offers her comprehending self as the patient foil to his willfull outbursts." During the shooting of the picture, the actual Mrs. Spence came out from Ames, Iowa, to observe the filming. After returning home, she sent Martha a note greeting her as "a third new daughter." The widow also sent the actress a hymn book that the Reverend Spence had given his fiancée during their courting days.

One Foot in Heaven consolidated Martha's film stardom. After its completion, Martha, the wife of Carleton Alsop, took a sabbatical to await the birth of her first child. On September 16, 1940, she had married Alsop, a radio-film producer who had given Martha her earliest radio jobs. The couple lived on a San Fernando Valley ranch, where visitors discovered that the actress was by no means a typical housekeeper. A maid handled the mundane chores while Martha relaxed smoking a pipe. She once told the press, "We have a very competent housekeeper—thank heavens! In fact, do you know what my mother said about me? She said she was convinced that the reason I became an actress was that I hated to wash the dishes!" In April of 1942, a boy, Carleton, was born, and afterward, Martha decided to return to acting. With no attractive roles available in Hollywood, she accepted a Broadway offer to star in *The Willow and I,* which opened in December 1942 and closed within a month.

Upon returning to Hollywood, Martha, who was now in her late twenties, found herself in an unusual position. There just were not many roles available that fitted her particular screen image. In *Our Town* she had been an ethereal image part of the time, and in *Cheers* and *One Foot* she had plied the gambit of aging oncamera. Her advisors decided she needed a new screen guise and began having her photographed in the cheesecake mold, in bathing suits and

473

sprawled seductively across beds. In line with her new look, she began accepting roles that were by no means comparable to her earlier successes. She was among the guest stars in *Stage Door Canteen* (1943), showed some good comedy sense in a minor screwball comedy, *Hi Diddle Diddle* (1943), mainly memorable for bringing back to the screen a long absent Pola Negri and was in *In Old Oklahoma* (a.k.a., *War of the Wildcats*) (1943). The latter film featured a great brawl between John Wayne and Albert Dekker, but wasted Martha as a "progressive" teacher-writer of the old West.

Martha correctly read the handwriting on the celluloid wall and returned to New York. Broadway, at least, was happy to have her. She starred in the successful *Soldier's Wife* (October, 1944), which ran for a season, and replaced Margaret Sullavan in *The Voice of the Turtle* in September, 1945. The footlights have been the site of much of her following career, and she has participated in over a dozen New York plays. Among the more successful were *The Number* (October, 1951), *The Male Animal,* a revival (April, 1952) in which she later toured, *The Remarkable Mr. Pennypacker* (December, 1953), *The 49th Cousin* (October, 1960), and replaced Maureen O'Sullivan in *Never Too Late* on April 27, 1964. She has also done much summer stock, touring in *Future Perfect* (1961), *The Complaisant Lover* (1962), and *Tchin-Tchin* (1963); and she toured in 1965 in *The Subject Was Roses,* after replacing Irene Dailey on Broadway.

Since the mid-1940s, Martha's film career had continued *very* sporadically. In 1947 she appeared in the English-made *So Well Remembered,* based on the James Hilton novel about an up-from-poverty humanitarian (John Mills) whose vicious wife leaves him and tries to prevent his social improvements. Martha played the wife, a completely different role for her, and she proved to be a most lethal bitch oncamera. *Strange Bargain* (1949) saw her standing by her husband (Jeffrey Lynn) when he is involved with the underworld; *When I Grow Up* (1951) found her with child problems with a runaway·Bobby Driscoll; *The Desperate Hours* (1955) found her as Fredric March's wife again, this time in a story of an average American household held captive by a group of desperate criminals (led by Humphrey Bogart); *The Ten Commandments* (1956) and *Sayonara* (1957) were both big films, but her roles were minor. Her next two films were *Eighteen and Anxious* (1957), an exploitive feature which cast her as a mother whose daughter elopes, becomes pregnant, is widowed, and then cannot prove her marriage because of a license

misprint; and *Ben-Hur* (1959), as Charlton Heston's understanding mother.

While movies have been few and far between, Martha has been very active in radio (especially on "Lux Radio Theatre"), in television, as well as in the theatre. She first appeared on the video medium on November 2, 1950, on "Airflyte Theatre," and has since appeared on dozens of shows. From 1954–57 she was the narrator and story editor of the Monday-to-Friday series "Modern Romances" for NBC. She greatly enjoyed the assignment. In fact, while making *The Desperate Hours* in Hollywood she was supplied with a stage and crew at Paramount in order to continue her hostessing segments of the show. When she went to Europe to appear in MGM's *Ben-Hur* she was forced to relinquish her "Modern Romances" chores. She has guest-starred on most of the top TV shows, including "Robert Montgomery Presents" and "Ironsides." In 1974 she appeared on the video special *Portrait: The Man from Independence* as Harry Truman's (Robert Vaughn) mother.

In 1946 Martha and Alsop divorced, and later that year she married Mel Powell, the pianist and composer of both classical and popular music, by whom she has had a daughter.

Martha still remains very active in the theatrical field. In 1969, she served as a co-director of the Plumstead Playhouse, a group established by cinema performers who wanted an opportunity to foster stage work. One of the shows was a revival of *Our Town,* which featured Henry Fonda, Ed Begley, Margaret Hamilton, Mildred Natwick, John Beal, and Elizabeth Hartman. In 1973, the Plumstead group sponsored the new edition of the musical *I Do, I Do,* starring Carol Burnett and Rock Hudson. In 1974 Martha was among the cast of the telefeature *Thursday's Game* in which Gene Wilder and Bob Newhart were two married men who over-enjoy their once-a-week night of freedom. Ever anxious to perpetuate the classics of the American theatre, Martha joined in the mid-1975 revival of *The Skin of Our Teeth,* playing Mrs. Antrobus with Alfred Drake as her stage husband.

While it is unfortunate that Martha never became a consistent star in films, at least she rarely allowed Hollywood to waste her in films that would have served her talents poorly. The dramatic ability so well displayed in *Our Town* is still there, nurtured by years in the theatre and on television. One can only wonder how she felt voicing such a line of dialog in *Airport '75* as—describing co-passenger Gloria Swanson to her companion nun—"She must be an actress or something worse."

MARTHA SCOTT

Our Town   *(UA 1940)*
The Howards of Virginia   *(Col 1940)*
Cheers for Miss Bishop   *(UA 1941)*
They Dare Not Love   *(Col 1941)*
One Foot in Heaven   *(WB 1941)*
Stage Door Canteen   *(UA 1943)*
Hi Diddle Diddle   *(UA 1943)*
In Old Oklahoma (a.k.a., War of the Wildcats)   *(Rep 1943)*
So Well Remembered   *(RKO 1947)*

Strange Bargain   *(RKO 1949)*
When I Grow Up   *(EL 1951)*
The Desperate Hours   *(Par 1955)*
The Ten Commandments   *(Par 1956)*
Sayonara   *(WB 1957)*
Eighteen and Anxious   *(Rep 1957)*
Ben-Hur   *(MGM 1959)*
Charlotte's Web   *(Par 1973) (Voice only)*
Airport '75   *(Univ 1974)*

Zachary Scott

"Zachary Scott gives another of his prize heel characterizations to carry majority interest in the plot and is well on his way to making himself the most hissable heavy on the screen," said *Variety*, reviewing Scott's performance in *Danger Signal* (1945), his fifth film. Dan Duryea also fitted this description, but Scott's typical screen heavy was more in the Joseph Schildkraut tradition: Ruthless, sleek, and sophisticated. Schildkraut was foreign and more effete than Zachary, but Scott was an American prototype. He was the best of the well-bred domestic scoundrels in Hollywood films in the mid-forties and epitomized it to the nth degree in his role as Monte Beragon, the unscrupulous Malibu Beach heel in *Mildred Pierce* (1945).

Zachary Thomson Scott, Jr. was born in Austin, Texas, on February 21, 1914, the son of Dr. and Mrs. Zachary T. Scott. His father was a distinguished physician and surgeon and was a leading advocate of tuberculosis research, as well as president of the National Tuberculosis Association. His mother, Sallie Lee Masterson, was a member of a family of Texas ranchers. Zachary's family can be traced back to the year 1694 when his ancestors settled on land in Fredericksburg, Virginia. One of his ancestors, Colonel Fielding Lewis, married George Washington's sister, Betty, and manufactured the first American guns used by the Continental Army.

Though from a well-to-do family, Zachary attended public school in Austin and was required to earn his own spending money. While he was in high school he worked as a soda jerk in a neighborhood drug tore. He retained this job through his first two years at the University of Texas. He had been active in dramatics in high school, and at the University he was president of the Curtain Club and appeared in many of their productions. He was also a prominent member of the school's track team. At age nineteen he dropped out of school and, with his parents' permission, went to New Orleans and signed on as a seaman on a freighter headed for England. He earned one dollar a day chipping paint and scrubbing down decks. During the three weeks at sea one crew member stabbed another and the ship was blown off course during a three-day storm before the vessel finally dropped anchor at the Thames River.

Scott's longing to be a professional actor had increased over the years, and when he was in London he found his chance by joining the English Repertory Company. His first professional acting stint was as the juvenile in *The Outsider.* He later joined the Theatre Royal in Bath (1933–34). He had hopes of attending the Royal Academy, but instead satisfied himself with working for a year and a half in lesser surroundings, appearing in more than twenty plays. He also managed to visit much of the Continent during his breaks from shows. During his British stay his Texas accent was a source of constant embarrassment to him, but

With Louis Hayward in Ruthless *(EL 1948)*

With Joan Crawford in Mildred Pierce *(WB 1945)*

he found that it sometimes worked to his advantage when he claimed that he was from Australia. He left England for America a few days before his twenty-first birthday.

After arriving in New York, he was offered a screen test, but Zachary was bent upon making good on the stage first, so he declined the offer. His dream of a stage success did not come immediately or easily. While visiting his family in Austin, he was in an automobile accident which broke his jaw and put him out of commission for four months. After he was able to talk again he obtained a job as an oil rigger and then returned to college to obtain his B.A. degree. On February 21, 1935, he wed Elaine Anderson, whom he had met in school. Scott and Elaine had a daughter, Waverly, who was cared for by a nurse while the two parents were still attending college classes. Zachary and Elaine would be divorced in 1950 and she would later wed author John Steinbeck.

During his senior year in college Zachary attended a party at the home of a friend, Stark Young, and was introduced to Alfred Lunt and Lynn Fontanne, who were then on a national tour. Young had spoken very highly of Scott to the Lunts, as did Richard Whorf, another guest. The Lunts suggested that summer stock was the best way to get started in the theatre in this country and recommended Zachary to Lawrence Langner of the Theatre Guild and to casting director John Haggott. Haggott said he could not promise anything, but informed Scott that he should come to New York again and give it a try. Scott did just that and was signed by the Westport Country Playhouse to play the bar boy in *Anna Christie* (1939), followed by *Easy Virtue* (1940) with Jane Cowl, in which Scott was a fifty-year-old butler. Miss Cowl liked him and suggested that he not use the name "Zach" professionally, that his full first name was less harsh. After a dress rehearsal of this play, Miss Cowl sent for Scott. It seemed that as she made her exit in the final scene of the play, instead of his speaking his final goodbye partly to the audience, he turned fully upstage and watched her exit. Miss Cowl said to him, "Young man, I expect to see you a star in your own right sometime. No one told you to sacrifice your last line to me, but if you had done it any other way you would have misportrayed a butler and infuriated your leading lady." Scott always treasured this remark.

Scott next appeared in the Chinese play, *Circle of Chalk* (1941), for the New School of Social Research. The play starred Dolly Haas and was a hit of a kind. From this he went into *The Damask Cheek*, which opened at the Playhouse Theatre on October 22,

With Jay Gilpin and Betty Field in The Southerner *(UA 1945)*

478

1942, and starred Flora Robson as well as featuring Celeste Holm and Myron McCormick. This play closed prematurely due to the star's illness, and then Zachary went into the ill-fated Billie Burke vehicle, *This Rock* (1943). On June 16, 1943, he opened, in the lead male role at the Booth Theatre in *Those Endearing Young Charms,* with Virginia Gilmore and Blanche Sweet. Scott was most pleased when, on opening night, he received a congratulatory note from Jane Cowl who had remembered her prediction of a few years before at the Westport Playhouse.

The play and Scott received favorable reviews and a few evenings after the opening, Warner Bros.' Jack L. Warner saw the show and was very enthusiastic over Scott's performance. By the end of the second act Warner had begun negotiations with Scott's agent, and by the end of the third act negotiations were completed and awaited only Scott's approval. Zachary Scott signed his Warner Bros. contract in August, 1943, without even the formality of a screen test. By November, he was in front of the cameras at the Burbank studio playing the title role in *The Mask of Dimitrios* (1944). He was a complete cinema novice but well on the road to fame as the suave villain of this Eric Ambler adventure. The *New York Times* argued that Zachary, outshone by co-players Sydney Greenstreet and Peter Lorre, presented "the rascally Dimitrios as a blue-steel American gangster type," while the *New York Herald-Tribune* found Scott "a genuine addition to the ranks of film actors."

The following year Scott was loaned to United Artists and director Jean Renoir to play the sharecropping farmer in *The Southerner* (1945). This is the film most critics believe contains Scott's best performance. The *New York World-Telegram* stated, "This young newcomer has achieved one of the acting triumphs of the season with his man of great charm laced with determination." The *New York Times* found him "excellent and outstanding, at once restrained and powerful." As important a role as it was, as critically acclaimed as Scott was, Warner Bros. still did not give him the opportunity to expand his talents further in other varied assignments.

Not that Scott could scoff at his key role in *Mildred Pierce,* a film engagingly, if flamboyantly, directed by Michael Curtiz. His direction focused less on the ambiance of southern California than it did highlighting the role played by Joan Crawford in what proved to be an Oscar-winning performance. The film's opening sequence, which has Scott shot by an unseen hand and muttering "Mildred. . . ." as he falls down dead, is one of the most vividly remembered scenes in a melodrama. Scott was so impressive and believable in this type of role that it was difficult for produ-

cers and audiences alike to ever accept him in any other type of characterizations.

Warners kept Zachary busy, usually in B features, and only occasionally cast him differently than his profitable stereotype. He played a romantic author in *Stallion Road* (1947), and at least was sympathetic in *The Unfaithful* (1947). Zachary was loaned out again, this time to MGM for *Cass Timberlane* (1947), with Spencer Tracy and Lana Turner, where he was back playing his old conniving screen self. He made *Ruthless* (1948) on loanout also, and this film gave Scott his best role since *Mildred Pierce.* He performed the title scoundrel astutely. The *New York Times* disagreed, however: "Never a trace of guilt or remorse shows through the character, either in the writing or in the performance of Zachary Scott. Nor is it a good performance, as Mr. Scott acts without expression and is about as flexible as a statue."

Scott then made two westerns and two comedies for Warners. The outdoors stories were far superior to the comedies, for they, at least, were somewhat action-filled. *South of St. Louis* (1949) was superior to *Colt 45* (1950) due to two very colorful performances provided by Scott and Alexis Smith. Miss Smith and Scott appeared together onscreen three other times: In *Stallion Road, Whiplash* (both 1948), and in one comedy, *One Last Fling* (1949). In the latter, both performers floundered dismally. His other Warners' comedy, *Pretty Baby* (1950), was no better.

In 1949 he co-starred again with Joan Crawford this time in *Flamingo Road.* He played a weak, well-bred deputy sheriff with high political ambitions, and Miss Crawford was the ex-carnival entertainer whom he weds. Scott and Crawford again played well together, but the hard-biting feature was hardly the success of *Mildred Pierce.* MGM then borrowed him again for *Shadow on the Wall* (1950), and in their change-of-pace roles, both he and Ann Sothern did nicely. In *Born to Be Bad* (1950) for RKO, Joan Fontaine was the ruthless one with Scott as one of the men she uses and discards.

Before Warner Bros. dismissed Scott, he made one more feature for them, as the local playboy in the Ruth Roman-Richard Todd mystery entry, *Lightning Strikes Twice* (1951). He left his home lot to freelance, do television, and to return to his first love, the stage. Scott did make a short-term pact with Twentieth Century-Fox, where he made two motion pictures: *The Secret of Convict Lake* (1951), in which he was at his nastiest and shared acting honors with Ethel Barrymore and Ann Dvorak, and *Let's Make It Legal* (1951), in which he was involved in adult shenanigans and a love triangle that found him and Macdonald Carey vying for Claudette Colbert's love.

That same year he went on tour playing the male lead in the national company of *Bell, Book and Candle.*

Two years after his divorce, on July 6, 1952, Zachary married actress Ruth Ford and adopted her daughter Shelley from a previous marriage. By the mid-fifties, his screen career was on the wane. He made a number of undistinguished features both here and in Britain and his roles in them were equally undistinguished. In *Bandido* (1956) he did not even receive star billing. Robert Mitchum, Ursula Thiess, and Gilbert Roland were featured above the title with Scott's name in the credits below. He played a gun runner and his dialog was typically old Zachary Scott, as when he sneers at his wife (Thiess), "Don't get your pretty head shot off. I may need it—just once more—for old times' sake."

Since he could no longer obtain decent movie jobs, he spent most of his time plying his craft on stage and on television. He recreated his role of Monte Beragon in *Mildred Pierce* with Virginia Bruce, on "Lux Video Theatre," and starred in *The Scarlet Pimpernel* (1960), and as Mr. Rochester in *Jane Eyre* (1961), the latter two for "Family Classics" on CBS-TV. He did stock again at the Westport Playhouse in 1954 and also toured in *The Moon Is Blue* (1954–55). In 1956 he played the King in the New York City Center's revival of *The King and I,* his first and only stage musical. "Scott is somewhat handicapped by a hoarseness of voice and a tendency toward Italian dialect in his speech," said *Women's Wear Daily.* "We felt he played the king with more brashness and more bravura, but with less subtlety, than [Yul] Brynner. But, despite that, in his own way he did manage to create a viable characterization of the volatile peremptory and barbaric monarch of Siam." Scott did not shave his head for the role of the king because he was only playing it for three weeks and did not think it was worth the alteration.

The following year he returned to England to costar with Margaret Lockwood in *Subway in the Sky* at the Savoy Theatre and appeared for the first time with his wife in *Requiem for a Nun,* a play written especially for them by William Faulkner. *Requiem* opened at the Royal Court in London, on November 26, 1957. About two years later they played it on Broadway to mixed reviews and, thus, for only a short run. *Variety* reported, "Zachary Scott scowls and looks fierce as the lawyer, a role the author doesn't clearly define or explain." Before bringing the play to New York, the Scotts performed it in nine other countries including Mexico. Scott was very loyal to this play and Miss Ford has stated, "Zack's been extraordinary in his dedication. All these years he's put this play first before anything else. I doubt the money he's lost in other things, movies and TV and the stage, too, could be calculated." The Scotts appeared together in two plays at the Spoleto Festival in Italy in 1962.

Zachary's last stage appearances were in a *A Rainy Day in Newark,* which opened on Broadway on October 22, 1963, and which went right down the drain. He then undertook a summer tour as Henry Higgins in *My Fair Lady* during 1964. He also appeared in the Luis Bunuel film *The Young One* (1961), which led Paul V. Beckley (*New York Herald-Tribune*) to advise his readers, "I understand Bunuel actually misled Scott as to his lines and action in order to obtain a certain spontaneity." In his final film, a rather helterskelter Jerry Lewis farce, *It's Only Money* (1962), Zachary provided a take-off of his own stereotyped, sneering screen image.

Offscreen, Zachary was quite removed from his celluloid image. He was a sensitive and very charming man, whose hobby was art collecting, and who loved to cook. The screen's charming, oft-moustachioed scoundrel died on October 3, 1965, of a brain tumor, following a long illness after cranial surgery. He passed away at Sweetbrush, his family home, in Austin, Texas.

Of his image as a superior screen scoundrel, Zachary once said, "Looking evil is really an occupational disease. It is not so much that the face looks so wicked by itself, it is just that you associate it with evil."

ZACHARY SCOTT

The Mask of Dimitrios   (WB 1944)
Hollywood Canteen   (WB 1944)
The Southerner   (UA 1945)
Mildred Pierce   (WB 1945)
Danger Signal   (WB 1945)
Her Kind of Man   (WB 1946)
The Unfaithful   (WB 1947)
Stallion Road   (WB 1947)
Cass Timberlane   (MGM 1947)
Ruthless   (EL 1948)
Whiplash   (WB 1948)
South of St. Louis   (WB 1949)
Flaxy Martin   (WB 1949)
Flamingo Road   (WB 1949)
One Last Fling   (WB 1949)
Guilty Bystander   (Film Classics 1950)
Colt .45   (WB 1950)
Shadow on the Wall   (MGM 1950)

Born to Be Bad   (RKO 1950)
Pretty Baby   (WB 1950)
Lightning Strikes Twice   (WB 1951)
The Secret of Convict Lake   (20th 1951)
Let's Make it Legal   (20th 1951)
Stronghold   (Lip 1952)
Wings of Danger   (Lip 1952)
Appointment in Honduras   (RKO 1953)
The Treasure of Ruby Hills   (AA 1955)
Shotgun   (AA 1955)
Flame of the Islands   (Rep 1955)
Bandido   (UA 1956)
The Counterfeit Plan   (WB 1957)
Flight into Danger   (Anglo Amalgamated 1957)
Man in the Shadow   (Anglo Amalgamated 1957)
Natchez Trace   (Panorama 1960)
The Young One   (Vitalite 1961)
It's Only Money   (Par 1962)

Kent Smith

Joan Crawford said of Kent Smith when he was playing the role of Martin Blackford opposite her in Warner Bros.' *The Damned Don't Cry* (1950), "He's such a good actor, he doesn't get half the credit he deserves!" Thus, Miss Crawford capsuled Kent Smith's career, which resembles a theatrical Baedeker, beginning in childhood as an assistant to Blackstone the Magician. It has extended from the audience of the Gaiety Theatre in New York to most probably last night's drama telecast. An able, hard-working professional actor with a most genial nature, Smith has never attained the status reached by his co-founders of the University Players in West Falmouth, Massachusetts (Henry Fonda, Margaret Sullavan, James Stewart, and Joshua Logan).

Born Frank Kent Smith on March 19, 1907, to hotel owner James E. Smith and his wife Charlotte, young Smith graduated from Phillips Exeter Academy in 1925, and matriculated at Harvard (Class of '29). He played many roles with the University Players in West Falmouth during the summer, and for their winter season at the Maryland Theatre in Baltimore, in addition to appearing with the Wardman Park Hotel Children's Theatre in Washington, D.C.

His first commercial theatre appearance was for David Belasco as the juvenile lead in *Blind Window* which opened at Ford's Theatre in Baltimore on August 15, 1929, and closed out of town. The flop

dashed the hopes of a young actor named Clark Gable, who was featured in the Belasco production. Kent made his Broadway stage debut at the Lyceum Theatre on October 14, 1932, as Lieutenant Chase in *Men Must Fight,* then opened and closed *Heat Lightning* (September, 1933), and on October 24, 1933, he was Juan Manuel Lorezana in *Spring in Autumn,* starring Blanche Yurka and featuring his pal, James Stewart. After a brief run as Karl Hoffman in *The Drums Begin,* he won recognition and glowing notices as Kurt von Obersdorf with whom the self-centered, youth-seeking, foolish wife of *Dodsworth* (February, 1934) falls in love. Smith stayed with the show for 315 performances and continued on the road tour until Gregory Gaye relieved him for newer adventures in the theatre. Kent's versatility kept him constantly occupied in the theatre: From playing Apollodorus on the summer circuit in *Caesar and Cleopatra* to Jack Dunois, Bastard of Orleans, in Katharine Cornell's *Saint Joan.* Prior to his first association with the Cornell contingent, Smith made his screen debut as Woode Swife in Metro-Goldwyn-Mayer's Philo Vance mystery of murder by hypnotism, *The Garden Murder Case* (1936). He returned to Miss Cornell's company under her husband Guthrie McClintic's direction as Phineas McQuestion in *Wingless Victory.*

On January 15, 1937, Kent married a young woman who was not in the theatre or films, Elizabeth V. Gillette, and returned to the Cornell aegis on March

With Anna Sten in Three Russian Girls *(UA 1943)*

With Rhys Williams and George Brent in The Spiral Staircase *(RKO 1946)*

10, 1937, as James Morell in Shaw's *Candida*. He spent that summer as leading man at Elitch Gardens in Denver, Colorado, and returned to Broadway to play Duffy in *The Star Wagon* (September, 1937), with Lillian Gish. Kent then succeeded Dennis King as Torvald opposite Ruth Gordon in the successful revival of Ibsen's *A Doll House*, as well as in Clemence Dane's adaptation of Friedrich Hebbel's play, *Herod and Marianne*, which starred Katharine Cornell and opened on September 27, 1928, at Washington, D.C.'s National Theatre. The play was notable only for being the American stage debut of the great German actor Fritz Kortner, but the script was abandoned on the road. After playing the title role of *Jeremiah* (February, 1939), Smith was reported to have signed for Paramount's *Back Door to Heaven* (1939) in the role of John Shelley. However, in the released version of this study of work-weary kids, it was Van Heflin who played the part. However, Kent Smith was back on Broadway at the Henry Miller Theatre on December 27, 1939, as Peter Thor in *Christmas Eve*. For the next two years Smith kept busy in the theatre, with Ethel Barrymore in *International Incident* (April, 1940), and with Jane Cowl in *Old Acquaintance* (December, 1940). Then RKO enticed thirty-three-year-old Kent to Hollywood and assigned him to *The Cat People* (1942).

Val Lewton's well-constructed, slight-budgeted horror production for RKO started with a tight, frightening script by DeWitt Bodeen and was directed imaginatively by Maurice Tourneur's son, Jacques. The film generated considerable excitement as its seventy-three minutes of black and white sequences unraveled its werewolf-like theme in which a human being turns into a murderous cat. Smith played Oliver Reed, a young maritime designer whose life is endangered by his bride Irene (Simone Simon), a mysterious Serbian who is transformed into a deadly, vicious cat. Two years later RKO hoped to repeat the success of its original cat fable with *The Curse of the Cat People*, again with Smith in the sequel trying to prevent Simone Simon from turning his daughter into a deadly feline. The follow-up was not equal to the original.

For RKO's *Hitler's Children* (1942), Kent was Nicky, joining Tim Holt and Bonita Granville in the sleeper film of the year. *Forever and a Day* (1943) was over two years in the making and most of the talent involved were British. It was an episodic cavalcade of generations of a London town house, cast with many stars, and all its proceeds were contributed to the war effort. Smith was Gates T. Pomfret, a newspaper correspondent who learns the history of the old house from Ruth Warwick during a London air raid. Kent was then Maureen O'Hara's patriotic brother, Paul

Martin, in *This Land Is Mine* (1943), one of the hard-hitting studies of Third Reich tyranny. After playing John Hill, an American flyer tended by Russian nightingale Anna Sten in *Three Russian Girls* (1943) at United Artists, plus a part in a weary programmer for RKO, *Youth Runs Wild* (1944), Kent joined the United States Army Air Force as a weatherman with the rank of private first class. Before his honorable discharge in 1945 he appeared in several government training films. And in 1945 he became the father of a daughter.

Kent's first film following his departure from the service set the tone for his movie career. In RKO's chilling, well-cast, and well-produced mystery, *The Spiral Staircase* (1946), he played the kindly, somewhat stodgy Dr. Parry, who is romantically attracted to mute Dorothy McGuire. This was followed by a supporting role of Hoopendecker in Robert Riskin's implausible smalltown saga, *Magic Town* (1947), which displayed the non-chemistry of leads Jane Wyman and James Stewart. On loanout to Warner Bros., Kent was Kenneth Bartlett in *The Voice of the Turtle* (1947) and played Dr. Richard Talbot, the idealistic soul led down the primrose path by songstress Ann Sheridan in *Nora Prentiss* (1947). Between films, he returned to the stage as defense attorney Reverdy Johnson, appearing with Dorothy Gish in *The Story of Mary Surratt*, and, as Anthony's friend, Enobarbus, gave a fine rendition of the running, cynical commentary on the tragedy of *Antony and Cleopatra* (Godfrey Tearle and Katharine Cornell). Back in Hollywood Kent was Lew Wengler in Susan Hayward's *My Foolish Heart* (1949) and, then, society architect Peter Keating in Warners' dialog-ridden production of Ayn Rand's novel, *The Fountainhead* (1949).

Extending his considerable talents to a new medium, Kent appeared on television in 1950's "Philco Playhouse" telecast of *The End Is Known* and then was Helen Hayes's leading man in the video version of *Victoria Regina*. He also appeared with Miss Hayes at the Martin Beck Theatre in New York for seventy-eight performances as Yancy Loper in Joshua Logan's production of *The Wisteria Tree* (March, 1950). Kent's performance as Yancy fused all the conflicting characterizations of Chekhov's protagonist Vermolay Lopakhin (of *The Cherry Orchard* on which *Wisteria Tree* was based) into a blustering, uncouth, domineering yet basically shy man. His role of Joe Saul in John Steinbeck's short-lived play, *Burning Bright* (October, 1950), with Barbara Geddes, provided him with one of his most believable roles in the theatre. Next, he was splendid in Lillian Hellman's play, *The Autumn Garden* (March, 1951). It starred Fredric March, Florence Eldridge, Jane Wyatt, Kent, and Ethel

With Ann Shoemaker, Jane Wyman, Wallace Ford, and Harry Holman in Magic Town *(RKO 1947)*

Griffies. Kent was the alcoholic, sarcastic bank clerk Edward Crossman. In the brief engagement of Ibsen's *The Wild Duck* at New York's City Center, Smith was Gregers Werle in a cast that included Maurice Evans, Mildred Dunnock, and Diana Lynn.

Kent tossed off continental charm as if he was palace born in the national touring company's version of *Call Me Madam,* with Elaine Stritch (May, 1952, to April, 1953). He gave a surprisingly light performance as Cosmo Constantine and sang surprisingly well in his first musical. He then essayed another musical role in the James Barton part in *Paint Your Wagon* at the Dallas State Fair. Prior to the professional discovery of his singing talent, Kent made a film with Loretta Young for Columbia, *Paula* (1952), but then retreated back to television, appearing as the Neanderthal man in *And Adam Begot,* plus appearing on most of the major dramas telecast, including the "Hallmark Hall of Fame" telecast of *King Richard II* (in which he had played Bolingbroke two years previously at Manhattan's City Center). He was seen also as Doc Stacey, with Charlie Ruggles, Frank McHugh, and Ed Begley, in *The Muldoon Matter* on the "Motorola TV Hour."

The first "legit" theatre on the west coast in twenty seven years was a million-dollar conversion of a former radio station. To open the new Huntington Hart-

ford theatre in Hollywood, Helen Hayes was asked to appear in James Barrie's *What Every Woman Knows,* the delightful comedy she had first played on Broadway in 1926, then revived several times throughout the years, as well as performing it for the screen in 1934. The new Huntington Hartford Theatre opened in September, 1954, with Miss Hayes again as Maggie Wylie guiding her humorless, overbearing Scotsman-husband John Shand, played to perfection by Kent Smith. The two leads took *What Every Woman Knows* on tour and experienced a brief run at New York's City Center at the close of 1954.

For the next two years Kent appeared occasionally on television. His theatre work during this time found him playing Angelo in *Measure for Measure* for the American Shakespeare Festival at Stratford, Connecticut, and replacing Anthony Ross as the Professor in *Bus Stop,* the long-run hit at the Music Box Theatre, after a run on the road starring in the comedy *The Tender Trap.* After a supporting role with Dana Andrews, in the lower-case western *Comanche* (1956), Smith played Warwick to Siobhan McKenna's *Saint Joan,* and was seen on television as a wealthy bachelor marrying Martha Scott in *Give and Take* on "Robert Montgomery Presents." Among his many other TV appearances were as Shelley Winters' husband on a "Wagon Train" episode, and his joining Claudette Colbert in the bizarre two-part telecast of *The Last Town Car* on "G.E. Theatre."

He was in Warner Bros.' emasculated screen version of James Mitchener's novel *Sayonara*, about marriages between American servicemen and Japanese woman. Smith retained his military status as General Charles Lane, killed early and impersonated by Glenn Ford in the frequently funny film, *Imitation General* (1958). Kent was Cyril Lounsberry double-crossing Alan Ladd and Ernest Borgnine in a western revamping of *The Asphalt Jungle* (1950), entitled *The Badlanders* (1958), and remained at MGM for a stock role in a dated gangster film called *Party Girl* (1958).

While other actors went hungry for work, Kent remained active. He was a police psychiatrist solving eleven muggings in United Artists' *The Mugger* (1958). In Henry King's talky, complex tale of a Napa Valley family, *This Earth is Mine* (1959), with Rock Hudson, Claude Rains, Jean Simmons, and Dorothy McGuire, Smith was Francis Fairon. As always he gave sensible performances even in movies of dubious cinematic value. On TV's "Naked City" he was George Blake, trying to clear himself of murder in *One to Get Lost,* and, acting with Jane Greer and Robert Webber, he was Gilbert Hughes in Alfred Hitchcock's TV episode *A True Account.*

In December, 1959, Kent was reunited with his former University Players' colleague, Margaret Sullavan. Together they opened at New Haven's Shubert Theatre on December 28, 1959, in *Sweet Love Remembered.* Their personal notices were good, but the play was found wanting, and then, on New Year's Day of 1960, Margaret Sullavan died from an overdose of sleeping pills. It was revealed that the fifty-year-old actress had been half-deaf for some time. *Sweet Love Remembered* closed despite efforts to substitute Arlene Francis in the female lead role. Kent returned to television as Jess Foladaire on "Wagon Train" in the episode *The Lita Foladaire Story,* had the token role of Stanley Baker in Columbia's *Strangers-When We Meet* (1960), and during the summer of 1960, starred with Arlene Francis on the straw-hat circuit in the boudoir romp of the Greek gods, *Amphitryon 38.* Smith's performance as Jupiter lusting after Amphitryon's wife Alkmena was a choice bit of acting, and he belied his fifty-odd years in his handsome costume as the Greek diety.

Television occupied much of Kent's time from 1960 to 1961. Assignments in feature films became less attractive, such as his role as Dr. Fain in support of Troy Donahue, Connie Stevens, and Dorothy McGuire in *Susan Slade* (1961). Nevertheless, after com-

pleting three television series segments, he replaced Melvyn Douglas in the national touring company of Gore Vidal's *The Best Man.* He was Harvard graduate, ex-Rhode Island governor, ex-secretary of state, and presidential hopeful William Russell. Playing his wife, Alice, in the play, was a very capable, chic actress named Edith Atwater. After seventeen years of marriage, Kent had divorced Betty Gillette in 1954, and, on March 10, 1962, following the closing of the touring *The Best Man* in Philadelphia in February, 1962, he and Edith Atwater were married.

During 1962, Kent was seen on the screen in Buena Vista's *Moon Pilot* in the type of stock assignment he handled so competently, as a Secretary of the Air Force. Among his many TV appearances that year was the *I Saw the Whole Thing* episode of "Alfred Hitchcock Presents," one of the few video segments actually directed by Hitchcock himself.

When he wasn't on the small screen, Kent returned to the big screen. In the past he had played the parts of generals, but he was an officer of a new sort when he became "The General" visiting the brothel of Madam Irma (Shelley Winters) in the not-very-fulfilling screen treatment of Jean Genet's avant-garde play, *The Balcony* (1963). Smith appeared almost monthly on a major television show during 1964 and for Warner Bros. he gave a sincere performance leading *Youngblood Hawke* (1964) to ruin after discovering his wife is having an affair with the young man. As a change of pace from that Delmer Daves outing, he became the Secretary of War with shoulder-length hair in Raoul Walsh's deadly and dull *A Distant Trumpet* (1964), which starred a rather wooden Troy Donahue. In movies, he found work as Uncle George in the Ida Lupino-directed *The Trouble with Angels* (1966), and the next year was an attorney in the muddled courtroom feature *A Covenant with Death* (1967). His true acting ability was given scope as Andrew Oxley, a newspaper editor who commits suicide after the disclosure of his past to his son in *Death of a Gunfighter* (1969).

At an age when most men contemplate retirement, Smith defies his age with his still virile, if grayed appearance and continues to make telling appearances on television, such as District Attorny Thomas Paine concealing the exposure of a vampire-type in *Night Stalker* (1972). In contrast, was his delightful performance as an aging conspirator with Rosalind Russell and Douglas Fairbanks, Jr. in *The Crooked Hearts,* a 1972 telefeature, and, after more than thirty years he was back with the evil felines in an "ABC Movie of the Week" called *The Cat Creature* (1973), with Gale Sondergaard, Stuart Whitman, and John Carradine. In

486

1974 he was in the TV movie *The President's Gang* (1974), filmed in San Francisco, with Lloyd Bridges and his son Beau.

Unlike Lillian Hellman's Edward Crossman of *The* *Autumn Garden*, Kent Smith knew a great many things he wanted to do but also knew what he wanted to do first, and that was to act. The gentleman has succeeded admirably.

KENT SMITH

The Garden Murder Case   *(MGM 1936)*
The Cat People   *(RKO 1942)*
Hitler's Children   *(RKO 1942)*
Forever and a Day   *(RKO 1943)*
This Land is Mine   *(RKO 1943)*
Three Russian Girls   *(UA 1943)*
Youth Runs Wild   *(RKO 1944)*
The Curse of the Cat People   *(RKO 1944)*
The Spiral Staircase   *(RKO 1946)*
Magic Town   *(RKO 1947)*
The Voice of the Turtle   *(WB 1947)*
Nora Prentiss   *(WB 1947)*
Design for Death   *(RKO 1948)* (Narrator)
My Foolish Heart   *(RKO 1949)*
The Fountainhead   *(WB 1949)*
The Damned Don't Cry   *(WB 1950)*
This Side of the Law   *(WB 1950)*
Paula   *(Col 1952)*
Comanche   *(UA 1956)*
Sayonara   *(WB 1957)*
Imitation General   *(MGM 1958)*
The Badlanders   *(MGM 1958)*

Party Girl   *(MGM 1958)*
The Mugger   *(UA 1958)*
This Earth is Mine   *(Univ 1959)*
Strangers When We Meet   *(Col 1960)*
Susan Slade   *(WB 1961)*
Moon Pilot   *(BV 1962)*
The Balcony   *(Continental Distributing 1963)*
Youngblood Hawke   *(WB 1964)*
A Distant Trumpet   *(WB 1964)*
The Young Lovers   *(MGM 1964)*
The Trouble with Angels   *(Col 1966)*
A Covenant with Death   *(WB 1967)*
Games   *(Univ 1967)*
Kona Coast   *(WB 1968)*
The Money Jungle   *(Commonwealth United 1968)*
Death of a Gunfighter   *(Univ 1969)*
Assignment to Kill   *(WB 1969)*
The Games   *(20th 1970)*
Pete 'N' Tillie   *(Univ 1972)*
Lost Horizon   *(Col 1973)*
Maurie   *(National General 1973)*

77

Craig Stevens

Fame came late to Craig Stevens. For almost twenty years he played not very good routine film roles. The few times he had starring parts they were in grade C melodramas at the Warner Bros. factory in the early 1940s. In 1942 he was top-billed in *Spy Ship, Secret Enemies,* and *The Hidden Hand,* a trio of productions that were mere fodder for the action picture houses. After completing his war service he returned to Hollywood and was kept in minor roles of the "tennis, anyone?" variety.

The six foot, two-inch dark and handsome man did not come into his own until producer Blake Edwards cast him as television's "Peter Gunn" in 1958. As the suave and sophisticated criminal hunter, he was likened by many critics to Cary Grant. There is a slight resemblance, but Craig does not feel the comparison is justified. Neither does his wife, actress Alexis Smith. Craig insists, "I was never offended. In fact, I was rather complimented by it. What I didn't like was that people said the character of Peter Gunn was created to be like Grant. That just isn't true."

After the "Gunn" series concluded its run (it is still in syndication here and abroad and Craig made a theatrical feature of the property in 1967), he continued as one of videoland's most popular guest stars. He also has found time and the opportunity to appear in Broadway shows and in stock. Noted stage director Morton DaCosta describes Craig as "almost a boy scout in the theatre, and if that makes him sound square, he isn't really. He's a terribly modest man with a dry, cryptic sense of humor."

Craig was born Gail Shikles, Jr. on July 8, 1918, in Liberty Missouri, which is near Kansas City. His father was a school teacher who retired in 1958. Craig was a pre-dental student at the University of Kansas and was quite serious about obtaining his D.D.S. degree. He was also a basketball star at the University, but, like many others before and after him, he found his life's work through the avenue of college dramatics. "My speech teacher doubled as the drama coach," Craig remembers, "and he persuaded me to try out for a role in a school play. I thought acting was a silly, sissified thing but after my first part I was sold." A talent scout, traveling through Missouri, spotted him in a University production and persuaded him to go to Hollywood to attend an acting school at Paramount studios.

He studied at Paramount for six months, in 1939, until the studio's drama coach informed him, "You're a nice kid and a lousy actor. Go out and learn your trade." Craig then returned to Kansas City and worked with a local stock company, hoping to gain some experience. After a while he enrolled at the Pasadena Playhouse in California and then toured the Pacific coast with a traveling stage company.

Warner Bros. signed him to a long-term contract in 1941, giving him little more than a walk-on role in *Affectionately Yours* (1941), starring Merle Oberon and Dennis Morgan. Other people with bits in the film were Alexis Smith, Faye Emerson, and William Hopper. Besides performing a few other ultra-minor screen assignments, Craig spent most of his time

Publicity pose ca. 1946

studying at the studio school with other contract hopefuls. One of these was lithesome Alexis Smith. They knew each other slightly from the school and had appeared together onscreen, besides their bits in *Affectionately Yours,* in *Dive Bomber* (1941), though they had not appeared in the same scene. *Dive Bomber* was Alexis' first major film and she was then given the lead in the less well-mounted, *Steel Against the Sky* (1941), with Lloyd Nolan. The role of Nolan's younger brother, the film's third lead, was not yet cast and the studio was going to choose a young actor from their drama school.

Alexis was then very friendly with Faye Emerson and Charles Drake and did all within her power to get Drake the part. It was assigned to Craig Stevens. "I thought him a nice, good-looking young man," says a smiling Alexis, "but I wanted Charlie to get it." However, Craig and Alexis fell in love, and they were married on June 8, 1944, as soon as Craig returned from the Air Force. *Variety,* reviewing *Steel Against the Sky,* said, "Stevens, shouldering the love interest, is a newcomer who shows considerable promise. He handles himself well and is a good romantic type."

Because he was drafted in 1942, Craig lost out on a good role opposite Bette Davis in *Old Acquaintance* (1943), for which he was being groomed. Gig Young, fresh from Barbara Stanwyck's *The Gay Sisters* (1942), played the role of the young man infatuated with the older Miss Davis. On Craig's return from service (he appears briefly in uniform in the 1943 film *This Is the Army*), Alexis was a big star on the Burbank lot, which naturally presented some domestic problems. He began pressing hard to make a success of his acting career but the studio kept giving him nondescript roles, as in *Too Young to Know* (1945), *Humoresque* (1946), and *That Way with Women* (1947). "Alexis was very understanding," explains Craig. That is one of the reasons they have been married so long. Each respects the other and there have been a number of balance changes in their professional lives. The last film the two appeared in together was *The Doughgirls* (1944), in which he was a war hero.

In 1948 Craig played Stephen Foster in a tenminute Warners' short subject called *Memories of Melody Lane.* It briefly touched on Foster's career and included songs such as "Camptown Races." After appearing in Jane Wyman's *The Lady Takes a Sailor* (1949), and *Night unto Night* (1949) with Ronald Reagan and Viveca Lindfors, his contract terminated, and like scores of other performers, he was let go.

As a freelance film performer, Craig's movie assignments did not noticeably improve, but at least he

With Jack Mower (second from right) in Spy Ship *(WB 1942)*

appeared in two better-than-average features at Twentieth Century-Fox: *Where the Sidewalk Ends* (1950) and *Phone Call from a Stranger* (1952); in the latter, however, he was upstaged by Evelyn Varden as his selfish mother. He starred as a detective opposite Joyce Holden in Allied Artists' crime drama, *Murder without Tears* (1953), but very few people saw this film. After playing straight man to Bud Abbott and Lou Costello in *Abbott and Costello Meet Dr. Jekyll and Mr. Hyde* (1953) and helping Jane Russell decorate *The French Line* (1954) in 3-D, he returned to the stage in a role of which he is most proud, a twenty-six-week engagement as *Mr. Roberts,* in Los Angeles.

His career has since been dominated by stage and television work. He joined with Joan Bennett in *Susan and God* and did *Remains to be Seen* with Sally Forrest, among other stage plays. He was a steady performer on television in the 1950s and made two series pilots which never sold: ''The Mighty O'' and ''Tales of the Texas Rangers.'' Alexis and he did their first musical together, when they toured in the national company of *Plain and Fancy* (1956). Craig was under negotiation to star in the national company of *Bells Are Ringing,* when Blake Edwards told him to get a crew cut because he was going to play the wel-dressed, two-fisted ''Peter Gunn.''

''Peter Gunn'' premiered on NBC-TV on September 22, 1958, with the lovely Lola Albright as his co-star, and Herschel Bernardi as a tough-skinned police detective. The program was a smash hit and turned Craig into a national celebrity. *TV Guide* reported, ''Craig Stevens is tall, handsome and rugged. He underplays the role with a touch of the Ivy League—if such derring-do can be called underplayed.'' The show ran for three seasons, two on NBC and one on ABC. It could have continued, but its producer, Blake Edwards, wanted to turn the thirty-minute series into an hour show. The sponsors refused and Edwards preferred dropping it. Craig's continued identification with ''Gunn'' makes his other television series less well remembered. He was a public relations man in TV's ''Mr. Broadway'' in 1964 and was the lead of ''Man of the World'' (1962), a British series which was filmed all over Europe. As the photographer-adventurer in the latter property, he filmed twenty-six one-hour segments. It was a very pleasant chore, one that Alexis especially enjoyed because she accompanied her husband on the Continental excursions. Of his belated fame, Craig has said, ''I love the recognition. I like privacy, too, but to tell the truth, I'd be terribly upset if no one asked for my autograph or wrote me a fan letter.''

With (right) John Ridgely, Cliff Clark, and Jack Mower in Secret Enemies *(WB 1941)*

With Lloyd Nolan and Edward Ellis in Steel Against the Sky (WB 1941)

Craig finally made his Broadway stage debut in the musical *Here's Love*, which opened at the Shubert Theatre on October 3, 1963. In this lesser Meredith Willson show he played an ex-Marine turned lawyer. He and co-star Janis Paige played the roles originally created onscreen by John Payne and Maureen O'Hara in *Miracle on 34th Street* (1947). Despite his proven talents in the tour of *Plain and Fancy* and his TV outing with Miss Paige in a video special, *Happiest Day* (1961), Craig surprised New Yorkers by his agility in musical comedy. "I've never had a formal music education," said Craig at the time, "but I've always been able to sing passably well. I'm a baritone, a little on the high side maybe, and I can do more than just get by." The *New York Times* called him "handsome and breezy as the hero, not a notable singer, but efficient." The producers of the "Mr. Broadway" series bought him out of his *Here's Love* contract for $30,000.

When Craig had to come east for *Here's Love,* the Stevenses sold their California home and purchased a Fifth Avenue apartment. Alexis loves New York because she finds it "stimulating." Craig prefers the west coast, however, because "that's where the work is." They again bought a home in California and maintain an apartment in New York, where Alexis

has been working recently in *Follies* and *The Women.* In 1968, Craig and Alexis starred in the national company of *Cactus Flower* and one reviewer said, "Stevens has the kind of looks from which matinee idols are made and his dramatic abilities extend far beyond the rock-faced image he created in *Peter Gunn* on television." A very talented actress, Alexis held back in most of her onstage scenes with Craig, making sure that she never stole the spotlight from him. It was very commendable of her but wrong for the show's values. The Stevenses have also worked together in stock in such shows as *King of Hearts, Critic's Choice,* and *Any Wednesday.* In a 1971 segment of "Marcus Welby, M.D." they portrayed a wealthy couple whose love for one another leaves no room for them to display affection for their child.

These days, Craig is one of television's most active performers, and, if there is a dramatic series on which he has not guest-starred, it is indeed a rarity. He has done several video commercials and has appeared in many made-for-television movies, including: *McCloud* (1970), *The Snoop Sisters* (1972), *The Elevator* (1974), and *Killer Bees* (1974). In the latter telefeature he played Gloria Swanson's son. Any possibility that *Nick and Nora,* a March, 1975 segment of "ABC Wide World" would develop as a new *The Thin Man*

492

series, fell apart upon airing. While Craig as Nick Charles was a smooth, sophisticated detective, Jo An Pflug as wife Nora and the script were "hopelessly adrift." In the summer of 1973 he toured as Henry Higgins in *My Fair Lady,* quite a departure from his usual roles. In mid-1975 he toured for thirteen weeks in a one-man stage revue (Ogden) *Nash at Nine.* Whenever he has free time from his acting chores, he builds furniture and keeps in shape by playing tennis and golf. In the fall of 1975 Craig joined the cast of NBC-TV's series "The Invisible Man," starring David McCallum, in the regular role of Walter Carlson.

His last theatrical feature film to date is *The Limbo Line* (1968), a British-made espionage film that was shunted to American television. Said the British *Monthly Film Bulletin* of this Samuel Gallu-directed feature, "Hackneyed dialogue, feeble direction and ludicrous histrionics from most of the cast give the impression of something left over from the worst days of the Cold War."

Looking back at his unfruitful early Hollywood days, Craig is not bitter. "Oh, I haven't forgotten the heartache. It's just suddenly become unimportant." He has been constantly annoyed at people's amazement that he and Alexis have been married since 1944. Now when asked how long they have been wed, he simply replies, "a few years."

CRAIG STEVENS

Affectionately Yours *(WB 1941)*
Law of the Tropics *(WB 1941)*
Dive Bomber *(WB 1941)*
Steel Against the Sky *(WB 1941)*
Now Voyager *(WB 1942)*
Spy Ship *(WB 1942)*
Secret Enemies *(WB 1942)*
The Hidden Hand *(WB 1942)*
This is the Army *(WB 1943)*
Hollywood Canteen *(WB 1944)*
The Doughgirls *(WB 1944)*
Since You Went Away *(UA 1944)*
Resisting Enemy Interrogation *(U.S. Army 1944)*
Roughly Speaking *(WB 1945)*
Too Young to Know *(WB 1945)*
God is My Co-Pilot *(WB 1945)*
Humoresque *(WB 1946)*
The Man I Love *(WB 1946)*

Love and Learn *(WB 1947)*
That Way with Women *(WB 1947)*
The Lady Takes a Sailor *(WB 1949)*
Night unto Night *(WB 1949)*
Blues Busters *(Mon 1950)*
Where the Sidewalk Ends *(20th 1950)*
Drums in the Deep South *(RKO 1951)*
The Lady from Texas *(Univ 1951)*
Phone Call from a Stranger *(20th 1952)*
Murder Without Tears *(AA 1953)*
Abbott and Costello Meet Dr. Jekyll and Mr. Hyde *(Univ 1953)*
The French Line *(RKO 1954)*
Duel on the Mississippi *(Col 1955)*
The Deadly Mantis *(Univ 1957)*
Buchanan Rides Alone *(Col 1958)*
Gunn *(Par 1967)*
The Limbo Line *(London Independent Producers 1968)*

Television viewers of the 1950s developed a strong liking for Gale Storm as impish "My Little Margie" and zany "Oh, Susanna." But film-goers of a decade prior could have confirmed that the effervescent, sweet Miss Storm was a pretty bundle of diversified talent, who was very much worth watching. During the World War II years she had served as demi-queen of Monogram Pictures, cavorting amiably through such exploitive film fare as *Foreign Agent* (1942), *Where Are Your Children?* (1943), and *Revenge of the Zombies* (1943). Perhaps the peak of her Poverty Row reign was in *Sunbonnet Sue* (1945), joining with Phil Reagan and George Cleveland in a tacky reminiscence of 1890s' New York when the Bowery was a place to visit and not to avoid.

Josephine Owaissa Cottle was born in Bloomington, Texas on April 4, 1922, but shortly after her birth the Cottles moved to Houston, Texas, where Josephine attended school. It was her high-school teacher who prodded the girl into entering the local "Gateway to Hollywood" contest, which, if won, would lead to her traveling to the movie capital to appear on Jesse L. Lasky's CBS radio program, "Gateway to Hollywood." If she succeeded on the show, which used established stars like Claudette Colbert, Edward G. Robinson, and Cary Grant to bolster the fledgling talents, it would mean a screen appearance with RKO Pictures and a possible term contract, under an agreement between producer Lasky and Leo Spitz, the latter then president of RKO.

Gale was successful and won a trip to Hollywood where she was heard on the Lasky radio show. Both she and Lee Bonnell, her male counterpart on the program, landed contracts with RKO, and both were christened by Lasky (who enjoyed this particular task) with new professional names. She emerged Gale Storm and he became Terry Belmont. Gale liked her new moniker, but Terry Belmont reverted to his real name.

She was given a six-month contract with RKO and made her debut as Effie with Jimmy Lydon and Freddie Bartholomew in *Tom Brown's School Days* (1940). In this rewritten version of the English classic it was Cedric Hardwicke as the famed Dr. Thomas Arnold, headmaster of Rugby, who took the limelight, while the critics complained that having such as Billy Halop in the cast made the economy production seem more like "The Dead End Kids Go Swank" than a recreation of the well-loved Thomas Hughes novel. Gale's appearance as Effie provided her with minimum oncamera time and little chance to display her pleasing personality. After a secondary role in RKO's *One Crowded Hour* (1940), the studio dropped her option and she started to freelance.

Meanwhile, RKO kept Bonnell busy in such B films as *Footlight Fever* (1941), *Parachute Battalion* (1941), *Lady Scarface* (1941), and *Look Who's Laughing* (1941). Gale bounced around the lesser studios in

Publicity pose ca. 1948

With Frankie Darro, Frank Sully, Marcia Mae Jones, and Jackie Moran in Let's Go Collegiate (Mon 1941)

minor roles: With Bob Steele and Robert Livingston in Republic's *Saddlemates* (1941), with Roy Rogers in two westerns, and with another "Gateway to Hollywood" winner, John Archer, in *City of Missing Girls* (1941). Neither Gale nor Lee's careers were progressing beyond the celluloid grade B and C movies, but their intense romance culminated in marriage on October 5, 1941, in Houston, Texas, and they honeymooned in Lee's home town of South Bend, Indiana.

Lee enlisted in the Coast Guard, and was stationed at San Francisco. During the service years Gale continued to prowl and plod across the screen in inferior movies, mostly for Monogram. The marriage of Lee and Gale was an union of two deeply religious people who worked at their marriage and made it one of Hollywood's most successful. While Lee was in the service, their first son, Phillip Lee, was born on March 19, 1943, followed three years later by Peter Wade on May 29, 1946. Bonnell, after his discharge from the military, deserted acting and went into the insurance business, realizing far greater success than he had had in the movies.

Gale continued to suffer through such tripe as *Where Are Your Children?* One critic, reviewing this quickie about juvenile delinquency, insisted the film was both juvenile and delinquent. At least in *Campus Rhythm* (1943), Gale's singing talents were given

some showcasing as she played Joan, a radio singer who decides to continue her college education. She sang "It's Great to Be a College Girl," "Walking the Chalkline," "Swing Your Way through College," and "College Sweetheart," the latter assisted by Johnny Downs. In 1945's Monogram picture *They Shall Have Faith* (a.k.a., *Forever Yours*), Gale, who could still pass for a younger girl, was a socialite who contracts infantile paralysis, but remains a good sport throughout the ordeal. Supporting her in this antiquated tearjerker were such stalwarts as C. Aubrey Smith, Mary Boland, Conrad Nagel, and the seemingly ever-present Johnny Downs. The cast even included western star John Mack Brown, here as an Army major who helps her regain her health.

In 1945, Gale was among the many stars invited to President Franklin Delano Roosevelt's birthday party in Washington, D.C., and, along with Margaret O'Brien, Myrna Loy, and Veronica Lake, she posed for a photograph with the first lady, Eleanor Roosevelt. Monogram had released a mildly entertaining musical called *Sunbonnet Sue,* the title having no relationship to the film's storyline of the daughter of a Bowery saloon owner who makes peace with their snobbish uptown society relatives to keep pop's saloon open. During these "heavy" proceedings, Gale is romanced by policeman Phil Regan, and, for diversion, there are such tunes as "Sunbonnet Sue" and such standards as "The Bowery," "By the Light of the Silvery Moon," and "Ain't You Comin' Out Tonight." Gale's erratic film career continued with a lightweight farce, *G. I. Honeymoon* (1945), in which she was a newly married woman whose husband (Peter Cookson) is recalled to camp immediately following the marriage ceremony.

To celebrate its invasion into the territory held by high-priced productions, Monogram's Allied Artists division blew their budget on what was, for them, an expensive cast for *It Happened on Fifth Avenue* (1947). Gale was Trudy, the willful daughter of the domestically feuding O'Connors (Ann Harding, Charles Ruggles). She becomes involved with loveable vagrant Victor Moore and is romanced by bland but available Don DeFore. The *New York Times,* who rarely reviewed Gale's previous low-budgeted efforts, found her "pretty and pert" in this assignment. Gale made her first visit to New York City with husband Lee to publicize the film. Shortly after her personal appearance for *It Happened on Fifth Avenue,* she gave birth to her third son, Paul William, on August 1, 1947.

Gale's film ventures became almost annual outings in unmemorable roles including another Hollywood fantasy on the life of Billy the Kid called *The Kid from*

Texas (1950), in which Billy (Audie Murphy) is hopelessly in love with Irene Kain (Gale), whose husband Billy has killed (Albert Dekker). Gale was Kate Mallory in a rather routine police patrol drama, *Between Midnight and Dawn* (1950), and, then, for the same studio, Columbia, she was Cathy in *The Underworld Story* (1950), featuring Dan Duryea. Over at Universal she was adequate as Julie Martin, niece of acerbic prima donna Eve Arden, who is determined to marry Donald O'Connor in *Curtain Call at Cactus Creek* (1950), a spoof of creaking stage melodramas performed in the wild, wild West. For Columbia's *Al Jennings of Oklahoma* (1951) Gale cast opposite Dan Duryea (as Jennings) in a distinctly fictionalized version of the would-be bandit's life. After two other outdoor dramas, Gale left the screen to become nationally known and beloved as television's "My Little Margie," although she had already appeared on TV, on such programs as "Pantomime Quiz" (playing charades with Jackie Coogan, Vincent Price, and Hans Conried), and "Bigelow Theatre." In the latter, she had joined with Gene Raymond in the episode *Mechanic on Duty* in which, as a female mechanic, she decided how much to charge each customer by their appearance.

"My Little Margie" was the brain child of Hal Roach, Jr., and was conceived as a summer replace-

With Margie Hart in Lure of the Islands *(Mon 1942)*

ment for the "I Love Lucy" show. Roach cast Gale as Margie and, for her father, Vern Albright, he persuaded retired actor Charles Farrell to make a comeback. Farrell had successfully teamed with Janet Gaynor in the silent *Seventh Heaven* (1927) and in numerous talkies. The show debuted on CBS-TV on June 16, 1952, and originally was scheduled to last only as long as the thirteen-week summer season. However, it caught on with the public and Gale and Farrell made 126 episodes of "My Little Margie" for television, as well as appearing in many segments on the radio series of the show. The Albrights, Vern and Margie, were a hit in both media. Gale also found time to appear with Robert Hutton in "The Unexpected" episode, *The Puppeteers,* and, for TV's "Footlight Theatre", she eloped to Las Vegas with reformed gangster Richard Denning in *The Hot Welcome.*

In January, 1953, Gale was elected honorary mayor of Sherman Oaks, California (she served two terms and was succeeded by Liberace!). Charles Farrell was then in his third term as mayor of Palm Springs, California where his Racquet Club was located. Between harried schedules, Gale found time to sing the role of Letitia in the west-coast charity production of Gian-Carlo Menotti's opera, *The Old Maid and the Thief.* By May of 1953 she had readied a nightclub act and appeared at Las Vegas' Thunderbird Hotel, making a

tremendous hit during her four-week debut. Her recordings started selling, and "I Hear You Knocking" and her first four records for Dot Records sold close to four million copies. She eventually made six LP albums for the Dot label. As the residuals from re-runs of "Margie" continued, Gale branched out in a dramatic role as Elizabeth, a woman rebuilding her life after her husband is killed in the war on the *Tomorrow Is Forever* episode of "Robert Montgomery Presents." The last "Margie" episode was completed in April, 1955, and Gale started to appear as a guest on most of the major variety shows. She also gave a telling performance as Hope Foster with Keith Andes on *Johnny, Where Are You?* for "Ford Theatre."

In 1956, energetic, very youthful-looking Gale signed for another series called "Oh, Susanna", in which her role was to be Susanna Pomeroy, social director for the S.S. *Ocean Queen* (filmed mainly aboard the Pacific liner S.S. *President Wilson*). The series featured fluttering, funny ZaSu Pitts as "Nugey," the luxury liner's addled beautician. Between the filming of the various episodes of the new TV series, Gale continued to make recordings for Dot and taught Sunday School at the Hollywood Beverly Christian Church. By 1957, Gale maintained a rigorous schedule working on the "Oh, Susanna" series; that same year she insisted on personally attending

With Rick Vallin in Nearly Eighteen *(Mon 1943)*

her husband's bout with pneumonia, and on November 12, 1958, gave birth to her fourth child, a girl, who was named Susanna for the TV series. All four of Gale's children appeared with her on television: Phillip on "My Little Margie" and Peter, Paul, and baby Susanna on "Oh, Susanna." "My Little Margie," "Oh, Susanna," and 1958's "The Gale Storm Show" (a revamping of "Oh, Susanna") were making Gale a comparatively wealthy woman, as she received both a percentage and the usual residuals on the re-runs of each show.

Gale did a summer music-tent show in *Finian's Rainbow* in 1963 (she had done *Wildcat* in an earlier season), and the following year she was seen as "Honey" with Linda Darnell, Mickey Rooney, and Elizabeth Montgomery in ABC's TV series "Burke's Law." She returned in 1965 for another "Burke's Law" segment as "Nonnine" with Gene Barry (series star), Nick Adams, Edgar Bergen, and Debra Paget, and made two appearances as a guest on the "Mike Douglas Show." Her Dot Record recordings and albums (including "Gale's Great Hits") sold well and became as popular as a group of "Soundies" films she had made several years before, singing such 1940s favorites as "Between the Devil and the Deep Blue Sea," "Almost Like Being in Love," "Ain't Misbehaven'," and a dozen others.

In September, 1968, Gale became a grandmother when the wife of her son Peter Bonnell had her first child and, after rumors of ill health, she opened on April 6, 1971, at Fort Worth's Windmill Theatre in *Cactus Flower* for five weeks, before moving to Dallas for another five-week run. The show continued to do good business when it toured the east coast. During the fall of 1972 Gale was back in the theatre playing *A Rainy Day in Newark* and, recently, she has toured in Neil Simon's hit comedy *Plaza Suite,* and such other staples as *No Hard Feelings* and *Forty Carats.*

Some years ago, the usually calm, composed, and collected Miss Storm dissolved into tears while dining with husband Lee at Hollywood's Knickerbocker Hotel. She had received a call at the table, "This is Ralph Edwards, and this is your life, Gale Storm." She cried throughout the show as her full and happy life paraded before her and millions of television viewers. Especially touching to the startled Gale was the tribute paid her by Dr. Cleveland Kleihauer, pastor of the Hollywood Beverly Christian Church. Dr. Kleihauer said, "Her deep spiritual feeling has made of her a wife and mother, not just another married woman." Then Ralph Edwards added, "You, Gale, have put your family, your husband, and your home before your career, and as a result, your career shines more brightly. Hollywood and Texas may well be proud to call you their own."

No one is going to argue that with Ralph Edwards.

In his declining years, Jesse L. Lasky was pleased to receive a letter from one of his former "Gateway to Hollywood" winners who had rejected Lasky's re-christening as Terry Belmont. The letter from Lee Bonnell stated: "Since you were instrumental in not only our meeting but in helping us to embark on our careers in the motion picture field, Gale and I owe you a debt of gratitude beyond repayment. We would love to have you meet our three sons and baby daughter, whom I think you may take some credit for indirectly."

Lasky was justifiably proud of the Bonnell family.

GALE STORM

Tom Brown's School Days   *(RKO 1940)*
One Crowded Hour   *(RKO 1940)*
Saddlemates   *(Rep 1941)*
Gambling Daughters   *(PRC 1941)*
Jesse James at Bay   *(Rep 1941)*
City of Missing Girls   *(Select 1941)*
Let's Go Collegiate   *(Mon 1941)*
Red River Valley   *(Rep 1941)*
Smart Alecks   *(Mon 1942)*
The Man from Cheyenne   *(Rep 1942)*
Rhythm Parade   *(Mon 1942)*
Foreign Agent   *(Mon 1942)*
Lure of the Islands   *(Mon 1942)*
Freckles Comes Home   *(Mon 1942)*
Where Are Your Children?   *(Mon 1943)*
Campus Rhythm   *(Mon 1943)*
Cosmo Jones, Crime Smasher   *(Mon 1943)*

Revenge of the Zombies   *(Mon 1943)*
Nearly Eighteen   *(Mon 1943)*
They Shall have Faith (a.k.a., Forever Yours)   *(Mon 1944)*
Sunbonnet Sue   *(Mon 1945)*
G. I. Honeymoon   *(Mon 1945)*
Swing Parade of 1946   *(Mon 1946)*
It Happened on Fifth Avenue   *(AA 1947)*
The Dude Goes West   *(AA 1948)*
Stampede   *(AA 1949)*
Abandoned   *(Univ 1949)*
The Kid from Texas   *(Univ 1950)*
Between Midnight and Dawn   *(Col 1950)*
The Underworld Story (a.k.a., The Whipped)   *(UA 1950)*
Curtain Call at Cactus Creek   *(Univ 1950)*
Al Jennings of Oklahoma   *(Col 1951)*
The Texas Rangers   *(Col 1951)*
Woman of the North Country   *(Rep 1952)*

79

Sonny Tufts

Today the name Sonny Tufts may evoke a smile or comment on his ambitious but limited acting ability or even be used as a whimsical barometer for dubious talent. But his arrival on the Hollywood scene in the early 1940s was timely, for many leading men had enlisted in the service or were being drafted. Enthusiastic Sonny was exempt from the war due to college football injuries.

Peter Tufts missed the Mayflower's sailing, but he did arrive in America from England in 1683 to start the Tufts family of Boston where, years later, another Tufts, Charles, founded Tufts College. On July 16, 1911, Mr. and Mrs. Bowen Tufts, Jr. became the parents of Bowen Charlton Tufts III who was called "Sonny" from birth. At the exclusive Exeter prep school Sonny organized a band, playing drums and alternating as vocalist. He soon decided he would become a singer, breaking with the family tradition of banking. He continued his stand of independence by breaking another family tradition by attending Yale rather than Harvard, despite his mother's telegram, "Yale may be for some people, but not for us."

Despite his family, Sonny did go to Yale, majoring in anthropology, spending two years in the freshman class, playing a few parts for the Yale Dramatic Society, Skull and Bones. One of his classmates was Winthrop Rockefeller. Sonny was the fifth oar "power house" on Yale's rowing crew and for their football team, he later claimed to have been their greatest "waiting tackle."

While at Yale he organized a band and every summer booked his group, with himself as drummer and vocalist, on Mediterranean cruises, making twenty-five round trips. Graduating from Yale in 1935, he decided to study for a career in opera and spent six months studying voice in Paris, plus many more months in New York City interpreting opera scores that led to an audition with the Metropolitan Opera Company. However, an investigation of the moderate salaries paid beginners in opera sent Sonny scampering into the more lucrative fields of musicals and supper clubs.

In 1937 Leonard Sillman tried his proposed *New Faces* before Noël Coward in a room at the Hotel Elysee in New York City. Coward's enthusiasm for the audition prompted him to suggest to Sillman that the young producer get Elsa Maxwell to produce the show. Maxwell agreed, arguing, though, that *New Faces* was really old hat, but approved highly of the new title for the revue, *Who's Who.* Under that name the musical show opened at New York's Hudson Theatre on March 1, 1938, with a cast including Rags Ragland, Imogene Coca, and young singer Sonny. The revue lasted a mere twenty-three performances, and Tufts went into another disaster-prone show, *Sing for Your Supper.* He then deserted the theatre for a

With Helen Brown in Swell Guy (Univ 1946)

Publicity pose with Betty Hutton for Cross My Heart (Par 1946)

four-year career as a supper club singer in such spots as the Glass Hat, the Beachcomber, the Belmont Plaza, and Palm Beach's Patio Club.

In 1942, it occurred to Sonny that he should give Hollywood a try. His westward migration was underwritten by his college chum, millionaire sportsman Alexis Thompson. Tufts and his wife, former dancer Barbara Dare (with whom he had eloped to Fort Lee, New Jersey in 1937), arrived in California, and Sonny eventually wangled a screen test. For his audition he did a scene from the Charles Boyer-Irene Dunne film *Love Affair* (1939), which he turned into a gag. The joked-up test interested Paramount director Mark Sandrich who tested the jovial Tufts again with Paulette Goddard, and although Richard Denning was originally scheduled for the part, Tufts was given the role of Kansas in *So Proudly We Hail* (1943).

The six-foot, four-inch, two-hundred-pound, blond, blue-eyed Sonny did quite well as Paulette Goddard's Marine on Bataan (a role he recreated on November 1, 1943's "Lux Radio Theatre" with the film's stars: Claudette Colbert, Veronica Lake, and Miss Goddard). Bosley Crowther (*New York Times*) was among those to enthuse of Sonny's screen debut: "A strapping new actor by the name of Sonny Tufts does wonders to give credibility and warmth to the scenes in which he plays. As a gawky and shy marine private with whom Miss Goddard pairs off, he conveys the essential illusion of being the genuine thing."

Following his initial success at Paramount who signed him to a contract, he was loaned to RKO for a comedy based on wartime Washington, D.C. The film was *Government Girl* (1943), starring Olivia de Havilland, and was a first directorial effort of screen writer Dudley Nichols. Tufts returned to Paramount with glowing notices for his natural, easy-going performance in the Nichols' comedy. He continued his screen image of a well-meaning, happy-go-lucky, if fumbling lug (in the tradition of Paramount's Eddie Bracken), to often surprisingly good reviews, as Windy in *Here Come the Waves* (1944), with Bing Crosby and Betty Hutton, and with Paulette Goddard in *I Love a Soldier* (1944). In *Miss Susie Slagle's* (1945) Sonny was Pug Prentiss, studying medicine at Johns Hopkins Medical School while romancing boarding house maid Joan Caulfield. Then, as half-hero, half-heel Jim Duncan, he gave a colorful performance in Universal's *Swell Guy* (1946), co-starring Ann Blyth. For one of Paramount's least successful remakes of Owen Wister's *The Virginian* (1946), Tufts played the role of trouble-maker Steve, and then Paramount recast him opposite Olivia de Havilland as Army Lieutenant Torchy losing Olivia to the Navy (Ray Milland)

in a comedy *The Well-Groomed Bride* (1946). The year before Tufts had made a token appearance in Paramount's all-star *Duffy's Tavern,* as a rival with Brian Donlevy for the affections of Paulette Goddard and helping Betty Hutton, Cass Daley, Bing Crosby, and Diana Lynn satirize the song, "Swinging on a Star." In the studio's third, and final vaudeville feature of the forties, *Variety Girl,* Sonny was himself.

In *Blaze of Noon* (1947), directed by John Farrow, Tufts was Ronald McDonald, one of four brothers flying the mail, and he was returned Seabee Kevin O'Connor hoping to marry Barry Fitzgerald's pert daughter Diana Lynn in *Easy Come, Easy Go* (1947). His Paramount contract ended with a praiseless B picture remake of Carole Lombard's farce, *True Confession* (1937), which was gussied up unsuccessfully as *Cross My Heart* (1947), with Sonny as the well-meaning attorney Olivier Clarke, and Betty Hutton as his over-imaginative girlfriend. Although Tufts was permitted to sing in several films, Paramount's resident crooner was Bing Crosby and the Studio made no effort to build up the one-time Metropolitan Opera aspirant into a major musical star. James Agee, however, commenting on Tufts' singing, thought he could become almost as good as Crosby, with almost as broad a range.

Sonny's film career deteriorated after leaving Paramount, although as gang leader Vince Alexander in United Artists' *The Crooked Way* (1949) he offered one of his soundest screen performances. In the summer of 1949, Tufts returned to the stage, touring the straw-hat circuit in the comedy, *Petticoat Fever.* After the supporting role as Victor Mature's fellow football player Tim McCarr in RKO's *Easy Living* (1949), Sonny's private life garnered more notice than his screen activities. In 1950 he made headlines when he was sued for $25,000 for allegedly biting stripper Barbara Gray Atkins in the thigh, and two weeks later dancer Marjorie Von sued him for $26,500 for the same rash appetite. During the summer he was sued by Mrs. Adrienne Formarr, who asked ten thousand dollars for Tufts' mauling, molesting, and pinching of her in a local restaurant. Miss Von settled for six hundred dollars and a bitten thigh, and Miss Atkins dropped her suit before it reached the courts.

On May 31, 1951, Sonny was jailed on a drunk charge after his wife's complaint, filed days before in a separate maintenance suit, charged he drank too much and was squandering their community funds. His wife Barbara had left him two years before when his drinking got out of hand and he was picked up drunk from a Sunset Strip sidewalk. By this time, Sonny was well on his way to becoming the joke legend that he is today.

With Dorothy Vernon, Charles Arnt, Constance Purdy, and Veronica Lake in Miss Susie Slagle's *(Par 1945)*

His appearances in impoverished films like *Cat Women of the Moon* (1954) or *Serpent Island* (1954) —the latter dealing with voodoo in the Caribbean— were negligible. Tufts felt he was making something of a comeback when he was signed for the part of Tom MacKenzie in Billy Wilder's top-grossing *The Seven Year Itch* (1955), starring Marilyn Monroe and Tom Ewell, and when he returned to the stage as the male lead in a musical *Ankles Aweigh* with Betty and Jane Kean. However, prior to that show's Boston opening, he was dropped, claiming to the press that his part "just didn't come off."

Somehow, everything seemed to go wrong for Sonny all the time. Back in 1951 he had played charades on CBS's "Pantomime Quiz" with Gig Young, Pamela Britton, and Andrea King, but generally, video work eluded him, and his reputation for drinking increased. After staying sober for a year, he was crushed when he lost the part of Jim Bowie that he had hoped to play in John Wayne's *The Alamo* (1960). Richard Widmark got that important assignment in the would-be epic western. When "The Virginian" began its second season on television in 1963, Tufts was seen as Frank Trampas killed by Judge Garth (Lee J. Cobb) in self defense, a flashback preamble that explained why young Trampas (Doug McClure) had arrived at Shiloh Ranch—for revenge.

For "Bob Hope's Chrysler Theatre" in the fall of 1964, Tufts was Monk, one of three prospective husbands (with Rod Cameron and Aldo Ray) to whom marriage broker Hope planned to marry off Jill St. John, Marilyn Maxwell, and Rhonda Fleming, in the episode *Have Girls—Will Travel.* Thereafter, Sonny spent a few years in Texas but returned to Hollywood and made *Land's End,* a pilot film for an unsold television series (set in Baja California), with Rory Calhoun and Gilbert Roland as co-players. In 1966 Sonny was a guest on the TV "Merv Griffin Show," and when he made his entrance, comedienne Totie Fields suggested that he sit down before he fell down, whereupon the studio orchestra improvised "Show Me the Way to Go Home." Sonny exchanged banter with host Griffin and good-naturedly accepted a great deal of kidding, and then received the show's biggest laugh when he turned to fellow guest, Tab Hunter, telling him he was really "a young Sonny Tufts." Later that year, Sonny entrenched his position in the constellation of camp by appearing as a leading participant on a syndicated video special on the subject of "Trivia." For TV's "Laugh-In," Sonny popped in and proved, again, that he could laugh at himself.

On June 4, 1970, Sonny Tufts died of pneumonia at St. John's Hospital in Santa Monica, California. The following Sunday, memorial services were held for Bowen Charleton Tufts, III in All Saint's Episcopal Church in Beverly Hills, and he was buried the following day. His easy-going charm and determined individuality enlivened the forties and he seemingly never ceased to have the knack of laughing at Boston's bad boy, Sonny Tufts.

SONNY TUFTS

So Proudly We Hail   *(Par 1943)*
Government Girl   *(RKO 1943)*
Here Come the Waves   *(Par 1944)*
In the Meantime Darling   *(20th 1944)*
I Love a Soldier   *(Par 1944)*
Bring on the Girls   *(Par 1945)*
Duffy's Tavern   *(Par 1945)*
Miss Susie Slagle's   *(Par 1945)*
Swell Guy   *(Univ 1946)*
The Virginian   *(Par 1946)*
The Well-Groomed Bride   *(Par 1946)*
Variety Girl   *(Par 1947)*
Blaze of Noon   *(Par 1947)*
Easy Come, Easy Go   *(Par 1947)*
Cross My Heart   *(Par 1947)*

The Untamed Breed   *(Col 1948)*
The Crooked Way   *(UA 1949)*
Easy Living   *(RKO 1949)*
The Gift Horse (a.k.a., Glory at Sea)   *(Independent Film Distributors 1952)*
No Escape   *(UA 1953)*
Run for the Hills   *(Jack Broder 1953)*
Cat Women of the Moon   *(Astor 1954)*
Serpent Island   *(Astor 1954)*
The Seven Year Itch   *(20th 1955)*
Come Next Spring   *(Rep 1956)*
The Parson and the Outlaw   *(Col 1957)*
Town Tamer   *(Par 1965)*
Cottonpickin' Chickenpickers   *(Southeastern Pictures 1967)*

80

Martha Vickers

The entrance of players into the world of Hollywood filmmaking has had many strange and unusual paths calculated to separate the meek from the brave, if not always the untalented from talented. Errol Flynn entered American-produced films wheeled onto the set of *The Case of the Curious Bride* (1935) on a morgue table as a dead body. Flynn later claimed that many people considered it his best part onscreen. Seventeen-year-old Martha MacVicar made her feature-film screen debut as inauspiciously as Mr. Flynn, as a corpse in *Frankenstein Meets the Wolf Man* (1943), one of several potpourri thrillers made by the chiller kingdom known as Universal Pictures.

Born Martha MacVicar on May 28, 1925, at Ann Arbor, Michigan, to James S. and Frances MacVicar, she attended schools in Chicago, Miami, Dallas, St. Petersburg, and Long Beach, California. In the last place she became a model for still photographer William Mortensen. Her posing for Mortensen led to a screen contract with David O. Selznick. Selznick never used her in a film and her contract was taken over by Universal where she had the rigid function role in the previously mentioned Lon Chaney, Jr.-Bela Lugosi opus. She was Evelyn Ankers' sister Dorothy Colman in *Captive Wild Woman,* and stuck it out at Universal for four additional entries, including *The Mummy's Ghost* in which she had a bit part.

Transferring to RKO, Martha had better luck. She

was Sally, the ingenue in *Marine Raiders* (1944), with Pat O'Brien, Robert Ryan, and Ruth Hussey in the leads. Martha registered recognition as an artist's daughter, Barbara, with Tom Conway as the dapper sleuth in *The Falcon in Mexico* (1944).

Moving to her third studio, Warner Bros., Martha also shortened her surname by dropping the "Mac" and adding an "s" and, as Martha Vickers, she was cast as Lauren Bacall's wild and unruly sister, Carmen Sternwood, in Howard Hawks' *The Big Sleep* (1946). Martha realistically played the bedeviled, blackmailed, drugged, murder-involved, dissolute Carmen, of whom Bogart's Philip Marlowe says, "You're cute . . . very cute. But I am cuter." Many newspaper sources rated her role in *The Big Sleep* as hitting a new high in screen viciousness—Martha's portrayal of the thumb-sucking, nymphomaniacal Carmen was a chilling performance. It was to remain her best and only high-charged dramatic role, the high point of her brief motion-picture career.

Warners did not follow through with other dramatic roles for Martha, who was being touted as a young Bette Davis. Instead, she was cast in a musical, for which she studied voice and dancing, though she hardly was expert in either department. *The Time, The Place, and the Girl* (1946) was a Technicolor refurbishing of a 1907 Broadway musical that Warners had produced in 1929 as a film. With new songs by Arthur Schwartz and Leo Robin that were adapted by Frederick Hollander, the film had Martha as Victo-

Publicity pose 1946

ria Cassell, an heiress pushed by her opera-conductor grandfather (S. Z. Sakall) into a romance with Dennis Morgan. Obviously, it is Sakall who finances a huge musical show to promote Martha and feature her new friends, Morgan, Jack Carson, and Janis Paige. Martha was unexpectedly okay singing and dancing the hit song, "A Gal in Calico" with Morgan and Carson, joining the boys and Paige for "A Rainy Night in Rio," and teaming with Morgan and Carmen Cavellaro's Orchestra in "Through a Thousand Dreams." Following her musical debut Martha was shuttled into the supporting role of Virginia Brown with Ida Lupino and Robert Alda in *The Man I Love* (1946), and, then, joined Jack Carson and Janis Paige in a lightweight comedy, *Love and Learn* (1947). During the spring of 1947, Warners sent Martha east and she made personal appearances at their Manhattan flagship theatre, the Strand.

In 1947, Warners' post-World War II passion for remakes dredged up an early George Arliss film *The Millionaire* (1931). The script was re-fashioned as a vehicle for Sydney Greenstreet, cast as an irascible, bored millionaire masquerading as an unlikely garage mechanic. Greenstreet was visibly uncomfortable and miscast in the lead, and Martha played the role Evelyn Knapp had done in the much better Arliss version. Both Greenstreet and Martha joined Eagle-Lion's *Ruthless* (1948), in which Martha was cast as wealthy Susan Duane, one of several discarded lovers of ruthless lover Zachary Scott.

Pint-sized Mickey Rooney had begun his enormous marriage-go-round on January 10, 1941, when nineteen-year-old Ava Gardner became Mrs. Mickey Rooney (#1). The stormy and explosive union continued until Rooney moved out on January 13, 1943, and, by May, Ava was the first Ex-Mrs. Mickey Roo-

ney. A year later, Mickey was in the Army at Camp Seibert near Birmingham, Alabama, where he met Miss Birmingham of 1944, Betty Jane Rase. A whirlwind, one-week engagement punctuated by booze, remorse, and premeditated rebound, culminated in marriage on September 30, 1944. During the four-year run of this second marriage, Rooney became the father of Mickey Jr. and Timothy. This marriage collapsed in February, 1948, but life seemed more meaningful when he met five-foot, four-inch, auburn-haired Martha at a Hollywood party shortly after the New Year.

Martha's plans to marry Hollywood automobile dealer Al Herd on September 15, 1945, had never materialized, but in 1948, she had become the wife of publicist A. C. Lyles, Jr. That marriage soon ended in divorce. Both Martha and Mickey found solace together, commiserating with each other over their crushed marriages until, five months later, they decided to wed. Martha insisted on a church wedding but requests to various churches for ecclesiastical nuptials were denied until, finally, the North Hollywood Unity Church accepted them for a wedding ceremony on June 3, 1949. Mickey described Martha as gentle, ladylike, and a saving hand in his state of private and professional limbo. He had her wedding ring inscribed "Today, Tomorrow, and Always. Mr. to Mrs."

Hollywood's staggering lack of interest in Rooney's great talent, his constant unemployment, and complicated private life led to marathon drinking and the gradual deterioration of a third marriage in Rooney's modest Encino, California home. Reflecting on his matrimonial ties to Martha, Rooney claims, "The marriage ran down like a toy whose spring had worn out and dissolved in a solution of Scotch and water." One and a half years after the long-sought North Hol-

With Creighton Hale and Sydney Greenstreet in That Way with Women *(WB 1947)*

With Laurie Lind in Alimony *(EL 1949)*

lywood ceremonies, Teddy Rooney was born, but the birth of Martha's son by Rooney could not hold together the floundering marriage, and on June 11, 1951, divorce case #D–416,884 was filed by Martha Vickers Rooney, charging the actor with "extreme cruelty." On September 24th of that year, Martha informed Judge Clarence L. Kincaid in Superior Court that she saw her husband not more than one or two nights a week and that Mickey had a very bad temper when anyone disagreed with him. The divorce was granted, giving Martha custody of their son Ted Michael, seventeen months old, a hundred fifty dollars a month for his support, and a descending scale of alimony, starting at two thousand dollars a month and declining to three hundred dollars a month in eight years. The alimony ceased when Martha married Chilean polo player Manuel Rojas on October 1, 1954, in Mexicali. Martha and Rojas had two daughters, but that marriage also ended in divorce.

The few motion pictures Martha made after her marriage to Rooney, including the prophetic *Alimony* (1949), were weak B pictures. In 1954, she turned to television, appearing effectively on "G. E. Theatre"'s *That Other Sunlight* as Helen, who restores confidence to disabled veteran David Brian; she also appeared as Susan, with Arthur Franz on *The Last 30 Minutes* for "Ford Theatre." Then, again for "Ford" she was Nancy, who helps accused bribe-taking cop Arthur Kennedy prove his innocence in *Night Visitor*. She also made two "Fireside Theatre" appearances, one with George Brent and Angela Lansbury in *The Indiscreet Mrs. Jarvis,* a tale of a wife's secret past, and another as Tom Drake's wife, Julie, in a story of a penniless couple finding refuge in an empty house.

Martha's final screen appearance was as Mary Hoag, wife of the (Purgatory, Arizona) terror in the western, *Four Fast Guns* (1959) a weakly scripted program movie made by the Phoenix, Arizona Film Studio with James Craig as the male lead. Martha's final video work was on two segments of Nick Adams' "Rebel" series.

In later years very little was heard of Martha. Then, on November 2, 1971, following a lengthy illness, she died at the Valley Presbyterian Hospital in Hollywood. She was only forty-six years old.

MARTHA VICKERS

As MARTHA MacVICAR
Frankenstein Meets the Wolfman   *(Univ 1943)*
Hi 'Ya Sailor   *(Univ 1943)*
Top Man   *(Univ 1943)*
Captive Wild Woman   *(Univ 1943)*
The Mummy's Ghost   *(Univ 1944)*
This is the Life   *(Univ 1944)*
Marine Raiders   *(RKO 1944)*
The Falcon in Mexico   *(RKO 1944)*

As MARTHA VICKERS
The Big Sleep   *(WB 1946)*

The Time, the Place, and the Girl   *(WB 1946)*
The Man I Love   *(WB 1946)*
Love and Learn   *(WB 1947)*
That Way with Women   *(WB 1947)*
Ruthless   *(El 1948)*
Alimony   *(El 1949)*
Bad Boy   *(AA 1949)*
Daughter of the West   *(Film Classics 1949)*
The Big Bluff   *(UA 1955)*
The Burglar   *(Col 1957)*
Four Fast Guns   *(Univ 1959)*

81

Dooley Wilson

In the more liberated 1970s, blacks are more willing to discuss how their race was exploited by Hollywood in the non-equal-rights days of the 1940s. Some concerned black men and women in the entertainment world insist the best cure is simply to demand television stations not screen World War II-vintage material which used black actors in minor and stereotyped roles. Other black performers, such as Lena Horne, have spoken up with candor and justified bitterness at how a studio (MGM in her case) could tempt and twist a performer into performing personally and racially degrading parts.

Ironically, over the years, one black player has done more by example for the equal rights cause onscreen than most of the offscreen activism of all black actors put together. He was Dooley Wilson and the film was Warner Bros.' *Casablanca* (1942).

Perhaps no motion picture produced during the 1940s is today as popular, as revered, or has become such a legendary classic as *Casablanca*. After more than thirty years, this film still withstands the passage of time. "Rick's Place" is identifiable today, invoking fond, nostalgic memories of a film based on an unproduced play that James Agee once called the "world's worst." The Michael Curtiz-directed picture reflects a time when the world was more innocent, permitting strong sentiment to be clearly defined in sharp terms. Fundamental to the picture is the idea that Humphrey Bogart's devious Rick, owner of the most important night spot in the North African city,

could be friends with, and consider as an equal, his black piano player, Sam (Dooley Wilson). It was certainly an innovation for Hollywood, and for that matter, the world at large.

Arthur Dooley Wilson made his professional debut at the age of twelve in his native Texas, where he was born in 1894, appearing with the "Rabbit Foot" Minstrels over a period of years before migrating to Chicago, where he joined the Pekin Stock Company. With the Pekin troupe he once played a role in white face with an Irish brogue and met another budding black actor, Charles Gilpin, who eventually found fame as Eugene O'Neill's *Emperor Jones*. Wilson arrived in New York City with S. H. Dudley's Smart Set Company, playing all the vaudeville circuits, from Keith's to Pantages' to the Orpheum to the Sun. After World War I, he joined James Reese Europe's Society Musicians and Entertainers and left for Europe in 1919 to tour England, France, Holland, Belgium, and Italy. Leaving the group, Dooley organized his own quintet known as The Red Devils, playing Maxim's and Dubonnet's in Paris, and Ciro's in London. He even became the first black to hold a charter from the French Government when he purchased and opened the Tempo Club at 14 Rue Richelieu in Paris. He returned to the United States in 1930 and decided to end his career as a singing drummer for a more precarious undertaking, the legitimate theatre.

With Frank Sinatra and Michele Morgan in Higher and Higher *(RKO 1943)*

With Elaine Shepard and Gordon Oliver in Seven Days Ashore *(RKO 1944)*

Dooley's legitimate stage debut was for the Federal Theatre in productions of Orson Welles and John Houseman, playing Androcles in the Federal Theatre's production of *Androcles and the Lion.* He played the title role in *Booker T. Washington,* William Ashley's play, for a long, successful run in Harlem and at the New York World's Fair of 1939. In the same year, he became an enthusiastic participant in the Rose McClendon Workshop Theatre organized by Dick Campbell and his wife, the late Muriel Rahn. Profits from the workshop's production paid the salary of Theodore Komisarjevsky, of the Moscow Art Theatre, who was the drama teacher, and there came to the workshop's Auditorium at the 124th Street Library such future great black performers as Canada Lee, Ruby Dee, Ossie Davis, Frederick O'Neal, and Jane White. When Steinbeck's *Of Mice and Men* toured, Dooley replaced Leigh Whipper as "Crooks." Ethel Waters, remembering his glowing performance as *Booker T. Washington,* recommended him for the part of "Little Joe" Jackson in the delightful Vernon Duke-John Latouche-Lynn Root musical, *Cabin in the Sky* (1940).

As Ethel Waters' wayward husband, Little Joe, Dooley gave a strikingly comic portrayal of an eager sinner bewildered by his sins. After being slashed by a razor in a dice game, he lies on his death bed and becomes a contestant between the Devil—Lucifer, Jr. (Rex Ingram)—and the Lawd's General (Todd Duncan) for his soul. The injured man's wife, Petunia (Waters), is close by, praying him onto the side of the Angels and hoping for a reprieve of six months so he can redeem his erring ways. Wilson's ingratiating personality and bewildered demeanor was a perfect balance for the ebullient Ethel's great portrayal of Petunia. Unfortunately, Wilson's next effort in the theatre, as a voodoo butler, Franklin, in an eight-performance flop called *The Strangler Fig,* is best summed up by a character in the play who exclaimed midway through the murder mystery, "Good God, what a mess!" The critics agreed that he felt he knew of what he spoke.

With the formation of the Negro Actor's Guild of America, Wilson became a member of the executive board and committee, along with Todd Duncan, Paul Robeson, Bill Robinson, Ethel Waters, Louis Armstrong, Marian Anderson, Fredi Washington, Leigh Whipper, and Bing Crosby. The Guild was instrumental in exerting considerable influence in the theatre world for better roles for black actors and pressed for the elimination of racially out-of-date sequences then rampant in the entertainment media. During the run of *Cabin in the Sky* in Los Angeles, Dooley was offered a small part in MGM's comic spoof of spy films

that was also to be Jeanette MacDonald's last long-term contract picture at that studio. *Cairo* (1942), a bottom-of-the-bill entry directed by W. S. Van Dyke II, was given little critical applause, and the majority of praise went to Ethel Waters (replacing a rebellious Lena Horne) as MacDonald's maid. Then came *Casablanca,* where, as Sam, Wilson's slickly smooth performance was the most humanizing aspect of Michael Curtiz' tautly directed film.

Within the 102-minute black-and-white feature, Dooley's Sam sings "Knock on Wood," and rotund Sydney Greenstreet (as the deliciously corrupt Ferrari) offers to buy him for his club, The Blue Parrot. However, Bogart retaliates with "I don't buy or sell human beings." Later, Wilson wheels his small, gaily decorated piano to a table where Ingrid Bergman, as Ilsa, initiates a memorable line that has come down through the years, "Play it Sam. Play 'As Time Goes By.'"*

From the memorable *Casablanca,* Wilson's film career sadly descended to a series of nothing roles such as Shadrach Jones in Paramount's dreadful *A Night in New Orleans* (1942), Moses in Rosalind Russell's *Take a Letter, Darling* (1942), and, peaking only slightly, Gabriel in Twentieth Century-Fox's thinly disguised dramatization of Bill Robinson's life, with Lena Horne and Robinson in *Stormy Weather* (1943). Dooley's ingratiating performance in the Robinson opus was followed by singing a few songs and having his accordian playing dubbed (as had his piano-playing in *Casablanca*) in Universal's bomb, *Two Tickets to London* (1943). After typical "colored" roles in *Higher and Higher* (1943) and *Seven Days Ashore* (1944), he returned to New York where he enjoyed a lustrous club engagement at the Greenwich Village Inn in April, 1943. His next theatrical assignment was as Pompey, a slave, in Harold Arlen's melodious *Bloomer Girl* (1944), in which Dooley stopped the show nightly with his singing of "The Eagle and Me" and "I Got a Song," both of which can still be heard on the original cast recording.

He returned to Hollywood for five more pictures. The best of these was Twentieth Century-Fox's *Come to the Stable* (1949), in which he was Anthony James aiding a brace of enthusiastic nuns, including Loretta Young and Celeste Holm. His last film was for Pine and Thomas at Paramount in a minor role as Rainbow in *Passage West* (1951).

When in New York, Dooley and his wife Estelle lived at the Dunbar Apartments on West 150th Street,

*With words and music by Herman Hupfield, "As Time Goes By" was originally introduced by Frances Williams in 1931's musical version of *Up Pops the Devil* called *Everybody's Welcome,* and was first recorded by Rudy Vallee.

and their neighbor was Bill Robinson. Dooley's career declined, although he did appear with Ethel Waters on her "Beulah" show, and in July, 1951, he was again telling audiences "We gotta be free—the eagle and me" in his original role of Pompey in *Bloomer Girl,* with Dick Haymes and Frances McCann at San Francisco's War Memorial.

A singing drummer, best remembered as the piano player at "Rick's" although in real life he could not play a note—and a fine actor capable of captivating film and theatre audiences around the world, Dooley Wilson died on May 30, 1953, at this home in Los Angeles. His life and career stated his philosophy, "I like to make a man laugh. I like to make him feel good. I think that's a great thing!"

With Bill Robinson and Lena Horne in Stormy Weather *(20th 1943)*

DOOLEY WILSON

Cairo *(MGM 1942)*
Casablanca *(WB 1942)*
A Night in New Orleans *(Par 1942)*
Take a Letter, Darling *(Par 1942)*
Stormy Weather *(20th 1943)*
Two Tickets to London *(Univ 1943)*
Higher and Higher *(RKO 1943)*

Seven Days Ashore *(RKO 1944)*
Triple Threat *(Col 1948)*
Racing Luck *(Col 1948)*
Free for All *(Univ 1949)*
Come to the Stable *(20th 1949)*
Passage West *(Par 1951)*

82

Teresa Wright

One of the most enduring aspects of the Hollywood scene is "professional prostitution"—a concept as unappealing as it is unfortunately genuine. The recounting of the progress of many actresses' careers are all too familiar: Beginning with the ever-popular casting couch, moving into the overhauling department where hair is teased, teeth are capped, figures are disciplined, hairlines are plucked, noses are bobbed, being stuffed into a revealing bathing suit for some hopefully well-circulated cheesecake shots; and, finally, landing a film role. With actual film exposure usually comes the procedure of becoming chummy with columnists, moving into a fitting domain in the exclusive cinema colony, subsequently choosing roles with a mascara-tinged eye more on vanity than artistic challenge, and then endless decades of chasing after eternal youth and economic security. These aspects of movie-star life are all cliches, but very much the ingredients of the success of loads of Hollywood girls who have come and gone (or refuse to go) since silent film days.

In 1941, a refreshing break in the rouged and girdled brigade of compromised and accoutremented starlets arrived in the form of one Teresa Wright. She managed to achieve a degree of stardom almost solely on the basis of acting talent. In the 1940s she became a performer of top import without the obvious kowtowing to lecherous talent agents, cheesecake hawkers, or vulturous gossip writers. When Teresa arrived in Hollywood as a Samuel Goldwyn discov-

ery in 1941 to begin work on *The Little Foxes,* she made no effort to become a typical captivating Hollywood actress. She was drably garbed, had a hairstyle that kindly could be termed undisciplined. Her stockings bagged at the ankles, and she did not own a pair of high-heeled shoes. She quickly made it evident to industry executives that she was not about to change her demeanor. She vociferously refused to accede to photographers' demands for leg art, freely stated that gossip columns and their librettists were absolute horrors, and moved into a humble apartment above an equally humble garage. She made it clear that she only wanted roles that tested her dramatic ability. Amazingly, she *almost* became a top star.

She was born Muriel Teresa Wright in the Harlem section of New York City on October 27, 1918. While she was still quite young, her parents separated, and for a time she lived with various relatives in New York and New Jersey. Finally, her father enrolled her at the exclusive Rosehaven School in Tenafly, New Jersey, where she received her first exposure to the arts of acting and dancing. While there was some theatre blood in her family—an Uncle Harry had been a stock company actor and her father had once played Little Eva bedecked with his own cascade of blonde curls—little Muriel resented any encouragement for a potential career in the theatre. She took such advice to imply that she was

With Judith Anderson in Pursued *(WB 1947)*

With David Niven in Enchantment *(RKO 1948)*

not reasonably bright enough to succeed at any other type of profession.

This idea changed when she saw Helen Hayes give a performance of *Victoria Regina*. Muriel Wright had been going to school in Connecticut, and then went to the Columbia High School in Maplewood, New Jersey. Miss Hayes's admirable stage performance inspired the girl to become her school's leading actress, and by graduation she was convinced she wanted to be in the theatre.

After apprenticing during the summers of 1937 and 1938 at the Wharf Theatre in Provincetown, Massachusetts, Miss Wright moved to New York. As there was already a Muriel Wright in Actors Equity, the aspiring actress decided to use her middle name Teresa, even though she disliked it. On the advice of a friend, Doro Merande, who was then in *Our Town*, Teresa auditioned for the Thornton Wilder play as understudy to the leading role of Emily. She won the part, playing the small role of Rebecca in the meantime. When Martha Scott, the original Emily, went to Hollywood, Teresa took over the assignment. She later toured in the show, playing the lead. The highlights of the road engagement were performances at Maplewood, New Jersey (her home town), and in Providence, the dwelling place of Mr. Wilder, who personally coached and entertained the cast there.

Our Town had finished its engagements by the summer of 1939, and Teresa accepted an offer to perform that hot season with the Barnstormers of Tanworth, New Hampshire. Among her assignments at that summer stock theatre was the role of Emily in *Our Town*. When she returned to New York in the fall, she was among the flock of performers auditioning for Howard Lindsay's and Russel Crouse's *Life with Father*. Teresa read for the part of the ingenue, Mary Skinner. Producer Oscar Serlin had originally conceived of the stage role with Mary as a blonde, but he was taken by the young brunette's abilities. After five callbacks, Teresa won the coveted role. *Life with Father* opened on November 8, 1939, for the first of its 3,224 performances, became an instant classic, and Miss Wright remained in the cast for over a year.

Meanwhile, in Hollywood, producer Sam Goldwyn had purchased the rights to the successful Lillian Hellman play, *The Little Foxes*. While a number of the New York cast (Carl Benton Reid, Dan Duryea, Charles Dingle, Patricia Collinge) had been retained for the film version, Bette Davis was chosen for the lead over the stage's Tallulah Bankhead. Goldwyn also wanted a *new* face for the role of Alexandra, the young lady who finally rejects her vitriolic Southern family. He told the press he "wanted a girl who could

look sixteen, demure, and un-actressy, yet be enough of an actress to play dramatic scenes with Bette Davis." Scouts were sent east to locate such a talent, and found her at a *Life with Father* performance in the form of Teresa Wright. (Goldwyn had originally planned to use Virginia Gilmore, under contract to him, for the important part.) Producer Oscar Serlin, who had taken a personal liking to the girl, agreed to let her leave the play, but only after he personally constructed her Hollywood contract. What resulted was a bizarre product of a mind that obviously harbored great respect for Teresa, a contempt for the cinema's usual methods of "building" a starlet, and a strange ability for discovering phallic symbols.

Among the contractual clauses was Number 39, which read:

The aforementioned Teresa Wright shall not be required to pose for photographers in a bathing suit unless she is in water. Neither may she be photographed running on the beach with her hair flying in the wind. Nor may she pose in any of the following situations: in shorts, playing with a cocker spaniel; digging in a garden; whipping up a meal; attired in firecrackers and holding skyrockets for the 4th of July; looking insinuatingly at a turkey for Thanksgiving; wearing a bunny cap with long ears for Easter; twinkling on prop snow in a skiing outfit while a fan blows her scarf; assuming an athletic stance while pretending to hit something with a bow and arrow. . . .

The five-year contract, which also prohibited Teresa from appearing in leg art or general cheesecake poses, allowed her time off for one play a year. The very strongly worded demands made quite a few people in Hollywood hopeful of seeing the idealistic little actress (5'2") fall on her face.

No such thing happened. Her performance in RKO's *The Little Foxes* was quite well received. *Newsweek* Magazine wrote that the actress "turns in a sensitive performance that shares first honors with Bette Davis' Regina Giddens." There was also a good deal of gossip talk, that said Teresa "stole the film" from Davis, which was not quite the case. Both Teresa and Patricia Collinge were Oscar-nominated as a result of their performances in that film, but each lost the Best Supporting Actress Academy Award to Mary Astor of *The Great Lie*.

After returning to the stage for mentor Serlin in *The King's Maid*, a play that was so dismally rated in its Boston tryout that it never opened in New York, Teresa was loaned to MGM for *Mrs. Miniver* (1942). She played Dame May Whitty's granddaughter, who falls in love with and marries Richard Ney, he the on-screen son of Greer Garson and Walter Pidgeon. So fully did she realize the Allied image of the well-bred, likeable, worthwhile human being, that she won another Best Supporting Actress nomination.

Less than a month after the release of Mrs. Miniver, Samuel Goldwyn released The Pride of the Yankees (1942), in which his starlet portrayed the wife of Lou Gehrig (Gary Cooper). Columnists took note that the actress had to finally consent to wearing high heels to bring her 5'2" height closer to Cooper's 6'2½". Nevertheless, it was an excellent performance by Teresa. One of the best joint scenes that the two stars enjoyed was the one in which the romantically-inclined couple playfully wrestle about, as well as the later scene in which Coop's Gehrig first feels the symptoms of his fatal paralysis. Both Cooper and Teresa won Oscar nominations.

Therefore, at the Oscar ceremonies of 1942, Teresa found herself in an enviable position. She was nominated for both Best Actress and Best Supporting Actress. Greer Garson won the Academy Award for Mrs. Miniver, and Teresa, in the supporting category, for the same film.

Teresa rejected a role in Goldwyn's North Star (1943), and Anne Baxter was borrowed from Twen-tieth Century-Fox to replace her. By the time Teresa went to Universal to star in Alfred Hitchcock's Shadow of a Doubt (1943), she was considered a big enough star to receive top billing over Joseph Cotten. This low-keyed film is one of Hitchcock's most engaging productions, perfectly contrasting the snide superiority of a widow murderer (Cotten) with the wholesome quaintness of the just-plain-folks California family with whom he stays. Teresa appeared as the young niece who comes to suspect her "Uncle Charlie" of having committed some foul deeds. It was one of those greatly enjoyable films in which nearly everybody disagreed over who stole the limelight. Some picked Cotten for his silky villainy, some, Hume Cronyn for his portrayal of the nosy mystery-story fan. Many filmgoers agreed with Time Magazine when it penned, "The show is really Miss Wright's." (She would later repeat her Shadow of a Doubt role on "Lux Radio Theatre" with William Powell as her co-star.)

With just three films, Teresa had become a major Hollywood name. She had done it in accord with her own stipulations: No fraternizing with the fourth estate and none of the suggestive poses with a turkey, etc. that her contract prohibited. Her oft-repeated objections to starlet photo-posing became a matter of much speculation by the more acid wags in Holly-

With Greer Garson, Claire Sandars, Christopher Severn, and Richard Ney in Mrs. Miniver *(MGM 1942)*

wood, who openly insinuated that her objections were not so much artistic as they were protective. If such remarks were made to goad the actress into wiggling into a swim suit, they were almost successful. Teresa angrily retaliated that some of her friends "tell me I have a very nice figure." She soon re-evaluated her position in the movie business, but still refused to pose in anything but the usual clothes, reasoning that such photographic sessions would be "boring." On May 23, 1942, she wed Niven Busch, a screen writer, which resulted in her leaving her Beverly Hills garage for the comforts of Busch's San Fernando Valley home. (Later, when Busch wrote the screenplay for David O. Selznick's *Duel in the Sun,* 1946, it is rumored he wrote the role of Pearl—which Jennifer Jones played—with Teresa in mind.)

Meanwhile, Goldwyn announced his actress star for two upcoming projects: *The First Cold,* which was never made, and *Casanova Brown* (1944), which should not have been made. The latter cast Gary Cooper as a single man who suddenly finds himself with a baby. The results were supposed to be funny and cute, but actually fell flat in both categories. In 1945, Goldwyn lent Teresa to Paramount for *The Trouble with Women.* Paramount flanked her with two of the studio's more popular leading men, Ray Milland and Brian Donlevy, and the script was at times rather funny. However, Teresa was not ideally cast as a determined newspaper reporter. The film, like a number of other frothy comedies shot during wartime, was delayed in its release, finally appearing in mid-1947.

There followed in 1946, the actress' most famous and best film, *The Best Years of Our Lives.* Goldwyn lavishly and tastefully produced this epic of the post-World War II rehabilitation of veterans. (His legendary remark about the film was, "I don't care if the film doesn't make a nickel. I just want every man, woman, and child in America to see it.") Bosley Crowther (*New York Times*) judged that it was the sort of film that "can be wholly and enthusiastically endorsed not only as superlative entertainment but as food for quiet and humanizing thought." Teresa was Peggy Stephenson, the soft, gentle daughter of G.I. Fredric March, who falls in love with Dana Andrews after his wife (Virginia Mayo) brutally cheats on him. Crowther praised Teresa's "lovely quiet performance" in the *Times.* She was never again to appear in so excellently mounted a film.

The Best Years of Our Lives completed Teresa's Goldwyn contract. However, she did work for Goldwyn again, in *Enchantment* (1948), with David Niven, a picture billed as "just about the most wonderful love story ever filmed." It was a quite moving picture that proved to be not too maudlin. She also appeared in Columbia's *The Men* (1950), the now famous saga of returning disabled veterans, in which she was Marlon Brando's faithful girl friend. In MGM's *The Actress* (1953), based on Ruth Gordon's screenplay on her own play, *Years Ago,* Teresa played the mother. Interestingly enough in this George Cukor-directed production thirty-four-year-old Teresa played the mother of twenty-three-year-old Jean Simmons (as Ruth Gordon) and the wife of fifty-three-year-old Spencer Tracy. Along the way, Teresa appeared in some admittedly poor films: She somehow wound up

With Ray Milland and Brian Donlevy in a publicity pose for The Trouble with Women *(Par 1947)*

in a Sam ("King of the B's") Katzman western for Columbia called *California Conquest* (1952), which showed her to worse advantage than had *The Imperfect Lady* (1947), in which she was wildly miscast as a Victorian belle of the music halls who is tarnished in a scandal.

In 1952, Teresa and husband Niven Busch were divorced. They had two children and she had appeared in two of his screenplays: *Pursued* (1947) and *The Capture* (1950). When Teresa appeared in the Don Siegel-directed quickie, *Count the Hours* (1953), co-starring Macdonald Carey, the director later revealed that Teresa had been so lofty during filming that her imperious attitudes toward this low-budget production had caused him to rate her a minus factor in the filming.

With film work being gradually abandoned, and her lifestyle changing, Teresa became quite active in television. She has appeared in some fifty programs, including such work as a "Playhouse 90" production of *The Miracle Worker* (1957) and *The Margaret Bourke-White Story* on "Sunday Show" (1960), both of which earned her Emmy nominations. In addition she has been in such other diverse offerings as playing in the "Hallmark Hall of Fame" version of *The Devil's Disciple* (1955) and a "Climax" show entitled *The Gay Illiterate* (1956), in which, ironically, she played Louella Parsons. In the 1974 telefeature *The Elevator*, she was reunited with her *The Best Years of Our Lives* co-star, Myrna Loy, in a tense study of eight terrified people trapped in an elevator that is threatening to plunge thirty stories to the ground at any moment.

During her post-screen-lead years she has been rather active on the stage. She has done extensive stock work in regional theatres (*The Heiress, The Rainmaker,* for instance) in the U.S. and Canada, and finally returned to Broadway on December 17, 1957, in *The Dark at the Top of the Stairs.* In this William Inge drama, Robert Coleman *(New York Daily Mirror)* weighed, "Teresa Wright is eminently right as the wife who, believing that her husband [Pat Hingle] doesn't understand her, learns that others have their problems." She later toured in the 1960s in packages of *Mary, Mary, Tchin-Tchin,* and *The Locksmith,* and most recently returned to Broadway on January 25, 1968, in *I Never Sang for My Father,* as the woman who is disowned by her family for marrying a Jew. She subsequently appeared off Broadway in *Who's Happy Now,* and, in October, 1970, gave a concert reading entitled *A Passage to E. M. Forster* at New York's Theatre de Lys.

On December 11, 1959, Teresa married playwright Robert Anderson, author of such plays as *Tea and Sympathy, You Know I Can't Hear You When the Water Is Running,* and *I Never Sang for My Father.* They own a farm in Brewster, New York, where she spends most of her time.

It is only very occasionally that Teresa performs in the media these days. She was Jean Simmons' mother onscreen (again) in *The Happy Ending* (1969), and appeared in the fall of 1971 with the Long Wharf Theatre of New Haven in a revival of *You Can't Take It with You.* She was seen on television in the 1972 telefeature, *Crawlspace,* and on the James Stewart's television series, "Hawkins" in 1974. In mid-1975, Teresa garnered excellent reviews portraying the distraught wife of Willy Loman (George C. Scott) in the Broadway revival of *Death of a Salesman.*

One thing is certain, the Teresa of the 1970s is still a firm believer in the effectiveness of non-glamour. Not too long ago, she was at Lincoln Center Library studying a copy of the manuscript of *The Effects of Gamma Rays on Man-in-the-Moon Marigolds,* preparatory to a stock engagement of the show. She arrived at the reference center garbed in a loose-fitting, drab dress, topped by a coolie-style hat tied with a ribbon under her chin. If not for the telling voice, one might have easily mistaken her for some eccentric woman several years her senior.

TERESA WRIGHT

The Little Foxes   *(RKO 1941)*
Mrs. Miniver   *(MGM 1942)*
The Pride of the Yankees   *(RKO 1942)*
Shadow of a Doubt   *(Univ 1943)*
Casanova Brown   *(RKO 1944)*
The Best Years of Our Lives   *(RKO 1946)*
Pursued   *(WB 1947)*
The Imperfect Lady   *(Par 1947)*
The Trouble with Women   *(Par 1947)*
Enchantment   *(RKO 1948)*
The Capture   *(RKO 1950)*
The Men   *(UA 1950)*

Something to Live For   *(Par 1952)*
California Conquest   *(Col 1952)*
The Steel Trap   *(20th 1952)*
The Actress   *(MGM 1953)*
Count the Hours   *(RKO 1953)*
Track of the Cat   *(WB 1954)*
The Search for Bridey Murphy   *(Par 1956)*
Escapade in Japan   *(Univ 1957)*
The Restless Years   *(Univ 1958)*
Hail Hero   *(National General 1969)*
The Happy Ending   *(UA 1969)*

Gig Young

There is something very strange about the extensive career of Gig Young. Some facet of his likeable, bouncy, yet sophisticated personality makes audiences continually enjoy watching him get romantically jilted or emotionally stepped upon on the big screen. His blithe, blase air has somehow encouraged leading ladies to wipe their high heels on him ever since his days as a minor Warner Bros. star of the 1940s. The names of actresses who, at one time or another have left Mr. Young in the final reel of a picture for another man reads like a who's who of the Hollywood distaff side. In fact, at one stage of Doris Day's melodious career, she was waggishly described as the actress who makes movies in which she ditches Gig Young.

Even when Gig is away from his characteristic romantic assignments, he has fared best when playing a loser. Critics and audiences took notice when James Cagney verbally pummeled him in *Come Fill the Cup* (1951) for being an irresponsible alcoholic. He lost the bid for Best Supporting Actor that year, but in 1969 he won an Academy Award for *They Shoot Horses, Don't They?* by etching a sharp delineation of the miserable promoter who whips himself into a phoney frenzy as the master of ceremonies of a sweaty dance marathon.

He was born Byron Ellsworth Barr in St. Cloud, Minnesota, on November 4, 1913. His father was a chef for a St. Cloud reformatory, and managed, in his spare time, to develop his own home canning business. The Depression finished that enterprise and the family relocated to Washington, D.C., where Mr. Barr took work with a food brokerage company. Young Byron attended McKinley High School. He can now rather jokingly recall that he was an extremely shy child, but reasons, "I think all actors were shy children." Schooling was no joy for the youth and he offhandedly recalls, "I only had one teacher who ever liked me. I was so happy she did that I used to give her dimes." He also recollects, "I can't remember a time when I didn't want to be an actor. I acted in high-school plays and after I graduated I acted at night with an amateur group. During the day I worked for the Hill-Tibbets Ford Agency."

When he was twenty-three, his family moved to North Carolina where his father had accepted a post with the Tennessee Valley Authority. At this point, Byron realized he *must* be an actor and he decided there could be no better testing ground than the famed Pasadena Playhouse. He used his small savings to bankroll his trip to California. He auditioned for the Playhouse, won a small part in an upcoming production, and before long had a scholarship. To supplement his income, he worked as a garage mechanic and parking lot attendant. Under the name Ronald Reed, he accepted a job with the non-Equity Beaux Arts Theatre in Los Angeles. For thirty dollars a week he played Abie in *Abie's Irish Rose*. ("On open-

With Arthur Kennedy, James Brown, and John Ridgely in Air Force *(WB 1943)*

With Eleanor Parker in The Woman in White *(WB 1948)*

ing night stink bombs were thrown at us," says the actor). But it was his continual exposure in the Playhouse productions that brought him to the attention of a Warner Bros. scout who took note of his looks and his progress. The actor soon signed a player's contract with the Burbank studio.

Still using the name Byron Barr, (he also used Bryant Fleming), the young hopeful began a series of nondescript, unbilled bits at Warners. He was in *Here Come the Cavalry* (1941), a promotional short subject for the studio's lavish Errol Flynn epic of soldiers versus Indians, *They Died with Their Boots On* (1941). In the feature version, Flynn sends Byron back to the fort with a message. Other appearances included *Dive Bomber* (1941)—in which he was a test pilot who gasps, "Yes Sir," while in a pressure chamber—*One Foot in Heaven* (1941), in which he took out a marriage license, and he played as one of Henry Fonda's students in *The Male Animal* (1942). Finally, in James Cagney's *Captains of the Clouds* (1942), he was a student pilot along with Michael Ames (a.k.a., Tod Andrews).

Among Byron's other chores at Warners was to assist other players in screen tests. When he played opposite Alexis Smith in her bid for a role in *The Constant Nymph* (1943), he acquitted himself so well that director Edmund Goulding put the stock player's name on the test as well as Miss Smith's. Shortly after that, director Irving Rapper ran the test, liked what he saw, and gave the young man the part of a young artist in *The Gay Sisters* (1942), a showcase vehicle for Barbara Stanwyck and her onscreen siblings, Geraldine Fitzgerald and Nancy Coleman. When preview audiences indicated on their cards how much they liked Gig Young, the actor took the name professionally. (It was a good thing as there was another actor—with Twentieth Century-Fox—at this time named Byron Barr.)

Young got a spattering of fan mail for *The Gay Sisters,* and Warners gave him a good part in *Air Force* (1943), the semi documentary film that followed the training and adventures of a Flying Fortress crew. He played Lieutenant Williams, a novice flyer who has to jump into the pilot's seat when the latter is killed. Gig displayed a believable and liberal acting ability in this important production. Craig Stevens, under contract to Warners, went into service, Gig was given the role of Rudd Kendall in *Old Acquaintance* (1934), featuring Bette Davis in one of her earlier matronly roles. He played the polished, young suitor of Dolores Moran, the daughter of Miriam Hopkins, Davis' long-time "friend."

After this Vincent Sherman-directed tearjerker, Young was caught up in World War II and joined the Coast Guard, serving in the Pacific for three years. As he puts it, he performed in that theatre of war "without any particular distinction."

When he was released, Warners was waiting to continue his contract. His first post-war feature was *Escape Me Never* (1947), which starred Errol Flynn and Ida Lupino. It was a rather bland romance story which supplied Miss Lupino with the cinema footnote of being the first actress onscreen to walk out on Young. Next came *The Woman in White* (1948), a distorted but still intriguing version of the Gothic tale featuring a fine Eleanor Parker performance in a dual role. This completed Young's Warners contract, and he chose not to renew it. "I was tired of playing Errol Flynn's spoiled brother, or the guy who loses the girl," he said. While departing that studio took care of his first professional objection, it hardly proved to be a panacea for the latter.

Gig had to wait three years for a role to come along that would advance his career. After costuming in MGM's *The Three Musketeers* (1948) and fighting John Wayne in Republic's *Wake of the Red Witch* (1948), he was disillusioned enough with freelancing to sign with Columbia. In a display of typical studio politicking, the company promised him the lead opposite Rita Hayworth in the upcoming *The Loves of Carmen* (1948). However, that role went to Glenn Ford, and, apparently, Gig's major roles in *Lust for Gold* (1949) and *Tell It to the Judge* (1949) were chopped down in the release prints. Young retaliated by going on suspension, and kept rejecting roles until he wore out his welcome. His status began slipping in Hollywood, and he was forced to take work he did not want. An example of this was his replacement of Howard da Silva in a dull RKO western, *Slaughter Trail* (1951), when da Silva's unpopularity with the House Un-American Activities Committee got him fired from the feature after shooting had already commenced.

The downward spiral for Gig finally ceased when a trip to Warners to sell an outboard motor to a gate guard led him to being tested for the role of Boyd Copeland, the emotionally weak nephew of publisher Raymond Massey in *Come Fill the Cup*. Gig's performance as the weak-willed husband of Phyllis Thaxter gained him more notice than any other film to that time, and reaped him a Best Supporting Actor nomination (won that year by Karl Malden of *A Streetcar Named Desire*). Particularly memorable is the scene in which he prowls like a wild beast through his apartment in search of liquor, and, unsuccessful in his search, has to be restrained from a suicide attempt.

At MGM, Gig continued his on screen romantic

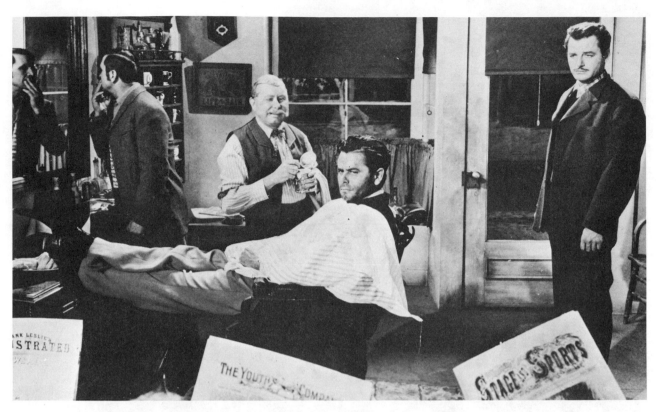

With Percy Helton (barber) and Glenn Ford in Lust for Gold (Col 1949)

losing streak: Jane Greer to Peter Lawford in *You and Me* (1952), Elizabeth Taylor to Fernando Lamas in *The Girl Who Had Everything* (1953), and Joan Crawford to a blind Michael Wilding in *Torch Song* (1953). This last film settled his Culver City contract, and Young plotted a new career strategy by defecting to the Broadway stage. On December 17, 1953, he made his debut in the comedy, *Oh, Men! Oh, Women!,* of which the *New York Times* wrote, ''Gig Young gives an immensely amusing performance as the rebellious husband to a peevish wife; he has a number of comic inventions to keep the character alive.''

Thereafter, whenever Young's film career has grown stagnant, he has wisely returned to the stage. In November, 1956, he returned to Broadway for a New York City Center engagement in *Teahouse of the August Moon,* opened in November, 1960, in *Under the Yum Yum Tree,* and in October, 1967, played in another specious sex farce *There's a Girl in My Soup.* (He was replaced in this long-running show by Lawrence Hugo.) Away from Broadway, he has starred in Philadelphia in *September Tide* (1958), which never made it to New York, in *Nobody Loved an Albatross* at the Drury Lane Theatre in Chicago (1966), and has done packaged stock versions of *The Music Man* (1966), *The Odd Couple* (1967)—as the

slob, surprisingly—and *On a Clear Day You Can See Forever* (1968).

Back in Hollywood, Young faced more of the same ''other man'' roles. In Warners' *Young at Heart* (1954), he outdid himself by losing not one girl, but three (Doris Day, Dorothy Malone, Elizabeth Fraser). In Twentieth Century-Fox's *Desk Set* he lost Katharine Hepburn to Spencer Tracy (hardly a contest), and when he lost Doris Day to Clark Gable in Paramount's *Teacher's Pet* (1958), it was such an expert summation of Young's unlucky-in-love image that he won another Oscar nomination for Best Supporting Actor. This time, he lost the award to Burl Ives of *The Big Country*. Up to this point, Young had been able to intersperse his celluloid farces with some dramatic screen work (for instance, 1955's *The Desperate Hours*), but after *Teacher's Pet* he recalls, ''I was offered nothing but comedies. Comedy is harder to do than drama, since comedy roles involve the offbeat, not merely the basic emotions. I like to play both comedy and drama.''

There followed the films that brought Young the most prominence up to that time: The ''sex comedies'' of the late 1950s and the early 1960s, which, in point of truth, often seemed carbon copies of themselves and might just have easily been done by simi-

523

With Katharine Warren, Robert Cummings, and Rosalind Russell in Tell It to the Judge *(Col 1949)*

larly pigeon-holed Tony Randall. *The Tunnel of Love* (1958) found Gig getting his wife pregnant repeatedly while neighbors Richard Widmark and Doris Day tried to adopt a child. *Ask Any Girl* (1959) saw him acting the playboy and losing Shirley MacLaine to his older brother, David Niven. *That Touch of Mink* (1962) added Cary Grant to the formula, along with the ubiquitous Miss Day, and *Strange Bedfellows* (1964) co-starred him with Rock Hudson and Gina Lollobrigida. (Guess who won the girl in that Universal comedy offering?) The films were all very popular and provided a perfect, if unvaried, showcase for Gig's light farce expertise.

Gig's countenance became a familiar sight on television. Jack Warner personally chose him to host the video series, "Warner Bros. Presents," in 1955, and after years of appearing as a guest star he was seen in another series, when, in 1964, he joined with Charles Boyer and David Niven as one of the very debonair con men in "The Rogues."

As the 1960s closed, the movies grew far too blunt in their treatment of sex to foster any more of the Doris Day-type comedies. The films in which Young had primarily earned his bread and butter became a joke with the suddenly matured public. The expert farceur's career might well have evaporated had it not been for the enterprising Marty Baum, Gig's former agent, who had become the new president of ABC Pictures. When *They Shoot Horses, Don't They?* was scheduled for production, Baum demanded that Gig play Rocky, the seedy dance marathon host who tackily exhorts the crowd with "yowza, yowza, yowza." The backers, as well as Jane Fonda, the film's star, were described as "shocked and furious" at Young being given such a focal role. They presumed that his forte was comedy and, in recent years, he had gained a reputation as being at the mercy of personal problems. Red Buttons was in the same boat as Young, in his portrayal of the aging sailor in the film. He recalls: "Marty did ram Gig and myself down the throats of the producers. Gig and I were like two guys in death row waiting for the pellet to be dropped. We kept reassuring each other we'd be great. We had to be, for Marty's sake." Young quickly discovered he was not wanted on the production when "the second day I got to the set I discovered I was supposed to do a twenty-page scene I hadn't been told to prepare."

Nevertheless, Gig scored triumphantly in the role and his performance can be ranked as truly memorable. *Variety* reported, "Puffy-eyed, unshaven, reeking of stale liquor and cigarettes, Gig Young has never looked older, worse, or acted better." A particularly well-played scene in the film found him calming a hysterical girl (Susannah York) in a shower by dint of his own onscreen personality. In April, 1970, Gig accepted the Oscar presented to him on the telecast by Katherine Ross. Young made a slightly fluffed but movingly sincere acceptance speech, especially thanking Marty Baum, "who believed in me when no one else did."

Young's career since has been vastly anti-climactic. He had a nice-sized role in *Lovers and Other Strangers* (1970), also engineered by Marty Baum for ABC Pictures. Gig was a mistreated grandfather in that well-received comedy. He then played a misanthrope in *The Neon Ceiling* (1971) a telefeature in which he was pursued by a looney Lee Grant. He was in a tour of *Harvey* with Shirley Booth, but due to an illness he had to be replaced on the road. (He did *Harvey* again in early 1975). He was an emcee at a Cannes Film Festival, and is still quite a draw in regional theatre, although there have been whispers of complaints from audiences who claim that Gig's acting has obviously been diluted by the effects of strong liquid refreshments. Marty Baum came to his professional rescue again in 1974 by casting him as a dissolute bounty hunter in Sam Peckinpah's *Bring Me the Head of Alfredo Garcia.* Then he replaced Jose Ferrer in the Italian-made feature, *A Black Ribbon for Deborah* (1975), and after completing another "Gig Young role" in the telefeature *The Great Ice Rip-Off* (in which the plotline required him to dress up like a woman for several sequences), he returned to Rome for a role in the Bradford Dillman feature *Michele* (1975). Back in Hollywood Gig was among the familiar faces cast in the film epic *The Hindenburg,* a Robert Wise-directed feature starring George C. Scott, Anne Bancroft, Gig, Roy Thinnes, Burgess Meredith, and Robert Clary. In *The Turning Point of Jim Malloy,* a 1975 telefeature based on John O'Hara's short stories of Gibbsville, Pa., Gig was on tap as the reporter-turned-alcoholic. *Daily Variety* acknowledged of his performance, "Young pulls off greatest coup but also has help of well-constructed role."

Privately, Young is a charming fellow, well-liked, and possessing a realistic attitude toward his unusual career. He simply states that he "picked the best from the lousy parts they offered me." He enjoys discussing his professional experiences and has invariably kind remarks to make about his co-stars, from Elvis Presley to Sophia Loren.

Offscreen, he has been unlucky in love. His first wife was Sheila Stapler, a fellow performer, whom he wed in 1939. "It was the longest lasting of my marriages," says Young. "It lasted eight years, but some of those eight were war years, when I was in the Coast Guard, and we weren't together." His next spouse

525

was Sophia Rosenstein, a drama coach at Warner Bros. They wed in early 1950; she died of cancer in late 1952. Wife number three was Robert Montgomery's actress daughter Elizabeth, whom Gig married in December, 1956. The couple divorced in January, 1963, "for no particular reason" claims Young. The actor's fourth spouse was Elaine Whitman, a real estate agent he married in September, 1963. In 1964, she gave birth to a daughter, Jennifer. After Young divorced Miss Whitman in 1966, he contested his paternity of Jennifer.

Despite all his matrimonial problems, Gig still enjoys the company of ladies. And, most of all, despite the many ups and downs of the past four decades, he is still very much hooked on acting.

"Acting is the exaggeration of life, and if you can blow it up and still make it look real, the better your performance. Any actor who loves what he is doing can't take his mind off it."

GIG YOUNG

As BYRON BARR or BRYANT FLEMING:
Misbehaving Husbands *(PRC 1940)*
Dive Bomber *(WB 1941)*
Sergeant York *(WB 1941)*
One Foot in Heaven *(WB 1941)*
They Died with Their Boots On *(WB 1941)*
The Man Who Came to Dinner *(WB 1941)*
Navy Blues *(WB 1941)*
You're in the Army Now *(WB 1941)*
The Male Animal *(WB 1942)*
Captain of the Clouds *(WB 1942)*

As GIG YOUNG
The Gay Sisters *(WB 1942)*
Air Force *(WB 1943)*
Old Acquaintance *(WB 1943)*
Escape Me Never *(WB 1947)*
The Woman in White *(WB 1948)*
Wake of the Red Witch *(Rep 1948)*
The Three Musketeers *(MGM 1948)*
Lust for Gold *(Col 1949)*
Tell it to the Judge *(Col 1949)*
Hunt the Man Down *(RKO 1950)*
Target Unknown *(Univ 1951)*
Only the Valiant *(WB 1951)*
Come Fill the Cup *(WB 1951)*
Slaughter Trail *(RKO 1951)*

Too Young to Kiss *(MGM 1951)*
Holiday for Sinners *(MGM 1952)*
You for Me *(MGM 1952)*
The Girl Who Had Everything *(MGM 1953)*
Arena *(MGM 1953)*
The City that Never Sleeps *(Rep 1953)*
Torch Song *(MGM 1953)*
Young at Heart *(WB 1954)*
The Desperate Hours *(Par 1955)*
Desk Set *(20th 1957)*
Teacher's Pet *(Par 1958)*
The Tunnel of Love *(MGM 1958)*
Ask Any Girl *(MGM 1959)*
The Story on Page One *(20th 1959)*
That Touch of Mink *(Univ 1962)*
Kid Galahad *(UA 1962)*
Five Miles to Midnight *(UA 1963)*
For Love or Money *(Univ 1963)*
A Ticklish Affair *(MGM 1964)*
Strange Bedfellows *(Univ 1965)*
The Shuttered Room *(WB–7 Arts 1967)*
They Shoot Horses, Don't They? *(Cin 1969)*
Lovers and Other Strangers *(Cin 1970)*
Bring Me the Head of Alfredo Garcia *(UA 1974)*
A Black Ribbon for Deborah *(Italian 1975)*
Michele *(Italian 1975)*
The Hindenberg *(Univ 1975)*

Staff

JAMES ROBERT PARISH, New York-based freelance writer, was born in Cambridge Massachusetts. He attended the University of Pennsylvania and graduated as a Phi Beta Kappa with a degree in English. A graduate of the University of Pennsylvania Law School, he is a member of the New York Bar. As president of Entertainment Copyright Research Co., Inc. he headed a major researching facility for the film and television industries. Later, he was a film reviewer-interviewer for *Motion Picture Daily* and *Variety*. He is the author of such volumes as *The Great Movie Series, The Fox Girls, The RKO Gals,* and *Actors Television Credits,* and *Hollywood's Great Love Teams.* He is the co-author of *The MGM Stock Company, Liza!, The Great Spy Pictures* and *Film Directors Guide: The U.S.* Mr. Parish is also a film reviewer for national magazines.

LENNARD DeCARL was born in New York City and is a graduate of the School of Performing Arts and Hofstra University. A professional actor and stage director, he has appeared extensively in the theatre, films, and television. He has also written for the publication, *Films in Review.*

WILLIAM T. LEONARD is currently Research Director for the Free Library of Philadelphia Theatre Collection. He has contributed articles to several publications, including *Films in Review* and *Classic Film Collector,* has written reports for proposed culture centers and was one of the principal contributors of data for the American Film Institute's catalog volume, *Feature Films: 1921–30.* During World War II, he wrote and appeared in the play *Hurry Up and Wait,* done by the Special Services, Air Corp. He has recently collaborated on the book *Film Directors Guide: The U.S.,* and is presently engaged in compiling, collating, and developing a comprehensive history of the theatre in Philadelphia (The First Two Hundred Years). Mr. Leonard is a member of the American Library Association.

GREGORY W. MANK, a film buff since the age of three, is a graduate of Mount St. Mary's College, Emmitsburg, Maryland, with a B.A. in English. He has contributed articles to such cinema journals as *Films in Review* and *Film Fan Monthly,* and is currently working with Mr. Parish on an upcoming book, *The Tough Guys.* Mr. Mank is an actor and acting instructor with the Baltimore Actors Theatre.

JACK ANO is a veteran reporter on the film scene. From 1965–1973 he was New York editor of the trade magazine, *Film Bulletin,* and has continued as a feature writer, columnist, and reviewer with that publication. He also has been a freelance publicity writer on *Walking Tall* and other major motion pictures and an encyclopedia editor at Columbia University Press and Grolier, Inc.

T. ALLAN TAYLOR, godson of the late Margaret Mitchell, has long been active in book publishing and is presently production manager of one of the largest abstracting and technical indexing services in the United States. He was editor on *The Fox Girls, The Paramount Pretties, The RKO Gals, The Slapstick Queens, The Great Spy Pictures, Hollywood's Great Love Teams,* and other volumes.

Since a very early age, Brooklynite JOHN ROBERT COCCHI has been viewing and collating data on motion pictures and is now regarded as one of America's most energetic film researchers. He is the New York editor of *Boxoffice* Magazine. He was research associate on *The American Movies Reference Book: The Sound Era, The Fox Girls, Good Dames, The MGM Stock Company; The Golden Era,* and many other books. He has written cinema history articles for such journals as *Film Fan Monthly* and *Screen Facts.* He is co-founder of one of New York City's leading film societies.

New York-born FLORENCE SOLOMON attended Hunter College and then joined Ligon Johnson's copyright research office. Later she was appointed director for research at Entertainment Copyright Research Co., Inc. and is presently a reference supervisor at ASCAP's Index Division in New York City. Miss Solomon has collaborated on such works as *The American Movies Reference Book: The Sound Era, TV Movies, The Great Movie Series, The George Raft File,* and others. She is the niece of the noted sculptor, the late Sir Jacob Epstein.

Index

540